# Facing the Enemy

## A History of Anarchist Organization from Proudhon to May 1968

*By Alexandre Skirda*

*Translated by Paul Sharkey*

AK PRESS

Facing the Enemy:
A History of Anarchist Organization from Proudhon to May 1968
        ISBN  1 902593 19 7


Library of Congress Cataloging-in-Publication Data
    A catalog record for this title is available from the Library of Congress.


British Library Cataloguing-in-Publication Data
    A catalogue record for this title is available from the British Library.


The English translation of *Autonomie individuelle et force collective*
*(Les anarchistes et L'organisation de Proudhon à nos jours)* Paris, 1987 A. Skirda.

Published by:

AK Press                          AK Press
P.O. Box 12766                    674-A 23rd Street
Edinburgh, Scotland               Oakland, CA
EH8 9YE                           94612
www.akuk.com                      www.akpress.org

In Conjunction With:

Kate Sharpley Library             Kate Sharpley Library
BM Hurricane                      PMB #820
London, England                   2425 Channing Way
WC1 3XX                           Berkeley, CA
www.katesharpleylibrary.org       94704

*Translated by Paul Sharkey.*
*Design and layout work donated by Freddie Baer.*

*The production of this book was made possible in part by a generous donation*
*from the Anarchist Archive Project. For more information, please contact:*

Anarchist Archive Project
P.O. Box 381323
Cambridge, MA
02238

# TABLE OF CONTENTS

"To lay the foundations for the liberty of individuals by organizing the initiative of the masses."

— P. J. Proudhon, *Confessions of a Revolutionary*, 1849

"I have this staunch belief that the time for theoretical discourse, in print or through the spoken word, has passed. Over the past nine years, within the International more ideas than were needed to rescue the world were devised, if ideas were all that were needed to save it, and I challenge anyone to come up with a new one.

The time for ideas is past, it is now time for deeds and action. What counts above all else today is the organization of the forces of the proletariat. But such organization must be the doing of the proletariat itself."

— Mikhail Bakunin, *Letter to the Comrades of the Jura Federation*, 1873

"What we have to get into our noggin is that we can expect no support. Only our biceps can set us free."

— Emile Pouget, *Le Père Peinard*, October 1894

"Anarchism is not some beautiful dream, some philosophical abstraction, but a social movement of the toiling masses. For that very reason, it has to garner its forces into one broad organization constantly acting as reality and the strategy of the social class struggle require."

— *The Organizational Platform of the Group of Russian Anarchists Abroad*, 1926

"It will be readily appreciated that I cannot remain indifferent to the nonchalance and negligence currently obtaining in our circles. On the one hand, it prevents the creation of a coherent libertarian collective that would enable anarchists to take their proper place in the revolution, and on the other, it permits a making-do with fine phrases and grand notions, while shying away when action is called for…. Responsibility and collective discipline should not cause alarm: they are the fellow travelers of the practice of social anarchism."

— Nestor Makhno, *On Revolutionary Discipline*, 1926

"A revolutionary organization is first and foremost a means of effective action by the proletariat in its process of liberation, and cannot ever represent an end in itself. It is a catalyst radicalizing the struggles waged, a living laboratory of experiences and analyses, a forum for comparisons, information, liaison and coordination. Its essential role is to echo, centralize and make exemplary all the militant work achieved by its members."

— The Groupe Kronstadt, Paris, 1971

# I. THE BANKRUPTCY OF SOCIALISM AND THE SETBACKS OF ANARCHISM

The age of modern revolutions was ushered in by the French Revolution. It cast a long shadow over the whole nineteenth century. Thus, other Bastilles were stormed and, gradually, by dint of master-strokes and insurrections, culminating in the extraordinary effervescence of 1848 and the rising of the Paris Commune in 1871, the revolutionary vision took shape. Since then, its supporters have been ceaselessly preoccupied with the prospects of its realization. Now, lots of difficulties have come to light over the attempts and the experiments conducted on its behalf. These reside equally in devising as precise a definition as possible of its objectives and in the plotting of a strategy to bring these about.

Thus, while this century is drawing to its conclusion and ought, according to the predictions of some of these socialist "prophets," to have witnessed the attainment of the "emancipation of humankind," we are in a position to state, without fear of contradiction, alas, that the promises that this century inspired at its beginning have not been honored. In particular, it is becoming more and more apparent that the extraordinary technological and scientific development that has marked our times has brought only bitter disappointments or tragic disillusionment to those who staked their hopes for liberation upon such advances. In the face of the obstinacy of facts, History has marked time and gone into a spin only to skid in every direction. Whenever its mask has fallen away, it has been noticeable that the grand preludes to revolution have been followed by pale, ordinary dawns.

In view of such dawns, far from radiant and choral, are we to conclude that the very notion of social revolution has become obsolete? Absolutely not. Speaking for ourselves, we are convinced that it remains, instead, the sole prospect for a *genuinely* humane society. And this regardless of the nitpickers, obscurantists and brainwashers of every type: in spite of fashions and fads, the socialist disguises and Marxist-Leninist crimes; despite the renegades from their class, the indifferent and the apolitical know-nothings who imagine that they can escape unscathed by holding aloof from social warfare.

But how are we to explain away the deviation and repeated setbacks suffered by the revolutionary ideal, its fall into disgrace and the "globally negative" verdict passed against it by a large segment of the earth's population? The correct answer to that would require a protracted and minute scrutiny of a whole series of factors and disparate influences. We hope ultimately to conduct such an inquiry, but for now, we shall make do with offering a few, very condensed comments.

First of all, there was a certain confusion surrounding the very notion of revolution. Socialist ideologues took it as synonymous sometimes with the "right to work" (1848), sometimes with the worker's right to the full product of his labor, then with mere rational organization of a society of producers, or even, first and foremost, prior conquest of the power of the state. The object being to set the tiller of society for a course suited to the interests of the "most numerous and largest" class — the proletariat — but in fact entrusting it to the care of those charged with representing its "historic calling." This trend fostered the emergence of a new "socialist" class: the Capitalists of Expertise or brain-workers.

Whenever one looks at the result of this deep-seated infatuation with industrial growth, one finds that it has brought the workers on the ground only crumbs, rendering their lot, certainly, more bearable than before, but every whit as precarious, as we today can readily appreciate. This aspiration to mere "administration of things" by good "governance of men" has been dependent in the minds of socialists and their acolytes upon a "catastrophist" analysis of the evolutionary trend of the capitalist system. The latter being destined, by their reckoning, for an early grave, as the victim of its countless contradictions, all that was needed was patience and that became the cardinal virtue of "scientific" socialism. It ought to be stated and stressed that this creed was shared, in a different form, by anarchists and honest revolutionaries, as well as by a goodly number of proletarians. Hence, by contrast, their impatience and their somewhat naive belief in a spontaneous revolution and immediate transformation of social relationships. They were encouraged in this course by those who declined to "legislate for the future." That was an astute and profitable ploy for disguising the ambition of a new ruling class and for dodging the issue of the real balance of forces existing between the revolutionaries and their designated or potential enemies. This sapping of vigilance led many proletarians to hurl themselves, often recklessly, into insurrectionist ventures. And this without their being sufficiently conversant with or critical of the orientation of their efforts or the recuperation of the gains achieved through their struggles by the new enemies within, who had been unduly underestimated up to that point. This could be seen at the time of the great workers' bloodletting in June 1848, the Paris Commune, Russia and the Ukraine in 1917–1921 and latterly in Spain in 1936–1939.

We should also note that a concentration upon economic conditions, these being regarded ultimately as the keystone of any overhauling of society, has gone hand in glove with ascendancy of the gregarious element over the individual, thereby banishing a more comprehensive, subversive appreciation of the relations of domination. Anarchism alone has been the exception to this, since it has instead taken the circumstances of the individual as its revolutionary project's point of departure and arrival. According to the anarchist viewpoint, the individual is more than just a producer and a consumer: he is also a human being endowed with a critical awareness and aspiring to social harmony through the interplay of individual autonomies.

The lack of precision in the ideologies of the nineteenth century has been mirrored in the "dance of labels": turn and turn about, each faction has styled itself "Collectivist," "Revolutionary-Socialist," "Communist" and "Social Democratic" until the process of decanting has left us with the exponents of a supposedly "scientific" state socialism and the federalist autonomists, who went on to become the anarchists or libertarian communists. Thus, the former were long convinced that capitalism's collapse was inevitable given the simple ripening of objective conditions, and that this merely needed speeding up a little by taking control of the state machinery. It is as plain as day that the system has proved itself livelier than anticipated and that it has even managed to recuperate all this feigned contestation in an intelligent manner. As for the conquest of state power, it has merely led socialists of every hue to perpetual denials, by dint of huge concessions, compromises and quite simply shameful compacts with the virtual enemy — the capitalist bourgeoisie — while purporting, say, to run capitalism better than the capitalists! All to the detriment of their ultimate aims, which are endlessly postponed to a more distant and indefinite future date.

In the view of one segment of these state socialists, as the system has refused to perish, it has become a matter of urgent necessity that the subjective conditions of the proletarian "Prometheus" be taken in hand and his endeavors overseen. So it was that the Blanquist concept of the revolutionary minority, overhauled and done up in "sauce tartare" by Lenin, spawned an organization of a new type: the Bolshevik party. Regarding itself as the sole repository of the historical interests of the industrial proletariat, and therefore awarding itself the right to act on its behalf and in its place, this party imposed itself sixty odd years ago, exercising a preferential option over the whole world revolutionary movement. With the disastrous results of its hegemony we are all familiar: everywhere that it succeeded, it has, far from eradicating economic and social inequality, merely added to and entrenched it. Weak and aging autocrats have been supplanted by ruthless and all-powerful party-crats. In short, the class struggle which started life with an eye to liberation, has, among the state socialists, reformists and totalitarians alike, turned into a commonplace "competition for office." A pleasing but very telling formula.

As regards the second factor in our alternative — the subject of this book — which is to say the anarchists or libertarian communists, they have always called for the direct assumption by the exploited of control of their fates, quite independently of any party or state tutelage. Along with the abolition of private and state capitalism alike, as well as elimination of all forms of political domination, so that these may be replaced by an economic and social arrangement wherein the production of consumer goods and human relationships would be directly related to the real needs and wishes of men and women, banded together into freely federated autonomous communes. For a long time this ideal has been dismissed as utopian, but it was implemented on a trial basis — and in spite of extremely difficult circumstances — during two revolutionary experiments, one in the eastern Ukraine in 1917–1921, and the other in libertarian Spain in 1936–1939. This demonstrated that the utopians were not the ones so considered, but rather the ones who reckoned that everything could go on as before, with the system of exploitation undergoing a little tinkering here and there: which boils down in fact to keeping it alive and endlessly fending off its inevitable collapse.

Yet, although anarchism emerged as the radical factor of a genuinely revolutionary vision and though its critical contentions have been borne out repeatedly by historical trends and thus retain their incontestable actuality, the methods advocated and the organizational practice espoused have sometimes led to misunderstandings or even to impasses. Coherence and cohesion have frequently been lacking. And that is the nub of the problem. Torn between strident individual autonomy and a sometimes lumbering collective approach, libertarians have regularly failed to leave a definitive liberating imprint upon events and upon the movement of history. Can this shortcoming be attributed to an unfavorable setting, to inescapable objective laws, to human nature, or is it to be put down to a congenital handicap, some "soft underbelly" in the doctrine and to a deficiency that is susceptible to remedy? We might launch into a lengthy dissertation upon each side of the argument, but anarchist ideas are rooted chiefly in the will to be and to do in each and every one of us. Thus, it seems to us to be a matter of priority that we should seek out the subjective explanations for this defect by means of an exploration of anarchist thinking, as demonstrated over the past century or more, marrying this closely to the sundry social and practical organizational experiences which it may have spawned. It will be no part of our intention to offer a complete inventory of anarchist ideas, but rather to focus upon some of the clearest expressions of these, most closely associated with the revolutionary project. We shall of course be setting these in the social and historical contexts from which they could not be isolated in any case, and our emphasis shall be upon the stumbling blocks and obstacles that they have encountered. In the light of that thoroughgoing investigation, we will then attempt to update the facts of the matter.

## II. FROM STIRNER'S INDIVIDUAL TO PROUDHON'S PRODUCERS

Anarchist ideas surfaced during the 1840s, by way of a backlash against the socialist and communist professions of faith that had recently come into vogue. Let us note the paradox: the latter were conceived in opposition to "bourgeois" individualism, and they sought the good of the "greatest number." In turn, anarchism made a stand against the societal pretension to overrule the individual and called for him to be freed from the constraints of the mass-state. In the estimations of Stirner and Proudhon who best expressed that backlash at the time, the individual is a flesh and blood being, the basic unit of society, a nonpareil, having nothing in common with the abstract "complete" man of historical or religious evolution whom the advocates of communitarian or statist gregariousness, to wit, the Saint-Simonians, Fourierists, Cabetians and other ideologues of sociability, had sought to impose. Especially as, in the vision of the latter, certain individuals had been destined to play a special, elite role, as "prophets" in short, and, as such, had a definite tendency to claim certain merit for themselves and a destiny that, in the long run, turned them into a caste or ruling class. Pending the advent of the paradisiacal promised land of the communist society, you understand.

Stirner adopted a quite different tack: as far as he was concerned, the individual was the "unique one," the "egoist" operating in accordance with self-interest, without thereby trespassing against the interests of others or ruling out any form of freely embraced association, but refusing state supervision in any guise. Such association was a contract entered into with other autonomous individuals, on a basis of absolute reciprocity and for a specified duration, being therefore subject to cancellation at any time:

> If I can make use [of some other being] I come to an arrangement with him and I join with him, so as to bolster my power by means of such arrangement, and accomplish more, thanks to our conjoined strength, I see absolutely nothing in that other than a multiplication of my capability and I let it endure only as long as it represents a multiplication of my capability. But, thus understood, that is association.[1]

Stirner's individual is no longer a "labor force" subject to the will of the collectivity: he "makes use of association and abandons it without a care for duty or loyalty, once he reckons that there is no longer any advantage to be derived from it." There is no implication there of sacrifice, for he gives his consent solely where he stands to benefit, out of self-interest. As far as sacrifice is concerned, he "sacrifices only that which is not within his power, which is to say he sacrifices nothing at all."

We should point out that Stirner drew a distinction between revolution and revolt. Whereas the former:

> …comprises an overturning of conditions, of an existing state of affairs (status quo) regarding the State or society, it is in consequence a *political* or *social* act. To be sure, the second has as its inescapable consequence a transformation of conditions, but it does not spring from that. Finding its origin in men's dissatisfaction with themselves, it is no strapping-on of shields, but rather a revolt of individuals, an uprising heedless of the *institutions* which might arise out of it. The revolution has as its object new *institutions*, but revolt induces us to no longer *countenance* being organized, but to look instead to self-organization and invest no glowing hopes in "institutions." It is a fight against the established order, then, since, in the event of success, this collapses unaided, so it is merely the difficult extraction of the self from that order.

Whereas, in the view of Stirner, the labor force of the individual ought to free itself from the tutelage of society, Proudhon espoused the line that the individual is, above all, the producer who is dispossessed of his product by the bourgeoisie, the ruling class. Proudhon believes in the validity of the association and federation of men, who, after having built up with one another their producers' and consumers' groupings, in accordance with their needs and wishes, represent a collective strength inimical to the state and the proprietors. Once these latter have been stripped of their privileges, their power will be exhausted and the exploitation of man will give way to a society cleansed of all government: Anarchy.

Again, Proudhon's line was that each individual is "unique" in his way: he is possessed of a basic capability: his will — his free choice — which creates the aspiration to dignity and independence and represents the *indispensable* condition for his freedom:

> It should not be thought, as the contemporary communists or socialists do, that man has value only thanks to society, that he is the product thereof, that it confers a function, a specialization upon him, that he is indebted to it for everything and that it owes him nothing. That arrangement leads on to *the demise of the personality,* to Oriental or Caesarist absolutism. It enslaves the individual, so that the mass may be free. That is tyranny, not association. No example exists of a community which, having been founded in enthusiasm, has not ended in imbecility.[2]

These extremely lucid words have since assumed a lot of import and they breathe new life into the interest one might bring to a man who could still write that "man does not wish to be organized, mechanized: his inclination is for disorganization, for restoration of the element of chance."[3]

This approach is underpinned by his ethical intent: the "dignity" and integrity of each individual, in the name of a justice defined as "spontaneously generated and reciprocally guaranteed respect for human dignity, regardless of the person or the circumstance involved and of whatever the risk to which its defense exposes us."[4] Such an appreciation establishes between men a bond of connection and solidarity that lays the foundation for real fraternity among them, assured by mutual consideration for their autonomy as individuals.

In a broader context, it is no longer a matter of social harmony between all existing classes, nor of association between capital and labor, but, instead, of irreconcilable opposition between them, of the imperishable contest between them. Here, Proudhon finds himself in the company of Marx, upon whom he undoubtedly exercised an influence: the affirmation of an absolute struggle between classes, the importance of labor, the development of the forces of production and relations of production, the role of science, the ideo-realist principle (which may be taken as equivalent to the materialist conception of history in Marx). In addition, they subscribed in common to a deep-seated atheism (although in the one the part of providence was taken by the quest for justice, and, in the other, by the direction of history). Despite these analytical coincidences, they were nonetheless divided by a tremendous disagreement: the finality of the class struggle. Marx regarded this as merely an historical permutation whereby the proletariat supplants a bourgeoisie that has begun to falter or defaulted upon its progressive vocation: in spite of all of which, its gains retain their validity. Proudhon's view was that it spelled a profound and irremediable breach: the bourgeoisie's role has come to an end and it is at *its* expense that the proletariat must advance, by moving outside of the bourgeoisie's terrain and being careful not to prop it up by getting involved in its shams of democracy. Here we have the inception of the notion of abstention from politics and the idea of all-out struggle on the economic terrain: hence the necessity of the working class being organized beyond the dominant influence and of its autonomous development receiving every encouragement. A precept that led first to anarchist theory and later to revolutionary syndicalism. The Proudhonian formula, "the workshop must supplant government," encapsulates this outlook. It is also to be noted that whereas in the view of Marx the proletariat was represented exclusively by the workers in large industry, Proudhon extended the definition to include the workers in small undertakings, the poor peasantry and virtually small craftsmen with no employees.

Shortly before his death, Proudhon was to review his creed: "All my economic ideas, elaborated over a period of twenty-five years, can be summed up in these three words: *agricultural-industrial federation*; all of my political views can be stripped down to a similar formula: *political federation* or *decentralization*."[5]

In order to encompass that goal, he advocated "the initiative of the masses, through a concert of citizenry, through the experience of the workers, through the onward march and diffusion of enlightenment, revolution through freedom." By means of a sequence of revolutionary acts, one will arrive at "the abolition of all powers, spiritual, temporal, legislative, executive, judicial and proprietorial."[6] The collective strength that he calls for is like the double of the "multiplied strength" of Stirner's Egos, albeit conceived in more enduring terms and temporally and spatially more systematic. This is why we find him deploring the failure in 1848 of the Clubs (popular societies par excellence just like the sections of 1793, likewise pre-figuring the Russian soviets) to play a more significant role, and that it occurred to no one to develop and strengthen them.

Thereabouts or just after, several 1848ers put their signatures to the birth certificate of anarchy. We might mention the *Manifeste de l'anarchie* (Manifesto of Anarchy) of Anselme Bellegarrigue, the very first anarchist periodical, published in 1850, wherein the writer targets voluntary servitude, very much in the tradition of Etienne de la Boétie: "Up to this very day, you thought that there were such things as tyrants! Well, you were mistaken; there are only slaves: where none obeys, none commands."[7]

As for Joseph Déjacque, he vehemently and poetically abused hierarchy and its muse, authority: "You toothless hag, tight-fisted shrew, snake-wreathed Medusa, Authority! Get thee behind me, and make way for freedom!... Make way for the people in direct possession of their sovereignty, for the organized commune."[8] As an emigrant to the United States, Déjacque was to launch a French language newspaper in New Orleans called *Le Libertaire*, forerunner of the journal of the same name set up in 1895 by Sébastien Faure and Louise Michel.

The better to appreciate the import and interest of these libertarian beliefs, let us recall the circumstances of the time: France was suffering under the reaction led by Louis Napoleon; slavery for blacks was still the rule in the United States; the serfdom of the Russian "white negroes" would persist until 1861 in the empire of the tsar; industrial mechanization was proceeding by leaps and bounds, as was the penal servitude in the factory; in the arts, the blandest academicism ruled the roost and among the most "advanced' social teachings, the church party and state socialism predominated. In short, the outlook was more than bleak.

## Endnotes to Chapter Two.

1. Max Stirner, *L'unique et sa propriété,* Oeuvres Complétes, Lausanne, Ed. L'Age d' Homme, 1972, pp. 347 et seq.

2. P. J. Proudhon, *De la justice dans la révolution et l'Eglise* (Paris, 1858) Tome 1, p. 117.

3. Ibid., Tome III., p. 228.

4. Ibid., Tome I, p. 225.

5. P. J. Proudhon, *Du principe fédératif Paris,* 1957, Riviére, p. 361.

6. P. J. Proudhon *Confessions d'un révolutionnaire pour servir à l'histoire de la révolution de février* (Paris, 1852) p. 35 and 37.

7. A. Bellegarrigue, *L'Anarchie, journal de l'ordre* (Paris, No. 1, April 1850) p. 6.

8. J. Déjacque, *A bas les chefs!* (Paris: Champ Libre, 1971) (La question révolutionnaire) p. 47.

# III. BAKUNIN: THE PROGRAMS OF REVOLUTIONARY ANARCHISM

It was at this point that the man dubbed "the demon of revolt" burst upon the revolutionary scene in Europe, a man who was profoundly to tax the minds of his day: Mikhail Bakunin. A veteran of the barricades in 1848, sentenced to death, then reprieved thrice over, imprisoned for eight years, he managed in 1861 to escape from his exile in Siberia. Far from being broken by his lengthy period in detention, he threw himself recklessly into the revolutionary fray. After an unsuccessful attempt at a landing in Poland with an eye to bringing assistance to local insurgents, he visited London in 1864. There he met Marx, at the latter's request, and Marx suggested to him that he join the nascent International. The encounter was a friendly one: Marx excused himself from the charge that he had peddled slanders about his interlocutor. In addition, he wrote to Engels a short while after that the Russian fugitive "pleased [him] greatly, I found him improved on his former self ... in short, he is one of those rare men whom I have met after 16 years who has moved forward and not gone backwards."[1] There was no hint of the formidable quarrel that would soon see them pitted one against the other.

Bakunin did not join the International right away, for he was preoccupied with the prospects of more immediate action and still believed in the formula of secret organization, which had been a widespread option for decades. It goes without saying here that in those days there was no country in which it was possible openly to profess revolutionary opinions. So he traveled to Italy, which he reckoned might be fertile ground for his schemes, and devoted all of his energies to organizing national and international networks. To this end, he drew up several programs and charters for secret societies: in several languages and sometimes with variations. All of these writings were of course in manuscript form and for a long time they were to remain scattered among Bakunin's correspondents and friends. It is only recently that most of these have been made accessible to the public. They cover the years between 1864 and 1872 and have thus far been little used by biographers of Bakunin. As a result, his organizational activities have remained little known. For that reason we shall be dwelling a little upon them.

The earliest program, dating from 1864, the so-called Florence program, is a program for the "International Revolutionary Brotherhood" or "Alliance."

According to his biographer, H. E. Kaminsky, this text of Bakunin's is, for anarchism, the "companion piece" to Marx's *The Communist Manifesto*.[2] Indeed, taking up and radicalizing Proudhon's analyses and positions, Bakunin laid down the basic principles of revolutionary anarchism. This text has been underrated for the good reason that it remained for a long time in manuscript, until Max Nettlau reprinted it in copygraph form in his monumental study and some biographers began to take note of it. Given the import of this foundation charter, we reckon we might be well-advised to quote lengthy extracts from it.

Finding fault with the religiosity of Mazzini and other social clericalists, Bakunin asserts that the first duty of the revolutionary is to be atheistic and to demand on behalf of the world and of man "all that religions have located in the heavens and attributed to their deities." Following which, morality, stripped of "all theology and all divine metaphysics" has no source other than the "collective conscience of men." Inimical to the "principle of authority" and all its applications and implications, "both in the realm of the intellect and morality, and in the realm of politics, economics and society," the revolutionary anarchist acknowledges that justice is embodied in "realization of the fullest freedom and most perfect equality in law and in fact."

In one passage of remarkable transparency, he defines the anarchist conception of social and political organization:

> He [the revolutionary] should be federalist like us, both within his country and without. He should understand that the advent of liberty is incompatible with the existence of states. Consequently, he should desire the destruction of all states and at the same time that of all religious, political and social institutions: such as formal churches, standing armies, centralized authorities, governments, unitary parliaments, state universities and banks, as well as aristocratic and bourgeois monopolies. So that upon the ruins of them all there may be erected the free society of men, which will no longer be organized, as is presently the case, from the top down and from center to circumference, along lines of enforced unity and concentration, but rather upon a basis of the free individual, free association and the autonomous commune, from the ground up and from circumference to center, along lines of free federation.
>
> In theory as well as in practice, and in the fullness of its consequences, he must embrace this principle: every individual, every association, every commune, every province, every region and every nation enjoys an absolute right of self-determination, of association or non-association, of allying itself with whomsoever it may choose and of breaking off its alliances without any regard for so-called historical rights, or the convenience of its neighbors; and let him be firm in his conviction that only when they are formed by the omnipotence of their inherent attractions and needs, natural and consecrated by freedom, will new federations of communes, provinces, regions and nations become truly strong, fecund and indissoluble. [3]

FACING THE ENEMY

Let us look at another passage where the rights of nationhood are analyzed in the most up-to-the-minute fashion:

> Thus [the would-be member of the Alliance] must reduce the so-called nationality principle, an ambiguous principle, replete with hypocrisy and snares, the principle of the historic, ambitious state, to the much greater, simpler and sole legitimate principle of liberty: each individual or collective body, being free or deserving freedom, and no one has the right to impose his dress, his customs, his language, his opinions and his laws upon him; each should be absolutely free in his home.

It goes without saying that this national freedom does not lead to a "parish patriotism": quite the opposite:

> All such narrow, ridiculous, freedom-killing and consequently criminal notions of greatness, ambition and national glory, good only for the monarchy and the oligarchy, are today equally good for the big bourgeoisie, because they serve their purpose in deceiving the peoples and exciting them one against the other, the better to enslave them.

And another crucial point:

> As labor is the sole producer of society's wealth, anyone who enjoys it without working is an exploiter of another man's labor, a thief, and as labor is the fundamental basis of human dignity, the only means whereby man truly wins and creates his freedom, all political and social rights should henceforth belong to workers only.

There we find the guideline from which revolutionary syndicalism was to spring.

Similarly, with regard to the peasant problem:

> The land, nature's free gift to every man, cannot be and must not be the property of any man. But its fruits, as the products of labor, should go only to those who till it with their own hands.

Let us underline the break with Proudhon's patriarchal and familial outlook: woman and child are deemed individuals equal to man in every particular:

> Woman, different from man, but not his inferior, intelligent, hard-working and free as he is, must be declared his equal in all political and social rights: in the free society, religious and civil marriage should be replaced by free marriage and the upkeep, education and instruction of all children should be borne equally by everybody, at society's expense, without the latter's having need, in protecting them against both stupidity and negligence, or the ill-will of the parents, to take them away from these, children belonging neither to society, nor to their parents, but to their future freedom.

On the subject of freedom, let us take note of this passage where Bakunin offers this very splendid definition of it:

It is untrue that a man's freedom is curtailed by that of all other men. Man is not truly free except when his freedom, freely acknowledged and reflected, as if by a looking-glass, by the free conscience of all other men, discovers in their freedom confirmation of its infinite extension. Man is truly free only in the midst of other equally free men: and as he is free only insofar as he is human, the enslavement of just one man on earth, being an offense against the very principle of humanity, is a negation of the freedom of all.

Thus, the freedom of the individual is attainable only in a context of equality of all. The attainment of freedom in equality in law and in fact is justice.

Apropos of the realization of the social revolution, one might think that the Paris Commune of 1871 had been inspired by the plan drawn up by Bakunin:

Even as it takes root everywhere, the revolution will of necessity assume a federalist character. Immediately following the overthrow of the established government, communes will have to reorganize themselves along revolutionary lines, equipping themselves with leaders, an administration and courts that are revolutionary, built upon universal suffrage and upon the real accountability of all officials to the people. In order to defend the revolution, their volunteers will at the same time serve as a communal militia.

However, no commune was to be left isolated, else it would perish and so it stood in "need of spreading the revolution beyond, of raising rebellion in all neighboring communes and, as these rise up, of federating with them for the sake of their common defense." The delegates or deputies sent out by each commune to "an agreed meeting point" were to be "invested with imperative mandates, accountable and liable to recall." "Revolutionary propagandists" and not "official revolutionary commissars with sashes of any sort" were to be dispatched to the provinces and to all insurgent communes and associations.

Let us underline that nearly all these standpoints and all the principles set out were not the personal inventions of Bakunin: for the most part, they had been subterranean devices since 1830. On the other hand, the expression given to them and the synthesizing of them all were quite new and this was no coincidence: Bakunin had read widely among Saint-Simonian, Fourierist and Proudhonian writings. Furthermore, he had been "enlightened" by his personal experiences of 1848. So it was under the inspiration of theoretical maturation and the fruits of social experimentation that he drafted the program.

Bakunin drafted another version of this program for some Swedish friends: it was from Sweden, in fact, that he had mounted his expedition to bring reinforcements to Poland, at the time of the 1863 rising and he was concerned to retain logistical support for further actions regarding Russia. An explanation is required of the secret form of organization advocated: given the circumstances of the day, that was the only practical chance for those who sought to change the world. In addition, Bakunin had been influenced by a brief and disappointing flirtation with Freemasonry, and above all by the conspiratorial usages of the former Mazzinian Italians who had defected to him. Deep down, he believed only in mass action and retained his June 1848 views on that subject: however, by his reckoning, it was vital that there should be some secret organization in existence to serve as a sort of … general staff" in the revolution. An anonymous and secret general staff that would take great care not to supplant the people in its struggle for emancipation. In this, it was very clearly differentiated from the Blanquist type of secret society, "which was governed quite differently and organized in a quite despotic fashion, worthy of the imperious mind of Louis [Blanqui]." The intent of the Bakuninist project was utterly different: it was not a matter of establishing the dictatorship of one man or of a group of conspirators, nor of one place or town over the rest: absolute, and so to speak, dictatorial centralization was out of the question:

> I want the order and calm in affairs to be the result, not of a single will, but of the collective wish of lots of associates scattered through each country and every country. This is to be replaced with the covert but powerful action of all concerned the lead of a single center.... — But for this decentralization to become possible a real organization is needed, and there is no organization without a degree of regulation — which is, in the end, nothing but the outcome of a compact or mutual undertaking.[4]

In addition, the approach was also a stark contrast: the ultimate aims of Bakunin's Brotherhood were openly declared, and the shroud of secrecy extended only to the means. Whereas everything was a secret among the Blanquists: ultimate aims, methods and internal structures alike, all were in the ken of just one man — the revolutionary dictator — an idea inherited directly from the Jacobins and from Babeuf.

In a later program for the secret revolutionary organization, the "International Brotherhood" (1868), Bakunin rounded even more violently on the Jacobin or Blanquist conception of revolution. It was a critique of which we can, with hindsight, note the still telling accuracy:

> We should not be surprised if the Jacobins and the Blanquists who have become socialists more through necessity than through conviction, and for whom socialism is a means and not the end of the Revolution, since they desire dictatorship, which is to say, centralization of the state and since the state will lead them by inevitable, logical necessity to a reconstitution of property, it is only natural, we say, that, not wishing to make a radical revolution against things, they dream of bloody revolution against men. But such a bloody revolution rooted in

construction of a mightily centralized revolutionary state would have as its inevitable outcome, as we will prove anon, the military dictatorship of a new master. So victory for the Jacobins or Blanquists would be the death of the Revolution.

We are the natural enemies of these revolutionaries, these future dictators, regulators and tutors of the Revolution, who, even before the present monarchist, aristocratic and bourgeois states have been destroyed, are already dreaming of the creation of new, revolutionary states every bit as centralistic as and more despotic than the states in existence today, and are so habituated to the order created by some authority from the top down, and have such a tremendous horror of what strikes them as disorders and which are nothing more than frank, natural expression of popular life, that even before a good, salutary disorder is produced by revolution, they are already dreaming of the termination and muzzling of it through the action of some authority that will have nothing revolutionary about it except the name, but which will in effect be nothing more than a new reaction in that it will be in fact a further sentencing of the masses of the people governed by decrees, to obedience, to immobility, to death, that is, to enslavement and exploitation by a new, quasi-revolutionary aristocracy.[5]

## Endnotes to Chapter Three

1. Quoted by Jean Ionguet (Marx's grandson) in *La politique internationale du Marxisme* (Paris 1918) p. 130.
2. H. E. Kaminsky, *Bakounine, la vie d'un révolutionnaire* (Paris: Aubier-Montaigne, 1938), p. 213.
3. Program reprinted by Daniel Guérin in his anthology *Ni Dieu, Ni Maître* (Paris: Maspéro, Tome I), pp. 167–223.
4. M. Bakounine, *De la guerre à la Commune* (Paris: Anthropos, 1972). Letter of December 4, 1868 to A. Richard, pp. 435–436.
5. Guérin, ed. *Ni Dieu, Ni Maître* p. 219.

# IV. BAKUNINIST ORGANIZATION

Bakuninist organization was designed only to embrace around a hundred international brethren, plus a variable number of national brethren in each of the countries of Europe, at most two or three hundred for the largest one. These were profiled as "committed, energetic, intelligent individuals and above all sincere friends of the people, and not ambitious or vain types, persons capable of serving as intermediaries between the revolutionary idea and popular instincts."

Moved by an ethical zeal, these revolutionaries were to wield "not some ostensible power, but a collective dictatorship of all Alliance members ... a dictatorship with no sashes, no titles, no formal rights and all the more powerful for having none of the appearances of power." [1]

Although Bakunin is careful to stipulate that "if you while away your time playing at Committees of Public Safety and at formal dictatorship, you will be gobbled up by the reaction that you yourselves will have created," the use of the term "dictatorship," even when drained of all meaning by the context in which it was used, lends itself to all sorts of ambiguities. Let us take a look at Arthur Lehning's view of these "invisible pilots in the eye of the revolutionary storm":

> Bakunin was concerned with inspiring with his ideas a tiny band of men of real, effective impact, but also with communicating to them his lust for action. They in turn had to operate in the quarters and at the level where they engaged in their activities, that is, in the context of the organization and principles of the International. The innermost circle consulted with one another and with Bakunin. In this way, he was in touch with militants from a variety of countries and maintained personal relations with them either through correspondence or through occasional encounters. He was thus able to coordinate propaganda and, if need be, action. In the labor movement and especially in the revolutionary movement, there was nothing out of the ordinary about this mode of operating. [2]

James Guillaume, a close associate of Bakunin, bears witness to the nature of this organization, which had nothing in common with the old secret societies where one was obliged "to obey orders coming from above." This one was simply the "free coming together of men who joined forces for collective action, without formalities, without solemnity, without mysterious rites, simply because they trusted one another and agreement struck them as preferable to acting in isolation."[3]

In the Bakuninist organization, the bond between one member and another was trust. If it were to be infiltrated by one spiteful member, the whole edifice would thereby be contaminated. Bakunin discovered this to his cost, following his dealings with Sergei Netchaiev. Russian, son of a serf, a student persecuted by the tsarist government, Netchaiev nurtured a deadly hatred for the whole established order and balked at no method, conscionable or otherwise, provided it could be of service to his ultimate objective: the destruction and eradication of tsarism. He began by immersing himself in the student opposition campaigns and then, once having secured control over these, diverted them into a huge conspiracy against the regime. He even scheduled a date for the decisive uprising — 1870 — quite a plausible date, for that was the year when the peasants, recently freed from serfdom, still faced a heavy burden in the requirement upon them to buy back their own land from their erstwhile masters. Casting around for support and backing for his plans, Netchaiev arrived in Switzerland, met Bakunin there and, painting him a glowing picture of an apocalyptic uprising in the land of his birth, bamboozled him and abused his trust: he got his hands on a substantial sum (the Bakhmetiev fund) and enmeshed the old rebel in his questionable intrigues.

On his return to Russia, the long-awaited great day failed to dawn, and, caught in a trap of his own making, Netchaiev murdered a student whose only offense had been to question his authority and the substance of his schemes. A police investigation did not take long to shed light upon the sordid murder, thanks to the ready assistance of Netchaiev's own accomplices and, more tellingly, members of his organization.

The episode blew up into a tremendous scandal that tainted the entire Russian revolutionary milieu. Bakunin, especially, was accused of having incited Netchaiev, and he was credited with the paternity of *The Catechism of the Revolutionary*, a sort of Macchiavellian conspirator's handbook discovered on one of Netchaiev's accomplices. However, the tone and the content of this text have nothing in common with Bakunin's radicalism, especially in the notion of people's squalid manipulation of one another. The influence of the Russian Blanquist, Tkachev, and of the memoirs of the Babouvist Buonarotti upon the document has since been properly authenticated, especially in recent years, through the researches of Michael Confino, Arthur Lehning, Pirumova and the latest soviet biographer of Bakunin, Grafsky. Nonetheless, several Western historians, to this very day, persist in depicting Bakunin as the sire of Netchaiev's "Jacobin jesuitry."

In any event, Netchaiev managed to flee to Switzerland and offered a version of the case that presented himself in a more favorable light, accusing the murdered student of having sought to denounce him to the authorities. Despite that, Bakunin now saw through him and distanced himself from him in a crucial letter likewise uncovered just a few years ago by Michael Confino. Its concealment can be explained in terms of Bakunin's preoccupation with its not being made public property, lest it damage the scheming Netchaiev — who was in dire straits at the time, being threatened with extradition — out of what might be described as blind anti-tsarist solidarity.

In that letter of severance, Bakunin announces to Netchaiev that:

the system of mystification which has increasingly become your main and sole approach, your method and quintessential weapon, is disastrous for the cause itself ... But we have to organize this community of revolutionaries and moralize it. Whereas you, thanks to your system, are corrupting it and nurturing within it traitors to yourselves and exploiters of the people ... following the jesuitical system, you systematically kill every personal human sentiment, any personal feel for justice in them — as if sentiment and the sense of justice could be anything other than personal — you nurture falsehood, mistrust, grassing and betrayal in them.

Not that Bakunin tended to idealize "virtuous" revolutionaries: he had no illusions about them: they did not act out of pure "conscience, nor considered reasons," but because of their own situation in the society. If one were to place them in a:

situation where they might exploit and oppress the people: one could with certainty affirm that, yes, they will exploit and oppress it without a second thought. As a result, there are among them very few innately virtuous. Capitalizing upon the disastrous situation that makes them virtuous in spite of themselves, we should then arouse, educate and bolster that virtue in them, making it impassioned and conscious by dint of constant propaganda and by force of organization. Now, what you are doing is the precise opposite.

On this occasion, he redefined the aim and the missions of revolutionary organization: "to assist the people's self-determination on a basis of absolute equality, and full and multifarious human freedom, without the slightest interference from any authority, even should it be provisional or transitional, which is to say, without the mediation of any state." Yet again he recalled that we "are the sworn enemies of all formal power, even if it is a[n ultra-revolutionary] power: foes of any publicly acknowledged dictatorship, we are social-revolutionary anarchists."[4] In order to dispel any ambiguity, he vehemently reaffirmed that reciprocal trust between revolutionaries could only be established through:

absolute sincerity on the part of all members. All jesuitry is banished from their dealings, as are craven mistrust, perfidious monitoring, and spying and informing on one another: there must be an absence and strict prohibition of all criticism behind one's back. If a member has something to say against any other member, he should say it at the general meeting and in that member's presence. Joint and fraternal monitoring of each by all: a monitoring that is by no means irksome, petty-minded, nor above all rancorous, must replace your system of jesuitical inquisition, and become a moral education, a mainstay of the moral strength of each member and the groundwork for that mutual fraternal confidence upon which the entire inner and outer strength of the Society depends. [5]

However, he did grant Netchaiev that his jesuitical approach — lying, trickery, mystification and, as the need arose, violence — could be deployed against the enemy. This gives rise to another ambiguity, for the notion of "enemies" can fluctuate somewhat — as we have seen many a time since then — and, especially as a result of opposition, lots of erstwhile friends have been seen to turn into implacable enemies in the here and now, so it seems we should have our reservations about this, (assuredly circumstantial) concession that Bakunin made to Netchaiev.

In fact, after having probed the outer limits of his organizational principles, Bakunin appeals in the last resort to his absolute yardstick: ethical passion (a wink of the eye for Fourier). As the guiding light of the revolutionary's conscience and his actions, it is nonetheless dependent upon the sobering influence of the "fraternal monitoring of each by all," in such a way that "oneness of thought and action" may be achieved. However, those internal relations are not the stuff of imagination: far from it, they are governed by very specific statutes and regulations, in which Bakunin had invested his most scrupulous efforts.

For instance, let us look at the secret regulation of the "Alliance of Socialist Democracy," dating from 1868. The crucial structure is represented by the "Standing Central Committee," of which the General Assembly is the highest expression. Members are inducted only if unanimously endorsed. A central bureau a few members strong represents the Alliance's executive organ — outside of the General Assemblies of the Central Committee at any rate — it has especial charge of keeping in contact with the national committees and bureaus, if need be sending them extraordinary delegates for the purposes of propaganda or action, as requested by the central branch. A complementary structure, the Vigilance Committee, sees to it that no one exceeds his mandate. One of the tasks entrusted to it was to draw as many labor organizations as possible into the International Workingmen's Association, so that the Alliance's work "may be confined to the political and revolutionary development of said Association."

The regulations of the "International Brotherhood," another of Bakunin's organizations, adopted essentially the same model of internal operation, except that the general assemblies became congresses required to attract a majority of the membership and disbarred from reaching decisions except by simple majority vote in the case of day-to-day business, or a two-thirds majority in matters of importance. The Central Committee and National Committees remained: the latter could be broken down into an Executive Bureau and a Vigilance Committee. A unanimous vote was required for the admission of new brethren. The National Committee was deemed based on three brethren from among the membership. Expulsions were decided by a simple majority, but were required in every instance to be ratified by the ensuing Congress.

In a later program for that same International Brotherhood, Bakunin notes that preparing for the revolution is not the sole mission of this organization. Even when the revolution gets underway, it will have to remain in existence so that it may substitute its strictly concerted and covert collective action for "any government or formal dictatorship, the latter being inevitably impelled to stamp out the revolutionary movement in the masses and to result in the reconstruction of the political, directorial, tutelary and thus necessarily bureaucratic, military, oppressor and exploiter state — which is to say of a new bourgeois rule." Yet another remarkable intuition about an appreciation of the necessity for an enduring revolutionary organization, dedicated to critical monitoring activity.

A little further into the same program, Bakunin spells out the supreme law on which his approach to organization is founded:

> always and everywhere to substitute collective thinking and collective action for all individual ventures [for, in his eyes] in the social revolution, there will be room only for collective thinking, resolution and action. [6]

On the basis of all this data, we now have a fairly clear appreciation of what Bakunin's organizations or Brotherhoods might have been: in fact, they amounted, given the circumstances of the times, to specifically anarchist organizations and, indeed, in the estimation of some, furnish the prototype for libertarian communist organization such as we today might conceive of it.

It is plain that as far as Bakunin was concerned this specific organization was to confine itself to its prescribed role as an "unseen" general staff. It never occurred to him that it should *replace* the effective action of the genuine revolutionary forces, namely, at that time, the workers and the most precarious segment of the proletariat, in the West, the lumpen-proletariat: in Russia, the peasants and vagabond outsiders, free Cossacks and déclassé individuals of every description, up to and including outlaws (not to be confused with the underworld in the Western sense of the term).

Apropos of the workers, he reiterated the Proudhonian line: they had to organize themselves "beyond the parameters of bourgeois radicalism." He further statated

> [The] basis for that organization is to hand: it is the workshops and the federation of workshops: the creation of strike funds, tools in the fight against the bourgeoisie, and federation of these not merely at

national level, but also internationally: and the creation of Chambers of Labor, as in Belgium. [7]

As for the Russian peasantry, he urges that they avail of the vestiges of the rural commune in order to proceed directly to the free society. He also registers the potential located in a segment of the young bourgeoisie and aristocracy, which may effectively commit itself to the revolution by "going to the people," that is, serving it through socially purposeful occupations such as teachers, doctors, agronomists, etc. Advice that was widely taken up in Russia around the time.

In Russia and in the West alike, all these writings by Bakunin wielded overwhelming influence in the 1870s. Which gives the lie to the view, (widespread among his political detractors or certain so-called "bourgeois" historians, eager to kowtow and hire their pens to the powerful of their day), according to which Bakunin was supposedly incapable of setting out his innermost thoughts on the aims and the means of social revolution in a coherent fashion. Lest we get marooned on the generalities, let us offer a sample of that school of "historians" which flourished during the years from 1950 to 1960, in the figure of Henri Arvon, "university lecturer, doctor of letters." This gentleman has made a specialty of assailing anarchism "from within," that is, making it the object of seemingly objective researches that are in point of fact very negative in outlook. Let us look at his little book *Michel Bakounine ou la vie contre la science* [*Mikhail Bakunin or Life versus Science*] … (quite a program there!). Let us lift from it a few telling passages:

> In the picturesque gallery of nineteenth century revolutionaries, Mikhail Bakunin, the "Storm petrel," appears to embody subversive activity with all of its romantically intoxicating and historically inefficacious self in the last century.… In 1870, he was the soul behind a rising in Lyons, thereby tasting for a few hours the intoxicating delights of quasi-dictatorial power … immediate and, it must be said, often disastrous consequences of that revolutionary activity.…" [And here comes the punch-line] "Seemingly bereft of all connection with a line of thought that would allow it to survive, Bakunin's teaching has an anachronistic, somewhat eccentric, and in certain respects reactionary ring to it in this day and age. [8]

Arvon of course credits him with the authorship of Netchaiev's *Revolutionary Catechism* and grants that he wanted to live up to its supposed device: "Full speed ahead into the mire." But let us look at a few more florid opinions:

> Riddled as it is with mistakes, Bakunin's thought … chaotic mind, prey to sometimes inadmissible passions[?] … the lode-stone utopia of Bakunin's teaching is anarchy.

From a reading of this philo-Stalinist diatribe, one can understand how such writers could have poisoned minds for decades against the nature and meaning of anarchist doctrine. Let us discard that "output" and note, paradoxically, that Bakunin has undergone a sort of rehabilitation at the hands of soviet historians in recent years. The latest study, by V.G. Grafsky, which appeared in 1985 plainly contradicts Arvon: Grafsky stresses the positive contribution of Bakunin to the struggle against tsarism and the underlying values of bourgeois society. His comment is supported by a dense exposition of his ideas and stances, often with the aid of generous quotations, and a few telling pages from *The Knouto-Germanic Empire* and *Statism and Anarchy* are given as appendices. Quite obviously, his differences with scientific socialism, which is to say, with Marx and Engels, are not glossed over but are in fact dealt with rather well. The innovation, Bakunin's anti-authoritarian socialism, is examined at some length. There is no snappy assessment but rather, as we said, an intentionally objective scientific evaluation. All the same, we should keep our feet on the ground, for this is the homage of an enemy, and, as behooves him in this instance, there is an unfavorable or patchy exposition of Bakunin's ideas, filtered through the Marxist-Leninist "lens":

> "Mikhail Aleksandrovich Bakunin, Russian revolutionary, is one of the most prominent representatives of revolutionary populism and anarchism. His genuine and impassioned hatred of all oppression and his readiness to give his all for the success of the social revolution drew many revolutionaries and persons of democratic leanings to his side. At the same time, his muddled and wholly illusory view of the concrete paths leading towards social emancipation helped turn him into an adversary of the ideas of scientific socialism.
>
> His name is linked with the birth and diffusion of the ideas of what is termed collectivist anarchism.... The strongest facets of his teachings were the denunciations of exploitation and of all the possible forms of oppression in contemporary societies, of religious obscurantism, the slavishness of liberal science as well as the advocacy of revolutionary methods of struggle versus bourgeois reformists. [9]

Grafsky finally justifies his choice of subject by invoking Bakunin's actuality, due to anarchism's resurgence in the West, which would, he suggests, account for the crisis by which the latter has been beset for some years now. In any event, let us note the respect and urge to explain that are nowhere to be found in Arvon's work, much less that of his colleague, Jacques Duclos, a GPU-loving messenger boy, who had strained his constipated bowels to bring us his *Ombres et lumière — Bakounine et Marx (Shadows and Light — Bakunin and Marx)*, better forgotten.

## Endnotes to Chapter Four

1. Bakunin, *Á la guerre de la Commune* op. cit., pp. 471–472.
2. *Archives Bakounine* published by Arthur Lehning, Leiden, 1961–1982, seven tomes published in eight volumes. That edition has been taken up by Editions Champ Libre under the

name *Oeuvres complètes de Bakounine* eight volumes so far. That being the most up-to-date text, it is the one we quote here. In the present instance the reference is to Volume 7, page XXXI.

3. James Guillaume, *L'internationale: Documents et souvenirs* Tome I, (Paris, 1905), p. 130.

4. Michael Confino, *Violence dans la violence*: *Le débat Bakounine-Netchaiev*, (Paris: Maspéro, 1973), pp. 106–149.

5. Ibid.

6. Bakunin, *Oeuvres Complètes,* Volume Six, p. 184–197 and 368–370.

7. Bakunin, *De la guerre á la Commune,* op. cit., p. 465.

8. Henri Arvon, *Bakounine* (1966), pp. 9–14. Among his other publications, we might point to Arvon's execrable book on anarchism in the "Que sais-je?" series. Lately, Arvon has turned out two books on the American (libertarian) Anarcho-capitalists. That "motherlode" must look a better bet to him than his Bakuninophobia!

9. V. C. Grafsky, *Bakunin* (in Russian) (Moscow, 1985), pp. 5–7 and 104–105.

# V. THE ALLIANCE, THE IWMA AND THE CLASH WITH MARX

While it may not be acceptable to Bakunin-hating historians as an extenuating circumstance, let us reiterate that most of the cited writings of Bakunin remained unknown until publication of the erudite works of Michael Confino and Arthur Lehning. Not that that prevented them from wielding undoubted influence over the people who were cognizant of them. The finest proof of this was the Alliance, which came to boast seventy International Brethren (out of a targeted one hundred) and in its Geneva branch in 1868 it included 145 members. It was its members also that founded the impressive Spanish section and the active Italian section, both of them affiliated to the IWMA.

In fact, following the refusal of the London-based General Council of the International Workingmen's Association to accede to the first application from the Alliance for admission en bloc, the latter decided to wind up its secret international organization and retained only its public section in Geneva. We know that Marx cited the continued existence of the secret Alliance as his chief ground for excluding Bakunin and James Guillaume. What was the real reason behind it? Whereas ongoing contacts between Alliance members persisted, largely on account of the personal relationships that had been struck up, and whereas the Spanish branch, the Alianza, held on to its clandestine structure (that being deemed well-suited to local conditions of struggle), it seems certain, according to Arthur Lehning, that the Alliance was no longer operating as a secret organization and, that, as a result, Marx's accusation was quite without foundation. Furthermore, it was not borne out by the report from the commission of inquiry established at the congress in The Hague, and Marx was forced to resort to making a personal allegation against Bakunin before he could be sure of the support of the members of that commission. Apropos of that, we should underline something that was going to have significant organizational repercussions: that celebrated five-strong commission of inquiry included an agent of the French police, Van Heddeghem (alias Walter) who, in fact, made himself scarce when the time came for presentation of the commission's report and a vote on it, either so as to leave that base task to "greater narks than him," or lest he attract attention to a minor figure like himself, for he was later to express regret that Benoit Malon had not been included in the "tumbrel" of those excluded. [1] We might add that among the "prosecution" witnesses called against

Bakunin and the Alliance there was yet another French provocateur, one Dentraygues (alias Swarm), likewise a member of the Marxist clique. We shall see anon the perverse and damaging effects of this police infiltration of the Marx camp.

It seems plain then that Bakunin's Alliance had indeed been wound up in its secret format. That said, the likelihood is that Marx was sincere in believing that it was still extant. He himself had been a member of several secret societies and, according to Arthur Lehning, Bakunin was similarly convinced in 1872 that Marx was still in clandestine concert with the six former members of the Communist League — the German secret society that had existed during the years 1847–1850 — who sat alongside him on the General Council in London at that time.[2] Moreover, Bakunin must assuredly have still had in mind the odd conversation that he had had with Marx in 1848:

> I met [Marx] in Berlin. Mutual friends forced us to embrace each other. [Bakunin had been accused by the Rhine Gazette then run by Marx of being a "Russian agent," so he bore him a grudge — author's note.] And then, in the middle of a conversation half in jest and half in earnest, Marx told me: "Are you aware that I am presently the head of a secret communist society so tightly disciplined that had I said to one of its members: 'Go kill Bakunin,' he would have killed you" to which I replied that if [his] secret society did [not] have anything better to do than kill people who displeased him, it could not be anything other than a society of lackeys or laughable braggarts.[3]

As we have seen, the Alliance was regarded by Bakunin as a specialist revolutionary organization, so we can now examine the terms in which he thought of his relationship with the IWMA, the mass labor organization (which by that point had nearly two million members, 1,200,000 of these in Europe):[4]

> The Alliance is the necessary complement to the International.... But the International and the Alliance, while pursuing the same ultimate goal, simultaneously pursue different aims. One has as its mission the gathering of the laboring masses, the millions of toilers, transcending differences of nation and country, into one immense, compact body: the other one, the Alliance, has as its mission the endowment of those masses with a genuinely revolutionary direction. The programs of them both, while not at all in conflict, are different even as the degree of their respective developments are different. That of the International, were it but taken seriously, enshrines in germ, but only in germ, the entire program of the Alliance. The Alliance's program is a further expounding upon the International's.[5]

Thus the International was intended only to marshal the laboring masses from the various trades bodies and from every country, on a broad political footing that was indeterminate, for had its "founders given to that great Association a ... socialist, philosophical, definite and positive political doctrine, they would have been in error." [6] In Bakunin's view then, it was a trade union international *ante literam*, having as its sole mission the defense of the working class's interests on its chosen terrain — the economic — and, thereafter, to nurse its class consciousness forwards in a revolutionary direction. That was no obstacle to the former members of the Alliance beavering away within it towards a radicalization of the movement as a whole: quite the opposite. But that was to reckon without Marx and the growing influence he wielded over the General Council in London. It was thus inevitable that they would clash.

We shall not be going into here all of the antagonisms and disagreements that set the two men one against the other, for that would take us too far from our subject, so we shall tackle only their differences in matters strategic and organizational.

Remember that in Marx's view the masterminding of the workers' movement could emanate only from the communists, they being:

> the most determined segment of the workers' parties, the faction that always gives a lead and above all which "from the point of view of theory" has this advantage over the rest of the proletarian mass, that it understands the conditions, progress and general outcomes of the workers' movement. [Furthermore, he argued, an] important part of the bourgeoisie is coming over to the proletariat, and in particular those among the bourgeois ideologues who have attained a theoretical grasp of the overall movement of history. [7]

It was plain then that, being unable to secrete its own leaders, the proletariat had to look to these "bourgeois ideologues" for guidance. On this point, Marx was merely abiding by the Jacobin and socialist tradition of the first half of the nineteenth century: so he could not help but espouse a centralistic organizational model and express utter incomprehension when Bakunin talked about "free organization of the laboring masses from the bottom up," and described that bluntly as "foolishness." [8] His activity within the ranks of the Communist League in 1848 demonstrated that choice: when some members got into difficulties with the German police, he inveigled some of his supporters into giving him carte blanche in deciding the organization's fate:

> ...The current circumstances imperiously require an energetic leader from the [communists'] society, for which a discretionary authority is, for the moment, an essential. [The Central Committee of the Society of Communists] determines:
> *Article 1:* The Central Committee is transferred to Paris.
> *Article 2:* Society member Karl Marx is hereby vested by the Brussels Central Committee with discretionary authority to assume temporary central control of all of the society's affairs, being answerable to the Central Committee that awaits establishment and to the forthcoming congress.

*Article 3:* The Committee charges Marx to establish in Paris, just as soon as circumstances will permit and from among the most suitable of the society's members, a new Central Committee of his choosing, and to draft on to it even those members of the society who may not be domiciled in Paris.

*Article 4:* The Brussels Central Committee is hereby disbanded.

Thus determined in Brussels, March 3, 1848.

The Central Committee [signatures of Engels, C. Fischer,<br>Cigot, H. Heingers, K. Marx][9]

A little while after that, Marx, along with Engels, announced that the organization had been wound up: they had not even consulted the rest of the membership! In that first day into organization one can just make out, beneath the surface, the approach that he was about to adopt inside the IWMA. His tack stayed the same, in keeping with what we might please to term his "narcissistic centralism!" Thus he had the General Council afford him carte blanche in the drafting of addresses and circulars on its behalf: new members were brought on to the General Council using a co-optation arrangement, leaving him a free hand, and any time that he needed to be sure of a majority, as at the congress in The Hague, he issued his supporters with blank credentials. If you want something done right, do it yourself, so the saying goes, and here we see the perfect illustration of that. Another instance of impropriety: at the time of the London Conference in 1871, the delegates from the IWMA sections had only ten votes, whereas the members of the General Council had thirteen! Similarly, Marx, along with his alter-ego, Engels, claimed to represent several countries: Russia, Germany, Spain, Italy, and Denmark, and this without either one of them being required to make their reports to the general secretary of the IWMA's London Council! However, in using this heavy-handed bureaucratic approach, Marx and Engels had no thought of representing a "party" in the organizational sense, but intended primarily to keep the fate of the workers' movement under close supervision so as to monitor its overall progress, Nor was it out of mere vanity, egocentricity or even some cult of personality — not that they were lacking in arrogance — that they acted this way: it was quite simply that they were convinced that they held a patent on the scientific truth of the future of society!

This ideological certitude is clearly mirrored in Marx's letter of March 28, 1870 to the Brunswick Committee — the Central Committee of the German Social Democratic Workers' Party. He affirms there the necessity of the IWMA General Council's remaining in London, on account of his "being at present in the happy position *of having direct control of this great lever of the proletarian revolution,*" as he considered England. As a result, he was against the setting up of a Regional Council for England, for that would be "madness, we might even say a crime, to let it [that great lever] fall into merely English hands?" How come? Because the "English have all the *wherewithal* needed for the social revolution. What they lack, is the *generalizing mind* and *revolutionary passion*. Only the General Council can supply that, and thereby accelerate the truly revolutionary movement in this country and, consequently, *everywhere*." [10] It is understandable that the English were, in the long run, to weary of being handled like a "lever" and that the leader of the trades unions, John Hales, should have talked about "broken irons" when describing his breaking loose of Marx's over-bearing tyranny and with the IWMA General Council obedient to it. [11]

It was all very natural too, that at the congress in The Hague, Marx and Engels were to get up to their old tricks of 1848 again by suggesting to the proletariat that it set itself up as a political party and assume "the conquest of political power" as its "primary duty," and thus convert the IWMA General Council into a sort of "center for national political parties — or 'governing body.'" (Marx)

It's hardly surprising then that Marx should have seen Bakunin as a threat to the well-nigh discretionary power he wielded on the General Council, and should have credited Bakunin with dark designs, including a scheme to re-move that Council to Geneva, which would mean, he argued, that "the Interna-tional would fall under Bakunin's dictatorship." His desire to dispose of this dangerous rival led him to hold him in the most utter contempt, as a person as well as theoretically:

> [Bakunin's program at the IWMA congress in Lausanne] is empty chatter, a rosary of hollow ideas that try to be sensational, in short, a bland concoction devised for the sole purpose of producing a certain effect at a given moment.... What a grotesque program is this hotch-potch of tired clichés.... As for Bakunin himself, one of the most igno-rant of beings in the matter of social theory, he suddenly looks like the founder of a sect. But the theoretical program of this Alliance is an unadorned farce.

Nor should it come as any surprise to find Marx now bent solely upon, to borrow his own words, "excommunicating" the Russian revolutionary. In addi-tion, as far as he was concerned there could be no question of conforming to some "ongoing audit," however "fraternal," on the part of the rank and file of the IWMA, much less be called to account by it.

We should also note that, unlike Bakunin, Marx was no man of action: Marx operated at the level of analyses, policy statements, decrees, circulars and other "communications." For instance, although he saluted the Paris Com-mune with a great fanfare, he proved utterly incapable of organizing a demon-stration by the IWMA in London in support of the Communards.

It was indeed as a desk-bound individual that he dreamt up the Messianic role of the working class, lionized as history's demiurge. On this point, his criticism of Bakunin's pronouncement that "workers who have become repre-sentatives of the people have ceased to be workers" is very telling: Marx's retort was that that was an impossibility "any more than today's manufacturer ceases to be a capitalist because he becomes a town councilor!"

More familiar with real men and real society, Bakunin had no illusions about worker representation, for he had noted that the mass had a tendency to choose representatives whom it failed, either through indifference or out of apathy, to keep under "continuous monitoring." Which inevitably lead on to a source of depravity for all who find themselves invested with any social authority, by virtue of the fact that:

> by dint of self-sacrifice and devotion, they have slipped into the sweet habit of command, and, through a sort of natural and almost inevitable hallucination in all people who cling too long to power, they have ended up imagining themselves indispensable. In this fashion, from the very ranks of those so frankly popular sections of the construction workers, a sort of governmental aristocracy has imperceptibly arisen. [12]

According to Bakunin, such inertia on the part of the working class could also be credited in his day, although we might as readily apply this to our own times, to the utterly self-serving and:

> corruptive [propaganda] of priests, governments and all bourgeois political parties, not excepting even the reddest of these [who] have spread a host of false ideas among the toiling masses, and those blinkered masses are unfortunately all too often enthusiasts of lies that have no purpose other than to reduce them, voluntarily and stupidly, to service of the interests of the privileged classes, to the detriment of their own interests. [14]

Which is a long, long way from the Marx's idealization of the worker as the "new Prometheus!" Not that such idealization is gratuitous, for it goes hand in hand with (in his view) decisive reinforcement in the shape of "defectors" from the bourgeoisie, those "ideologues" who would supposedly help the worker to rise above his ignorance and steer him along the path of his historical vocation, even should they have to stand in for him in order to assist him down the "right" road. It was on the basis of that analysis that Marx justified his own role inside the IWMA. Here too Bakunin subjected him to a robust criticism:

> From the moment that the International Association would split into two groups — the one comprising the vast majority and made up of members the sum of whose onus would be blind faith in the theoretical and practical wisdom of their leaders: and the other made up only of a few dozen individuals — leaders — that institution, which ought to emancipate Mankind, would turn into a sort of oligarchic state, the worst of all states: and what is more, that clear-sighted, expert and adroit minority that would shoulder, along with all responsibilities, all the rights of a government that would be all the more absolute for its despotism being diligently concealed under the show of an obsequious respect for the will and for the resolutions of the sovereign people, a resolution which that government always injects into the so-called will of the people

— that minority, as we say, obedient to the needs and conditions of its privileged position and prey to the fate of all governments, would soon grow more and more despotic, maleficent and reactionary.[15]

Bakunin's conclusion from that was that the IWMA could never become a tool for emancipation unless it "will be emancipated itself first of all," by being no longer split into a "majority of blind tools and a minority of learned mechanics." That intuitive understanding was borne out at another level, a half century later, with the appearance of Marxist-Leninist "learned mechanics" who soon turned into the "engine-drivers of history," with tens of millions of workers for fuel.

Thus, organizational ideas and the implementation of them inside the IWMA, intersected with fundamental and diametrically opposed theoretical tenets, and could not help but lead to a clean break. It came at the IWMA congress in 1872. In the enforced absence of Bakunin (enforced by his being unable to cross Germany or France because of the threat that he would be arrested and imprisoned — as Marx knew very well) his adversaries had a field day with a majority of mandates procured in advance. In order to secure the exclusion of his rival, Marx nevertheless made the mistake of bringing the level of the debate down to personalities, charging Bakunin with fraud in connection with an obscure episode concerning an advance payment to Bakunin for a translation of Marx's own *Das Kapital* that had not been refunded to a Russian publisher. That crude gambit provoked a general reproof in the IWMA, even among the "Marxists" of that or a later vintage. Let us, for example, look at how this episode was judged a few decades later by one of Marx's adepts (and by no means the least significant one) Otto Ruhle, the German ultra-left communist:

> Marx had triumphed over his despised adversary, but, not content with severing all bonds of party fraternity between himself and his rival, he had indulged his hatred further by attacking his honor. Bakunin, at least if the Congress was to be believed, had omitted to pay Marx back a 300 ruble advance for a translation of *Das Kapital*: and Marx, the Marx who was immersed in a thousand shady deals and who had lived his whole life long on other people's money, made this out to be hanging offense.
>
> It was legitimate for him to battle for an objective policy to which he looked, to the exclusion of any other, for the liberation of the proletariat. He was within his rights to summon the International together to try to get rid of Bakunin, for Bakunin was doing all in his power to thwart him and his policy. But for him to seek to triumph objectively through recourse to methods as shameful as blackening his adversary was a dishonorable course that did not besmirch Bakunin but did besmirch its author. We see here the fatal aspect to his character: nothing ever took priority for Marx over his self-regard: not political matters, not the workers' movement, nor the interests of the revolution. That a gathering of international revolutionaries ready at the drop of a hat to blow private

property and bourgeois morality sky high should have driven out, out-lawed and expelled, on the denunciation of its leader, the most gifted, most heroic and most fascinating of its number because of some alleged infraction of the bourgeois laws of property, was one of the bloodiest jests in history.[16]

The severity of Otto Ruhle's unappealable verdict nonetheless strikes us as incomplete, for it relates only to the methods employed and not to the political intent to which these were of course secondary. Now, that political intent was not really broached at The Hague: the debate was side-tracked by this settling of personal scores. However, had it been broached openly, the outcome might have been very different: maybe even more favorable to Marx, as the clarification of the respective positions of anarchist collectivists and reformist state socialists was to demonstrate a few years later.

The course chosen by Marx was different though: pig-headedly, he capitalized upon his circumstantial majority to bolster considerably the omnipotent role of the General Council and to push through acceptance of the need to convert the sections of the IWMA into political parties, assigning them the mission of "conquering state political power." Then, seeing himself overridden by persons even more into centralist politicking than himself — his erstwhile allies, the Blanquists — he outmaneuvered them by formally transferring the residence of the IWMA General Council to … New York, that is, as far as possible from the European theater of operations. Furthermore, he entrusted it to the care of German émigrés, selected from among his most faithful supporters.

That desperate ploy did not save him from complete defeat: most of the sections of the IWMA disowned the decisions made in The Hague and kept up their contacts with the outcast Bakunin and James Guillaume. The Jura Federation stepped into the shoes of the General Council and pressed on with IWMA activity. In spite of a sham congress in Geneva in 1873, at which Marxists had to "pull mandates out of the ground" (Becker) lest they find themselves surrounded only by German-speaking Swiss, Marx's factional breakaway petered out and disappeared into the maw of history.

In reality, Marx re-enacted the Communist League stunt when control had slipped away from him. We should point out that all these events are common knowledge, duly recorded in the congress minutes or works devoted to the IWMA: not that that has prevented the misrepresentationists or other licensed manipulators, who have striven so hard for the past century to cover up that pitiable outcome that we today have to reiterate these stubborn facts: the IWMA did not fade away in 1872 — it was to founder only much later on reefs that we shall be examining anon — and it was the Marxist faction that was whittled down to its simplest expression, to wit, Germans only. So much so that several of Marx's staunchest and most loyal supporters, who had been just that for twenty years, like Eccarius and Jung, ended up criticizing his chicanery, denouncing his "dictatorship" and abandoning ship.

## Endnotes to Chapter Five

1. *The First International's Hague Congress* (minutes) (Moscow, 1972), p. 119.
2. Bakunin, *Oeuvres complètes,* Vol. II, p. 462.
3. Ibid., p. 127.
4. I. Tchernov, *Le parti républicain au coup d'état et sous le Second Empire,* (Paris, 1906), p. 482.
5. Bakunin, *La liberté,* texts presented by F. Munoz, (Paris: Pauvert, 1965), pp. 195–196 (Letter to Morago dated May 21, 1872, in Nettlau Archives).
6. Ibid.
7. Karl Marx, *Manifeste communists* Oeuvres I, (La Pléiade), pp. 174 and 171.
8. Marx, "Notes sur l'Etatisme et l'Anarchie de Bakounine" in Marx-Engels-Lenin, *Sur l'anarchisme et l'anarcho-syndicalisme* (Moscow, 1973), p. 169.
9. Quoted by Hem Day, *L'internationale de 1864* (Paris-Brussels: Libres propos, 1965), p. 30.
10. Karl Marx, Jenny Marx, and F. Engels *Lettres à Kugelmann,* )Paris: Editions sociales 1970), pp. 146–163, for all the quotations from Marx.
11. Letter from J. Hales to the Belgian Internationalists, *Bulletin de la Fédération Jurassienne,* No. 20–21, (November 10, 1872).
12. Marx-Engels-Lenin, *Sur l'anarchisme,* op. cit., p. 166.
13. *Bakunin Oeuvres,* Tome IV, published by James Guillaume, (Editions Stock, 1913), p. 19.
14. Mikhail Bakunin, *Le politique de l'Internationale,* (Paris: Vie Ouvriére editions, no date).
15. Bakunin, *L'organization de l'internationale* (Geneva, 1914), pp. 14–15.
16. Otto Ruhle, *Karl Marx,* (Paris: Grasset, 1937), pp. 320–321.

## VI. THE FEDERALIST IWMA: APOGEE AND DEMISE

Meeting in congress in Saint-Imier shortly after the congress in The Hague, the federalists opened by rescinding decisions taken at the latter, particularly those relating to the expulsion of Bakunin and James Guillaume, before going on to dismiss the New York General Council and adopt a clear and forceful stance on the central issue of political action by the proletariat:

*Resolution 3*
*The Nature of the Political Action of the Proletariat*

Considering

That seeking to foist upon the proletariat a policy line or uniform political program as the only route capable of leading it on to its social emancipation is an undertaking as absurd as it is reactionary.

That no one has the right to deny the federations and autonomous sections their incontrovertible right to determine for themselves and to abide by the policy line that they deem best, and that any such attempt would inevitably lead to the most disgusting dogmatism.

That the proletariat's aspirations cannot have as their object anything other than the establishment of an absolutely free organization and economic federation founded upon the labor and equality of all and absolutely independent of all political government, and that that organization and that federation cannot be other than the product of the proletariat's own spontaneous action, [the action] of its trades bodies and autonomous communes.

Being persuaded that any political organization cannot be anything but the organization of domination for the benefit of the classes and to the detriment of the masses, and that the proletariat, if it were to seek to take control of political power, would itself turn into a dominant, exploiting class.

The congress assembled in Saint-Imier declares:

1. That the destruction of all political power is the premier duty of the proletariat.

2. That any organizing of a so-called provisional and revolutionary political power in order to encompass that destruction cannot but be yet another trick and would pose as great a danger for the proletariat as all the governments in existence today.

3. That, rejecting all compromise in order to hasten the implementation of the social revolution, the proletarians of every country ought to establish, outside of all bourgeois politics, the solidarity of revolutionary action.[1]

Following which, the delegates from the Spanish, Italian, Jura, French and American federations entered into a pact of friendship, solidarity and mutual defense against the tendency of the "authoritarian party, which is the party of German communism, to substitute its rule and the power of its leaders for free development and for that spontaneous, free organization of the proletariat." They were joined a little later by the English, Belgians, Portuguese and Danes … on the strength of the emotion aroused by Marx's outburst against Bakunin and James Guillaume, we might say; for some of them, like the Belgians, the Dutch and the English were opposed more to Marx's methods than to his ideas and did not take long to rejoin the flock.

The steadfastness behind the adoption of positions by the Saint-Imier congress contrasted with the weakening of organizational ties discernible there: by way of a backlash against the authoritarian centralism of the erstwhile London General Council, those attending the congress called for absolute autonomy for the IWMA's federations and sections. In addition, they rebutted "any legislative or regulatory power vested in congresses," whether these were regional or general, and at which, in any case, the majority "must not force its resolutions upon the minority." They cited the example of the "Spanish organization as the finest to date;" strike action was indicated as the best weapon in the economic struggle, albeit employed "without illusions." A commission, as it happens, a section of the Italian federation, was charged with presenting a draft for a world-wide organization of resistance and an overall statistical scheme. That commission subsequently became the correspondence and statistical bureau.

Seeking to preclude any repetition of bureaucratic practices, these federalists, themselves the victims of what we might term the "Marx syndrome," went to the opposite extreme and denied the need for any serious organizational ties. Inevitably, their cohesion was to be eroded, their goodwill used up, their isolation from one another exacerbated and their centrifugal inclinations were to ring the death knell of every consistent attempt at unification.

Why did things turn out as they did? To be sure, the authoritarianism of Marx and the late General Council in London pointed to the route to be avoided. Assembled in congress in Sonvilliers the delegates from the Jura Federation drew the conclusion that:

the society of the future should not be anything other than the univer-
salization of that organization with which the International will have
endowed itself. So we should take care to match organization as closely
as possible to our ideal. How could we expect an egalitarian, free society to emerge from an authoritarian organization? Impossible. The International, as the future society in embryo, is required to be in the
here and now a faithful reflection of our principles of freedom and federation, and to expunge from its ranks any principle leaning towards
authority or dictatorship.[2]

Among the signatories to this we find the name of one Jules Guesde, who
was actively involved in the drafting of the text; however, he was to make his
name later as a "pure and hard-line" Marxist. That things were being taken too
far was plain: any extended connection or dynamic initiative was construed as an
authoritarian act. As evidence of that, let us take the line argued by Paul Brousse,
another one destined to back-slide later — at the Geneva congress of the IWMA
in 1873. Faced with a suggestion that an IWMA central commission be set up, he
retorted without batting an eyelid that any:

central commission, even one without powers, bereft of rights, having
naught but duties, strikes me as not without dangers. It will have its
creatures, its official propaganda, its official statistics, its pretensions.
It will avail of all possible means to establish its authority, to become a
government. In which it will succeed. Soon, under another guise, the
General Council that has just been laid low will in fact be restored ...
You seek to topple the authoritarian edifice, anarchy is your program
and you appear to shrink from the consequences of your undertaking.
Have no hesitation. You have delivered one blow of the axe and a portion of the edifice has fallen away. Deliver a second, a third, and the
edifice will come tumbling down. [3]

In point of fact what came tumbling down was the IWMA, succumbing under such anti-organization "axe blows," delivered, believe it or not, by the future
leader of the Possibilist Socialist Party and indeed Chairman of Paris City Council! Be that as it may, this was the general trend among the Jurassians: every
organizing endeavor or proposal was instantly categorized as an authoritarian
snare. Such assumptions could not help but lead to the same old negativity and,
to make matters worse, inevitably dishearten all well-meaning folk who cared
about consistent social action. The "Marx syndrome" settled in for a long reign.

True, the Jura's hostility towards all organization or coordination also rested
on another weighty consideration: the dangers implicit in police infiltration.
Remember that two agents provocateurs had played a crucial role in Marx's
chicanery against Bakunin. Deceived by their compliance, Marx had not hesitated to entrust to them the task of re-organizing the French section, along
with a certain Laroque. The latter was even commissioned to pick up money in
Bordeaux on the personal authority of Engels "without awaiting the yea or nay

of the General Council." The "bag-man" dropped out of sight a little while later, with his pockets full! Van Heddeghem, alias Walter, was put in charge of organizing the Paris branch, and afforded discretionary authority, for he was "entitled to suspend the organization or any member from his district, until such time as the General Council's decision was made known." He was quickly "arrested" and adopted one of the most pitiable attitudes: pleading extenuating circumstances, that he had been duped by the Internationalists who had abused his youth and lack of experience, but, having now seen them at work and knowing what they were made of, his only concern would be to expose them for what they were. Engels himself was forced to concede that he had been a "nark and maybe even a Bonapartist agent." As for Marx's other emissary, Dentraygues, alias Swarm, he turned out to be even more damaging. To quote Jules Guesde who denounced him vehemently in a famous article, "The Marxist Pro-consuls," carried in the Jura Federation's *Bulletin*:

> The Swarm who, after having assisted at the Hague congress in the expulsion of Bakunin and James Guillaume from our Association, then proceeded, off his own bat, to extend that expulsion to include comrade Paul Brousse [from Montpellier] has just revealed himself in his true light before the court in Toulouse.
>
> On the pretext of recruiting workers from our Midi to the International, and thanks to full powers from Marx, he acted as a beater of socialist game, driving it into the nets of Thiers's police. He it was who denounced the thirty-six victims from Toulouse, the four from Béziers, etc., and it is his evidence that convicts them now. His real name is Dentraygues. "You are the lynch-pin of the prosecution" the president of the court was able to tell him to his face, without drawing the slightest objection from him. [4]

Guesde used this blatant provocation as the basis for damning once and for all the "authoritarian system of organization of which Marx and the General Council are the mainstays," and he laid the blame on the "initiatory role that the Hague congress attributed to a central organization":

> *Leave the working class in every country to organize itself anarchically,* as best suits its interests and the Dentraygues will not be possible any longer.

> 1. Because the workers of each locality know one another and will never be exposed to dependence upon a man who might betray them, sell them out.

> 2. Because, even granted that the trust they may have placed in one of their own may have been misplaced, the traitor, being confined to his own branch alone, will never be able to betray more than one branch to the bourgeoisie's police.

The autonomy of its sections and federations is not just the spirit of the International, it is also its security.

Looking back, it is amusing to find the future guardian of Marxist orthodoxy at the forefront of the fight against Marx and the General Council. Be that as it may, his denunciation of the twin perils of centralism and police infiltration has become a touchstone for the organizational views of the autonomous federalists. That said, what a fiasco for Marx and Engels! Carefully covered up, of course, by all their hagiographers and exegetes.

Implicitly, there was another factor at work: the prospect that intellectuals might seize the reins of the workers' movement. Enjoying the essential skills and, above all, the requisite time to disport themselves inside the organization, they could not help but overwhelm the manual workers. Even at the IWMA's Geneva congress, in 1866, the delegates from Paris and several others from Switzerland had asked that manual worker status be a condition upon admission into the Association, for fear that "ambitious scheming types might worm their way into the Association, in order to achieve mastery over it in the short or long term and to turn it to the service of their personal interests, thereby distracting it from its goal." On the first occasion, that motion was rejected. The Parisians returned to it whenever the discussions turned to the statutes. Again to no avail. But the Parisian delegation was not to be put off: Friborg announced that "some fine day it may come to pass that the workers' congress will be made up for the most part of economists, journalists, lawyers, bosses, etc., a laughable situation that would wipe out the Association."[5]

That was a hypothesis that was not at all unfounded, if one looks at the leadership bodies of the so-called workers' organizations over the past near-century. Tolain, a delegate from Paris, even went further:

> Simple membership of the Association is one thing and living up to the role of delegate to the congress is a matter of much greater delicacy. The latter requires greater guarantees vis a vis the cause to be served. We hate no one: but, under present conditions, we have to see adversaries in all members of the privileged classes, whether that privilege is conferred by capital or by qualifications. The working class has long been accused of trusting to others for its salvation, of relying upon the state, etc. Today, it aims to side-step such reproaches: it seeks its own salvation, asking nobody's protection. Thus its delegates must belong neither to the liberal professions nor to the caste of capitalists.[6]

In this way, the gauntlet was plainly being flung down and the likelihood is that Marx and Engels, eminent representatives of the two categories cited, were being targeted openly by the Parisians. The majority at the congress, made up of English, German and Swiss delegates, rejected that proposal once and for all. Five years later, after having attended the conference arranged in London in 1871, Paul Robin, ex-Alliance member, also spotted the threat and alleged that the "workers will dispatch, into the Councils that enjoy or are moving towards enjoying authority, men of complete or comparative leisure, *rentiers* or privileged professionals, lawyers, journalists, teachers, doctors, liberated workingmen owning their own tools and having assistants." Applying that rule to himself, doctor as he was, Robin resigned from all responsible positions:

> Exercising one of those privileged professions, I will no longer consent to be appointed to any workers' council, administrative or supervisory. And I shall have to render to the cause of social revolution, to which I remain committed, whatever special services it may require of those in my profession.
>
> I shall have achieved my aim should the step I am taking with regard to myself become general practice: should the workers from now on have only one echelon, administrative councils under the constant supervision of the General Assembly or its special, temporary representatives. Councils composed of real workers suffering the ordinary conditions of contemporary industrialism, paid at the usual rate for the time that they will donate to the common affair, and assisted as the need may be by clerks, likewise paid, for whom they will be answerable. [7]

This was an extremely honest attitude that does its author credit but it was very poorly received by those to whom the admonishment was addressed, the General Council and Marx, who wasted no time in instantly expelling this "fly in the ointment." Robin was to persist with his militant activity alongside the Jurassians; he was subsequently to devote his time to his specialty — education — with enthusiasm and commitment. He was to be one of the neo-Malthusian apostles of eugenics, then, at the age of 74, choose to bid this life goodbye. In any event, he cut a fine figure in that age of renegadism and dereliction.

As for Bakunin, he took an active part in the Jura Federation's congresses in Sonvilliers and Saint Imier, and then in 1872 he revived the International Alliance of Social Revolutionaries and thereafter devoted his time to founding its Slav sections. Thus he drew up the programs for the Russian, Serb and Polish brethren, largely adopting, but in a more polished form, his earlier programs. He also wrote lengthy articles and letters to denounce the Marxist putsch inside the IWMA. In these we find remarkable prophecies about state socialism's future and the future of what he described as the "Knouto-Germanic" empire. Unfortunately the majority of these writings were to remain unpublished until recent years and thus did not have the desired influence upon the course of events. Plagued by health problems, the old lion took the view that his internationalist mission was over and he bade his comrades farewell in a very fine letter of October 12, 1873, which in fact came to be regarded as his testament. In it he thanked his comrades, especially the Jurassians, for having "retained their esteem, their friendship and their trust" in him, despite the "chicanery of our common foes and the infamous calumnies peddled against [him];" he thanked them for not having yielded to intimidation in the shape of the label

"Bakuninists" that had been cast up to them: such constancy had enabled them "to score a complete victory" over the "dictatorial designs of Monsieur Marx."

The victory of freedom and of the International over authoritarian intrigue "now complete," he reckoned that freedom of action "according to personal convenience had been restored to every individual": so he thought that he was within his rights to resign from the Jura Federation and the International. Especially in light of his health, his part from now on could not go beyond theoretical propaganda — which did not appear to him to be the number one priority in the short term, for he closed his letter with the assertion that:

> the time for ideas is past, and deeds and actions have come into their own. The priority today above everything else is the organization of the forces of the proletariat. But that organization should be the handiwork of the proletariat itself. Were I a young man, I would betake myself into the workers' circles and, sharing my brethren's life of toil, I would also share with them in this great labor of necessary organization. But neither my years nor my health permit me to do so.[8]

Thereafter he spent his time on personal matters, while drafting (in Russian) one of his major writings, *Statism and Anarchy*, a text that stands alone but was intended as the first part of a study intended to stretch to several volumes but which, alas, was never completed. Similarly, he wanted to buckle down to writing his memoirs but, seeking to solve his financial straits once and for all and assure his family's future, (his Polish wife and the three children she had had by the Italian Internationalist Cambuzzi for, in fact, his "marriage" was a marriage of convenience, and his wife enjoyed complete sexual freedom) he threw himself into a madcap venture, the La Baronata agricultural commune. He turned out to be a mediocre farmer and an atrocious manager, which led to his frittering away a substantial sum of money borrowed by his colleague Carlo Cafiero. This had a dramatic result: he fell out with his best friends and colleagues in the Jura: this falling-out did not become generally known to outsiders but it had a very damaging impact inside the Jura Federation. In desperation, Bakunin tried to throw his life away in an insurrection in Italy and almost succeeded in that, before coming to a dismal death amid rancor and illness. Up to the last, he retained his rebellious spirit in spite of everything and to a young Russian woman who nursed him he offered the counsel that "authority depraves, submission to authority debases."[9]

The IWMA that had survived held four congresses: Geneva (1873), Brussels (1874), Berne (1876) and Verviers (1877). This was its heyday, a period generally glossed over by historians of the workers' movement, yet a period that was crucial, for it was then that the real demarcation between reformist advocates of state socialism and the conquest of state power and revolutionaries, determinedly committed to the economic struggle, took place. So much so that it became impossible for them to coexist. The schism was consummated at the world socialist congress held in Ghent in 1877. The Germans, Dutch,

Belgians and English — or at any rate the federations representing them in the IWMA — at the instigation of the Belgian César De Paepe, came out clearly for participation in bourgeois institutions. The autonomists rallied around the Jura Federation did not quite advocate political abstention as lots of their adversaries sought maliciously to suggest, but, faithful to the Proudhonian idea, they condemned the embracing of participation in bourgeois parliamentarism as an objective to the detriment of the workers' economic struggle.

Caught between true believers and like-minded types on the one hand, and prey to international persecution on the other, the autonomists were to lose interest in the holding of international congresses. These were replaced by the congresses of the Jura Federation which also attracted other foreign autonomists. Thus there was no longer the old International but instead a movement rallied around a specific organization, albeit more informal than the Alliance and, over the years, increasingly remote from the laboring masses. Furthermore, an additional subdivision took place in the ranks into those who preached propaganda by insurrectionism and those less enthused by that.

As early as 1876, Malatesta, speaking on behalf of the Italian Federation, had issued a declaration in favor of propaganda by deed. The "act of insurrection, designed to assert socialist principles by deeds" was regarded as the most effective mode of propaganda and the only one which "without deceiving and corrupting the masses, can reach the deepest layers of society and draw the vital forces of mankind into the struggle sustained by the International."[10] An impromptu uprising in Benevento in Italy that year turned into a fiasco but failed to dishearten its instigators: quite the opposite indeed, but the strategy espoused by them was nevertheless repugnant to many others. This latter fact, plus the backlash from employers and the state whittled the membership of the Jura Federation down to a few dozen members — in contrast to the hundreds of its early days — and led to the collapse of the organization's clockmaking production cooperative. So much so that its chief exponent, James Guillaume, was obliged to move away to Paris in 1878, his departure signaling the end of the *Bulletin de la Fédération*. A new mouthpiece emerged in the shape of *Le Révolté*, published out of Geneva: Peter Kropotkin was its mainstay.

Geographical isolation played a part in the demise of the Jura Federation: for a time, refugee French Communards and several Russian and Italian Internationalists provided some sort of international liaison, albeit fraught with personal squabbles. Indeed, Jules Guesde, who went back to France in 1876, struck out on his own, diluting his views as the need arose and launching his own newspaper *L'Egalité*. Paul Brousse who stood by his extremist opinions clandestinely produced another French paper *L'Avant-Garde*. Benoit Malon and Gustave Lefrançais, for their part, began to distance themselves from the antiauthoritarians.

The amnesty granted to the Communards in July 1880 accelerated the demarcation process and signaled the end of an epoch. Guesde and Brousse, erstwhile friends, the Castor and Pollux of the federalist IWMA, joined forces to launch the *Parti Ouvrier Français* (French Workers' Party) on the basis of a minimum program that Guesde had obtained from his one-time *bête noire*, Marx, in London. Not that their alliance lasted long, for it came to a somewhat comical end; at the workers' congresses in Paris and Saint-Etienne in May and September 1882, the Broussists secured a majority and expelled the Guesdists! Not that that was the end of it: each of them set up his own party and sailed back and forth over a period of twenty years of "armed neutrality" before they found themselves in the same camp once more, along with Jean Allemane and the Blanquist Edouard Vaillant, with the founding in 1905 of the SFIO (French Section of the Workers' International) Socialist Party. Having become by then what once they had despised — electoralists — they set about conquering public office, with a degree of success: Brousse was to become chairman of the Paris city council and the Guesde minister of war in 1914–1916!

How are we to account for the trajectory followed by those who once would have railed against the conquest of state power and the stifling centralism of the Marxist General Council of the IWMA, only to end up themselves as the surest guardians of the capitalist order, while displaying the label "socialists?" There are the objective factors: capitalist production expanded considerably and reserved the leading role for the workers who became essential to its survival. Smarting from the bloody reverses they had suffered in 1848 and 1871, those workers leant more and more in favor of less violent remedies and let themselves be seduced into participation in bourgeois institutions, in hopes of improving their circumstances by that route. Socialists thus found themselves cast as the representatives of such aspirations. As for the subjective element in the defection of ultra-revolutionaries, that may be construed as young bourgeois reverting to type after their impulsive extravagances: but an "honorable" reversion, for all that. Especially as, being denied access to the tiller of society by the plutocrats, the intelligentsia discovered in socialism an ideal means by which to advertise its "special talents and capabilities." As a result, while supporting the workers' cause, it earned itself a sort of "legitimacy" in justifying its "wise choice," provided that it jettison the anarchist enthusiasms of its younger days, and hold itself ready to share in the "responsibilities" of state power alongside the once despised bourgeoisie.

The die-hard rebels believed that the collapse of the system was just around the corner and they believed they might even accelerate that collapse with a few spectacular insurrections or attentats, like the Russian populists who had believed that they might topple the autocracy by assassinating Alexander II. It was full steam ahead; at his trial in Lyon in 1883, Kropotkin reckoned that bourgeois society had at most another decade of life left in it!

To sum up: the workers' movement, at its inception united and homogeneous, progressively differentiated itself into several competing tendencies, each one striving on its own account to play upon the elements of evolution or revolution, economic and social. As the Great Score-Settling failed to arrive, they scuttled around looking for ways of hastening its arrival by laying the stress thereafter on subjective conditions. In this way the tendencies turned into specific organizations, the better to get across their ideological messages and extend their influence over the workers. This with the notable exception of the ones who would henceforth go under the name of anarchists who, believing the social revolution to be imminent, denied the necessity of organization at all, because, on the one hand, they were keen to start in the here and now abiding by the principles that would govern the society of their dreams, and, on the other, with the example of Marx in mind, they were wary of any half-structured organization.

### Endnotes for Chapter Six

1. *La Première Internationale* anthology of documents published under the supervision of Jacques Freymond, (Geneva: Droz, 1971), Tome E, p. 7 ff. for the quotations that follow.
2. Ibid., Tome III, p. 104.
3. Ibid., Tome IV, p. 53.
4. Alexandre Zévaès, *De L'introduction du marxisme en France* (Paris: Riviére, 1947), pp. 59–63 for all the quotations below.
5. J. Freymond, op. cit., Tome I, pp. 41 and 68.
6. Ibid., p. 80.
7. Bakunin, *Oeuvres complétes,* Volume Two, p. 391.
8. Bakunin, *Oeuvres complétes,* Volume Six, pp. 233–235.
9. Arthur Lehning, *M. Bakounine et les autres,* (Paris: 10/18 Books, 1970), p. 372.
10. J. Freymond, *La Première Internationale,* op. cit., Tome IV, p. 514.

## VII. PROPAGANDA BY DEED AND "ANARCHY ON THE PAYROLL"

In the eyes of anti-authoritarians, incompatibility with the reformist state socialists had become so blatantly obvious that their every thought was devoted to finding ways of demarcating their differences if only in terms of labels. At the time of the 1879 and 1880 congresses of the Jura Federation in Chaux-de-Fonds in Switzerland, at the suggestion of Carlo Cafiero and Peter Kropotkin, anarchist communism was espoused as their ultimate goal and collectivism described as a transitional form of society. The corollary of these objectives was "the abolition of all forms of government and the free federation of producer and consumer groups."

At a secret get-together in Vevey in Switzerland in 1880, thirty-two anarchist "political leaders" who included Kropotkin, Elisée Reclus, Pierre Martin and five other Frenchmen, set out the tactical methods to be used to bring about anarchist communism. They agreed to recommend propaganda by deed and adopted a program drawn up by the Swiss, Herzig, and the German, Otter:

1. Utter destruction of existing institutions by force.

2. Every possible effort must be made to spread the revolutionary idea and the spirit of revolt through deeds.

3. Desert the legal terrain in order to focus action upon the terrain of illegality, which is the only road leading on to revolution.

4. Technical and chemical sciences having already rendered services to the revolutionary cause, we should urge upon our organizations and the individuals belonging to these groups that they place great store by the study and applications of these sciences as a means of attack and defense.

5. The autonomy of groups and individuals is acceptable, but in order to retain unity of action, each group is entitled to enter into direct correspondence with the others, and in order to facilitate such relations, a central international information office is to be set up. [1]

For the time being, that program was kept secret and Jean Maitron, who reprints it in full in his monumental and unsurpassed thesis on this period, discovered it in the police archives, which would suggest that there was a police presence at that formal get-together, though there is no way of knowing whether that does credit or discredit to what emerged from it. Nevertheless, the organizational eccentricity espoused will be noted: autonomy was "acceptable," there was a "right to correspond" and an "information" office. Maybe the one accounts for the other. Otherwise, what we have projected in this formula is the picture of the society of the future, albeit in very hazy colors.

On the other hand, police involvement is crucial to the launching of the first French anarchist journal to have seen the light of day since the Commune, *La Révolution sociale*. The Paris prefect of police, Louis Andrieux, had made his name a decade before, by taking on Bakunin and the Lyon Communards. In his *Memoirs* he explains and accounts for his initiative. He opens with a startling argument that to this very day raises a lot of questions: "We know that the perpetrators of political crimes, when they remain unknown, are always agents provocateurs, and that it is always the police who are at the back of it."!

Disturbed by talk of propaganda by deed and by the plot to have the Palais Bourbon (Chamber of Deputies) blown up, and briefed on the anarchists' problems in bringing out a newspaper, he seized this opening to infiltrate those circles and "place Anarchy on the payroll." As this case is a model of the genre, let us quote the juicy story of this provocation at some length:

> The comrades needed a backer: but fiendish Capital was in no hurry to respond to their appeal. I shook that fiendish Capital by the shoulders and managed to convince it that it was in its interest to encourage the publication of an anarchist newspaper. One does not stamp out teachings by preventing them from springing forth, and the teachings gained nothing from being made known. Giving the anarchists their newspaper was like installing a telephone link between the plotters' back-room and the office of the prefect of police. One does not keep secrets from one's financial backer, and, day by day, I would be kept abreast of the most mysterious schemes. The Palais Bourbon would be spared: the representatives of the people could get on with their deliberations in peace.
>
> Do not think, also, that I crudely offered the encouragements of a police prefect. I sent along a well-dressed bourgeois to seek out one of the most active, most intelligent of them. My agent explained to him that, having made his fortune in the drug business, he wanted to devote a portion of his income to assisting anarchist propaganda. This bourgeois entering the lion's den aroused no suspicion among the comrades. Through him, I placed a security with the state funds and so the newspaper *La Révolution sociale* made its entrance.
>
> It was a weekly publication, my generosity not stretching to the expense of a daily newspaper. Mlle. Louise Michel was the star attraction of my editorial panel. Needless to say, "the great citizen-ess" was oblivious of the part in which I had cast her, and it is not without a

measure of confusion that I own up to the trap I had set for the innocence of some comrades of both sexes.

Every day, around an editorial table, the most respected representatives of the party of action would assemble: together, they would scan their international correspondence: they would consider the steps to be taken to do away with "man's exploitation of his fellow-man": the recipes that science was placing in the revolution's service were passed along. I was always represented at these councils, and if the need arose, I would put in my two pennies' worth, more than once acting as a lightning conductor.[2]

Instructive indeed! Note that "one of the most active and intelligent of them" was Emile Gautier, a leading light of the Paris movement at the time, a doctor of law and superb orator, but somewhat more gullible than the cobbler Jean Grave who had a better "nose" in this connection. Whenever Andrieux's agent, the Belgian Spilleux alias Serraux, turned up to put this "stroke" to Grave he at first hesitated, then made to agree under certain conditions, that is, that the paper was brought out but Serraux was soon sent packing. The "wheeler-dealer," in this instance, Andrieux, smelled a rat and concentrated instead on Gautier.[3] The latter nonetheless was alerted by the sight of the names and addresses of French anarchist groups and their members in the columns of the paper. By then the game was obvious and that led to the demise of *La Révolution sociale*, after 56 issues and almost a year on the scene. The role of "lightning conductor" mentioned by Andrieux is also worth looking into: in this instance it took the form of a sham anarchist outrage. After having considered the Banque de France, the Elysée Palace, the prefecture of police, and the Interior Ministry — all of which targets were easily ruled out by Serraux, Andrieux's man — the statue of Thiers recently unveiled in Saint-Germain was chosen "as a practice run." Let us have a look at the exact circumstances, as related with easy humor by Andrieux:

The comrades set off for Saint-Germain, carrying the infernal machine: this was a sardine can packed with fulminate and carefully wrapped in a handkerchief. I was aghast to learn of this plot: I knew what time they would be setting off for Saint-Germain: I knew what time the intended crime was scheduled for. What was I to do? The act had to go through if a crackdown was to be made possible. I had no hesitation in sacrificing the liberator of the nation in order to save the Palais Bourbon. When night fell, the comrades slipped into the darkness through the ageless trees: they followed the rue de la République as far as the rue de Poissy, where the statue loomed larger and heavier than life in a little square. The pale moonlight brightened the face of the bronze old man who looked down upon the plotters with a sardonic gaze.

One of them lifted the sardine can on to the plinth of the statue, between the legs of the armchair where a seated Mr. Thiers was unfolding something that must have been a geographer's map along his left thigh.

FACING THE ENEMY

A long fuse trailed from the pedestal. One of the comrades set it alight, while his colleagues scattered revolutionary proclamations on the ground: then, as the flame began slowly to edge along the fuse, the comrades took to their heels, racing down the hill: and as they raced on across the flat ground they clambered over the railway barriers.

Upon their arrival back in Paris they impatiently awaited the news from Saint-Germain. They had not stayed to watch the spectacular destruction they had wrought: they had no idea of the extent of the damage.

How disappointed they were when they learned they had, at best, rudely awakened a few peaceable inhabitants of the quiet town of Saint-Germain. The statue was untouched: the fulminate had failed to damage the bronze: a broad black stain was the only trace left by the outrage. I knew the names of the plotters: I had made the trip with them, by proxy at least: I had seen everything, heard everything.

According to Jean Grave, it was "two or three Southerners, recently arrived from Marseilles, men whose verbal revolutionism … signified their readiness to turn their hand to anything" who made the trip to plant that famous "sardine can," which caused only an "explosion of laughter." This time, we might add, for the procedure was repeated over and over again and often had unfortunate consequences. The lesson was not learned properly and there were always naive souls or imbeciles ready to be sucked into police provocations. Now, these narks have often had their defenders, as Grave stresses:

> Unmasking these narks would be so easy if all comrades were prepared to use a little common sense in their reasoning. But for many of them plain common sense goes out the window where propaganda matters are concerned. They drag in a host of elements unconnected with the issue, merely complicating and muddying it. … if you dare to attack 'their' chap, it must be out of jealousy or because he does not see eye to eye with you. [4]

Grave here is upbraiding those "Christian-minded" anarchists who refuse to "think ill of anybody." For all that, Grave has a tendency to play down the influence of narks upon the evolution of the movement, which appears a bit paradoxical of the man who had been so disparaged in anarchist circles for *flicomanie* (having cops on the brain). And yet, there were notable police plants at the time: in 1882, at the time of the riots in Montceau-les-Mines, the agent provocateur Brenin was unmasked: in Lyon, center of the libertarian movement at the time, an agent of the prefecture, one Valadier, managed to infiltrate the editorial panel of the anarchist newspapers, which were in any event subject to permanent censorship harassment, since a single newspaper was obliged, for instance, to change its name seven times in under two years!

Police plants have never been exclusive to anarchists, as some once attempted to have us believe — far from it! All revolutionary organizations of any importance have always been infiltrated by provocateurs and traitors. Starting with Grisel who "blew" Babeuf's Conspiracy of the Equals in 1796: then even the great Blanqui, the "Old Lag" who spent 33 years of his life behind bars, was compromised by the Taschereau document, uncovered in police archives in 1848, in which he denounced Barbès and his colleagues from the abortive rising in 1839 (unless this was only a ploy on his part designed to get rid of his rivals). During the 1848 revolution, the incoming prefect of police, Caussidière, was stupefied to discover that his own deputy, Delahodde, appointed secretary of the prefecture, as well as the captain of his guards, Chenu, were agents of the police of Louis Philippe planted inside the revolutionary secret societies years before; Delahodde had even served time in prison, the better to play the stoolie among fellow inmates who could scarcely distrust such a "pure" revolutionary.[5]

Inside the Russian revolutionary movement, renegadism, treachery or provocation amounted to what might be described as an often honorable tradition. We might start by mentioning Utin, the man who slandered Bakunin and was an unconditional supporter of Marx: quickly disappointed by the lack of prospects in Europe, he sought a pardon of the Tsar and went back to Russia. Leon Tikhomirov, one of the most prominent populists, did likewise in the 1880s. Yevno Azev, the head of the Social Revolutionaries' terrorist fighting organization, was a direct agent working for the Okhrana, the tsarist secret police. The Bolshevik paper *Pravda* was founded in 1912 by another agent provocateur, Zhitomirsky. Furthermore, Malinovsky, leader of the Bolshevik faction in the Russian Chamber of Deputies or Duma, although "beloved" by Lenin, was another Okhrana agent and was shot as such in 1918. Thus all these agents were often well placed and as a result had a crucial influence upon their organization or the course of events. Moreover, there is no reason to be startled by this, for all is fair in war: the bourgeois state protected itself however it could. Moscow's "workers'" state has since done a lot better, which is to say a lot worse, conjuring ready-made phony anti-Bolshevik organizations into existence, manipulating them as has suited its needs and also penetrating most of the Russian émigré associations.

We should note that Andrieux was quick to reveal his manipulation, just four years after the event, probably to pre-empt his being held accountable for eventual "mishaps," for his *La Révolution sociale* had done nothing but talk about bombs, arson and explosions. So he had to cover himself against those who succeeded him in the prefecture of police. The oddest reaction to his disclosures came from Jules Guesde: Guesde later accused him of having "sired" anarchism in France. Thus, Guesde, who had once denounced Marxist centralism inside the workers' movement as a conduit for police infiltration, switched his rifle to his other shoulder!

In 1880, not all the bridges between socialists had yet been burned. At the Le Havre congress, the few anarchists present even managed to have a motion passed, advocating "libertarian communism as the ultimate objective." It was only at the Paris congress on May 22, 1881 that the split really came. It came over an organizational issue, which may seem odd for anarchists: they decided to address the congress only on behalf of their groups rather than in any personal capacity. When the socialists turned down this proposal, they held a congress of their own from May 25 to 29, 1881, the date of the official foundation of the French anarchist movement.

The London international congress, in July that year, set the seal upon the split. Thirty-one delegates, all of them described by a number rather by their names, represented 56 federations and 46 non-federated sections or groups. Among these delegates were Louise Michel, Peter Kropotkin, Emile Pouget and the celebrated Serraux, Andrieux's "nark." Two crucial motions were passed. One, carried by a "slim minority," concerned the establishment of an international information office (!) based in London and comprising three titular members and three deputies. Its existence was to remain notional. The other and unquestionably more important motion, had to do with propaganda by deed. It repeated the Vevey motion virtually word for word:

> Congress expresses the wish that affiliated organizations should bear the following suggestions in mind: as a matter of strict necessity, every possible effort must be made in the form of acts to spread the revolutionary idea and the spirit of revolt to that great fraction of the laboring population that does not as yet participate in the movement and deludes itself about the morality and efficacity of lawful methods. In departing from the lawful parameters within which we have generally remained thus far, in order to remove our action to the terrain of illegality which is the only path leading to revolution, we must have recourse to methods consonant with that objective.... It is absolutely necessary that we focus our efforts in that area, bearing in mind that the simplest of actions against existing institutions says more to the masses than thousands of printed and floods of spoken words, and that propaganda by deed in the countryside is even more important than in the towns. Congress recommends to all organizations and persons affiliated to the International Workingmen's Association that they place great store by the study of the technical and chemical sciences as a means of defense and attack.[6]

This last recommendation is mind-boggling: the use of explosives to trace out a path for social revolution! Seductive though the strategic notion of propaganda by deed may have seemed (and the same could be said of the economic, social, individual or other approaches that would translate libertarian aspirations into day to day practicalities — and a fair number of comrades were engaged in these areas), the reduction of it to the simple expression of "chemical and technical means" seems, with the benefit of hindsight, quite ludicrous, not to say aberrant.

Another inconsistency arose here: the congress claimed no right other than its right to offer a broad outline of what struck it as the best form for revolutionary socialist organizing, leaving "the secret organizations and others which might strike them as advancing the success of the social revolution" as a matter for the initiative of the groups themselves. All in all, this fitted in with the trend already apparent in the last few congresses of the Jura Federation. If the slightest doubt persisted about its refusal to adopt a definite stance, the London congress stipulated that it "is readily appreciated that the delegates from organizations which have sent representatives to London were not empowered to pass binding resolutions. It will be up to their groups and federations to make the final decision as to whether they accept them." How? By corresponding! For each affiliated group "will have the right to correspond directly with all the other groups and federations which might give it their addresses." A lamer recommendation would be inconceivable and the suggestion remained a "dead letter." We can appreciate how the recollection of Marx's centralistic General Council may have over-shadowed the delegates' deliberations, but this evasion of organizational responsibilities was simply suicidal and its boomerang effect was about to produce an eclipsing of libertarian ideas as the ideas of the majority revolutionary current, so much so that they would subsequently have to resort to other organizational and social methodologies in order to find expression.

It is noteworthy that Kropotkin did what he could to oppose these resolutions. He was somewhat inclined to advocate a return to the Bakuninist form of organization, at once secret and public, which is to say, a resurrection of the Alliance: on two occasions he also spoke up against the recommended study of "chemical sciences' as the favored method of propaganda by deed. In addition, he tried to focus attention upon the much more significant problem of "clandestine presses" in those countries where newspapers could not be published freely, and it was with great difficulty that he managed to get the congress to adopt a stance on revolutionary morality.

It is telling to note that his greatest opposition on those two points came from Andrieux's agent, Spilleux/Serraux, supported by other Parisian delegates from the 11th, 16th and 21st arrondissements of the city, including the famous "sardine can" bombers of that statue of Thiers. Naturally, Serraux moved that the term "morality" be stricken from the motion and steadfastly refused to see the establishment of any statistical or information bureau, or any bureau otherwise described, on the alleged grounds that that would mean the reconstitution, under one denomination or another, of an "authority." In the end, he moved that the congress be wound up without recommending a clandestine press and, to cover his tracks, he argued that it was "a duty upon us all to show solidarity with every revolutionary act." Whereupon one of his most obsequious followers, the delegate from Levallois-Perret, added to the confusion by saying that it is "hard to determine where the revolutionary act begins and where the bourgeois act begins." This was a splendid confusionist success, carried off without serious opposition from others at the congress like Louise Michel, Charles Malato, Emile Pouget, Grave, Malatesta, Merlino and other tried and tested revolutionaries.[7]

Let us note the presence at this congress in London of a representative from the Icarian commune in Iowa, in the United States, which had moved away from the original patriarchal and religious socialism of Cabet towards a libertarian communism. (Furthermore, in 1881 a newspaper called *Le Communiste libertaire* was published by Pierre Leroux's brother, Jules Leroux.)

From then on, except in Spain which followed its own Bakuninist, collectivist path, targeting the producers of field and factory, it was France that became the center of gravity of the international anarchist movement, thereby regaining the status she enjoyed in the nineteenth century as the "Homeland of Revolutionaries and Revolutions." The evolution of anarchist thinking in the Hexagon (France) was to march in step with international trends up until 1914. For that reason, we shall now focus our attention upon the French anarchism of that period.

Instances of "propaganda by deed" came fast and thick, anarchist ideas gained ground and in order to combat them the authorities seized upon the pretext of the London congress and indicted around sixty anarchists from Lyon and elsewhere in 1883, on charges of attempted reconstruction of the IWMA, which was still under ban in France. The accused in turn availed of the trial to indict the bourgeois order and give full vent to their propaganda. Kropotkin, Emile Gautier, Bordat and Pierre Martin used the witness box as a rostrum for hours on end, not that this prevented them from receiving several years in prison as their sentences in spite of it all. Emile Gautier, one of the most brilliant anarchist propagandists of his day, was entitled to special treatment: he was freed before completion of his sentence, upon undertaking to break with Anarchy. That was a promise that he kept, for he was thereafter to devote his energies to scientific publications far removed from chemistry and matters social. Only once did he retreat from his undertaking, much later on, when he wrote a preface to the memoirs of Coron, the one-time head of the Sûreté, who, it transpired, had been a childhood friend! Gautier took this paradox to extremes by "complimenting" the man who had had the celebrated anarchist burglars, Duval and Pini, arrested, upon his having retained "the seditious soul of his younger day" beneath the "tricolor sash of the head of the Sûreté," a compliment coming from a "staunch old friend who went to the bad"![8]

The movement slowed down: its newspapers came out in fits and starts: congresses were rejected as "leftovers from parliamentarism," because they laid down a "single policy line trespassing against the freedom of the federations." In spite of which, an attempted "International Anarchist Congress" was held in 1889 over a period of one week. As it had no pre-arranged agenda, it proceeded "amid the worst features of anarchy, in the vulgar sense of the term" (to borrow Jean Maitron's description). There was not a single resolution passed, no vote was taken, and it was, in fact, a "Donnybrook Fair." Which is scarcely surprising, for the prevalent notion in France at the time was as latitudinarian as could be:

> Unhindered entry and rights of discussion for every comrade, for, as soon as some individuals show up speaking on behalf of other

individuals, they will be tempted to believe that they are expressing a collective opinion and, when they leave, will go away persuaded that their view, their words carry more weight than if they were acting solely upon their own behalf: in short, they will be tempted to lay down the law....[9]

That sort of sophistry was the general rule, not merely for individuals remote from all social existence, but also for propagandists of some renown like Jean Grave, the editor-in-chief of *La Révolte*, who championed freedom of assent and freedom of initiative:

Individuals belonging simultaneously to several groups based on different acts of propaganda ... once their aim has been achieved, and the propaganda act been accomplished, the group dissolves, reforming on a new basis, those persons not accepting this new outlook breaking off and others being recruited and propaganda thus being carried out by groups continually undergoing transformations along these lines, accustoming individuals to bestir themselves, to act, without being bogged down in routine and immobility, thereby preparing the groupings of the society to come, by forcing individuals to act for themselves, to seek out one another on the basis of their inclinations, their affinities.[10]

Once he realized that he was living in times where the "shores of Anarchy" were not within sight, Grave was to overhaul that idyllic conception of propaganda activity. By that time, though, the damage had been done: atomization and the enthronement of individual autonomy as an absolute principle were to dilute and decompose the French anarchist movement. Jean Maitron estimates the number of militants in the entire country at somewhere between 600 and 800 during the 1880s, and reckons that by 1894 there were 1,000 active militants, 4,500 sympathizers and around 100,000 people receptive to anarchist ideas. Very few indeed, considering the goals in mind and the above all the advent of the much awaited society of the future.

This headlong flight from reality led to a plain dissociation from social struggles. The option for propaganda by deed, to the exclusion of every other tactic or stratagem, inevitably led to a divorce from the workers' everyday preoccupations. In order to gloss over that deficiency, anarchy took on the form of a religion, peddled by prophets and dreamers possessed. All that this mystical surge needed was its martyrs: and they would not be long in coming forward. In fact, the more the breakdown of society became desirable, the more unbearable became the ordinary, everyday ghastliness to some who then turned to acts that "make more propaganda in a few days than thousands of pamphlets" (to quote Kropotkin from *The Spirit of Rebellion*) without thereby unleashing the yearned for spontaneous uprising of the masses.

In fact, such practice signaled a complete breach with the traditions of association, union and solidarity built up in early decades of the workers' movement and of the federalist IWMA in particular. Quite the contrary: it made head-way as an abrupt backlash against such social values, as we can see from the anti-organizational trend that was to gain the upper hand in anarchist circles and speed the skid towards "bomb-ism."

## Endnotes for Chapter Seven

1. Quoted by Jean Maitron, *Histoire du mouvement anarchists en France (1880–1914)*, (Paris, 1951), pp. 73–74.

2. Louis Andrieux, *Souvenirs d'un préfet de police,* (Paris: L'Anarchie subventionnée, 1885), Tome I, p. 337ff. We should say that Louis Andrieux was the adulterine father of the Stalinist poet Louis Aragon, author of the notorious "We need a CPU" and of absurd paeans to Stalin "the father and sun of the peoples." As for his father, he was only a virtuous republican policeman; much given to womanizing and irregular habits, he made staunch enemies and the day came when, having gone to see the minister and told him: "I bring you glad tidings!," the response came: "I thank you for tendering your resignation!" (*Le Crapouillot* July 1837). This was one amusing detail that, as a good "humorist," he chose to pass over in silence in his memoirs.

3. Jean Grave, *Quarante ans de propaganda anarchists,* (Paris: Flammarion, 1973), pp. 401-405.

4. Ibid.

5. Jean Caltier-Boissière, "Les mystères de la police secrète" in *Le Crapouillot* (July 1936), pp. 114–117.

6. Report of the congress carried in *Le Revolté* No. 13, (August 20, 1881). Quoted also by J. Carin. *L'Anarchie et les anarchistes* (Paris, 1885), pp. 46–50.

7. Ibid.

8. Goron (former head of the Sûreté), *Mémoires,* Tome I, *De l'invasion à l'anarchie,* foreword by Emile Gautier, (Paris: Flammarion, no date), p. XIV.

9. Quoted by J. Maitron, op. cit., p. 106.

10. *La Révolte* No. 3, (1890).

# VIII. ANTI-ORGANIZATIONISTS AND BOMBERS

Author of a recent thesis on anarchist individualism, Gaetano Manfredonia, offers a very fine definition of the chief characteristic of this era:

> Individual initiative, free agreement, free communism, propaganda by deed, spontaneity of revolutionary action, such were the keynote ideas of anarchism's ideological profile in the 1880s, and they all harked back to the autonomous individual as the agent of social transformation.[1]

Against that sort of backdrop, what might the relations between these "autonomous individuals" be like? All but nonexistent, for there was no federation, no stable liaison, only groups getting together from time to time. In what sense? Emile Gautier explicitly spelled this out at his trial in Lyon:

> We have to be clear about what a group is. In Paris at any rate the anarchist groups are simple rendezvous where friends come together each week to discuss with one another matters of interest to them. Most of the time, indeed, there is hardly a new face to be seen there, beyond the small core of four or five faithful attendees.

In short, these were sort of encounter groups or anarchist "coffee mornings" — minus the drinks apparently. Lest he had not been properly understood, Gautier returned to the topic at his trial:

> An attempt has been made to use as an argument against such and such an anarchist group that there were stamps, that secretaries were appointed, that private meetings were held from time to time.... I defy the prosecution to produce anything of that sort against the Paris anarchist groups — the only ones with which I am familiar, the only ones of which I can speak with knowledge — I defy the prosecution to prove that these anarchist groups were anything other than rendezvous, mere temporary get-togethers, the personnel of which varied every time and to which any newcomer was admitted: therefore he was free to walk away also without further ado, without payment of any subscription, without his even being asked his name or his opinions.[2]

As a result, the anarchist group was wide open, implying no duty or obligation upon participants, nor did it require them to reveal names or occupations, nor to commit themselves to any activity of any sort. The individual remained fully free and autonomous within the group, and the group in turn enjoyed the same freedom and autonomy in the context of the federation, if there was one: there was no connection and no coordination involved. Better still, as Gaetano Manfredonia has remarked, "in the name of the principles of individual autonomy and freedom of initiative, every stable organizational tie was repudiated as being 'authoritarian' and thus anti-anarchist." Hardly surprising, therefore, if the mentally unbalanced or above all agents provocateurs turned up inside these groups, said whatever entered their heads and indulged in the most inflammatory and provocative speechifying. Even Jean Grave ended up exasperated that there were "crackpots" and confidence tricksters locked in interminable competition for the "right to diddle" the comrades. In fact, the illegalist option, a logical choice for revolutionaries confronted with a system which they called into question, was open to a variety of interpretations, even to the extent of introducing "individual recovery" (*reprise individuelle* or petty crime) as a stepping stone to emancipation, by means of murder if need be. Ravachol started off that way: he murdered an old recluse in order to get his hands on his "nest egg" (an action that may have been inspired by or at least placed on a par with the character Raskolnikov in Dostoyevsky's novel *Crime and Punishment*). Others indulged in a less criminal form of illegalist practice, and thus the common-law marriage (*union libre*), and the moonlight flit and other sharp practices came into vogue. All such practices were lumped under a general heading of everyday propaganda by deed, to be sure, but for many that idea was still best encapsulated by the "savage eloquence of dynamite." For years this did not get beyond verbal violence, but in the wake of police harassment, a cycle of murderous outrages was launched one first of May. In the space of two years, it was to cancel every inch of ground gained by libertarians and reduce anarchism to the caricature of the "mad bomber." The ground had been well prepared over a time by a number of loud-mouthed individualists on a retainer from the prefecture of police: those Martinets, the Georges Renards and the mysterious copywriter for *L'Internationale*, a rabble-rousing advocate of propaganda by deed, published out of London

> It is becoming essential that we make everything that science has placed at our disposal sing out loud and clear.... Thus to the theft, murder and arson that have naturally become our legitimate [?] methods for communicating our ultimatum to all the leaders of the present society, we will not hesitate to add chemistry, whose powerful voice is becoming absolutely necessary to our making ourselves heard above the hubbub of society, and to shaking the enemy's fortune into our arms, without squandering our side's blood.... Let us turn our attention to chemistry and set to the manufacture of bombs, dynamite and other explosive materials, a lot more capable than rifles and barricades of encompassing the destruction of the current state of affairs.[3]

That same journal even issued an *Anarchist Guide* which offered descriptions of methods for making such "anti-bourgeois products." It recommended the destruction by fire of all "paperwork" as a means of doing away with government! The unnamed author thus advised arson against ministry offices, tax offices, notaries' offices, all with the aid of inflammable "business circulars"! The provenance of this clumsy provocation was all too transparently obvious. Some people did not take the bait and that brought the worst abuse down on them: they were "petty anarchist popes," "mind-blinkerers," "gangs of doctors, lawyers and other bourgeois turn-keys," or "charlatans, vipers and the like." Jean Grave and *La Révolte* were especially targeted. A number of ordinary swindlers and house-breakers, allegedly operating in pursuit of a militant goal, but in fact for their own petty gain, found here a moral and revolutionary pretext for their skullduggery.

As for explosives, no longer was it a question of Andrieux's Marseilles-made "sardine can," but rather of serious, lethal devices — the instructions for use of which had been widely distributed by "well-meaning folk" — and there were hotheads or manipulated "innocents" to use them.

However, the model for this strategy, the Russian populist terrorists, ought to have served as a painfully instructive object lesson. To review the record: after a number of bloody attempts, they managed to assassinate Tsar Alexander II. True, he was no paragon of democracy and had only hinted at reforms; that said, however, he had abolished serfdom in Russia in 1861, maybe or even assuredly under pressure from events and the repercussions of defeat in the Crimean War against the Anglo-French in 1854–1855. Yet his assassination led his successor Alexander III to condemn his policy in its entirety and waste no time in enforcing a black reaction. This was also a blow to the subterranean campaign being conducted among the peasant masses by thousands of nameless revolutionaries who had taken up Bakunin's advice to go to the people and place themselves at their service. Seeking to accelerate history by a few heroic acts, the Russian terrorists had believed they could skip the requisite awakening of peasant masses still numb from two and a half centuries of serfdom. Here again we find the harm in the Blanquist conspiratorial approach: a tiny band of the "elect" substituting itself and making the choices for everybody.

In addition, this dismal policy was married to a stunning naivety: Zhelyabov, the terrorist leader, a prisoner at the time of the assassination of Alexander II, loudly claimed responsibility for the action when no one suspected him. The police promptly took an interest in his entourage, laid their ambush and thus rounded up the surviving perpetrators of the assassination! There was even a provocative corollary here too: one of the most prominent terrorists, Degaiev, betrayed his colleagues, thereby delivering the *coup de grâce* to the organization. Not that this stopped those who escaped from sticking to the same tactics: in 1887, an attempt on the life of Alexander III failed, and several of the conspirators were hanged, among them the elder brother of the man who was later to make his name as Vladimir Lenin. Several populists slipped through the net and fled abroad, first to Zurich and thence to Paris. It was at this point that a certain Abraham Hekkelman made a name for himself under the alias of Landesen with his revolutionary bombast. A few years before, he had come under suspicion from Vladimir Burtsev (the Sherlock Holmes of the Russian revolutionary movement) of being an agent provocateur. To no avail, so high did his reputation stand among his "Christian" comrades, as Jean Grave would have described them. This Hekkelman-Landesman character acquired so great a moral authority within the Paris group of the populists that on May 28, 1890 and with "fiendish care" he distributed several bombs among his main comrades. The following day, as if by coincidence, the Paris police mounted a search of the home of one of them and arrested 27 of them. Quite unperturbed, Hekkelman stayed calmly at home: before he could be persuaded to get offside, "it took urgent pressures from two naive militants, B. and S., both of them very well regarded in the [Russian] colony [in Paris]: they burst into Landesen's home one evening and *briefed* him about the arrests of their comrades and the suspicions hanging over him."[4] And so he dropped out of sight for a few years, long enough to build himself a new identity: he renounced Judaism, converted to the Orthodox faith and took a young Belgian bourgeois bride, Even so, he continued to render considerable services to the tsarist police, to the extent of being ennobled and, under the name of General Harting, being appointed the head of the police's foreign service. It was not until 1909 that he was finally exposed by Burtsev. Another tsarist secret agent turned up in the affair of the Liège anarchist group; it transpired that he was its explosives man and its leader! The hand of the Okhrana chief, Ratchkovsky, was plain in this: some years later, he would be credited with the fabrication of the *Protocols of the Elders of Zion*. One might think that such events, public knowledge in their day, would have opened the comrades' eyes to the perils of "bomb-ism." Not a bit of it: they made do with, at best, recognizing the limitation upon that method of struggle: thus, in 1891, Kropotkin noted that

> that was where anarchists went wrong in 1881. When the Russian revolutionaries had killed the tsar.... European anarchists imagined that henceforth a handful of zealous revolutionaries, armed with a few bombs, would be enough to make the social revolution.... An edifice built upon centuries of history cannot be destroyed by a few kilos of explosives.... (*La Révolte* No. 32, March 18–24, 1891)

Yet there was no self-criticism in this for he notes that the error was not without its usefulness, in that it enabled anarchists to "maintain their ideal in all its purity"! As far as the era of outrages that was to ensue was concerned, prominent anarchists refrained from offering any justification of them and, to borrow the words of Jean Maitron, "condemned [them] between the lines"!

May 1, 1891 was the start of it all. A police inspector of Levallois-Flerret displayed undue enthusiasm in meting out beatings to several anarchists guilty of having unfurled a red flag! A short while after the anarchists had been given harsh sentences — a travesty of justice that outraged their Paris comrades — the homes of the judge and the prosecutor who had handled the case were the targets for bomb attacks. Thanks to information laid by a female nark planted in his entourage, Ravachol, the perpetrator of the explosions, was quickly identified.[5] A spicy detail: the constabulary almost picked Ravachol up at his home in Saint-Denis, for he had just moved on, with the assistance of a brigadier of the gendarmerie whom he had offered some cigars! We might add that the handcart containing Ravachol's effects and pushed by the sympathetic officer included, in pride of place, a box of dynamite.[6] Ravachol was nonetheless arrested a short while later, because of his preaching, having attempted to convert to his way of thinking the waiter at the Véry restaurant who did not take kindly to the matter and noted his face, reporting him at the earliest opportunity. Some comrades took revenge by blowing up the Véry restaurant, followed by the Bons-Enfants police station and other places, this time with the loss of several lives. The era of "bomb-mania" was at its height. It created such panic that, odd to relate, the profession of magistrate became a risky one and magistrates came to be regarded as undesirables by their landlords, as the one-time head of the Sûreté, Coron, relates:

> Many [magistrates] were given notice, and whenever they showed up at other premises seeking to rent, they were shown the door, at times even rudely. There was one concierge who said one day, with great dignity: "Monsieur Dresch, the police inspector who arrested Ravachol, was left for several weeks with nowhere to stay but the house of a friend!"

Odd that the actions of anarchists should have had that effect, unless M. Goron was exaggerating greatly when he claimed that an anarchist "openly admitting his opinions, was, by contrast, received with open arms."[7]

Motivated by the same sacrificial heroics as the Russian terrorists, some anarchists thus began to carry out to the letter the "explosive" precepts of propaganda by deed, which had been preached on that scale for years to no avail. Countless acts of the sort, happily less lethal, the handiwork of more or less sincere imitators or even of maverick figures, aped Ravachol's example. Later, things took a turn for the worse with the bloody attentats of Emile Henry, Léauthier (who stabbed a Serbian diplomat while he dined because he reckoned he looked and dressed like a bourgeois!), Auguste Vaillant and Caserio. Now, this phenomenon was not beyond everyone's control, and the state authorities were not long in making it redound to their advantage. The memoirs of former police inspector Ernest Raynaud are extremely informative in this regard.[8]

According to Raynaud, one Puibaraud, inspector-general of the Interior Ministry civil service in 1893, played a key role in most of the political skullduggery and provocations of that time. Not that this Puibaraud looked the part: with "his great black moustache, his mop of white hair and his round, churchwarden's face, you would have sworn, upon seeing him, that he was a debonair bourgeois, a harmless pen-pusher," but "behind his podgy appearance [he hid] an acute farsightedness and a steadfast determination. He was an old hand, and had been around a bit," having made a "virtue of cunning." He managed to find himself an employer to match his understated talent, in the person of the minister and high-flying politician Charles Dupuy.

The year 1893 had seen the parliamentary regime shaken by the Panama scandal as its corruption and compromise stood exposed. Dupuy, a "firm-handed authoritarian," was called in to salvage its reputation. He tried a diversionary move, as is often the case in such circumstances, by ordering the closure of the Bourse du Travail on May 1, 1893. But that did not really turn out to his advantage; so he next installed the famous prefect of police, Lépine, and made his first use of Puibaraud in the "Norton papers" set-up, by means of which he disposed to two redoubtable adversaries, Millevoye and Déroulède.

What particularly worried Dupuy, again according to Raynaud, was the libertarian propaganda that was spreading openly and keeping minds in a state of latent rebellion. He told Puibaraud one day of the socialists and *coup d'état*-makers, "Leave them to me! I know where to lay hands on them, but I confess that I am frightened of this virus of anarchy that has invaded the body of society, wreaking great havoc there. It is that virus above all else that we have to eradicate. As I see it, the real danger lies there." In fact, the first anarchist attentats had been so well received, according to Raynaud, by the populace who acclaimed the propagandists by deed as "liberators," for those attacks had been primarily directed against "tyrants, sovereigns, heads of state, the well-to-do, magistrates and policemen." Furthermore, anarchy was very much in vogue among the literati and artists, if not in fashionable circles.

Puibaraud replied to Dupuy that he would undertake to exercise that danger, provided that he could have new legislation outlawing the anarchists and criminalizing their beliefs. Promoted director-general of detectives at the Prefecture, Puibaraud then set to work. Thus, when, on November 9, 1893, Vaillant tossed his bomb into the "crêpe-eaters of the Aquarium" (as the Chamber of Deputies had been nicknamed by *Le Père Peinard*), causing only a few slight injuries, Dupuy, who was chairing the Assembly displayed extraordinary sang-froid and even ventured the historic comment: "The proceedings continue!"

According to Raynaud, Dupuy, who had learned of the intentions of Vaillant (who had been driven to despair by society's iniquity) through one of Puibaraud's informants had, far from proceeding against him, ordered his minions to remedy his lack of wherewithal. So, a "house-breaker" comrade, conveniently released from prison, supplied Vaillant with the money and materials for his nail-bomb, manufactured in the Prefecture's municipal laboratory, so that they could rest assured as to its harmlessness. The entire political class, implicated up to its neck in the Panama scandal, was home and dry by the next day: the attentat had served as its lightning conductor and public attention had been diverted in the direction of the scapegoated "dangerous anarchists." Especially as Puibaraud laid on a whole flurry of phoney attentats in every quarter of Paris, bringing about a u-turn in the public's opinion of anarchists.

Hot on the heels of that, the "crêpe-eaters" now had only to vote through the *lois scélérates* of 1894 and that was that. Libertarian ideas were at last deemed thought crimes and the way was clear for massive repression: two thousand searches carried out across the country, dozens sentenced for the crime of Anarchy: finally, thirty celebrated anarchists were placed on trial. Against all the odds, that trial ended with the prosecution in disarray and the accused were set free. We might note one ridiculous incident during the proceedings. The prosecution counsel, Bulot, sworn enemy of anarchists, opened his mail while one hearing was in session, probably intending to peruse with relish the many letters denouncing anarchists that he received on a daily basis, when suddenly he leapt to his feet and asked for a recess: "I request a one-minute suspension of the proceedings. I have just unwrapped a package that I received through the post, and it contains fecal matter. I request leave to go and wash my hands." Which enabled one of the accused, Fénéon, to provoke general hilarity when he commented: "Not since Pontius Pilate have hands been washed with such solemnity." [9] That day the "party of mockery" made recruits, especially as the panic-stricken bureaucrats had taken their nit-picking to the lengths of placing a formal ban, with an eye to New Year's Day 1894, upon "the exercise of any industry involving furnaces or requiring the assistance of flammable instruments." [10] The scare had burned itself out: it was the end of an era. Having obtained what it was after, the bourgeois state had no further need of the "bomb madness" and such activities were to vanish from the records in the decades that followed.

As for Puibaraud, his provocative methods seriously upset his own colleagues from the Prefecture, and he was removed from office. Shunned by his decidedly ungrateful silent partners, he ended his life in oblivion, forgotten by everybody. We should say that the calling of the provocateur on the payroll was not always so peaceable. One Gustave Buisson, known as "le Petit Pâtissier" (the Little Pastrycook), having wormed his way into the Le Havre anarchist group, denounced several of its members who were arrested and convicted. Moving to Paris and believing his cover to be intact, he tried to carry on as a nark. Two Parisian comrades, café waiters at that (a profession that had a rather unsavoury reputation in these matters), lured him, on the pretext of some operation, to the banks of the Saint Denis canal, where they called him to account and executed him.[11] They were discovered and deported to penal servitude. Nevertheless, what they had done gave the Little Pastrycook's imitators food for thought and dampened their ardor.

The vast majority of anarchists, including Kropotkin, Reclus, Grave, Malato and Malatesta ended up dissociating themselves completely from the outrages. They were a bit late, for, unbeknownst to themselves, they had let their enemy's back-room boys prescribe their movement's policy line. So, for them, it was unquestionably a heavy defeat. They were to strive to learn from it, because, in the final analysis, it was from that point on that the movement got off the ground. Henceforth, there would be a clear dividing line between the social, libertarian communist current and the individualist anarchist trend, which was yet to be the object of much controversy.

## Endnotes to Chapter Eight

1. Gaetano Manfredonia, *L'individualisme anarchists en France (1880–1914),* duplicated doctoral thesis submitted to the Paris Institute for Political Studies, 1984, 559pp. The quotation is taken from p. 54.

2. *Le procés des anarchistes devant la police correctionnelle et la cour dapper de Lyon,* (Lyon, 1883), pp. 10 and 152.

3. Quoted by Félix Dubois, *Le péril anarchists*, (Paris, 1894), pp. 165–174.

4. Jean Longuet and Georges Silber, *Les dessous de la police russe: Terroristes et policiers,* foreword by V. Burtsev, (Paris: Librairie Félix Juven, 1909), p. 223. This whole period of subterfuge and police dirty work have been analysed in detail by Henri Rollin's remarkable book *L'apocalypse de notre temps*, (Paris: Gallimard, 1939) (extremely rare, having been destroyed as soon as the Germans entered Paris).

5. Jean Maitran, Introduction to *Ravachol et les anarchistes*, (Paris, 1964), p. 40.

6. M. Coron, *Mémoires,* op. cit., Tome I, p. 194.

7. Ibid., p. 204.

8. Ernest Raynaud, *Souvenirs de police: La vie intime des commissariats Payot,* (Paris, 1926), pp. 33–46.

9. Jacques Prolo, *Les anarchistes*, (Riviére, 1912), p. 62.

10. Henri Varennes, *De Ravachol a Caserio,* (Garnier, no date), p. 101.

11. Goron, *Mémoires,* op. cit., Tome IV, pp. 210–220.

## IX.  FROM THE FREE CONTRACT TO THE "ANARCHIST WORKERS' PARTY (CGT)"

After a year and a half of a repression that led several anarchists — Pouget, Malato, and Louise Michel — to seek safety in exile in London, an amnesty afforded the French movement the opportunity to spring back into life. Militant activity was at all times expressed primarily through periodicals: *Le Libertaire* founded by Sébastien Faure and Louise Michel, reappeared in 1895; *La Révolte* was replaced by *Les Temps nouveaux* with the irreplaceable and imperturbable Jean Grave at the helm; finally, under the alert authorship of Emile Pouget, *Le Père Peinard* embarked upon a new series.

In order to show off the coherence of anarchist ideas, prominent militants themselves brought out a whole series of publications, primarily under the imprint of the *Bibliothèque sociologique* of the Stock publishinghouse. These were often articles that were first blown up into pamphlets and then revised and expanded into book size. Peter Kropotkin, still in London because he was forbidden to enter France, also took part in this publishing venture. Taken together, these publications represent a solid theoretical grounding, and they anchored libertarian ideas firmly in many a head. However, we have to note the vagueness of the practical methods advocated: in a way, once the goals had been determined, it was up to each individual to shift for himself in the reaching of them. Freedom of initiative and the free contract between individuals were the panacea in matters of organization. Malato hinted very timidly at a "libertarian federation of workers and peasants ... an idea unfortunately hampered in its execution by a variety of factors, but which remains completely valid." What about those factors? Malato fails to make any further reference to them and makes do with the claim that:

> with its thousand centers of activity, groups, committees, federations, all autonomous but in constant liaison one with another and not afraid, should the circumstances so demand, to subordinate their personal preferences to the necessity for concerted action, anarchism is stronger and above all less vulnerable than authoritarian socialism with its hierarchy, its watchwords, its parliaments and its crude connections, which the government can sever with one saber blow.[1]

One seeks consolation where one may, but it is better to have something to "sever" than nothing at all, we might say. Like a good "*bouif*,"[2] Jean Grave drives his nail home into the question, but very gently for he has to wade through elementary banalities such as, say, conceding that:

> every time the human being seeks to accomplish something, he finds himself obliged to join his endeavors to the efforts of other like-minded beings, in order to afford his action the widest possible scope and all of the impact that they can bring to it. And, whatever they may say, that is what those who deny the usefulness of association are compelled to do. But the efforts brought jointly to bear, with an eye to deriving the greatest possible advantage from them, must, if their goal is to be achieved, be coordinated into collective action, with each individual taking up the part to which he is best suited, or which strikes him as most apt in his sphere of activity. Some may call that organization, some may prefer the description of contract, but what matter the name, provided the thing be accomplished.

As was his wont, that stance was immediately counter-balanced by the vision of

> seeing resurrected as a result (in these hopefully vast federations), central committees, shared minimum programs, and other authoritarian appendages that we imagined we had transfigured because we yoked them to new formulas and hung new names upon them.[3]

The fear of "regimentation" still held sway.

Little by little, though, the natural need to seek company, even if only for as long as a congress took, reappeared on the agenda. Especially as, whereas anarchists had repudiated the need to hold congresses, they had no objection to going along to disrupt the congresses of the socialists: thus, it was on those grounds that they were denied entry to the Zurich Congress (1893) and the London Congress (1896), when recognition of state socialism was made a prerequisite for participants. An anti-parliamentary congress was scheduled for Paris in 1900. Several submissions were drafted with that in mind. As the congress was banned, these appeared as articles or in pamphlet form. The very active Internationalist Revolutionary Socialist Students of Paris group (*Etudiants Socialistes Révolutionnaires Internationalistes de Paris* — ESRI) thus brought out its *Submission on the Necessity of Establishing Some Ongoing Understanding Between the Anarchist and Revolutionary Communist Groups*. It was hedged about by all sorts of provisos: it included the declaration that the authors had no designs upon "any kind of centralized organization, nor any kind of administrative authority." The groups would not be giving up any of their autonomy in this marriage of necessity: the professed aim was for them to be in contact with one another, to have suitable addresses and to correspond or possibly get together. The overriding reasons for getting together followed: "Nothing of any import" had been undertaken in respect of the struggle against the reaction: at critical moments, they had been forced to resort to bourgeois newspapers in order to issue summonses to libertarians: personal misunderstandings, taken together with the lack of liaison between the local groupings had occasionally resulted in the decline, if not the demise, of certain national movements.

Another drawback was stressed: newspapers were exclusively dependent upon their owners and their relations with the groups were more rather desultory or even hostile for "a man is master in his own home" [our quotation — A. Skirda]. When all was said and done, the authors wanted:

> something that will allow us to maintain contacts with one another — between the districts of a large city like Paris, between the different communes in a country, or even between comrades from different countries — as often as we may have the need. Let it go under the name of "understanding," "alliance," "union," "federation" or "correspondence bureau": the name is of little significance to us. But it will still be the first step towards an organization, we may be told, "and that organization may culminate later in centralization!"[4]

In the name of their libertarian principles, the authors ruled out the possibility of things following such a course. The Marx syndrome was still doing damage and cast a long shadow over minds as soon as organization was mentioned. All the same, was this not overstating things a bit and erasing all recollection of the Bakuninist Alliance or were the former members of that afraid of lifting the veil covering its structure and its mode of operation? Unless we are to rule out that hypothesis, it is none too easy to understand how the general disorganization of the anarchists failed to trigger some sort of a backlash and how the ESRI group could have been induced to close its submission with the stipulation that its appeal for unity was addressed only to those who were supportive of it (!) and that they hoped others would not place obstacles in its path!

Even this surprisingly timid proposal in favor of a correspondence bureau and a federation failed to find favor with Jean Grave. In a later report drawn up for the same banned congress, he opened by upbraiding the absurdity of those who had thus far, on one pretext or another, tried:

> to dragoon, to discipline and draw individuals into hierarchical and centralized arrangements that are bedecked with the name of organization, [and] among the anarchists, we have witnessed comrades asserting that, as they want nothing more to do with authority, so they want no more truck with organization.

He then notes the lack of cohesion that leads anarchists to "be a little bit indiscriminate in their fire, having no links of any kind and losing something of their strength as a result for want of solidity in affording their activity more consistency." However he did not bemoan that, for, by his reckoning, it was not "such a big problem," because it was:

> the wont of the authoritarian parties to decree agreement and federation, setting up organizations and groupings whose object was to ensure such union and unity of purpose.

As he saw it, federation would come about only through the progressive agglomeration of groups and not because some decision would have been made to set up a grouping charged with seeing to its organization. Also, in his view, agreement and relations did exist between the anarchist groups: what was lacking was to have these in a coordinated, consistent and generalized way. In passing, he congratulated himself upon the anti-militarist propaganda carried out over the past twenty years, this having made it possible for the Dreyfus Case to be played up! [5]

In Grave's view, had anarchists been "centralized or federalized at the outset of their propaganda, they would have lost in initiative and autonomy whatever they might have gained in unity." And what of the correspondence bureau to which reference had been made? Let us look at that: Grave himself had been in charge of one at the London Congress and wow! it had remained a dead letter. A distinction had to be made between cohesion and unification, which meant proceeding from the "top instead of from the grassroots up." Consequently, anarchists needed to become alive to the overriding necessity of it and acquire the necessary conviction the better to connect with one another. Likewise, he had no particular "aversion" to mention of an "anarchist party." Provided that the term was used to "designate merely a category of individuals who, possessed of a fund of shared ideas, therefore enjoyed a degree of effective and moral solidarity against their adversary: the bourgeois society." The counterbalance to that (again that even-handed style of his) came from rejection of any body "charged with expressing the ideas of the party":

> In any group, however tiny, there are always, of necessity, disagreements in the thinking of its component members. And whenever that group affirms a set of ideas as its own, that is only the mean of its thinking, for if they had set them all out, it would no longer be making an affirmation but a straightforward contradictory exposition of them. Now, how are you going to arrive at an official organ of the anarchist party expressing the thinking of the "anarchist party," when anarchists are not and cannot be in agreement on every particular?

It is to some extent understandable that Grave should have questioned the precept of delegation, but for him to postulate "necessary" disagreement between anarchists seems absurd, for if that were truly the case, what then would be the common ground that would justify their libertarian convictions? That is taking the cult of individuality a bit far, if one wishes to struggle for realization of its social ideal. This attitude is worth underlining, for it is what we might describe as a human constant which boils down to saying, according to the classic example, that a bottle is half empty when it is only half full. In organizational terms, it consists of advancing every possible and conceivable ground for not seeing eye to eye on anything, rather than stressing the grounds for a fundamental unity: in the final analysis, this is setting everybody systematically against everybody else. Leading on to complete disunion, and in roundabout fashion arriving at the prevailing motif of inegalitarian societies "the war of each against all": a position diametrically opposed to the revolutionary ethic peddled by the founding fathers of the anarchist doctrine, as we have seen above. Closed fist, or open hand — one has to choose!

This "negativist" position on organization is not merely the one adopted by Grave, he claims it as his own:

> A unity of views is unrealizable: then again, it would be harmful, because it would spell immobility. It is because we do not agree upon certain ideas that we discuss them, and that in discussing them we will discover others which we did not even suspect. A huge diversity of ideas, views, aptitudes is necessary for the organization of a harmonious social condition.[6]

That was far from being merely his personal opinion: it was the view held overwhelmingly in the anarchist circles of the time.

Despite the smugness that Grave radiates, the development of anarchist ideas was then unmistakably stagnant, especially as the yearned for "Great Day" had failed to arrive. In order to sidestep any charges of passivity, it became more convenient to rail against the "ignorance of the crowd" and the brutalization of the workers by the state and the reformist parties. Anarchy turned into an elitist concept: Grave talked about the "difficulties of making oneself understood by the crowd" and of "drawing it up to us and not descending to its level." Curious evolution from propagandist anarchist to libertarian anchorite!

Grave's final argument against organization: the danger that police repression posed for a central agency. It need only be "harassed" and its members would be scattered and above all "the exchange of correspondence one was trying to facilitate, hobbled." Given the modesty of the connection envisaged, such anxiety might seem exaggerated.

How are we to account for this attitude on the part of Grave, one of the leading figures in French anarchism at that time? He was a self-educated cobbler who had had an impoverished childhood, a real "son of the people" who became a zealous propagandist so persnickety about the orthodoxy of the doctrine that he came to be nicknamed "the Pope of Anarchy" by malicious tongues. His reasoning, standpoints and opinions often seem essentially correct but, as we have seen on several occasions, they added up to nothing when it came to practical action in the short term. For all his gifts as a writer, his emotional nature left him incapable of public speaking (just like the talented Emile Pouget). Perhaps it was this inhibition that gave him a complex and led him to take refuge in his work as a publicist — he was to edit excellent publications over a forty-year period — and to recoil from the slightest attempted interference.

With Fernand Pelloutier, we are confronted by a horse of a quite different color: he had his feet well planted in social soil. A convert from socialism to anarchism (as was Sébastien Faure, while Constant Martin was a convert from

Blanquism) in 1892, when the "Ravachol era" was at its height, he immersed himself completely in trade union affairs: he played a preponderant role especially in the founding of the Bourses du Travail, astutely fending off intrusion by Guesdist politicians. In his celebrated *Letter to Anarchists* in 1899, he offered a hard-headed assessment of the movement:

> Thus far we anarchists have conducted what I shall term practical propaganda [as opposed to the purely theoretical propaganda of Grave] without the shade of a unity of views. Most of us have flitted from method to method, without great deliberation aforethought, and with no spirit of consistency, at the whim of circumstances.[8]

He noted that anarchists' "wonderful" written propaganda had been followed up only by the most mediocre "active propaganda." Which he regarded as a great pity, for, as he saw it, the anarchist "has resources of energy and a proselytizing zeal that might be described as inexhaustible!"

What Pelloutier was asking for, then, was "that each of us (in the light of his own conscience) makes a firm option in favor of one particular mode of propaganda and the no less firm determination to commit to it all of the energy with which he has been endowed." Especially as the first general congress of the Socialist Party had just been held and the workers' unions had been remarkable by their absence, proof of their mistrust of parliamentarism and the usefulness of reforms. In fact, socialists of various persuasions had managed to find a temporary solution to the "abominable squabbling" between (in Pelloutier's words) the "Torquemada in the opera glasses and the would-be shooter of anarchists, [9] Lafargue and Zévaès." It should be said that that same year, 1899, had seen the sensational entry of a socialist, Millerand, into the bourgeois government of Waldeck-Rousseau, a government in which General Callifet — who had massacred the Communards in 1871 — had been appointed, by way of a counter-weight, Defense Minister! All to preserve the unity of the nation, threatened by the Dreyfus Affair. The "man who shot down the Commune shook hands with the defender of the shot": that naturally triggered a great storm, albeit a storm in a tea cup — for the reformists, and the appetite for power in many socialists, triumphed in the end and they adapted to the good form of ministerial office. It was on these grounds that Pelloutier argued that the existence of the Socialist Party was "precious" in the extreme, and that "if it did not exist, we would have to invent it, given the way its haughtiness and its impertinence make political socialism hateful in the eyes of the unionized masses." There followed a few extremely pertinent and relevant lines about the Socialist Party which "is not going to be just another political party, paralyzing the energy and spirit of initiative that we seek to inject into the union groupings, but will in addition be a counterrevolutionary party, tantalizing the people's appetites with anodyne reforms, and the trades associations, forswearing ... will again put their trust in the unrealizable promises of politics."

Pelloutier then went on to offer this remarkable profile of the anarchists:

Outcasts from the Party, because they are no less revolutionary than Vaillant and Guesde, as steadfast in their advocacy of the suppression of individual ownership, we are, in addition, something they are not: rebels around the clock, men truly godless, masterless and nationless, irreducible enemies of every despotism, moral and material, individual or collective, that is to say, of laws and dictatorships (including that of the proletariat) and keen enthusiasts of self-improvement.

In his estimation, that last point was a crucial complement to the economic struggle, so that the awakening of the workers, who, after having "long believed themselves condemned to the role of instrument, seek to become intelligent creatures so that they may be at once the inventors and the creators of their endeavors."[10] That, he reckoned, was where anarchy came into its own. As for the unions, their duty was to "sow in the very belly of capitalist society the seeds of the free producers' groups through which it seems our communist and anarchist ideal must come to pass." We might also note the advocacy of the general strike, a point setting anarchists apart from the Guesdists and political socialists. For Pelloutier, it was the method par excellence whereby the society of oppression might be overturned, thus replacing the famous violent overthrow or the make-or-break Great Day.

Though he went to an early grave at the age of just 33 — the onerous task he had set himself played its part in his demise — Pelloutier is the founding father of revolutionary syndicalism, which really took off with the amalgamation of the various unions and the *Federation of the Bourses du Travail* into the General Confederation of Labor *(Confédération Générale du Travail* — CGT). Following his example, large numbers of anarchists henceforth gave of their best to this.

One of the ones that committed himself most to it was Emile Pouget. By no means an unknown in the anarchist movement, it could even be said that he was one of the founders of it in France, since he had belonged to it since 1879. He took part in the London congress in 1881, then was involved in the Louise Michel demonstration in 1883 that turned into looting of the breadshops. It was while attempting to rescue "good old Louise" from the hands of the police that he was arrested and sentenced along with her in connection with the riots. After a three-year prison term, he was freed and in 1889 launched an extremely popular publication, *Le Père Peinard*, an anarchist reincarnation of the French revolution's firebrand *Le Père Duchêne*, which had been revived once before, in 1871 at the time of the Paris Commune. Pouget displayed a heck of a journalistic gift, writing in popular style. Let us take a look at the program of this old "shoe-mender":

It's as familiar as the villainy of generals: less long-winded than the 1793 Constitution, it was summed up, a little over a century ago, by the Old Man, Father Duchêne: "I don't want anyone shafting me!" To the point. No weasel words there. And that declaration, more incisive than the Declaration of the Rights of Man and the Citizen, answers everything, encapsulates everything, does for everything. The day when the common folk are no longer being shafted is the day when bosses, governments, priests, magistrates and other blood-suckers are pushing up daisies. And on that day the sun will shine upon everybody and there will be a place at the table for everybody.

But, damn it, it won't all happen in one go! The time is long gone when quails fell from out of the heavens, ready roasted and wrapped in vine leaves. Come that day, if we want Society to smile upon us, we have to shift for ourselves and rely upon our own efforts alone.

This blunt, rough-and-ready talk not only made him a hit with his readership, but also brought Pouget and the paper's administration lots of brushes with the authorities. During his enforced exile in London in 1894, Pouget had acquainted himself with the British trade unions and come to appreciate their capacity for standing up to capitalism. As soon as he returned to France he set about spreading the syndicalist gospel:

If there is one group where the anarchos should be making inroads it is of course the Trades Council.… The problem is as follows: "I'm an anarcho, I want to plant my ideas, now where would they prosper best?" "I already have the factory and the drinking den.… I'd like something better: somewhere where I can meet proles who have some grasp of the exploitation we suffer and are racking their brains to come up with some remedy for it. Does such a place exist?" Yes, by God. And there is only one: the trades association!

Pouget set about encouraging his colleagues into the unions — some of them were reluctant, if not downright hostile — for the "big cheeses would kick up some stink if it turned out that the anarchos, whom they reckoned they had muzzled, were seizing upon the opportunity to worm their way into the unions and spread their ideas there without any great to-do, or airs and graces." [11] As good as his word, he became increasingly involved in the CGT, becoming its assistant general secretary and editor in chief of its mouthpiece *La Voix du Peuple*. He also continued to elaborate upon its theory and practice in numerous articles and a few crucial pamphlets. His syndicalism was of a distinctly libertarian hue: its prime and principal target was "elimination of wage-slavery and the employer." This struggle was waged exclusively on the economic terrain, in stark opposition to the Guesdist politicians' strategy of going after political power. And it was with some reason that the elderly James Guillaume regarded this CGT as the "continuation" of the federalist anti-authoritarian International of Bakuninist tradition. Enriched, this time around, by the experience accumulated over upwards of twenty years of anarchist militancy. Along with his colleagues, Pouget devised a clear, well-defined strategy and tactics. In keeping with the First International's device of "the emancipation of the workers will be the workers' own doing," that strategy relied upon direct action, eschewing any intermediary or substitute for the workers' own determination to fight and win. The latter was founded upon the "...personal worth of each individual and thereby genuinely carried out an educational task, while also carrying out a commission to bring to bring about change." [12]

In this way the proletariat was released from the sheepish status in which leaders and property owners were their shepherds. As Victor Griffuelhes, another revolutionary syndicalist theorist (with his roots in Blanquism) put it, direct action meant that "happiness is not a gift but something to be earned and worked for."

The main tactical method adopted was the strike, the "gymnastics of rebellion," whether partial and local or general and expropriatory: in either instance, it was not at all spontaneous but carefully cultivated. The general strike was not envisaged as a wholly peaceful process: violence was, so to speak, inescapable, so it tended to be revolutionary and insurrectionary, thereby supplanting the Blanquist coup de main and the armed uprising which had been regarded as the only ways of overthrowing the old order. [13]

At the suggestion of Emile Pouget and Paul Delesalle, the CGT's Toulouse congress in 1897 approved two other significant weapons of labor struggle: the boycott and sabotage. The first meant the "placing upon the Index, an interdict placed upon an industrialist or businessman, inviting workers not to consent to work for him and, in the case of a trader under boycott, inviting customers not to use his shop": it was also a way of defending oneself against the greed of intermediaries trying "on the backs of the consumer, to lay claim to the improvements secured by the producer." The counterpart of this was the union label, signifying conformity with union conditions. As for sabotage, that was the implementation of the maxim: "Poor work for poor pay"; it hit the boss "where it hurt, namely, in the wallet." [14]

All of these ideas underpinned revolutionary syndicalism and signaled the ascendancy of anarchists inside the CGT from 1902 to 1908, so much so that one of the later generation of CGT leaders, Lucien Niel, wrote that the CGT had ceased to be a trades body and turned into an Anarchist Workers' Party! That wisecrack is not completely bereft of truth, but it comes as a surprise if we examine the organizational thinking and internal operation of the CGT. The first point that strikes us is that among the anarchists and their supporters, who were then in the majority in the Confederation, there was an utter repudiation of democracy. For example, at the Bourges congress in 1904, they rejected the reformists' motion in favor of proportional representation. Let us see how Emile Pouget accounted for this seemingly paradoxical stance:

> The confederal organization's methods of action do not draw their inspiration from the vulgar democratic idea: they are not the expression of the consent of a majority indicated by means of universal suffrage. That could not be the case, in most instances, for it is rare for a union to encompass the totality of workers: all too often, it embraces only a minority. Now, if the democratic mechanism was operating inside

the workers' organizations, the dissenting voice of the unconscious and non-unionized majority would bring all action to a standstill.

But the minority is not prepared to abdicate its demands because of the inertia of a mass whose spirit of rebellion has yet to awake and spring to life. As a result, there is a duty upon the conscious minority to act, without regard to the refractory mass — on pain of their being forced to kowtow, as the unconscious ones do. [16]

Also, according to Pouget, the mass had no grounds for complaint, for, amorphous though it might be, it would be the first beneficiary of the minority's action: whereas the militants were entitled to bear the full brunt of the struggle, often failing in the fray. Unlike universal suffrage which entrusts:

the helm to the unconscious ones, the foot-draggers (or rather to their representatives) smothers the minorities who carry the future within them" [the syndicalist approach led to] "the diametrically opposite result: the drive comes from the conscious, the rebels, and all well-meaning folk are summoned to action, to participation in the movement.

In the political sphere, Pouget reckoned that there was more justification for proportional representation because under:

the simplistic mechanism of universal suffrage, the unconscious big battalions come together and crush the conscious minorities, so there is more of a justification for proportional representation in that it enables these latter to show themselves.

In spite of this repudiation of all democratism, the CGT's structures and modus operandi could not have been more democratic and federalist. Comprising of two sections, the Trades Federations and the Bourses du Travail, it was run by a Federal Committee made up of the delegates from each of its affiliated organizations: these delegates could be recalled at any time for they were in permanent contact with the group from which they received their mandate. Sovereignty was vested in Congress. Voting there was on the basis of mandates, not in proportion with the membership of each body or affiliated organization, but by grouping — this was a rejection of the democratism sought by the reformists who accounted for a majority of the membership numerically but controlled only a minority of the organizations represented. Congress could endorse or reject the reports presented by those officers whom it had commissioned to carry out certain duties: the general secretary, his assistant, the editors of the CGT mouthpiece *La Voix du Peuple,* and other committees and commissions. These officers were full-time officials and were paid, albeit very poorly, and were described as "officials."

Thus, the CGT was a mass organization embracing a conscious and active minority, with openly professed libertarian aims and methods tailored to the social and economic circumstances of the day. In its operation, it departed from that utter rejection of delegation which had come to be the tradition among French anarchists.

We can see here a resurgence of the anti-authoritarian current of the First International and even, informally, of the Bakuninist Alliance, embodied this time by the anarchists who assumed the leadership of the CGT, though they were not specifically organized to do so. After a hiatus of thirty years, and the blind alleys of propaganda by deed, anarchism was returning to its Proudhonist and Bakuninist roots, at last successfully jettisoning the Marx syndrome which had had such an inhibiting effect thus far. But was such social and economic intervention by anarchists unanimously welcomed in anarchist ranks? Not at all: that was far from the case, as we shall now see.

## Endnotes to Chapter Nine

1. Charles Malato, *Philosophie de l'anarchie,* (Paris: Stock, 1897), p. 236.
2. Slang or trade term for shoe-mender.
3. Jean Grave, *L'Anarchie, son but, ses moyens,* (Paris: Stock, 1899), pp. 220–222.
4. Etudiants Socialistes Révolutionnaires Internationalistes de Paris *,Rapport sur la nécessité d'établir une entente durable entre les groupes anarchistes et communistes révolutionnaires,* (Paris, 1900).
5. In fact, the period was profoundly marked by that Affair: it gave rise to a confused turmoil in which a revolutionary cat would have had great difficulty identifying her kittens! The root cause of it all was the unjust conviction of a captain, (a millionaire and son of a millionaire in the francs of the day) on account of his Jewish faith. Many anarchists let themselves be dragged into this questionable episode: Sébastien Faure even set up a daily newspaper with the backing of Jewish capital, and good comrades wrote for it. It is questionable whether libertarians seized upon the issue the better to attack and discredit the army, the very army whose commanders had waded deep in the blood of the Communards. Thus, it was a sort of revenge from beyond the grave, albeit in a very roundabout fashion. But let us move on.
6. Jean Grave, *Organisation, initiative, cohésion,* (Paris, 1900), pp. 3–15.
7. Jean Grave, *L'Anarchie, son but, ses moyens,* op. cit., pp. 34– 45.
8. Fernand Pelloutier, *Le congrés général du Parti Socialiste Français,* (December 2–8, 1898) preceded by his *Lettre aux anarchistes,* (Paris: Stock, 1900). pp. III–IX.
9. Pelloutier used these labels for Jules Guesde and Edouard Vaillant respectively.
10. F. Pelloutier, "L'organisation corporative et l'anarchie" in *L'Art social,* 1896, quoted by Victor Dave in F. Pelloutier, *Histoire des Bourses du Travail,* foreword by Georges Sorel and biographical outline by Victor Dave, (Paris: Costes, 1921), pp. 18–19.
11. "A roublard, roublard et demi" in *Le Père Peinard,* (October 1894).
12. *Encyclopédie du mouvement socialists* part one, (January 1912), article by V. Griffuelhes on direct action, pp. 12–17.
13. E. Pouget gave an excellent description of this imagined revolutionary process in his social novel, written in partnership with Pataud, *Comment nous ferons la révolution,* (Paris, 1911).
14. E. Pouget, *La Confédération Générale du Travail,* (Paris: Ed. Riviére, undated-1908?), pp. 44-46.
15. J. Prolo, *Les anarchistes,* op. cit., p. 72.
16. E. Pouget, *La CGT,* op. cit., pp. 36-37.

# X. THE INDIVIDUALISTS, THE RUSSIAN REVOLUTION OF 1905 AND THE CONGRESS OF AMIENS (1906)

Although the majority of French anarchists committed themselves to the CGT's trade union action, some remained staunchly opposed to that. They regarded the trade union as powerless to carry out the revolution and favored, say, the wildcat to the organized strike, for, in the latter instance, if the demands made resulted in negotiations or agreements, that involved, they argued, compromise with the employers and the state. As a result, (the argument went) syndicalism undermined the will to revolution and nursed a sectional mentality, to the detriment of the class as a whole and, particularly, those whom the system tossed onto the scrap heap: the unemployed, the hoboes (there were nearly 400,000 gentlemen of the road in France around 1900), seasonal workers, even the ones with a police record and the prostitutes or any unprotected worker.

Figures of some renown, like Sébastien Faure, Jean Grave and Ernest Girault were numbered among these opponents of syndicalism but, for the most part such opponents were recruited from among the individualist anarchists. With the appearance of the first French translations of Stirner, the old verbose, provocative and suspect individualism was, so to speak, validated and made more coherent. Anarchy was no longer a social teaching but rather a philosophy and the art of a "lifestyle." Indeed, the "Bengal lights" of propaganda by deed having failed to inspire the *Slave's Awakening* (to take the title of one anarchist publication), a change had swept over anarchists, the individualist anarchists especially. While standing by their advocacy of libertarian communism, they had no wish to postpone their emancipation to some far-off tomorrow and took the line that a start had to be made by regenerating individuals one at a time, by making a "revolution of minds," and freeing them from the noxious influence of the established society, so as to lay the foundations of an anarchist society right now. Thus, for the most active of them, new fields of activity were opened up: education, not restricted to children but targeting adults also, by means of evening classes: the question of birth control and neo-Malthusianism, including eugenics and abortion: vegetarianism — veganism, for the most radical, with no eggs or dairy products acceptable: anarchist colonies and so-called "free space" where an attempt was made to live in as anarchistic a fashion as possible: finally, anti-patriotic and anti-militarist activities on more systematic lines than hitherto.

Disappointed by the masses' lack of enthusiasm for their subversive schemes, the individualists completely withdrew into themselves. They denied the existence of social classes, acknowledging individuals only: some of the latter would be willful and aware, the others passive and unconscious. These latter seemed every bit as dangerous as the exploiters, for, by their submission and resignation, they were their accessories and accomplices. In 1905, one of the editorial staff of *L'Anarchie*, the individualists' weekly newspaper, even took the workers scornfully to task for being worse than sheep because "on a sheep farm, whenever a move is made to shear a sheep, it tries to escape and has to be tied. No need of that where the worker is concerned: he offers his own back."[1] In the view of the individualists, the anarchist should not be molded by his environment, but should instead be the one who molded it.

Around this time two personalities emerged from among the individualists: Albert Libertad and Paraf-Javal. A duo connected as if they were twins, they were the motivating forces behind the *causeries populaires* (Popular Talking-Shops) based in the rue du Chevalier de la Barre in Montmartre. They peddled and, on occasion, acted upon the new doctrine of liberation of the individual. Paraf-Javal pushed a "scientific" version of anarchy, worked out almost mathematically: his exposition was based upon logical and unprejudiced analysis of a phenomenon, a free examination that turned, by its conclusion, into a fundamental and categorical theorem. Thus the freethinker is the man whose thinking is *a posteriori,* working from physical knowledge, unlike the "brute," with his unexamined, *a priori* opinions.[2] Libertad was in his thinking a touch less simplistic and above all else was possessed of a real journalistic talent. As the founder of *L'Anarchie*, the individualists' official platform, he forcefully upbraided all oppressors and impostors, while not sparing their confederates, the resigned types, and he sang the praises of the individual's "joie de vivre" freed of all impediment through pursuit of his real needs and aspirations. We might note particularly his original application of the Taylor system to real life: he urged a "stoppage in useless gestures" as a means of shrugging off phony activities and harmful acts. These included all useless and parasitical trades, the object of which was laughable luxury, arbitrary supervision, defense of the state and the accumulation of wealth. On that basis and himself working irregularly as a proofreader of libertarian or kindred publications, it will be appreciated that Libertad had but little sympathy for syndicalism, which did not at all suit the trades plied by his followers.

Despite their undeniable outrageousness, all these notions flying in the face of conventional wisdom might have had a certain interest to them, had their inventors not been associated with a "muckraking" (Libertad's phrase) exhibitionist ethos, inevitably resulting in personal or factional squabbles and controversies. Which led Paraf-Javal to devise a theorem for "mock-anarchists": "Most were only brutes, for the *scientific* anarchists are the only true authentic ones," scientific anarchists being those individuals "determined to be freethinkers in all circumstances and capable of being so." Out of which sprouted attacks upon his erstwhile "twin" in anarchy, as Libertad and his colleagues were characterized as "ignorant every last one of them, filthier and more pathological than the bulk of their contemporaries whom they label as bourgeois ... (they are) often addicted to alcohol and tobacco, and megalomaniacs."[3] These seemingly crackpot disagreements degenerated dramatically, however: increasingly violent punch-ups pitted the disciples of the respective "feuding brothers" against one another, and after Libertad's death in 1908 from an improperly-treated anthrax infection (and not from a police beating as the legend has claimed), the score-settling by revolver cost lives. Paraf-Javal gave ground, drifted away from anarchist circles and went off to bring the good news to what he reckoned was a more likely audience: the Freemasons (he came to wield complete control of one lodge, before setting up his own Masonic sect, where he broke new ground by replacing the three symbolic dots in the form of a triangle by a hyphen!)

Although highly critical of the social and trade union focus of the majority of their comrades, the individualists did not systematically oppose this, as Ernest Armand, one of their main theoreticians, asserts:

If he joins a trade union, the anarchist enters into it only as a member of a given trade, in the legitimate hope of securing through collective action some improvement in his individual lot: but, should he secure a reduction in working hours or an increase in pay, he will see nothing anarchist about that. In economic terms, in current circumstances, every anarchist copes as best he can: one by working for an employer, another by operating outside the law, another by availing of the trade union, still another by operating inside a communist colony, but then only in matters related to the communist colony and on condition that the undertaking is genuinely communist; none of these ways of getting by is any more 'anarchist' than any other: they are "make-shift," no more, no less.[4]

Thus, Libertad earned his livelihood as a proofreader: Paraf-Javal, after having pronounced that the "trade union is a grouping wherein the brutalized are classified according to trade, in an effort to render the relations between employers and workers less intolerable. One of two things will happen: either they would succeed, in which case trade union work is harmful," made honorable amends for it by writing this time that he supported entry into the unions in order to "show the unionized that they are brutalized and to try to induce them to cease being such. I set an example myself at one time and entered a trade union."[5] And yes, fine phrases and persuasive arguments would not fill a man's belly in the existing society, and in order to get by, he had either to play along as a wage slave, or try to "live as an anarchist comrade" along with other comrades by coming together into cooperatives or communities for living and working, or even be an "economic refractory," that is, operate "extralegally" to borrow Ernest Armand's phrase, or, to put it another way, carry out individual recuperation or illegalist activity: house-breaking, counterfeiting, or some other pursuit officially designated as criminal.

Self-evidently, it was for the latter two courses that those individualists who were at daggers drawn with bourgeois society opted. Several colonies were launched and survived for varying lengths of time, only to founder either because of the hostile surroundings or as a result of internal mismanagement, or indeed due to the absence of real affinity between the participants. Among the production cooperatives, the printworks held out the longest. As for illegalism, that was nothing new but rather the continuation of the pioneering activity of Duval and Pini. At the turn of the century, Alexandre Jacob and his "workers by night" were the finest representatives of that. Whereas, for Jacob, such activity was selective and targeted only outstandingly parasitical representatives of the bourgeoisie, to the extent that he set aside ten percent of the proceeds of his burglaries for the anarchist movement's propaganda, in his colleagues the motivation quickly turned into personal profit and they had no care for helping their libertarian comrades, let alone offering any ideological justification for their entirely criminal pursuits. Far from bringing emancipation, "individual recuperation" led eventually to a dead-end street, to an almost inevitable promiscuity with the underworld, with its whole train of provocateurs, narks and dirty deals. Armand in particular was the victim of a shady affair involving counterfeit money (and sexual liaison as well) which earned him a five-year prison sentence.[6]

Mauricius, an individualist anarchist prominent at the time, and who tells of the unfortunate mishap that befell Armand, records a provocation along similar lines in which he himself was almost ensnared.

Being at the time editor of *L'Anarchie*, and having no idea how to come by the money needed for publication of the paper, he was approached by one Pierre-Napoléon Jacob (no relation to the famous, well-respected illegalist of the same name) who suggested to him that he get by vià the methods he had theorized about in the columns of *L'Anarchie*: "I will practice illegalism, placing my sword of Brennus in every balance, including the balance of miseries, mine own alone being of any import to me as I reckoned." A declaration which, as Mauricius notes, leads to the "filling of the prisons," and he says further: "I declined. So he sent his wife to me. She was a fine-looking woman, the flesh is weak, she drew me to her place and then, in the wake of her amorous displays she showed me a fine 20-franc coin that looked the part: 'Seven francs,' she told me, 'I can get you as many as you like.' I made my escape, having realized what was afoot."

The story does not stop with this "post-carnal" insight on the part of Mauricius, which he may with hindsight have exaggerated a little, for, a few months later, we find this Pierre Jacob and his temptress of a wife hauled up before the assizes, charged with the manufacturing and passing of counterfeit money. In their defense, they stated that they "were agents of the prefecture of police, to which they had been seconded at 150 francs per month and that they had only manufactured the counterfeit coinage in order to gain acceptance in anarchist circles!" Called as a witness, the head of the "anarchist squad" at the prefecture acknowledged that they were indeed informants but claimed ignorance of their cover as "counterfeiters"!

On the strength of several such episodes and the fates of most of the anarchist "expropriators," Mauricius claims that:

> housebreaking, counterfeiting money, swindles, even pimping (for even that was practiced in certain anarchist circles at the time) as a means of economic self-liberation was a puerile and dangerous utopia. As I wrote in my *Confessions*, illegalism liberated nobody, it led them to the court of assizes.[7]

To be sure, expropriation of the expropriators was also practiced during these same years by Russian revolutionaries, not just by anarchists, but also by the Social Revolutionaries and even the Bolsheviks, as a means of securing the wherewithal to prosecute their struggle, and there are differences of nuance here, but let us note that there too, in most cases, things either backfired, with the expropriators holding on to the loot for themselves, or blew up into a huge scandal as a result of police provocation over there as well (as in the case of the Bolsheviks caught red-handed in the act of cashing stolen bonds). Finally, let it be noted that, insofar as our subject is concerned, individualist anarchist illegalism failed as far as most of those who embarked upon it were concerned, and then went on to an even more unfortunate and bloody dénouement with the "tragic bandits" a few years later.

The century's first revolutionary upheaval took place in Russia in 1905. In the wake of the Empire's military defeat at the hands of Japan, revolutionaries threw themselves into the attack on tsarism. Partly through concession and reform and partly through savage repression, the autocratic tsar managed to regain control of the situation. Despite the recession of the revolutionary tide, anarchists multiplied, in view of the minimalism of the Social Revolutionaries and Social Democrats, a minimalism that was one of the reasons why the revolution failed. Some fifty anarchist groups sprang up across the Empire, embracing tendencies similar to those existing in France: individualists, libertarian communists and syndicalists. The movement came to be a phenomenon of some importance, attracting thousands of members, often former Social Revolutionaries, Social Democrats or Bundists (the Bund being the Jewish Workers' Social Democratic Party) who had it in mind to conduct a radical and pitiless struggle against tsarism's henchmen. However, the Russian libertarian movement ran into the same problems as its French counterpart: inadequate liaison between groups, police provocateurs and illegalist excesses, all added to the crackdown upon the armed struggle.

In organizational matters, the prevalent tendency was at first the one existing in the West, especially as its chief exponents were the Russian anarchists in exile: free contracts between individuals within a group and free union between groups, in accordance with their wishes or choices. Congresses were desirable, but the decisions reached were binding only upon those who might be in agreement with them. The role of liaising between and coordinating the federated groups could not be fulfilled by committees, for these "always have a tendency to become, like any government, a brake upon further development, and quickly at that." Voting was ruled out, unanimity being deemed the only solution: if the matter was too important for either camp to make concessions, the only option was to split. The group retained complete autonomy and freedom in its activity. Every publication represented nothing more than the viewpoint of the publishing group and there was no question of a central organ of the movement. All these prescriptions were laid down at a gathering in London in 1906 of Russian libertarian communists in exile. In a way, this was a theoretical updating of anarchism in the light of the Russian revolution of 1905 and quite in keeping with the overall orientation of the movement worldwide. Among the authors of the reports and submissions, let us note names such as Peter Kropotkin, Zabrezhnev (future editor in chief of *Pravda*), I. Vetrov (who was to become an historian of some renown in the 1920s) and above all Maria Korn who drafted three of the reports, on the matter of politics and economics, on organization and on the general strike.[8]

Yet there were other active militants inside Russia itself pressing for a quite different organizational approach. Assimilating the benefits of what he considered the best of French anarchism, namely the revolutionary syndicalist theses of Emile Pouget, Novomirsky drafted an anarcho-syndicalist program (this being the first use of the term "anarcho-syndicalist"). He recommended an umbrella organization for Russian anarchists, and indeed internationally. Well-=informed about events and trends abroad, and committed to direct action and insurgency in Russia, Novomirsky strove to make his analysis as concrete as possible and to move away from the usual abstractions and generalizations. The organization he advocated was to be distinguished from a club, where debates and discussions might take place, and be a "political organization in the best sense of the term, for it must seek to become the political force necessary to break the organized violence for which the state stands."

That character, it seemed to him, was best expressed through use of the term "Party": all "anti-authoritarian socialists should unite into a Workers' Anarchist Party. The next step would be the formation of a vast union of all revolutionary elements under the black flag of the International Workers' Anarchist Party. Only then will anarchists represent sufficient strength to struggle against reactionaries, overt or covert."

This party stood apart from the propaganda or debating clubs, which made do with nurturing consciousness, while the party set itself the task of "combining the actions of its members" and had need of a set theoretical platform, in the absence of which, it is "impossible to achieve unity of action." Consequently, the program was "the *sine qua non* for all activity by the Party of Labor," which would no longer confine itself to propagating but also organize the actions of its members.

[This] Anarchist Party is the only *revolutionary* party, unlike the conservative parties which seek to *preserve* the established political and economic order, and the *progressive* parties which seek to *reform* the state in one way or another, so as to reform the corresponding economic relations, for anarchists aim to *destroy* the state, in order to do away with the established economic order and reconstruct it upon new principles.

This anarchist organization has nothing to do with Lenin's concept whereby the Party depends chiefly upon statutory constraints and where its members become mere functionaries. Nor has it anything in common with the Social Democratic notion, whereby organizing means establishing a Central Committee above individuals. The anarchist organization is *the free union of individuals struggling for a common goal.*[9]

Again according to Novomirsky, the Anarchist Party's program had to be complemented by a tactical plan suited to the everyday needs of the workers. In the context of the Russia of his day, that tactic had to consist of extending the revolutionary period initiated in 1905 for as long as feasible, by all means available, to wit: replying with revolutionary terror to the government's terror, targeting both their henchmen and those behind the repression, the capitalists and the big landowners. Expropriations of banks and state establishments would supply the requisite funds.

This direct armed struggle had to be matched to an economic organization of the workers by means of the most widespread revolutionary trade unions in every town across the country.

To sum up, Novomirsky spelled out four points:

1. It is essential that we devise a clear program and tactics, and, on the basis of these general principles and tactics, unite all the wholesome elements of Russian anarchism into a single federation: the Workers' Anarchist Party.

2. It is vital that it differentiate itself organizationally and theoretically from all the questionable elements which peddle and practice the theory of theft as "a means of struggling for anarchism."

3. We need to make participation in the revolutionary syndicalist movement the central objective of our work, so that we can make that movement anarchist.

4. Our practical watchword: an extended boycott of all state establishments, particularly the army and parliament, and the proclamation in villages and towns of workers' communes with soviets of workers' deputies, acting as industrial committees, at their head.[10]

With hindsight, we can note that this program was to become the agenda a decade later, at least up until the Bolsheviks' coup d'état.

Whenever Novomirsky sought to dissociate himself from "dubious elements" in the anarchist camp, he was referring to those who laid claim to the label anarchist as a cover for their petty "individual recuperation" activities, or indeed for carrying out "motiveless" acts of terror in the style of Emile Henry, that is, murdering bourgeois or people at random.

In Novomirsky's view, the latter activity was not, in certain instances, completely free of police "motives," as these provocations played right into the hands of the authorities, enabling them to treat revolutionary acts as terrorism.

In any case, aside from the organizing of workers' communes and revolutionary trade unions, which was impracticable due to the tsarist repression, all the remainder was implemented by most of the anarchist groups in the Russian Empire. Though their losses were heavy, they were to succumb only because outnumbered after 1910, while planting the seeds of revolutionary action that were able to sprout in 1917.

Let us digress in order to point out that the organizational issue lay at the root of the split between Lenin and his supporters ("the Bolsheviks"=the majority) and Martov and his supporters ("the Mensheviks"=the minority) inside the Russian Workers' Social Democratic Party at its 1903 congress. The debate had centered upon the definition of what constituted a party member, with Lenin taking a more restrictive line than the generous definition of his opponents. That article from the party statutes became the focal point of the controversy between the protagonists for many a long year up until 1917. As for the functioning of the Party, its pyramidal format — with the Central Committee at the apex making all the decisions — was not a matter of controversy. The same centralistic trend obtained in all the other parties and organizations in the Russian Empire — the Social Revolutionaries, the Polish, Latvian, Ukrainian, Georgian and other Social Democratic Parties. The tsarist secret police, the Okhrana, capitalized upon this fact to infiltrate its agents and, often very successfully, neutralize the activities of these parties.

In France also the police managed to plant Henri Girard in high office inside the CGT. Exploiting his foibles — as a heavy drinker and womanizer, with the debts that that inevitably implied — they managed to get this erstwhile socialist worker appointed as a replacement for the general secretary of the CGT's Committee for the General Strike, a post that he retained for ten years until his death in 1902.[11] In fact, the government found it to its advantage to keep the apple of discord handy, in the shape of the watchword of general strike that divided syndicalists and socialists. In the end, this parting of the ways crystallized at the CGT's congress in Amiens in 1906 where the charter adopted could not have been more explicit:

> The CGT embraces, outside of all political affiliations, all workers conscious of the struggle to be waged for the elimination of wage slavery and the employer. Congress takes the view that this declaration is a recognition of the class struggle which, on the economic terrain, pits the workers in rebellion against all the forms of exploitation and oppression, material and moral alike, deployed by the capitalist class against the working class.[12]

Syndicalism set itself the two-pronged mission of improving the workers' well-being through the achievement of short-term aspirations such as reductions of working hours and the raising of wages, as well as paving the way for the comprehensive emancipation that could only be accomplished by means of expropriation of the capitalist. The general strike was the main method envisaged, and the trade union, as a mutual aid group, was destined in the future to become the agent of production and distribution, the basis for the reorganization of society.

Outside of their trade union activities, the union membership had a completely free hand to involve itself in any form of philosophical or political campaigning, without thereby carrying those campaigns into the union itself. The congress went on to repudiate any and all interference from "parties or sects." Its concern was to differentiate itself once and for all from all socialists and other politicians seeking to throw a halter over trade union struggles: however, anarchists or at least some anarchists were also targeted, as was noted the following year at the Anarchist Congress in Amsterdam. Syndicalism, turning itself into the "Party of Labor" (to borrow from Pouget's pamphlet of the same name) announced that it was quite capable of conducting the class struggle unaided upon its chosen terrain, that is the economic terrain, at a remove from all the influences of politicians or ideologues, and was therefore sufficient unto itself. This was, in a sense, a resurrection in a French setting of the First International, quite in line with Bakunin's last counsel.

## Endnotes to Chapter Ten

1. *L'Anarchi,e* No. 26, October 5, 1905, "Réflexions" by Redan, quoted by J. Maitron, op-cit., p. 395.

2. Paraf-Javal, *L'Absurdité des soi-disant libres-penseurs: les faux-libres-penseurs et les vrais,* (Paris: Edition du Groupe d'études scientifiques, 1908), p. 4.

3. Ibid., "Théorème des anarchistes libres-penseurs," p. 8 and "Une variété de faux-libres-penseurs, les faux anarchistes," p. 9. See also René Bianco, *Paraf-Javal, une figure originale de l'anarchisme français,* (Marseilles, 1980), p. 13.

4. *L'Anarchisme comme vie et comme activité individuelles: Rapports présentés au congrès libertaire d'Amsterdam par E. Armand & Mauricius,* (Paris: 1907), p. 8.

5. Quoted by J. Maitron, op. cit., p. 255.

6. E. Armand, *Sa vie, sa pensée, son,* oeuvre, La Ruche ouvrière, (Paris, 1964). *E. Armand tel que je l'ai connu* by Mauricius, pp. 104–124.

7. Ibid.

8. *The Russian revolution and Anarchism* (reports and findings of 1906) published in 1922 (in Russian) by the Federation of (Russian) Anarchist Communist Groups in the United States and Canada, 60 pages.

9. Novomirsky, *The Program of Anarcho-syndicalism* (in Russian), (Odessa, 1907), pp. 172–173.

10. Ibid., p. 184.

11. Robert Brécy, *La grove générale en France,* (Paris: EDI, 1969), *Un apôtre nommé Judas,* pp. 66–70, and Maurice Dommanget, *La Chevalerie du Travail française 1893–1911,* (Lausanne: Editions Rencontre, 1967), pp. 98–101.

12. Roger Hagnauer, *L'actualité de la Charte d'Amiens,* preface by Pierre Monatte, (Paris, 1956), p. 5.

# XI. THE INTERNATIONAL ANARCHIST CONGRESS IN AMSTERDAM (1907)

In 1906 Holland's Libertarian Communist Federation and Belgium's Libertarian Communist Grouping had jointly floated the possibility of summoning an international congress. The first named organization assumed responsibility for the actual mounting of a week-long congress: the second published, under the editorship of Henri Fuss, five issues of a *Bulletin of the Libertarian International*, the purpose of which was to draw up an agenda and to publicize the submissions handed in. Somewhere between sixty and eighty delegates, attending in an individual capacity or representing the anarchist federations of a number of countries, were present at the Congress. The largest number came from the host country and from neighboring Belgium and Germany. Among the best known participants we might list the names of Errico Malatesta and Luigi Fabbri (Italy), Emma Goldman (United States), Nikolai Pogdaev and Wladimir Zabrezhnev (Russia), Domela Nieuwenhuis and Christian Cornelissen (Holland), Henri Fuss, Georges Thonar and Emile Chapelier (Belgium) and Rudolf Rocker and Alexander Schapiro (London Jewish Anarchist Federation). The French delegation was tiny, for many of the French were still hostile to the holding of congresses, specific or otherwise. Even so, some anarchist syndicalists from the CGT were present, people like: Pierre Monatte, Benoit Broutchoux, R. de Marmande and Amédée Dunois (who was, bizarrely, the delegate for francophone Switzerland, although he was a Parisian through and through); Pierre Ramus (Austria), although living in London, was also there; Dr. Friedeberg headed a sizable German delegation; and, by their presence, natives of Bohemia (Czechoslovakia), Poland, Bulgaria, Serbia and Argentina afforded an undeniably international and representative character to the Congress. Although it was felt that the taking of a head count was interesting, it was agreed that majority decisions would not be binding upon either the majority or the minority: this was in accordance with the well-established practice of the anarchist movement.

The Congress described itself as being the fourth in number after the socialist congresses in Zurich (1893), London (1896) and the banned congress that should have been held in London (in 1900). In fact, as a homogeneously anarchist congress, it might be regarded as the second in number after the London Conference (1881) at which the dire decision had been to go for propaganda by deed. The implicit task facing this congress was precisely to draw the lessons from that and to eliminate its damaging effects. The agenda adopted was a good reflection of that preoccupation:

1. Anarchism and syndicalism.
2. General strike and political strike.
3. Anarchism and organization
4. Anti-militarism as a tactic of anarchism.
5. Integral education of children.
6. Productive association and anarchism.
7. The revolution in Russia.
8. Alcoholism and anarchism.
9. Modern literature and anarchism.
10. Libertarians and a world language.
11. Anarchism and religion.
12. Anarchism as individual living and activity.

Four other items, reserved for the supporters of international relations, were to be dealt with during the last two non-public sessions:

1. Organization of the Libertarian International.
2. Drafting of a statement of anarchist-communist principles.
3. Creation of an international bulletin, an information organ.
4. The goal of the new International.[1]

The inaugural proceedings went ahead with around a thousand people in attendance; the Internationale was sung. It fell to the German Dr. Friedeberg to deliver the first speech. He vehemently berated the German Social Democracy and its sole method of action, "corruptive parliamentarism." Instead of which he called for direct action in every guise and methodical diffusion of the idea of the revolutionary general strike. He was followed by ten other speakers, including Malatesta, Emma Goldman, Rogdaev, Pierre Ramus and Cornelissen.

The next day, Monday, August 26, 1907, a reading was given to the submissions regarding the current status of the anarchist movement in various countries. Three hundred comrades, delegates included, attended the evening session, which closed with the final report on activity in England, from Karl Walter. The following day the congress appointed its chairman for the day and two assessors, before the floor was made available to Amedée Dunois to broach the prickly question of organization. He opened by dismissing the opposition to organization on the part of most anarchists as outmoded and overtaken by events. In bygone days, organization's supporters might have been suspected of "backward-looking ulterior motives and authoritarian designs." "Individual initiative" was alleged to have been sufficient; the reality of the class struggle would have been denied and misrepresented as "conflicting views for which it was the very task of propaganda to prepare the individual." That was how anarchism had lost sight of the "terra firma of reality and practical action and been washed up on the desert isle of individualism." Organization was no longer thought of as anything other than "forms inevitably oppressive of the individual" and all collective action had been systematically shunned. But in France things had moved on: syndicalism and anti-militarism now occupied pride of place. Anarchism had become a "revolutionary theory, a specific program for the transformation of society, the most perfect theoretical expression of the tendencies of the proletarian movement," and was not any longer the "ultimate elaboration upon the old bourgeois individualism." Dunois even defined it as "integral and primarily associationist federalism."

The speaker dismissed the individualist argument against organization: "I cannot see how an anarchist organization might harm the individual development of its members. No one, in fact, would be under any obligation to enter it, nor, having entered, would they be obliged to quit." According to him, that line of argument did not stand scrutiny, for it might as easily be deployed against any form of society. As he saw it, the syndicalists' objection had more substance to it. The existence in France of a labor movement with a plainly revolutionary outlook was the "major fact upon which any attempt at anarchist organization risked stumbling, if not foundering." Indeed, unlike "opinion groupings, tiny chapels into which none but the faithful would venture, the trade union movement had not lost hope that it might yet encompass the proletariat in its entirety within its supple, accommodating frameworks." Consequently that was where anarchists belonged, lest they be separated from the people, the "essential driving force of every revolution." Unless they, like the Social Democrats, had "interests different from those of the proletariat to pursue — the interests of party, sect or clique?" Was it not the role of anarchists to draw nearer to the proletariat (and not the other way round) to live its life, to "earn its confidence and incite it by word and example to resistance, revolt, revolution?" That said, Dunois resolved the issue by venturing the idea that the role of anarchists, who thought themselves the "most advanced, most daring and most liberated fraction of that militant proletariat organized within the unions, is to be at all times at its side and, from its very ranks, to fight in the same battles." If they were to keep faith with their vocation as educators and exhorters of the working class, anarchists nonetheless had to band together with one another so as to "endow their trade union activity with maximum force and continuity." The stronger they were, (and they could only be strong if they banded together) the "stronger also will be those currents of ideas that we might direct through the labor movement."

Did this mean that they could make do with the task of educating militants to "keeping the sap of revolution alive in them, letting them acquire self-knowledge and contacts with one another?" Would they not have some "activity of their own to pursue 'directly?'" By his reckoning the answer was yes, and he supplied a precise definition of the role of the active revolutionary minority:

The social revolution can only be the handiwork of the masses. But every revolution is of necessity attended by acts which, by their very

FACING THE ENEMY

nature — technically, so to speak — can only be the work of a tiny few, of the boldest and most enlightened fraction of the proletariat on the move. In every district, so every region, in times of revolution, our groups would form many little fighting organizations designed to carry out delicate specialist measures for which the broad masses are most often unsuited.

What Dunois was getting at was that affinity groups, wherein the members are well-known to and trust one another, are better suited to carrying off daring and decisive operations which the masses cannot possibly accomplish spontaneously. Not that there should be any substitution for the wishes of the latter. He also nominated anarchist propaganda as the essential, ongoing object of the group's activities, theoretically as well as practically. Such activity had been conducted on an individual basis hitherto and so the point was to ensure that it was tackled on a more collective and consistent basis. In France and despite the large numbers of anarchists, the chief obstacle remained the lack of agreement and organization. What was needed was an anarchist movement that would marshal "on a common footing, all those forces which have thus far been fighting a lonely fight." This would spring from joint action by anarchists, from their

concerted, coordinated action. Needless to say, the anarchist organization would not presume to unite all those elements which profess, very mistakenly at times, to subscribe to the idea of anarchy. It would be enough for it to rally around a program of practical action all those comrades subscribing to our principles and desirous of working with us.

This strikes us as a crucial address by Amedée Dunois and it bears at once the stamp of the best Bakuninist spirit and a precise and clear vision of the tasks devolving upon revolutionary anarchists. Some of those at the Amsterdam Congress were not quite of our opinion, as the contributions that followed made plain. Georges Thonar, for example, abdicated his right to address the congress, saying that he subscribed to every word of Dunois's speech, but he declared himself opposed to any vote being taken and asked congress to align itself with his position. That contradictory attitude created uproar: Malatesta immediately spoke up in favor of a vote being taken, finding no reason why one should not proceed. Monatte followed suit, saying that he failed to see what there was in the taking of a vote that was anti-anarchist, or, to put it another way, authoritarian, as there was no question of equating it with parliamentary voting or universal suffrage. Voting was a regular practice inside the unions and, truth to tell, he saw absolutely nothing in that that was contrary to anarchist principles. He berated those "comrades who, on every item, even the most trivial, felt impelled to raise issues of principle."

Christian Cornelissen reckoned that voting was to be condemned *only* if it imposed an obligation upon the dissenting minority: de Marmande agreed with that reasoning, and the controversy was defused. Then an individualist, Croiset, spoke out against Dunois: he saw anarchy as opposed to any system of organization, for this had the "inevitable result of always placing limits upon the freedom of the individual, to a greater or lesser extent," and, by shouldering the "pointless ambition of being practical" anarchists had stepped on to organization's slippery slope. (!?) As Croiset argued it, anarchist ideas had to "cling to their ancient purity rather than seek to become more practical." That caricature of a response drew no support. Siegfried Nacht spoke along the same lines as Dunois and called for action which alone could educate the people and invest it with a "revolutionary mentality." However, he rather curiously described the role of the masses in the future revolution as being that of the "foot soldiers of the revolutionary army," whereas the anarchist groups, "specializing in technical tasks, will be its artillery"! What a pity he failed to mention its general staff and its cavalry (which was to play a considerable, not to say, primary part in the Mexican and Russian revolutions)!

Other speakers expressed some misgivings about Dunois's submission, without however daring to contradict him. Emma Goldman pronounced herself "in favor of organization, in principle" but had misgivings about a possible "exclusivism" and insisted that the autonomy of the individual, the essential principle of anarchy, be respected. She would countenance organization on one condition only: that it be "founded upon absolute respect for all individual initiatives and place no obstacle in the way of their interplay or evolution." We may note the incongruousness of that word "all," the source of all the possible and conceivable confusions which Goldman seems to have overlooked.

It appears that the clarity of Dunois's statement of position had left the antiorganizationists in disarray, but there was a lingering opposition and it was Errico Malatesta who took it upon himself to disarm it. Deliberately conciliatory, he put the differences over the organization issue down to semantics: basically, he was convinced, everybody was of the same mind about it. According to him, all anarchists, regardless of whatever tendency they belonged to, were, to some extent "individualists." But the converse was very far from being true. The category first named included those who "claim for every individual human being the right to integral development, their own as well as their neighbor's." The second category embraced those who "have a care only for their own individuality and never have any hesitation in sacrificing others to it. The tsar of all the Russias is numbered among the latter."

Malatesta went on to spell out a few home truths about individualism thus understood, describing as a "colossal nonsense" Ibsen's assertion that: "the most powerful man in the world is the loneliest of men!" Because what sets the individual free, "what allows him to develop all his faculties, is not solitude but association." Although cooperation was indispensable, he nevertheless reckoned that association ought to leave full autonomy to its affiliated individuals, and the federation should respect that same autonomy in the groups. He called for organs that would be expressions of the groups and not of individuals, for in that way each opinion might be freely measured alongside all the rest. Apropos of authority and authoritarianism, they had to be clear: anarchists took up arms against the authority of the state, but if they were faced with a "purely moral authority emanating from experience, intelligence or talent, then, anarchists though we all may be, there is none among us who will not respect such authority."

He closed his address with a curious axiom: whether they were "organizers," federalists, or individualists opposed to organization of any sort, what distinguished them was not some alleged authoritarianism, on the grounds they would be having a bureau and taking decisions in the case of the former, in the case of the latter, the actual authoritarianism of many groups wherein the "absolute freedom of the individual" was noisily proclaimed — it was above all else the fact of their "doing nothing or next to nothing." From which he concluded that:

> words divide and action unites. It is high time we all set to work together in order to exercise some effective influence over social events.... So let us strive to make a reality of the Anarchist International. If we are even to begin to issue an urgent summons to all comrades to struggle against the reaction, as well as display revolutionary initiative when the time comes, we must have our International!

The discussion resumed with the seventh session of the congress on the morning of August 28th. A number of speakers picked up and refined certain details of Malatesta's address, and then Amedée Dunois's motion — amended by Emma Goldman in the matter of individual initiative, and by Malatesta and the Czech Vohryzek in the matter of the organizational format envisaged — was put to a vote. A second motion, from Ramus, was more or less a repetition of the first, and took only 13 votes in favor and 17 against, with all the rest abstaining: as a result it was rejected. The Dunois motion was passed by 46 votes against a single dissenter. This marked the arrival of anarchism as a social theory and not a philosophy of the individual. It was a significant milestone in the movement's history, so we shall reprint it in its entirety:

> The anarchists assembled in Amsterdam, August 27, 1907.

> Considering that the ideas of anarchy and organization, far from being incompatible, as has sometimes been claimed, are mutually complementary and illuminate one another, the very precept of anarchy residing in the free organization of the producers;

> That individual action, important though it may be, could not make good the absence of collective action, of concerted movement: "any more than collective action could make good the absence of individual initiative;" (Emma Goldman's addendum)

> That organization of militant forces would assure propaganda of fresh wings and could not but hasten the penetration of the ideas of federalism and revolution into the working class;

> That labor organization, founded upon identity of interests, does not exclude an organization founded upon identity of aspirations and ideas;

Are of the opinion that the comrades of every land should place on their agenda the creation of anarchist groups and the federation of existing groups.

### The Vobryzek-Malatesta addendum

The anarchist federation is an association of groups and individuals, wherein no one may impose his will, nor diminish the initiative of another. Vis-à-vis the current society, it has as its goal the alteration of all moral and economic conditions and, to that end, it supports struggle by all appropriate means.

That last amendment adds nothing and wanders off into generalities, which is not like Malatesta: he probably endorsed it as a gesture to Vohryzek and in an effort to settle the debate.

Be that as it may, that resolution on anarchist organization represents an historical milestone and a libertarian publication of the time asserts that it will:

no longer be feasible for our social-democratic adversaries to invoke out ancient hatred of organization of any sort to banish us from the socialist camp without further ado. The anarchists' legendary individualism was publicly slain in Amsterdam by the anarchists themselves, and all the bad faith of certain of our adversaries will not be enough to resuscitate it.[2]

The eighth session, on the afternoon of August 28, was held in camera: the public and journalists were not admitted. On the agenda was the practical organization of the International. After several elliptical addresses, including one by Emma Goldman who suggested a bulletin as the sole link, instead of the envisaged five-member International correspondence bureau, everybody agreed upon its creation. Its powers consisted of the creation of international archives accessible to comrades, and keeping in touch with anarchists from different countries, either directly, or through the agency of the three comrades chosen by the federations or groups from the countries involved. Individuals could be members of the International, provided that they had been vouched for by an organization, by the Bureau or by comrades known to it. A resolution to that effect was passed by the Congress. Emma Goldman's motion commending the bulletin only, picked up only four votes. London was fixed as the Bureau's seat: among the five members appointed to it were Malatesta (despite his protestations!), Rudolf Rocker and Wilquet (Germans), Alexander Schapiro (Russian), and John Turner (who was not even at the congress!).

To judge by this specific outcome, the organizational mountain diligently erected during the congress turned out to be a molehill: the Bureau appointed looked to be a mere formality, as did its role. It was to be active after a fashion until 1911, then was swallowed up by the countryside!

Regarded as the oldest advocate of organization and collective action, Malatesta welcomed the creation of the International as "affirmation of the desire for shared solidarity and struggles." The Bureau's existence struck him as being of "lesser importance." As he saw it, the most important thing was "the desire to struggle alongside one another and the intention to keep in touch so that we do not have to go looking for one another when the time comes to act, with the risk that the moment may pass before we have found one another"![3]

Its appetite whetted by the spicy hors d'oeuvre on organization, Congress moved on to the main dish on the menu: the relations between revolutionary syndicalism and anarchism. The ninth session, on the evening of Wednesday, August 28, opened before a packed hall. Pierre Monatte, a member of the CGT national committee, took the rostrum. Then 25 years old, he was already a veteran labor activist, steeped in trade union activity. He gave a masterly exposition of the nature and aims of the revolutionary syndicalism that had asserted itself in the face of socialism, and of anarchism indeed, not so much theoretically as through its actions and so "it is in actions rather than in books that we have to search for it."[4]

All the same, it was anarchism that had been the chief inspiration behind syndicalism, anarchism that "dragged the workers' movement down the revolutionary road and popularized the idea of direct action." In its turn, syndicalism had "recalled anarchism to a feeling for its labor origins." It was inside the CGT that these two currents were best embodied, for the "greater good of them both." Monatte launched into a lengthy description of the CGT, its activity, its modus operandi and its distinctive identity in the worldwide workers' movement. The Confederation had successfully fended off political intruders and government attempts to seduce it: its chief weapon was direct action, that is, "acting on its own behalf, reliance upon none but itself," wholly in keeping with the First International. He catalogued the various forms that this might assume — strikes, sabotage, boycotts, etc. — as well as the revolutionary superweapon, the general strike. Syndicalism had breathed life back into the revolutionary spirit which had withered in the face of the verbosity, or worse still, electoralism and parliamentarism of Guesde or the governmentalism and ministerialism of Jaurès, on the one hand, and the revolutionism of anarchists "disdainfully beating the retreat into the ivory towers of philosophical speculation" on the other. Thus it was "important that the Proletarians of other lands should learn from the syndicalist experience of the French proletariat." According to Monatte, it was incumbent upon anarchists wheresoever there was a workers' movement to make that experience known. In that way the class struggle could be prosecuted "in all its fullness and to maximum effect." He referred to the famous declaration by the congress of Amiens that — "syndicalism is sufficient unto itself' — which was sometimes misinterpreted by certain anarchists, when all that it meant was that the "working class, having reached the age of majority, aims at long last to shift for itself and no longer looks to anyone else for its emancipation." What anarchist "could find fault with such a loud affirmation of the will to act?"

Syndicalism "does not waste time promising the workers an earthly paradise. It asks them to go out and win it, assuring them that their actions will never be quite in vain. It is a training school for determination, energy, purposeful thinking. To an anarchism too long withdrawn into itself, it holds out the prospect of fresh promise, fresh hopes." As a result, Monatte called upon libertarians to commit themselves to syndicalism. He made no bones about its having flaws that needed to be eliminated, especially this tendency on the part of individuals to:

> entrust the chore of struggling to their union, their federation, to the Confederation, to appeal to strength of numbers, when their individual energies would have sufficed. By constantly appealing to the will of the individual, his initiative and his daring, we anarchists can mount a vigorous backlash against this harmful tendency to have constant recourse, in little things as in big, to strength of numbers.

Trade union bureaucracy was also a problem, but all that could be eliminated or put straight by a "constantly vigilant critical spirit."

The congress's tenth session, on the morning of August 29, found it drawing together the questions of syndicalism and the general strike. Siegfried Nacht caused an incident by accusing the individualist Croiset of having, the evening before, furnished Amsterdam's bourgeois pressmen with information concerning the in-camera proceedings that day. The congress was outraged. Croiset took the floor to admit to the charge, and accepted the reprimands that might be issued to him over his "culpable thoughtlessness." The bulk of those at the congress censured him.

The afternoon session resumed with a motion on the Russian Revolution which was passed unanimously, before the debate on Monatte's submission continued. Cornelissen expressed reservations: anarchists ought to support syndicalism and direct action, but on one condition: that these be revolutionary in their objectives, that they "never cease to aim at the transformation of the existing society into a libertarian communist society."

In support of his argument, he invoked the case of the Amsterdam and Antwerp diamond cutters, and workers in England and the United States, all of whom had used direct action in order to secure special privileges for themselves: he also spoke out against direct action that was directed against modernization of the means of production.

Errico Malatesta followed him in the speaking order. Amid utter silence in the auditorium, he spent quite some time taking issue with Monatte; he announced that he was dissenting from Monatte's conclusion to the effect that "syndicalism is a necessary and sufficient means of social revolution," or, to put it another way, that "syndicalism is sufficient unto itself." He first of all drew a distinction between the workers' movement and syndicalism: one was a *fact*, the other a *doctrine*, a system. Moreover, he was quite in favor of them both, unlike these intellectual anarchists who had walled themselves up inside "the ivory towers of pure speculation." He even supported trade unions "wide open to all workers, without regard to opinions, absolutely *neutral* unions." However, it was in order to spread their ideas that anarchists should get involved in these, using them as a means to an end, the "best of all the means open to us, of course," whereas syndicalists tended, instead, to make an end of that means, posing a "threat to the very existence of anarchism." Now, even if it "decked itself out in the utterly useless label of revolutionary, syndicalism is only and will be only a legalistic, conservative movement, with no accessible goal other than the betterment of working conditions." In support of this, he cited the case of the great American trade unions. Once radically revolutionary in their weaker days, they had, as they had grown in size and wealth, turned into plainly conservative organizations "solely preoccupied with making their members privileged persons in the factory, workshop or mine, and persons a lot less hostile to employer capitalism than to the unorganized workers," the very people lashed by the social democrats as the "ragged proletarians" (*Lumpenproletariat*) and whom anarchists defended not less, but rather more than the rest.

According to Malatesta, the mistake made by Monatte and the revolutionary syndicalists arose from a "too simplistic notion of the class struggle": they thought that the economic interests of all workers — of the working class — would be all of a piece and that all it took was for the "workers to look to the defense of their own interests for them to be defending, in so doing, the interests of the entire proletariat against the bosses." As he saw it, it did not work that way: within the working class itself, as within the bourgeoisie, there was competition and contention. What is more, certain workers were closer to the bourgeoisie than to the proletariat: aside from the examples cited by Cornelissen, Malatesta chose the example of workers using violence against "scabs" who were every bit as exploited as themselves! Here, in our estimation, Malatesta was overstating things a bit and displaying his actual ignorance of the class struggle, but apparently he was determined at all costs to head off the competition from the revolutionary syndicalists and any argument would do there. So he seized upon the point made by Monatte regarding the danger in paid trade union officials, as a danger comparable with parliamentarism! Even the general strike held no charms for him: it would come to nothing, unless accompanied by an insurrection…. Anyway, the general strike was pointless unless it was active, that is, unless it turned work to its own service. To sum up, he deplored the fact that many comrades had let themselves be consumed by the workers' movement for "yet again, workers' organization, the strike, the general strike, direct action, boycotts, sabotage and armed insurrection itself, are but means. Anarchy is the end." And anarchy was far more than the interests of a class: anarchy aimed at the "complete liberation of mankind, presently enslaved on three counts — economic, political and social." So, Malatesta closed, we should steer clear of "any unilateral, simplistic method of action": syndicalism therefore could not be the only means, much less "should it make us lose sight of the only goal worth the effort: Anarchy!"

It appears that Malatesta did not listen properly to Monatte's address, or was grievously mistaken about the reality of French revolutionary syndicalism, for the criticisms he offered and the analogies he drew — illogically, we might add — were off the mark. It was more a case of his pursuing an agenda of his own, offering his own interpretation of the International's tradition and invoking a highly abstract Anarchy. It was to that that Henri Fuss set about replying: Fuss stipulated that it was "impossible not to regard the organized proletariat as fertile soil for propaganda" and a "straightforward means;" henceforth the class struggle proceeds upon the economic terrain and "the time is past when revolution consisted of seizing a few town halls and decreeing the new society from some balcony" (a reference to the Benevento insurrection in 1874 in which Malatesta had been a participant and which had ended in fiasco). Fuss went on: "The social revolution towards which we are marching will consist of the expropriation of a class. Henceforth, the fighting unit is no longer, as once was the case, the opinion group, but rather the trades group, the workers' union or syndicate. The later being the agency best suited to the class struggle. The essential thing is that it should be nudged progressively in the direction of the expropriating general strike, which is what we invite comrades from every country to do."

The Frenchman Benoit Broutchoux, an anarchist worker militant forged in the hard school of the miners of the Nord, also voiced objections and offered a "formal rebuttal of Malatesta's theories."

Pierre Ramus likewise failed to identify with Malatesta's misgivings: revolutionary syndicalism's direct action methods were properly anarchist, so syndicalism was "contained within anarchism" and not the other way round. However, syndicalism could not be sufficient unto itself: anarchism, having supplied it with its weaponry, now had to endow it with a philosophy and an ideal, until such time as it would become anarchism itself and be capable of self-sufficiency. He closed by declaring: "Let us be anarchists first and above all else: let us then be syndicalists. But not the other way about."

Monatte's response was a lively one: through the "bitter criticisms" which Malatesta had leveled at these newfangled revolutionary notions, he believed he could make out "a voice echoing from the distant past." To these fresh ideas whose "brutal realism unnerves him, Malatesta has at best opposed only the tired old thinking of Blanquism which flattered itself that it could make the world anew by means of a successful armed insurrection." He rebutted the accusations of revolutionary minimalism and announced that "our anarchism is worth as much as yours and it is not our intention that you should shove our beliefs down our throats." While the experience of syndicalism might have, in certain countries, given rise to "errors and deviations, we have the experience there to prevent us from repetition." And if, instead of "loudly carping about syndicalism's vices past, present or even future, anarchists were to involve themselves more closely in its activities, any misgivings there might be would be exorcised forever."

Nevertheless, the spell was broken: the dissension voiced was to leave its mark on the movement and create a gulf between the two sides. The debate was considered closed and at the thirteenth session on Friday, August 30, four motions were voted on, and all four were carried by a very wide margin even though they contradicted one another in places! The first motion, submitted by

Cornelissen-Vohryzek-Malatesta, backed by Rogdaev, Emma Goldman, Wilquet, de Marmande and Knotek, was carried by 33 votes to ten. It was of course in favor of unions as both "fighting organizations in the class struggle for improved working conditions and as unions of producers that might further the transformation of capitalist society into an anarchist communist society." Any inhibition arose out of the "anarchists' task, which is to represent the revolutionary element within those organizations, to propagate and support only those forms and manifestations of 'direct action' (strikes, sabotage, boycotts, etc.) which are inherently revolutionary in character and make a contribution towards the transformation of society," as well as from the fact that anarchists "regard the syndicalist movement and the general strike as powerful revolutionary instruments, but not as substitutes for the Revolution" and thought that "destruction of capitalist and authoritarian society can be accomplished only by means of armed insurrection and violent expropriation and that recourse to a more or less general strike and the syndicalist movement ought not to blind us to more direct methods of struggle against the military might of governments."

This was tantamount to taking very little account of the extremely violent struggle conducted by the CGT against the army and police, which at that very moment were being deployed by the French government to break and repress strikes and demands with some bloodshed. There was, as it were, a dichotomy between the sentiments expressed and the reality of events. The authors of the motion posed as lecturers and instructors in revolution before proletarians committed to the class conscious active minority represented by the CGT.

The second of the motions, tabled by the German Friedeberg, was even more stand offish: it made a clear distinction between the class struggle and the emancipation of the proletariat by means of the ideas and aspirations of anarchism which "aims — above and beyond the short-term aspirations of classes — at economic and moral redemption of the human person, at a setting wherein authority has no place and not at some new power, that of a majority over a minority." A curious amalgam was constructed of the parliamentarism of Marxist socialism with the trade union movement and the strike for political rights — all of it irrelevant and none of it so much as breathed during the debates. This motion closed with a reference to the anarchist spirit which "might pervade the syndicalist movement and lead it on to the advent of a society free of all authority." It was passed, though, by 36 votes to six.

Amedée Dunois's submission, endorsed by Monatte, Fuss, Nacht, Fabbri and K. Walter, recalled the reality of the class struggle waged by the mass of producers, the specific and basic agency of which was the trade union organization, destined to turn into a production group and to be "in the present society the living embryo of the society of tomorrow." It committed the

> comrades from every country, without losing sight of the fact that anarchist action is not wholly contained within the framework of the union, to participate actively in the autonomous movement of the working

class and to develop within the trade union organizations the ideas of rebellion, individual initiative and solidarity which are the very essence of anarchism.

Passed by 28 votes to seven, this was complemented by the Nacht-Monatte motion (endorsed by the very same signatories) on the expropriatory general strike which was held to be a "remarkable incentive to organization and the spirit of revolt in the present society and the format in which the emancipation of the proletariat can be effected." This had nothing to do with the political strike, and was suggested as the main route to "destruction of the present society and expropriation of the means of production and their produce." As a result, it was by way of a dismissal of Malatesta's reservations, his insurrectionist tactics and clear intention to see the general strike as serving the interests of the working class alone. Nevertheless, the motion was carried by 25 votes.

Moving on through the agenda, Emma Goldman moved a resolution in favor of "acts of revolt by individual and whole mass alike." Although that was open to a number of interpretations — as an endorsement of individual or terrorist attentats, or indeed insurrectionist movements — (which is to say, that damaging old propaganda by deed) and although there was no debate that could have dispelled that vagueness, the motion was rushed through unanimously. In fact, the congress was well behind schedule on its agenda, and there was no time left for dissecting the meaning of words. It was decided that the anti-militarist item would be dealt with at the anti-militarist congress that was underway simultaneously in the neighborhood. The following item on *Alcoholism and Anarchism* was dealt with by the teacher Van Ree: he was against not merely the abuse of alcohol but even moderation in its use, and in fact he railed against the drinking of diluted "health" beverages. This item was postponed until later, probably time enough for "a wee drink," to give tempers time to cool and time for fuller consideration of the matter!

The item on *Productive Association and Anarchism* was touched upon briefly by the Dutchman Samson who declared himself in favor of production cooperatives and libertarian colonies which might be of service to the workers with an eye to their emancipation. *Integral Education of Children* was handled by de Marmande whose conclusion was that the Bourses du Travail and Workers' Unions were best placed to decide upon the character of the educational provision for workers' children. As the rapporteurs upon *Anarchism as Individual Living and Activity* (E. Armand and Mauricius) were not present, that item on the agenda was skipped. The items on alcoholism, productive association and Esperanto did not result in the passage of resolutions, due to lack of time to discuss them, and Errico Malatesta delivered the congress's closing address, at its seventeenth and final session Saturday, August 31. He offered congratulations upon the holding of this first congress which had "opened the way to fruitful union.... To be sure, differences of opinion have emerged among us: however, these relate only to secondary matters. We are all in agreement in affirming our essential principles," and he called upon his comrades to work away at propaganda and organization "with more confidence and energy than ever."

A round of applause "greeted these resounding words. Enthusiasm was at a peak. Faces were lit up by joy"(read the minutes) and everybody stood up to sing the Internationale.

The revolutionary syndicalists present at the congress held two meetings to launch a common Press Bureau serving all of the international trade union organizations, pending a "practical internationalism for the maintenance of the closest solidarity connections." (Dunois).

So much for this important international anarchist congress. Important on a number of counts: it was the first real congress of the sort since the London congress in 1881: it allowed ventilation of the issues preoccupying the libertarian movement, especially the matters of organization and revolutionary syndicalism, determining its social practice and signaling its internal divisions. It also provided the occasion for a physical get-together of militants internationally, who had hitherto known one another only as names and could now get down to open comparison of their various modes of activity. On the other hand, the concrete results of it were limited, the links forged in this way rather loose, and no real decision leading to concerted practical undertakings was arrived at. Which explains why there were no other congresses for many a long year: the organizations and most of the individual militants were absorbed by their national and day-to-day tasks, and that was a great pity in the years leading up to 1914, when international connections were so sorely needed if the looming threat of war was to be defused.

## Endnotes for Chapter 11

1. Congrès anarchists tenu è Amsterdam, août 1907: *Compte-rendu analytique des séances et résumé des rapports sur l'état du mouvement dans le monde entier.* (Paris, 1908), 116 pages.
2. Ibid., p. 57.
3. Ibid., p. 4.
4. Ibid., p. 62ff.

## XII. LIBERTARIANS IN THE CGT AND THE ILLEGALISTS (BONNOT AND COMPANY) IN ACTION

While certain anarchists preened themselves upon their "orthodoxy" as a way of bolstering their claims to revolutionary pre-eminence, those anarchists committed to revolutionary syndicalism inside the CGT took it upon themselves to espouse a tactic of direct class warfare. The real difference between the two schools really lay there at that level, the direct product of their contrasting organizational beliefs. The former trusted almost exclusively to individual initiative and the "spontaneous" receptivity of the masses, while the latter abided strictly by the organizational practice of a class-conscious active minority. That practice was founded upon the autonomous activity of each affiliated union, connected and coordinated with the other unions in the Confederation by the Confederal Committee, which was not a leadership organ but, according to E. Pouget:

> an agency for coordinating and widening the revolutionary action of the working class: it is, therefore, the very opposite of democratic bodies which, with their centralization and authoritarianism, stifle the life force out of their component units. In the CGT, there is cohesion, not centralization: there is drive and not direction: Federalism is omnipresent: at every level, the various bodies — from the individual member, Union, Federation or Bourse du Travail, right up to the confederal branches — are all autonomous. Which is what makes for the CGT's radiating power: the drive comes not from the top, but from any point and its vibrations are passed on by being widened to encompass the confederal masses.[1]

As for the Union Council, it carried out the decisions made by the union's general assembly which was at all times sovereign. All union members should attend these assemblies: should they neglect to attend, they have to acquiesce in the decisions reached. "It cannot be otherwise, without a relapse into the dangers of democratism, where the witless and spineless hobble the vigorous. Thus, there can be no appeal against the decisions of the general assembly, however many may have been present." The CGT's national congresses, organized at two yearly intervals, were the equivalents of the general assemblies of the grassroots unions: they encouraged a "useful distillation of the currents of opinion evolved and the clarification of guidelines."[2]

All such clarification carried some weight, for it was a way of distinguishing this revolutionary minority — a worthy continuation of the IWMA — from the Blanquist style of revolutionary minority which deliberately supplants its mandators, and of banishing some anarchists' misgivings about the nature and purpose of the CGT, misgivings that did not seem, at that point, to have any foundation.

This may have been all very fine on paper, but what was the reality? Well, the struggle waged through direct actions and variations upon that theme — strikes, boycotts — was telling in its results. Pouget gives figures for strikes and actions mounted between 1890 and 1905: the percentage of strikes that ended favorably rose from 56 percent in the years 1890–1900 to 62 percent in the 1901–1904 period, rising to 65.67 percent for the year of 1905. The number of strikers benefitting increased even more plainly: 23.38 percent for 1890–1900, 79 percent for 1901–1904 and 83.24 percent in 1905.[3]

It was at this point that the French bourgeoisie chose to hand over to radical and Jacobin politicians of "leftist" backgrounds, that is, more "knowledgeable" about their subject and thus capable of smothering this victorious onslaught by the organized working class. Clemenceau (the former mayor of the commune of Montmartre in March 1871, implicated in the business of the cannons that launched the Paris Commune) became the "Beast of the Interior Ministry" and then, in 1906–1908, Prime Minister. "France's number one cop" as he described himself, displayed his talent for repression: prison terms totaling 104 years were handed down, 667 workers were wounded and 20 killed, and 392 dismissed from their jobs, in the years 1907–1908 alone.[4] 1908 was the watershed year: following the massacre of workers in Draveil-Villeneuve Saint Georges, in which the provocateur Métivier (a CGT official in the pay of Clemenceau) played a capital role, twelve CGT leaders, chosen from among the most militant, were arrested: Griffuelhes, Pouget, Delesalle, Janvion, Monatte, Merrheim and other less celebrated names. Also, whether for motives like those or because of their anti-militarism, the CGT leaders were regularly jailed, then acquitted or sentenced to prison terms.

Clemenceau meant to bring the CGT to heel, through the use of the stick or the carrot. Just prior to the Marseilles congress at the end of 1908, he had his two bêtes noires, Griffuelhes and Pouget, thrown in jail. His gambit was simple: by exposing the alleged irresponsibility of these die-hards, he sought to isolate them from the rest of the leadership — among whom he had, in Latapie, a henchman — and secure a moderation of the CGT's approach. His plan was only partly successful: the congress failed to disown the imprisoned leaders, but Griffuelhes stepped down as general secretary, as did his right-hand man, Pouget, after the confederation's treasurer, Albert Lévy, had tried to make things impossible for him during his period of absence. Griffuelhes was subsequently to be cleared of all suspicion of embezzlement, but was nevertheless to remain in retreat, spending his time on theoretical studies and his own trade union activities.

After a reformist interlude, quickly terminated by the blunders of the new general secretary, Lucien Niel, it was a libertarian militant, Léon Jouhaux, son of a Paris Communard and grandson of a (shot) 1848 rebel, that stepped into the breach on a provisional basis.

Far from drawing the teeth of the CGT, the government crackdown proved a spur to its expansion: its membership grew from 100,000 in 1902, to 400,000 in 1908 — out of a total unionized population of 900,000 workers. Its fight for the eight-hour day, against employment bureau, for a day off work each week, for wage increases and improvements in working conditions — a fight often crowned with success — made it the representative of the finest of the labor movement's aspirations to emancipation.

Clemenceau's heavy-handed approach having failed to produce the desired results, the renegade ex-socialists Aristide Briand and Viviani, taking up cabinet office and the premiership, set about corrupting the CGT by introducing reforms relating to workers' pensions, collective bargaining agreements, compulsory arbitration and business size: all of them things forcefully rejected by revolutionary syndicalists. So much so that the latter launched an offensive against this social offensive: in March 1909, there were two consecutive postal workers' strikes, followed by a failed attempt at a general strike; in 1911, there were strikes by railway workers, Newfoundland seamen, dockers and construction workers; in 1912 there was the strike by registered seamen that brought the commercial ports to a standstill; in 1913 came the general strike by the miners of the Nord; in February of the following year, there was a further general strike by miners, excepting the departments of the Nord and the Pas-de-Calais. The CGT systematically snubbed all draft reforms presented by the government or emanating from the parliament. Its membership climbed back to 600,000 in 1912, and by January 1, 1914 stood at 839,931.[5]

Obviously it was not all wine and roses in the CGT: far from it. Personal squabbles arising out of personality clashes or differences of temperament, (Griffuelhes, for example, was coarse to say the least and that made him staunch enemies) divided the leadership. The reformist minority — supporters of joint action with the Socialist Party — was still significant and was bolstered by the affiliation of the powerful Miners' Federation. Trade union bureaucracy ensconced itself, being bound up with the charisma of leaders who were re-elected over and over again or confirmed in office by the rank and file membership: most of the affiliated Federations had no thought for anything beyond their short-term sectional interests and were indifferent to the demands of other Federations, and even more so to overall revolutionary aspirations. Let us quote from the hard-nosed analysis of the anarchist miner, Georges Dumoulin, who became a CGT officer:

> Everyone was in hot pursuit of advantages down twisted parliamentary paths. Class mentality was ill-defined and even worse expressed. It was no longer coordinated direct action, it was desultory sectional

action that was to produce, one after another, the strike of the railway workers, the seamen and then the miners, all three heavily influenced by the politicians.

I shall pass quickly over this pre-war situation, but the disease had deeper roots. The mass of the union membership was afflicted by the same disease as its leaders. Let me go further. Jouhaux drafted a report in which mention was made of the "immorality of the working class." Alcoholism was a greater scourge than ever in the ports and demoralizing working methods were still in vogue among union members. In the construction industry [the backbone of the CGT at the time — A. Skirda] the preference was for a fat wage packet — for a better standard of living, with no improvement of the individual conscience. Merrheim and Lenoir reported the same scourges among metalworkers. Among jewelers, hairdressers and waiters, horseracing was a big thing. A proletariat corrupted by envy, still clinging to its class instinct but increasingly losing its soul.

An ignorant proletariat unable to read, with no urge to read or reading only filth. Militants playing interminable card games with their drinking pals.

Dumoulin was even more scathing about the mass of non-unionized workers, among whom:

It was common practice to make capital out of another man's actions. It was well understood that good wages were the result of trade union action but they reaped the benefits without lifting a finger. They provided the audiences for public meetings. These were the people who badmouthed the CGT in order to keep in with the boss.... They joined the union because it might be momentarily of use in securing a fat wage packet. They stopped paying their dues because, once that fat wage had been extracted, they no longer had any use for the union.[6]

Mistakes, the corruption of the leadership, union members and the non-unionized, in short the entire proletariat, according to Dumoulin, eroded class consciousness.

Yet we should introduce a few nuances into this very dark portrait, drawn in June 1918, that is, before the armistice in November 1918, for it is also the expression of its author's personal anger at the proletariat's lack of preparedness in the face of war in 1914. Sure, all of it is true and fair comment, but all the same it should not be allowed to conceal the lingering revolutionary resolution of many CGT militants. Furthermore, the anarchists in the CGT were well aware of all these failings and did what they could to remedy them. The essential point is that the CGT adhered strictly to the Charter of Amiens, keeping the socialist or government politicians at a distance, and that its revolutionary options were staunchly upheld, in principle at any rate.

For their part, the anarchists who gave the CGT a wide berth pressed on with their well-meaning propaganda activities, expressed virtually entirely in the written word and remained as inimical as ever to organization in any form. Jean Grave went on bringing out his publications and, typically, working in his usual idiom, the paradox: "An individual seeking to stand alone against the crowd would soon be trampled. Then again, trying to unite men behind a general program is condemning them to disintegration the moment they might need to go into action!"[7] At best, he noted that the "proselytizing spirit that moved the earliest anarchists is wanting in the newest ones, and it is to that want that we must ascribe the inertia of most of those who profess to be anarchists."

He held the individualists chiefly responsible for this: "failed bourgeois, lacking only the capital or they would be the most accomplished examples of exploitative loutishness." All of this, he argued, was due to "half-assimilated ideas." If, on occasion, he was prepared to concede that anarchist activity was in a dormant state, this was not to be explained in terms of dispersion of effort but rather attributed to "the indolence, the apathy, the indifference of the vast majority of individuals and to the fact that in them ideas have not yet attained that status of convictions."[8] For his part, he remained convinced that it was absurd:

> to seek to get anarchists to put their heads together with a view to a common action program. There are differences of temperament, of character that involve different ways of looking at things. And each of these ways of seeing and acting has as much right to exist and be observed as any other.

So it was not desirable that anarchists should put their heads together in order to "thrash out a common program, for this could only be feasible at the expense of initiatives and the birth of original ideas." The least that we can say about him is to note that his stance was increasingly isolated and out of step in anarchist circles and removed from the course of events.

Kropotkin, too, was isolated, in England; elderly and ailing, he was also restricted in what he could do. Even so, he published the results of his researches into the French Revolution, *Mutual Aid* "the positive and sure source of our ethical notions" and the "best guarantee of further evolution" of the human species.[9] In so doing he set out clearly the essentials of libertarian communist theory: we might single out his excellent definition of the method employed:

> Anarchy represents an attempt to apply the generalizations derived from the inductive-deductive method of the natural sciences to the evaluation of human institutions. It is likewise an attempt to guess, on the basis of that evaluation, mankind's march towards liberty, equality and fraternity, in order to secure the greatest possible measure of happiness for every single component of human societies.[10]

Divorced, in his English exile, from all social practice, he failed to appreciate fully the latent dangers of statism and was emphatic that state communism was an impossibility, as he had so "often demonstrated that it would serve no purpose to labor this point."[11] As for a specifically anarchist organizational practice, that is startlingly missing from his writings of this time.

In spite of everything, in the wake of the Amsterdam congress, a number of attempts at organization had been made in France. The anarchists from the north of the country met in congress in December 1907: the concrete outcome of which was the establishment of the newspaper *Le Combat* with an editorial committee tantamount to the "federative bureau of a Federation not actually in existence"! In June 1908, a federation was set up in the Paris region. That venture was taken up the following year on a more serious basis: a statement of principles was published, broadly reiterating the motions passed at the Amsterdam congress. Organizationally, it comprised branches linked by a federal committee made up of one delegate from each group, assisted by a deputy: each group had only one vote, regardless of its numerical size. A general assembly held at four monthly intervals was envisaged. Subscriptions were payable monthly by the groups in proportion with the numbers of their members. That federation stumbled along and one of the most active anarchists of the day, G. Durupt, complained that there was no "atmosphere" there any more and that the groups were "awash with stammerers." Much of the blame for this he attributed to Jean Grave's disorganizing influence. A plan emerged for a "Libertarian Party," affording generous autonomy to its groups, at the suggestion of the insurrectionist wing of the Socialist Party and the disciples of Gustave Hervé, but that, too, was stillborn. In 1910, an Anarchist Communist Alliance was launched; but its over-flimsy structures led to its collapse. Its place was taken in June 1911 by a Communist Federation: this soon changed its name to the Anarchist Communist Federation. Louis Lecoin was its secretary. In September 1912, it was considering a membership card and monthly dues stamps. At the same time regional congresses were held. These all looked forward to a national congress in Paris in 1913 which would at last lay the foundations of the long awaited Anarchist Confederation.[12]

This sudden preoccupation with "serious" organization was not fortuitous. It reflected a plain determination to dissociate from the individualist anarchists who had just been making headlines with the spectacular exploits of Jules Bonnot and his pals. Indeed, since the demise of Albert Libertad in 1908, *L'Anarchie* (the newspaper he had founded) had led a desultory existence as director after director took it upon himself to keep it afloat. In theoretical terms, Paraf-Javal discredited himself in the eyes of his comrades for referring his differences with Libertad's disciples to the "bourgeois courts": so it was André Lorulot who stepped first into the breach. Lorulot was involved with the libertarian colony in Saint-Germain from 1905 to 1907, then been a regular contributor to *L'Anarchie* and sampled imprisonment for anti-militarism. Setting aside the class struggle and the principle of organization, he scarcely differed from the libertarian communists. If anything, he laid more emphasis upon vigilant observance of real solidarity between individuals, based upon reciprocity and naturally culminating in communism:The individualist anarchist accepts solidarity as a lever, a weapon, a new force. It is not a dogma to be respected nor a duty by which to abide — it is an interest that one is wise to heed. Conscious solidarity proceeds through selection, it is not indiscriminate in its fraternity. In order to retain its utilitarian value, it selects its associates on the basis of the principle of reciprocity.

Communism is that form of social relations that levels economic barriers and destroys all obligation in respect of production and consumption. It is the most integral form of comradeship, the most advantageous solidarity, the one that best allows individual interests to coordinate. There can be no real mutual aid without communism.[13]

Such genuine fraternity was anarchist comradeship. It remained individualist because the starting point of it all had to be the individual affecting himself and his surroundings. "In order to make the revolution around him, he must first of all be capable of making it within himself," he averred, in the tradition of Libertad. Just like Libertad, he berated the resigned accomplices of the system. And the proletarian did not find favor with him either:

He bows before the rich exploiter, licking his boots with servility. Turn and turn about: criminal soldier, spineless worker, collaborator of the police, mainstay of every despotism, the people cannot overnight acquire the capacity to live out its fate with pride, logic and solidarity.[14]

This was one of the reasons why, he argued, anarchist attentats had proved incomprehensible to the "uncultivated mind of the witless masses." Self-education and rebellion were the virtues he preached: refusing to sacrifice the present to some hypothetical revolutionary future, the individualist anarchist had to drain from his existence all of the delights that it had to offer him. "Living his life," free of all slavishness, of all impediment. But what if the impediment was these "witless proletarians?" On the answer to that he remained evasive and found illegalism acceptable only if it was "interesting, seriously pursued with a minimum of risk and with gratifying benefits."[15]

Other theoreticians and editors of *L'Anarchie*, like Ernest Armand and Le Rétif (Victor Serge to be) were deliberately more individualistic, making light of solidarity and in the name of a demented cult of the "ego" they encouraged all manner of extravagances, including "economic rebels." So much so that they ended up uncovering zealous disciples of "living with no care for the cost, by any method whatever" until the paper's editorial offices were visited from time to time by weird individuals jumping around "pop-eyed" to demand with "much gesticulation, a bomb, a Browning, some weapon to spill bourgeois blood, to deal some blow,"[16] without anyone's quite knowing whether these were provocateurs or "nut cases." In short, some people were not content with Lorulot's "cosy" illegalism and preferred to indulge in "house-breaking," petty larceny or even carrying out "con operations." Then on to the scene comes a "lad" from Lyon, a peerless mechanic and expert driver with nerves of steel: Jules Bonnot. He fell in with some individualists driven to despair by an iniquitous society and looking for some "big job" to rescue them from it. In December 1911, in the Rue Ordener in Paris, they set upon a bank messenger before going on to commit further attacks, using an automobile every time, and quick to shoot anybody who stood up to them or even to "bump off" witnesses (as Garnier put it). Among their victims were a rentier in his nineties and his maidservant; a driver working in a garage; a traffic policeman; an uncooperative motorist and two bank clerks, not to mention several others who were wounded. These "motorized bandits" held the front pages of newspapers on the lookout for a sensational story, this style of criminal activity and holdups using an automobile being a real innovation. Rewards were posted, and the network of informers was at full stretch. But the "grapevine" did not take long to discover who was involved: the perpetrators of these bloody attacks were quickly traced, and some of them picked up on "information received." His back to the wall, Bonnot gunned down the number two at the Sûreté, Jouin, before making a run for it and perishing after a lengthy siege. "Turned in," Valet and Garnier were also besieged for a long time in Choisy-le-Roi where the police were reinforced by Zouaves from the army! For them too, it ended in death. A huge dragnet rounded up their close associates and a trial was held in February 1913.

The significant, and also the telling, point is the attitude adopted by the individualist theoreticians, who might be held responsible for the illegalist craze. Lorulot was to say the least unforthcoming, and had indeed always been hostile to violent activities: the only thing for which he might be taken to task was the contempt in which he held the witless accomplices of the system. Even so, he, alone of them all, ventured to wonder, after Callemin, Soudy and Monnier had been executed, whether:

> we did not have some indirect, unwitting responsibility in this carnage. Not by preaching illegalism which, no offense to our detractors, few of us did, but by urging struggle, rebellion and life upon natures that were pathological, impetuous, simplistic or unbalanced. But no, the fault lies with human speech which can germinate in different soils and produce the most varied fruits.

In this way he acknowledged the tree as legitimate, but not its "fruits."

Armand broke ranks by writing that he had thought of the illegalist in abstract terms whereas in fact he was *a-legal*. Aside from this splitting of hairs, he would not condemn the illegalists and even tried to show his solidarity. Le Rétif, on the other hand, himself facing charges of receiving two stolen revolvers, began to play along with the crowd in berating the illegalists, swearing the he had always been against them. As he was to make a habit of this sort of behavior, namely, damning today what he was idolizing yesterday, let us see the fox at his work, in this impassioned tirade which was carried by *L'Anarchie* on January 4, 1912, the very next day after the incident in the rue Ordener:

> That a wretched bank messenger should be shot down in broad daylight is proof that men have at last grasped the virtues of audacity.... I

have no fear in admitting it: I am on the side of the bandits. I find theirs to be a beautiful role: maybe I see them as men. Also, I see naught but boors and puppets. The bandits spell strength. The bandits spell daring. The bandits demonstrate their steadfast determination to live.

Whereas the others suffer the proprietor, the employer and the cop, and vote and protest against iniquities and go to their deaths like they have lived, wretchedly. Be that as it may, my preference is for the fighter. He may go to his grave younger, he may know the manhunt and penal servitude: he may well finish up beneath the abominable kiss of the widow. It is a possibility! I like the man who accepts the risks of open struggle: he is manly. Then, whether he be victor or vanquished, is his fate not to be preferred to the sullen vegetation and interminably slow agony of the proletarian who will go to his death brutalized and broken, without ever having known the benefits of existence?

The bandit has a go. So he has some chance of winning. That is enough. The bandit is a man![18]

In his *Memoirs*, Le Rétif — the troubadour of the "manliness" of the bandits, who was to turn into Victor Serge — the minstrel of Bolshevism, seems to have suffered an "amnesia" attack regarding these youthful writings. At his trial, he was to pass himself off as a "theoretician" who had blundered into a situation not of his making, and he was to put his conviction down to heretical opinions (whereas the charge was receiving) and to his refusal to cooperate with the police authorities. The latter does him credit: somewhat less creditable was the attitude he displayed when Lorulot showed up at the hearing, as a character witness: he insisted that Lorulot too be charged for having mixed with and harbored the illegalists. Disappointed in his petition, he was to accuse Lorulot openly of informing!

Another prominent individualist, Mauricius, brazenly championed the cause of the "tragic bandits," publishing an apologia for their "offense"[19]: "driven by the implacable logic of facts, we will erase society's crimes by crimes against society." Although this may have been rather nebulous and something of a literary device, he was to make himself scarce for a time, before he was arrested and then acquitted in 1915.

However, it was patently clear that Bonnot and his comrades came from the individualist anarchist circles. In addition, they abided strictly by the precepts laid down by Libertad and the "scientific" school: teetotalers and vegetarians, extremely fussy about their appearance, they practiced calisthenics in prison. That said, they refused to cite anarchy as a cover for their foul crimes: this was not for the cause (partly at any rate) like the crimes by Jacob and his "workers by night": they were active, but for their own ends and it was on that count that they were judged severely by most anarchists. We should note, further, that the vast majority of these illegalists were in their twenties and that their operations were handled very amateurishly: "jobs" were carried out on the spur of the moment, there was no discretion, and no real organization to follow up operations (scarcely surprising when dealing with individualists!). They were, in short, bicycle and car thieves who graduated too fast to bank robberies and attacks. In the end they bravely paid the price for their actions. In terms of lethality, theirs was a drawn match with society: nine dead on each side. The "braid-wearers," the professional killers would shortly be conducting an incomparably worse slaughter.

We shall leave the last word on illegalism to Victor Méric: its "ravages among thousands of enthusiastic youngsters were beyond reckoning. For having sacrificed to the illegalist idol, anarchists filled the penal colonies and prisons: they had become the stuff of jailers and 'screws.' A rather odd way of living to the full."[20]

These dismal affairs made plain the dissolution of the individualist milieu. Many lacked elementary courage and, concerned only for themselves, "had no hesitation in grassing" and making "deals." Not a thought was given to the theory of it all.

In popular imagination, the anarchist was already the planter of bombs, and now that the "bandit" was added to the picture, the French anarchist movement felt threatened in its very existence. There would have to be a closer check kept upon the use of the label "anarchist" and demarcation from these criminal "deviationists." The congress in August 1913 set to it. It drew around 130 delegates from 60 groups (24 from Paris and 36 from the provinces), and a few individualist trouble-makers who, in a move unique in anarchist annals, were expelled from the gathering.

It should be pointed out that Mauricius, their spokesman, had arrived bearing a submission on his view of anarchism, which conflicted unduly with that of the congress. For example, lest the "rights of the individual be snuffed out," he refused, when it came down to organization, to countenance a vote, the emergence of a majority view and the appointment of working parties. He saw all that as simply a threat of "dragooning and kowtowing to a group of leaders." The principles of delegation and mandate, put into effect at the congress, represented for him the "biggest joke played on anarchists in fifty years."[21] Let it be noted that Jean Grave was particularly insistent that Mauricius should be expelled.

The Anarchist Revolutionary Communist Federation (FCRA) was established at the congress on the basis of a theoretical consensus that Sébastien Faure took it upon himself to set out in a declaration that he read to the gathering: anti-militarism, anti-parliamentarism, trade union action and condemnation of individualism, the latter being henceforth separated by an "unbridgeable abyss" from libertarian communism. Regional federations were created and these were founded upon the untouchable precept of the independence of individuals within the group and the groups' autonomy within the regional or national Federation. Such loose connections ruled out sufficiently consistent activity, allowing only lobbying campaigns like the campaign against extension of the term of compulsory military service to three years, and against militarism as a whole. Thus all of its activities boiled down to propaganda by means of newspapers, pamphlets and sundry published materials. The practical undertaking of waging a social and economic struggle against the system devolved in fact upon the CGT. And that was how the position stood on the eve of the conflagration in 1914.

## Endnotes to Chapter 12

1. E. Pouget, *Le parti du travail,* (Paris: Bibliothéque syndicaliste, undated), p. 28.
2. E. Pouget, *Le syndicat,* (Nancy: Bibliothéque de documentation syndicaliste, undated), pp. 22–23.
3. E. Pouget, *La CGT,* op. cit., pp. 51–54.
4. Edouard Dolléans, *Histoire du mouvement ouvrier,* (Paris: Armand Colin, 1948), Tomeff, p. 145.
5. Alexandre Zévaès, *La CGT,* (Paris: Editions du journal 'La Concorde,' 1939), p. 72.
6. G. Dumoulin, *Les syndicalistes français et la guerre,* in Alfred Rosmer, *Le mouvement ouvrier pendant la guerre: De l'Union sacrée A Zimmerwaid,* (Paris: Librairie du travail, 1936), pp. 523–542.
7. Jean Grave, *Réformes, Révolution,* (Paris: Stock, 1910), p. 36.
8. Jean Grave, *L'entente pour l'action,* (Temps nouveaux, 1911), pp. 5–13.
9. P. Kropotkin, *L'entr'aide,* (Paris: Alfred Costes, 1938), p. 326.
10. P. Kropotkin, *La science moderne et l'anarchie,* (Paris: Stock, 1913), p. 132.
11. P. Kropotkin, *Communisme et anarchie,* (Paris: La librairie sociale, undated), p. 10.
12. Jean Maitron, *Histoire du mouvement anarchists,* op. cit., pp. 416-421.
13. André Lorulot, *L'individualisme anarchists et le communisme,* (Romainville, 1911), p. 10.
14. André Lorulot, *Les théories anarchistes,* (Paris: Giard et Brière, 1913), p. 238.
15. *L'Anarchie,* No. 42, January 25, 1906, quoted by J. Maitron, op. cit., p. 395.
16. Victor Méric, *Les bandits tragigues,* (Paris: Simon Kra, 1926), pp. 142–143.
17. *L'Anarchie,* No 419, (April 24, 1913), cited by J. Maitron in "De Kibaltchiche à Victor Serge" in *Le Mouvement social,* No 47, (1964), p. 68.
18. Le Rétif, "Les bandits" in *L'Anarchie* No. 352, (January 4, 1912).
19. Mauricius, *L'apologie du crime,* (no place, undated), p. 16.
20. Victor Méric, *Les bandits tragigues,* op. cit., p. 153.
21. Mauricius, *Mon anarchisme,* report submitted to the Paris Congress (Paris: Editions de l'Anarchie, August 15, 1913), pp. 4–5.

# XIII. THE SACRED UNION AND
## "THE WAR TO END ALL WARS"

Franco-German rivalry had been at a peak since 1905. Ever since the war in 1870, they had been at odds: French patriots had the famous blue line of the Vosges mountains, symbolizing the two lost provinces of Alsace and Lorraine, forever in mind. To that was added a frantic competition to win African colonies, as well as the anxiety of British imperialism, worried about the preservation of its "pearl" of the Indies and other assets from the covetousness of the Germans and Turks. For its part, the Austro-Hungarian empire had the Serbian irredentists to contend with. And it was from that quarter that the spark came: the heir to the Austrian throne was assassinated by Serbian nationalists in Sarajevo. Austria declared war on Serbia and, thanks to the system of alliances, their respective allies found themselves at daggers drawn. In August 1914 the whole of Europe combusted. What was the line adopted by the workers' organizations of the protagonist nations?

First and foremost, there was Germany, the country where the socialist movement was strongest. The Social Democratic party had 110 (out of a total of 400) deputies in the parliament and nearly four million voters. The trade unions directly under its control numbered over three million members. Now forty years of class collaboration had so integrated the Social Democracy and its national bourgeoisie that on August 4, 1914, it unanimously, in a frenzy of enthusiasm, voted credits for the war! In December 1914, Karl Liebknecht was to stand alone in voting against further credits and, in March 1915, only Otto Ruhle joined him in voting against the budget proposals. How are we to explain away that stance, so much at odds with all the resolutions from the international congresses of the socialist parties? Well, there was the difficulty of trying to mobilize the German working class at the very time when military mobilization was underway, and the implacable repression that would ensue (Karl Liebknecht was subsequently to be sentenced to a four year prison term for his opposition to the war) and, above all, the threat of annihilation of all Social Democrat activity, so laboriously built up over decades. Then there was the general feeling, widespread among the rich and powerful German trade unions, that there was a close identity between the interests of workers and capitalists in the empire's industrial and commercial expansion. Finally, there was the important consideration of the concept of a defensive war against the barbarian hordes of tsarism, which stood for feudalism and reaction; in which respect the Social Democracy was quite in keeping with the Russophobia of Marx who reckoned, from 1848 on, that Germany should wage a "revolutionary" war against Russia.

In the Russian Empire which was burgeoning economically, the workers' movement was expanding in terms of numbers and political significance; on the eve of the declaration of war, a strike wave had affected 250,000 workers in St. Petersburg. The autocracy was wrestling with all of the contradictions arising out of the survival of feudal privileges alongside economic growth and nationalist movements in its many colonies (Finland, Poland, Ukraine, Caucasus, Asia, etc.). There was nothing like a little war to restore national unity and revive the faltering authority of the state, is what Nicholas II and his entourage were saying. And their gamble largely succeeded: many Social Democrats, not least Plekhanov, rallied to the defense of their homeland in the face of the threat from German imperialism. The Social Revolutionaries joined them en masse: some anarchists like Kropotkin and Tcherkessov, though living in exile, also embraced the cause of the Entente, in hopes of an overhaul of the regime in the wake of victory. A tiny number of Social Democrats — Lenin was their mentor — advocated revolutionary defeatism instead, that is, anticipated that victory for the Central powers would precipitate the collapse of tsarism and open up the prospect of social renewal.

In Britain, the trades unions, more than three million members strong, and with fifty Labor MPs, were hostile to the war and participated only reluctantly. Several European nations opted for neutrality: Italy (to begin with at any rate), Holland and the Scandinavian countries and Spain and Portugal.

In France the problem was rather more ticklish. There was no problem with the socialists who, in spite of the assassination of Jaurés, the "apostle of peace," readily reverted to the rhetoric of the soldiery of the Year II of the Revolution and the Paris Communards to repel the German invader. (Note that in Europe the danger always emanated from the East: was this perhaps some vestige of the ancient fear of barbarian invasions, going back to the beginning of the Christian era?) Gustave Hervé, the Socialist Party's insurrectionist, who had planted the "tricolor flag in the shit," turned into a rabid jingoist. Jules Guesde and Marcel Sembat joined the government of Sacred Union. The reason was quickly grasped: here too this was a "defensive" war. Except that, "the better to defend themselves," everybody was attacking: the French scurried off to liberate Alsace and Lorraine; the Germans invaded Belgium so as to outflank the French positions (and avert the loss of 100,000 men, as the German Social Democrat deputy, Dr. Koster, was to explain while deploring the hostility from the Belgian workers for, had they but played ball, they could have had universal suffrage, legislation protecting women and children and social services, in short, a "welfare society").[1]

The "fatherland" card was harder to play when it came to the CGT, the libertarian mass organization to which many members of the French proletariat looked for a lead. Ever since its inception, it had been violently opposed to the army and to militarism. Yvetot and others of its leaders had been jailed time and time again on charges of anti-militarism. The CGT had regularly denounced the arms race, the introduction of a three-year term of compulsory military service, budget allocations to the army, belligerent speechifying and other ancillary threats. It had played a preponderant part in the success of a demonstration by 150,000 Parisians on the Pré-Saint-Gervais against the army and militarism on March 16, 1913. In its defense it should be noted that every time it attempted to mount a joint campaign with its German counterpart against war, the Germans, wholly in thrall to the Social Democracy, had declined, on the grounds that this was a matter to be handled through the political process, that is to say, through the good offices of their respective socialist parties! Nevertheless, for years past, the CGT's policy had been set out clearly: in the event of war being declared and a general mobilization being decreed, an insurrectionary general strike would be called. To be sure, in July 1914, under Jaurès's influence, there was some back-sliding: its anti-militarism was exchanged for a peace campaign. There is some significance to this nuance, for the backsliding continued in the manifesto of July 29, 1914: the CGT invoked its opposition to war, but at the same time emphasized Austria's guilt (coming very close to the official government line); it called for popular demonstrations throughout the land for peace. Two days later, following the assassination of Jaurès, contrary to all expectations, it was not outrage at the French warmongers that prevailed, but appreciation that war was a "fait accompli" and "a crisis on the way." At Jaurès's funeral on August 4th, Jouhaux delivered his famous address and did a U-turn: he spoke at some length about Jaurès in very eulogistic terms (scarcely justified by their political disagreements) before announcing that:

> we did not want this war.... We shall be the soldiers of freedom in order to win for the oppressed a regimen of freedom, so as to create harmony between peoples through free agreement between the nations, through an alliance between the peoples. That ideal will make it possible for us to succeed.[2]

This was a discreet but real defection to the patriotic cause, and it was for that reason that Jouhaux was feted by everybody, left and right alike. This was the celebrated "Sacred Union." Set alongside the old anti-militarist struggles, this was the world turned upside down, so how are we to explain it away? Jouhaux himself was later to say that above all else what he wished to avert was that his words should supply the pretext for any crackdown on the working class and that that was what lay behind his speaking. In fact there was the ominous threat of the "Carnet B," that is, the list of three thousand, and some, revolutionary militants on the books of the police as dangerous individuals to be rounded up immediately upon the outbreak of war. The Minister of War, General Messimy, had publicly threatened to "tie [the CGT leaders] to the execution stake" and ship anti-militarist militants off to concentration camps. And these were no idle threats, for the army was omnipotent at that point. The CGT's assistant secretary, Dumoulin, an opponent of the Sacred Union, did not mince his words: he stated that it was funk that induced the majority of the CGT's confederal committee to make its U-turn: "they were afraid of war, afraid of repression, simply because they were men like other men."[3] Himself called up and posted to Verdun, to share the harsh life of the private soldier, he delivered himself of this pained and deserved comment in August 1915:

> At the start of the war, as during the few days leading up to the decla-
> ration of it, the impotence of the peace party was equally plain in ev-
> ery part. Nowhere had anti-militarism succeeded in eradicating either
> national pride or race prejudice. Our anti-militarism, more strident than
> the pacifism of the German workers, failed to neutralize the poison
> peddled in great profusion by the lying press among the masses of
> ignoramuses unreached by all wholesome propaganda. Where we went
> wrong was in overestimating the impact of our anti-militarism and our
> militants would have done well to shoulder the blame for our power-
> lessness instead of shifting that blame on to the shoulders of the Ger-
> man labor leaders.[4]

Dumoulin further adds that the CGT had not taken an adequate interest in the play of diplomatic alliances. Sure, there were secret clauses, and it would not have been easy to get wind of them. However, Dumoulin patently underplays the culpability of the German Social Democracy, which is blatant. In spite of every-thing, the CGT leadership was also to blame and there is no way to disguise that fact by invoking outside factors. Despite the jingoistic mania, there was a worker minority ready to take action, and if the CGT confederal committee had cast caution to the wind and declared a general strike against mobilization, it would first of all have been true to itself and to the strategy pursued for years past, and a proletarian backlash might have dampened the warmongers' enthusiasm. In addition, the military chiefs in charge of the mobilization had anticipated a de-sertion rate of ten percent and were delighted to have had a desertion rate of only two percent![5] As Jouhaux explained, the likelihood was that the CGT lead-ership was not merely afraid for itself but feared a "Saint Bartholomew's night" massacre of its best militants.

That said, and without excusing the conduct of Jouhaux and the CGT confederal committee, we might look at the opinion of Monatte who remained opposed to war:

> I will not take the confederal bureau to task for having failed to un-
> leash a general strike against the mobilization order: no! We were pow-
> erless, one and all: the tidal wave passed and we were swept away.[6]

Even Merrheim, the chief adversary within the CGT of the Sacred Union, was to concede in 1919 that:

We were in utter disarray, lost our heads: how come? Because at that point the working class of Paris, caught up in a formidable tide of nationalism, would not have allowed the security forces the chore of shooting us. They would have shot us themselves.[7]

Be that as it may, Jouhaux became a Commissioner of the Nation and, along with all of the other CGT leaders, was a close confederate of the government in its war effort, right into 1917.

As for the anarchists, wrong-footed by the speed of events, they did not have the time to react collectively, for want of a real federal organization, so the decisions were made on an individual basis. Some complied with the mobilization order, others deserted and left the country. Sébastien Faure bravely published texts hostile to the war and to the Sacred Union, but the main event was the appearance in February 1916 of the Manifesto of the Sixteen (in fact, fifteen, the place name having been mistaken for the name of a signatory) in favor of the Entente powers against Germany. Among the signatories were militants of some repute: Kropotkin, Grave, Malato, Paul Reclus, Marc Pierrot, Cornelissen and Tcherkessov. Their statement was countersigned by about a hundred other anarchists, half of them Italians. Although this was very much a minority in the international anarchist movement, it did that movement great damage. To account for this disconcerting stance, we have to look to the past and compare Karl Marx's stance at the time of the Franco-Prussian war in 1870, when he wrote to Engels that the:

> French need a good drubbing. If the Prussians are victorious, the centralization of state power will be of service to the concentration of the German working class. Furthermore, German preponderance will shift the European workers' movement's center of gravity from France to Germany; and we need only compare the workers' movement in those two countries from 1868 up to the present to see that the German working class is superior to the French in theoretical terms as well as organizational. The ascendancy upon the world stage of the German proletariat over the French proletariat would simultaneously give our theory the ascendancy over Proudhon's.[8]

That letter had just been made public through James Guillaume's book *Karl Marx, Pan-Germanist*, and would have provoked the wrath of the older generation of anarchists who already despised Marx as the gravedigger of the international and hated his heirs, the German Social Democracy for the very same reason. That subjective, emotional factor has to be taken into account if we are to grasp the spirit of the times. Likewise, the fact that the French Republic was under threat from emperors and their aristocratic hangers-on is another point to be included in the reckoning (although the Russian aristocracy was a somewhat embarrassing ally to have in that respect).

As hostilities erupted everybody was firmly convinced that this would be a short war. In France, certain zealots imagined that they would be in Berlin within three weeks, on the strength of the heartening immensity of the massive Russian army. As the hostilities grew prolonged and part of France was overrun and an atrocious trench war involving countless masses of humanity and heavy loss of life ensued, this gung-ho attitude gave way to a critical perspicacity. Many people now had their eyes opened to how they had been taken in by "brainwashing." It was no longer a question of waging "the war to end all wars" — to bring everlasting peace! — but rather of acting as guinea pigs for all sorts of murderous machinery and letting oneself be slaughtered so that a few generals might strut around bedecked with medals. The "fresh and joyous" war turned into a great butchery for everyone in which lots of men met their deaths while still in their prime.

On the Russian front, initial successes quickly gave way to unspeakable disasters. All of the shortcomings of the autocracy were sensationally exposed to public gaze: the ineptitude of the High Command, the virtually non-existent logistics, the speculators and fence-sitters enriching themselves beyond belief in the rear. With an eye to easing the pressure on the western front, the Russian generals dispatched troops equipped with decrepit rifles and only a handful of cartridges against impregnable German positions bristling with machine guns and artillery, and that without any prior softening up by artillery barrage, very often for want of shells! The "grim reaper" had a field day: the millions of dead and wounded on the Russian front inspired a rising tide of indignation. At the beginning of 1917, an incident of no great import — the refusal by a Cossack unit to break up a demonstration by the hungry in Petrograd — brought the 300-year-old Romanov regime tumbling down like a house of cards. It was replaced by a provisional government. When that too proved powerless to stop the slaughter, it was overthrown by a few thousand soldiers and some Petrograd workers. Lenin and his Bolshevik supporters, as well as his allies, the Left Social Revolutionaries, established a new government, the Soviet of People's Commissars, before signing a separate peace deal with Germany and the Austro-Hungarian Empire in February 1918.

Russia's defection from the Entente camp was made good by the entry into the war of the United States, but the morale of the "poilus" (French equivalent of the British "Tommies") sank, because by now the futility of the carnage was apparent to all and they were, in any event, influenced by the outbreak of the Russian revolution. In April 1917, there were mutinies along the French front: these were harshly repressed. On that same occasion, the power of the generals was turned against pacifists in the rear. Hervé's erstwhile lieutenant, Almereyda, tossed into prison, was found "suicided" in his cell.

Sébastien Faure who, in spite of the censors, managed with the aid of Mauricius to bring out the pacifist journal *Ce qu'il faut dire*, fell victim to a crude police frame-up: he was indicted for "moral turpitude," that is, for having pinched the bottom of a teenaged girl! Faure, who for twelve years had been the outstanding educator from the La Ruche children's settlement! Despite the absurdity of the charges, he was sentenced to a six-month prison term.[9] Cut to the quick psychologically, it was only thanks to the unstinting assistance of his comrades that he recovered from this blow. Armand, individualist or not, spoke out against the wartime carnage: he was charged with having aided the desertion of one Raymond Bouchard, a dubious character addicted to drugs who had earlier led to the sentencing of the pacifist Gaston Rolland to a fifteen-year term of penal servitude for having harbored him. Armand "went down" for five years!

The indomitable Louis Lecoin, gardener and dauntless anarchist, who had already a conviction against him for having refused to march (he was then in the army) against striking railway workers in 1910, plus a further five-year prison term for his anti-militarism, threw himself into a flat-out campaign along with some colleagues for an immediate peace, the moment he was released from prison in November 1916: only to be re-arrested and re-convicted. Aged 24 in 1911, he was to spend a total of eight years out of the next ten in prison! Dozens of other anarchists, including Lepetit (who served two years) were convicted of pacifist propaganda. Thanks to the "Clemenceau" approach (Clemenceau the "strike-breaker" having returned to power in the interim). What is more, outraged by this repression, an anarchist called Emile Cottin opened fire on the "Father of Victory" on February 19th, hitting him with two bullets. He was at first sentenced to death, then, on the lobbying of Clemenceau himself, to ten years in prison when, just one month earlier, Villain, who had *killed* Jaurès, had been acquitted! [10]

We might do well to remember that there were some anarchists of integrity — these were in fact the larger number in the movement — who did not fail to live up to their beliefs, contrary to the notion peddled by Bolshevik detractors whose constant preoccupation was with harping upon the stance adopted by the "Sixteen" who went over to the Sacred Union.

## Endnotes to Chapter Thirteen

1. Alexandre Zévaès, *La faillite de l'Internationale,* (La Renaissance du livre, Paris, 1917), pp. 143–144.
2. Annie Kriegel & Jean-Jacques Becker, *La guerre et le mouvement ouvrier français,* (Paris: Armand Colin, 1964) , pp. 135–143.
3. G. Dumoulin, *Les syndicalistes français et la guerre,* quoted by A. Rosmer, op. cit., p. 530.
4. G. Dumoulin, *Carnets de route (Quarante années de vie militante)* (Lille: Editions de l'Avenir, 1938), p. 76–77.
5. Edouard Dolléans, *Histoire du mouvement ouvrier,* op. cit., Tome ff, p. 221.
6. Ibid., p. 222.
7. Quoted by Etienne Martin-Saint-Léon, *Les deux CGT. Syndicalisme et communisme,* (Paris: Plon, 1923), p. 20.
8. James Guillaume, *Karl Marx pangermaniste,* (Paris: Armand Colin, 1915), p. 85.
9. *Une infamies L'affaire Sébastien Faure, les dessous d'une odieuse machination,* (Paris, undated), 32 pages.
10. Paul Savigny, Louis Lecoin, Emile Cottin, Alphonse Barbé, Eugène Bévent, *Les anarchistes et le cas de conscience,* (Paris: La librairie sociale, 1921), 32 pages.

# XIV. THE "MIRAGE OF SOVIETISM" AND ANARCHISM IN CRISIS

The establishment in October 1917 of what was sold as soviet power lies at the root of one of the most tragic misunderstandings of this century. Ever since the February 1917 revolution which had toppled tsarism, the soviets (or "councils") had become the grassroots organs of the Russian workers' direct democracy. In the face of the impotence of the provisional revolutionary government made up of liberals and Social Revolutionaries, a government led towards the end by the capricious Kerensky, a dual power situation had increasingly favored those who called for "all power to the soviets on the spot and at the center," with, as its corollary, the demands of "the land to the peasants, the factory to the worker," and, above all, "immediate peace, with no annexations and no tribute." Lenin was remarkably skillful at adapting to these watchwords and above all putting them to use in carrying out the coup d'état of October 1917, purportedly in the name of the soviets but in fact for the exclusive advantage of his party and its sole decision-making organ: the central committee. That substitution was quickly spotted but in the light of the circumstances it was considered a temporary expedient. The Russian anarchists, who were quite numerous if insufficiently organized, supported and even cooperated with the Bolsheviks. In fact, their interpretation was that the Bolsheviks had jettisoned the entire social democratic inheritance and gone over to the libertarian theses. With the passage of time, they came to realize that this was not in fact the case, and that the heads of Lenin and his faithful followers were still crammed with the centralist and statist outlook. However, civil war, foreign intervention and the threat of a return to the despised old order induced them to keep their criticisms to themselves and led to their taking an active role in the defense of what they termed "the revolution's gains," all under the guidance of the Bolshevik party. It was only at the end of 1919, when victory over the Whites became likely and the new Bolshevik authorities made plain their hegemonic ambitions and set about blatantly repressing them, that many anarchists severed their links, although they did not all take up arms against the Bolsheviks. After the crushing in March 1921 of the Kronstadt sailors' revolt, such reservations as they had turned into open hostility and the breakdown was complete. Obviously, by then it was too late, for the new authorities were solidly entrenched in position, could call upon a mighty state machinery of control and repression and were able to face down any internal challenges without too much difficulty. We ought to make it clear that this phenomenon of rallying around the Bolsheviks was not exclusive to anarchists, but was equally the case among all the other old revolutionary tendencies: the Social Revolutionaries, the Mensheviks, the Bundists (Jewish Workers' Social Democratic Party) or indeed dissident social democratic factions. (Hitherto hostile to Lenin, Trotsky went over to his camp after his return to Russia in 1917.) This second edition of an allegedly revolutionary Sacred Union, in the name of the "mirage of sovietism" was, when all is said and done, even more damaging to the Russian and worldwide revolutionary movement.

Returning to Russia after forty years in exile, Kropotkin quickly grasped how things stood and in a celebrated *Letter to the Workers of Western Europe* on June 10, 1920, he set out his analysis of the position. First, he railed against any armed intervention in Russia by the Entente powers, in that this would be directed primarily against the Russian social revolution, which he related to its English and French predecessors, and which, he argued "seeks to build a society in which the entire product of the combined efforts of labor, technical expertise and scientific discovery would go to the community itself. Any intervention [he wrote] would only reinforce the Bolsheviks' dictatorial methods and render the country hostile towards the Western nations." He regarded the independence of the Russian empire's former colonies, Finland, Poland, the Baltic nations, the Ukraine, Georgia, Armenia, Siberia, etc., as irreversible. By his reckoning the Russian revolution was trying to venture where the French revolution had not gone, namely, into the realm of *de facto equality*, meaning economic equality. Unfortunately, these efforts were the work of a "strongly centralized party dictatorship" which was, to some extent, the heir of Babeuf's centralistic, Jacobin outlook. He believed that it was all about to end in fiasco and provide an object lesson in *"how not to introduce communism*, even for a people grown weary of the old regime and offering no active resistance to the experiment conducted by the new governments." The idea of the soviets, he went on, was a "great idea," especially as these should be made up of "all who play any real part in the production of the nation's wealth through their own personal endeavors." In the shadow of a party dictatorship, they became meaningless, especially if there was no press freedom and no election campaigns to decide their composition. Such a dictatorship was "the death knell of the new construction." The new bureaucracy created by the Bolsheviks was even worse than that of the French which "requires, for example, the involvement of forty officials just to sell off a tree felled across a national route by some storm." Western workers had to learn from this, for "appealing to the genius of party dictators" was the best "means of not carrying out the revolution and of rendering its achievement impossible." He cautioned against such leadership and closed with a call for a great International that would not be a mirror image either of the second or of the third, both of which were directed by a single party, but would embrace trade unions worldwide — all who created the world's wealth — in order that these might "deliver themselves from their present subjection to Capital."

In 1920, during a visit by a foreign comrade, the aged apostle of libertarian communism further declared that the "communists, with their methods, instead of setting the people on the road to communism, will end up making them hate the very mention of it."[1] An all too accurate forecast, alas! although Lenin did not use the term communism until 1918, in the obvious hope of shrouding his theoretical gobbledy-gook (which the French social democrat Charles Rappoport at the time was to label bluntly as "Blanquism served up in a tartar sauce") with that noble title.

Kropotkin's analysis was shared by the vast majority of Russian anarchists, but a not inconsiderable number of them nevertheless opted to carry on cooperating with the Bolsheviks, though stopping short of formal affiliation to their party. This was the case with, among others, our old acquaintance Kibaitchitch, formerly Le Rétif, the fellow who marveled at the "manliness of the bandits," that onetime director of *L'Anarchie* and erstwhile theoretician of individualist anarchism, henceforth to be known as Victor Serge. His patron, Zinoviev, the president of the Communist International, entrusted him with the uneasy task of explaining away his defection. Which he did in a pamphlet published in France in 1921, *The Anarchists and the Experience of the Russian Revolution*.[2]

In his foreword, this guy has the nerve to argue that several foreign anarchist militants — including Lepetit and Vergeat, who mysteriously vanished during their return journey to France, a disappearance upon which Serge could certainly have shed "his" little light — had "agreed" with the thinking he was setting out in his pamphlet. Even so, he notes that in several countries "a number of anarchist militants, have felt it their duty to espouse with regard to Russia's proletarian dictatorship a frankly hostile attitude that most often is revealing of inexperience and a traditionalism loaded with dangers"! He therefore was taking it upon himself to spell out a few "elementary truths." After the "experience of war and revolution, our ideas stood in need of a complete and methodical overhaul," yes, but in the light of what? Of the "new fact" in History, "the victory of the October revolution ... the victory of the soviets ... the victory of the social revolution." That progression is a good reflection of the official Bolshevik falsehood that their coup d'état was synonymous with ideas that were the very reverse of it: soviets and social revolution. Then comes an enormous lie of Serge's own: "the social revolution in Russia is largely the work of Bolshevism." He himself had not reached Russia until the beginning of 1919, so he was scarcely in a position to judge, but it was so convenient to peddle that official version that he was to lose no time in spreading it in France through his two mythomaniacal works: *The Year I of the Revolution* and *The Year II of the Revolution*. His definition of Bolshevism is a fair return for his mess of pottage: "a leftward movement of socialism — bringing it close to anarchism — prompted by the will to carry out the revolution right away. Will to revolution: the essence of Bolshevism is encapsulated in those three words." Some performance that, to reduce the social revolution to the power cravings of a tiny caste of doctrinaire intellectuals! All of it is only playing with words, something in which he was a past master already, as we have had occasion to see. But there is a more serious aspect to this when he goes on to justify the Bolshevik terror:

> From the vantage point of those who made it (the Revolution), it is a tough, dangerous undertaking, sometimes a dirty business into which one has to wade up to one's knees, sleeves rolled back, braving the urge to retch. It is a matter of cleansing the earth of the scum of the old world. One will have to shift the filth by the shovel-full: and there will be a lot of blood among that filth.

One can hear an echo of Netchaiev talking about "revolution full steam ahead, through blood and mud." Red terror was to be implemented "on pain of death," as one "weakness could have spelled defeat." Defeat would have ushered in the White terror "a hundred times more ghastly." Here Serge cites the example of the Paris Commune, when the Versailles forces allegedly shot down in a fortnight three times as many victims as the Red terror had claimed in Russia in three years of revolution! Like Pinocchio's, his nose must have grown considerably with this enormous lie: Latsis, the Chekist ideologue himself acknowledges that the Red terror claimed nearly one million seven hundred thousand victims, many of them peasants and workers. Without blinking, Serge slashes that figure to a mere ten thousand victims of "mud and blood." And here we are faced with deliberate lying, for he was well placed, in Petrograd, to know what lay behind the regime's statistics.

Next comes a walk down the memory lane of the individualist anarchist: contempt for the masses "corrupted by the old regime, relatively uneducated, often unthinking, racked by the feelings and instincts of the past." This is all leading up to a justification of revolutionary dictatorship: "I confess that I cannot think how one could be a revolutionary (except on a purely individual basis) without conceding the necessity of the dictatorship of the proletariat." "*Over* the proletariat" he should have said, for the sake of accuracy. Lest the reader has failed to grasp his meaning, he goes on later to rehearse the essentials of his new credo:

> Suppression of so-called democratic freedoms: dictatorship, backed up, if need be, by Terror: creation of an army: centralization for war of industry, supply, administration (hence the statism or bureaucracy): and lastly dictatorship of a *party*.... In this redoubtable chain reaction of needs, there is not a single link that can be dispensed with, not one link that is not strictly dependent on the one before it and does not determine the one that comes after it.

Let us quote his refrain: "Every revolution is a sacrifice of the present to the future." One might wonder if this is the same Kibaltchitch, the erstwhile Le Rétif, talking here. The shades of his old chums from the Bonnot gang must have started upon reading such lunacy! We can understand how Victor Serge-Kibaltchitch, having zealously embraced his new faith, had to demonstrate his loyalty and justify his membership in the Bolshevik party, that "vigorous, innovative minority required to make good, through constraint, the deficient education of the backward masses (!?)," but even so, what a betrayal of the ideals of his youth and what abject surrender to his squalid mission! Not that this sad fellow was to stop there, for he acted as the official escort to foreign anarchists and revolutionaries visiting the red Mecca, sometimes poisoning their minds and reporting back to his masters. The most startling thing was to find him, fifteen years or so later, posing as a victim of Stalinism!

Among those anarchists who threw in their lot with the Bolsheviks, very few, fortunately, plumbed those depths of servility. Most of them either left the party, if they had joined it, or distanced themselves from it following the repression of the Kronstadt revolt, the prohibition upon factional work inside the party and the ensuing introduction of the NEP. This was especially true of Alexander Berkman and Emma Goldman.

The "mirage of sovietism" had an impact every bit as pernicious abroad, most especially in France. Government censorship, alongside denunciation of the Bolsheviks as accomplices of the Germans, up until 1919, made a substantial contribution to this. According to the precept that "the enemies of my enemies are my friends," many who opposed the Great War thought they detected genuine and consistent pacifists in Lenin and his disciples. The myth of "soviet power" was the finishing touch in persuading the most revolutionary elements, a goodly number of them anarchists.

So much so that the first *Parti communiste*, French Section of the Communist International, was set up at the start of 1919: it recognized the "temporary dictatorship of the proletariat." It was comprised almost exclusively of anarchists — and the oddest thing is that one discovers one-time individualists converted into fervent supporters of Bolshevism. In November 1918, Lorulot wrote that "in time of revolution, a measure of dictatorship is necessary"; in 1921 he was at it again and worse: the "iron dictatorship of the proletariat" was to be "a dictatorship of elites over brutes." Mauricius and even Armand admitted feeling a "certain sympathy" for the Bolsheviks; Charles-Auguste Bontemps also reckoned that dictatorship was "an evil but a necessary evil" in helping to "establish a communist system."[3]

At its congress of December 25–28, 1919, the *Parti communiste* turned itself into a Communist Federation of Soviets, which is testimony to the preponderant influence of the anarchists, in that its structure was federalist: the rank and file soviets made up regional soviets and these in turn appointed a central soviet, the whole thing reflecting the desire for ongoing rank and file supervision. Needless to say Moscow did not at any time recognize the existence of either of these communist organizations, for it reserved its favors for the party that emerged from a split at the Tours congress of the Socialist Party. Be that as it may, they still remain a rather telling indication of the spell cast upon many libertarian comrades by this "mirage of sovietism." In addition, most of these returned to the anarchist orbit, with the notable exceptions of certain revolutionary syndicalists and CGT anarchists, belonging to the anti-Jouhaux minority: people like Monatte, Rosmer, Amedée Dunois, etc. The latter took a lot longer to see the error of their ways.

Meanwhile, as the flow of information began to improve, and corroborating evidence became more plentiful, the Bolshevik regime's soviet mask fell away and everyone was able to see it for what it truly was. The better to dissociate itself from them, the Anarchist Communist Federation of 1914 changed its name, as soon as it was reformed, to the Anarchist Union (UA), which was blatantly and relentlessly hostile to the Bolsheviks from the end of 1920 onwards.

Dumoulin and Merrheim, the two leaders of the CGT's anti-Sacred Union minority, were not taken in by Lenin like Rosmer and Monatte were. Merrheim had met him face to face at Zimmerwald in 1915 and had quickly got the measure of the man: "He is a Guesdist, a hundred times more sectarian than all the Guesdists put together, which is no mean feat," his sole ambition being "dictatorship over everything and everybody, his own dictatorship, even should it set civilization back by a century." The labor militant discerned in the "mysticism of Lenin's adorers" the very same sentiment that had motivated the enthusiasts of General Boulanger two decades earlier, that same unthinking ardor of persons "searching for a savior, the man who will make their revolution for them."[4] Dumoulin, who returned to the fold alongside Jouhaux and became the "strong man" of the Confederal Committee, was violently opposed to the "Muscovites" and was the chief architect of the 1921 trade union schism with the pro-Bolshevik minority and its anarchist allies. The latter in turn broke away from Lenin's disciples in 1924. Thus the CGT, like the international workers' movement, finished up split into three factions: Jouhaux's CGT, affiliated to the Amsterdam Trade Union International, the Bolshevised CGTU, affiliated to the Red International of Labor Unions, and the Revolutionary Syndicalist CGT (CGT-SR) of Pierre Besnard and the anarcho-syndicalists, affiliated to the Berlin-based International Workers' Association.

The French and worldwide anarchist movement, already stretched to the limit by the war, found itself even more divided in the face of the new situation created by the advent of Bolshevism. The congress of the Anarchist Union did not meet until November 1920, nearly seven years after the preceding one (1913). An international congress had been planned for September 1914, but did not take place until December 1921 when it met in Berlin. Anarchists had been caught wrong-footed by events, not to say completely overwhelmed by them. The obvious cause of that was the lack of proper liaison and quite simply of real organization: one can only speculate what an organization in the Bakuninist Alliance might have achieved: general guidelines might have been adopted and made known, some practical policy line laid down and put into effect, with regard both to the war and to the Bolshevik phenomenon. Instead of which, there was a lengthy hiatus, followed by a general fragmentation of forces. At the Lyon congress of the Anarchist Union, Mauricius, recovered from his Bolshevik rapture, following a nine-month stay in Russia, urged his comrades to draw up an agrarian and industrial program, lest anarchists be caught even more off guard by future revolutionary crises. Another delegate to the congress even moved that training schools for militants be established: broadly speaking, emphasis was laid upon the crucial importance of scrutiny of issues of a political, agrarian and industrial nature.

As for the individualists, they were increasingly sidelined from congresses and organizations. Anyway, Lorulot finally bade farewell to anarchism and devoted himself exclusively to attacking clericalism: Armand declared without equivocation that he was no revolutionary and thereafter devoted his energies to his hobbyhorse of "loving comradeship," venturing so far as to set up an "International for the fight against bodily possessiveness, sexual jealousy and amorous exclusivism"! Just as seriously, he called for personal ownership of the means of production to be vested in the individual and became the "pope" of a tiny sect from which all consideration of society was excluded, "guile" being regarded as the only means open to the "liberated" individualist to break free of it.

Now, affirmation of individual autonomy had not been exclusive to the individualists, but was, rather, as we have seen, a constant motif in the international anarchist movement and particularly in the French movement. That notion, married to the autonomy of the group within the organization, relied upon the untouchable principle of the free agreement. So that was where the real difficulty lay. In an article entitled "Let's Get Organized," Louis Lecoin labored the need for a "well-ordered cohesion" as a means of repairing the movement's ineffectuality. Another leading militant, Georges Bastien, wrote: "Only through organization will we achieve maximum results in terms of propaganda and action." Appreciating, in 1925, the diffidence on the part of certain dogmatic champions of individual autonomy, he anathematized them by asserting that they were "scared of seeing their ego trampled underfoot in an organization. That is the reason behind their rejecting it categorically or in some roundabout fashion, by quibbling over every minuscule detail. It all makes regular association repugnant to them."[5] The need for a specific and coherent and cohesive organization was consequently making itself felt more and more, even if it meant revision of certain of anarchism's traditional values. This was the task that several survivors from the Russian and Ukrainian anarchist movement who had taken refuge in Paris that year were to set themselves.

The anarchists' most enormous defeat was sustained in Russia. Throughout 1917, their ranks had swollen incessantly, until they numbered tens of thousands of supporters in the Anarchist Federations of Petrograd and Moscow (each of which issued its daily newspaper) as well as across all the important cities in the land. Their role in the July Days of 1917 — the abortive rising against Kerensky — in every strike wave and of course in the fighting in October 1917, (the fruits of which were claimed by the Bolsheviks all for themselves) indicate the crucial influence they wielded at that point. And yet they were too slow to develop mistrust of the new Leninist authorities, paying them no heed in a sense, busying themselves with the immediate implementation of the social and economic changes of which they had long dreamt. Not that they remained unorganized: in Moscow they set up 50 Black Guard detachments with one overall command and thousands of members. The onslaught came from the quarter they least expected: on the night of April 12–13, 1918, Moscow's 26 anarchist clubs were stormed by units acting upon the orders of the Bolsheviks and their Left Social Revolutionary allies. Seeking to avert fratricidal fighting, 600 anarchists surrendered. By the autumn of 1918, the Black Guards in Moscow reckoned they were strong enough to consider overthrowing Lenin, and were only deterred from doing so by the threat of counterrevolution. In fact, the Sacred Union around the Bolsheviks in the face of the threatened restoration of the old regime was to cloud the issue and help to ensure that libertarians were progressively and irreversibly pushed into the background.[6] At the time, Kropotkin deplored the lack of liaison between anarchists and floated the idea of establishing an "anarchist party" so as not to "remain with arms folded." He used the word "party" in a sense different from that of the politicians' usage of it, and only because the word "group" struck him as a bit lame and inadequate in the circumstances. In fact, it was an anarcho-syndicalist party, uniting a "band of honest, dedicated anarchist militants capable of setting aside their personal vanities," that he wanted and he regretted that he was not young enough any more to give it his all. Let us note that he gave priority to person-to-person contacts and correspondence over the press and printed matter.[7]

In the Ukraine, things took a different course. There the Bolsheviks were, to begin with, all but nonexistent and they relied upon the extraordinary Makhnovist insurgent movement driven by the local anarchist groups. In short, they had, shall we say, a lot more problems securing their mastery of the situation. We might mention that a powerful anarchist confederation, the Nabat (Tocsin) confederation, had been in existence in the Ukraine for several years: its apotheosis was to have been a pan-Russian anarchist congress in Kharkov in November 1920, but this was nipped in the bud by the Leninists who quickly realized the implicit danger.

Nabat's organizational structure and modus operandi are also worthy of note: a denominational organization, it set itself the exclusive task of spreading libertarian ideas among the workers. Militants and sympathizers were organized into groups or circles: on a recommendation from group members, sympathizers could be accepted as participants in the organization. Groups got together to form regional or urban federations which in turn came together to make up the Confederation. Every group appointed a secretary, whose task it was to oversee its activities and keep in touch with other groups and organizations. The regional and urban federations set up a secretariat, appointed at a general assembly. This secretariat undertook to supply the groups with the necessary literature, propagandists and agitators, and took charge of the overall activity of the federation. Delegates from the groups made up the federation's soviet, which took care of all organization business: its decisions were carried out by the federation's secretariat. The Confederation's secretariat was elected by a congress of all affiliated anarchist organizations and its term of office lasted until the following congress. Its duties were to bring out a press organ, publish writings, organize propagandist training schools, convene congresses and keep in touch with anarchist organizations from other countries. Organizational discipline arose out of the moral duty upon every member to implement the organization's principles and tasks. In particular, responsibility had to be assumed for any action taken. Any intervention on behalf of the group had first to be debated and endorsed by a general assembly of that group. Officers had regularly to report back on the implementation of the tasks entrusted to them.

The Nabat Conference, involving anarcho-syndicalists and libertarian communists, drew attention to the abuse of the name "anarchist" by all sorts of dubious types and recommended that these be exposed by word of mouth, or in leaflets or in print. On this point, it issued a reminder that no anarchist worthy of the name could belong to any Cheka, militia, or tribunal, or be a jailer or play any part in other institutions of a repressive nature. Likewise, no anarchist could be a director or officer of institutions of the bureaucratic-authoritarian type. These practical resolutions, lifted from a significant body of other resolutions reached at the first Nabat Conference on November 12–16, 1918, are indicative of the seriousness of the sort of organization set up and explains why it prospered for over three years. We do not have sufficient information about the other organizations existing at the time in Russia or elsewhere in the country, but there is no doubt that, had they broadly corresponded to Kropotkin's wishes and Nabat's principles, the course taken by events might have been very different.[8] That, at least, was the profound conviction of the members of the Group of Russian Anarchists Abroad, based first in Berlin, then in Paris, and counting Piotr Arshinov and Nestor Makhno among its membership. This group was to make strenuous efforts to analyze the precise reasons for the anarchist movement's defeat in Russia and to draw lessons theoretical and practical from that for the benefit of the movement internationally. There was a happy coincidence there with the concerns of the French comrades traumatized by the defections of the Sacred Union and the growing Bolshevization of the workers' movement.

## Endnotes to Chapter 14

1. *Les Temps nouveaux,* No. 19–21, March 1921, special issue devoted to Peter Kropotkin, pp. 14–17.
2. Reprinted in Alexander Skirda *Les Anarchistes dans la revolution russe Paris*, La Tête de Feuilles, 1973, pp. 129–161.
3. Cited by Jean Maitron, *Le mouvement anarchists en France,* (Paris: Maspéro, Tomen, 1975), pp. 41–55.
4. Max Hoschiller, *Le mirage du soviétisme,* foreword by A. Merrheim, (Paris: Payot, 1921), pp. 21–22.
5. Cited by J. Maitron, op. cit., p. 81.
6. For further details, see A. Skirda, *Les anarchistes dans la révolution russe,* op. cit.
7. Camillo Berneri, "Kropotkin," *Noir et Rouge* (January 1964), pp. 13–14 and *P. A. Kropotkin and His Teaching* (in Russian), (Chicago, 1931), p. 204.
8. *The First Conference of the Anarchist organizations of the Ukraine on November 12–16, 1918, in Kursk* (published in Russian in Argentina).

# XV. THE ORGANIZATIONAL PLATFORM OF THE *DYELO TRUDA* GROUP

Since Nestor Makhno is a rather familiar figure, we shall provide instead a few biographical details regarding Piotr Arshinov (real name, Marin). He was a locksmith by training: his working life had begun as a railwayman in the Eastern Ukraine. By the age of seventeen in 1904, he was a sympathizer with the thinking of the Bolshevik faction of the Russian Social Democratic Labor Party, but quickly realized that they were not equal to the revolutionary situation in which the country then found itself, and so he became a libertarian communist. Armed struggle by way of resistance to the relentless repression from the tsar's henchmen was then on the agenda: so, at the age of just nineteen, on December 23, 1906 he blew up a building housing members of a police punitive expedition. Several Cossack officers and gendarmes perished in the rubble. A little later, on March 7, 1907, he publicly gunned down with his revolver the boss of the Alexandrovsk railway workshop, who had been responsible not merely for the oppression of the workers for years past but also for having denounced 120 of them during the strikes and insurrections of 1905 and 1906 (around a hundred of these had either been sentenced to death or to penal servitude). Arrested and condemned to death, Arshinov managed to escape in incredible circumstances, thanks to assistance from his comrades, and resumed his activities. Recaptured and sentenced to death once again, he managed to pull off another escape. Nothing daunted, he continued his activism, smuggling weapons and anarchist literature across the border from Austria. Apprehended in 1910, he contrived, by a happy conjunction of circumstances, thanks to deft use of a range of aliases, to escape suspicion in connection with some of his terrorist acts and was merely sentenced to political servitude in the Butyrky prison in Moscow. [1] There, he made the acquaintance of Makhno and the pair established solid bonds of friendship and like-minded ideas. They even decided that some day they would publish a libertarian communist theoretical review, the lack of which was sorely felt at that point.

February 1917 opened the prison gates to the survivors from those heroic days. Arshinov stayed in Moscow and was intensely involved in the work of the local Anarchist Federation. While staying in the city in May–June 1918, Makhno promptly asked Arshinov to come back to the Ukraine, where they could carry on the struggle as a team. He arrived back at the beginning of 1919 and immediately assumed a position of importance in the Makhnovist movement's cultural commission, seeing, among other things, to publication of the insurgents' newspaper. He stuck with the movement until the end of 1920 and was then commissioned to write a history of it. He carried out this commission — not without some difficulty, for he had to redraft the opening of his book four times after the initial manuscript had been seized by the Cheka in the course of search operations — while living underground in Moscow. He made his way to Berlin by clandestine means, had his book published there and immersed himself in the activities of the Russian anarchists in exile there. So it came about that he joined them in publishing an initial review (in Russian) *The Anarchist Messenger*, of which seven issues appeared between July 1923 and May 1924. Having come across Nestor Makhno again, after the latter had had a devil of a time fleeing across Europe from the provocations of the Cheka, the pair of them decided to flee beyond the danger by settling in Paris. There they founded the review *Dyelo Truda* (The Cause of Labor) in 1925, which was to carry excellent studies and analyses. A number of their compatriots lent a hand in this: so did some Poles — Walecki, Ranko (Goidenburg) and Ida Mett (Gilman) who had a perfect command of Russian. Their collective deliberations led to their publication in June 1926 of the *Draft Organizational Platform for a General Union of Anarchists*: this was to be a watershed in the history of anarchism. For a long time it would be known as the "Arshinov Platform", for the introduction to it had borne his signature, he being the group's secretary. But this was a misnomer, for it was a collective undertaking, the expression of their fundamental ideas: in addition, several other texts bore the collective signature of the group, as we shall see from a chronological scheme of their appearance in *Dyelo Truda*.

Piotr Arshinov's *Our Organizational Problem* appeared in August 1925 and, in a way, signaled the beginning of the process. In it, he examined the political situation in Russia, noted the ravages caused by Bolshevism, but offered an apology for the anarchist movement which, as the revolution had proceeded, had been overtaken theoretically and organizationally, all too often confining itself to "positions that were, yes, correct, but too general, acting all at once in a diffuse way, in multiple tiny groups, often at odds on many points of tactics." Keeping a cool head, he steadily examined all of the prospects offered by the Bolsheviks, the Russian socialists and the liberals. The former could only tread the path of "prolonged exploitation and enslavement of the masses." The only point was to find out if they would share their power with the bourgeoisie. The second group listed, statists every one, seemed like the "parties of socialist promises, nothing more"; as for the liberals and out-and-out monarchists, they would go even to the lengths of joining forces with the Bolsheviks, just to recover a morsel of their lost privileges. Anarchists were still the only real exponents of social revolution, dragging the workers' movement forwards and not backwards. Simple:

> awareness of that should multiply our strength percent ten-fold and encourage us in a protracted, bitter struggle. The proletariat's path is

a winding, tiresome one: more than once, weariness and doubt will grip the revolutionary ranks: but, as difficult as that path may be, none among us should funk the struggle and abdicate by embracing submission to the present order of things. May the spirit never die! That popular saying should now, more than ever, linger in the mind of every worker and every revolutionary fighter.

Arshinov underlined the "differences, dissensions, absence of solidarity and collective responsibility" that had hitherto prevented the anarchist movement from playing a crucial part in social struggles. The only solution lay in "common organization of our forces on a basis of collective responsibility and collective methods of action." [2]

Chernyakov, a Russian anarchist very much to the fore during the revolution, published an article *The Immediate Task* wherein he advocated the creation of an anarchist party, which would of course have no authoritarianism about it and nothing in common with the statist socialist parties.[3] It would be modeled on the Bakuninist Jura Federation. Voline replied to this in the following edition: he rejected the use of the term "party" which was overloaded with suggestions of aspirations to state power. This was no ritualism, for he recalled that the mere act of appointing a chairman to preside over a meeting had, until very recently, been deemed anti-anarchist. That said, he invoked the Ukrainian Nabat (in which he had been involved for a time) as the organizational model. Voline returned to the theme again in an article in which he reviewed the activities of Nabat and in particular the declaration and resolutions passed at its Kursk conference. He had been commissioned to write a theoretical platform, something he had not been able to accomplish, but he gave a glimpse of it by suggesting that the common denominator compatible with each anarchist tendency — the communist, the syndicalist and the individualist — be retained, and the rest discarded. This was in rough the *Synthesis* that he was to propose along with Sébastien Faure in the years to come. The organizational issue struck him as being of secondary importance, although Nabat should again be the inspiration: "union, on a basis of federalism, with some of the elements of a natural, free and technical centralization, which is to say, (and let us not balk at the words) fusion between fraternal and free discipline and collective responsibility." and Nestor Makhno's piece in the same edition of the review focused on the very theme of discipline.[4]

At that time, it was still possible to correspond with comrades left behind in the USSR, even the deportees among them, and in every edition of the review, a rubric was set aside for them. Some of them called for a more developed sense of organization, for that seemed indispensable and prudishness with regard to it struck them, from where they sat, as incomprehensible or puerile.

Not until issue no. 10 in March 1926 was there any collective response forthcoming from the Group of Russian Anarchists Abroad to Voline's articles on synthesis. The latter was systematically rebutted as incoherent and ill-informed about anarchist history (a sideswipe at Voline's late conversion to libertarian thinking, a little before 1914). The article *The Organizational Issue and The Notion of Synthesis* (reprinted in full as an appendix to this book) states that it was not a question of turning the doctrine upside down, as its spinal column was still "libertarian communism," but of drawing one's inspiration from the "material amassed by anarchism over the years of its life process and its social struggle."

It was in issue No. 13–14 of June–July 1926 that the first part of *The Organizational Platform* saw the light of day. At the end of that issue, Ida Mett reported on the meeting of June 20, 1926, the date on which the *Platform* emerged and the first birthday of the review. Several French, Italian, Bulgarian and other comrades (Chinese among them) were invited along on that occasion.

Arshinov spoke first, as the secretary of the group, rehearsing its work and introducing the *Platform* as the child of the collective deliberations which had led it towards a homogeneous ideological and tactical outlook. The speaker added that the work accomplished by the group could be of significance for international anarchism, in that it was blazing a trail in the selection and marshaling of anarchist forces and that there was no other way of ensuring their expansion worldwide. Makhno followed Arshinov, drawing attention to the absence of anarchist influence among the peasants prior to the revolution, which he ascribed to the nonexistence of an organizational mentality or thought for coordination among anarchists, on the one hand, and to their prejudices about what they supposed to be the petit-bourgeois character of the peasantry, on the other. He reckoned that *Dyelo Truda* was doing vital work in working out answers to the revolutionary and political tasks of the anarchist movement. Next, Maria Korn spoke briefly to welcome the work undertaken by *Dyelo Truda* and wish it success. Sébastien Faure spoke when his turn came to declare that he too had long been calling for a solid anarchist organization. However, it was not his belief that it could embrace the exponents of contrary tendencies. In conclusion, he recalled that he had been in the French anarchist movement for the past 35 years and failed to see where this crisis was with which it was alleged to be afflicted. A Bulgarian comrade spoke up to align himself with the *Dyelo Truda* scheme, for an attempt at a synthesizing anarchist organization in Bulgaria had come to nothing. The Chinese comrade declared that there was such a disparity between the social, economic and political settings in Europe and China that the same approach simply would not be appropriate. In Europe, technological and cultural progress was such that anarchists should be active rather than talkative. As time was running out, the meeting stopped at that point, although there were several other listed speakers.

Publication of the *Platform* continued in the subsequent issues of the review. What did it amount to? The arguments set out in those early articles in *Dyelo Truda* were reiterated and expanded upon. The chief reason for the anarchist movement's lack of success was the "absence of firm principles and consistent organizational practice." Anarchism had to "marshal its forces into an active general organization, as required by reality and the strategy of the social struggle of the classes," which was in tune with the Bakuninist tradition and the wishes of Kropotkin. This organization would lay down a general tactical and political line for anarchism, leading on to an "organized collective practice." To these ends, a homogeneous program was needed. The *Platform* represented only a broad outline of this, an outline needing exploration and expansion by the whole body of the General Union of Anarchists. The *Platform* falls into three parts: a general part, affirming and reaffirming the basic principles of libertarian communism — class struggle, the necessity of a violent social revolution, repudiation of democracy, negation of the state and authority, the role of anarchists and the masses in the social struggle and social revolution, the transitional period and trade unionism; the constructive part dealt with matters of industrial and agrarian production, consumption, then defense of the revolution; finally, the concluding part was given over to the principles of anarchist organization, dependent upon ideological unity, tactical unity or collective methods of action, collective responsibility, federalism and the powers of the Executive Committee of the General Union of Anarchists. (See the complete text in the appendices.)

In issue No. 16 of the review in September 1926, Ida Mett returned to the matter of the *ideological direction of the masses*. As she explained, this was to be understood as the duty upon anarchists to make their conception of revolution the predominant one among the workers, and not to aspire to take over state power as the political parties did. The following month, she reported on a discussion session given over to the *Platform* : that meeting was a follow-up to the one cut short on June 20th. Arshinov was the first to speak, repeating his finding that there was no specific ideology or detailed organizational principles. He asked whether this was to be laid at the door of objective circumstances or blamed upon the anarchists themselves? He inclined to the latter answer. He cited the example of Kronstadt: had there been an anarchist organization in existence at the time of the revolt of March 1923, the revolt might have been spread to all parts of the country and things might have taken a different turn. Similarly, right now, for want of an organization, anarchists were powerless to intervene on behalf of those Russian workers hostile to the Bolsheviks. In spite of the efforts made by isolated individuals and groups, the anarchist movement was threatened by disintegration. A number of comrades, with none of the revolutionary experience of the Russians and Italians, consoled themselves with saying that the Revolution would set their movement to rights. Pie in the sky! Quite the contrary: the revolution would annihilate those who would not have organized themselves in time, anarchism was the ideology of the working class and its best tactic, so it had to present a united front, theoretically as well as organizationally. The Dutchman Cornelissen retorted that if the movement had not been able to come up with a solution to the organization problem in thirty years, it was too late to do so now, for every day brought pressing situations.

Voline then piped up to express the view that, on the contrary, it was not too late to resolve this problem, but that there had to be a prior clarification of doctrine. He invoked the Nabat experience. In contrast, he detected in the organizational principles of the *Platform* a Bolshevik deviation: namely, party, program, the policy line and direction of the masses.

Several other libertarians present spoke up on a variety of points, without really dealing with the agenda, as Arshinov noted in his final address. He pointed out that in spite of their argumentative aspect, the criticisms that had been voiced had not been thought through and that nothing had been offered as an alternative to the criticized proposals. As far as he was concerned, it was hard to answer to comrade Yudov's reasoning: "The Group of Russian Anarchists Abroad expounds the notion of a revolutionary class struggle and strategy, which means that it has designs on power." He could only refer the critic to more comprehensive explorations of semantics. If it had not been possible to devise a solution to the organizational problem over a thirty-year period, as comrade Cornelissen had said, it was not too late to do it now and it was unrealistic to rely upon the trade unions to handle the economic aspect of the revolution, unless these were anarchist in outlook. He replied to the charge of Bolshevik deviation leveled by Voline, by saying that in terms of theory, anarchism had nothing in common with Bolshevism and the state socialists, which fore-armed it against that danger; furthermore, it had no designs upon the conquest of state power. The notion of ideological direction of the masses was not at all a contradiction of anarchism: on the contrary, that was where its mission lay, otherwise it had no raison d'être. Nor was it true that the Russian revolution and Bolshevism had demonstrated the harmfulness of ideological direction of the masses: instead it was the statist approach that had been so exposed. The novelty in the approach of the *Dyelo Truda* group lay in its aspiration to "organize the ideological influence of anarchism over the masses, not as a weak and intermittent factor, but as a constant in the workers' social revolutionary struggle." On which note the meeting came to an end.

Issue No. 18, in November 1926 carried a *Platform Supplement*, containing replies to a first series of questions (put by the old Kropotkinist, Maria Korn, alias Isidine, real name Maria Goldsmidt). There were six of these questions and they related to: majority and minority in the anarchist movement; the structure and essential features of the regime of free soviets; the ideological supervision of events and of the masses; the defense of the revolution; freedom of the press and freedom of speech; the anarchist principle: to each according to his needs. (See the complete text of this *Supplement* in the appendices.)

In *Dyelo Truda*'s Issue No. 20–21, of January–February 1927, there were several articles marking the tenth anniversary of the Russian revolution of February 1917. Linsky's article registered the current unfeasibility of establishing independent workers' organizations in the USSR, due to the omnipotence of the GPU. He drew comparisons between the situation of the Russian workers and that of German workers in 1916–1917, and found only the factory committees capable of any response: anarchists had to radicalize these as much as possible against the Bolshevik regime. Maxim Ranko, in another article, stressed the ideological differentiation necessary in anarchist ranks if they were to create an anarchist International capable of having an impact upon the course of events. Arshinov replied to questions from a certain F (Fleshin?) on the anarchists' role in the wake of the social revolution, on the threat of a new war and on individual terrorism. His most intriguing answer, it seems to us, concerned the definition of soviets, which were envisaged as being, unlike the Bolsheviks' soviets of worker and soldier deputies, worker and peasant producer and consumer organizations. As for the Terror, that could not be the work of an individual, but rather the maturely considered policy of an organization in the light of the precise situation in the country where it took place.

Under the heading *The Struggle for the Spirit of Organization* the review carried a report on a further meeting held along with Polish and Bulgarian comrades. Arshinov had spoken on behalf of the Group of Russian Anarchists Abroad: he indicated that the discussion about the organizational issue had been in progress in Paris for nearly a year and that two schools of thought were already evident regarding the group's draft *Platform*: one for organization, the other disorganization. Which fitted in with three attitudes adopted with regard to the *Platform*: one positive, one with reservations and the last one individualist and "devil may care." The first of these attitudes was, for the moment, the most widespread; the second showed itself in the questions put by Maria Korn in the *Supplement*; as for the third, it took the line that anarchism should be able to be the *vade mecum* of every person and thus that there was no need for "organizations," much less any *Platform*. Voline was the most typical representative of this anti-organizationist school of thought: also, he was at that very moment working on a reply to the *Platform*, with an eye to exposing its anti-anarchistic contents. Although there was little prospect of that being anything to get worked up about, we look forward to seeing what it would be like. In reply, Arshinov once again rehearsed all of the strong points of the *Platform*. Makhno spoke after him: he endorsed what Arshinov had said and would have liked to answer the criticisms from "our opponents through misunderstanding," but these had failed to take up the invitation to take part in the meeting, and he found it difficult to criticize them in their absence. In any event, their irresponsibility, organizational and political alike, could only lead them into a swamp where they would not be able to do any more than "carp." It had long been plain that the movement needed to marshal its forces, failing which it could never have any influence upon revolutionary developments, even when these might boast an unmistakably libertarian character. It was because the "opponents through misunderstanding" had never bothered about that and had absolutely no intention of doing so, that they had begun to seek out anything in the *Platform* that might be construed as anti-anarchist. The only people they could recruit would be elements who had blundered into the anarchist movement by accident, not having lived through the chastening experience of the Russian revolution. Their political and organizational irrelevancy was plainly exposed — the Ukrainian exile went on — when they attempted to rebut the lessons of our revolutionary experience, bought at the price of "our blood, our heart and our nerves."

An old militant from the Bulgarian movement took over then and explained that it was precisely this "devil may care" attitude on the part of certain anarchists that had shown itself to be the chief obstacle to the expansion of libertarian ideas in Bulgaria. Another Bulgarian stipulated that above all else the problem of organizing the anarchist movement should not be mixed up with the problem of organizing the society of the future. These were two extremely important matters that had to be dealt with separately. One Grisha Br. broached the issue of majority and minority: he failed to understand why it was the minority that had to defer to the majority and not vice versa. Arshinov's answer to that was that this was not a matter of principle, but rather a matter of practical common sense: otherwise, no policy line would be possible. The meeting closed with unanimous support for continuation at other meetings of the debate on the issues raised by the *Organizational Platform*.

In the April–May 1927 edition, No. 23–24, Arshinov reviewed the review's two years of existence and its organizational approach. He stressed the backing it had received from every quarter and, in order to differentiate himself from all the disorganizing elements, he employed, for the first time, the expression "Libertarian Communist Party," which alone could afford anarchism the opportunity to take up its rightful place in the ranks of struggling Labor. In the very same edition, following its appearance in a French translation and the reactions, favorable or unfavorable, that it had elicited, Arshinov devoted a lengthy article to the *Organizational Platform*. For some, it was an "historic step forward in the development of the anarchist movement: for others, it is a curse." There was nothing startling in that, for the "authors of the *Platform* started from the fact of the multiplicity of contradictory tendencies in anarchism, not in order to set themselves the task of blending them all into one, which is absolutely impossible, but in order to make an ideological and political *selection* of anarchism's homogeneous forces and at the same time *differentiate themselves* from anarchism's chaotic, petit-bourgeois (liberal) and rootless elements." That selection, as well as the differentiation, could only be effected through the union of all theoretically homogeneous anarchists into one "revolutionary political collective, in a General Union of Anarchists, or, to be more specific, in a *Libertarian Communist Party* which, as we see it, amounts to the same thing." Next, Arshinov turned to Jean Grave's objections: Grave found unity of action acceptable but was hostile to centralization of it. In Arshinov's view, that sort of attitude was the result of a misunderstanding or differing interpretation of words. The entire chapter of the *Platform* dealing with federalism was quite explicit and the sort of centralization it had in mind could readily be understood. Apropos of the minority, Grave depicted its concessions to the majority as subordination and suggested agreement in its place. The latter, though, could only come about through concessions from the minority or indeed, if they were considered too important, a parting of the ways was the only solution. Similarly, Grave's misgivings about the *Executive Committee* of the Union/Party simply reflected his ignorance of anarchist organizational endeavor. If he acknowledged the need for serious collective effort, bound up with the existence of a general anarchist organization, he had to accept the necessity for organs like the *Union's Executive Committee*, as well as for collective organizational responsibility, discipline, etc.

Arshinov rebutted a further objection regarding the use of expressions like "class struggle" or "working classes" — an objection that sprang from the belief that there would be no classes in the anarchist society of the future, and thus no class struggle. This was quite simply a refusal to acknowledge the *present* reality, which was independent of the wishes of anarchists themselves. Although aspiring to a classless society, all our hopes are pinned upon the aspirations of workers who have the most interest in *social truth*. That is why their class struggle is one of anarchism's underlying principles. Denial of that boiled down to "rejoining the swamp of bourgeois liberalism, which has often happened to anarchists who came to us from the ranks of the bourgeoisie but failed to grasp the revolutionary spirit of Labor."

Certain comrades from Europe and North America have seen fit to draw attention to the apparent contradiction between our negation of the transitional period and the assertion that achievement of the libertarian communist society would not follow immediately upon the social revolution, but would be a protracted process of hard work and social creativity. That contradiction is merely apparent and, yet again, arises from a faulty understanding of the notion of the transitional period. Obviously, libertarian communism could not be introduced immediately and would be the product of steady and protracted construction. It is essential that one have in mind a clear picture of the ways and means involved in that construction, working from the basis of a realism that signifies not anarchism's weakness but rather its strength and has nothing to do with the notion of a transitional period, which implies a time lapse between the revolution and the advent of the free society embodied in a political and economic system. He referred to the example of the Bolsheviks, whose dictatorship had no time limit and might last anything up to a century. We anarchists are against that notion of the transitional period, for it presupposes the survival of state power and exploitation of the workers. We stand for social revolution and for the *process of direct social reconstruction*. Arshinov concluded his article by putting this question: can the text of the *Platform* be amended in any way in order to take account of the comments and criticisms made by these ones or those ones? He answered in the negative, for there would assuredly be bickering at every step over the points needing amendment. Only an anarchist congress establishing a General Union of Anarchists could do that.

In issue No. 25 of *Dyelo Truda* in June 1927, Chernyakov returned to the question of the Libertarian Communist Party, the establishment of which he regarded as the only viable alternative to the empty chatter and individual efforts of groups and the squandering of time, energy and manpower. In that fashion, the anarchist revolution would drive out Bolshevism. Nestor Makhno himself brought out a substantial article on *The Defense of the Revolution*, largely sharing his personal experiences.

It was at this point that we reckon the expository stage of the *Dyelo Truda Organizational Platform* came to its conclusion. Now that a French translation of the document had been made available, as well as a number of articles in *Le Libertaire* from Arshinov, Makhno, Walecki and Ranko, its arguments were quite well known and the real debate could begin.

## Endnotes to Chapter 15

1. In 1927 Arshinov was to issue a pamphlet (in Russian) *Two Escapes* relating these activities: this was to lead one of the former chiefs of the Okhrana, then also an émigré in Paris, to describe him as one of the most dangerous terrorists on his wanted list.
2. *Dyelo Truda,* No. 3, (August 1925).
3. Ibid., No. 4, (September 1925).
4. Ibid., No. 5, (October 1925) and No. 7–8 (December 1925–January 1926). See Makhno's article in the anthology *The Struggle Against the State and Other Writings*, (J.-P. Ducret, 1984), pp. 75–76 (English edition published by AK Press and translated by Paul Sharkey).

# XVI. THE CONTROVERSY ABOUT THE *PLATFORM*

The earliest polemic brought a confrontation with Voline, who had made the translation into French. In *Le Libertaire* Ranko took him to task for mistranslation or misrepresentation of certain terms and expressions. The suggestion was even made that an "expert" comrade be appointed before whom both sides could verify their grounds for recrimination. But, on the day arranged, Voline failed to show up for the rendezvous.[1] The fact is that relations between Voline and Makhno, and later, Arshinov, had recently begun to worsen. Up to then, Voline had been a full member of the Group of Russian Anarchists Abroad and a regular collaborator in *Dyelo Truda*. What could have been the cause of the friction between them? Assuredly, certain personal and ethical derelictions towards Makhno on the part of Voline[2]; probably also, the plain differences of opinion over the *Synthesis* that Voline had been trying to peddle for some years past, continually harking back to his Nabat experiences. Invocation of that was rendered less credible when *Dyelo Truda* carried a letter from one of the Nabat founders who had stayed behind in Russia, describing the Confederation's modus operandi in terms contradicting Voline's accounts: (see the appendices for the full text). Their social origins were also at odds: Voline was a bourgeois intellectual, painstakingly reared by governesses who taught him the foreign languages in which he was fluent (German and French), while both Arshinov and Makhno were of very humble extractions, did not have the same glibness of expression and thus did not enjoy the same audience among their comrades. There was also Voline's dalliance in Masonic lodges, which fitted in very well with his idea of *Synthesis* but was criticized by those who saw class collaboration in it. There was also, paradoxically enough, a difference in anarchist culture and not quite in the way one might have expected: Arshinov and Makhno had been anarchists for more than twenty years and were conversant with all the classics — which they had studied, especially while convicts — whereas Voline was Social Revolutionary in his provenance and had swung around to libertarian ideas only a short while before 1914, under Kropotkin's influence. In short, there were all sorts of likely reasons for feuding between the erstwhile comrades in arms of the years 1919–1920. As is often the case, life as exiles and its attendant difficulties added enormously to their differences of opinion.

The Group of Russian Anarchists Abroad thus published a statement in *Dyelo Truda* in December 1926, to expose the mischief-making of a certain Maisky, whom Voline had introduced into the group in 1924, and who had since been expelled for wrecking and unethical activity. Not that that prevented Voline from providing a reference for this character, who had allegedly abused the trust of his comrades. The Group issued a public reprimand to Voline — which did not settle accounts between the two sides: far from it.

The *Reply of Some Russian Anarchists to the Platform*, published in April 1927, was endorsed by seven names: Sobol, Fleshin, Schwartz, Mollie Steimer, Voline, Lia, Roman, and Ervantian. But these multiple signatures fooled no one: Voline was its author, as was obvious simply from its persistent references to Nabat and his characteristic style. It was a closely written 39-page pamphlet, using lengthy extracts from the *Platform* and offering a painstaking criticism of all of its essential points. There were fundamental differences of view, as over the weakness of the anarchist movement, which could not be explained away, the *Reply* argued, in terms of the absence of an organization or collective practice, but rather was due to a number of other factors:

a) the haziness of several ideas fundamental to our outlook:

b) the contemporary world's difficulty in assimilating libertarian ideas:

c) the mind set of the contemporary masses who let themselves be taken in by demogogues of every hue:

d) the widespread repression of the movement as soon as it begins to show signs of real progress:

e) anarchists' irrational reluctance to resort to demagoguery:

f) anarchists' repudiation of all artificially constructed organization, as well as all artificial discipline.

One crucial source of discord was the refusal of the *Platform*'s authors to take the *Synthesis* under their notice. Another source of friction: the notion of an Anarchist Party, which was promptly taken as synonymous with the idea of the classical authoritarian political party. The *Reply* next tackled the idea of anarchism being a class concept, for it was, they maintained, also human and individual. Direction of the masses and of events was suspected of disguising an ambition to lord it over the masses, instead of "serving them, being their collaborators and their aides."

With regard to the transitional period, the *Platform*, argued the *Reply*, rejected it "platonically, phraseologically" while it "acknowledges it more than anyone on our ranks": it was alleged to be, in reality, an "attempt to explain away that idea and graft it onto anarchism." The constructive portion of the *Platform* was subjected to the same virulent criticism, with everything depicted in a negative light. On the matter of the defense of the revolution, arming of the workers and isolated local detachments, rather than an insurgent army with an overall command structure, was the recommendation. The lesson of the Russian revolution here was not heeded: the armed workers had quickly turned into Red Guards, even against their will, and isolated armed detachments were easily dispatched by regular armies. But the *Reply* had a different intention in mind: it aimed to demonstrate, at all costs, the anti-anarchist character of the *Platform* and no exaggeration was spared, not even the allegation that the insurgent army had almost naturally turned into the Red Army! Complete with its political police, or Cheka, to which, it was alleged, the *Platform* was looking forward. The purpose of the *Reply* was to push the idea that the *Platform* sought "the creation of a directing political center, the organization of an army and a police at the disposal of that center, meaning, essentially, the introduction of a transitional political authority in the state mold."

The organizational portion of the *Platform* was subjected to the same pseudo-orthodox wrath: the *Reply* divined in it an aspiration to a centralized Anarchist Party that would leave the Bolsheviks in the shade. In conclusion, the *Reply* did not beat about the bush: "Yes, the ideological essence is the same among the Bolsheviks and platformists alike." This Platform was only a "disguised revisionist lurch towards Bolshevism and acceptance of a transitional period"; it was all "unacceptable: its underlying principles, its essence and its very spirit."

That over-the-top attack was too systematic and partisan to be taken seriously: it gave off the stench of a settling of personal scores. How could the authors of the *Platform*, especially Arshinov and Makhno, be painted as crypto-Bolsheviks? When they had fought the Bolsheviks with guns in hands, and seen their finest colleagues murdered by Bolsheviks? There was a moat of blood separating them. On the other hand, Voline had several times kept up ambiguous contacts with the Bolshevik authorities. Not that that was the most important point. The striking thing about the *Reply* was the absence (leaving aside the idealized Nabat) of any reference to the ideas and practices of the anarchist movement. All the same, the authors of the *Platform* themselves stated that they had invented nothing new, and merely taken on board the movement's accumulated ideas and real-life experiences. We ourselves have seen that Bakunin had already dreamt of a specific organization with "unity of thought and action," which is to say, a collective method of action, and "ongoing fraternal supervision of each by all," equivalent to the *Platform*'s notion of "collective responsibility." For anyone with sufficient knowledge of the movement's history, the kinship between the *Platform* and Bakunin's Brotherhoods ought to have been obvious and beyond discussion. Such discussion was paying undue heed to the partisan criticism and denigratory intent characterizing the *Reply*.

The Group of Russian Anarchists Abroad did not go into these historical or personal considerations: a few months later it published an *Answer to Anarchism's Confusionists*. In this, the acerbic criticisms of the *Reply* from Voline and company were refuted item by item, the inconsistency between them exposed for all to see. (See the complete text in the appendices.) The charge of

"Bolshevizing anarchism" was slated as a base calumny. Now, that argument was to be common currency among all future detractors of the *Platform*. However, some common-sensical views were expressed at the time, like this by L.G. which appeared in *Le Libertaire*:

> The *Platform*, as offered for discussion, is not presented as some unassailable credo: I and many another find much in it that is very debatable. The *Reply* which I have just been reading contains just as many points of error: let me quote just one, so as not to clutter up the paper: the error of seeing dogs, cats, wolves and lambs lying down in the same organization, the better to achieve the end, says the *Reply*. I find that laughable, for, in that grouping, there would be nothing but bitter squabbles, backbiting and hatreds. I sense in this *Reply* a lot of prickliness with no feeling for tolerance. I wish they would leave out of all this a little of all this long-winded peroration about what tomorrow will bring and be more down to earth in their propaganda right now.[3]

Two years later, Voline, Fleshin, Steimer, Sobol and Schwartz were to publish a tirade against *Dyelo Truda* which was accused this time of waging a campaign against the highbrow anarchists. The worker-peasant anarchism of the review was described as "real anarcho-hooliganism" (!?) on a par with anti-Semitism![4] The jarring little detail is that, all this carping aside, they were unable to come up with a single text finally setting out their own views. Not that there was anything surprising in that, for such behavior was, all in all, rather commonplace: incapable of coming up themselves with anything positive or constructive, certain individuals, anarchists or otherwise, professing to belong to the most radical tendency, on paper at least, were quick to light, microscope at the ready, upon any achievement, to pronounce it good or bad. These unwelcome "busy bees," on the other hand, paid no heed to the fetid stench in which they lived and disported themselves. Reality and the gusts of history swept them aside never to return, but it is important to appreciate that this phenomenon exists and crops up again from time to time.

Meanwhile, the discussion-meetings organized by *Dyelo Truda* on the theme of the *Platform* continued at regular intervals. Militants from all parts of the globe attended the one on February 12, 1927: Arshinov, Makhno, and four other members representing the Russian Group; Pierre Odéon from the anarchist youth of France; Ranko was delegated by the Polish group; there were several Spaniards, including Orobon Fernandez, Carbé and Gibanel; and a number of exiles attended in an individual capacity, like Ugo Fedeli, Pavel (a Bulgarian), Chen (a Chinese), Dauphin-Meunier (a Frenchman), etc. The meeting was held in the back room of a Paris cafe: several languages were used ... Russian, German and, of course, French.

Arshinov gave the first address, as usual, rehearsing the theses of his group and adding that implementation of them was of equal concern to France and the international movement. Being, for the most part, refugees, it was hard for them to act on French soil, as they lacked a social base and it was desirable that some French-language international organ be set up which would tackle the essential questions of the movement. A Spaniard spoke next and intimated that the Spanish movement had similar preoccupations. Odéon announced his backing for the *Platform* and asked if those present had a mandate to arrive at decisions. Ranko came right out with a proposal that a provisional committee be set up with an eye to the creation of the Anarchist International. Several of those present expressed reservations; however, an acting commission, made up of Makhno, Ranko, and Chen, was established. That commission issued a circular to all interested parties on February 22, 1927, reviewing the steps taken on the basis of the Russian Group's *Platform*. There followed an invitation to an International Conference in a cinema in Bourg-La-Reine on March 20th.

Before a sizable turnout, Makhno spelled out all the key points contained in the *Platform* by way of a program. His listeners reacted in a variety of ways. Luigi Fabbri suggested a minor amendment and was backed by the French and Spaniards. Agreement was reached upon the principle of the anticipated international organization, on the basis of the following points, i.e. recognition that:

1) the struggle of all the downtrodden and oppressed against the authority of state and Capital, as the most important factor in the anarchist system;

2) the labor and trade union struggle as one of the most important of anarchists' methods or revolutionary action;

3) the necessity in every country of a possible General Union of Anarchists sharing the same ultimate aim and the same practical tactics, resting upon collective responsibility;

4) necessity of anarchists having a positive action and construction program for the social revolution. [5]

Just as they were settling down to discuss this motion from the Italians, the room was invaded by French police who arrested everybody. Some informer or opponent of the *Platform* had tipped off the police that some conspiracy was afoot. The scheme was not completely aborted, though, for the acting secretariat, made up of Makhno, Ranko and Chen issued a letter on April 1, 1927 which took it as read that an International Libertarian Communist Federation was now in existence, and espousing unadulterated the points put forward by the Russian Group, prior to their amendment by the Italians. This was rushing things a little and was especially clumsy in its handling of the Italians, who wasted no time in making it known that they could not associate themselves with the project "for the time being." Others who had taken part in the conference expressed similar views. Thus, undue haste (or, if one prefers, zeal) on the part of Makhno and Ranko stymied the plan.

At the autumn 1927 congress in Paris of the (French) Anarchist Union, supporters of the *Platform* defeated the advocates of the *Synthesis* and other recalcitrants. The supporters of the *Synthesis*, led by Sébastien Faure, broke away to set up the Federal Association of Anarchists (*Association Fédérale des Anarchistes*). Faure, that old tribune, was not against organization as such, nor was he one to rest on his laurels, but he wanted a "solid, powerful organization, capable of binding together, at a time determined by the gravity of the circumstances, all those forces of revolt represented by numerous, energetic groupings" and a "proletariat swept into decisive action by a succession of disturbances, agitations, strikes, riots, insurrections."[6] Thus, Faure had nothing in common with the dilettantism of a Voline and, for some time, he had been paying a heavy personal price. He rejected the arguments of the *Platform* because he found them unduly sectarian and preferred a certainly sentimental "happy family" single-mindedness, or, as he himself jokingly termed it a "general festival of hugging and kissing": he was quite a likable fellow and full of goodwill. The old anarchist sensed that anarchists would soon be in sore need of goodwill and mutual assistance, for the prospects of social and military confrontation were plentiful. [7]

In Italy, Mussolini's fascism had been ensconced in power for some years already and reaction ruled the roost. Errico Malatesta was under house arrest, his correspondence censored. Even so, he managed to get wind of the *Platform* and he drew up a critical review that appeared in *Le Réveil anarchiste* in Geneva, first of all, before being issued in pamphlet form in Paris. Although he too was an advocate of organization, he would countenance neither the notion of collective responsibility nor the existence of an Executive Committee. By his reckoning, the authors of the *Platform* were "obsessed with the Bolsheviks' success in their homeland: they sought, after the manner of Bolsheviks, to bring anarchists together into a sort of disciplined army which, under the ideological and practical direction of a few leaders, might march in step against existing regimes and which, having secured material victory, might direct the constitution of the new society." In *Dyelo Truda*, Arshinov published *The Old and the New in Anarchism*, wherein he replied to Malatesta's objections and reiterated with infinite patience the main features of the approach of the Russian Group (see the complete text in the appendices). Makhno also sent a long letter to Bakunin's old comrade, putting their disagreements down to a misunderstanding. It was nearly a year before Malatesta learned of it (on account of the censor), and he promptly replied to it. Maybe translation had obscured the meaning of the words, but he was still hostile to collective responsibility, suggesting moral responsibility instead, and against the existence of an Executive Committee which he likened to a "government good and proper" with its attendant police and bureaucratic powers! Again, Makhno answered him:

> It is my belief that a properly social movement, such as I hold the anarchist movement to be, cannot have any positive policy until such time as it has discovered more or less stable forms of organization which will furnish it with the wherewithal it needs for struggle against the various authoritarian social systems. It is the absence of such wherewithal that has ensured that anarchist action, during time of revolution especially, has degenerated into a sort of localized individualism,

all because the anarchists, in declaring themselves foes of "all and every constitution" have seen the masses drift away from them, for they inspire no hope in the prospect of any practical achievement.

In order to fight and to win, we need a tactic the character of which ought to be set out in a program of practical action.... In the realm of practical achievement, autonomous anarchist groups should be capable, in the face of each new situation as it presents itself, to settle upon the problems to be resolved and the answers to devise to these, without hesitation and without amendment to anarchist aims and anarchist mentality.[8]

Malatesta later shifted a little on "collective responsibility," which struck him as "better suited to some barracks," for he understood it to imply "the blind submission of all to the wishes of a few." He conceded that it was, perhaps, a matter of semantics, but that if it was a question of "the agreement and fellowship that should obtain between the members of an association ... we would be close to agreeing."[9] It was assuredly his isolation and a semantic problem that must have led the movement's grand old man into this misapprehension.

Pierre Besnard, the leader of the CGT-SR and theoretician of anarcho-syndicalism, had no such misgivings about collective responsibility: in the entry he wrote for the *Encyclopédie anarchiste* under responsibility, he made it the fundamental organizational principle of libertarian communism. It did nothing to banish the individual responsibility of all the group's members: there was no contradiction between these. They were complementary and overlapped:

Individual responsibility is the *original* form of responsibility: it springs from consciousness. Collective responsibility is its *social and final* form. It broadens the responsibility of the individual to the collectivity: in extending it thus, according to the principle of natural solidarity which is, at the same time, a physical law as applicable to the component parts of society as to the component parts of any body, animate or inanimate, it makes each individual answerable to the collectivity as a whole, for his actions. And through reciprocity, *through supervision,* it makes the collectivity accountable before all its individual members. Like federalism itself, of which it is indeed one of the prime elements, collective responsibility operates in two directions: ascending and descending. It makes it an *obligation* upon the individual to answer for his actions to the group, and the latter answerable to the individual for its own.

Thus, it can be said that the two forms of responsibility are mutual determinants. *Collective responsibility is the consecration and refinement of individual responsibility.*[10]

Besnard saw it as something positive, something that made the organization both methodical and supple, with optimum powers of *contraction* and *relaxation*.

Marie Isidine also published a critique of her own of collective responsibility (which she rejected in favor of moral responsibility) in *Organization and*

*Party*. She was primarily taking issue with the principle of the majority decisions which the minority would have to apply without jibbing. Arshinov provided her with a reply a little later. (See the two texts in the appendices.)

Makhno rounded upon the criticisms that sought to play up the allegedly anti-anarchistic character of the *Platform*. In particular, he rounded on Malatesta's criticisms regarding tactical unity, and he made a stand against the use of just any tactic by just about any member of an anarchist organization, a stance that he ascribed to the old Italian agitator. Such a dispersion of effort could not produce anything and, in time of revolution, it was scarcely the way to link up with the masses, he noted.[11]

The very same edition of the review carried a piece by Khudoley, a Russian anarchist who had stayed behind in the USSR and was an enthusiastic supporter of *Dyelo Truda*. Khudoley emphasized the innovation in the *Platform*'s having afforded priority to the political over the economic, that is, to the ideological grouping united around the trade union. Thus, the Libertarian Communist Party was, as he saw it, "the conscious minority steering the revolutionary movement towards libertarian objectives through its example." The workers' and peasants' organizations, the unions and cooperatives were the "active minority carrying out the revolution." He invoked Bakunin as the forerunner of this idea. The name "General Union of Anarchists" created the belief that all anarchists should feel obliged to belong to it, when this was not the case. Khudoley's own preference was for the term "party," it being more precise, for it embraced only *some* of the anarchists, on the basis of theoretical affinities and a common desire to affiliate to it: this did not at all imply a breach with the other anarchists in the movement. In short, those who supported a homogeneous theory were free to organize themselves as a party. In the last analysis, Khudoley was startled to find so much brouhaha about a scheme that every individual was free to accept or reject.

Also in the same edition, Arshinov published a summary overview of the debate provoked by the *Platform*. He listed the four types of reaction to it: hostility, incomprehension, deliberate or involuntary ignorance, and sympathy or even enthusiasm. In the light of the intended aims, he found the results to be meager, but the low ebb of anarchism in many countries could be one explanation of that. That being the case, the *Platform* had been the only attempt made in ten years to make some practical and positive progress towards developing the movement. However he did quote a very critical letter from a comrade inside Russia:

> In my opinion, you have overstepped the mark by pushing for the organization of a party. As I see it, your thinking goes like this: the Bolsheviks have won, thanks to their organization, which means that we too should have one. Of course, our army will be, not red, but black, our CPU will not be statist but something else, our party will be, not centralist, but federalist. With a number of comrades here, I am not at all in agreement with you. Your efforts to lift the movement out of the swamp of cant, by making use of the experience of recent years are

very praiseworthy.... But by my reckoning, you have succumbed to the Bolshevik temptation.

That correspondent nonetheless had to stress the value of the review, its serious approach and its levelheadedness in tackling issues; for him and for his friends, this was a sign that anarchism was alive and well.

Arshinov mentioned other disagreements over several points in the *Platform*: production, defense of the revolution or indeed the use of certain terminology. However, he noted that thus far the hostile reactions had missed this essential point: "appreciation of our approach to the question of organization and the method espoused to resolve it." Above all, the *Platform* was an attempt to find a solution to a specific practical problem. Anybody not afraid to look the current state of the movement in the face would grasp that without any difficulty. In the Russian anarchist movement, for instance, there were two tendencies in existence at the time: the confusionist tendency in the United States with the review *Rassvyet* (Dawn) which had ambiguous dealings with reactionary Russian émigrés; and there was another — mystical — tendency in Moscow. A whole range of other tendencies or nuances still coexisted within the movement and had nothing to do with revolutionary working-class anarchism. This was nothing new and had always been the case and it was the reason why the movement had never been able to act in a united and concerted fashion. Its actions had been contradictory and even antagonistic, nullifying all practical endeavor. The milieu was so awash in such contradictions, there was no point trying to unify or "synthesize." The only way to leave this chaos behind and restore the movement's health was to select a core of active militants on the basis of a homogeneous and definite theoretical and practical program, and thereby effect an ideological and organizational differentiation. That was what the *Platform* was about. An organization united on its theory and tactics (a party) would deliver our movement from all glaring contradictions, (internal and external alike), which put the workers off, demonstrate the potency of libertarian communism's ideas and tactics and, without question, rally around itself the revolutionary element of the peasantry and working class. Finally, those who did not see eye to eye with this approach and thinking could come up with their own, so that the alternative might be made known.

In the second part of his text, Arshinov replied to the objections voiced on several points. With regard to production, some had found the proposed unity to be at odds with decentralization, and that the peasant and worker soviets, and the factory and workshop committees better suited to a regime of free soviets than to the idea of the anarchist commune. Unity of production meant that that whole process was communistic, the property of all and not of individuals or private groups, for that would mean the restoration of capitalism. Such unity did not at all involve centralism: quite the opposite in fact. If we had been against decentralization, that was simply lest it mean the welfare of specific groups competing with that of others. As for the soviets' role, that was executive and technical, whether in relation to production or to consumption. They had nothing in common with political soviets, whose members played no part in production. In the *Platform*, there was only an outline of the first stage of the journey along the road to achieving the anarchist commune: if there were mistakes or inexactitudes there, the collective intelligence of the movement would spot them and set them right. The authors were the first to look for them, for they were concerned not to conceal problems but to resolve them, and in the most authentic anarchist spirit at that. Moreover, they would be resolved by means of the collective thinking and practice of the movement.

As for organization, the most criticized thing was the "party" format, because it appeared to fly in the face of anarchist principles. That allegation was ill-founded, for it was wrong and absurd to think that a party must, of necessity, be an authoritarian organization with designs on power. It was merely a getting together of persons sharing the same specific beliefs and pursuing the same specific ends, which need not necessarily mean the conquest of power. The much anathematized Executive Committee was, as its title implied, merely executive, that is, it carried out the technical tasks entrusted to it by congress; also, it had always existed among anarchist organizations — the anarchist trade union international, for example, had an equivalent in the shape of its secretariat. In conclusion, Arshinov noted that most objections rested either upon a misapprehesion or some deliberate misrepresentation: as a result, he recommended the former to read the *Platform* more attentively, and the latter to admit their impotence. At which point he closed his audit of the three years of sundry discussions and controversies.

That edition of the review carried a group letter from the Moscow anarchists, signed by Borovoy, Barmash and Rogdaiev, saluting the endeavors of *Dyelo Truda* as nothing more than was to be expected of revolutionary anarchists. That may have been the signal for it, but the GPU mounted a swoop upon anarchist circles in the USSR, hitherto very grudgingly tolerated by the regime. The signatories to the letter to *Dyelo Truda*, Khudoley and dozens of others, were rounded up, jailed or deported. Naturally, all links with the West were severed and forbidden. Curiously and in an associated way, Arshinov was arrested by the French police who charged him with engaging in political activities incompatible with his political refugee status: he was expelled to Belgium in January 1930. Under the concerted blows of the Stalinist and French republican repression, *Dyelo Truda*'s work of clarification and liaison was finished in Europe. After a few months delay, the review re-emerged, this time in Chicago in the USA. Arshinov continued to contribute to its columns, albeit fitfully. All of a sudden, there came a bombshell: he brought out a pamphlet where, referring to the Lenin of *The State and Revolution*, he conceded the necessity of the dictatorship of the proletariat, the only way out of the movement's historical and theoretical impasse. In the wake of the Spanish revolutionary upheaval in 1931, he envisaged only one option for the Spanish anarchists: the establishment of a dictatorship of the proletariat or evolution in the direction of reformism and opportunism. That startling analysis was matched by an even more dismaying piece of advice: that contact should be established with the embassy of the USSR and with communist parties around the world!

That backsliding, though, was counterbalanced by some virulent articles against Bolshevism and against Stalin which came out at the same time. How can we explain away this glaring paradox? The testimony of Nikola Tchorbadiieff, close friend of Makhno and Arshinov, with whom he shared lodgings in Vincennes for several years, furnishes us with the only logical solution. Following his deportation, which had been put back for a time, thanks to lobbying from several French VIPs, Arshinov found himself in dire material and personal straits with his wife who was weary of life in exile. Disheartened by the continual controversies and depressing vista of the anarchist movement, Arshinov had contacted Sergo Ordzhonikidze, who was at that time close to Stalin, and whom Arshinov had known 20 years before when they were cellmates in prison. Ordzhonikidze had undertaken to help him get back to his homeland, but naturally there were specific conditions upon that: he would have to abjure all his criticisms of Bolshevism and sever all ties with the anarchist movement. This is what Arshinov had made up his mind to do, not without some headaches, for he found it hard to turn his back on all his activities, not just the twenty-five years as a militant anarchist, but also the five years of constructive endeavors through *Dyelo Truda*. Also, in the two pamphlets he issued acknowledging the existence of the dictatorship of the proletariat and a "workers'" state in the USSR, there was no self-criticism of his activities, merely a detailed audit of the negative picture of anarchism in various countries around the world, to the extent that in nearly 50 pages of text there were only three or four genuinely politically compromising phrases, like that recommendation to make contact with the Soviet embassy and defend the workers' state against the rising danger from the worldwide reaction. Before he returned to the USSR in 1933, Nikola Tchorbadiieff put to him this question: "Have you become a Bolshevik?," to which Arshinov replied: "Do you think I could?" and explained away his return in terms of the lack of prospects for militant activity in France and Europe, whereas in the USSR he was ready to join even the Communist Party in order to be able to carry on working on anarchism's behalf.[12]

Thus, it had more to do with an act of personal despair than any real political conversion. In any event, Arshinov was to be shot in Moscow in 1937 on charges of having sought "to rebuild anarchism in Soviet Russia." As a result, it would appear that he had put his clandestine action plan into effect, which we regard as rather in keeping with his fanatical working class anarchism, his militancy and his strong personal determination, qualities that he had previously demonstrated time and time again.

What a gift to the opponents of the *Platform*! By his actions, their worst enemy was confirming their accusations beyond anything they could have hoped for. And they made a real meal of the fact. It was Max Nettlauwho perhaps went the furthest. Although he had never met him personally, Nettlau coolly asserted that Arshinov had never been an anarchist: he allegedly had clung to his Bolshevik beliefs since 1904 and had been attracted to anarchism only on account of its radical and terrorist aspects. For one reason or another, he was supposed to have forgotten to return to the fold in 1917, but he was now putting that omission straight and Nettlau wished him "bon voyage," while wishing good riddance to this obstacle to going around in circles.[13]

As we see it, this was jumping the gun a little, for, although he had indeed been official spokesman for the *Platform*, Arshinov was not the sole author of it and so a cause-and-effect relationship needed to be established between that text — whose underlying theme was a relentless condemnation of Bolshevism — and his return to the USSR. In fact, there is something that should be kept in mind all the time if one truly wants to understand the *Dyelo Truda* approach: the fact that from 1906 to 1921, for more than 15 years, Makhno and Arshinov had been operating inside the anarchist movement, first by means of direct action, then in prison and finally in the revolution and that extraordinary Ukrainian insurgent movement known as the Makhnovist movement. So it was the lessons and insights of all their militant and fighting activity that they had set down on paper in the *Platform*. If one wanted to reject that document, then one also had to throw out "the baby with the bathwater," that is, repudiate what was, along with Spain in 1936–1939, the most radical revolutionary experiment of the century. On those grounds we regard all the nit-picking of the *Platform*'s critics as out of place and above all inconsequential: calling its authors to "account," overemphasizing the merest hints and doggedly sniffing out the "evil" — the celebrated Bolshevization of anarchism — from between the lines of a text as limpid as any rock pool. An attitude that does not look beyond a relative or absolute "negativism," the crippling bane of a certain anarchist tradition.

What then was so extraordinary about this famous *Platform*? In order to banish the continual confusion and dispersion of anarchist ideas and anarchist efforts, it argued for the elaboration of a coherent theory and resultant cohesion in action: that necessarily involved the devising of a libertarian communist program and a consistent policy line. All of that should have been a collective undertaking and not the handiwork of a few recognized leaders or chiefs. In fact, it amounted to a reversion to the Bakuninist traditions of the Alliance and the Brotherhoods, illuminated by the first hand militant historical experiences of the document's authors. Who could challenge that? Always the same old figures, the usual ditherers, the incorrigible blatherers, all those who in the end had something to lose, be it their petty vanity, or ultimately cozy position in established society. That said, the loudest opposition came from the Russian émigré community — which had nothing in common with the Makhnovist Ukrainian peasantry — and a handful of anarchist elders. Here the Marx syndrome which had done such damage before 1914, was replaced to advantage by the obsession with Lenin and his monolithic party, so much so that the mere mention of "party" was like mentioning the rope in the home of a hanging victim! Perhaps Arshinov, Makhno and their colleagues ought to have been more circumspect, used euphemisms, scattered question marks all around and "walked on eggshells" when, like "good Cossacks" they had in fact become obstreperous and given the harebrained dreamers of anarchy a taste of the saber!

Arshinov's defection did not stop Makhno trying to spread the keynote ideas of the *Platform*. He made a ringing appeal to the congress of the Revolutionary Anarchist Communist Union (UACR) in Paris in 1930.[14] To no avail: the platformists found themselves in a minority of seven groups to fourteen. It is true that Arshinov had found them prone to a centralist deviation, a sort of literal application of organizational principles without regard for their spirit. All the same, it was not until 1934 that a "sacred union" was established within the Anarchist Union (the adjectives "communist" and "revolutionary" having been dropped in the interim) in view of an increasingly worrying international situation and the attempted *coup de force* by the far right in France on February 6, 1934. At that point, a homogeneous platformist tendency was set up under the name of the Libertarian Communist Federation (FCL). Later, the Popular Front and developments in Spain were to polarize attention and efforts in such a way that practical unity would override theoretical dissensions.

## Endnotes to Chapter Sixteen

1. *Le Libertaire,* Nos. 103, (March 25, 1927) 106, 107 and 112 (May 27, 1927).

2. See my book, *Nestor Makhno, le cosaque de l'anarchie,* pp. 323–326 and Nestor Makhno, *La lutte contre l'état,* op. cit., pp. 136–143.

3. *Le Libertaire,* No. 133, (October 21, 1927).

4. *Golos Truda* (Voice of Labor), (November 1, 1928).

5. According to the account by Ugo Fedeli in *Volontà* No. 6–7, (January 15, 1949).

6. S. Faure, *Les anarchistes, qui nous sommes, ce que nous voulons, notre revolution,* (Paris 1925?), p. 15.

7. See "La synthèse anarchists" in *Le Trait d'union libertaire* the AFA bulletin, No. 3, (March 15, 1928). For an examination of the synthesist press of the time and of the discussion of the *Platform* in *Le Libertaire,* see the master's thesis by Elisabeth Burello, *Le problème de l'organization dans le mouvement anarchists de l'entre-deux-guerres (1926–1930): Le débat sur la Plate-forme* Paris, Center d'histoire du Syndicalisme, (1972: typescript) 155 pages.

8. Errico Malatesta, *Anarchie et organization* (Paris, 1927), reprinted several times since then, and see especially E. Malatesta, *Articles politiques,* (Paris, October 18, 1979), which also contains the correspondence with Makhno, excepting the second letter, which appeared in *Le Libertaire* No. 269, (August 16, 1930).

9. *Le Libertaire,* No. 252, (April 1, 1930).

10. P. Besnard, *La responsabilité La brochure mensuelle,* (September 1933) and in *L'encyclopédie anarchiste* edited by S. Faure.

11. *Dyelo Truda,* No. 48-49, 1929.

12. P. Arshinov, *Anarchism and Dictatorship of the Proletariat* (in Russian), (October 1931), 16 pages and *Anarchism and Our Times* (in Russian), (January 1933), 30 pages. See Nikola Tchorbadiieff's testimony in the video film we made with Marie Chevrier: *Nestor Makhno raconté par son ami Nikola* (Paris, 1987), 36 mm.

13. Max Nettlau, "From the '*Platform*' to 'close contact' with the proletarian state in the USSR" (in Russian), in *Notes on the History of Anarchist Ideas* (Detroit, USA, 1951), pp. 370-379.

14. Reproduced by Jean Maitron in *Le mouvement social,* No. 83, (1973), pp. 62–64. As for the review *Dyelo Truda* it was to continue publication for nearly another 30 years in the United States.

# XVII. THE CNT-FAI IN SPAIN IN 1936-1939

If France was the homeland of anarchy, Spain was its "promised land"—even in the days of Bakunin it had been held up as an example to be followed. Libertarian collectivism had been around there for decades of indefatigable activity. The National Confederation of Labor (CNT), an openly anarchist trade union, founded on November 1, 1910, and modeled on the French libertarian CGT, had had designs on hegemony: in 1919, it had given all Spanish workers three months to affiliate to it, on pain of being declared traitors and suffering the consequences. Having retreated a little while later from that overbearing posture, it had nonetheless attracted increasingly overwhelming masses of workers: by 1936, their number was reckoned at around two million. As for the Iberian Anarchist Federation (FAI), it had come into existence in July 1927, on the initiative of groups living as refugees in France. Forced underground until 1931, it operated as a specific organization watching over the CNT's doctrinal orthodoxy. Relying upon grassroots affinity groups, it bore a closer resemblance to a conspiratorial organization along the lines of Bakunin's Alliance than to the General Union of Anarchists advocated in the *Platform*. It was only later and especially during the years 1937–1939 that dual CNT-FAI membership was made virtually obligatory upon militants. Here we may cite the incident that befell Pierre Besnard, the French anarcho-syndicalist leader. Invited to an international anarchist congress in Barcelona in 1937, he found himself asked whether he was in fact a member of the French Anarchist Federation (FAF) — set up in 1936 but in competition with the Anarchist Union (UA) — before he could take part in the congress without creating "difficulties with certain anarchist comrades."[1] Unable and refusing to fulfill that condition, he declined to attend the congress.

If the *Platform* project was of interest to anyone, then it was the Spanish movement: all of the issues spelled out or broached in writing in *Dyelo Truda* lay at the heart of the preoccupations which exercised the Spanish comrades. In late 1927 or early 1928, a Spanish translation of the *Platform* was issued in pamphlet form by the *Prisma* group from Béziers. That translation was based on the French text, that is, retained the terminology and passages queried by *Dyelo Truda*. We learned of this text from Frank Mintz and he has indicated that another partial translation appeared, along with unfavorable commentary, in *La Protesta* in Buenos Aires.[2] He adds that:

the particular circumstances of the Iberian movement made discussion very difficult, if not nonexistent, In exile, following the involvement of certain anarchists in a coup de main alongside some Catalanists on the Spanish border in 1926, then the mobilization on behalf of Sacco and Vanzetti, and the campaign to release Ascaso and Durruti, not to mention activities on behalf of Spain itself, one finds no hints of a debate on the *Platform*. [3]

However, at the request of several regional committees in Spain, it had found its way on to the agenda of the foundation conference of the FAI. As a Spanish translation was not yet available, it could not be debated and the matter was put back until the follow-up meeting. The testimony of an FAI member bears out this impression of ignorance:

> The *Platform* had little impact on the movement, in exile or in the interior. Advocates, very few. You know how we were all "radicalized" at that time and how reserved we were about any amendment or revision. The *Platform* was an attempted overhaul designed to invest the international anarchist movement with coherence, breadth and a realistic outlook, in the light of the experiences of the Russian revolution and, above all, of the Ukraine. Today, in the wake of our own experiences, it seems to me that that attempt did not receive its proper appreciation.[4]

Several Spaniards had, as we have seen, participated in the discussion meetings organized by *Dyelo Truda*. In 1927, as they emerged from French jails, Ascaso and Durruti had had lengthy talks with Nestor Makhno about his experiences in the Ukraine. The exiled Makhno had passed on the lessons he had derived from all his activity, and he had probably spelled out the sense and contents of the *Platform*. Also, he was to keep abreast of the situation inside Spain, and in 1931 there was even a possibility of his going off to lead a guerrilla campaign in the north of the country. Although known in broad outline, it would thus appear that the *Platform* had not been read and above all not been debated. Here we should take account of another factor: a certain "isolationism" in the Spaniards. In view of their long lineage, and their own wealth of experience, they must have felt disinclined to take "lessons" from outsiders, and they displayed great confidence in their own capabilities, not to say a superiority complex vis à vis the international workers' movement that had caved in so pitifully in 1914.

To complete this cursory survey of the possible influence of the *Platform* over the Spanish libertarian movement, let us quote from César M. Lorenzo, author of a standard reference volume on the period: he writes that *Los Solidarios*, a famous group of activists like Durruti, Ascaso, Garcia Oliver, Jover, Vivancos and others "merely noted that the *Platform* squared with their own views."[5] We have our reservations for, thanks to an input of Garcia Oliver, we can see how these comrades deviated somewhat from the notion of the role ascribed to the anarchists' specific organization, inclining instead towards a typically vanguardist strategy; they openly advocated its designs:

upon the seizure of political, administrative and economic power, with the aid of its own trade unions once the old state with organizing production and distribution in the new libertarian society, would therefore be an insurgent non-statist power of the trade union type, operating from the periphery towards the center and comprising of a range of federated revolutionary committees, in a sort of democratic "dictatorship of the proletariat," silencing the forces of the right, the former proprietors, the Church, etc. As a transitional authority guaranteeing revolutionary order, it would not imply a dictatorship in the ordinary sense of the word: guided by libertarian ideology (and not by Marxism, a dogmatic teaching devoid of humanistic content) it would elevate popular liberty, the initiative of the masses, and would invite other leftist organizations to cooperate in its work of regeneration. [6]

But how was this "seizure of power" to be accomplished? Not by means of the specific organization or even the trade union organization, but rather by a "revolutionary army," a "centralized trade union militia, endowed with a respected national command."

Thus, the divergences from the *Platform* were great, and the role that the latter ascribed to the specific organization was purely political with regard to the proletariat's grassroots agencies, while this "revolutionary army" supplanted it entirely. It was, to paraphrase Charles Rappoport's definition of Leninism, "Blanquism in Catalan sauce!" But it was this that was strictly put into effect in July 1936, as we shall see.

Meanwhile, *Los Solidarios* were to be labeled as "anarcho-Bolsheviks" by their adversaries inside the CNT. Not that that stopped them from taking a crucial hand in the June 1931 congress of the CNT in the elimination of the Marxists, Freemasons and reformists from the leadership bodies of the CNT, then affiliating to the FAI and helping shape its outlook. They were to call for "unflagging class warfare, a tough line on the Communist Party and reformism, Social Democratic or libertarian alike." Among the supporters of the latter, we might mention the "Thirty" (Treinta), headed by Peiró, who sought to take a more constructive line, but were labeled as "reformists." According to them, the libertarian ideal:

> retained its fundamental validity but certain prejudices and wrong-headed tactics which had been eulogized up until then had to be jettisoned. In particular, intellectuals and technicians had to be attracted, production and consumer cooperatives created, their revenues being used on propaganda, the training of educated militants and the construction of workers' cultural centers. A solid and disciplined organization also had to be founded and the ignorance and fanaticism of the bulk of anarchist militants tackled: he deplored their ignorance of Marxism and of anarchism itself, which was, above all else, tolerance, anti-dogmatism and nobility, and whose premier interest lay in morals and philosophy.[7]

Mikhail Bakunin (1814–1876)

James Guillaume (1844–1916)

Peter Kropotkin (1842–1921)

Pierre-Joseph Proudhon (1809–1865)

Louise Michel (1835–1905)

Elisee Reclus (1830–1905)

Peter Kropotkin at the trial of the anarchists of Lyon, January 1883

Militants from *La Guerre Sociale*
(photo from the archives of Emile Pataud)

The office of Endehors newpaper. Engraving published in *Illustration*, No. 659, (February 10, 1894). Clockwise from left: Tabarant, Zo d'Axa, A. Hamon, Jean Grave, Bernard Lazare, Octave Mirbeau, L. Matha (?), Malato.

The newspaper, *La Dynamite,* edited by Ravachol, did not hide its program: "Dynamite is the language of French."

Emily Henry (1872–1894)

Proudhon in 1848

Pierre Ramus (1882–1942)

Fernand Pelloutier (1867–1901)

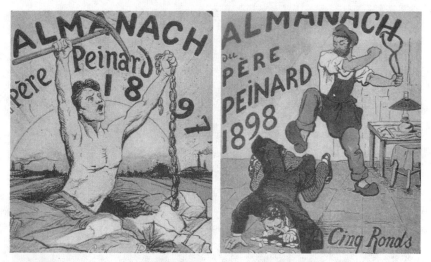

Covers from the 1897 and 1898 Père Peinard

Sèbastien Faure (1858–1942)

Drawing of Emile Pouget by A. Delannoy published in *Men of the Moment*, No. 27 (no date)

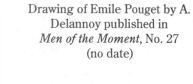

Drawing of Emile Pataud by A. Delannoy published in the *Men of the Moment*, No. 67, (May 1, 1909)

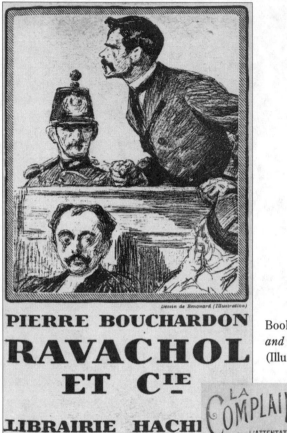

Book cover for *Ravachol and Company* (Illustration by Renouard)

French songsheet cover celebrating the bomb which Vailliant threw into the Chamber of Deputies.

Nestor Makhno and Alexander Berkman, Paris, around 1927

Ernest Armand (1872–1962)

Alexander Berkman and Rudolf
Rocker, Paris, France, in 1920s

Gaston Leval (1895–1978)

Daniel Guérin (1904–1988)

Mollie Steimer (1897–1980)

Senya Fleshin (1894–1981)

Senya Fleshin,
Voline, and
Mollie Steimer

The vast majority of the CNT's anarchists were somewhere between these two competing tendencies. However, it is to the activist tendency that we have to chalk up the uprisings of 1932 and the ensuing years, which culminated in the Asturias Commune (in concert with the UGT and the socialists), all of them ruthlessly and bloodily repressed by the authorities, right-wing and left-wing alike. In fact. let us note the libertarians' decisive involvement in the Spanish legislative elections: in 1931, casting their votes for the left, they brought down the monarchy; in 1933, disappointed with the left in power, they tipped the scales in the other direction and, by abstaining, smoothed the way for the right; finally, spoiling for a fight, in order to secure an amnesty for 30,000 political prisoners (arrested after the uprisings) they cast their votes to bring the Popular Front success in February 1936. And, to cap all those uprisings in which they had been engaging for years past, on July 19, 1936, they found themselves faced with a rising by rebel Nationalists! — and were obliged to stand by "republican legality"! Driven by their heady ardor and madcap heroics, they outdid themselves by securing victory in Barcelona and Catalonia, where they assumed full control. Elsewhere in the country, the outcome was less clear cut. and a good half of the country fell to Franco and his Moorish troops. Even so, the anti-fascists and the CNT held the wealthier half of the country. That was when their problems started and their theoretical deficiencies became flagrantly obvious: how were they going to set about assuming effective power without establishing a state, in the "bourgeois" sense of the word, that is, what were they to put in place of the government, its ministers, its civil service, the police, the army and all the other accoutrements of the state? Hitherto, it had been merely a question of introducing a libertarian communist republic, of replacing "government of men by administration of things," establishing a free federation of communes, with the producers and consumers getting themselves organized with one another, and now they had to tackle, in addition, the defense of the revolution, without alienating potential allies such as the socialists, Catalan republicans and POUMists (dissident communists) previously their bitterest foes — and also without influencing, in an international context, the British and French "democracies." In short, every one of the pressing and essential points that the recent CNT congress in Zaragosa on May 1–10, 1936, had been careful to side-step, preoccupied as it had been with defining the "confederal conception of libertarian communism." Ascaso and Garcia Oliver had tried to suggest to that congress that confederal militias be established which would be capable of breaking any army revolt, only to hear Cipriano Mera taunt them: "Maybe comrades Ascaso and Garcia Oliver could let us know what color of general's braid they would like?"[8]

By a twist of fate, it was Mera himself who was to wind up as a real general, as commander of the Fourth Army Corps, and he was to brook no departure from discipline nor from respect for rank. The former members of the *Los Solidarios* group, now banded together as *Nosotros*, had intended to lay the foundations of an insurgent army by unifying the CNT-FAI defense committees which had been around since 1931 but which had no coordinating agency or command. That point, with which the *Platform* and Nestor Makhno had dealt ought to have been under consideration by the ordinary membership for some years.

As soon as its victory in battle had been secured, the CNT in Barcelona came together in plenary assembly on July 20 and 21, 1936, and came up with a halfway house solution: the regional government or Generalitat, was retained as a shop window for diplomatic purposes, while a real revolutionary authority was established in the shape of a Central Committee of Anti-Fascist Militias. Comprising, to begin with, fifteen members drawn equally from the three predominant leftist factions: the CNT-FAI, the Marxists (the Stalinists of the PSUC were lumped against their wishes with the POUM) and the Catalan republicans. The Central Committee soon subdivided into several committees and commissions, with responsibility for: provisions, education, investigation (security), and justice, and there was an Economic Council which played a fundamental role in production and administrative organization. Control patrols monitored public order, and these were made up of 700 men (325 of them anarchists), run by an eleven-member (four of them anarchists) central committee. All the key positions in these committees were held by anarchists. Garcia Oliver was the "soul and indefatigable driving force" of the Central Militias Committee, and appeared as "the very essence of the unchallenged revolutionary leader"; in fact he carried out what he had been preaching along with *Los Solidarios* ten years earlier.

The Central Militias Committee was a face-saver for all of the member organizations of the antifascist camp, while it cemented their unity. That said, each organization also had its own armed groups, its columns serving on the front and even its own police and prison. Throughout Catalonia, revolutionary committees organized along roughly the same lines took their districts and their economic and social lives in hand.

Prompted however by urgent concerns, such as the procurement of arms from the national government in Madrid as well as from abroad, the CNT leadership called these revolutionary structures into question and sided with a classical government, first in Catalonia and then in Madrid.

What alternative was there and how was it posed? The answer to that question is crucial, for collaboration with the "bourgeois" government was to become the Achilles heel of the Spanish libertarian movement. It was all thrashed out at a plenum of local and *comarcal* federations of the libertarian movement in Catalonia at the end of August 1936. Unconventionally, that plenum which was attended by all responsible militants not away at the front, met in camera. Remember that the founding of the Central Militias Committee was already a trespass against the doctrine that called for immediate implementation of libertarian communism, but it was a lesser evil for the anarchists were masters of the situation. Yet the grassroots organs of the CNT-FAI had yet to have their say. Now, after protracted discussions, it was Garcia Oliver who formulated the choice facing them: "Either we collaborate, or we impose a dictatorship." Historian César Lorenzo, reporting this episode, comments with the assertion that "in fact, there was no question of a reversion to the old apolitical tradition and the 'a-cratic' ideas that had been completely overwhelmed and overtaken by events, but which certain folk doggedly championed against Hell and high water."[9] That latter comment indicates that some found the "medicine" hard to swallow. All the same, it had to be done, and they could not glibly walk away from what had been the raison d'être and motivating force of several generations of militants. Nor was the alternative mentioned by Garcia Oliver very precise either: how could the label "dictatorship" be hung on power assumed by anarchists — who were in a position of hegemony at that point — with the complaisance of virtually the entire working population? Plainly, that was a misapplication of the term. Nevertheless, Garcia Oliver, with the backing of his old colleagues from *Los Solidarios* and *Nosotros*, was in favor of the CNT's taking power, with "all of the risks and dangers that that implied." He "hoped to see the political parties ousted, the UGT (the socialist trade union) humbled, the Generalitat abolished and the Central Committee of Militias, after a reshuffle, strengthened in its remit, emerging as the supreme authority." Consequently, it would have been something between the Committee of Public Safety, in the tradition of Bakunin the insurgent, and the Bolshevik Soviet of People's Commissars of October 1917. Take your pick. Most of the CNT leaders opted for collaboration, that is, participation in the autonomous Catalan government. Diego Abad de Santillan, the main advocate of that option, was to explain later that his main consideration had been to procure arms, hard currency and raw materials for industry and, in order to do that, they had to withdraw their "backing for people's power."

This decision to participate in the Generalitat government was ratified by the regional congress of CNT unions on September 24–26, 1936, in the presence of 505 delegates representing 327 unions, in the course of a closed "secret" sitting. On September 27th the "news burst like a bombshell" (Lorenzo). The one difference was that henceforth the Catalan government would be termed the "Generalitat Council." There were three CNT "councilors" on it.

Now that they had bitten the bullet, it only remained to do likewise in other regions of the country and indeed, at national level. With the notable exception of Aragon, which was in the firing line. Zaragoza, a stronghold of anarcho-syndicalism, had been lost to the enemy through the fault of a CNT leader, Abos, who had chosen to place his trust in the civil governor, Vera Coronel, and the military governor General Cabanellas, on the basis that they were fellow-masons of his, and he had managed to "sell" the lies of his "lodge"[10] friends to the majority of his comrades. The upshot was a disaster: handed over, unarmed, to the rebels' repression, somewhere between 15,000 and 30,000 revolutionaries paid with their lives for the nonchalance and ingenuousness of a few "officials." In response, the Aragonese anarchists became more radical and unbending. They had no hesitation in forming a Council of Aragon, made up exclusively of anarchists, with Joaquin Ascaso, Francisco Ascaso's younger brother, as its president. What the Catalan anarchists had not dared do was done by the

Aragonese. However, these would later be obliged to pass through the Caudine Forks* of the central state and adulterate their actions.

After the September 15, 1936, national Plenum, the CNT requested the establishment of a National Defense Council, comprising five CNT delegates, five UCT delegates and four republicans. This was a logical follow-up to the policy of anti-fascist unity that had been adopted and it took into account the true balance of economic and social forces, on a federalist basis comparatively consonant with anarchist principles, for the state was no longer made up of ministries, army, police and officers: everything had had its name changed and now they were "departments, war militias and popular militias and military technicians." The CNT's general secretary, Horacio M. Prieto, doggedly opposed this scheme because of its "utter lack of realism, given the foreign powers and the international aspect to the war." He managed to talk the national Plenum of the regional federations on October 18th into open and direct collaboration with the government as it stood. The organizational corollary to that reformist option was a strengthening of the powers of the CNT national committee which, "ceasing to be appointed by the local federation of its place of residence, was thereafter made up of permanent delegates from the regional federations and by a larger number of specialist administrative members." César Lorenzo, who is, by the way, the son of Horacio M. Prieto, notes that "the CNT was thereafter equipped with a central, complex and effective agency freed from pressures from local militants." Indeed, a royal road was opened up for the bureaucratization of the CNT.

Like the frog who jumped into the water to escape from the rain, the CNT-FAI leaders, or at least most of them, were afraid to make the revolution, arguing that they were more concerned with winning the war first, and moved from retreat to evasion, from compromise to capitulation. The slippery slope came to its inevitable end: dissolution of the Barcelona-based Central Militias Committee, militarization of the militias, growing Stalinist influence, elimination of the POUM, dissolution of the Council of Aragon, destruction of the collectives, the May Events of 1937 in Barcelona (when the CNT leadership robbed the insurgents of their victory over the Stalinist provocateurs).

The CNT-FAI's structures mirrored and followed this political retreat: the National Defense Committee lost its autonomy to wind up as merely the military branch of the Confederation's national committee. On April 2, 1938, a regional assembly of the CNT, the FAI and the FIJL (Iberian Federation of Libertarian Youth) was held in Barcelona. Garcia Oliver was critical of the disorder and lack of discipline obtaining within the movement and proposed the establishment of an Executive Committee which "would wield full authority, overseeing and directing everything: the press, the confederation's troops, the

---

* Two mountain passes in southern Italy in the Apennines between Benevento and Capua through which Spanish refugees traveled.

economy." This was unanimously endorsed. That Executive Committee of the Libertarian Movement of Catalonia, made up of just ten members, was "entitled to expel individuals, committees, unions and federations which refused to abide by its decisions. Its executive powers applied to front and rear alike. It intended to press on relentlessly with militarization, to step up production by all means and to facilitate the entry of the CNT into the central government, the Generalitat and every one of the administrative ramifications of the state. To assist it in its functions, the Committee appointed a military commission and a political commission."[11] This was out and out Bolshevism, or the word has no meaning. This was a heresy that the CNT national committee could not countenance. Although himself a "great bureaucratizer," Horacio M. Prieto let it be known that the Catalan regional committee alone counted for nothing and this Executive Committee, which had the endorsement of no congress, could not have any independent existence of its own. In the light of that opposition, the plan was in fact withdrawn.

In August 1938, Horacio Prieto published a series of articles making public certain ideas of his which had been peddled a year before to a narrower circle. According to him:

Libertarian communism could not be anything other than a distant objective, an aspiration, and anarchism a moral code and a philosophy. In order to arrive at that communism, a lengthy period of transition was necessary, during which libertarian achievements were possible, though not in any systematic way. We had to display opportunism, suppleness and have no hesitation about participating in government, in all high offices of state and even in Parliament with the intention of taking power. We had to engage permanently in politics rather than circumstantially as hitherto: revolutionary apoliticism was a dead duck.[12]

The die was cast and libertarian communism postponed until the kalends*, if not relegated to the museum of antiquities and utopia. Apparently, the FAI was to turn itself into an electioneering political party and see to it that the CNT's interests were represented. Later on, Prieto was to dub this "possibilism," reaching across the Pyrenees and the decades to link hands with Paul Brousse's policy. However, he failed to carry with him the majority of the national plenum of regional federations of the Libertarian Movement, held in Barcelona on October 6–30, 1938: it had been summoned to consider this scheme and determine the strategy to be adopted. We might also note the existence of the Auxiliary Policy Committees (CAPs), bodies launched in June and July of 1937, whose mission it was to brief "militants on all matters that overspilled the strictly trade union framework and advise them on as to *the best way to operate politically*"[13] (our emphasis). Made up of the best known militants, these CAPs became the "real leadership organs of the CNT" (Lorenzo). As we can see, the CNT's federalism was

---

* The first day of the ancient Roman month from which days were counted backward to the ides.

only a smoke-screen and there was a real Jacobin-style democratic centralism that increasingly prevailed in its organizational practice.

The "officers" decided everything and did so alone. Once the mistake that had given rise to all the rest, the entry into the Generalitat government, had been made, complications had eaten away at doctrine, good intentions and revolutionary determination. Defeat had become inescapable, because it already had a foothold inside the revolutionary camp. Yet again, the lessons of previous experience were not heeded: the most radical revolutionaries — the anarchists or their like — stand alone against everybody and it is only by fighting against all sides at once, that is, by carrying out the most comprehensive social revolution, that victory is made possible. Stopping in midstream amounts to digging one's own grave, as was said long ago by Saint-Just.

Needless to say this appetite for "politicking" was not appreciated by all of the CNT-FAI's members and militants. There were the Friends of Durruti Group (denounced as "provocateurs" by the CNT leadership), and the Iron Column (prevented by the regional committee in Valencia from giving the Stalinists what they had coming to them) which resisted militarization for a long time. When, beset from all sides, it was forced to give in on March 1937, only 3000 to 4000 out of its roughly 20,000 men stayed behind "all the rest having chosen to desert rather than become soldier-robots." The same was true of other columns too, but not on the same scale.[14]

Be that as it may, it has to be placed on record that the vast majority of grassroots militants passively countenanced the zigzag tactics of their leaders. How are we to account for that? First, there was the need to attend to the most pressing business, namely, the war against fascism and the defense of a minimum of the revolution's gains, in addition to undue confidence in their leaders. Such charisma that dulls the critical faculties is the enemy of the revolutionary. Bakunin said as much, and once again we see the results of it. Among the leadership, those who had their misgivings — like Durruti — opted to go off and fight instead of bandying words. We will never be able to gauge the measure of the loss suffered in the death of Francisco Ascaso, who was a perfect partner to Buenaventura Durruti. Had Ascaso survived July 19, 1936, the likelihood is that through his daring, his recklessness and his ingenuity he might have changed the face of the military situation, by, say, quickly taking Zaragoza. Durruti's death was a catastrophe, militarily as well as politically. As Abel Paz has written, he was killed a second time when he was credited with a concocted phrase that could be turned to anyone's service: "Renounce everything, save victory!" We might quote the episode, related by Paz, of the Bank of Spain's gold: Pierre Besnard had insistently cautioned against a repetition of the error made by the Paris Communards of 1871 who had not dared to make use of the gold in the Bank of France. Better still, the Frenchman had located a consortium of arms dealers who undertook to supply all the modern weaponry needed, upon receipt of negotiable cash, of course. Durruti devised a plan to raid the bank holding the gold in Madrid, with the 3000 men from the anarchist Tierra y Libertad column, to ship it to Barcelona and then proceed with the deal. It was Diego Abad de Santillan who carelessly leaked it to the CNT national committee which, frightened by the tension that it would create between Madrid and Barcelona, aborted the plan by publicly exposing it. Durruti gave Santillan a real tongue-lashing but the game was up. That is the sort of thing that can determine the fate of a revolution: the lack of resolution and above all lack of daring of a handful of "leaders." [15]

However, it was the rank and file, the rabble, the people, the humble folk, the dregs, whatever one prefers to call the peasants and workers of Catalonia, Levante, Aragon, Andalusia, Castile and elsewhere, that saved anarchism's honor by taking their fate into their own hands, by organizing fantastic collectives, when even those who had never heard tell of, or were hostile to libertarian communism, put it enthusiastically into effect here and there. According to Gaston Leval, there were around 1600 collectives, more or less. Each one, like each one of the little townships organized along communal lines, would deserve a book to itself, again according to Leval (the son of a Paris Communard who died in the USSR). All these creative activities, these ventures, the changes to human relationships amounted to a "miraculous blossoming." It is "fully cognizant of the meaning of words, without hyperbole, and with no demagogic intent that I say again: 'Never in the history of the world as we know it to date was a comparable social undertaking ever carried out.' And in a few months at that, if not a few weeks or even a few days, depending upon the example." [16] We should correct the old propagandist (the CNT's delegate to the Profintern Congress in Moscow in 1921) by reminding ourselves of the similar achievements of the Makhnovist insurgents in the Ukraine in 1917–1921. We might also give a mention to the extraordinary militias from the anarchist columns, who, in sandals and overalls, armed with a few poor quality rifles and aboard ramshackle trucks, set off to conquer a brave new world. There is no question here of lumping these fighters and agents of social revolution with the category of leaders who "played at politics." While not seeking to diminish the responsibility of the latter, we should bear in mind the widespread hostility that greeted the revolution of July 19, 1936, on the international stage, the ongoing arms blockade enforced by the Western powers and Stalin, and especially the shameful conduct of the French Popular Front government of Leon Blum, who "backed down" in the face of Hitler and Mussolini by agreeing to nonintervention, when the merest effort on his part would have guaranteed a rapid victory for the republican camp in Spain. As for the French workers, they were reveling in "holidays with pay," the mess of pottage bought with their lack of solidarity, at a time when — for want of arms — their brethren across the Pyrenees were being slaughtered.

Might a more daring policy on the anarchists' part have changed that hostility? Here let us quote from Victor Alba, author of a history of the POUM:

Had the CNT embarked upon the conquest of power in Catalonia — and it could have taken it in under twenty-four hours, had it so desired — the situation would have changed in the remainder of the republican zone. Political elimination of the communists might have been bartered for British, Czech and French arms (by way of an answer to the Soviet arms blackmail), or Moscow could have been forced to choose between abandoning the Spanish revolution or helping it, even if the communists were not in control of it, in exchange for the political existence of the latter being preserved, albeit properly monitored.[17]

Nothing is that certain, but it was worth a try. But let us not get into rewriting history; let us derive this conclusion from it: that every single instance of alliance between anarchists and leftist or Stalino-Leninist politicians — like in the Ukraine and in China in 1925–1930 — ended in political and physical defeat for the anarchists. In any event, the defeat of 1939 signaled the long eclipse of libertarian ideas, and it was only after nigh on thirty years in the wilderness that they were to explode back on to the scene in May 1968.

Despite their slight numbers, French anarchists did their best to help their Spanish comrades. A Sébastien Faure *centuria* went off to fight alongside the Durruti Column, a small quantity of provisions and arms (two truckloads each week) were regularly dispatched across the Pyrenees, and an intensive propaganda campaign mounted on the Spanish revolution's behalf. A wholly libertarian Committee for Free Spain was replaced, at the urging of Spanish comrades, by a French section of International Anti-Fascist Solidarity (SIA) with comprehensive support ranging from left-wing personalities and CGT unionists like Jouhaux, Dumoulin and René Belin. The SIA had up to 15,000 members, published a weekly paper, which had 5,500 subscribers by February 1939 and organized mass rallies. It was above all around this latter date, corresponding to the end of the Spanish Civil War, that solidarity was needed to overcome the hostility of the French government and the apathy of a large fraction of the population. Of the 500,000 Spanish refugees, the anarchists were the most unprotected: republicans and socialists found it easier to secure asylum in Mexico and South America. Dumped in horrifying conditions on the coast and in the hinterland of Roussillon, they paid an additional penalty (160,000 deaths from disease, malnutrition or cold) for their social revolution and general indifference. Aid from French comrades and a part of the local populace eased their circumstances a little.

The Hitler-Stalin Pact and the outbreak of hostilities in September 1939 once again exposed the organizational and practical frailty of the anarchists. Despite the publication in large numbers of pacifist appeals and tracts by Louis Lecoin and Nicolas Faucier, who were promptly jailed, comrades were forced to fend for themselves in order to "save their skins" in a conflict that was none of their doing. Some went into exile in Switzerland or elsewhere, as best they could; others went underground with all of the attendant risks; Maurice Joyeux, for all his resourcefulness, was jailed yet again and by 1945, when he was thirty-five years old, he had spent nearly ten years in military prisons.[18] Others, who were conscripted, agreed to serve and perished in the fighting, like Frémont, the secretary of the French Anarchist Union.

Caught in the crossfire, Spanish anarchists threw themselves into the fight against the German occupier and his Vichy accomplices. Some of them — like Juan Peiró, the ideologue of the Thirty (Treinta) in 1931 — were handed over to Franco and, having declined to compromise, were shot (as was Companys, the erstwhile president of the Generalitat in Barcelona). Some were deported to German concentration camps. Significant numbers of Spanish libertarians joined the Maquis in the southwest and played a crucial part in the liberation of that region. Others, having fled to North Africa, joined General Leclerc's Second (Free French) Armored Division and entered Paris as liberators, aboard tanks daubed with names like "Durruti" and "Ascaso." They all had justified expectations of being rewarded upon their return with an opportunity to liberate their native land next, but to no avail, for the reckonings of the western Allies had determined otherwise.

## Endnotes to Chapter Seventeen

1. Pierre Besnard's report as secretary of the IWA to the International Anarchist Congress, *Anarchosyndicalisme et anarchisme*, (undated), 16 pages.
2. In its literary supplement of January 1927, plus the four succeeding issues.
3. Frank Mintz's text, sent to the writer: "The influence of the Arshinov *Platform* on the Spanish language libertarian movement," three typewritten pages.
4. Ibid.
5. César M. Lorenzo, *Les anarchists espagnois et le pouvoir 1868–1969*, (Paris: Le Seuil, 1969), pp. 60–61. This book has been depicted several times as the author's apologia for the stance taken by his father, Horacio M. Prieto, an enthusiastic revisionist and advocate of political collaboration by the CNT. As for ourselves, we regard it as a relentless arraignment of that same "collaboration," by dint of the detail and comprehensiveness of its information, and especially the objectivity of the author.
6. Ibid.
7. Ibid., p, 64.
8. Ibid., p. 94.
9. Ibid., p. 121–125. All of the quotations and references below refer to this book.
10. Ibid., p. 140–141.
11. Ibid., p. 292–293.
12, Ibid., p. 294.
13. Ibid., p. 294–300.
14. Ibid., p. 188. A column was made up of centuries, themselves divided into ten groups of ten militians, who appointed their delegates, who, together, made up the column's War Committee.
15. Abel Paz *Durruti, le peuple en armes*, (Paris: La Tête de Feuilles, 1972), pp. 384–388.
16. Gaston Leval, *L'anarchisme et la revolution espagnole in Anarchici e anarchia nel mondo contemporaneo*, (Turin: Fondazione Luigi Einaudi, 1971), pp. 118–123.

17. Victor Alba, *Histoire du POUM,* (Paris: Champ Libre, 1975), pp. 266–267. We ought to point out that CNT-FAI mistrust of the POUM could be justified in terms of the intentions and severe criticisms leveled against anarchism by the POUM leader Joaquin Maurin, such as: "The final elimination of anarchism is a difficult task in a country where the workers' movement has been carrying a half-century of anarchist propaganda around with it. But we will have them...." in Joaquin Maurin, *L'anarcho-syndicalisme en Espagne* (Paris: Librairie du travail, 1924), p. 47, and "An anarchist who manages to see clearly, to stand up straight, to learn, automatically ceases to be an anarchist," in J. Maurin, *Révolution et contre-révolution en Espagne,* Paris: Editions Rieder, 1937), p. 124.

18. See M. Joyeux, *Mémoires d'un anarchists,* Volume I (up to 1945), (Editions du Monde Libertaire, 1986), 442 pages.

# XVIII. THE OPB AND THE FCL (LIBERTARIAN COMMUNIST FEDERATION)

The French anarchist movement was re-formed amid the euphoria of the Liberation in 1945. An Anarchist Federation was established under good auspices: it was a matter of "wiping the slate clean of the methods of action from another age, the failure of these being beyond dispute." In spite of some hesitation, more rigorous organizational principles were adopted, leaving "far behind them all past errors in relation to libertarian organization." Among the decisions made then, we might note the revival from 1913, 1927 and the FCL (Libertarian Communist Federation) of 1935, of the obligation upon members to possess membership cards and subscription stamps, after the practice of the trade unions. Majority rule was formally introduced into the operation of the organization and its groups, as well as at congresses. Three committees came into existence: a National Committee, the body for coordinating groups and members (it had a general secretary): a Propaganda Committee, in charge of bringing out the federation's newspaper: and a Youth Committee, designed to induct sympathizers and new recruits. The Federation had three officers: two administrators and one at the newspaper (Georges Brassens, not yet famous as a singer, would be one). Alongside it, an anarcho-syndicalist trade union confederation, the French CNT (CNTF), was to be launched along the lines of the Spanish CNT (indeed, many, if not most, of the CNTF members were drawn from the Spanish CNT). The two organizations would work hand-in-hand. Their newspapers had print runs in the tens of thousands: the weekly *Le Libertaire* printed an average of nearly 50,000 copies (and one of its editions, covering the Renault strike in 1947, printed 100,000). However, both organizations were to shrink, drift apart and dwindle to tiny cliques within just a few years. Let us look at the reasons for this.

The national and international context played a crucial part in it. The heady unanimity of the Resistance and the dream of a new Popular Front gave way to open hostilities between socialists and communists: the strikes of the miners and at Renault, which bordered on insurrection, were firmly defused by the French socialists in power. The "Prague Coup" during which the Stalinists seized total power without a shot being fired, when, under the Yalta agreements, they had only observer status in the country, opened the eyes of many to Stalinist designs. All of these events of necessity had a demobilizing effect and led, on the one hand, to an evaporation of goodwill, and, on the other, to a climate of great tension, due to the risk of the "cold war" heating up.

However, to put things in their historical context, Stalinism was then "in control and sure of itself" inside the workers' movement. It was also in the ascendant among intellectuals and made the running for its regiment of "fellow travelers," the most famous of whom was the Existentialist Jean-"Baptiste" (as Céline dubbed him during one diatribe) Sartre, who saw nothing wrong with covering up the facts about the totalitarian regime existing in the USSR, lest those facts "sow despair in Boulogne-Billancourt, (the site of the Renault plant)!" True, the author of *The Flies* was also keen to draw a veil over his dramatic activities under the Occupation when he staged his plays in front of stalls filled with German officers.

The atmosphere, then, was one of confrontation. The Anarchist Federation set up a "self-defense group," under the supervision of its general secretary, Georges Fontenis. To begin with, this was a core of experienced and reliable militants, whose task it was to ensure that provocateurs found no access to the organization. Its existence was common knowledge, although its operation and composition were kept secret. On this score, there was complete confidence in the general secretary, who was elected and re-elected in 1946, 1947, 1948 and 1950. From 1950 on, a fraction of the self-defense group began to hold separate meetings, turning its attention to internal matters and resolving to fight back against certain Anarchist Federation members. Its aim developed into elimination of individualists, Freemasons and other opponents of class struggle and social anarchism. It endowed itself with a structure, espoused a statement of principles, collected its own dues and adopted the name OPB (Thought-Battle Organization) by way of a tribute to Camillo Berneri, the Italian anarchist murdered by the agents of Mussolini or Stalin in Barcelona in May 1937. At its outset, the OPB comprised fifteen Parisian members and two correspondents in the provinces. Significantly, its existence was kept a sworn secret inside the FAF. Some of its members subsequently left it and in 1954 they published a document disclosing its ins and outs: this document came to be known as the Kronstadt Group Memorandum. Let us examine its analysis:

> At its head the OPB had a three-member bureau. Compulsory subscriptions furnish it with solid funding, used for example to cover OPB members' traveling expenses. Admission to the OPB is by means of co-optation after the would-be militant's past has been investigated and on the recommendation of two sponsors. Plenary assemblies of the OPB take place every fifteen days, sometimes weekly. Attendance at these is obligatory upon everyone. The decisions reached there are binding upon everyone, including those who voted against them ... In the groups, OPB militants should hold the secretaryships: encourage, by example, the fly-posting and street sale of *Le Lib(ertaire)*, and seek out likely persons for acceptance into the OPB. Also in the groups,

OPB militants push through motions all carrying the same sense in the run-up to Congresses.[1]

Little by little the original commission to spread social anarchism and stand apart from the "individualists" and "liberals" in the organization, was extended to cover also those who were described as "woolly," "deadweight" and even "traditional anarchists." Thanks to its tactic of entryism into the groups and positions of responsibility, the OPB had, by 1952, captured most of the Paris region (the most important one in the country) and provoked an initial wave of defections at the Bordeaux congress that year: the defectors included notables like Maurice Joyeux, the Lapeyres, Maurice Fayolle, Arru, Vincey, etc., and hostile groups. On the occasion of the congress, in a new departure, the principle of voting by mandate was carried by a large majority. The OPB was victorious all along the line. Let us look at how the *Memorandum* accounts for this phenomenon, which is there described as "bureaucratic centralism":

Thus, making capital out of the passivity of the mass of militants and methodical noyautage, one faction managed to control and direct the Federation as a whole. Let us summarize the process that culminated in the establishment within the Federation of a power concentrated in a graduated pyramid, which directed the most important cogs of the organization.

This procedure is oddly reminiscent of the "holding" system that allows a tiny number of share-holders to "hold" a wider and wider circle of companies, in which they hold a minimal, but active number of votes.

A. The chief Paris groups "hold" the 2nd Region (Paris) and the Federation by taking over the vast majority of positions of responsibility (the National Committee, etc.) and commission seats.

B. The OPB "holds" the main groups in the Paris region by monopolizing group offices.

C. The OPB Bureau "holds" the OPB whose members are reduced to the role of compliant henchmen.

D. Fontenis "holds" the OPB through his predominant position as Secretary in the organization. It will be readily understood how the priority of the Fontenis faction has come about. Its monolithic thinking and disciplined cohesion have made it capable of a strategy and tactic easily overruling scattered militants trusting to the organization's federalism. The OPB alone had the capacity to operate simultaneously inside numerous groups in order to nudge them from within in a specific direction. The OPB alone has been in a position to monopolize initiatives and activity inside the groups, then in the name of the groups. The OPB alone was able to guarantee itself a de facto monopoly over the Federation's administrative and ideological activities. The OPB alone was that redoubtable instrument capable of putting a seeming democracy to use in service of the needs of a hidden dictatorship. Thus the Federation, instead of being the expression of the grassroots militants as a whole through democratically elected bodies, became the creature of just one man, supported and abetted by bodies standing by to act from center to periphery. That is the very inverse of the federalist, or even of the democratic, process and Stalinism was one of the finest examples of that.[2]

According to the Memorandum, this precise mechanism explained how one "single, determined" individual could, thanks to cunning and chicanery, take over a revolutionary organization. Going into a more detailed description, the *Memorandum* compared the OPB to a political bureau (politburo) and its secretary, Georges Fontenis, to a "guide," setting the seal upon the internal dichotomy within the organization between the leader, with his claim to patent rights over the devising of the policy line, and the membership, mere enactors of his wishes. To make this ascendancy comprehensible, the *Memorandum* stressed the "particularly dangerous assets" of G. Fontenis, namely his "personal worth," his profession (teacher), his capacity for attending the local on a frequent basis and his ability to make lots of trips around the country, in short, his omnipresence, availability and gift for making himself indispensable. In addition, his charisma ensured that he had the unfailing support of the faithful. According to the *Memorandum*, the success of Fontenis's designs was attributable primarily to the "militants" lack of revolutionary vigilance and to the passive failure of many of them to exercise their right to criticize with regard to actions that may have seemed dubious to them."

A second wave of expellees — including Prudhommeaux, Louvet, Fernand Robert and Beaulaton regrouped into an Anarchist Entente, on an individualist basis. After a referendum, the FAF changed its name to the FCL (Libertarian Communist Federation). It fitted itself out with new commissions: Studies, Labor, Control and Disputes. It was before the latter that the squabble between Fontenis, the National Committee and the Kronstadt Group was settled on January 1, 1954. Serge Ninn chose the very same day to reveal the existence of the OPB, regardless of his undertaking upon entry never to make that public. Fontenis, who was there at the time, declared:

At the end of 1950, there was indeed, a secret organization, the OPB. Had there not been an OPB, there would not be any FCL today. Tremendous efforts were made in 1950. We kept *Le Libertaire* afloat. Never mind the FA. The Third Front policy was first devised in the OPB. I regret nothing of the work achieved. Those who have left did not leave on my account. Anyway, the OPB was wound up after the Paris congress in 1953. I await the cataloging of that organization's misdeeds, even with regard to old militants. Accused, let me now act as the accuser. The OPB survived up to and including the most recent congress. Insofar as Ninn and Blanchard [a member of the Kronstadt Group — author's note] were in opposition, the OPB was dissolved as soon as the FCL was established. The OPB, as understood up to that point, no longer had any *raison d'être*.

The OPB was necessary and I am not in the least embarrassed. Did we dictate decisions to the commissions? No. Broad lines, broad decisions, yes. Proof that the OPB had no intention of taking the organization over at the Paris congress, is the fact that it appointed not one of its own members to the Disputes Commission. The OPB did exist, and its handiwork is laudable. I formally deny that the OPB wields a dictatorial influence over the life of the organization. I deny that within the OPB, there was any Fontenis dictatorship. Who, other than I, had the contacts and capacity for work?[3]

He went on to say that the OPB had been wound up because the danger it posed outweighed the advantages it offered. Why "was it not disclosed? That must be obvious. The OPB was not in crisis and did not systematically whittle away at the numbers of FA militants." In conclusion, the Disputes Commission "reprimands comrade Fontenis for his attitude, which consisted of factional work in the run-up to the congress. It expresses the formal desire that there will be no repetition of such conduct."[4]

What are we to think about such a phenomenon, startling in an anarchist movement? Have the annals anything similar to offer? Can an analogy be traced with Bakunin's secret societies, especially the Alliance? The historical context was very different: these were forced into clandestinity and were targeted on outsiders or against political adversaries rather than against like-minded fellow strugglers. The analogy with Blanquist secret societies strikes us as plainer. There is also some similarity with the Pact agreed between Pierre Besnard and seventeen other revolutionary syndicalist militants in February 1921, with an eye to combating the increasing hold of Moscow and the Third International upon the CGT. Among the articles of that Pact there was a pledge "to disclose the committee's existence to none" and "to strive by every means in our power to see that at the head and in all the essential ramifications of the Revolutionary Syndicalist Committee (CSR), and chiefly at the head of the CGT, once it is in our power and under our control, we ensure the election to the highest profile positions of responsibility, whether theoretical or concerned with practical action, of purely revolutionary syndicalist personnel, autonomists and federalists."[5] Its existence was made public on June 15, 1922, and Pierre Besnard had to explain himself over it. The most tangible result of it was the elimination of Monatte, but it failed utterly in the attempt to conquer first the CGT and then the CGTU, where the communists ended up supplanting it. That example aside, we cannot discover anything comparable with the existence of a secret internal organizational faction, like the OPB, other than bodies of the same sort current in Bolshevik circles, especially among the Trotskyists, those great adepts of "entryism."

To justify his approach and also perhaps to excuse the methods used, Fontenis published a series of articles in *Le Libertaire* under the rubric *Essential Problems*. Some of these were reprinted as a pamphlet entitled *A Manifesto of*

*Libertarian Communism*. It was issued by *Le Libertaire* and prefaced by an "Introduction" from the Publications Commission. We should note that the circumstances of its publication were queried by Roland Breton, a member of the Kronstadt Group. He had drafted a motion expressing the view that the pamphlet was merely the personal views of a comrade and not the view of the Federation: he even queried the existence of the Publications Commission and indeed the publication by *Le Libertaire*, as no decision had ever been taken with regard to the matter. In his view the most significant point was that this "pamphlet had never been submitted for discussion by the organization, much less adopted as the opinion of the movement."

Even so, let us proceed to examine this document which the FCL would adopt at its 1953 congress as its fundamental text. The Publications Commission in its "Introduction" explains that the "capitalist system has passed its peak and that all cosmetic solutions and pseudo-[state communist] solutions" had failed, and thus it seemed "necessary and urgent that the libertarian communist analysis and solution be set out in a manifesto." That assertion is as relevant today as ever, but the "urgency" seems a lot less, as the situation depicted goes right back to the 1920s, and for a sick man, capitalism is in rather splendid health, thank you very much, in spite of all its crises and fevers: the revolutionary workers' movement, on the other hand, has been in declining health. Be that as it may, the "Introduction" goes on to say that the *Manifesto* was drafted by G. Fontenis "at the request of virtually the totality" of militants, that he had no thought of "devising a new doctrine," nor of being "original at all costs," but rather aspired only to pen a "modest anthology." For such a fundamental text, it is unusual that it should have come from the pen of a single militant, capable though he may be, even if it had been "retouched, corrected, revised in the light of observations, endorsements, and criticisms offered by militants and the readership of *Le Libertaire*." This unusual circumstance would endorse what the *Memorandum* had to say about G. Fontenis's predominance inside the FCL in matters of policy making.

Despite the professed reluctance to break new ground, this *Manifesto* offers what is in many respects a revisionist analysis compared with anarchist teaching as known up to that time. Careful to differentiate himself at all costs from traditional anarchism, the author uses notions and expressions that are, on occasion, ambiguous. After having repeated several times over that, say, anarchism is not "a philosophy of the individual, or of man in general," he asserts that anarchism is precisely that, but "in a particular sense," for it is, in its aspirations and goals "human, or, if you will, humanist." [6] In this way he contrasts the philosophical tendency against the social teaching, when, as we have seen amply demonstrated, the latter is an historical advance upon the former, without doing away with it, though. His definition of social classes and of the proletariat seems somewhat contradictory. The proletariat is first very properly described as the "range of individuals who have only an executive role to play in production and in political terms", then it boils down to its "most determined, most active fraction, the working class properly so called," then goes on to talk about something "broader than the proletariat and embracing other social strata which have to be committed to action: the popular masses which include the small peasants, the poor artisans, etc." Finally, he mentions the "working class's supremacy over other exploited strata," touching upon a possible interpretation of the "dictatorship of the proletariat," for which he substitutes "direct worker power." Among the tasks facing the latter is the defense of the revolution against the "fainthearted, that is, against the backward exploited social strata (certain categories of peasants, for instance)." All of it very vague and liable to confusion, especially with these categories of "fainthearts" and "backward types," all very subjective and liable to spread ever outwards: this was the way, for example, that the Bolsheviks were able to shift revolutionary consciousness away from the class to the party and to the party's leadership organs.

The rebuttal of Bolshevism's keynote ideas, such as "dictatorship of the proletariat," or the so-called "workers' or proletarian" state and the "transitional period," is not really convincing. The first of these was rejected as the rule of a minority over the majority and the opposite advocated, but Fontenis deemed the expression "improper, imprecise, open to misunderstandings." He saw the "proletarian" state exercising "organized constraint, made necessary by the inadequacy of economic development, the underdevelopment of human capabilities and initially at least waging a struggle against the vestiges of the formerly ruling classes defeated by the revolution or to be more exact defense of the revolutionary territory within and without." This explanation is highly questionable: we have seen how that "worker" state was the chief obstacle to genuine economic development and, even more so, of "human capabilities," which it squanders senselessly. As for the battle against the "vestiges" of the late system of exploitation, that boiled down to relentless police repression that did not stop at the physical elimination of entire classes (like the poor peasants who resisted collectivization in 1930–1940) and all sorts of recalcitrants. Apropos of the transitional period, Fontenis makes a distinction between the higher and lower stages of communism: the former, otherwise known as socialism, is characterized by a certain poverty that "means the ascendancy of the economic over the human, and thus some lingering limitation," which translates as "egalitarian rationing or redistribution through the agency of monetary bills of limited validity." Such a setup would still be marked by "notions or rank" and "wage differentials," albeit minimal, for it "would incline towards the greatest possible equalization, equivalence of circumstances." Pipe dreams! Punctured by all historical experience, in Russia and elsewhere. On the contrary, wage differentials or even gradations of redistribution have been the source from which a new class of exploiters has sprouted. Bakunin predicted as much with stunning clarity, as did others after him, and it seems astonishing that Fontenis should not have been aware of that. The inconsistency arises out of Fontenis's refusal to describe this "lower communism," leading on to "perfect communism," as a "transitional period," his view being that this term is inaccurate.

As regards organizational practice, the *Manifesto*'s author borrows willy-nilly from the *Platform* of *Dyelo Truda*, while playing up the vanguardist aspect.

There is a telling change in title between the article that appeared in *Le Libertaire* and the corresponding chapter in the pamphlet: "relations between the masses and the revolutionary organization" becomes "relations between the masses and the revolutionary vanguard." Yet the vanguard is described in exactly the same terms as in the *Platform*. It is neither ahead of, nor outside of the class or the masses, it "aims only to develop their capacity for self-organization" and deliberately takes up its position in their midst, for if it floats free of them, it "becomes a clique or a class." Be that as it may, the revolutionary anarchist specific organization becomes the "knowing, active vanguard of the popular masses." We might add that this latter expression is also loaded with all sorts of potential confusions, and conclude from that that a "revolutionary organization or party" so conceived was an attempt to embody the hegemonic revolutionary consciousness of the active anarchist minority, and set up shop in direct competition with the "phony" French Communist Party (PCF).

Thus far, the *Manifesto* and Fontenis's plan have been construed as an attempt to "Bolshevize" anarchism, for the belief was that they were both addressed to anarchists. On the other hand, if we were to take them as specially geared towards the labor militants of the day who were under the sway of Stalinism-Leninism, or even towards the sympathizers and dissidents of the PCF, then it is possible to decode the *Manifesto* in the opposite sense: as an attempt to "anarchize" these. In which case the confusions, contradictions or, if one prefers, the "obscurities" in the text suddenly become clear, when viewed through the lenses of such a readership. Subsequent events — the unbridled workerism, the outbidding of CGT and PCF slogans, the active commitment to the anti-colonialist struggle (the Algerian war), to begin with, and then the running in the legislative elections of 1956 and the comeback by André Marty, excluded from the PCF — appear to validate this construction.

It is plain that the mimicry of the Communist Party was part and parcel of an intention to overtake it on its left and on its stamping ground, the working class: but the FCL had neither the stomach nor the wherewithal for that task. That said, we cannot agree with Jean Maitron when he writes that it was a "synthesis between anarchism and a measure of Leninism," and "consonant with a platformist line but going further than Arshinov's theses."[7] In our view, it was rather an extreme attempt to promote social anarchism on the back of labor disputes, with the obsession with "impact" overtaking respect for a certain libertarian tradition. And this was not the only such instance that history has to show us; we have seen Emile Pouget's rejection of democratism within the CGT and the attempts at dictatorship with trying to convert the FAI into a political party during the Spanish Revolution. As we see it, the ancestry of this, in theoretical terms, can be traced to a certain anarchistic Blanquism (and let's not forget that Blanqui, towards the end of his life came up with the device "Neither God nor Master," making it the title of one of his publications). In support of this argument we should note that neither Pouget, nor Besnard, Garcia Oliver nor Horacio M. Prieto nor Fontenis ever, so far as we are aware, joined a Bolshevik organization. Which would necessarily have been their fate had they been drawn towards that teaching by their deepest convictions.

As regards the affinities between Fontenis's *Manifesto* and the *Platform* of the *Dyelo Truda* group and Arshinov's positions, they are unquestionably there, in the espousal of the class struggle as the driving force behind social struggles, as well as organizational principles. However, we have seen how Fontenis and his friends put them into effect through the OPB. Also, the *Platform* does not credit the working class with the same significance as Fontenis does: the former sees it only as a component part of the proletariat consisting essentially of the poor peasantry. Which may be explicable in terms of different historical make-ups of Russian and French society. The essential point on which they part company remains the option they chose to exercise: the *Platform* invited public debate inside the anarchist movement and relied upon collective deliberation and consciousness to move things forward; whereas Fontenis and his disciples resorted to underhand and bureaucratic ploys to impose their views.

The FCL's activities against the Algerian war resulted in the censoring and confiscation of *Le Libertaire*: heavy fines swallowed up its funds, leading in short order to the demise of the paper and the loss of its premises. In addition, its increasingly "heretical" policy choices led to disaffection among those militants who had remained faithful to libertarian communism. While there was no formal "death" certificate, it vanished from the political scene during the years 1957–1958.

We have quizzed ourselves as to the why and the wherefore of this extraordinary experiment in the anarchist movement's history, and we also approached Georges Fontenis for some basis on which to answer these questions. He very kindly replied to our inquiries and spelled out with concision the raison d'être of the OPB. His letter to us is reprinted as an appendix to this book. Let it be noted that he stands by and claims responsibility for matters concerning the OPB but appears to have his reservations about the evolution of the FCL in the 1954–1956 period. He has promised a detailed book in which he will "go over it all in detail and in a spirit of self-criticism." We will wager that that book will be very useful in arriving at a better understanding of certain aspects of this period which remain in obscurity.

### Endnotes to Chapter Eighteen

1. *Memorandum from the Kronstadt Group*, a 67-page pamphlet, (Paris, 1954), pp. 9–10.
2. Ibid., p. 20.
3. Ibid., p. 47–48.
4. Ibid., p. 52.
5. Quoted by Jean Maitron, op. cit., Tome II, p. 62.
6. G. Fontenis, *Manifeste du communisme libertaire,* (Editions Le Libertaire, 1953), 32 pages reissued in 1985 by Editions L.
7. J. Maitron, op. cit., p. 92.

# XIX. LIGHT AT THE END OF THE TUNNEL: MAY 1968

All the people who had either been expelled from the FAF while it was under the control of the Fontenists or who had walked out of it under their own steam came together towards the end of 1953 to relaunch the FAF, the Fontenist organization having taken the name FCL. Traumatized by their singular experience, they adopted very loose organizational ties, allowing a variety of strands and tendencies all professing to be anarchist to coexist with one another:

> a) the possibility and necessity of all tendencies working in concert; b) autonomy (i.e. absence of authority) for each group; c) abolition of all centralizing (National Committee-type) agencies; d) personal responsibility (never collective); e) the movement's organ to be above tendencies, with everybody at liberty to bring out his own organs … as well as to engage in any activity in the context of culture, research, action or anarchist propaganda; f) cordial and open relations with movements moving in an anarchist direction on a particular point.[1]

Social classes no longer played the same role in the struggle: their place was taken by "mind-sets." In the end, detailed statutes were drawn up and a Protective Association set up to fend off any new coup de force against the organization. The Louise Michel group from the Montmartre district of Paris, and the Sébastien Faure group from Bordeaux were the mainstays of the new FAF and of its mouthpiece *Le Monde Libertaire*.

Following an attempt in 1949 to have it made a ward of the FAF, the CNTF recovered its full freedom of action, but the fact that most of its membership was made up of Spaniards, hobbled politically by their refugee status, led it to withdraw into itself and focus upon the Iberian question. Its newspaper, *Le Combat Syndicaliste*, increasingly served as a vehicle for the Spanish CNT, until eventually it came to be published in the Spanish language (save for the front and back pages).

Several dissenting groups from the FCL, the Kronstadt Group for one, came together under the name of the CAAR (Anarchist Revolutionary Action Groups) and published an irregular magazine *Noir et Rouge*.

In their 1957 Statement of Principles, they also took on board the experience of the FCL, while coming out clearly for the platformist approach:

In the realm of direct action, the anarchist-communist organization is agreeable to alliance with proletarian militants or groups of militants in joint activities, for short-term or limited objectives, provided that the object of the struggle represents a step forward in the direction of workers' emancipation. In any event, it reserves the right to put forward its own positions.

Participation in our organization's work must be voluntary. It should, though, involve sufficient sense of responsibility for the inclinations and aversions of each individual to be freely and voluntarily subordinated to the interests of an adequate organization so that the coordinating of groups' activities may be handled effectively.

The anarchist communist specific organization comprises of a federation of affinity groups which have come to an agreement upon the principle of ideological unity, with an eye to presenting a united front of anarchists committed to the social struggle. Ideological unity is not made up of rigid principles, but will be susceptible to revision by way of necessary adaptation to an economic and social situation.

Unity of ideology implies unity of tactics. As we see it, tactical unity is recognition by the movement as a whole of the success of such and such a method in the hands of such and such a group, and a voluntary commitment from the rest to espouse it as their own. It is the acknowledgment by all groups that there is a need to use a common tactic with regard to such and such a specific problem which everybody recognizes they face in common. Moreover, it is consonant with federalism that each group should operate as it sees fit.

In this way, we will devise the basis upon which free individuals may organize themselves for effective action, while remaining free. In that spirit, with the ideals and in pursuit of the goal set down in this statement, let us press forwards, freely and in solidarity, in brotherhood.[2]

Meanwhile, the war in Algeria was raging, May 1958 had come and gone and General De Gaulle had been hoisted into power. Most anarchists did what they could, and their efforts were not negligible, for their solidarity with draft evaders and deserters was roundly affirmed (an underground railroad was to smuggle nearly 600 of these out to Switzerland). Anarchists also had a presence in all the street demonstrations, especially in 1961 and 1962. Some were involved in support networks for the Algerian FLN (this was by no means a unanimous choice, and, with the benefit of hindsight, we might query the point of it). The movement slowly clawed its way back. Some of the CAAR decided to return to the FAF and set up shop as the UGAC (Union of Anarchist Communist Groups); another faction carried on with the task of "clearing the ground" which had begun with the review *Noir et Rouge*, and published studies of the class struggle, revolutionary anti-clericalism, Freemasonry, nationalism, Marxism and the experiments in self-management in Spain, Israel (the kibbutzim), etc.

Following the death of Paul Zorkine, (a Montenegrin by birth and one-time member of the Yugoslav maquis), who was its leading light, as well as the retirement of his close colleague Henri Kléber, the UGAC went into a spectacular U-turn. Taking the line that no worthwhile activity was feasible inside the FAF, the UGAC reasserted its autonomy and espoused a somewhat bizarre strategy. Forswearing all autonomous activity, it presented itself as a component part of an "International Revolutionary Front" embracing other "revolutionaries," such as the Trotskyists of the Fourth International revolutionary Marxist school of thought (the Pabloists) and some pro-Chinese Swiss! In its *Letter to the International Anarchist Movement* published in 1966, it noted that that the revolution's center of gravity had shifted towards the Third World nations (colonial or colonized countries) and that it "would be dangerous for anarchists not to have a presence there." It also wondered if the "peoples achieving freedom are not also freeing the whole human race too."[3] In a way, it detected the new world proletariat in the Third World and turned Western workers into "bourgeois." Self-management, in existence in Algeria and in Yugoslavia (?!) (and later they would even detect the germ of it among the Vietnamese NLF!) was, in their view, the example to follow. The *Letter* concluded that "should our appeal, alas, go unheeded, we say plainly that anarchism will slide into reformism, in the most sordid complicity, and that, in any event, it would perish historically. Who would claim our inheritance?"[4] Instead, it was the members of the UGAC who were to slide more and more into absurdity and renegadism: clinging to their flirtation with "revolutionaries" in the name of a mythic, much touted self-management, they were, from 1968 on, to find a niche in associations made up of dissident Stalinists and a few bureaucrats hard up for fellow travelers. We might quote the opinion of some ex-members who abandoned it to its unenviable fate: "it locks anarchists into the caboose of a Leninist-powered revolutionary movement. That sort of thinking is either astoundingly naive or an addle-minded partisanship." [5]

That same year, the historian Daniel Guérin attempted to marry anarchism and Marxism (chalk and cheese): "By taking a bath in anarchism, today's Marxism can emerge cured of its pustules and regenerated."[6] To this end, he devised a "libertarian Marxism," praising it to the skies. And Maurice Fayolle came up with a real innovation by going into a scrupulous analysis of some of the key points of anarchism. We might dwell especially upon the distinction he draws between *decision-making power* and *executive power* in organizational matters. It is this distinction that sets the anarchist representative apart from a bureaucrat, for his mandate entitles him merely to carry out the directives or specific mandate entrusted to him by his organization. Fayolle also has an interesting, if traditional, approach to the role and behavior of the minority:

First: in no event may the minority, in the name of a false (barrack-style) discipline, be obliged to implement the decisions reached by the majority: the latter and the latter alone bears the responsibility for implementing those. On the other hand, the minority refrains (and this is where the real discipline comes into it) from obstructing the decisions reached by a majority at congress. It simply reserves its own right and chance of overturning that majority to its own advantage.

Second: for this proposition to be a practical reality, the minority (even should it amount only to a single individual) must be able to express itself freely at every level and in every organ of the movement, without the majority's being able to veto that on any pretext whatsoever.[7]

At about that time, the student world was in turmoil over all sorts of petty problems (visiting rights to the female quarters in the university residences, polemics with a few outmoded mandarins, etc.). On the Nanterre campus, members of the "non-group group" — an outgrowth of the review *Noir et Rouge* — and of the Enragés (Angries), close to the Situationists, provoked incidents which, spilling over into the Latin Quarter, in Paris, degenerated into violent clashes with the forces of law and order. All so-called leftist and revolutionary organizations were caught unprepared, sometimes absurdly so: on May 6, 1968, in the Rue Soufflot, as a peaceful demonstration was drawing to an end there, we heard a bespectacled character (probably a trainee teacher) calling upon everyone to "come and draw up leaflets under the workers' supervision at the Ecole Normale Supérieure, right around the corner!" Then came May 10th and the night of the barricades, crucial in the course of events. We can speak as an eyewitness in saying that no member of any of the Trotskyist, Maoist or Stalinist PCF grouplets (the UEC — Union of Communist Students) had any hand in it. Quite the contrary. All of those who were there to begin with attempted — before cowardice made them withdraw — as "heavyweight, responsible revolutionaries" to stop "provocateurs" from digging up the cobblestones and getting on with an enthusiastic and well worked out occupation of the place. Needless to say they were unceremoniously bundled aside. Not that that stops them from claiming all the credit for May 1968 for themselves these days. The protagonists of that watershed event were for the most part young people — most of them students or former students — reverting instinctively to the old revolutionary traditions of Paris cobblestones.

Those anarchists present on the spot that night did their duty as revolutionaries: they threw up several barricades and manned them into the early hours, especially the barricades controlling access to the Rue Mouffetard, the Rue Blainville, Rue Thouin, Rue de l'Estrapade, Rue du Pot de Fer, Rue Lhomond, and Rue Tournefort. They received welcome reinforcement from members of the FAF and the crowd coming from the Mutualité hall, where there had been a gala night on behalf of *Le Monde Libertaire*, with Leo Ferré at the top of the bill. Later, some of them took an active part in the Student-Worker Committees based at the Censier campus — the Committees from Citroen, Renault, and Thomson-Houston and others, when it was necessary to make a move right from the first to get the occupations and strikes rolling. This was a hard thing to do, for these factories were controlled by trade union pickets; even so, the results were extremely heartening. There were committees of all sorts; we recall one "sham" one at Renault, one evening two young Renault workers were brought before it, and it transpired that there was nobody of it except about thirty students or intellectuals, probably pro-Maoist, dreaming about the "workers' citadel," but devoid of any real connection with it. So it became necessary to vet and authenticate the identities of people and indeed to proceed with the bodily removal of Trotskyists from the FER (Federation of Revolutionary Students) and of PCF members who had had the effrontery to try to set up shop in Censier. The committees there occupied the third and fourth floors and they worked more effectively than at the Sorbonne, which had turned into an oriental bazaar of leftism. We should mention the launching by one comrade of a Paris-Province Committee, which dispatched agitprop teams and materials in every direction, including handbills and posters from the fine arts faculty, whose workshops had been made available right from the start at the request of that committee.[8] Stewards, in the shape of about ten members, were placed in charge of monitoring the comings and goings inside the Censier site. This had its uses in deterring "suspect" elements. Other comrades mounted a wall-newspaper and a standing discussion group at the Gobelins crossroads. All of this carried on for three weeks, day and night, with bed and board provided on the spot (throughout this time there was a canteen, known as the CLEOPS, and a Student-Peasant Committee organized by students from the Agricultural Institute, assisted by sympathetic truckers, saw to it that it was kept supplied regularly). That was only one of the examples to which we could testify personally, but there were other libertarians as well who gave unstintingly of themselves during May and whom it might be interesting to publicize some day.

The presence of anarchists was very noticeable during the May 13th and Charléty stadium marches, on account of the large number of black flags on display. The many libertarian slogans and subversive graffiti on the walls, the "adaptation" of advertising hoardings and other areas rehabilitated revolutionary lyricism. Subjectivity bounced back with a bang and all things became possible. However, despite some attempts to coordinate the Action Committees and at parallel economic organization, there was not sufficient collective determination to come up with a solution capable of replacing the eroding power of the state. The Stalinists of the CGT, in keeping with their counterrevolutionary vocation, did what the Gaullist government could not quite manage: by fraudulent votes, they forced a return to work at the RATP (Paris Autonomous Transport Authority), and overnight the system was placed back on its feet. Yet, for those who had been caught up as participants in the events, there could be no turning back the clock and the libertarian ethos of May restored their vigor and enthusiasm.

Written off as being on its deathbed, if not consigned already to the graveyard of history, anarchism became extraordinarily relevant again and aroused equally widespread curiosity, This fact made it possible to publish books on that topic and in comparatively significant numbers: of course, these were not all of the same quality, but it helped rescue a few famous writers from oblivion (writers like Déjacques, Coeuderoy, Proudhon, Bakunin, etc.) and above all to vindicate the true value of anarchism's historical experiences. The movement bookshops were inundated by a swarm of bulletins, pamphlets, handbills and posters.

In organizational terms, initially the stress was upon spontaneity, but as that retreated into limbo, it gave way to attempts at more enduring organizations. Let us allow Maurice Fayolle to draw the lessons from the events:

> In May–June 1968, we paid a high price for our 15 years of absenteeism and organizational vacuum. The ceaseless activities of a few comrades and a few groups could not make good that deficit And, at a time when Paris was bedecked with black flags, we glided through these events like ectoplasm through a mist, that is, without reaping all of the benefits which other leftist formations drained from them. Had we, at that point, had a worthwhile organization, like the FA of the years following the 1939–45 war, with its structures and its weekly newspaper, France today would have over two hundred organized groups and a press with a huge print run, in short, a numerous and very coherent anarchist movement which might make its voice heard in this country.[9]

We would not have posed the question in just those terms … of competing with the left, and of numerical terms strength … but would have focused more broadly upon the measure of the impact of libertarian ideas, though there were not enough militants to take them on board, but that boils down to essentially the same thing, for Maurice Fayolle reckons that the "infantile malady" of anarchism — its disorganization — proved a handicap to the movement when eminently favorable circumstances "the likes of which happen only rarely in a hundred years" came to pass. The "praiseworthy efforts of a few comrades and a few groups will have done little but rescue other people's chestnuts from the fire." Fayolle's analysis was to prove his testament, for he passed away a short time later. So let us focus all of our attention upon it. It regards organization as an *instrument* and not, of course as an end in itself. However, it is not an *indispensable instrument*. The essential points about it are that decisions should be made at a *collective* level, by *the* body of the membership. They must be made "not at the top, but at the bottom, not at the center but at the periphery." Given the geographical size and the difficulty of bringing groups together on a consistent basis, there must, necessarily, be delegates to take decisions at congresses, these latter being the seat of the organization's sovereignty. There must be no confusion between congress and "colloquium," an opportunity to exchange ideas. In order to guard against the accountability of coordinating or executive bodies turning into leadership powers or some immovable bureaucracy, there would have "to be constant monitoring by the grassroots and a frequent rotation of officers."

At the same time, one autonomous group, the Kronstadt Group (nothing to do with the group of the same name that issued the *Memorandum*) brought out a *Draft of Organization Principles* [10] for a libertarian communist organization. This was the product of around a decade of experience and as such attempted to derive lessons from that. Following an outline declaration regarding the nature and role of a revolutionary organization,[11] it went on to assert that there should be many such organizations, that is, that there may be several of them styling themselves revolutionary, but that "none may claim a monopoly": all of them "should aim towards unification in the act of revolution, thereby basing themselves upon comprehensive grassroots struggle bodies, embryonic Workers' Councils." This meant a break with the organizational chauvinism that had been so widespread hitherto, as well as a repudiation of all vanguardism. It was then specified that such an organization "as a means, ought to be matched with a fixed goal, which is to say that from its inception and as it develops, it must do away with the mental and social separations and divisions between the givers and the followers of orders, and not permit the reproduction of the pyramidal relationships existing in established society. *And not fight alienation through formats that alienate.*"

This *Draft* stipulated that it "goes without saying that affiliation to a revolutionary organization is incompatible with membership of any other organization whose nature and methods would not suit revolutionary aims." Organizational practice was directly inspired by the *Platform*, with its phrasing brought up to date. There was mention of a policy line underpinning the organization's collective approach. By policy line we should understand a range of general and particular standpoints on basic relevant issues: this would not be set in concrete because it would be subject to "permanent exchange of the analyses and experiences of the membership as a body." There was a basic underlying point in that decisions arrived at collectively would be binding upon all members. The organizational operation was highly detailed: in fact, it reiterated all of the essentials of earlier organizational practices: the *Statutes* of Bakunin's Alliance, the quintessence of platformist documents and the experiences of the 1960s (see especially the text partly reprinted as an appendix). That *Draft* formed the basis for the creation of the Libertarian Communist Movement (MCL), an assemblage of about a hundred militants, Georges Fontenis among them. He had surfaced again in May 1968 on the Action Committee in Tours: in fact, he was commissioned to draw up the organization's basic charter. A little later, negotiations were entered into with the Revolutionary Anarchist Organization (ORA) which had been formed on the basis of Maurice Fayolle's thinking. The ORA at first was affiliated to the FAF and then, following a falling-out over the organization of the International Anarchist Congress scheduled to be held in Paris in 1971, became autonomous.

The organizational creeds of the two organizations were close (see the appendices for the ORA's organizational compact), but personal differences and splitter maneuvers ruled out amalgamation. The ORA carried on with its theoretical deliberations, which it offered in the form of reports to the Paris International Congress in August 1971, without any positive response, for that congress spent its time settling political and personal scores (Augustin Souchy, the aged, German anarchist acting as the delegate for the Cuban Anarchist Federation, was shamefully expelled, accused of being in cahoots with the CIA!).

We should note that the ORA's organizational practice met with some measure of success, especially in the creation of about a hundred *Front Libertaire* circles, up until this expansion was compromised and halted by a whole flurry of political and police provocations,[12] on the one hand, and by a somewhat zombie-like vision of militant activity, due to an exaggerated leftism, on the other. We might note as well the predominant role played by a "historic core" of ORA founders, which operated as a hidden policy leadership, even though they were well-known to and above all tolerated by most of the organization.

The years 1970–1976 were, as a result, racked by numerous splits or straight-forward disappearances (such as the demise of the review *Noir et Rouge*).[13] In the final analysis, the ORA and the OCL (formerly the MCL) ended up being supplanted by two more enduring organizations: the OCL (heir to the ORA) and the UTCL (Union of Libertarian Communist Workers, tinged with councilism and Marxism) which, to this day, profess to be of the libertarian communist persuasion. This reversal from the thousands of militants who have made that claim since 1968 is striking. How come? It may perhaps be attributable to a period of digestion of ideas, needed if confusionism was to be avoided, and also to the overall context of the country, with lots of people retreating into their personal concerns, and most of all to the absence of any credible libertarian alternative to the established system.

For the past decade or so, the French anarchist movement has been more sober and there have not been any more of these upheavals. The most important organization, the FAF, has rounded the horn by endowing itself with good propaganda resources: a radio station, a weekly paper and a superb bookshop. In addition, it has overhauled its basic principles, acknowledging the existence of the class struggle, of which "the object ought to be the establishment of an anarchist society": it "urges workers and the exploited as a whole to fight the mediation that runs counter to their class interests, and to opt for direct action (that is, for actions determined and carried out without intervention of inter-mediaries) and coordination along federalist lines." While linking up with so-cial anarchism, it nevertheless retains the organizational character of a synthesis, repudiating collective responsibility and advocating that responsibility be personal. It depends upon several dozen groups, some of which are very firmly established locally, and which often publish superbly produced periodicals.

Alongside these, there are the anarcho-syndicalists — scattered around the various trade unions — and a number of groups connected with the publication of reviews, magazines and quality newspapers. To which we might add several libertarian cooperatives: bookshops, restaurants, printing-works (eight of them in France at one point) and even self-managing farms. It is to be regretted that information about all these ventures does not circulate more freely: we hope that this oversight may be repaired so that this libertarian cooperative trend can flourish.

For anyone who experienced the years in the wilderness between 1958 and 1968, all such signs and ventures — indicative of the movement's life — are gratifying, and so let us not be too persnickety and regret that there is not more intervention in social struggles. We just hope that there can be level-headed and positive collaboration by all who subscribe to anarchism in every sphere.

## Endnotes to Chapter Nineteen

1. Quoted by Roland Biard, *Histoire du mouvement anarchists 1945–1975,* (Paris: Editions Galilée, 1976), pp. 112–113.
2. Quoted in *Noir et Rouge: Anthologie,* (Paris: Spartacus and Acratie, 1982), pp. 28–29.
3. *Lettre au mouvement anarchists international* published by the UGAC, (Montreux, Switzerland, 1966), pp. 26–27. The UCAC later turned into the TAC (Anarchist Communist Tendency).
4. Ibid., p. 69.
5. *Continuons le débat, bulletin anarchiste-communiste,* No. 1, (November 1970), p. 3.
6. Daniel Guérin, *Pour un Marxisme libertaire,* (Paris: Robert Laffont, 1969), p. 17.
7. Maurice Fayolle, *Réflexions sur l'anarchisme,* (Paris: Publico, 1965) pp. 26 and 42.
8. The first poster, a one-off, showed a chicken with Pompidou's head, complete with a worm in its mouth, and was sent anonymously to the provinces, despite the repeated requests from some necrophiliac collectors of revolutionary ephemera.
9. Maurice Fayolle, *Contribution à l'élaboration d'un manifeste anarchists révolutionnaire in L'organization libertaire,* No. 6, (June 1970), pp. 32-33.
10. Six page text, published at the beginning of 1971. The Kronstadt Group had been in existence from 1969 to 1971 and numbered about ten members, including, at one time or another, Daniel Guérin, Roland Biard and the present author, who was in fact chiefly responsible for drawing up the *Draft.*
11. Reprinted at the opening to this book.
12. We might mention the case of a certain Marco, a Spaniard who had fled to France as a draft dodger: he was exposed at a Paris gathering of the ORA for having thrice had criminal charges against him dropped: the majority of those present, "Christian-minded" folk as Jean Grave might have described them, refused to expel him. They had cause to regret this, for this Marco suddenly "discovered" Marxism and the Lenin of *The State and Revolution* and managed to take a dozen followers with him when he went over to the Trotskyist JCR (which went on to become the Ligue Communiste we know today). A little later, he was behind the authorities' banning of that organization when he brought a rifle into its premises on the very morning of the search that drew the thunderbolt from the courts! This time he was denounced on an international scale! The ORA was also lacking in vigilance in several other "shady" affairs, which resulted in a rush of defections from it.
13. Which Christian Lagant, another who perished tragically, explained away in terms of "our own disorganization (theoretical problems; lack of common analyses; inability to take May 1968 on board and draw the necessary political conclusions from it; practical difficulties; also our inability to overcome our division into manual- and brain-workers, which did exist despite our being "thinkers," and thus our failure to ensure proper rotation of material tasks) was to steer us into failure," in *Notes sur la composition sociale, l'évolution du mouvement libertaire de 1950 à nos jours* (undated) p. 8.

# XX. MATCHING ENDS AND MEANS

In the course of our look at anarchist thinking and anarchist organizational and social practice, we have chosen to focus upon three countries — France, Russia and Spain — which have struck us as being, historically, fertile ground for anarchism. In addition, these are relatively well-known examples. Now, in order to get a more comprehensive view of our theme, we would also have had to tackle the anarchist movement, which has occasionally been very powerful at certain points in history, in countries like Bulgaria, Italy, Portugal, China, Korea, Japan, Mexico, Argentina with its FORA, not to mention the United States. This was not feasible, due to lack of space and time. (We would have had to write a book ten times the length of this one.) Furthermore, we have refrained from commenting overmuch upon the writings and attitudes we have cited — most of them little known and not readily accessible — for the very same reasons, and we leave it to the reader to arrive unaided at the critical opinions that are needed. All because of the limitations we have imposed upon ourselves.

One considerable problem to be resolved relates to the usage of an elastic terminology which is occasionally dated in historical terms and occasionally mutilated in translation, for precise equivalents are not readily available. Purely anarchist jargon also creates problems. "Anarchist" and "libertarian," two synonyms of roughly the same vintage — from 1840–1850 — are in common currency: on the other hand, with regard to "anarchist communist" and "libertarian communist" — likewise contemporary terms, from 1876 and 1881 — we have chosen to favor the latter, meaning both "common ownership and the free commune," over the former, which has become vaguely equivalent to "anarcho-Bolshevik." Plainly, the term "communism" has been perverted by the Bolsheviks, who, however, did not adopt it until very late on, in 1918, but the same could be said of "revolution," the meaning of which has been comprehensively mauled. Optimum precision is to be desired, for mix-ups or misunderstandings can give rise to real tragedies, if one thinks of the example of the "soviet," let alone "soviet power," sweeteners that Lenin used in order to establish his totalitarian dictatorship. One should not toy with words for they can kill: that is one of the lessons to be learned there. They should be invested or reinvested with their original import.

For anarchists, certain words are taboo, and rightly so: words like "chief," "party," "center" and "state." Others are, in our estimation, misapplied: "Marxism" especially, which is systematically equated with Leninism-Stalinism, when it is mainly applicable to economic analyses and, strictly speaking, to the pre-1914 German Social Democracy. "Bolshevik" is regularly used instead of "Jacobin" or "Blanquist." "Politics" is taken in its politicking sense, when often it ought to be read in its Aristotelian sense of "civic life." "Power" has become synonymous with central power and the state, when the making and implementation of any decision is an act of power: there is power over the self, over one's life, and power over others, rule over others. As we have seen, Fayolle thus draws a distinction between powers of decision-making and executive powers. In short, we need to know what we are talking about, and a regularly updated dictionary might be very useful. Let us, then, bear such nuances in mind before we tackle any text, and our reading and understanding of it will be all the better for that.

Likewise it should be obvious by now that a libertarian organization is not some tool acting in obedience to orders emanating from on high or from some central point, but rather a theater for the implementation of mutual aid and a way of blending individual endeavors, so as to bestow upon them, in so doing, greater social impact. Should that organization be permanent, ad hoc, specific or broadly-based? Let us answer with a statement of the obvious: it all depends on the aim. Here, we reckon we must not forget to distinguish between varieties: there are propaganda-type organizations, affinity organizations, social struggle organizations or armed struggle organizations, depending on whether the point is to publicize libertarian ideas, bring out some magazine or newspaper, organize some trades or trade union group, or mount a popular uprising. It all depends, too, upon the conditions in which one finds oneself: whether one is in one of the couple of dozen nations in the world where formal freedoms exist that "genuinely" permit propaganda, or elsewhere in the vast majority of the planet, where the mere words anarchy and freedom are banned from everyday usage. Thus there is an adjustment to be made between the organization's open or clandestine nature and a strategy and tactics adapted to the local reality. We should specify, though, that violent activities — armed, or terrorist activities — we regard as not merely uncalled for, but indeed worthy of condemnation in countries where there is toleration of the free spread of ideas.

That said, as we have seen, organization adds up to more than a sum of individuals: it represents a strength of numbers — a synergy — that can get a real purchase on reality. Should it lack suppleness, mobility or dynamism, it inescapably turns into a lumbering machine, if not open bureaucracy. How can we strike a harmonious balance between the conscious, autonomous individual and the organizational approach? The individual is at one and the same time the strength and the weakness of anarchism: like Aesop's language, it can be both the best and the worst of things. When it comes down to a solution, we confess our own preference for Bakunin's: "ongoing fraternal monitoring of each by all." That, it seems to us, is the only antidote to any descent into bureaucracy. At that stage, an organization is only as good as its individual members: if these abjure all critical faculties and are lacking in vigilance, even the best of organizational statutes avail nothing. Leaders, chiefs and guides are made by the passive, the inert, the "mealy-mouthed." Let us not deceive ourselves: organizational and social practice is not for angels and many often fall for the easy way out. We might add the inevitable gap between thought, the spoken word, the printed word and the deed, to underline the vital necessity for clarity on everyone's part, that being the sole guarantee of the degree of consistency between those four levels of expression and action. Here we must be plain and categorical: a promise made and an undertaking given should be honored; otherwise, nothing can be achieved. Acting upon them is an absolute necessity if the wasting of time and energy is to be avoided.

Practical operational structures are a lesser evil in mediation between individuals: their implications cannot in any way be kept check by the acceptance of the rules of the organizational game; voting, delegation, specific and imperative mandates. The right attitude and fraternal intent should antedate the internal relations. Thus, majority and minority should be capable, should the need arise, of making the requisite concessions: otherwise all concerted activity remains impossible. There should be a greater sensitivity to what unites rather than to that which divides. In any event, things would be same in the yearned for free society. If the common denominator among anarchists is the refusal to kowtow to systems of oppression, a negative attitude, this ought to be counterbalanced by the will to unity, a positive attitude. Obviously, spirit and letter are not the same thing, although the one inspires the other. All organizational fetishes — card-carrying, subscriptions stamps, meeting-mania, etc., — strike us as obsolete and dangerous, and therefore to be avoided: they could profitably be replaced by the intensive and consistent communication of information.

As a sometimes minuscule minority in mass society, revolutionaries fight for themselves as much as for everyone. Being an anarchist is not just a matter of striking rebellious poses against every trespass against one's autonomy — every healthy individual is perfectly capable of that — but, in terms of behavior, which is its ethic acted out, is a matter of being true to oneself and others. This is how the rebel breaks free of the ruler/ruled schizophrenia of contemporary society. Libertarian communism, the most rounded form of direct democracy, is a collective assertion of his determination to exist.

# TEXTS AND DOCUMENTS

## INTRODUCTION

Our interest in the *Platform* dates from 1964, when we embarked upon our investigation of the Makhnovist movement. That document struck us as the condensation of the experiences accumulated within that movement by its two main authors — Arshinov and Makhno — although, to judge by the testimony (collected during 1970–1971) of Ida Mett, a member of the *Dyelo Truda* group, there were many involved in the discussion of it. As early as 1967, we came up with a translation of these basic libertarian communist texts. It was also necessary to trace its theoretical ancestry, its posterity and its relevancy, and above all to make known the Ukrainian insurgent movement that was their inspiration.

This we have now done with our book *The Cossack of Freedom* and the anthology of Nestor Makhno's *Political Writings*. The *Platform* and the controversy it triggered are thus part and parcel of that extraordinary historical experience and they help focus attention upon the crucial issue in anarchism: its organized practice.

We ought to remember that the original translation by Voline was called into question as "bad and clumsy," the translator having failed to "bother to adapt his terminology and vocabulary to the mentality of the French movement." We have searched for what could have prompted such criticisms and we discovered in fact that there are several terms that have deliberately been travestied: *napravieniye*, which means both "direction" and "orientation" has been systematically translated as the former: likewise the word *rukovodstvo*, meaning "conduct," and its derivative "guidance, leadership, direction, administration" have been systematically rendered as "leadership." An even more blatant instance is the closing expression of the *Platform*, *zastreishchik*, meaning "instigator," which has been rendered as "vanguard." In this manner, by deft touches, the document's underlying meaning has been tampered with. All of which is annoying, for the translator, Voline, then went on to become the main detractor of the *Platform*. For our own part, we have adhered as closely as possible to the literal meaning and we hope we have been faithful to its spirit.

We have added a number of other texts and articles in chronological order, to afford a better picture of the debate initiated. We should have liked to add the *Reply* from Voline and his friends but its extreme length and the prospect of having to contend with possible copyright difficulties deterred us from doing so. Maybe somebody else will have more success there? The better to convey the relevance of the issue, we thought of reprinting the Kronstadt Group's *Organizational Principles* and the *Organizational Contract* of the Revolutionary Anarchist Organization (ORA), both of them dating from 1971. They could give some idea of the practicalities of the operations of a libertarian communist organization in the *Platform* tradition. Finally, until such time as his book becomes available, the letter from Georges Fontenis offers an outline explanation of that extraordinary phenomenon, the OPB.

— Alexandre Skirda

## Endnote to the Introduction to Texts and Documents

1. *Le Libertaire,* No. 106, (April 15, 1927).

# Document No. 1
# The Problem of Organization and the Notion of Synthesis

Several comrades have had their say in the columns of *Dyelo Truda* regarding the question of anarchist principles and organizational format.

Not that they all approached the problem from the same angle. The essence of this matter, as spelled out by the editorial staff of *Dyelo Truda*, consists of the following:

We anarchists who agitate and fight for the emancipation of the proletariat, must, at all costs, have an end of the dissipation and disorganization prevailing in our ranks, for these are destroying our strength and our libertarian endeavors.

The way to go about this is to create an organization that might not perhaps enfold all of anarchism's active militants, but assuredly the majority of them, on the basis of specific theoretical and tactical positions and would bring us to a firm understanding as to how these might be applied in practice.

It goes without saying that the tackling of this issue should go hand in hand with the elaboration of theoretical and tactical positions that would furnish the basis, the platform for this organization. For we should be wasting our time talking about the need to organize our forces and nothing would come of it, were we not to associate the idea of such organization with well-defined theoretical and tactical positions.

The Group of Russian Anarchists Abroad has never lost sight of this latter question. In a series of articles carried in *Dyelo Truda* its viewpoint has been spelled out in part on the important particulars of the program: anarchism's relationship to the toilers' class struggle, revolutionary syndicalism, the transitional period, etc.

Our next task will be to arrive at a clear formulation of all these positions of principle, then to set them all out in some more or less rounded organizational platform which will serve as the basis for uniting a fair number of militants and groups into one and the same organization. The latter will in turn serve as a springboard to a more complete fusion of the anarchist movement's forces.

That then is the route we have chosen to a resolution of the organizational problem. It is not our intention to proceed on this occasion with a total re-examination of values or elaboration of any new positions. Our view is that everything necessary for the construction of an organization founded upon a given platform can be found in Libertarian Communism which espouses the class struggle, the equality and liberty of every worker, and is realized in the anarchist Commune.

Those comrades who champion the notion of a theoretical synthesis of anarchism's various currents have quite another approach to the organizational question. It is a pity that their view is so feebly spelled out and elaborated and that it is thus hard to devise a thoroughgoing critique of it. Essentially, their notion is as follows: Anarchism is divided into three strands: communist anarchism, anarcho-syndicalism and individualist anarchism. Although each of these strands has features particular to itself, all three are so akin and so close to one another that it is only thanks to an artificial misconception that they enjoy separate existences.

In order to give rise to a strong, powerful anarchist movement, it is necessary that they should fuse completely. That fusion, in turn, implies a *theoretical* and *philosophical* synthesis of the teachings upon which each of the strands is founded. It is only after theoretical synthesis of these teachings that we can tackle the structure and format of an organization representing all three tendencies. Such then is the content of the synthesis thus conceived, as set out in the "Declaration on anarchists' working together," and in a few articles by comrade Voline carried by *The Anarchist Messenger* and *Dyelo Truda* (Nos. 8 and 9). We are in total disagreement with this idea. Its inadequacy is glaringly obvious. For a start, why this arbitrary division of anarchism into three strands? There are others as well. We might mention, say, Christian anarchism, associationism, which, be it said in passing, is closer to communist anarchism than to individualist anarchism. Then again, what precisely is the consistency of the "theoretical and philosophical" discrepancies between the aforementioned three tendencies, if a synthesis between them is to be devised?

For one thing, before we talk about a theoretical synthesis of communism, syndicalism and individualism, we would need to analyze these currents. Theoretical analysis would quickly show the extent to which the wish to synthesize these currents is harebrained and absurd. Indeed, does not talk of a "synthesis between communism and syndicalism" signify some sort of contrast between them? Many anarchists have always regarded syndicalism as one of the forms of the proletarian revolutionary movement, as one of the fighting methods espoused by the working class in fighting for its emancipation.

We regard Communism as the goal of the laboring classes' liberation movement.

So, can the end be in contradiction with the means? Only the wobbly reasoning of some dilettante intellectual ignorant of the history of libertarian communist thought could place them side by side and seek to arrive at a synthesis of them. [That is, Voline — A.S.] For our own part, we are well aware that libertarian communism has always been syndicalist in that it regards the existence and expansion of independent professional organizations as a necessity for the social victory of the toilers.

So it could only be, and was in reality only a matter, not of a theoretical synthesis of communism and syndicalism, but rather of the role that syndicalism should be assigned in communist anarchism's tactics and in the social revolution of the toilers.

The theoretical inadequacies of the supporters of the synthesis is even more striking when they seek to arrive at a synthesis between communism and individualism.

In fact, what does the anarchism of individualists consist of? The notion of the freedom of the individual?

But what is this "individuality"? Is it the individuality of the individual in general or the oppressed "individuality" of the toiler?

There is no such thing as "individuality in general," because, one way or another, every individual finds himself objectively or subjectively in the realm of labor or else in the realm of capital. But isn't that idea implicit in libertarian communism? We might even say that the freedom of the individual qua toiler is realizable only in the context of a libertarian communist society that will take a scrupulous interest in social solidarity as well as in respect for the rights of the individual.

The anarchist commune is the model of social and economic relations best suited to fostering the development of the freedom of the individual. Anarchist communism is not some rigid, unbending social framework which, once achieved, is set and sets a term to the development of the individual. On the contrary: its supple, elastic social organization will develop by growing in complexity and constantly seeking improvements, so that the freedom of the individual may expand without hindrance.

Similarly, anti-Statism seems to be one of the fundamental principles of communist anarchism. In addition, it has a real content and a real expression.

Communist anarchism rejects statism in the name of social independence and the self-management of the laboring classes. As for individualism, on what basis does it refute the state? Assuming that it does! Certain individualist theoreticians champion the right to private ownership in personal relations and in economic relations alike. But wheresoever the principles of private property and personal fortunes exist, a struggle of economic interests inevitably comes into being, a statist structure created by the economically more powerful.

So what remains of individualist anarchism? Negation of the class struggle, of the principle of an anarchist organization having as its object the free society of equal workers: and, moreover, empty babble encouraging workers unhappy with their lot to look to their defenses by means of recourse to the personal solutions allegedly open to them as liberated individuals.

But what is there in all this that can be described as anarchist? Where are we to find the features in need of synthesis with communism? That whole philosophy has nothing to do with anarchist theory or anarchist practice: and it is unlikely that an anarchist worker would be inclined to conform to this "philosophy."

So, as we have seen, an analysis of the theoretical tasks of the synthesis leads into a dead end street. And we find the same again when we examine the practical aspect of the issue. We have to choose between two options:

Either the tendencies named remain independent *tendencies*, in which case, how are they going to prosecute their activities in some *common organization*, the very purpose of which is precisely to attune anarchists' activities to a specific agreement?

Or these tendencies should lose their distinguishing features and, by amalgamating, give rise to a new tendency that will be neither communist, syndicalist nor individualist…. But in that case, what are its fundamental positions and features to be?

By our reckoning the notion of synthesis is founded upon a total aberration, a shoddy grasp of the basics of the three tendencies, which the supporters of synthesis seek to amalgamate into one.

The central tendency, the spinal column of anarchism is represented by communist anarchism. Anarcho-individualism is at best only a philosophical/literary phenomenon and not a social movement. It often happens that the latter is drawn into politics and ends up as a bourgeois fad (like Tucker and other individualists).

The above does not at all mean that we are against concerted endeavor by anarchists of varying persuasions. Quite the opposite: we can only salute anything that brings revolutionary anarchists closer together in *practice*.

However, that can be achieved practically, concretely, by means of the establishment of liaison between ready made, strengthened organizations, In which case, we would be dealing only with specific *practical tasks*, requiring no synthesis and indeed precluding one. But we think that, the more that anarchists clarify the basics — the essence of libertarian communism — the more they will come to agreement on these principles and erect upon that basis a broad organization that will provide a lead in socio-political matters as well as in the realm of trade union/professional matters.

As a result, we do not in any way see a link between the organizational problem and the notion of synthesis. If it is to be resolved, there is no need to get carried away by vague theorizations and expect results from that. The baggage that anarchism has amassed over the years of its life process and social struggle is more than sufficient. We need only take proper account of it, applying it to the conditions and exigencies of life, in order to build up an accountable organization.

The Group of Russian Anarchists Abroad.
The Staff of *Dyelo Truda*. From *Dyelo Truda* No. 10, (March 1926).

## DOCUMENT NO. 2:
## THE GROUP OF RUSSIAN ANARCHISTS ABROAD
## THE ORGANIZATIONAL PLATFORM OF THE GENERAL
## UNION OF ANARCHISTS (DRAFT) JUNE 20,1926

### INTRODUCTION

Anarchists!

For all of the cogency and unquestionably positive character of libertarian ideas, of the clarity and integrity of anarchist positions with regard to the social revolution, and finally the heroism and countless sacrifices contributed by anarchists in the struggle for libertarian communism, it is very telling that the anarchist movement has, in spite of all this, always stayed weak and most often featured in the history of workers' struggles, not as a determining factor, but rather as a fringe phenomenon.

This contrast between the positive basis and incontrovertible validity of libertarian ideas and the wretched condition in which the anarchist movement is forever mired, is explicable in terms of a range of factors, the chief one being the absence of hard and fast principles and of a consistent organizational praxis.

In every country, the anarchist movement is represented by some local organizations, often espousing a contradictory theory and tactics, with no forward planning, nor continuity of militant endeavor, habitually evaporating almost without leaving any trace behind them.

Such a condition in revolutionary anarchism, if we take it as a whole, cannot be described as anything other than a "chronic general disorganization."

Like the yellow fever, this disease of disorganization has invaded the organism of the anarchist movement and has had it on the rack for some decades.

It is not in doubt, however, that this disorganization has its roots in a number of shortcomings of a theoretical order: notably in a mistaken interpretation of the principle of individuality in anarchism: that principle being too often mistaken for the absence of all accountability. Those enamored of asserting their "ego" solely with an eye to personal pleasure cling stubbornly to the chaotic condition of the anarchist movement and, in defense thereof, invoke the immutable principles of Anarchy and its theoreticians.

Now, the immutable principles and the theoreticians demonstrate the very opposite.

Dispersion and dissipation spell ruination. Close union is the guarantor of life and of development. That law of social struggle is equally applicable to classes and to parties.

Anarchism is not some beautiful dream, nor some abstract notion of philosophy: it is a social movement of the toiling masses. For that reason alone, it must gather its forces into *one umbrella organization, forever acting as the reality and the strategy of the social struggle that the classes require of it.*

Kropotkin said: "*We are convinced that the formation of an anarchist party in Russia, far from doing prejudice to the common revolutionary endeavor, is instead desirable and useful in the highest degree.*" (Foreword to Bakunin's *Paris Commune*, 1892 edition)

Bakunin too never opposed the idea of an anarchist umbrella organization. On the contrary: his aspirations with regard to organization, as well as his activities within the First WorkingMen's International, entitle us to look upon him as an active advocate, indeed, of such an organization.

Broadly speaking, nearly all of the active militants of anarchism were against all dissipated action and dreamed of an anarchist movement bound together by a commonality of end and means.

It was during the Russian revolution of 1917 that the need for an umbrella organization made itself felt most plainly and most imperiously. It was during the course of that revolution that the libertarian movement displayed the greatest degree of dismemberment and confusion, The absence of an umbrella organization induced many of anarchism's active militants to defect to the ranks of the Bolsheviks. It is also the reason why many other militants find themselves today in a condition of passivity that thwarts any utilization of their resources, which are moreover often of great importance.

We have a vital need of an organization which, having attracted most of the participants in the anarchist movement, might prescribe for anarchism a general tactical and policy line and might thereby serve as a guide for the whole movement.

It is high time that anarchism emerged from the swamps of disorganization to put paid to the interminable dithering in the most important theoretical and tactical matters, and set off in search of a clearly conceived goal and pursued an organized collective practice.

It is not enough, though, to register the vital necessity of such an organization: it is also necessary to settle upon a means of establishing it.

We repudiate as theoretically and practically inept the idea of creating an organization using the recipe of the "synthesis," that is to say, bringing together representatives of the various strands of anarchism. Such an organization, having embraced motley elements (in terms of their theory and practice) would be nothing more than a mechanical assemblage of persons with varying views on all issues affecting the anarchist movement: that assemblage would inevitably break up on impact with life.

The anarcho-syndicalist approach does not resolve anarchism's organizational difficulty, for it fails to give priority to it and is interested only in penetrating and making headway into workers' circles.

However, even with a foothold there, there is nothing much to be accomplished there, if we do not have an anarchist umbrella organization.

The only approach leading to a solution of the problem of an umbrella organization is, as we see it, recruitment of anarchism's active militants on the basis of hard and fast positions: theoretical, tactical and organizational, which is to say on the more or less rounded basis of *a homogeneous program*.

The drafting of such a program is one of the chief tasks with which the social struggle in recent years has confronted anarchists. It is to that task that the Group of Russian Anarchists Abroad has dedicated a significant fraction of its efforts.

*The Platform of Organization* published below, represents, in outline, the skeleton of just such a program. It should serve as a first step towards the gathering of libertarian forces into a single, active revolutionary grouping poised for action: the General Union of Anarchists.

We have no illusions about this or that deficiency in this present *Platform*. Beyond all doubt, deficiencies it does possess, as in fact does any practical new departure of note. It may be that certain essential positions have been left out, or that certain others have not been dealt with adequately, or that still others may be there, but in too much detail or with undue repetition. All of which is possible. But that is not the most important point.

What matters is that the groundwork be laid for a general organization. And that is the aim achieved, to a requisite extent, by the present *Platform*.

It is up to the whole collectivity — the General Union of Anarchists — to go on to expand upon and explore it so as to turn it into a definite program for the whole anarchist movement.

On another score also we have no illusions. We anticipate that several representatives of individualism, so-called, and of "chaotic" anarchism are going to attack us, foaming at the mouth and charge us with having infringed anarchist principles.

Yet we know that these individualist and chaotic elements take the phrase "anarchist principles" to mean the cavalier attitude, negligence and utter absence of accountability, that have inflicted all but incurable injuries upon our movement, and against which we struggle with all our energy and enthusiasm. That is why we can, with equanimity, ignore attacks emanating from that quarter.

Our hopes are vested in other militants: in those who have kept faith with anarchism, who have lived out the tragedy of the anarchist movement and are painfully searching for an escape.

Finally, we have high hopes of the anarchist youth, born in the shadow of the Russian revolution and absorbed, from the outset by the round of constructive problems and who will assuredly insist upon the implementation of positive organizational principles in anarchism.

We invite all the Russian anarchist organizations scattered across the globe, as well as isolated militants, to come together into a single revolutionary grouping, on the basis of a common organizational Platform.

May this *Platform* furnish all of the militants of the Russian anarchist movement with a revolutionary watchword and rallying point! May it lay the foundations of the General Union of Anarchists!

Long live the Social Revolution of the world's Toilers!

— The Group of Russian Anarchists Abroad
For the Group, Secretary Piotr Arshinov, June 20, 1926

## GENERAL PART

### 1. Class Struggle, Its Role and Its Meaning
**"There is no ONE mankind. There is a mankind made up of classes: slaves and masters."**

Like all of its predecessors, the capitalist and bourgeois society of our day is not "one." It is split into two very distinct camps, differing socially in their position and function: the proletariat (in the broadest sense of the word) and the bourgeoisie.

The lot of the proletariat has, for centuries now, been to bear the brunt of taxing physical labor the fruits of which devolve, however, not to itself, but rather to another, privileged class that enjoys property, authority and the products of learning (science, education and art): the bourgeoisie. The social enslavement and exploitation of the toiling masses form the basis upon which modern society stands and without which that society could not exist. This fact gave rise to a secular class struggle sometimes assuming an open, violent form, sometimes undetectable and slow, but always, essentially, directed towards the transformation of the existing society into a society that would satisfy the toilers' needs, requirements and conception of justice.

In social terms, the whole of human history represents an unbroken series of struggles waged by the toiling masses in pursuit of their rights, their liberty and a better life. At all times in the history of human societies, that class struggle has been the principal factor determining the shape and structures of those societies.

The political and social system of any country is primarily the product of the class struggle. The structure assumed by any society shows us the position at which the class struggle has finished or presently stands. The slightest change in the tide of the battle between the classes and the relative strengths of the contending classes inevitably produces amendments to the fabric and structures of the society.

Such are the general, global implications and import of the class struggle in the life of class societies.

## 2. The Necessity of a Violent Social Revolution

The principle of the enslavement and exploitation of the masses through violence lies at the root of modern society. All of the manifestations of its existence: economics, politics, social relations, repose upon class violence, whose auxiliary agencies are the authorities, the police, the army, the courts. Everything in that society: every undertaking considered separately, as well as the whole state system, is nothing but a bulwark of capitalism from which the toilers are forever being monitored, and where forces designed for crushing any movement by the workers that may threaten the foundations or even the tranquillity of the present society, are on constant stand-by.

At the same time, the arrangement of that society deliberately keeps the toiling masses in a condition of ignorance and mental stagnation: it forcibly prevents the raising of their moral and intellectual levels, the more readily to lord it over them.

The advances of modern society: the technological evolution of Capital and the amelioration of its political system, reinforce the might of the ruling classes and make the struggle against them increasingly difficult, thereby postponing the crucial moment when Labor achieves emancipation.

Analysis of modern society leads us to the conclusion that violent social revolution is the only route to transformation of capitalist society into a society of free workers.

## 3. Anarchism and Libertarian Communism

Among the oppressed, the class struggle spawned by the enslavement of the toilers and their aspirations to freedom engender the idea of anarchism: the idea of the complete negation of the social system based upon the class and state principles, and of the replacement of these by a free, stateless society of self-governing toilers.

Thus anarchism was born, not of the abstract deliberations of some sage or philosopher, but out of the direct struggle waged by the toilers against Capital, out of the toilers' needs and requirements their aspirations towards liberty and equality, aspirations that become especially vivid in the most heroic stages of the toiling masses' life and struggle.

Anarchism's leading thinkers: Bakunin, Kropotkin, and others, did not invent the idea of anarchism, but, having discovered it among the masses, they merely helped refine and propagate it through the excellence of their thinking and their learning.

Anarchism is not the outcome of personal endeavor, nor the object of individual quests. Likewise, anarchism is not at all the product of humanitarian aspirations, A "singular" humanity does not exist. Any attempt to make anarchism an attribute of the whole of humanity, as it presently stands, or to credit it with a generally humanitarian character, would be an historical and social falsehood that would inevitably result in justification of the current order and of fresh exploitation.

Anarchism is broadly humanitarian only in the sense that the ideals of the toiling masses tend to sanitize the lives of all men, and that the fate of humanity today or tomorrow is bound up with that of enslaved Labor. Should the toiling masses prove victorious, the whole of humankind will know a rebirth. If they should fail, violence, exploitation, slavery and oppression will prevail in the world like before.

The inception, unfolding and realization of anarchist ideals have their roots in the life and struggle of the toiling masses and are indissolubly bound up with the fate of the latter.

Anarchism aims to turn today's bourgeois capitalist society into a society that will guarantee workers the product of their labors, freedom, independence and social and political equality. Libertarian communism will be that other society. It is in libertarian communism that social solidarity and free individuality find their fullest expression, and that those two notions develop in perfect harmony.

Libertarian communism reckons that the sole creator of social assets is labor, physical and intellectual, and, as a result, that labor alone has any entitlement to govern the whole of economic and social life, That is why it neither excuses nor countenances the existence of non-laboring classes in any way.

As long as such classes survive contemporaneously with libertarian communism, the latter will not own any obligations towards them. Only when the non-laboring classes make up their minds to become productive and willing to live in the communist society on the same footing as everyone else, will they take up a place comparable to everyone else's, that is, resembling the position of free members of society, enjoying the same rights and the same duties as every other laboring member of it.

Libertarian communism seeks the eradication of all exploitation and violence, whether against the individual or against the masses. To that end, it lays down an economic and social groundwork that knits all of the country's economic and social life into a harmonious whole, guarantees every individual parity with every other and affords the utmost well-being to everyone. This groundwork is the common ownership, in the form of socialization, of all of the means and instruments of production (industry, transport, land, raw materials, etc.) and the construction of economic agencies on the basis of equality and self-governance of the laboring classes.

Within the parameters of this self-governing toilers' society, libertarian communism lays down the principle of every individual's (not of the individuality "in general," nor the "mystic individual" either or of the concept of individuality, but rather of the concrete individual instead) equality in worth and in rights.

It is from this principle of equality and also the fact that the labor value supplied by each individual cannot be either measured or estimated that the underlying economic, social and juridical principle of libertarian communism — *"From each according to his means, to each according to his needs"* — follows.

## 4. The Negation of Democracy

Democracy is one of the forms of capitalist and bourgeois society.

The basis of democracy is the retention of the two antagonistic classes of modern society, the class of Labor and that of Capital, and of their *collaboration on the basis of capitalist private property. The expression of this collaboration is parliament and representative national government.*

Formally, democracy proclaims freedom of speech, of the press, of association, as well as universal equality before the law.

In reality, all these freedoms are of a very relative nature: they are tolerated as long as they pose no challenge to the interests of the ruling class, that is to say, of the bourgeoisie.

Democracy leaves the principle of capitalist private property untouched. In so doing, it leaves the bourgeoisie its entitlement to hold within its hands the entire economy of the country, all of the press, education, science and art: which, in fact, makes the bourgeoisie the absolute mistress of the country. Enjoying a monopoly in the realm of economic affairs, the bourgeoisie is free to establish its unbounded power in the political realm also. Indeed, parliament and representative government are, in democracies, merely executive organs of the bourgeoisie.

As a result, democracy is merely one of the facets of the bourgeois dictatorship, concealed behind the camouflage of notional political freedoms and democratic assurances.

## 5. The Negation of the State and Authority

The bourgeoisie's ideologues define the state as the organ regulating the complex political, civil and social relations between men within modern society, watching out for the latter's law and order. Anarchists are in perfect agreement with that definition, but they look beyond it, asserting that underpinning that order and those laws is the enslavement of the vast majority of the people by an insignificant minority, and that that is the precise purpose of the state.

*The state is at one and the same time the organized violence of the bourgeoisie against the toilers and the arrangement of its executive organs.*

The left-wing socialists and, in particular, the Bolsheviks also look upon Authority and the bourgeois state as the servants of Capital. But they take the line that Authority and the state can, in the hands of the socialist parties, become a powerful weapon in the struggle for the emancipation of the proletariat. On those grounds, these parties are for a socialist Authority and a proletarian state. Some (the Social Democrats) seek to win power by peaceful, parliamentary means: others (the Bolsheviks, the Left Social Revolutionaries) by way of revolution.

Anarchism regards these two theses as profoundly in error and harmful to the drive to emancipate Labor.

Authority always goes hand in glove with exploitation and enslavement of the masses of the people. It arises out of that exploitation, or is created in the latter's interests. Authority without violence and without exploitation loses all raison d'être.

The state and Authority rob the masses of initiative, murder the creative spirit and the spirit of free activity, nurturing in them the slavish mentality of submission, of patience, the hope of climbing up the ladder of society, of blind faith in leaders, of the illusion of a share in authority. Now, emancipation of the toilers is feasible only through the process of direct revolutionary struggle by the laboring masses and their class organizations against the capitalist system.

The conquest of power by the social democratic parties, by parliamentary methods, in the context of the present order, will not advance the task of emancipation of Labor by a single step, for the simple reason that the real power, and thus the real authority, will remain with the bourgeoisie which will have control of the whole of the country's economy and politics. The role of the socialist authorities will in that case be confined to reforms, *to improvement of that same bourgeois regime.* (Examples: Mac Donald, the Social Democrat parties of Germany, Sweden and Belgium which have attained power in a capitalist society.)

The taking of power through social upheaval and the organization of an alleged "proletarian state" cannot further the cause of genuine emancipation of Labor either. The State, supposedly erected at first for the purpose of defending the revolution inevitably ends up by becoming swollen with those needs and characteristics peculiar to itself, and becomes an end in itself, spawning specific privileged castes upon which it relies: it forcibly subjugates the masses to its needs and those of the privileged castes and thus restores the groundwork of capitalist Authority and the capitalist State: habitual enslavement and exploitation of the masses by violence. (Example: the Bolsheviks' "workers' and peasants'" State.)

## 6. The Role of Anarchists and the Masses in the Social Struggle and Social Revolution

The principal forces of social revolution are: the urban working class, the peasant masses and a segment of the working intelligentsia.

*Note*: — While being, like the urban and rural proletariat, an oppressed and exploited class, the working intelligentsia is comparatively less united than the workers and the peasants, thanks to the economic privileges which the bourgeoisie awards to certain of its members. That is why, in the early days of the social revolution, only the less well-off strata of the intelligentsia will take an active part in it.

The anarchist conception of the role of the masses in the social revolution and in the construction of socialism is tellingly different from that of the statist parties. While Bolshevism and its kindred currents take the line that the toiling mass is possessed only of destructive revolutionary instincts, and incapable of creative and constructive revolutionary activity — the main reason why the latter should be placed in the hands of the men making up the government or the Party Central Committee — anarchists think instead that the toiling mass carries within itself vast creative and constructive potential, and they aspire to sweep aside the obstacles preventing these from showing themselves.

Anarchists in fact look upon the State as the chief obstacle, usurping all the rights of the masses and divesting them of all their functions in economic and social life. *The State must wither away, not "one day," in the society of the future, but right away. It has to be destroyed by the workers, on day one of their victory, and must not be restored in any guise whatsoever.* It is to be replaced by a federalist arrangement of toilers' production and consumption organizations, federatively connected and self-governing. That system rules out both Authority and the dictatorship of any party whatsoever.

The Russian revolution of 1917 specifically exemplifies this approach to the process of social emancipation through the creation of the system of workers' and peasants' soviets and of factory committees. Its dismal error was not to have liquidated the organization of State Power at the opportune moment: the provisional government, to begin with, and then Bolshevik power. The Bolsheviks, capitalizing upon the trust of the workers and peasants, reshaped the bourgeois state in accordance with the circumstances of the time and then, with the aid of that State, killed off the creative activity of the masses: by strangling the free system of soviets and factory committees that represented the first steps in the direction of construction of a state-less, socialist society.

Anarchists' action may be viewed as failing into two phases: the one *before* the revolution, and the one *during* the revolution, In both, only as an organized force with a clear-cut idea of the goals of their struggle and of the pathways leading to accomplishment of those goals will anarchists be in a position to live up to their role.

The fundamental mission of the General Anarchist Union, in the pre-revolutionary era, must be to prepare the workers and peasants for the social revolution.

By denying formal (bourgeois) democracy, Authority and the state and proclaiming the full emancipation of labor, anarchism places the utmost stress upon the rigorous principles of the class struggle, awakening and nurturing class consciousness and revolutionary class intransigence in the masses.

It is precisely along these lines of class intransigence, anti-democratism, anti-statism and the ideals of anarchist communism that the libertarian education of the masses should be conducted. But education on its own is not enough. What is also needed, is a certain anarchist organization of the masses. If this is to be accomplished, we have to operate along two lines: on the one hand, by selecting and rallying revolutionary worker and peasant forces on a libertarian communist theoretical basis (specifically libertarian organizations), and on the other, pursue the association of revolutionary workers and peasants on an economic footing of production and consumption (revolutionary workers' and peasants' production organizations, free workers' and peasants' cooperatives, etc.).

The worker and peasant class, organized on the basis of production and consumption and imbued with the positions of revolutionary anarchism, will be the social revolution's premier fulcrum. The more such strata become consciously and in an organized way, anarchist, *starting right now*, the more will they demonstrate a determined libertarian intransigence and creativity come the revolution.

As for the working class in Russia, it is plain that after eight years of Bolshevik dictatorship, which has bridled the masses' natural appetite for unfettered activity, and the like, and demonstrated better than anyone the true nature of all authority, that class harbors within itself immeasurable potential for the formation of an anarchist mass movement. The organized anarchist militants must immediately and with all available resources set about cultivating that appetite and potential, lest these be allowed to degenerate into reformism (Menshevism). With like urgency, anarchists must dedicate all their efforts to organizing the poor peasantry, ground down as it is by the statist authorities, looking around for some release and harboring within itself vast revolutionary potential.

The anarchists' role in time or revolution cannot be confined to the mere dissemination of libertarian slogans and ideas.

Life can be seen as an arena not just for the dissemination of this or that idea, but also and equally as an arena for the struggle, strategy and aspirations of such ideas to the direction of social and economic life.

More than any other outlook, anarchism should become the guiding light of the social revolution, for it is only on the theoretical basis of anarchism that the social revolution will be able to encompass the complete emancipation of Labor.

The spearhead position of anarchist ideas in the revolution means *anarchist theoretical direction of events*. However, this theoretical driving force should not be confused with political direction by statist parties, culminating in State Power.

Anarchism aspires neither to winning of political power nor to dictatorship. Its chief aspiration is to assist the masses to choose the genuine path of social revolution and socialist construction. But it is not enough that the masses should embark upon the social revolutionary route. It is necessary too that *that construction upon the revolution and its objectives be sustained*: with the elimination of capitalist society in the name of the society of free toilers. As the experience of the 1917 Russian revolution has shown us, the latter task is no easy thing, principally on account of the many parties seeking to steer the movement in a direction leading away from social revolution.

Although the masses in social upheavals are prompted deep-down by anarchist tendencies and watchwords, the latter nevertheless remain diffuse, not being coordinated and as a result they do not lead on to the organization of the driving force of libertarian ideas, needed if the social revolution is to retain its anarchist orientation and objectives. This theoretical driving force can only find expression in a collective especially established by the masses for that express purpose. It is the organized anarchist elements and the General Anarchist Union that constitute that collective.

The theoretical and practical duties of that collective, in time of revolution, are considerable.

It has to display initiative and demonstrate complete commitment in every aspect of social revolution, encompassing the orientation and general tenor of the revolution, the civil war and defense of the revolution, the positive tasks of the revolution in the new production, consumption, the agrarian question, etc.

On all of these issues and on a number of others, the masses demand a plain and precise answer of the anarchists. And, just as soon as anarchists peddle a concept of revolution and of society's structure, they are *obliged* to come up with a plain answer to all such questions, and to link solution of those problems to the over-arching conception of libertarian communism and to commit all of their resources to its effective realization.

Only thus do the General Anarchist Union and the anarchist movement perform their spearhead theoretical function in the social revolution properly.

## 7. The Transitional Period

By the phrase "transitional period," the socialist political parties mean a specific phase in the life of a people, the essential features of which phase are: a break with the old order and the introduction of a new economic and political arrangement, an arrangement which, however, does not yet imply the full emancipation of the toilers.

In this respect, all of the minimum programs of the socialist political parties, for instance the democratic program of the opportunist socialists, or the communists' "dictatorship of the proletariat" program, are programs for the transitional period.

The essential feature of these minimum programs is that, one and all, they regard the complete realization of the toilers' ideals — their independence, their liberty, their equality — as, for the time being, impracticable, and that as a result they retain a whole series of the capitalist system's institutions: the principle of statist restraint, private ownership of the means and instruments of production, wage-slavery, and several others, according to the goals to which one program or another relates.

Anarchists have always been opposed on principle to such programs, taking the view that the construction of transitional arrangements that sustain the principles of exploitation and constraint of the masses lead inescapably to regrowth of slavery.

Instead of laying down minimum policy programs, anarchists have always championed the notion of immediate social revolution, that would strip the capitalist class of political and economic privileges and restore the means and instruments of production, as well as every other function of economic and social life, to the care of the toilers.

That is a position that anarchists have retained to this very day.

The idea of the transitional period, according to which the social revolution should culminate not in a communist society, but in a given system that retains elements and relics from the old capitalist system, is essentially antisocial. It threatens to result in the bolstering and expansion of such elements to their former proportions and sends events into reverse.

One sensational example of this is the "dictatorship of the proletariat" regime established by the Bolsheviks in Russia.

According to them, this regime was to be only a *transitional* stage in the march to total communism. In point of fact, that stage has in reality resulted in the restoration of class society, at the bottom of which, just like before, we find the workers and the poor peasants.

The center of gravity in the construction of the communist society does not consist of the feasibility of guaranteeing every individual, right from the early days of the revolution, boundless freedom to seek satisfaction of his needs, but resides in the conquest of the social basis of that society and the establishment of the principles of egalitarian relations between individuals. As for the matter of the greater or lesser abundance of resources, that is not a matter of principle but arises as a technical problem.

The underlying principle upon which the new society will be erected, the precept upon which that society will, so to speak, rest and which must not be tampered with even to the slightest degree is *that of the toilers' parity in relationships, liberty and independence.* Now that principle precisely encapsulates the premier essential requirement of the masses, in the name of which alone they rose up for the social revolution.

One has to choose: either the social revolution will end in the defeat of the toilers, in which case, we have to start all over again to prepare for another struggle, a fresh offensive against the capitalist system: or it will bring about the victory of the toilers, in which case, the latter, having seized the wherewithal to fend for themselves — the land, production and social functions — will set about the construction of the free society.

That will be the characteristic of the launching of the construction of the communist society which, once begun, will then proceed with its development without interruption, endlessly gathering strength and working towards perfection.

In that way, the toilers' takeover of productive and social functions will signal a plain dividing line between the statist era and the non-statist one.

If it wishes to become the spokesman for the struggling Masses, the emblem of a whole era of social revolution, anarchism must not accommodate its program to vestiges of the outmoded world, the opportunistic tendencies of transitional arrangements and periods, nor cover up its underlying principles, but should instead build upon these and put them to maximum use.

## 8. Anarchism and Trade Unionism

The tendency to contrast libertarian communism with syndicalism, and vice versa, is one that we consider artificial and bereft of all foundation and sense.

The ideas of anarchism and of syndicalism occupy two different planes. Whereas communism, which is to say the free society of equal toilers, is the goal of the anarchist struggle, syndicalism, which is to say the workers' revolutionary movement based on trades, is but one of the forms of the revolutionary class struggle. In uniting the workers on the basis of production, revolutionary syndicalism, like every trades association indeed, has no specific theory: it has no world-picture embracing all of the complicated social and political issues of the contemporary condition. It always mirrors the ideology of a range of political groupings, notably of those most intensively at work within its ranks.

Our standpoint with regard to revolutionary syndicalism follows from what has just been said. Without getting bogged down here with resolving in advance the matter of the revolutionary trades unions' role on the morrow of the revolution, that is, with knowing whether they are to be the organizers of all the new production, or will yield that role to workers' soviets, or indeed to factory committees, it is our view that anarchists should be involved in revolutionary syndicalism as one of the forms of the revolutionary workers' movement.

However, the question, as posed today, is not whether anarchists should or should not play a part in revolutionary syndicalism, but rather, how and to what end they should play that part.

We regard the whole foregoing period, right up to our own times — when anarchists entered the revolutionary syndicalist movement as individual militants and propagandists — as a time of artisanal relations with regard to the trade union movement.

Anarcho-syndicalism, looking around for some way of injecting libertarian ideas into the left wing of revolutionary syndicalism, through the creation of anarchist-type unions, represents, in this respect, a step forward: but not quite, as yet, an advance upon the empirical method. For anarcho-syndicalism does not necessarily link the drive to "anarchize" the syndicalist movement with the drive to organize the anarchist forces outside of that movement. Now, "anarchization" of revolutionary syndicalism, and inoculation against deviation in the direction of opportunism and reformism only become feasible if just such a linkage is established.

Regarding revolutionary syndicalism solely as a trades movement of the toilers possessed of no specific social and political theory, and thus, as incapable of itself resolving the social question, it is our estimation that the task of the anarchists in the ranks of that movement consists of developing libertarian ideas there and of steering it in a libertarian direction, so as to turn it into an army active in the service of the social revolution. It is important that we never forget that, if syndicalism fails to win the support of anarchist theory at the right time, it then leans, willy-nilly upon the ideology of some statist political party.

French syndicalism, which once upon a time shone on account of its anarchist watchwords and tactics, before falling under the sway of the Bolsheviks and, above all, of the opportunist socialists, is a telling example of this.

But anarchists' task in the ranks of the revolutionary labor movement can only be performed if their efforts there are closely bound up and compatible with the activity of anarchist organization outside of the trade union. To put that another way, we have to enter the revolutionary trades movement as an organized force, answerable before the anarchist umbrella organization for our work inside the trade unions, and receiving guidance from that organization.

Without burdening ourselves with the establishment of anarchist trade unions, we should seek to exercise our theoretical influence over revolutionary syndicalism as a whole, and in all its forms (the IWW, the Russian trades unions, etc.). We can only accomplish this aim by setting to work as a rigorously organized anarchist collective, and certainly not as little empirical groups bereft of organizational interconnection or theoretical common ground.

Anarchist groupings inside firms and factories, preoccupied with the creation of anarchist trade unions, campaigning inside the revolutionary trade unions so that libertarian ideas should prevail in syndicalism: groups receiving guidance in their activities from an overall anarchist organization — these are the forms and features of anarchists' attitude with regard to revolutionary syndicalism and its revolutionary trades movements.

## CONSTRUCTIVE SECTION

### The Problem of Day One of the Social Revolution

The essential objective of the world of struggling Labor is the foundation, through revolution, of a free, egalitarian communist society based upon the precept: "From each according to his abilities, to each according to his needs."

However, such a society will not come about of itself, but only by dint of a social upheaval. The accomplishment of it will seem like a more or less protracted social revolutionary process, steered by the organized forces of victorious Labor down a particular route.

Our task is to trace out that route right here and now, to frame the positive, practical problems that will confront the workers right from day one of the social revolution. The very fate of the latter will hinge upon proper resolution of them.

It goes without saying that the construction of the new society will only be practicable after the toilers have triumphed over the present bourgeois capitalist system and its representatives. There is no way that the construction of a new economy and new social relationships can be tackled until such time as the power of the state defending the rule of slavery has been smashed, until such time as the workers and peasants have assumed charge of the country's industrial and agrarian economy in a revolutionary arrangement.

As a result, the very first task of the social revolution is to destroy the statist edifice of capitalist society, strip the bourgeoisie, and more generally, all socially privileged elements, of the means of power, and establish throughout the will of the rebellious proletariat as articulated in the underlying principles of the social revolution. This destructive and belligerent facet of the revolution will merely clear the way for the positive challenges that make up the meaning and essence of the social revolution.

Those challenges are as follows:

1. To find a libertarian communist solution to the problem of the country's industrial output.
2. To resolve the agrarian problem in the same manner.
3. To resolve the problem of consumption (supply).

### Production

Bearing in mind that fact that the country's industry is the result of the efforts of several generations of toilers, and that the various branches of industry are closely interconnected, we look upon the whole of current output as one big workshop of toilers, wholly the property of all the toilers as a whole, and of no one in particular.

The country's productive machinery is global and belongs to the entire working class. This thesis determines the character and the form of the new production. It too is to be global, common in the sense of the products turned out by the toilers belonging to everybody. Those products, of whatever sort they may be, will represent the general fund for supplying the toilers, from which every participant in the new production will receive everything that he may need, on a footing of equality for everyone.

The new production arrangement will utterly dispense with wage slavery and exploitation in all their forms, and will in their place establish the principle of fraternal, solidarity collaboration of the toilers.

The intermediary class which in modern capitalist society performs intermediary tasks — commerce and the like — as well as the bourgeoisie, will have to play its part in the new production, on the very same basis as all other toilers. Otherwise, these classes will be placing themselves outside of laboring society of their own volition.

There will be no bosses, neither entrepreneur, proprietor nor proprietor-state (as one finds today in the Bolsheviks' State). In the new production, organizing roles will devolve upon specially created administrative agencies, purpose-built by the laboring masses: workers' soviets, factory committees or workers' administrations of firms and factories. These agencies, liaising with one another at the level of the township, district and then nation, will make up the township, district and thereafter overall federal institutions for the management of production. Appointed by the masses and continually subject to their supervision and influence, all these bodies are to be shuffled constantly, thereby embodying the idea of genuine self-governance of the masses.

Production unified, its means and its output the property of everyone, with wage slavery replaced by the principle of fraternal collaboration and equality of rights for all producers an established fact: production overseen by workers' management bodies elected by the masses: such is the practical first step along the road to the realization of libertarian communism.

### Consumption

This problem will surface in the revolution in two guises:
1. The principle of the demand for consumer goods.
2. The principle of the distribution thereof.

As far as distribution of consumer goods is concerned, solutions will hinge primarily upon the quantity of goods available and upon the principle of meeting targets, etc.

The social revolution, in tackling the reconstruction of the entire established social order, thereby assumes an obligation to look to everyone's essential needs. The sole exception being the group of non-producers — those who decline to play their part in the new production on counterrevolutionary grounds. But, broadly speaking, and with the exception of this last category of people, all of the needs of the entire population of the territory of the social revolution will be met out of the overall stock of consumer goods. Should the quantity of goods prove insufficient, they are to be allocated on the basis of greater urgency of need, which is to say, with children, the infirm and workers' families getting priority.

A much more difficult problem will be that of organizing the stock of consumer goods itself.

Without a doubt, in the early days of the revolution, the towns will not have stocks of all the basic essentials required by the population. At the same time, the peasants will have an abundance of the produce in short supply in the towns.

Libertarian communists cannot have any doubts as to the mutuality of relations between toilers in the towns and toilers in the countryside. They reckon that the social revolution cannot be accomplished except through the concerted efforts of the workers and the peasants. Consequently, solution of the problem of consumption in the revolution will be feasible only through close revolutionary collaboration between these two categories of toilers.

In order to establish such collaboration, the urban working class, once having assumed control of production, should immediately consider the basic needs of the countryside and endeavor to supply the everyday consumer goods, wherewithal and tools for collective cultivation of the land. Gestures of solidarity shown by workers towards the requirements of the peasants will elicit a like response from the latter who will, in return, collectively supply the towns with the produce of rural production, with pride of place going to foodstuffs.

Workers' and peasants' cooperatives will be the first bodies to cater for the food requirements and economic supplies of town and countryside. Commissioned later to handle more important, more ongoing tasks, notably that of furnishing the necessary wherewithal to guarantee and expand upon the economic and social life of the workers and peasants, these cooperatives will thereby be converted into standing agencies handling urban and rural provisions.

This solution to the provisions problem will enable the proletariat to establish a standing fund of provisions which will have a favorable and crucial impact upon the fate of the whole of the new production.

### The Land

In the solution of the agrarian question, we consider the peasant toilers — those who exploit no one else's labor — and the wage-earning rural proletariat as the main creative revolutionary forces. Their mission will be to carry through the new allocation of lands, so that the land may be put to use and cultivated along communist lines.

Just like industry, the land, exploited and cultivated by successive generations of toilers, is the product of their common endeavors. It also belongs to the toiling populace in its entirety, and to no one in particular. As the common and inalienable property of the toilers, the land cannot be subject to purchase or sale or leasing either: so it cannot furnish the means to exploit another man's labor.

The land is also a sort of common popular workshop where the community of toilers produces life's sustenance. But it is a type of workshop wherein every toiler (peasant) has, thanks to certain historical circumstances, fallen into the habit of performing his labor for himself, of working independently of the other producers. While, in industry, the collective mode of labor is essentially necessary and the only feasible one, in agriculture it is not the only feasible method in our day. Most peasants work the land self-reliantly.

As a result, when the land and the wherewithal to work it pass to the peasants, with no possibility of sale or lease, the issue of the patterns of usufruct and of cultivation (communally or on a family basis) will not be wholly and definitively resolved right away, as it will be in industry's case. To begin with, we will very probably resort to both of these patterns.

It will be the revolutionary peasants themselves who will determine the definitive pattern of land cultivation and usufruct. There can be no outside pressure in this matter.

However, since we consider that only a communist society, in whose name the social revolution will in fact have been made, can rescue the toilers from their condition as slaves and victims of exploitation, and endow them with a full measure of freedom and equality: and since the peasants account for the overwhelming majority of the population (nearly 85 percent in Russia) [In 1926, that is. — A. Skirda] and since, as a result the agrarian system adopted by the peasants will be the crucial factor in determining the revolution's fate: and, finally, since private enterprise in agriculture leads, just like private enterprise in industry, to commerce, accumulation, private ownership and the restoration of capital — it will be incumbent upon us as a duty to do all in our power right now to ensure that the agrarian question is resolved along collective lines.

To this end, we should, starting now, conduct forceful propaganda among the peasants on behalf of a collective agrarian economy.

The foundation of a specific Peasant Union of libertarian outlook will be of considerable assistance in this undertaking.

In this regard, technical advances are going to have enormous significance in speeding the development of agriculture and likewise the achievement of communism in the towns, above all in industry. If, in their dealings with the peasants, the workers will operate not as individuals or as separate groups, but rather as a huge communist collective embracing whole branches of industry: if they, furthermore, give consideration to the essential needs of the country-side and if they supply each village, not just with everyday necessities, but also with tools and machinery for collective cultivation of the land, that will assuredly nudge the peasants towards communism in agriculture.

### Defense of the Revolution

The question of defending the revolution also relates to the problem of "day one."

Essentially, the revolution's mightiest defense is a happy resolution of its positive problems: the problems of production, consumption and the land. Once these matters have been fairly resolved, no counterrevolutionary force will be able to induce change or hesitancy in the free regime of the toilers. Nevertheless, the toilers will, in spite of everything, have to face a harsh struggle against the revolution's foes, in order to defend and cling to its actual existence.

The social revolution, which threatens the privileges and the very existence of the non-toiler classes of the existing society, will inevitably provoke from these a desperate resistance that will assume the guise of a vicious civil war.

As the Russian experience has shown, such a civil war will not be a matter of a few months but rather of several years.

Happy though the toilers' first steps may be at the outset of the revolution, the ruling classes will nonetheless retain a huge capacity for resistance for quite some time to come.

Over several years, they will unleash attacks on the revolution, trying to snatch back the power and privileges of which they have been stripped.

A sizable army, military expertise and military strategy, capital the victorious toilers will have to face them all.

If they are to preserve the gains of the revolution, the latter will have to set up organs for defense of the revolution, in order to field a fighting force, that is equal to the task, against the onslaught of the reaction. In the earliest days of the revolution, that fighting force will be made up of all the workers and peasants in arms. But that makeshift armed force will only be viable in the earliest days, when the civil war will not yet have reached its peak and the two opposing sides will not yet have established regularly constituted military organizations.

In the social revolution, the most critical juncture is not the one when Authority is cast aside, but the one that comes after that, that is, the one when the forces of the ousted regime unleash a general offensive against the toilers and when the point is to safeguard the gains achieved.

The very character of that offensive, as well as the technique and extension of the civil war will compel the toilers to create specifically military revolutionary units. The nature and underlying principles of these units must be laid down in advance. In rebutting statist and authoritarian methods of governing the masses, we are ipso facto rebutting the statist manner of organizing the toilers' military strength, or, to put that another way, the principle of a statist army founded upon compulsory military service. It is the volunteer principle, in accordance with the basic tenets of libertarian communism, which should provide the basis for the toilers' military formations. The detachments of insurgent partisans, workers and peasants, which carried out military action during the Russian revolution, might be cited as examples of such formations.

Yet voluntary service and partisan activity should not be construed in the narrow sense of the terms, that is as a struggle waged by worker and peasant units against a local enemy and operating without coordination with one another in the shape of an overall operational plan, each unit acting off its own bat, at its own risk and peril. Partisan action and partisan tactics should be guided, in the time when they are fully developed, by a common revolutionary strategy, Like any war, civil war could not be waged successfully by the toilers except by application of the two principles fundamental to all military activity: unity of operational planning and unity through single command. The most critical time for the revolution will be the one when the bourgeoisie will march as an organized force against the revolution.

That critical point will force toilers to have recourse to these principles of military strategy.

In this way, given the requirements of military strategy, and also of the counterrevolution's strategy, the revolution's armed forces will inevitably have to amalgamate into a broad revolutionary army with a shared command and a shared operational plan.

The following principles will be the basis for that army:

a) *The class nature of the army.*
b) *Volunteer service* (all constraint will be utterly banished from the undertaking of defending the revolution).
c) *Free revolutionary (self-) discipline*: (revolutionary volunteer service and revolutionary self-discipline are perfectly mutually complementary, and will make the revolution's army psychologically stronger than any state army.)
d) *Utter subordination of the revolutionary army to the worker and peasant masses*: in the shape of common worker and peasant bodies throughout the land, hoisted by the masses into positions overseeing economic and social life.

To put this another way: the revolution's defense agency, charged with combating the counterrevolution on the open military fronts as well as on the fronts of the civil war within (plots by the bourgeoisie, hatching of counter-revolutionary action, etc.), will be wholly the responsibility of the workers' and peasants' productive organizations, to which it will be answerable and by which it will be directed *politically*.

Observation — While it must of necessity be structured in accordance with specified libertarian communist principles, the army itself should not be regarded as a point of principle. It is merely the consequence of military strategy in the revolution. a strategic measure to which the toilers will be drawn inescapably by the very process of civil war, But that measure should be the focus of attention even now. It must be diligently examined, so that, in the endeavor to protect and defend the revolution, all irreparable delay may be avoided, for delays in times of civil war, can prove damaging to the outcome of the whole social revolution.

## ORGANIZATIONAL PART
## THE PRINCIPLES OF ANARCHIST ORGANIZATION

The broad constructive positions set out above represent the organizational platform of anarchism's revolutionary forces.

This platform, containing a specific theoretical and tactical outlook, represents the minimum around which all the militants of the organized anarchist movement must be rallied as a matter of urgency.

Its task is to rally around itself all of the wholesome elements of the anarchist movement into one umbrella organization, continuously active and operational: the General Union of Anarchists. The resources of all of anarchism's active militants will have to be directed into the creation of this organization.

The underlying organizational principles of a General Union of Anarchists will have to be as follows:

*1. Ideological unity*. Ideology represents that force which directs the activity of persons and of organizations along a specific route towards a specific goal. Naturally, it ought to be common to all persons and all organizations affiliating to the General Union. All of the activity of the General Anarchist Union, broadly, as well as in its details, should be in perfect and constant accord with the ideological principles professed by the Union.

*2. Tactical Unity or Unity of Collective Method of Action*. The tactical means employed by the individual members or groups from the Union should likewise be unitary, that is to say, be strictly consonant with one another as well as with the overall ideology and tactic of the Union.

That there should be a common tactical line in the movement is of crucial importance for the existence of the organization and of the entire movement: it rids it of the damaging impact of several mutually antagonistic tactics and focuses all of the movement's forces, making them follow a common direction culminating in a specific objective.

*3. Collective Responsibility.* The practice of operating off one's own bat should be decisively condemned and rejected in the ranks of the anarchist movement.

The realms of revolutionary, social and political life are pre-eminently collective in nature.

Revolutionary social activity in those realms cannot be based upon the personal responsibility of individual militants.

The general anarchist movement's executive body — the Anarchist Union — taking a decisive stand against the tactic of unaccountable individualism, introduces into its ranks the *principle of collective responsibility*: the Union as a body will be answerable for the revolutionary and political activity of each of its members: likewise, each member will be answerable for the revolutionary and political activity of the Union as a whole.

*4. Federalism.* Anarchism has always repudiated centralist organization in the realm of the masses' social life as well as in that of its political action. The system of centralization relies upon the stunting of the spirit of criticism, initiative and independence of every individual and upon the masses' blind obedience to the "center." The inevitable natural upshot of this system is slavishness and mechanization in social life and in the life of parties.

Contrary to centralism, anarchism has always professed and advocated the principle of *federalism*, which reconciles the individual's or the organization's independence and initiative with service of the common cause.

By reconciling the idea of the independence and fullness of each individual's rights with service of social requirements and needs, federalism thereby opens the door to every wholesome manifestation of the faculties of each individual.

But very often the federalist principle was warped in anarchist ranks: it was too often taken to mean primarily the right to display one's "ego," with no obligation to heed one's duties towards the organization.

This misrepresentation disorganized our movement in the past. It is high time that it was ended firmly and irreversibly.

Federalism means free agreement of individuals and organizations upon collective endeavor geared towards a common objective.

Now, such agreement and federative union based thereon become realities, rather than fictions and dreams, only if the essential condition is fulfilled that all parties to the agreement and to the Union fully honor the obligations they assume and abide by the decisions reached in common.

In a social undertaking as vast as the federalist basis upon which it is constructed, there can be no rights without obligations, just as there cannot be decisions without implementation thereof. That is all the more unacceptable in an anarchist organization which takes upon itself alone obligations with regard to the toilers and their social revolution.

As a result, the federalist type of anarchist organization, while acknowledging every member of the organization's right to independence, to freedom of opinion, initiative and individual liberty, charges each member with specific organizational duties, insisting that these be rigorously performed, and that decisions jointly made be put into effect.

On that condition only will the federalist principle be alive, and will the anarchist organization function properly and move towards the goal it has set.

The idea of the Anarchist General Union raises the problem of coordination and compatibility of the activities of all of the forces of the anarchist movement.

Each organization affiliated to the Union represents a living cell that is part of the overall organism. Each cell will have its secretariat, carrying out and theoretically shaping the organization's political and technical activity.

With an eye to coordinating the activity of all of the Union's affiliated organizations, a special body is to be established: *The Executive Committee of the Union*. The following functions will be ascribed to that Committee: implementation of decisions made by the Union, which the latter will have entrusted to it: theoretical and organizational oversight of the activity of isolated organizations, in keeping with the Union's theoretical options and overall tactical line: scrutiny of the general state of the movement: the maintenance of working and organizational ties between all of the organizations of the Union, as well as with outside organizations.

The rights, responsibilities and practical tasks of the Executive Committee will be prescribed by the Congress of the General Union.

The General Union of Anarchists has a specific and concrete goal. For the sake of the success of the social revolution, it must above all choose and absorb from among the workers and peasants the most revolutionary personnel most endowed with critical spirit.

Espousing social revolution and being, to boot, an anti-authoritarian organization, which seeks the immediate abolition of the class society, the General Union of Anarchists likewise relies upon the two fundamental classes of the present society: the workers and the peasants. It will also facilitate those two classes' quest for emancipation.

As regards the workers' trades and revolutionary organizations in the towns, the General Union of Anarchists will have to escalate all of its efforts so as to become their spearhead and theoretical mentor.

It sets itself the same tasks where the exploited peasant mass is concerned also. As a fulcrum playing the same role as the workers' revolutionary trades unions, the Union will strive to build a network of revolutionary peasant economic organizations, and, furthermore, a specific Peasant Union built on anti-authoritarian principles.

Emanating from the heart of the mass of the toilers, the General Union of Anarchists takes part in all aspects of their life, always and everywhere bringing the spirit of organization, perseverance, activity and belligerence.

Only thus can it fulfill its role, its theoretical and historical mission in the toilers' social revolution and become the organized instigation of their process of emancipation.

## DOCUMENT NO. 3
## SUPPLEMENT TO THE ORGANIZATIONAL PLATFORM (QUESTIONS AND ANSWERS) NOVEMBER 2, 1926

As was to be expected, the organizational platform of the General Union of Anarchists has sparked very lively interest among several militants of the Russian libertarian movement, While some wholeheartedly subscribe to the overall idea and fundamental theses of the "Platform," others frame criticisms and express misgivings about certain of its theses.

We welcome equally the positive reception of the platform and the genuine criticism of it.

For, in the endeavor to create an overall anarchist program as well as an overall libertarian organization, honest, serious and substantial criticism is as important as positive creative initiatives.

The questions we reprint below emanate from just that sort of serious and necessary criticism, and it is with some satisfaction that we welcome it. In forwarding them to us, their author [Maria Isidine — note by A. Skirda] — a militant of many years' standing, well respected in our movement — encloses a letter in which she says: "Obviously, the organizational platform is designed to be discussed by all anarchists. Before formulating any final opinion of this 'platform' and, perhaps, speaking of it in the press, I should like to have an explanation of certain matters which are insufficiently explicit in it. It may well be that other readers will find in the 'platform' a fair degree of precision and that certain objections may only be based on misunderstandings. It is for that reason that I should like to put a series of questions to you first of all. It would be very important that you reply to these in a clear manner, for it will be your replies that that will afford a grasp of the general *spirit* of the 'platform.' Perhaps you will see a need to reply in your review."

In closing her letter, the comrade adds that she wishes to avert controversy in the columns of the review *Dyelo Truda*. This is why she seeks above all elucidation of certain essential points from the platform, This sort of approach is very fair. It is all too easy to launch into polemic in order to come out against a view with which one thinks one is in disagreement. It is even easier to trouble oneself solely with polemicizing without bothering to frame any *alternative* positive *suggestion*, in place of the targeted view. What is infinitely harder is to *analyze* the new proposition *properly*, to *understand* it, so that one may go on to arrive at a well-founded opinion of it. It is exactly this last, most difficult course that the author of the questions below has chosen.

Here are those questions:

1. The central point of the *Platform* is rallying the bulk of the anarchist movement's militants on the basis of a common tactical and policy line: the formation of a General Union. Since you are federalists, you apparently have in mind a Union that will link autonomous groupings. Now, you also have in mind the existence of an Executive Committee that will have charge of the "ideological and organizational conduct of the activity of isolated groups," That type of organization is to be found in all parties, but it is possible only if one accepts the *majority principle*. In your organization, will each group be free to prescribe its own tactics and establish its own stance vis-à-vis each given issue? If the answer is yes, then your unity will be of a purely *moral* character (as has been and still is the case inside the anarchist movement). If, on the other hand, you seek organizational unity, that unity will of necessity be *coerced*. And then if you accept the majority principle inside your organization, on what grounds would you repudiate it in social construction?

It would be desirable that you further clarify your conception of federalist liaison, the role of Congresses and the majority principle.

2. Speaking of the "free regime of soviets," what functions do you see these soviets having to perform in order to become "the first steps in the direction of constructive non-statist activity"? What is to be their remit? Will their decisions be binding?

3. "Anarchists should steer events from the theoretical point of view," says the platform. This notion is insufficiently clear. Does it mean simply that anarchists will do their utmost to see that (trade union, local, cooperative, etc.) organizations which are to build the new order are imbued with libertarian ideas? Or does it mean that anarchists *will themselves take charge* of this construction? In the latter case, in what would that state affairs differ from a "party dictatorship"?

It is very important that this matter be clarified. Especially as the same question arises regarding the role of anarchists in the trade unions. What is the meaning of the expression: *enter the unions in an organized manner*? Does it mean merely that the comrades working in the unions should come to some agreement in order to establish a policy line? Or does it mean that the anarchist Executive Committee will prescribe the tactic of the labor movement, rule on strikes, demonstrations, etc., and that those anarchists active in the unions will strive to capture positions of leadership there and, using their authority, foist these decisions on the ordinary membership of the unions? The mention in the "Platform" that the activity of anarchist groupings active in trade union circles is to be *steered by an anarchist umbrella organization* raises all sorts of misgivings on this score.

4. In the section on defending the revolution, it is stated that the army is to be subordinated *to the workers' and peasants' organizations throughout the land, hoisted by the masses into positions overseeing the economic and social life of the country*. In everyday parlance, that is called "civil authority" of the elected. What

does it mean to you? It is obvious that an organization that in fact directs the whole of life and can call upon an army is nothing other than a *state power*. This point is so important that the authors of the "platform" have a duty to dwell longer upon it. If it is a "transitional form," how come the platform rejects the idea of the "transitional period"? And if it is a definitive form, what makes the "platform" *anarchist*?

5. There are some questions which, while not dealt with in the "Platform," nevertheless play an important part in the disagreements between comrades. Let me quote one of those questions:

Let us suppose that a region finds itself effectively under the influence of the anarchists. What will their attitude be towards the other parties? Do the authors of the Platform countenance the possibility of violence against an enemy *who has not had recourse to arms*? Or do they, in keeping with the anarchist idea, proclaim *undiluted freedom of speech, of the press, of organization, etc., for all*? (Some years ago, a similar question would have seemed out of place. But at present certain views of which I am aware prevent me from being sure of the answer.)

And, broadly speaking, is it acceptable to have one's decisions implemented by force? Do the authors of the "platform" countenance the exercise of power, even if only for an instant?

Whatever the group's answers to all these questions, I cannot keep mum about one idea in the "Platform" which is openly at odds with the *anarchist* communism that it professes.

You speculate that once the wage system and exploitation have been abolished, there will nevertheless remain some sorts of non-laboring elements, and these you exclude from the common fellowship union of toilers: they will have no title to their share of the common product. Now this was always the principle at the very basis of anarchism "To each according to his needs": and it was in that principle that anarchism always saw the best guarantee of social solidarity. When faced with the question: "What will you do with the idlers?," they answered: "Better to feed a few idlers for nothing than to introduce, merely on account of their being there, a false and harmful principle into the life of society."

Now, you create, for political reasons, a sort of idler category and, by way of repression, you would have them perish of hunger, But apart from the moral aspect, have you stopped to consider where that would lead? In the case of every person not working, we will have to establish the grounds on which he does not work: we will have to become mindreaders and probe his beliefs. Should somebody refuse to perform a *given* task, we will have to inquire into the grounds for his refusal. We will have to see if it is not sabotage or counterrevolution. Upshot? Spying, forced labor, "labor mobilization" and, to cap it all, the products vital to life are to be in the gift of authorities which *will be able to starve the opposition to death*! Rations as a weapon of political struggle! Can it be that what you have seen in Russia has not persuaded you of the abominable nature of such an arrangement! And I am not talking about the damage that it would do to the destiny of the revolution: such a blatant breach of social solidarity could not help but spawn dangerous enemies.

It is in relation to this problem that the key to the whole anarchist conception of social organization lies. If one were to make concessions on this point, one would quickly be hounded into jettisoning all the other anarchist ideas, for *your* approach to the problem makes any *non-statist* social organization an impossibility.

It may be that I may have to write to the press about the "Platform." But I should prefer to put that off until all these gray areas have been elucidated.

Thus, the organizational *Platform* spawns a series of substantive questions set out in the letter just quoted, notably: 1. the question of *majority and minority* in the anarchist movement; 2. that of the *structure and essential features of the free regime of soviets*; 3. that of *the ideological steering of events and of the masses*; 4. that of *defense of the revolution*; 5. that of *press freedom and freedom of speech*; and, 6. the construction to be placed upon the anarchist principle of *to each according to his needs*.

Let us tackle them in order:
1. *The question of majority and minority in the anarchist movement.* The writer broaches this by linking it to our idea of an Executive Committee of the Union. If the Union's Executive Committee has, besides other functions of an executive nature, also that of "steering the activity of isolated groups from a theoretical and organizational point of view," must that steering not be coercive? Then: are groups affiliated to the Union to be free to prescribe their own tactics and determine their own stance with regard to each given matter? Or are they to be obliged to abide by the overall tactic and the overall positions to be laid down by the Union's majority?

Let it be said, first of all, that in our view, the Union's Executive Committee cannot be a body endowed with any powers of a coercive nature, as is the case with the centralist political parties. The General Anarchist Union's Executive Committee is a body *performing functions of a general nature in the Union.* Instead of "Executive Committee," this body might carry the title of "Chief Secretariat of the Union." However, the name "Executive Committee" is to be preferred, for it better encapsulates *the idea of executive function* and that of initiative. Without in any way restricting the rights of isolated groups, the Executive Committee will be able to steer their activity in the theoretical and organizational sense. For there will always be groups inside the Union that will feel burdened by various tactical issues, so that ideological or organizational assistance will always be necessary for certain groups. It goes without saying that the Executive Committee will be well placed to lend such assistance, for it will be, by virtue of its situation and its functions, the most au fait with the tactical or organizational line adopted by the Union on a variety of matters.

But if, nevertheless, some organizations or others should indicate a wish to pursue their own tactical line, will the Executive Committee or the Union as a body be in a position to prevent them? In other words, is the Union's tactical and policy line to be laid down by the majority, or will every group be entitled to operate as it deems fit, and, will the Union have several lines to start with?

*As a rule*, we reckon that the Union, as a body, should have a *single* tactical and political line. Indeed, the Union is designed for the purpose of bringing an end to the anarchist movement's dissipation and disorganization, the intention being to lay down, in place of a multiplicity of tactical lines giving rise to intestinal frictions, an overall policy line that will enable all libertarian elements to pursue a common direction and be all the more successful in achieving their goal. In the absence of which the Union would have lost one of its main raisons d'être.

However, there may be times when the opinions of the Union's membership on such and such an issue would be split, which would give rise to the emergence of a majority and a minority view. Such instances are commonplace in the life of all organizations and all parties. Usually, a resolution of such a situation is worked out.

We reckon, first of all, that for the sake of the unity of the Union, the minority should, in such cases, make concessions to the majority. This would be readily achievable, in cases of insignificant differences of opinion between the minority and the majority. If, though, the minority were to consider sacrificing its viewpoint an impossibility, then there would be the prospect of having two divergent opinions and tactics within the Union: a majority view and tactic, and a minority view and tactic.

In which case, the position will have to come under scrutiny by the Union as a whole. If, after discussion, the existence of two divergent views on the same issue were to be adjudged feasible, the co-existence of those two opinions will be accepted as an accomplished fact.

Finally, in the event of agreement between majority and minority on the tactical and political matters separating them proving impossible, there would be a split with the minority breaking away from the majority to found a separate organization.

Those are the three possible outcomes in the event of disagreement between the minority and the majority. In all cases, the question will be resolved, not by the Executive Committee which, let us repeat, is to be merely an executive organ of the Union, but by the entire Union as a body: by a Union Conference or Congress.

*2. The free regime of soviets.* We repudiate the current (Bolshevik) soviet arrangement, for it represents only a certain political form of the State. The soviets of workers' and peasants' deputies are a state political organization run by a political party. Against which we offer *soviets of the workers' and peasants' production and consumption organizations*. That is the meaning of the slogan: free regime of soviets and factory committees. We take such a regime to mean an economic and social arrangement wherein all of the branches and functions of economic and social life would be concentrated in the hands of the toilers' production and consumption organizations, which would perform those functions with an eye to meeting the needs of the whole laboring society. A Federation of these organizations and their soviets would dispense with the state and the capitalist system, and would be the chief pivot of the free soviets regime. To be sure, this regime will not instantly represent the full-blooded ideal of the anarchist commune, but it will be the first showing, the first practical essay of that commune, and it will usher in the age of free, non-statist creativity of the toilers.

We are of the opinion that, with regard to their decisions relating to the various reams of economic and social life, the soviets of the workers' and peasants' organizations or the factory committees will see to those, not through violence or decrees but rather through common accord with the toiling masses who will be taking a direct hand in the making of those decisions. Those decisions, though, will have to be binding upon all who vote for and endorse them.

3. *Anarchists will steer the masses and events in terms of theory.* The action of steering revolutionary elements and the revolutionary movement of the masses in terms of ideas should not and cannot ever be considered as an aspiration on the part of anarchists that they should take the construction of the new society into their own hands. That construction cannot be carried out except by the whole of laboring society, for that task devolves upon it alone, and any attempt to strip it of that right must be deemed anti-anarchist. The question of the ideological piloting is not a matter of socialist construction but rather of a *theoretical and political* influence brought to bear upon the revolutionary march of political events. We would be neither revolutionaries nor fighters were we not to take an interest in the character and tenor of the masses' revolutionary struggle. And since the character and tenor of that struggle are determined not just by objective factors, but also by subjective factors, that is to say by the influence of a variety of political groups, we have a duty to do all in our power to see that anarchism's ideological influence upon the march of revolution is maximized.

The current "age of wars and revolutions" poses the chief dilemma with exceptional acuteness: revolutionary events will evolve either under the sway of statist ideas (even should these be socialist) or else under the sway of non-statist (anarchist) ideas. And, since we are unshakable in our conviction that the statist trend will bring the revolution to defeat and the masses to a renewed slavery, our task follows from that with implacable logic: it is to do all we can to see that the revolution is shaped by the anarchist tendency. Now, our old way of operating, a primitive approach relying upon tiny, scattered groups, will not only not carry off that task but will, indeed, hinder it. So we have to proceed by a new method. *We have to orchestrate the force of anarchism's theoretical influence upon the march of events.* Instead of being an intermittent influence felt through disparate petty actions, it has to be made a powerful, ongoing factor. That, as we see it, can scarcely be possible unless anarchism's finest militants, in matters theoretical and practical alike, organize themselves into a body capable of vigorous action and well grounded in terms of theory and tactics: a General Union of Anarchists. It is in this same sense that the drive to pilot revolutionary syndicalism in theoretical terms should be understood. Entering the trade unions in an organized manner meant entering *as the carriers of a certain theory, a prescribed work plan*, work that will have to be strictly compatible in the case of every anarchist operating within the trade unions. The Anarchist Union is hardly going to trouble itself to prescribe tactics for the labor movement or draw up plans for strikes or demonstrations. But it is going to have to *disseminate* within the unions its ideas regarding the revolutionary tactics of the working class and on various events: that constitutes one of its inalienable rights. However, in the endeavor to spread their ideas, anarchists will have to be in strict agreement, both with one another as well as with the endeavors of the anarchist umbrella organization to which they belong and in the name of which they will be carrying out ideological and organizational work inside the trade unions. Conducting libertarian endeavors inside the trade unions in an organized manner and ensuring that anarchist efforts coincide have nothing to do with authoritarian procedure.

4. The writer's voiced objection to the program's thesis regarding *defense of the revolution* is, more than any other, rooted in a misunderstanding.

Having stressed *the necessity and inevitability*, in a civil war context, of the toilers' creating their revolutionary army, the platform asserts also that that army will have to be subordinated to the overall direction of the workers' and peasants' production organizations.

Subordination of the army to these organizations does not at all imply the idea of an elected civil authority. Absolutely not. An army, even should it be the most revolutionary and most popular of armies in terms of its mentality and title, cannot, however, exist and operate off its own bat, but has to be answerable to someone. Being an organ for the defense of the toilers' rights and revolutionary positions, the army must, for that very reason, be wholly subordinate to the toilers and piloted by them, *politically* speaking. (We stress *politically*, for, when it comes to its military and strategic direction, that could only be handled by military bodies within the ranks of the army itself and answerable to the workers' and peasants' leadership organizations.)

But to whom might the army be directly answerable, politically? The toilers do not constitute a single body. They will be represented by manifold economic organizations. It is to these very same organizations, in the shape of their federal umbrella agencies, that the army will be subordinated. The character and social functions of these agencies are spelled out at the outset of the present answers.

The notion of a toilers' revolutionary army must be either accepted or rejected, But should the army be countenanced, then the principle of that army's being subordinated to the workers' and peasants' organizations likewise has to be accepted. We can see no other possible solution to the matter.

5. *Press freedom, freedom of speech, of organization, etc.*

The victorious proletariat should not tamper either with freedom of speech nor of the press, not even those of its erstwhile enemies and oppressors now defeated by the revolution. It is even less acceptable that there be tampering with press freedom and freedom of speech in the context of the revolutionary socialist and anarchist groupings in the ranks of the victorious proletariat.

Free speech and press freedom are essential for the toilers, not simply so that they may illuminate and better grasp the tasks involved in their constructive economic and social endeavors, but also with an eye to discerning all the better the essential traits, arguments, plans and intentions of their enemies.

It is untrue that the capitalist and social opportunist press can lead the revolutionary toilers astray. The latter will be quite capable of deciphering and exposing the lying press and giving it the answer it deserves. Press freedom and freedom of speech only scare those like the capitalists and the communists who survive through dirty deeds that they are obliged to hide from the eyes of the great toiling masses. As for the toilers, freedom of speech will be a tremendous boon to them. It will enable them to listen to give everything a hearing, judge things for themselves and make their understanding deeper and their actions more effective.

Monopolization of the press and of the right to speak, or the limitation of these by their being squeezed into the confines of a single party's dogma, put paid to all confidence in the monopolists and in their press. If free speech is stifled, it is because there is a desire to conceal the truth: something demonstrated sensationally by the Bolsheviks, whose press is dependent upon bayonets and is read primarily out of necessity, there being no other.

However, there may be specific circumstances when the press, or, rather, abuse of the press, may be restricted on grounds of revolutionary usefulness. As an example, we might cite one episode from the revolutionary era in Russia.

Throughout the month of November 1919, the town of Ekaterinoslav was in the hands of the Makhnovist insurgent army. But at the same time, it was surrounded by Denikin's troops who, having dug in along the left bank of the Dniepr in the area around the towns of Amur and Nizhnedneprovsk, were shelling Ekaterinoslav continually with cannon mounted on their armored trains. And a Denikinist unit headed by General Slashchev, was simultaneously advancing on Ekaterinoslav from the north, from the area around Kremenchug.

At the time, the following daily newspapers were appearing in Ekaterinoslav, thanks to freedom of speech: the Makhnovist organ *Putsk Svobodey* (Road to Freedom), the Right Social Revolutionaries' *Narodovlastiye* (People's Power), the Ukrainian Left Social Revolutionaries' *Borotba* (Struggle), and the Bolsheviks' organ, *Zvezda* (Star). Only the Cadets, the then spiritual leaders of the Denikinist movement, were without their newspaper. Well now! Say the Cadets would have wanted to publish just then and in Ekaterinoslav their own newspaper which without any doubt would have been an accessory to Denikin's operations, would the revolutionary workers and insurgents have had to grant the Cadets the right to publish their newspaper, even at a time when its *primarily military* role in events would have been apparent? We think not.

In a civil war context, such cases may arise more than once. In these cases, the workers and peasants will have to be guided not by the broad principle of freedom of the press and free speech, but by the role that enemy mouthpieces will be undertaking in relation to the ongoing military struggle.

Generally speaking though, and with the exception of extraordinary cases (such as civil war) victorious labor will have to grant free speech and freedom of the press to left-wing views and right-wing views alike. That freedom will be the pride and joy of the free toilers' society.

Anarchists countenance revolutionary violence in the fight against the class enemy. They urge the toilers to use that. But they will never agree to wield power, even for a single instant, nor impose their decisions on the masses by force. In this connection their methods are: propaganda, force of argument, and spoken and written persuasion.

6. The proper interpretation of the anarchist principle: *"From each according to ability, to each according to needs."*

Without question, this principle is the corner-stone of anarchist communism. (See the "Platform.") No other economic, social or legal precept is as well suited to the ideal of anarchist communism as this one. The platform also says that "the social revolution, which will see to the reconstruction of the whole established social order, will thereby see to it that everyone's basic needs are provided for."

However, it is a broad declaration of principle on the problem of an anarchist regime. It has to be distinguished from the practical demands of the early days of the social revolution. As the experiences of the Paris Commune and the Russian revolution have shown, the non-working classes are beaten, but not definitively. In the early days a single idea obsesses them: collecting themselves, overthrowing the revolution and restoring their lost privileges.

That being the case, it would be extremely risky and fatally dangerous for the revolution to share out the products that would be available in the revolutionary zone in accordance with the principle of "To each according to his needs." It would be doubly dangerous for, aside from the comfort that this might afford the classes inimical to the revolution, which would be morally and strategically unconscionable, new classes will immediately arise and these, seeing the revolution supply the needs of every person, would rather idle than work. Plainly this double danger is not something that one can ignore, For it will quickly get the better of the revolution, unless effective measures are taken against it. The best measure would be to put the counterrevolutionary non-working classes usefully to work. In one sphere or another, to one extent or another, these classes will have to find themselves useful employment of which society has need: and it is their very *right* to their share in society's output that will *force* them so to do, for there are no rights that do not carry obligations. That is the very point that our splendid anarchist principle is making. It proposes notably to give to every individual in proportion to his needs, provided that every individual places his powers and faculties in the service of society and *not that he serves it not at all.*

An exception will be made for children, the elderly, the sick and the infirm, Rightly, society will excuse all such persons from the duty to labor, without denying them their entitlement to have all their needs met.

The moral sensibilities of the toilers is deeply outraged by the principle of taking from society according to one's needs, while giving to it according to one's mood or not at all: toilers have suffered too long from the application of that absurd principle and that is why they are unbending on this point. Our feeling for justice and logic is also outraged at this principle.

The position will change completely as soon as the free society of toilers entrenches itself and when there are no longer any classes sabotaging the new production for motives of a counterrevolutionary nature, but only a handful of idlers. Then society will have to make a complete reality of the anarchist principle: "From each according to ability, to each according to needs," for only on the basis of that principle will society be assured of its chance to breathe complete freedom and genuine equality.

But even then, the general rule will be that all able-bodied persons, enjoying rights over the material and moral resources of society, incur certain obligations in respect of production of these.

Bakunin, analyzing this problem in his day, wrote in the maturity of his anarchist thinking and activity (in 1871, comrade Nettlau reckons): "Everyone will have to work if he is to eat. Any man refusing to work will be free to perish of hunger, unless he finds some association or township prepared to feed him out of pity. But then it will probably be fair to grant him no political rights, since, although capable of work, his shameful situation is of his own choosing and he is living off another man's labor. For there will be no other basis for social and political rights than the work performed by each individual."

— The Group of Russian Anarchists Abroad<br>
November 2, 1926

## FOREWORD: THE CRUX OF THE MATTER

The debates provoked by the "organizational Platform" have thus far focused chiefly upon its various arguments or indeed the draft organization proposed by it. Most of its critic as well as several of its supporters have at no time been clear-sighted in their appreciation of the matter of the Platform's *premises*: they have never tried to discover what were the factors that prompted its appearance, the point of departure adopted by its authors. And yet these are matters of the greatest importance to those who seek to understand the spirit and import of the Platform.

The recently published "Reply to the Platform" from Voline and a few other anarchists, purporting to be a wholesale rebuttal of the Platform, has — for all the effort invested in the undertaking, for all its claims to be reading "between the lines" — failed to rise above the level of a banal diatribe against arguments that are considered in isolation, and it has shown itself powerless to strike at the very heart of the matter.

Given that this "Reply" displays utter incomprehension of the theses of the Platform, misrepresenting them and using sophistry to counter them, the Group of Russian Anarchists Abroad, having scrutinized this would-be rebuttal, has once again identified a series of points that are being queried: at the same time, the Group has registered the political and theoretical inadequacies of the Reply.

The commentary below, entitled "Reply to anarchism's confusionists," is given over to an examination of their reply. It is not at all intended either as a complement nor as an addendum to the Platform: it is merely designed to clarify a few of its theses.

Nevertheless, let us avail of this opportunity to point out a few things for consideration by comrades who may take an interest in the Platform for organization of Anarchism: we believe that in so doing we will be helping to make its meaning and its spirit better understood.

We have fallen into the habit of ascribing the anarchist movement's failure in Russia in 1917–1919 to the Bolshevik Party's statist repression. Which is a serious error. Bolshevik repression hampered the anarchist movement's spread during the revolution, but it was only one obstacle. Rather, it was the anarchist movement's own internal ineffectuality which was one of the chief causes of that failure, an ineffectuality emanating from the vagueness and indecisiveness that characterized its main policy statements on organization and tactics. (We hope to demonstrate and develop this claim in a separate study, adducing the data and the documents to prove it.)

Anarchism had no firm, hard and fast opinion regarding the main problems facing the social revolution, an opinion needed to satisfy the masses who were carrying out the revolution. Anarchists were calling for seizure of the factories, but had no well-defined homogeneous notion of the new production and its structure. Anarchists championed the communist device: "From each according to abilities, to each according to needs," but they never bothered to apply this precept to the real world. In this way, they allowed suspect elements to turn this grand principle into a caricature of anarchism. (We might just remember how many swindlers seized upon this principle as a means of grabbing collective assets during the revolution for their own personal advantage.) Anarchists talked a lot about the revolutionary activity of the workers themselves, but they were unable to direct the masses, even roughly, towards the forms that such activity might assume: they proved unable to regulate reciprocal relations between the masses and their ideological center. They incited the masses to shrug off the yoke of authority: but did not indicate how the gains of revolution might be consolidated and defended. They had no clear cut opinion and specific action policies with regard to lots of other problems. Which is what alienated them from the activities of the masses and condemned them to social and historical impotence.

That is where we have to look for the prime cause of their failure in the Russian revolution. We Russian anarchists who lived through the ordeal of revolution in 1905 and 1917 have not the slightest lingering doubt of that.

The obviousness of anarchism's *internal ineffectuality* has impelled us to search around for ways that might afford it success.

Upwards of twenty years of experience, revolutionary activity, twenty years of effort in anarchist ranks, and of effort that met with nothing but failures by anarchism as an *organizing movement*: all of this has convinced us of the necessity of a new comprehensive anarchist party organization rooted in one homogeneous theory, policy and tactic.

These are the premises of the "organizational Platform." Should anarchist militants from other countries, with no first hand experience of the Russian revolution, but with any knowledge of it, however meager, be willing to examine carefully the climate within the anarchist movement in their own country, they cannot fail to notice that the *internal ineffectuality* that caused anarchism to fail in the Russian revolution is equally prevalent in their own ranks and represents a deadly threat to the movement, especially in time of revolution. They will then understand the significance of the step forward that the organizational

Platform represents for anarchism, from the point of view of ideas as well as that of organization and construction.

And they will then realize that only the trail blazed by the Platform can restore anarchism's health and fortify it among the masses.

— P. Arshinov

## RETORT TO THE REPLY OF SOME RUSSIAN ANARCHISTS TO THE PLATFORM

The Reply (of April 1927) from some Russian anarchists to the Platform is an attempt to criticize and utterly refute the "organizational Platform" published by the Group of Russian Anarchists Abroad.

The Reply's authors claim to be in disagreement, not with certain ideas set out in the Platform, but rather with the whole thing. It is precisely "the Platform as such ... its underlying principles, its essence, its very mentality" that are not, in our estimation, acceptable, they say: they reckon that it is not anarchism but Bolshevism which is set out therein. (pp. 30–37) The *ideological essence* of the Bolsheviks and the "platformers" is identical (p. 37). Unquestionably, they say (p. 29) "the "Platform' authors look upon these as indispensable: the creation of a *directing policy center*, the organization of an army and a police force at the disposal of that center, which, in essence means, *the introduction of a transitional political authority statist in character*." And the Reply is peppered with lots of other similar and similarly stunning assertions.

It is our belief that such assertions make it obligatory upon their authors that they adduce adequate evidence before they make them.

Indeed, this practice of making unfounded allegations may lead in the anarchist movement to questionable conduct: every anarchist, in the true sense of the word, ought thus to make a determined stand against this approach.

In the course of our exposition, we shall see in what measure the authors of the Reply have authenticated their claims and this may enlighten us as to the meaning and worth of the Reply.

Its authors open with the declaration that they are "wholly in disagreement with the group regarding several fundamental or important theses in the Platform." But in reality, the dissension relates to every one of the Platform's theses on organization and principle. To explain their difference of opinion, they go to a lot of bother, resort to lots of sophistry and come up with unlikely arguments of their own. Since they are a priori hostile to the entirety of the Platform, but have no explicit view of their own on any of the issues broached therein, this necessarily had to be the case. We can appreciate this if we examine their main objections. But there is more: we shall see too that the authors of the Reply, while rebutting certain arguments from the Platform, very often wind up reiterating those arguments, claiming them as their own and using them to counter the Platform.

One point: the best retort to their objections is the Platform itself and the reader will find a specific and definite opinion there on all of the issues broached.

We shall, in order to clarify the spirit and the current by which they are motivated, be dwelling only upon certain points from the Platform which the authors of the Reply have sought to rebut.

## 1. The Causes of the Anarchist Movement's Weakness

The Platform locates the main cause of the anarchist movement's weakness in the absence of organizing factors and organized relations within the movement, which plunges it into a state of "chronic disorganization." At the same time, the Platform adds that this disorganization itself nestles in a few shortcomings of an ideological nature. We can see these shortcomings in a whole range of petit-bourgeois principles which have nothing to do with anarchism. The disorganization prevailing in our ranks draws succor from ideological confusion. And in order to overcome such practical and ideological confusion, the Platform floats the idea of establishing a general organization founded upon a homogeneous program. In this way, the Platform lays the foundations for a general organization of anarchists and creates ideological homogeneity. The organization thus collectively created will be strong enough to free anarchism from its ideological contradictions and organizational inadequacies and to pave the way for a mighty anarchist organization banded around homogeneous principles, We see no other way of developing and fortifying anarchism among the masses. The Platform has pointed out that the approach of bringing the various strands of anarchism together into one "tenderly united family' will not restore the health of the anarchist movement, but will instead only weaken and befuddle it.

The criticisms from the Reply utterly repudiate the picture of the causes of the anarchist movement's weakness that the Platform has painted. They see the causes located in *"the vagueness of several ideas basic to our outlook*, such as: the notion of social revolution, that of violence, that of collective creativity, that of the transitional period, that of organization, and still others," Also, the authors of the Reply enumerate other matters on which not all anarchists see eye to eye. If they are to be believed, you would think that anarchists have no common view on any matter, and that we would first have to theorize about everything before going on to tackle the organization issue. We have heard these ideas and promises often by now. And, instead of threatening for the hundredth and first time to come up with a probing theoretical work, would the authors of the Reply not be better employed getting on with that task, bringing it to fruition and offering it as a counter to the Platform? Our conception of the principles of anarchism is quite different. We are well aware that there is agreement among anarchists on the major issues like the idea of social revolution, that of violence, collective creativity, dictatorship, organization, etc. Those who have thus far remained adversaries of social revolution, of revolutionary violence and of organization, will always be such, and it really would be too naive to begin the history of anarchism all over again just for them. As soon as somebody would come along and tell us that he does not accept the idea of the social revolution, someone else would announce that he is against revolutionary violence, and a third would express unhappiness with the very idea of communist anarchism and a fourth would speak up against the class struggle. Shouting in every instance that *"anarchism's principles"* are not precise enough is tantamount in fact to a failure to devise an overall theory. Didn't we have Bakunin, Kropotkin and Malatesta who were precise enough about anarchism's principles? There were anarchist movements in a variety of countries based on those principles. How can we claim that they are not clear enough?

True, there are many obscure points in anarchism. But those are of quite another character. The fact is that alongside unquestionably anarchist personnel, the movement contains a number of liberal tendencies and individualist deviations that prevent it from having a stable base. To restore the movement to health, it must be freed of these tendencies and deviations: but this purge is, to a very large extent, prevented by just those individualists, open or disguised, (and the authors of the Reply are undoubtedly to be numbered among the latter) who are part of the movement.

## 2. The Class Struggle in the Anarchist System

The Platform declares quite plainly that the "class struggle between labor and capital was at all times in the history of human societies the chief factor determining the form and structure of those societies," that anarchism emerged and developed on the terrain of that struggle, in the bosom of oppressed, laboring humanity: that it is a social *movement* of the oppressed masses: the attempt to represent it as a general humanitarian problem amounts to a social and historical falsehood. In the struggle between capital and labor, anarchism fights wholeheartedly and inseparably alongside the latter.

The authors of the Reply counter that clear and precise message with "anarchism is a synthesis of elements: class, humanitarian and individual." That is the view held in common by liberals fearful of relying upon the truths of labor, who are forever dithering ideologically between the bourgeoisie and the proletariat and looking for common humanitarian values to use as connections between the contending classes. But we know well that there is no mankind, one and indivisible, that the demands of anarchist communism will be met only through the determination of the working class and that the activity of mankind as a whole, including the bourgeoisie, will not come into that at all: consequently, the viewpoint peddled by the liberals who do not know how to pick a side in the world-wide social tragedy cannot have anything to do with the class struggle and thus with anarchism.

## 3. On the Problem of Direction of the Masses and Events from the Ideal Point of View

The Reply rather takes issue more the idea an authoritarian leadership of *its own devising* than with the idea set out in the Platform. And, broadly speaking, throughout the Reply, its authors strive to divine some hidden meaning to the enigmatic Platform and go on to paint a picture that might strike terror not just into anarchists but even into certain overly sentimental statists. Thus, the influence wielded in the realm of ideas by the anarchists over the revolutionary trade unions is turned by them into subordination of those unions to the anarchist organization. The method of a common revolutionary military strategy applied in defense of the revolution "becomes," in their interpretation, the idea of a centralized State's army. The notion of an executive committee of anarchist organization becomes, in their representation of it, that of a dictatorial Central Committee demanding unquestioning obedience. One might think that the authors of the Reply are too ignorant to be capable of grasping the essence of all these problems: Not a bit of it! All of the misrepresentations and alterations made by the latter are made to the same end: we shall demonstrate anon to what end our adversaries pretend to be alarmed by the expression "direction of the masses and events from the ideas point of view." But are they not then like those odd sorts who, being terrified by the idea of influence, are afraid of influencing themselves? Direction of the masses from the "ideas" point of view simply means the existence of a guiding idea in their movement. In the world of socialist struggle and socialist demands, such ideas are not numerous. But it is natural that we anarchists wanted the toilers' guiding idea to be the anarchist idea and not that of the social democrats for example, of those who have only recently betrayed the Viennese workers' revolutionary movement.

But, in order that the anarchist idea should become the lodestone of the masses, we have to develop well organized ideological activity which in turn necessitates an anarchist organization whose members spread very clear and coherent notions among the masses. All of which is so elementary and self-evident that it is embarrassing to have to spell it out again in this day and age to folk who claim to be conversant with anarchism. The authors of the "Reply" are, moreover well aware of that, since, after having misrepresented our point of view and peddled a mountain of absurdities regarding the General Union of Anarchists, they close by saying that the anarchists' role in economic organizations is to influence the masses morally and in terms of ideas, while that of specifically anarchist organizations would be to help them indeed from this "ideas" point of view. But is not saying that tantamount to borrowing the positions of the "Platform" after having blackened its name? What is the meaning of "influence and assist the masses from the ideas point of view"? Are anarchists going to render ideological assistance to a mob in the process of mounting a pogrom or of carrying out lynch law? All assistance afforded to the masses in the realm of ideas must be consonant with the ideology of anarchism: otherwise, it would not be anarchist assistance. "Ideologically assist" simply means: influence from the ideas point of view, direct from the ideas point of view. Bakunin, Kropotkin, Reclus, Malatesta — those are men who were, incontestably, ideological directors of the masses. But we aim to see that such direction, exercised occasionally, becomes a permanent factor: that is only going to be possible when there is an organization possessed of a common ideology and whose membership engage in ideologically coordinated activity, without being side-tracked or dispersed as has been the case hitherto. Those are the terms in which the question is posed. And it is in vain that the authors of the "Reply" will dream up sophisms in order to show that direction in the realm of ideas means authoritarian direction.

It is the masses of the people that will make the revolution themselves, say our adversaries. Understood. But they ought to know that the revolutionary mass is forever nurturing in its bosom a minority of initiators, who precipitate and direct events. And we are entitled to assert that in a true social revolution the supporters of worker anarchism alone will account for that minority.

## 4. The Idea of the Transitional Period

The "Platform" notes that the social political parties understand the term "Transitional Period" to mean a specific stage in the life of a people, the essential features of which period are: a breach with the old order of things and the installation of a new economic and political system, a system which as yet does not represent the complete emancipation of the toilers. Communist anarchism, however, repudiates transitional arrangements of that sort. It advocates a social revolution of the toilers that will lay the foundations for their free and egalitarian society.

It strikes us that the problem could not be posed any more clearly. But the authors of the "Reply" have contrived to discover the precise opposite in the "Platform." In their estimation, the "Platform" is, all in all, merely *an attempt to peddle this idea (of the transitional period) and to graft it on to anarchism*." And here comes the proof: the "Platform" looks forward to certain points, (there are some set out in the appendix to the "Platform") when the press (or rather the abuse thereof) of the class hostile to the toilers will have been shut down by struggling labor. And the authors of the "Reply" are cock a hoop: why, doesn't that amount to a "transitional period really"? Then again the "Platform" declares that the anarchist communist principle "from each according to his talents, to each according to his needs" in no way makes it incumbent upon labor in rebellion to feed everyone, including its avowed enemies who, for counterrevolutionary motives, would refuse to play a part in production and would dream of nothing other than decapitating the revolution. That principle merely means equality in distribution within the parameters of the egalitarian society: it does not at all apply to those who have placed themselves outside that society for counterrevolutionary motives. Furthermore, that principle means that every member of laboring society who profits from its services should serve it in accordance with his strengths and capabilities and not at all in accordance with his whims or indeed not at all. The authors of the "Reply" again raise a hue and cry: what about that, is that not the transitional period? They proclaim "the application of the principle of equal enjoyment of all available and freshly manufactured products, regardless of their quantity, by all the members of the collectivity, without exception, restriction or privilege of any sort." True, it is none too clear from this formula whether the rebel workers must feed the bourgeoisie that plays no part in production and uses its ingenuity to oppose them. But, since that formula is opposed to the labor principle of the "Platform," we have to conclude that the toilers do have a duty to maintain the bourgeoisie, even if they have not the slightest desire so to do.

We shall not enter into discussion of such a viewpoint. The working class itself will resolve it practically, come the social revolution. However we do believe that it will not shower the authors of the "Reply" with praise for the tender care with they have surrounded a bourgeois that refuses to work. Would the authors of the "Reply" not be better advised to devise some way of turning bourgeois into honest members of laboring society instead of watching out for them with such solicitude?

But the most impressive sleight of hand by the authors of the "Reply" comes only later. After having seen them rebut all of the positions of the "Platform," after having seen them dismiss its authors as shameful Bolsheviks, and their constructive system as a transitional political and economic state system — one would expect to find them presenting a bold outline of the post-revolutionary anarchist society, of the society in which everybody would find his every need met and which would have nothing in common with the one sketched in the "Platform," Not a bit of it, though. All one finds there is an admission that the creative endeavor of the social revolution *"will be a natural start to the formation of an anarchist society."* Now that declaration is borrowed, word for word, from the "Platform," which states "the victory of the toilers… will be the *start of the construction* of the anarchist society which, once outlined, will then, without interruption, follow its line of development, growing stronger and more rounded." In truth, with our adversaries, the right side of their minds has no idea what the left side is thinking and doing.

## 5. The Problem of Production

Nor do the authors of the "Reply" fail to raise categorical objections to us in relation to the problem of production as well. It is very hard to get an idea of what prompts their objections, as well as of what they are advocating in their exposition. The idea of *unified* and *coordinated* production set out by the "Platform" leaves them cold, as does the idea of agencies directing production and elected by the workers. In the idea of coordinated production they divine the specter of centralization and statism and they offer instead the idea of decentralized production.

The idea of unified production is clear: the "Platform" looks upon the whole of modern industry as one single, gigantic workshop of producers, created by the efforts of several generations of toilers and altogether the property of everybody and of no one in particular.

Particular branches of production are inseparably interconnected and they can neither produce nor even exist as separate entities. The *unity* of that workshop is determined by technical factors. But there is only one unified and coordinated production capable of existence in this mammoth factory: production carried out in accordance with an overall scheme prescribed by the workers' and peasants' production organizations, a plan drafted in the light of the needs of society as a whole: the products of that factory belong to the whole of laboring society. Such production is truly socialist.

It is very much to be regretted that the authors of the "Reply" omitted to explain how they envisage decentralized production. But we may suppose that they are talking about several independent productions, isolated industries, separate trusts and maybe even separate factories producing and disposing of their products as they see fit. The authors of the "Reply" declare that decentralized production will operate according to federalist principles. But, since the federated units will be nothing more than small private entrepreneurs (to wit, the united workforce of a single plant, trust or industry), production will not be at all socialist: it will still be capitalist, in that it is based on the parcelization of ownership, which will not take long to provoke competition and antagonisms.

Unified production is not centralized production directed from some authoritarian "center." Unified production is merely authentically communist production.

## 6. Defense of the Revolution

Examining the problem of the defense of the Revolution, the "Platform" remarks first that the most effective means of defending the revolution would be to find a radical solution to the problems of production, supply and the land. But the "Platform" also foresaw that solution of these problems will necessarily spark a bitter civil war in which the exploiter class will strive to retain or to regain its privileges. That is quite inescapable. The "Platform" indicates also that the class currently in power will in that war resort to "the methodology of all military action: unity of operational planning and unity of overall command." It goes on to say that the toilers will also have to have recourse to these methods of struggle, and all the armed units that will spring up voluntarily will have to amalgamate into a single army. This necessity does not make it impossible for local detachments to wage an independent fight against the counterrevolution. It does, though, require that a revolutionary worker and peasant army confront the broad front of the counterrevolutionary onslaught.

In order to combat the counterrevolution, the workers must possess their common operational plan and overall command. Otherwise, the enemy will attack them where they are weakest and least expecting it.

History is the best proof of this:

a) All popular revolutions were especially successful when the army ceased blindly to serve the ruling classes and threw in its lot with the rebels.

b) During the Russian revolution, it was those popular movements that managed to unite their armed forces, units of importance, to which military operations affecting an entire region were entrusted, that met with appreciable success. This was the case with the insurgent movement headed by Makhno. Insurgent groups that failed to understand this necessity perished in the face of a well organized enemy. There were hundreds of instances of that in the Russian revolution.

c) The Russian counterrevolution led by Koltchak, Denikin, Yudenich and others owes its military defeat chiefly to the fact that it failed to establish a single operational plan and united command for the counterrevolutionary armies: thus while Koltchak was (in 1918) near Kazan and making for Moscow, Denikin stayed in the Caucasus: but it was only when Koltchak was "liquidated" (in 1919) that Denikin rounded on Moscow. (*Note*: We are not speaking here of the partisan warfare waged by the peasants against Koltchak and Denikin and which brought the latter to military and social defeat.)

Insurgent revolutionary work during the civil war must know how to use the methodology of unity of operational planning and overall command of the revolutionary armed forces. Without that, the workers and peasants will be beaten by counterrevolutionary forces highly conversant with the military arts. The "Platform" pointed out how necessary it was that workers utilize that methodology as well as create a single army embracing all of the armed forces at the revolution's disposal. It goes without saying that the "Platform" insists upon this organization only for the duration of the civil war in the fight against the counterrevolution. Once that war ends, the revolutionary army has no further raison d'être and will fade away. To tell the truth, the whole chapter in the "Platform" that deals with defense of the revolution stressed only the need that workers will have to utilize the methodology of a common operational plan and common command. The "Platform" also labors the point that these methods as well as the idea of the revolutionary army are to be regarded only as a stratagem necessitated by civil war and in no way as anarchist principles. It strikes us that no sane and honest mind could find grounds there for accusing the "Platform" with pushing the idea of a standing, centralized army. But the "sages" of the "Reply" manage it nonetheless. They charge us with nothing more nor less than aspiring to create a centralized army placed at the disposal of the overall productive organizations directed, in their turn, by the Union/Party. We believe that anarchist circles are clear-sighted enough to grasp for themselves that this view is absurd and incoherent. The "Reply" proposes no hard and fast solution to the problem of defense of the revolution. After having, as is its wont, proffered the most motley shower of insults against the "Platform," the authors of it start to mumble something about union of the armed forces in the revolution, thereby aping the idea of the "Platform," albeit misrepresenting it as usual.

But it is by examining the necessity, announced by the "Platform," of the revolutionary army's being subordinated to the toilers' higher productive organizations that the authors of the "Reply" display a truly penetrating mind, a real masterpiece of farsightedness. How dare you, they exclaim, argue that that is not a transitional period? Precisely how subordination of the revolutionary army to the workers' and peasants' productive organizations constitutes a transitional period — that is the inscrutable enigma. The toilers' military forces will not in any way become an end in themselves: they will have only one way of implementing the formalities of the worker and peasant revolution. As a result, it is to the workers and peasants that the army should be answerable and by them alone that it should be directed politically. According to the authors of the "Reply," the revolutionary army, or indeed the armed groupings, should not be answerable to those organizations: they will lead an independent existence and fight as they deem fit. Thus are folk who have the effrontery to speak of things upon which they have never reflected hoist on their own petard!

## 7. Anarchist Organization

On this score too, the authors of the "Reply" are primarily concerned with misrepresenting the meaning of the "Platform." First of all they turn the idea of an Executive Committee into that of a Party Central Committee, a committee that issues orders, makes laws and commands. Anybody in the least degree slightest conversant with politics knows well that an executive committee and a central committee are two quite different ideas: the executive committee may very well be an anarchist agency: indeed, such an organ exists in many anarchist and anarchist-syndicalist organizations.

While rejecting the idea of a broad anarchist organization based on a homogeneous ideology, the authors of the "Reply" peddle the idea of a synthesizing organization wherein all of the strands of anarchism are gathered together into "one single family." To pave the way for the establishment of that organization, they propose to set up a newspaper in every country which would discuss and examine all controversial issues, from every angle, and thus bring about an entente between anarchists.

We have already spelled out our position regarding this notion of synthesis and we shall not rehearse our reasoning here. We shall confine ourselves simply to adding that the existence of discrepancies between the opinions of anarchists is due more to the lack of a periodical to act as a forum for discussion (there were some once). A forum for discussion will never manage to bring the divergent currents together, but it will assuredly clutter up the minds of the laboring masses. Furthermore, a whole swathe of individuals claiming to be anarchists has nothing in common with anarchism. Gathering these people (on the basis of what?) into "one family" and describing that gathering as "anarchist organization" would not only be a nonsense: it would be positively harmful. If that were to happen by some mischance, all prospect of anarchism's developing into a revolutionary social movement of the toilers would be banished.

It is not an indiscriminating mix, but rather a selection from the wholesome anarchist forces and the organization thereof into an anarchist-communist party that is vital to the movement: not a hotchpotch synthesis, but *differentiation* and exploration of the anarchist idea so as to bring them to a homogeneous movement program. That is the only way to rebuild and strengthen the movement in the laboring masses.

To conclude, a few words on the ethical *features* of the "Reply." In reality, it is not to the "Platform" that this "Reply" is addressed, but to a whole series of positions duly misrepresented in advance by the authors of the "Reply." There is not a single paragraph to which they reply without preamble. They always start off by ferreting out the Jesuitical recesses of the position and, after having concocted those, they put their objections to them. In their hands, the "Platform" has been turned into a fiendish conspiracy against the anarchist movement and against the working class. This is how they represent the thinking of the "Platform": "On top, *the leading party*, (the General Union of Anarchists); down below, the higher peasant and worker organizations directed by the Union; lower still, the inferior organizations, the organs of struggle against the counter-revolution, the army, etc." Elsewhere, they talk about "investigatory and political violence" institutions. A whole picture is painted there, a portrait of a police state, directed by the General Union of Anarchists.

One might well ask: why this recourse to all these lies? The authors of the "Reply" have read the "Platform." So they ought to know that the thinking behind the "Platform" boils down to the organization of anarchist forces *for the period of struggle against the capitalist class society*: its object is simply to spread anarchism among the masses and ideological direction of their struggle. The moment that the toilers will have defeated capitalist society, a new era in their history will be ushered in, an era when all social and political functions are transferred to the hands of workers and peasants who will set about the creation of the new life. At that point the anarchist organizations and, with them, the General Union, will lose all their significance and they should, in our view, gradually melt away into the productive organizations of the workers and peasants. The "Platform" contains a whole constructive section dealing with the role of the workers and peasants in the wake of the Revolution. By contrast, it says nothing about the specific role at that juncture of the World Union of Anarchists. And this is no accident, but rather a deliberate omission. Because all political and economic activity will then be concentrated, as we see it, in the toilers' organs of self-administration: in the trade unions, the factory committees, the councils, etc.

But, to credit the authors of the "Reply," it is only then that the Anarchist Communist Party comes into its own: positioned somewhere up above, it is to direct the "higher" and the "lower" toilers' organizations, the army, etc. That is their way of dealing with a document of which they propose to offer a critique, their way of treating the reader to whom they promised truth. The *irresponsibility* of these methods will surely startle any reader capable of reflection on matters political.

In scrutinizing the other reasons for the anarchist movement's weakness, the authors of the "Reply" point to this one: "The current state of mind of the masses who have neither the wherewithal nor the desire to *investigate, analyze and make comparisons* and who, consequently still and always plump for the easiest option, the course of least resistance according to the "ready-made' recipes on offer from demagogues of every hue."

Let us conclude our examination of the "Reply" by these remarkable utterances from its authors. Remarkable words in that they demonstrate the futility and hypocrisy of their speechifying about the creative potential "of the masses, their autonomous activity, the dire threat that ideological direction poses to that potential, etc. If the "Reply is to be believed, one gets the impression that the masses are not only incapable of finding the paths to their liberation, but also have not the slightest desire so to do, and prefer to follow the line of least resistance."

If that is how things really stand, things are going badly for anarchism, since it is by force that it has to draw the masses to its side. In setting themselves the target of rebutting the "Platform," regardless of cost, even should they have to fly in the face of reason, the facts and life itself, in order to achieve that, the authors of the "Reply" have been reduced to declarations like those.

We hope that we have proved, in the foregoing exposition, that the program of the authors of the "Reply" was quite without foundation and that they are typical specimens of the political incoherence in our movement. As for the ethical side of the "Reply," that cannot be described as anything other than an *object lesson in calumny*.

— The Group of Russian Anarchists Abroad
August 18, 1927

# DOCUMENT NO. 5
# PIOTR ARSHINOV — THE OLD AND THE NEW IN ANARCHISM (REPLY TO COMRADE MALATESTA)

In the Geneva anarchist magazine *Le Réveil* first of all, and later in pamphlet form, comrade Errico Malatesta has published an article critical of the *Organizational Platform* issued by the Group of Russian Anarchists Abroad.

That article has inspired puzzlement and regret in us. We had expected, and expect still, that the notion of organized anarchism may meet with dogged resistance from the supporters of chaos, so numerous in anarchist circles, for that idea obliges any anarchist participating in the movement to shoulder his responsibilities and confront the notions of duty and consistency. Whereas the favored principle in which most anarchists have been schooled thus far can be summed up by the following axiom: *"I do as I please and pay no heed to anything."* It is only natural that anarchists of that sort, imbued with such principles, should be violently hostile to any notion of organized anarchism and collective responsibility.

Comrade Malatesta is a stranger to this principle, and that is why his text has drawn this response from us. Puzzlement, because he is a veteran of international anarchism and has failed to grasp the spirit of the Platform, its essential character and its relevance, which flow from the demands of our revolutionary age. Regret, because, in order to keep faith with the dogma implicit in the cult of individuality, he has set his face (only temporarily, let us hope) against the endeavor which seems a crucial stage in the further spread and development of the anarchist movement.

Right at the outset of his article, Malatesta says that he subscribes to a number of the theses of the Platform or indeed reinforces them with the ideas he sets out. He would agree with us in noting that anarchists have not had and do not have any influence over social and political developments, for want of a serious, active organization, The principles embraced by comrade Malatesta correspond to the chief tenets of the Platform. One might have expected that he would also have examined, grasped and accepted a number of other principles set out in our draft, for there is a thread of coherence and logic running through all of the Platform's theses. Malatesta, though, goes on to express in trenchant terms his difference of opinion with the Platform. He raises the question of whether the General Anarchist Union anticipated by the Platform might resolve the problem of education of the toiling masses, answering that query in the negative. He advances as his grounds for this the allegedly authoritarian character of the Union which, according to him, would nurture the idea of submission to higher-ups and leaders.

On what can such a grave charge be based? It is in the notion of collective responsibility espoused by the Platform that he sees his chief grounds for framing such a charge. He cannot countenance the principle that the Union as a body is answerable for each of its members and that, conversely, each member is answerable for the policy line of the Union as a whole. Which means that Malatesta rejects the very principle of organization which appears to us to be the most essential thing if the organized anarchist movement is to be able to proceed with its development.

Thus far the anarchist movement has nowhere reached the stage where it is a popular movement organized as such. The blame for this cannot be laid at the door of objective circumstances, for instance the fact that the toiling masses might not understand anarchism or take any interest in it in times of revolution: no, the cause of the anarchist movement's weakness and instability resides essentially in the anarchists themselves. Not once to date have they attempted conduct either propaganda of their ideas or their practical activities among the toiling masses in an organized manner.

Strange as this may appear to comrade Malatesta, we staunchly affirm that the activity of the most active anarchists — of which he is one — necessarily displayed an individualistic character: even if that activity was marked by high personal responsibility, it was the business only of an individual and not of an organization. In the past, when our movement was new-born as a national or international movement, this could not have been otherwise: the foundations had to be laid for the anarchist mass movement: the toiling masses had to be called upon and invited to commit themselves to the anarchist mode of struggle. That was necessary, even if it was only the doing of isolated individuals of limited means. Those militants of anarchism fulfilled their mission: they drew the most active workers towards anarchist ideas. However, that was only half of the task. At a time when the number of anarchist personnel, coming from the laboring masses, grew considerably, it became impossible to confine oneself to isolated propaganda and practice, individually or in scattered groups. To continue thus would have meant marking time. In order to avoid slipping backwards, one had to press on. That is the precise explanation for the widespread decline in the anarchist movement: we had taken that first step but proceeded no further.

That second step consisted then and consists still of gathering anarchist personnel drawn from the toiling masses into an active collective capable of leading the organized struggle of the toilers with the aim of making a reality of anarchist ideas.

The question facing anarchists of every land is as follows: can our movement content itself with subsisting on the basis of the old forms of organization, local groups with no organizational linkage between them, each one operating off its own bat, with its own ideology and particular tactic? Or should our movement instead look to new forms of organization that would help it develop and put down roots in the broad masses of toilers?

The experience of the last twenty years, and more especially that of the two Russian revolutions — of 1905 and 1917–1919 — hint better than any "theoretical considerations" at the answer to that question.

During the Russian revolution, the toiling masses were won over to anarchist ideas: even so, anarchism as an organized movement suffered a complete rebuff in it. Whereas at the outset of the revolution, we were in the van of the fighting, as soon as the constructive phase arrived we found ourselves irreparably at a remove from this and, in the end, remote from the masses. This was not the work of chance: such an attitude flowed *inevitably* from our own powerlessness, in terms both of organization and of our ideological confusionism.

At the root of that failure was the fact that, throughout the revolution, anarchists proved unable to expound their social and political program, and courted the toiling masses only with fitful, contradictory propaganda: we had no stable organization. Our movement was represented by makeshift organizations sprouting up here and there, themselves unsure of what they wanted and which most often evaporated after a time, leaving not a trace. One would have to be desperately naive and stupid to think that the toilers could follow and join such "organizations" in time of social struggle and communist construction.

We have fallen into the habit of putting the failure of the anarchist movement in Russia in 1917–1919 down to statist repression by the Bolshevik Party: this is a great mistake. The Bolshevik repression hobbled the spread of the anarchist movement during the revolution, but it was not the sole obstacle. Rather, the *internal impotence* of the movement itself was one of the chief causes of that failure, an impotence that arose from the vagueness and indecision that characterized the sundry political statements regarding organization and tactics.

Anarchism had no set, hard and fast opinion on the essential problems of the social revolution: an opinion that was crucial in satisfying the appetite of the masses who created the revolution. Anarchists preached the communist principle: *"From each according to his ability, to each according to his needs,"* but they never troubled to apply that principle to reality, or indeed they allowed certain suspect elements to turn that great principle into a caricature of anarchism (let us just recall how many swindlers capitalized upon it so as to seize the assets of the collectivity for their own personal advantage). Anarchists talked a lot about the revolutionary activity of the toilers, but proved incapable of helping them, even by sketching out in rough the form that such activity should have assumed: they proved unable to regulate the reciprocal relations between the masses and their source of ideological inspiration. They encouraged the toilers to shake off the yoke of Authority, but they did not indicate how to consolidate and defend the revolution's gains. They lacked clear and precise ideas and a program of action on lots of other issues. It was this that distanced them from the masses' activity and condemned them to social and historical impotence. *There* is where we should seek the prime cause for their failure in the Russian revolution.

And we have no doubt that, if the revolution were to erupt in several European countries, anarchists will suffer the same failure, for there they are no less divided — if not in fact more divided — in terms of their ideas and organization.

The present age, when the toilers in their millions are entering the lists of the social struggle, requires of anarchists direct and plain answers to a whole series of questions concerning that struggle and the communist reconstruction that should follow it: likewise, it requires that anarchists assume collective responsibility for those answers and for anarchist propaganda generally. Should they not shoulder that responsibility, anarchists, like anyone else in such circumstances, are not entitled to engage in inconsequential propaganda among the laboring masses, which fight heedless of heavy sacrifices and the loss of countless victims.

These days, this is neither a game nor a matter of improvisation. So it is that, until such time as we have our General Anarchist Union, we will not be in a position to supply common answers to all of these vital questions.

At the start of his article, comrade Malatesta appears to welcome the idea of an anarchist umbrella organization being set up: however, by categorically rejecting collective responsibility, he makes realization of such an organization an impossibility. For it would be possible only if there was a theoretical and organizational concordance, representing a common platform on the basis of which numerous militants might come together. Insofar as they would accept that platform, the latter would become *binding* upon them. Anyone unwilling to accept these basic principles as binding will not, and indeed will not be willing to, become a member of the organization.

In this way, that organization would be the union of those who would share a common conception of the theoretical, tactical and political policy line to be observed, As a result, the practical activity of a member of the organization is naturally in complete harmony with the overall activity, and conversely the activity of the organization as a whole could not be at odds with the conscience and activity of each member, assuming he has accepted the program fundamental to the organization. It is this which characterizes the principle of collective responsibility: the Union as a body is answerable for the activity of each member, in the knowledge that he could only carry out his political and revolutionary work in the political spirit of the Union. Likewise, each member is fully answerable for the Union as a whole, since its activity could not be at odds with what has been determined by the whole membership. There is no hint here of authoritarianism, as comrade Malatesta mistakenly argues: merely the expression of an alert and responsible understanding of militant work.

It goes without saying that in summoning anarchists to organize themselves on the basis of a definite program, we are not thereby depriving anarchists of other persuasions of their right to organize howsoever they may deem fit, However, we are convinced that, as soon as anarchists have created an organization of importance, the hollowness and futility of the traditional organizations will become glaringly apparent.

…The principle of responsibility is taken by comrade Malatesta in the sense of the moral responsibility of individuals and groups, This is why he attributes to congresses and their resolutions the mere role of sort of friendly get-togethers, mouthing only platitudes.

That traditional way of thinking about the role of congresses does not stand up to the simplest test in real life. In fact, what would be the point of a congress that would merely express "opinions" and would not undertake to make these a reality in life? None. In a broad movement, a merely moral rather than organizational responsibility loses all value.

Which brings us to the question of majority and minority. Our thinking is that all discussion of this topic is redundant. In practice, it has long since been resolved. Always and everywhere, practical problems among us have been resolved by majority vote. Which is perfectly understandable, for there is no other way of resolving these things in an organization that is determined to act.

Out of all the objections voiced to the Platform, an understanding of the most important thesis therein — understanding of our approach to the organizational problem and how to resolve it — has thus far been missing. Indeed, understanding of this is extremely important and is of crucial significance with regard to a proper appreciation of the Platform and of the whole organizational endeavor of the *Dyelo Truda* group.

…The only way to banish chaos and breathe life back into the anarchist movement is a theoretical and organizational *clarification* of our ranks, leading on to *differentiation* and *recruitment* an active core of militants on the basis of a homogeneous theoretical and practical program. Which is one of the main aims of our text.

What does this clarification represent and how should it proceed? The absence of an agreed overall program has always been a lack sorely felt in the anarchist movement, and has helped leave it very often highly vulnerable, its propaganda having never been any too coherent and consistent in relation to the ideas professed and the practical principles advocated. Quite the contrary, it has often come to pass that what was propagated by one group is denigrated by another one. And this holds not only for tactical applications, but also for the underlying theses.

Some excuse such a state of affairs by saying that it is an index of the multiplicity of anarchist ideas. Fine, let us agree upon that, but of what interest is that multiplicity supposed to be for the toilers?

They struggle and suffer *in the here and now* and have immediate need of a proper conception of revolution that may speed them on their way to emancipation right away: they do not need any abstract notion, but a living idea that is a real, developed answer to their questions, while anarchists, in practice, often proffer many contradictory ideas, systems and programs, with the most significant rubbing shoulders with the trifling, or even at odds with one another. In such circumstances, it is readily understandable that anarchism has not managed, and, in the future *never will manage* to germinate in the masses and become one with them, in such a way as to provide the inspiration for their liberation movement. For the masses sense the pointlessness of contradictory ideas and instinctively give them a wide berth: even though, in time of revolution, they may act and live in a libertarian manner.

To conclude: comrade Malatesta reckons that the Bolsheviks' successes in their country have been giving sleepless nights to those Russian anarchists who issued the Platform. Malatesta's error consists of his having failed to take account of the extremely significant circumstance that the *Organizational Platform* is the product, not just of the Russian revolution, but also of the *anarchist movement in that revolution*. Now, there is no way that this fact can be overlooked if one wishes to resolve the problem of anarchist organization, its format and its theoretical basis. It is crucial that questions be asked about the place that anarchism occupied in the great social upheaval in 1917. What was the attitude of the insurgent masses to anarchism and anarchists? What was it about them that they prized? Why, in spite of that, did anarchism meet with failure in that revolution? What lessons have been learnt from that? All these questions, and many another, must inevitably arise to confront anyone who broaches the issues raised by the Platform. This, comrade Malatesta has not done. He has tackled the current problem of organization as an absent-minded dogmatist. Which is rather incomprehensible for those of us who have been wont to look upon him not as an ideologue but, rather, as a practitioner of real, active anarchism. He makes do with examining the degree to which such and such a thesis from the Platform is compatible or otherwise with anarchism's traditional viewpoints, then he rebuts them, finding them to be at odds with those old notions. It does not even enter his head that the reverse might be true, that it is these latter which might be at fault, and that that is reason for the appearance of the Platform. That is one way of explaining the whole series of errors and contradictions set out earlier in his text.

Let us note still another serious omission on his part: he fails to dwell at all upon the theoretical basis, or the constructive part of the Platform, focusing solely upon the organizational draft. Our text not only refuted the notion of synthesis and of anarcho-syndicalism as untenable and having failed, but it also proffered a scheme for *rallying anarchism's active militants on the basis of a more or less homogeneous program*. Comrade Malatesta ought to have dwelt in detail upon that approach: however he passes it over in silence as he also does the constructive section, although his conclusions are apparently applicable to the Platform as a whole. Which makes his article somewhat of a contradiction and unstable.

Libertarian communism must not languish in the doldrums of its past: it must rise above them by combating and overcoming its defects. The novelty of the Platform and of the *Dyelo Truda* group consists precisely of their being strangers to obsolete dogmas and preconceptions and that instead they strive to conduct their activity on the basis of real, current data. This venture represents the first ever attempt to fuse anarchism and real life, and to create anarchist activity on that basis. Only thus will libertarian communism be wrested from the talons of an obsolete dogma and invigorate the life-giving movement of the masses.

*Dyelo Truda*, No. 36, (May 1928), pp. 4–11

# DOCUMENT NO. 6
# THE "NABAT" ORGANIZATION IN THE UKRAINE, 1919–1920

Note by the editors of *Dyelo Truda: The article published below is lifted from a lengthy letter from a Russian anarchist, one of the founders and most active participants in the "Nabat" anarchist Confederation in the Ukraine: we shall not name him, for since 1920 he has been incarcerated without cease in Bolshevik prisons: in the Butyrki, in the Solovietzky islands … and is even now a deportee in Siberia.*

*The organizational and political structure of "Nabat" has hitherto been described only in the articles of Voline and, in his version, seems a rather loose organization founded upon friendly and harmonious relations, ignorant of organizational discipline and responsibility, and acknowledging no leadership echelon, in terms of ideas, in anarchist circles. Now we have the testimony of a comrade who sheds a different light on the organizational and political aspect of "Nabat.' Not only did the latter enforce strict organizational principles and collective responsibility, but in fact it struggled to impose these and tended to become the prototype of the structured organization for which the* Dyelo Truda *Group of Russian Anarchists is now campaigning. And we have the testimony of one of "Nabat's" founders and active participants to that effect.*

*Obviously, there were theoretical contradictions, on account of the aspiration of certain of its members that the Confederation should espouse the famous ideology of the anarchist synthesis. But that in no way undermined the strength of the "Nabat" structure.*

*It should be pointed out that the author of this piece has not dealt adequately with the centralist deviation of the French anarchists, regarding that deviation as a quite natural and useful backlash against the chronic chaos and disintegration that have prevailed in anarchist circles, and would therefore identify with that deviation. As for ourselves, however, we see it as a passing fad that will give way to a libertarian federalism strictly compatible with ideological and organizational accountability.*

*— The editors of* Dyelo Truda

Let me come back to the problem of the "Nabat," concerning which our exchange of views has been temporarily interrupted in our correspondence, for I have yet to reply on this matter to one of your last letters, due to the fact that, on account of circumstances not of our making, that latter was destroyed and I lost the thread of our discussions.

That said, I want to answer you in a couple of words regarding the background of this matter, for apparently you have not yet grasped the true nature of "Nabat," the circumstances in which it was established and how it resolved the problems that confronted it. What you term, if memory serves, the realistic idealism of "Nabat" represented its genuine, living aspect, its true essence. At first, "Nabat" had no definite standard program that could have resolved all of the movement's theoretical and practical questions. *It had not yet managed to draft one.* It had only begun to do so, operating on the basis of certain methodological principles. It had even made a little headway in this, particularly with regard to structure and organization. It was in fact an organizational Union rooted in a few broad principles, the aim being to carry out organizational work in concert with the best and most wholesome representatives of the various anarchist tendencies, with those sensible of the need for that. The Nabatovians as yet had no set program, but they did have a common outlook on the basis of which to resolve a series of points in that program: an outlook that was forged in the process of struggle, on the basis of lived experience of revolution, requiring immediate answers and solutions.

Tactical matters accounted for a large part of our concerns: the soviets, the toilers' Unions, the army, the insurgent movement, the peasantry and so on were all on the agenda. At the same level, the great theoretical issues of the movement's program were broached. Some were resolved, others were in the process of being resolved. An issue as important as the matter of the transitional period was forever being debated among us, and it was only at the September 1919 "Nabat" conference that it was resolved through the formulation of phase one of the communist reconstruction of society, which we strove with considerable difficulty to endow with an increasingly concrete content.

As regards organizational structures, a definite line was developed and implemented at two levels: first of all through a policy line rising above the various schools of anarchism: and then through organizational practice, through the rallying of the most determined, most dynamic militants with an eye to launching a healthy, well-structured movement with the prospect of a standardized program.

Such organizational construction depended upon the principle of "federalist centralism": it was, in a manner of speaking, a party, built upon this principle, with a single organizational framework, structured along federal lines. The component organizations and groups were well-disciplined and answerable to one another for the implementation of policy options. In particular, they regarded the resolutions and decisions reached at general assemblies, even by a simple majority vote, as binding.

In short, it was a well-structured and disciplined movement with a leading echelon appointed and monitored by the rank and file. And let there be no illusions as to the role of that echelon: it was not merely "technically executive," as it is commonly regarded. It was also the movement's "ideological pilot core," looking after publishing operations, and propaganda activity, utilizing the central funds and above all controlling and deploying the movement's resources and militants, who were, sad to say, none too numerous. In this way, "Nabat" was a well-structured party with a single, coherent platform. I say platform because we had not, as yet, any finalized standard program: we were drafting one as the revolutionary experience we were living was evolving. But the minimum basis for agreement that served us in our common endeavors was the same and binding upon all Confederation members. To the extent that the Secretariat was empowered to take steps to exclude from the movement any organization seriously departing from the movement's overall line, until such time as the following congress of the Confederation might make a final decision. Without fear of overstating the case, I believe that everything being done among you in France, and generally speaking, everything wholesome that is going to be accomplished in the anarchist movement *in the realm of organization*, cannot outdo the "Nabat" experience. Maybe a few operational details could be improved: that is all. It goes without saying that at present we may have differing views of the problems of the future party, its role and its place in the preparation and piloting of the toilers' social struggles, as well as its ties to the toilers' organized or spontaneous movements. That is quite obvious, but this is not because "Nabat" *erred* or resolved these matters differently, for at the time, it existed only *historically*, which is to say that it had been caught up in the whirlwind of revolution and had not yet reached its *maturity*, lacking the experience and the time to resolve these matters as perfectly as in the present moment.

...It is on the basis of these principles that our movement operated and grew, at the risk of being regarded as "heretical" and vilified by the "orthodox" chatterboxes of all sorts who decline to get involved in life. The orthodoxes screamed treachery, and raised a hullabaloo about a centralist party, etc. But then, as now, theirs was a voice from the past and from confusion, over which we must raise a huge cross so that we may gain a firm footing in the here and now and fight for the future to come.

— A Nabatovian, *Dyelo Truda* No. 32, (January 1928), pp. 12–16

## DOCUMENT NO. 7
## MARIA ISIDINE — ORGANIZATION AND PARTY

The problem of the organization of anarchist forces is of the order of the day. Many comrades explain the fact that, in the Russian revolution, the anarchists, despite being at all times in the forefront of the revolutionary battles, wielded only slight influence over the march of events, in terms of the lack of solid organization. Thus they posit the creation of such an organization, an anarchist party, as the premier requirement for more fruitful efforts in the future. This word "party" of itself triggers controversy: can there be such a thing as an anarchist "party"? It all depends on the meaning with which one invests the word.

The term "party" can be applied simply to the community of persons of *like minds, agreed with one another on the aims to be achieved and the means to be employed*, even if they are bound by no formal link, even if they do not know one another. The more united their thinking, the more they devise a similar solution to the particular issues that arise, and the more apt the use of the term "party" in relation to them, It is in that sense that the *Internationale* talks about the "great party of the toilers." and also in that sense that Kropotkin, Malatesta and other militants from our movement, especially from the older generation of its founding fathers, talk about the "anarchist party." In that sense, the "anarchist party" has always been with us: furthermore, in the anarchist movement, we have always had organizations, well-defined organizations indeed, such as standing federations of groups, embracing all the groups in a town, region or country. Such federations have always been the customary form of anarchist organization across the world.

In this respect, neither the scheme spelled out in the "Platform" of our Russian comrades, nor the mode of organization adopted by the Union Anarchiste at its last congress imply anything novel. But there is one novelty and it is this. The "Platform" aims to amend the *essential character* of the bond which has hitherto bound anarchist groups together, and to change this unspoken "constitution" that has always obtained in our ranks and which, uncontroversially, like something self-evident, lay at the root of every anarchist organization. In their yearning to tighten the bonds between militants, the authors of the "Platform" propose to launch a new model of anarchist "party," along lines espoused by the other parties, with binding decisions made by majority vote, a central leadership committee, etc. Such a party ought, as they see it, to cure the anarchist movement of most of the ills that beset it.

It is surprising to see that the experience of the Russian revolution, which has demonstrated with spectacularity the inappropriateness of a party dictatorship as the pilot of social life, has not just led these comrades to ask: what other organizations should have pride of place in the work of revolution, but, on the other hand, has inspired in them an aspiration to a strong, centralized party. And the same goes for our French comrades. We know that the *Union Anarchiste* at its congress in Orléans has adopted a declaration of principles by which it plainly broke ranks with the anarchists of the individualist school and proclaimed a series of basic propositions regarding both anarchism's social ideal and its campaign methods. At the most recent congress, that declaration has been endorsed as the foundation charter of the Union. That was not enough for the congress, and it saw fit to draw up *statutes*: and it is here that the centralizing tendency at odds not just with anarchist principles in general, but also with the text of the very "charter" that had just been adopted, showed itself.

From the outset, the Orléans declaration announces that the authority principle is the root of all social ills, that centralism has manifestly failed, politically and economically, and that the free commune and free federation of communes must form the basis of the society of the future: for its part, the commune should be simply the gamut of the various associations existing in the same area. All centralism is, as a matter of principle, stricken from social organization, which should be supple enough for each individual inside the association, and each association inside the federation to enjoy complete freedom. All of which is unanimously accepted by all anarchists, and, if the authors of the Orléans declaration have seen fit to enunciate these truths yet again, it was for propaganda purposes. And we were entitled to expect "statutes" consonant with these principles. But this was not the case: thinking to create something new, our comrades have ventured on to the beaten tracks of other parties.

For a start, in the Union, decisions are reached *by majority vote*. This question of majority is sometimes regarded as a mere detail, a handy way of resolving issues. Now, it is of capital importance, for it is inseparably bound up with the very notion of a society without power. In their critique of all forms of the State, even the most democratic, anarchists operate from the principle that *decisions taken by one group of individuals cannot be binding upon others, who have not reached them and who are not in agreement with them* — and it is of no matter whether they are reached by a majority or by a minority. It is of course pointless to enter here into a rehearsal of all the arguments, with which our literature is awash, against the majority principle: all comrades are conversant with these, especially as they make daily use of them to expose the fictitious character of popular representation under a parliamentary regime. How come then, that this principle, whose absurdity and unfairness are so plain where the future society is concerned, turns beneficial and fair when it is to be applied to our own circles? Either the majority is always entitled to prevail, or we should drop this arithmetic of truthfulness and look around for another one.

In their infatuation with organization, our comrades overlook the fact that, instead of strengthening union, the overruling of the minority will merely give rise to fresh intestinal struggles: instead of working productively, energies will be squandered on winning a majority in congresses, committees, etc. And understandably so: life inside a party is, in these conditions, easy only for the members of the prevailing majority: the others are stymied when it comes to their action. Moreover, the resolution from the congress of the Union states this very bluntly, by proclaiming that, while entitled to criticize the resolutions tabled, the minority ought not, once these had been passed, to impede their implementation. That means that the minority has to hold its peace or quit the party, and then, instead of a single party, we have two, usually more venomous with each other than with the common enemy. Another resolution from the congress states that there should be no criticism voiced outside of the organization and that nobody has the right to make use of the columns of *Le Libertaire* to criticize the decisions reached. Now, *Le Libertaire* is the official organ of the Union, and as such, should reflect all the views existing within the latter. It occupies a quite different position from that of an organ founded by a group of comrades pretty well agreed upon propagation of *their* views: these comrades are perfectly entitled not to accommodate opposing voices in their organ, in that they claim to represent no one but themselves. That is how things were in the old *Le Libertaire*, in *Les Temps Nouveaux* and virtually all the organs of the anarchist press. But whenever a newspaper styles itself the organ of the Union of the anarchist federations of the whole of France, all the members of that Union have that entitlement. Now, the resolution passed plainly shows that such an entitlement is acknowledged only where the majority is concerned.

Although our anarchist movement may be open to reproach on several counts, we have to give it its due: it has always been free of congressional intrigues, electoral chicanery, the artificial cultivation of majorities, etc. And that thanks solely to the principle that has prevailed within it up to now, to wit, that *decisions are binding only upon those who have taken them*, and may not be imposed upon those unwilling to accept them. The force of such decisions and the commitment given are all the greater for that, in that each man is more sensible of a decision taken by himself than of some decision reached without his input and very often contrary to his wishes.

We may perhaps be told: "if comrades band together on a properly thought out and well-drafted program, accepted by *everybody*, differences of opinion will relate only to details and the sacrifice asked of the minority will be minimal." This is far from always being the case. Every day life poses fresh problems, sometimes very important ones, but which were not foreseeable at the time when the compact was entered into: differing replies may perhaps be forthcoming to such problems. Thus, in days gone by the anarchists of France were split over the trade union movement, more recently over the war, and the anarchists in Russia — over the Makhnovist movement, the attitude to be adopted regarding Bolshevism, etc.: if, at those points, anarchists had been "banded together into a real party," would a congress decision upon questions of that gravity have been accepted by everyone? These matters are for the individual conscience and its conception of the revolution: in which case, can a mechanical decision taken by a majority prevail?

Still another tendency is emerging, with regard to the introduction of the majority principle and the limitation of the autonomy of the groups: it would like to see all anarchist initiatives overseen by a single organization of the hierarchical type, headed by a single Executive Committee. The statutes adopted by the most recent Union congress contain a series of propositions that sound queer to our ears. Take, say, groups belonging to the minority, which is to say, not accepting some resolution passed by the congress: that minority's right to criticize is indeed acknowledged (so far, at any rate) but its criticisms must be addressed exclusively to the Federation to which the group belongs (and to which it is obliged to belong if it wishes to be part of the Union) or to the central steering commission "which alone have the competence to give them a hearing and satisfaction." In other words, the minority is not entitled simply and openly to peddle its views among the comrades (not to mention the public): it has to address itself to the bodies named, following hierarchical procedure. Likewise, the unfettered initiative of groups tends everywhere to be replaced by the principles of election and delegation: no one must attempt anything at all unless he has authorization from the competent organization. A newspaper, a review, say, may not spring into life through the decision of a group or individual: they can only be published by Anarchist Federation delegates and must reflect only the thinking endorsed at its congresses. The same holds true for the publication of books or pamphlets, for lectures, clubs, even aid funds for imprisoned comrades. At first glance, this "organization" appears to certain minds to be a highly practical thing. But in point of fact such rules (if anarchist circles proved capable of abiding by them) would end up killing off the movement completely. Take a group of comrades intending to set up a propaganda newspaper and possessed of the wherewithal to do so: they have no right so to do: they must first seek the approval of the existing organization as a body and invite the latter to take charge of publication. Let us suppose that the latter agrees and appoints its delegates to that end: fortunately the ideas of the instigators are in tune with those of the organization's majority: then they need only yield possession of the planned publication and pass it on to others' hands (which is not always a good move either). But what if those delegates, speaking for the majority, are not of the same mind as the instigating group? Then the latter has but one option: to disown publication. And the newspaper never sees the light. Instead, whenever a group embarks upon a publication at its own risk and peril, those whose aspirations it meets rally around it, disseminate it, and magnify its scope for expansion. Others, of differing views, set up other organs, and such variety of the anarchist press, far from harming propaganda, simply works to its benefit.

Take a group of comrades who want to publish books or organize lectures. "On whose authority?" they are asked. "We first of all must find out if the existing groups agree to place you in charge of this and if they endorse your program." Work grinds to a halt. Discussion begins inside the groups on the drafting of a number of programs. In the end, as there is no way to keep everybody happy, the venture is aborted and its instigators are for a long time rid of their appetite for launching anything at all.

Only utter ignorance of the history and life of the anarchist movement could explain the eruption of such schemes for "organization." Everything valuable and lasting ever created in our movement has been the handiwork of groups and individuals well endowed with the initiative to press on without waiting for authorization from anybody. That is the way the finest organs of the anarchist press have created: the way that propaganda began in the trade unions that led on to the creation of revolutionary syndicalism: the way that the anarchist idea has survived, in its purity and its logic, inside certain groups of staunch convictions, in spite of all the desertions and betrayals. It does not lie within the power of any mechanical organization to replace this initiative. The role of an organization is to facilitate the work of individuals and not to hinder it: this is all the more true in the anarchist movement, which is not strong enough numerically to indulge in hindering the actions of its members and squander precious resources. Which is how the tendency that emerged at the latest Union Anarchiste congress will inevitably end up.

What the anarchist movement needs right now, is not so much new organizational formulas as a concrete, well-defined program of work to be undertaken, just as soon, in the wake of a successful revolution, there will be scope for every initiative in the endeavor to create the new society. Only familiarity with what they are to propose at that crucial point will guarantee anarchists the influence to which their ideas entitle them. For this, initiatives must not be stifled and minds snuffed out, but instead, a free and lively exchange of all views is to be encouraged. Otherwise, energies will be squandered on the pettiness of internal frictions and the real will not be advanced by a single step.

It is always easy to criticize, some comrades may perhaps object; it is a lot harder — and more useful — to put forward a practical mode of organization that would help rid our movement of what keeps it weak. Certain comrades seek to do that by creating a more or less centralized party, based on the majority principle: others — and the writer of these lines is one of them — believe that such a party would be more harmful than useful.[1] Of course, they do not deny either the need for anarchists generally to get organized, or the need to rid the movement of the flaws that stop it from acquiring the social influence to which its ideas entitle it. But what form of organization have they to offer in place of the one suggested by the "Platform," and upon what principles are they going to found that organization, which they would argue is more free, in order to achieve the same outcomes: agreement on principles, a prescribed policy of practical action, and appreciation by each individual of his duties towards the movement?

The fundamental error of those of our comrades who are supporters of the "Platform" resides perhaps in the fact that they look to a union of groups and even to a directing center for the rehabilitation of our movement, instead of looking to the *groups* themselves. It is not of the federation but rather of the groups which make it up that we can require such and such a policy line: the movement's center of gravity lies there: the federation will be whatever its component groups are. And whenever issues are broached and debated, not at the level of the federation, but at group level, solution of them will be greatly facilitated: a group can readily do what a huge organization cannot. The devising of a single policy line for a complete federation presents insuperable difficulties, for it presupposes decisions taken by majority vote and thus, inevitably, involves internal frictions. Recruitment of members and the elimination of undesirables whose presence compromises the movement, is a task that the federation's leadership body is incapable of carrying off with success. Any more than it capable of ensuring that the action of all its members conforms to anarchist principles. But all of that can be easily and naturally accomplished by each group within its own ranks. So the premier issue to be resolved is this one: what are the fundamental principles upon which an anarchist group can base its existence?

There is no way that a sweeping answer, good for all groups, can be given to that, for the answer might vary greatly according to the goals pursued by the group and the context in which it operates, depending whether the group was set up to tackle a particular practical task or general propaganda, whether it operates in a period of calm or a time of revolution, whether it operates openly or in clandestine fashion, etc., etc. But, even so, a few general considerations can be framed.

Take this first question: is it desirable that the group should comprise of comrades with a common conception of the anarchist idea, or can anarchists of varying persuasions (communists, individualists, etc.) really work in concert within it? This issue was raised at the most recent anarchist congress. Certain comrades reckon that, since each of the existing anarchist tendencies contains a kernel of truth, it would be better not to dwell upon their discrepancies but instead to "synthesize" everything that looks worthwhile, so as to arrive at a basis for joint activity. At first sight, this approach seems very logical and perfectly practicable, but upon reflection, it transpires that unity taken in that sense would be merely formal. Of course, circumstances may arise in which anarchists of differing shades of opinion will act in concert, but the same goes for all revolutionaries in general: the anarchists in fact collaborated with the Bolsheviks in the fight against the White armies. Such instances will always be frequent in times of revolution: such arrangements, most often tacit, are thus quite natural and necessary, but when it comes down to lasting activity in a period of calm, agreement upon basic principles is not enough. Suppose that an individualist anarchist, an anarchist communist and an anarchist syndicalist reach agreement upon declaring their opposition to the state and their approval of the communist form of property (assuming that the individualist agrees to it): of what practical significance would this be, since they immediately go their separate ways afterwards? The individualist is preoccupied with liberating the individual this very day, in the existing social context (colonies, living in nature, "free love," etc.): contemptuous of the masses and their movements, he is not going to identify with them. So what could he undertake in common with his communist colleague? Then again, a pure syndicalist comrade will place store only by labor movement tasks and will collaborate only with certain of his communist colleagues: he may even find himself at odds with them, on the issue of relations between the trade unions and the anarchist groups for instance. And so it all goes. In day to day action, the methods proper to such and such a tendency play such a significant role that agreement upon the general principles acknowledged by all is far from sufficient. When disagreements inside a group are substantial and do not relate merely to the use of certain labels, they hinder the action of the group, for the members, being united neither in their propaganda nor in their chosen methods, expend a lot of their energy upon internal wrangling. A truly united group, though, made up of comrades who have no need for further debate about the most essential points and who, come what may, are as one on propaganda and action, that sort of a group can become highly influential, even if it not large. By comparison, other groups of different mentality will founder: not that there is any loss in that, for there is nothing useful about trying to enfold the largest possible number of comrades within the same organization.

Random recruitment of members is, perhaps, the prime cause of the defects of most groups. Very often, people become anarchists all too easily and all too quickly, without having familiarized themselves with other schools of socialism, nor indeed with anarchism in the essentials of its theories: that way, in the future, for oneself and for comrades, lie sore disappointments, for, as one's knowledge expands and one's horizon widens, it may perhaps be found that one has gone astray and that one professed to be an anarchist only out of ignorance of everything else. One day, a Russian Social Revolutionary was asked, in my presence, at what point in his life he had ceased to be a Marxist: "When I began to read something other than Marx" was the answer.

Things may be a lot more serious if it is not just a matter of some theory that one accepts or rejects, but a cause to which one has devoted part of one's life and which one at some point feels incapable of championing because one had never given prior consideration to the criticisms of adversaries. Then again, the life of groups is often made difficult by an excess of practical mentality: one accepts such and such a comrade on account of the services he may render (as speaker, theoretician, administrator, etc.) without taking care to ensure that his overall moral or intellectual profile meets the group's requirements.

Plainly, such close scrutiny in the selection of members can be maintained only by the group and not by the federation, and no federal statute will ever be able to guarantee it. But, if it is implemented in the federation's component groups, the federation will find that many thorny questions resolve themselves.

In our conception, the bond between the various groupings is absolutely free and arises from their needs alone: there is no center, no secretariat entitled to dictate to the groups with which, in some shape and on some basis, they must unite. Links may be established for a wide variety of reasons: like-mindedness, concerted action, territorial contiguity, etc. Generally, the rule is that groups from the same region are in touch with one another, but it can happen (and we have seen examples of this) that a Paris group has closer bonds of solidarity with a London or Geneva group than with the group in the next district. Broadly speaking, set frameworks, where each group is obliged to belong to such and such a federation, and each federation to maintain links with its neighbor through the obligatory mediation of such and such a committee can (if such regulations really are observed) paralyze all action. A secretariat can be a very useful agency in the facilitation of communications, but it is merely a tool to be used when one feels it necessary.

The anarchist movement has always had congresses: they can be of very great importance if they arise from the activity of *pre-existing groups* which feel the need to share their work and their ideas. Certain especial features of our congresses relate to the very principles of anarchism. Thus, up to the present, comrades assembling for a congress did not necessarily have to be *delegated* by the groups: they could participate in an individual capacity.[2] Contrary to the practice in other parties, where delegates take away *from the congress* resolutions to which their mandataries have merely to submit, anarchist delegates bring *to the congress* the resolutions, opinions and tendencies of their respective groups. Congress is free to express an opinion of them — but that is all. The counting of the votes (should that be judged useful) is merely a statistical exercise: it may be interesting to know how many comrades, belonging to which grouping, come down on this side or the other. The importance of congresses is in no way diminished, and their work only grows more serious: instead of furnishing an arena for gambits designed to win a majority, they can devote themselves to making known the movement's status in different localities, its successes and failures, its different tendencies, etc. The resolutions cannot be anything more than indications, expressions of opinion, for the delegates to impart to their groups, which may adopt or reject them.

In short, this schema merely rehearses that which is familiar, things that might even seem too self-evident to need mention: but the present confusion of minds is such that one sometimes feels compelled to reiterate old truths. The *formal* connection between organizations is extremely loose here: because all of the emphasis is upon the intellectual and moral *internal* bonds. Furthermore, in this schema, the individual or group is formally free: the less subordination to anything, the more extensive and grave the moral responsibility. Here each member of the group is answerable for the action of the entire group — all the more responsible in that the resolutions are reached by common accord and not mechanically, by any majority vote. Moreover, the entire group is answerable for the deeds of each member of it, all the more so, also, in that it has recruited its members only discriminatingly, accepting only those who suited it. Then the federation as a body answers for the actions of each of its component groups — precisely because there is nothing to make the liaison engaged in any way binding, and because the groups know in advance with whom and for what purpose to join forces. And each group is answerable for the whole federation — precisely because the latter cannot do a thing without its assent.

There is more. Every anarchist, whether he wishes it or not, bears the *moral* responsibility for the actions of his comrades, even if no formal connection binds him to them: every act contrary to the anarchist idea, every contradictory posture, has repercussions for the movement as a body, and this extends the responsibility beyond the individual, beyond even his immediate group. And it is this consciousness of his responsibility that should be the great spur capable of maintaining the solidarity in anarchist circles. Maybe this is not always properly understood, and maybe that is the source of many of our movement's shortcomings, shortcomings that some would remedy by means of new forms of organization. We are not persuaded of the efficacy of these measures; our confidence is vested instead in other means, of a quite different nature, only a few of which we have touched upon here.

*Plus loin* No. 36, (March 1928), and No. 37, (April 1928)

## Notes to Document No. 7

1. Events have borne this out even more quickly than might have been expected: scarcely a few weeks had elapsed after the last congress of the "Union" and the organization has split in two. And *Le Libertaire* now manages to appear only with the greatest of difficulty.
2. This state of affairs was amended at the latest "Union Anarchiste" congress in respect of the introduction of the majority principle.

## DOCUMENT NO. 8
## PIOTR ARSHINOV — ELEMENTS OLD AND NEW
## IN ANARCHISM (A REPLY TO MARIA ISIDINE)

Comrade Isidine counters our conception of a revolutionary anarchist organization with the old conception corresponding to an age when anarchists had no real organization, but, by means of mutual understanding, came to agreement upon goals and upon the means of achieving them.

In fact, that old party was confined to analogous ideas and was bereft of authentic organizational format: it corresponded above all to the birth of the anarchist movement, when its pioneers were groping their way forward, not having been tempered by harsh experience of life.

Socialism too, in its day, had a difficult gestation. However, as the masses' social struggle evolved and became acute, all the tendencies that were vying to influence the outcome took on more precise political and organizational forms. Those tendencies which failed to keep in step with this evolution lagged far behind life. We Russian anarchists were especially sensible of this during the two revolutions in 1905 and 1917. Whereas, at their outset, we were in the van of the fighting, as soon as the constructive phase began, we found ourselves side-lined beyond recovery and, ultimately, remote from the masses.

This was not the result of chance: such an attitude flowed *inescapably* from our impotence, from the organizational point of view as well as from the vantage point of our ideological confusion. The current, of this decisive age, requires of us something more than a "party" devoid of organizational format and erected solely upon the notion of a beautiful ideal. These times require that the libertarian movement, as a whole, supply answers to a whole host of issues of the utmost importance, whether relating to the social struggle or to communist construction. They require that we feel a responsibility towards our objectives. However, until such time as we have a real and significant organization, it is not going to be possible for us to supply those answers, nor to shoulder those responsibilities. Indeed, the consistently distinctive feature of our movement is that it does not have a unity of views on these fundamental issues. There are as many views as there are persons or groups.

Certain anarchists regard this situation as reflective of the multifariousness of anarchist thinking: struggling labor has no idea what to make of this mixed bag, which strikes it as absurd. So, in order to rise above the morass of absurdity in which the anarchist movement has got bogged down, by loitering in the first stage of organization despite its numerical expansion, it is vital that a strenuous and decisive effort should be made: it must adopt the organizational formats for which it has long since been ripe: otherwise, it will lose its ability to hold its natural place in the fight for a new world. The urgent necessity of this new step is acknowledged by many comrades, the ones for whom the fate of libertarian communism is bound up with the fate of struggling labor. Comrade Isidine, if we understand her aright, is not to be numbered among the anarchists of whom we spoke earlier, but she is not a participant in our movement either: she takes part only in debate, in a critical way, and, to be sure, she helps its progress in so doing.

Let us now tackle the various critical points indicated by comrade Isidine. Everybody knows that any wholesome principle can, once denatured, serve a cause contrary to the one to which it was originally assigned.

In our ranks, this holds true for federalism: sheltering behind that cover, lots of groups and certain individuals perpetrated acts the opprobrium of which fell upon the movement as a whole. All intervention in such cases came to nothing, because the perpetrators of these acts of infamy sought refuge in their autonomy, invoking the federalism that allowed them to do as they saw fit. Obviously, that was merely a crass misrepresentation of federalism. The same might be said of other principles, and especially, of the principle of organizing a General Union of Anarchists, should it fall into the clutches of witless or unscrupulous persons. ... Comrade Isidine disagrees profoundly with the principle of majority. We on the other hand reckon that on this point debate is scarcely necessary. In practice, this matter has long been resolved. Almost always and almost everywhere, our movement's practical problems are resolved by majority vote. At the same time, the minority can cling to its own views, but does not hold out against the decision: generally and of its own volition, it makes concessions. This is perfectly understandable: there cannot be any other way of resolving problems for organizations that engage in practical activity: there is, anyway, no alternative if one really wants to act.

In the event of differences of opinion between the majority and the minority being due to factors so important that neither side can give ground, a split comes about, regardless of the principles and positions espoused by the organization prior to that moment.

Nor do we agree with comrade Isidine when she says that the mouthpiece of an isolated group can work out a policy line of its own, and that, in this way, according to her, the organ of the General Union of Anarchists should mirror all of the views and tendencies existing inside that union. In fact, the mouthpiece of a particular group is not the concern merely of its editorial team, but also of all who lend it material and ideological backing. Since, in spite of this, a well-determined policy line is needed by that, say, local, organ, it is all the more essential for the mouthpiece of the Union which carries a lot more responsibilities with regard to the anarchist movement as a whole than that particular organ.

To be sure, the Union mouthpiece must afford the minority a platform for its views, for otherwise the latter would be denied its right of free expression: however, while allowing it to set out its point of view, the Union mouthpiece must simultaneously have its own well-defined policy line and not just mirror the motley views and states of mind arising within the Union. In order to illustrate the example of a decision made by the Union as a body, but not enjoying unanimous backing, comrade Isidine cites the Makhnovist movement, anarchists having been divided in their attitudes towards it. That example, though, rather redounds to the advantage of the argument in favor of the ongoing necessity of a libertarian communist organization. The differing views expressed then are explicable primarily in terms of many libertarians' utter ignorance of that movement during its development: many of them were later powerless to analyze it and adopt a policy line with regard to a movement as huge and original as the Makhnovists. They needed a solid collective: had they had one at the time, it would have considered itself *obliged* to scrutinize that movement minutely and then, on the basis of that scrutiny, it would have laid down the stance to be adopted with regard to it. Which would have served libertarian communism and the Makhnovist movement better than the chaotic, disorganized stance adopted by anarchists with regard to the latter during its lifetime. The same goes for the problem of the war.

It comes to pass that differences arise in organizations over such matters, and in such cases splits are frequently the outcome. However, there is an argument for taking it as a rule that in such situations, the point of departure should be, not the individual conscience and tactics of every single anarchist, but rather the essential import of the theory, policy and tactics of the Union as a body. Only thus will the movement be able to preserve its policy line and its liaison with the masses.

Organization and the principle of delegation are not such impediments to the display of initiative as comrade Isidine believes. Quite the contrary: all wholesome initiative will always enjoy the backing of organization: the principles spelled out are not designed to stifle initiative but to replace the fitful activity of individuals operating randomly and occasionally, with the consistent, organized work of a collective. It could not be otherwise. A movement that survived only thanks to the initiative and creativity of various groups and individuals and which had no specific overall activity would run out of steam and go into decline.

For that very reason one of the fundamental tasks of our movement consists of contriving the circumstances that allow every militant not merely to demonstrate initiative, but to seize upon and develop it, making it an asset to the entire movement.

Thus far, and for want of an overall organization, our movement has not had such circumstances, thanks to which every authentic militant might find an outlet for his energies. It is common knowledge that certain of the movement's militants have given up the fight and thrown in their lot with the Bolsheviks, simply because they were not able to find an outlet for their efforts in the anarchist ranks. Moreover, it is beyond question that lots of revolutionary workers, who find themselves in the ranks of the Communist Party of the USSR, have no illusions left regarding Bolshevik rule and might switch their loyalty to anarchism, but do not do so because there is no overall organization offering precise guidance.

Comrade Isidine stresses one of the merits of the Platform, in that it has broached the principle of collective responsibility in the movement.

However, she thinks of this principle solely in terms of *moral* responsibility. Whereas, in a large, organized movement, responsibility can only find expression in the form of the *organization's collective responsibility*.

A moral responsibility that does not accommodate organizational responsibility is bereft of all value in collective endeavors, and turns into a mere formality devoid of all content.

What we need, comrade Isidine tells us, is not so much an organization as a definite practical policy line and a hard and fast immediate program. But each of those is unthinkable in the absence of prior organization. If only to raise issues of the program and its implementation, there would have to be an organization in place that might undertake to struggle towards their resolution.

At present, the *Dyelo Truda* Group of Russian Anarchists Abroad has given that undertaking, and enjoys the support in this of several anarchist toilers' organizations in North America and by comrades remaining in Russia.

In the pioneering work carried out by these organizations, there may well be certain errors and gaps. These must be pointed out and help given in the repairing of them, but there must be no lingering doubt as to the basis and principle upon which these organizations operate and struggle: the drafting of a definite program, a well-determined policy and tactical line for libertarian communism, creation of an organization representing and spearheading the whole anarchist movement: this is vitally necessary to it.

— *Dyelo Truda* No. 30-31, (November–December 1928), pp. 13–17

## DOCUMENT NO. 9
## GEORGES FONTENIS ON THE OPB

When the OPB came into existence in January 1950, it was merely the aspiration, the expression of the "platformist" tendency in the Fédération Anarchiste, which is a rather motley collection of appreciations of anarchism.

The operational considerations that underlay the need for the OPB inside the libertarian "magma," are *the necessity of a highly structured organization, tactical unity and the class nature of anarchism*.

The fact that it is a secret caucus within the Fédération Anarchiste makes the OPB highly effective in the struggle in theoretical terms (a return to the origins of Bakuninism, of the anti-authoritarian school of socialism in the First International, with the utilization of certain contributions of Marx and the dialectical materialist methodology) and in terms of responsibilities at every level.

Thus, in three years, it broke the ascendancy within the Fédération Anarchiste of the individualistic and "synthesist" currents which ensured a stagnation and confusionism that exasperated younger militants, members of the factory groups, and the traditionally platformist groups (Paris 18e, one group in Lyon, Narbonne, to name but a few). For we have to place the facts on record: the OPB is a backlash against the mentality of "deliquescence" (to borrow the expression of our Narbonne comrades) in other tendencies which, after their fashion, have organized themselves, settling at "get-togethers" upon their strategy for preventing Congresses from producing anything positive[1] and stressing a "humanistic" vision of anarchism that makes it transcendent of class and thus non-proletarian.

If the OPB succeeded in Bordeaux in 1952, in Paris in 1953, this was quite simply because it *represents the majority of the groups and militants* because, in a context of cold war and in the face of the French Communist Party's (PCF) hegemony within the working class, it saw its essential options through to success:

- *Proletarian combat* (the OPB's adversaries being primarily a collection of small businessmen and artisans, indeed of small employers and masonic-style intellectuals) designed to overthrow the hegemony of the PCF's ascendancy.
- *The Third Front* simultaneously opposing Stalin and Truman (at a time when the movement as a whole had opted for the US camp).

- *Anti-colonialism* which, in opposing the war in Indo-China and later the war in Algeria was to take a high toll of the FCL (after the departure of the "nothingarians" and "empty vessels," the platformist majority of the Fédération Anarchiste assumed the name FCL at the Paris Congress of 1953).

As for the constricting nature of the OPB's regulations, the fact is that, by way of a backlash against the rejection of a solid organization, there were some exaggerations that left a number of members unhappy. To this should be added personal rivalries, harassment by police and courts, the wearying effect of uninterrupted campaigning from 1950 to 1956, and also a certain mentality of "making the running" in some from 1954 onwards.[2] But that is a far cry from the exaggerations and half-truths with which the Kronstadt group's "Memorandum" (which was maliciously reprinted in 1968 by A. Lapeyre, a sworn enemy of the Platform) is peppered.

I cannot say any more on the subject in this short communication, but I wish to close by stating that, in spite of those who condemned the anarchist movement in France to a lingering degeneration and evaporation, the FCL, thanks to the OPB, salvaged its honor and managed, through many historical vicissitudes, to see to it that a libertarian communist current was established that has self-evidently endured to this very day.[3]

## Notes to Document No. 9

1. And from the first congress held in Paris on October 6–7 and December 2, 1945 at that. At the Dijon congress in November 1946, a split was just averted through my appointment to the position of general secretary. I shall be returning to this point in the detailed work I have under preparation.
2. Obviously, in the work I have promised, I will be returning to this in detail and in a spirit of self-criticism.
3. Letter to the author dated March 25, 1987.

## APROPOS OF GEORGES FONTENIS'S *MÉMOIRES*

In 1990, just as he had promised when we put some questions to him, Georges Fontenis published a book of memoirs on the FCL experience and has supplied further details of the structure of the OPB.[1]

Here let us make a personal statement, for certain people have taken us to task for even mentioning this matter: conversant and involved with the French anarchist movement since 1959, we had cause to know the authoritarian drift and mischief of the OPB, but always from word of mouth reports, because few of the militants from those times took the risk of putting pen to paper to explain this "extraordinary" phenomenon — and I employ that adjective in its proper and literal sense of "out of the ordinary." Such discretion struck us as irksome, as if it was a matter of drawing a veil over some shameful disease that had stricken the movement. For the purposes of our present study, we sought, without great success, to discover more about it: Fontenis's book, however, has shed some light and adduced enough information to enable us to pass definitive judgment upon this adventure. Indeed, it seems not so much a book of memoirs proper as a defense plea, except that the arguments adduced by the defense have back-fired and played into the hands of the prosecution! Let us examine them in order:

1. First, the style of the book: the narrative is clumsily constructed and virtu-ally incomprehensible to the uninitiated; there are obscure references, con-tinual repetitions and a lurching backwards and forwards in time, with details blown up out of all proportion and a rather annoyingly disingenuous moralistic tone, especially regarding slanderous allegations leveled at the stance of well known libertarian comrades during the period of the war and the Occupation between 1939 and 1944. Since several of these were acquaintances of ours and are no longer around to defend themselves, we are duty bound to defend them. Let us take the case of Nicolas Faucier, a comrade of high caliber, very active between 1925 and 1960. On page 66 of his book, Fontenis has this to say: "He entered the service of the Todt organization" [working on the Atlantic Wall defenses — A. Skirda], only to relate (page 73): "He refused the draft, was sentenced to three years' imprisonment and was then interned. He went on to escape and was to remain underground right up to the Liberation." What are we supposed to make of that? Especially when Fontenis, assuming the role of prosecuting counsel, comments (page 67): "We cannot feel satisfied with the lack of any explanation as to how Faucier the draft defy-er of 1939 turned up in the ranks of the Todt organization by 1943." We brought this innuendo to the attention of Nicolas Faucier and his reply was this splendid characterization of Fontenis's ploy: "I repudiate it, but even so I am annoyed for the sake of those who are no longer with us and who are not in a position to reply. Nursing a grudge as a way of covering up his own bankruptcy shames nobody except the one who resorts to such things…. How edifying this urge to sling mud as a way of making up for a deficiency of positive ideas."[2]

Likewise, in the case of Louis Mercier Vega, an outstanding comrade from the French anarchist movement of the years between the 1930s and the 1970s, a member of the Durruti Column's International Group in Spain in 1936 — somebody else we knew well and whom we hold in the highest regard — Fontenis takes him to task for refusing the call-up in 1939 only to enlist with the Gaullist Free French Forces in 1942. Whenever we mentioned one day the various rumors circulating about him, Mercier Vega too replied with this splen-did virile answer: "All this is said behind my back and never to my face." Since he took his own life in 1977, we can but honor his memory and fume at Fontenis's calumny. Other treacherous and contradictory remarks are peddled regarding Pierre Besnard, who is accused of having joined the Pétainist *Légion des Combattants* (Servicemen's Legion), before "…having been courted as a pos-sible minister of Labor (in 1945), coming within an ace of succumbing to the

Gaullists' siren song" (p. 83). Fontenis goes on to add this squalid misrepresentation of Pierre Besnard: "He was a utopian intellectual hungry for the limelight. Under the Occupation, he wrote a book, meant for the victors, whoever they might turn out to be, setting out his 'scheme' for organizing the world." This was Besnard's masterpiece, *Un Monde nouveau*, which had in fact been written prior to 1939 and reissued in 1946, something of which Fontenis cannot have been aware as it confounds his entire thesis.

Here again his allegations backfire against him. Although he himself was born in 1920, he says not one word about what befell him in the years between 1939 and 1945. He must have been in there somewhere, so why the veil of silence drawn over it? Or could it be that he would like to blacken other people's memory in order to exonerate himself? To put it bluntly: he may well be keen to point to the mote in others' eyes, but hasn't he overlooked the beam in his own? Be that as it may, he maintains a discreet radio silence in his book.

We were profoundly shocked by another episode related by Fontenis: after a libertarian comrade of some renown, Louis Louvet, had made some slighting remark about him, Fontenis went to see him with two goons in tow: and "spurred on by indignation" he struck him "a couple of almighty blows ... of some violence, for he staggered and fell." Maille took great care not to get involved (p. 348). Fontenis omits to mention that Louvet and Maille — whose acquaintance we made in 1960 — were old men in comparison with him. They could have given him a good 20 to 30 years. And he had two of his henchmen along to boot! And he dares to glory in this deplorable act of cowardice! The same misfortune befell Fontenis himself nearly twenty years later, but he does not brag about that in his book! Shocking and rather more than distasteful it may be, but it speaks volumes about the man.

2. Fontenis even seeks to rewrite the history of libertarian ideas and, like a fantasist, he dismisses as "proto-history" the entirety of the libertarian movement prior to September 15, 1872 and the Saint-Imier congress of the anti-authoritarian International, thereby throwing overboard the 1848 revolution and the plead of libertarian thinkers and militants like Proudhon, Coeurderoy, Déjacque and Bellegarrigue (to name only the French ones, and not counting Russia, with Bakunin, or Switzerland, or England, etc.) Wonder why? Fontenis supplies the answer with his constant references to Marx and Marxism which he praises to the skies, flying in the face of history, because, since the collapse of the Berlin Wall in 1989, these have been cast into the rubbish bin of history.

The anarchists are unfailingly accused of having ignored Marx and his teachings: let us cite a few examples of this: "phony theorization based upon refusal and negation: Marx's dialectical materialism and Bakunin's interpretation thereof [?] are ignored or forbidden"! (p. 30). "The anarchist texts from this period" (prior to 1914) "are exceptionally impoverished by comparison with "Marxist' analyses" (p. 36). "The ORA (Organization Révolutionnaire Anarchiste) broke free from the morass of the Fédération Anarchiste (Anarchist Federation) of the day [1971] and embraced a living conception of historical dialectical materialism (p. 46). Marx goes unread but "Marxism' is condemned (p. 51). Most of those [among the anarchists, he means — A. Skirda] who speak out or write have deliberately simplified Marx's thinking so that they need not take any heed of it ... Maurice Joyeux, a specialist in anti-Marxist idiocies. (p. 53). In fact, they have read nothing. Which is why we had to wait for what I regard as Maximilien Rubel's overstated theses about an "anarchist' Marx before there was any movement past a simplistic and mulish condemnation of anything resembling Marx's thought. Even Skirda was to wait for Rubel before moving past simplification [?] (p. 54). "Marxism' is repudiated without quite knowing what it is" (p. 117). And so it continues on pages 118 and 126. The whole book is studded with such charges, that anarchists are not familiar with Marx, have not read him, nor studied him, etc. The most entertaining point is that this blows up in Fontenis's own face, because Marx never used the expression "historical and dialectical materialism." It was Engels and above all Stalin who employed it as a general purpose term. To quote his own words, Marx merely devised a "materialist conception of history" (see his *1859 Foreword to Contribution to a Critique of Political Economy*). Fontenis has done a little "simplifying" through the Marxist-Leninist current from which he has drawn all of his ideological sustenance. Hence his criticism of French anarchists as "petits bourgeois" engaged in small trades, omitting to mention, on the one hand, that some of them were reduced to this as a result of repression by employers or by society at large, and, on the other, that traditionally, in France and elsewhere, the anarchist movement has always comprised mostly of proletarians, whereas it is common knowledge that Marxism has, instead, been primarily an obsession of bourgeois intellectuals.

3. Freemasonry: the statutes of the FCL (given on page 318 of Fontenis's book) prohibited "membership of a secret society, in particular in France, the Freemasons, membership of which is incompatible." Freemasonry stood accused of class collaboration and the blackest misdeeds: but as soon as Fontenis became a Freemason, it became a benevolent association of the kindhearted! Here he forgets to mention that it was thanks to his becoming a Freemason that he became eligible to teach again and the likelihood is that he is indebted to that for his having been able to build a good career and end up as a "regional teaching inspector," a startling appointment and promotion for someone purporting to be a dyed in the wool revolutionary! Moreover, if we must underline the baleful role of Freemasonry, we need only invoke all of the political-financial scandals of recent years, whether in Italy, with its famous P2 Lodge, or in France during the Socialists' hegemony under Mitterrand, and, subsequently, at present, under the Right. Of Freemasonry's wheeler-dealer nature, which is too embarrassing to admit, there can be no doubt.

4. The OPB: the chief focus of our study in this book. Fontenis defines it as a "militant order ... Intent upon binding participants in the OPB by a sort of compact requiring a degree of obeisance to the collective will" (pp. 168–169). It is not hard to work out who could have been the embodiment of that "collective will,"

namely, the "bargain basement," Stalin, Fontenis himself. He has forgotten nothing and learned nothing, if we are to go by his explanations and commentaries: "We declare loud and clear that the OPB, clandestine or not, was a necessity if we were to have done with the insidious cunning of the anti-organizers, anarcho-liberals and anarchy's 'purists'" (p. 169). May we point out that among the OPB statutes which he reproduces is one providing for "the possibility of suppression, that is, to put it at its most blunt, of murder! Every militant, active, on suspension, expelled or having tendered his resignation must observe absolute silence on the subject of the OPB and the militants belonging to it. Any dereliction in this respect entails whatever steps the OPB may deem appropriate and which may extend even to suppression, in the event of denunciation jeopardizing the security of its militants." Fontenis's comment today upon this passage is that it is indicative of a rather derisory penchant for dramatization and overestimation of the secret group and its members. In our view, the word "derisory" is a rather feeble description of such a flawed and criminal measure.

In an interview subsequent to the publication of his book, Fontenis conceded with rather more candor:

"Yes, there is no denying it. We slid into what might be called a certain "functional Leninism,' but you have to understand that we tended to borrow from elsewhere, from Lenin, not all of whose actions were so awful, what the last fifty years of anarchist tradition had failed to provide: for instance, scrupulous observance of commitments given, punctiliousness and assiduity [?]. That said, there was no 'scandalous excrescence.'" [3] One could not be any plainer: Fontenis's FCL and OPB were classic Bolshevism, taken to lampoonish extremes in some respects.

Naturally the sequel to this is not hard to guess: there were disagreements and refusals to bow to Fontenis's "will," which entailed resignations and expulsions, followed by a rearguard action; standing for elections, recruiting André Marty, (he who had been the "butcher of Albacete" in Spain), and some so-called clandestine activity that was, going by its results and Fontenis's present assessment as he satirizes the game of "professional revolutionaries" played out back then, quite puerile, and, at the last lap, total eclipse as Fontenis and his chief lieutenants wound up either in Trotskyist organizations or in Leninist ones like the Communist Party. It was a pathetic adventure, but one that proved extremely useful; in terms of what it had to teach us about how a secret organization animated and controlled by just one man, an out-and-out political police agency can lead to the self-destruction of what had been, at the outset, a libertarian organization.

What is the explanation for all this? In our view, the charisma of one militant gifted with certain talents, who, becoming gradually very sensible of his responsibilities abetted by the passivity, blind and deaf obedience of certain others, the lack of revolutionary vigilance in still others, comes to look upon himself as the "leader," a sort of guru figure, the organization becoming a closed sect until everything eventually implodes as human nature emerges as the stronger factor.

All of which leads us to revise our assessment of the FCL and OPB which we had initially analyzed, on the basis of inadequate data, as anarchistic Blanquism: but no, now everything is clear thanks to the revelations contained in Fontenis's book: they were only a bureaucratic, Stalinist aberration.

— Alexandre Skirda, April 1997

## Notes to Skira's Remarks on Georges Fontenis's *Mémoires*

1. Georges Fontenis, *L'autre communisme. Histoire subversive du mouvement libertaire*, (Mauléon, 1990), 396 pages.
2. Letters from N. Faucier to the author on February 10 and March 20, 1991.
3. Georges Fontenis interviewed in the January 20 – February 5, 1991 edition of *L'École émancipée, revue syndicate et pédagogigue* (pp. 32-33).

## THE GROUPE KRONSTADT, PARIS
## DRAFT LIBERTARIAN COMMUNIST ORGANIZATIONAL PRINCIPLES

1. The Libertarian Communist organization (OCL) is characterized by the collective approach of its members' militant practice, which is rooted in the organization's policy line, subject to the principle of ongoing monitoring of the analyses and experiences of the membership as a whole.

2. The OCL's policy line is defined by the following principles:
   a. *Theoretical coherence.* Which is to say strict homogeneity in the overall positions espoused by the organization, amended in the light of ongoing analysis of the evolution of the political reality, thereby eliminating the danger of a monolithism of fixed positions and accentuating the effectiveness of actions undertaken.
   b. *Practical cohesion.* The OCL seeks tactical unity through militant implementation of the overall policy line espoused by groups and regions at Congresses.
   c. *Ongoing collective responsibility.* In respect of external expression, each member is answerable for the organization's line. Similarly, the organization is answerable for and claims responsibility for the positions and actions adopted by each of its members, provided that these accord with the general line of the OCL.
   d. *Federalism.* The organization is only the emanation of its component groups — the group being the driving force behind the whole organization. However, the militants or group may not adopt positions contrary to the organization's line.
   e. *Fraternal ethic.* Within its ranks, the organization practices the ethical conception of libertarian communism. Fraternal relations — based on mutual trust, esteem and respect — link its militants as a body.

3. **Operational work plan.** Congress is sovereign in defining the organization's line. It lays down the plan of militant work, delegating and assigning commissions and responsibilities, updating the OCL's Declaration of political and organizational principles.
   Certain posts are allocated at congress:

*The Press and Propaganda Commission*: this is charged with the publication and distribution of all of the OCL's forms of public expression: newspaper, review, pamphlets, posters, handbills, along federal lines. It operates in close concert with the treasurer.

*The Secretariat* has the task of overseeing the organization's internal, external and international communications. It publishes the Internal Bulletin. It includes a treasurer. Its role is, consequently, merely technical and administrative.

The *IB* (Internal Bulletin) contains reports of the meetings of the various officers, commissions and the Liaison Council: also featured are reports on the activities of groups and regions, motions or guideline texts of the organization, internal or operational information, and a discussion forum, Reserved for the exclusive use of OCL members, its contents are confidential.

*Treasury*: This is fed by compulsory dues (set by the congress) levied from militants, subscriptions and the revenue from sales of publications.

The work of the commissions is monitored by congress. Members of the commissions are nominated by their group at the congress and elected by the latter.

The commissions may drop or add members, under the supervision of the Liaison Council.

Congress meets at least once per year. Extra-ordinary congresses can be convened following a referendum of the groups.

In the interval between two congresses, the OCL is represented by the Liaison Council, whose duty is to oversee implementation of the policy line laid down by congress, and to oversee the work of the commissions and officials. It pronounces upon proposals from the groups with implications for the whole organization.

The Liaison Council is made up of delegates from the groups or regions — but it is not necessary for a group to have a delegate on it, should its functioning, activity or geographical location not allow this.

The Liaison Council meets regularly — monthly — or, exceptionally, following a referendum of the groups. Only delegates from groups or regions can participate in its meetings: members of the commissions are also required to attend.

## 4. Organization chart.

*The group.* Is the basic unit, the nerve center of the organization. It comprises at least five members and at most 15. It brings militants together on the basis of locality, trade, school or practicality. The group is free to organize as it sees fit, but it should, however, include a coordinator/secretary and a treasurer. Posts should be rotated among the members. The group participates in the internal life of the organization, in the ongoing discussions and collation, culminating in the drafting of the OCL's operational scheme of work.

The group is required to conduct its activities within the parameters of this scheme.

The group is free to do what it will outside of the objectives of the scheme and may do so in the name of the OCL, provided it does not conflict with its line, and that the group undertakes to report its experiences and its outcome to the rest of the organization.

Around its outside activities the group organizes its sympathizers, maintaining contacts with those isolated members of the organization closest in geographical terms. It co-ordinates their activity within the OCL and is answerable for it.

Inter-group commissions can be set up for specific tasks.

*The Circle.* The group may give rise to the formation of circles, embracing active sympathizers who devote themselves to specific activities: propaganda work, external expression, running a study and debating circle.

Several groups together make up one *sector*, or, on a larger scale, one region. But the sector and the region are merely an internal link for operational work — they are not sovereign inside the organization, which is founded on the group alone.

There is a free hand in the organization of sectors and regions.

Together, the groups, sectors and regions make up the *Federation. In its functioning, the OCL is thus a body coordinating and planning the practices of its component groups.*

The OCL has no international boundaries, and federations may organize themselves into one International Libertarian Communist Federation.

*Methods of operation.*

All matters and decisions upon which there is not unanimity, at all levels of the organization: — group, region, sector, federation (congress) — and in the Liaison Council, will be put to a vote, following discussion. The majority view prevails in matters tactical and practical: in matters theoretical and strategic, and other important decisions (expulsions, admissions ...) there must be a three-quarters majority.

When there is profound disagreement between two positions on a fundamental issue, the only solution is a split.

*Decisions taken are binding upon all members.*

Voting is by mandates: in the Liaison Council, and in the congress, each group has three mandates, making possible representation of the various positions: one for, one against and one blank. At the level of the group, the sector and the region, voting is by head count.

5. **Supervision**. The OCL operates in accordance with the principles of permanent delegation and revocability.

The various posts taken up are monitored continually by the groups. Any post can be withdrawn, outside of congress, on a referendum of the groups, and registration of a majority against.

Accounts by post-holders of their stewardship should be provided continually in the IB, so that information may circulate as promptly and regularly as possible.

6. **Internal regulation**. Participation in the OCL is conditional upon membership of a group.

*The sympathizer:* takes an interest in the OCL's stance and takes part in the organization's practical activities through the group to which he is attached. He is briefed regularly on militant experiences and the organization's line by means of all of the OCL's external documents. But he may not hold any office and does not partake of the internal activities of the group or the OCL.

In principle, after a certain time, a mutual decision by the sympathizer and the group should be made regarding his membership, for it is not possible for an organization to have eternal sympathizers.

*The corresponding member:* He wholly subscribes to the OCL's positions and line, but cannot participate regularly in the activity of a group, either on account of geographical isolation or for personal reasons. He pays dues and participates as best he can in the group closest to his place of domicile.

However, isolated militants should strive to found a local group.

*The militant.* He is affiliated to his group. His membership is not an act of faith, but a significant commitment, entailing for him the obligation to partake of the activities of his group and of the whole organization, that is to say, to shoulder responsibilities there and report back on these, then to supervise the activities and responsibilities of his group and of the OCL.

*Affiliation* The admission of a sympathizer or a militant is left to the sole discretion of the group. It comes about through co-optation.

A group suing for admission into the OCL makes contact with the Secretariat and the nearest group, familiarizes itself with the Declaration of political and organizational principles as well as the line of the time, then is obliged to submit its comments upon the lot and a resume of its past and activities to the Secretariat, which circulates it to the groups. These latter give their opinions and verdict: for or against.

Following unanimous acceptance, the candidate group becomes a full-fledged affiliate: in the event of hostility from one or more OCL groups, the application is discussed at the next congress.

*Expulsion.* In the event of a serious breach of the OCL's political and organizational principles, a militant or a group may be expelled from the organization.

In the case of a militant, he is suspended by his group, which reports its grounds to the Liaison Council, if there is any challenge, until such time as the next congress endorses (or fails to endorse) the decision through a vote, with the group in question taking no part in the vote.

In the case of a group, the procedure is the same, except that suspension is decided by the Liaison Council.

## DOCUMENT NO. 11
## REVOLUTIONARY ANARCHIST ORGANIZATION (ORA)

### Organizational Contract

The organizational Contract is specifically defined by what is the essential basis of anarchism, to wit, a two-pronged assertion:
- the primacy of the individual.
- the necessity of living in society.

Within this framework, anarchism repudiates all authoritarianism: that of pure individualism with its repudiation of society, and that of pure communism which seeks to ignore the individual. Anarchism is not a synthesis of antagonistic principles, but a juxtaposition of concrete, living realities, the convergence of which must be sought in an equilibrium as elastic as life itself.

Thus, anarchism cannot be identified with a philosophy of immutable truths, nor with a doctrine of untouchable principles, but may be defined as a way of life whose basis is creative liberty and whose means is ongoing experimentation.

Our organization has no pretensions to a rigid ideological unity generating dogmatism. But on the other hand, it refuses also to be merely a motley collection of divergent tendencies, the frictions between which would inevitably lead to stagnation.
- Union on ideological common denominators, but not stodgy uniformity in the interpretation of them (ideological unity).
- Tolerance in ideas and coherence in action (tactical unity).
- Effective shared responsibility of all militants (collective responsibility).
- Non-hierarchical and non-centralist organization (libertarian federalism).

These are the essential points which are required a priori for participation in the life of the organization.

The organization is a federation of territorial or trades groups, and not a gathering of individuals. It has a specific character and is regarded as forming a whole in itself.

The man or woman who joins the organization does so with full knowledge of what is afoot and their affiliation represents a moral commitment towards the entire organization, just as the latter acknowledges a collective responsibility towards every new member.

## The Group

1) The Group is the basic cell of the organization, wherein the militant activity arising out of all decisions taken at congresses is concentrated.
2) The Group is autonomous in the sense that it can take, locally, all the decisions it may deem fit. That autonomy, though, is limited by the very fact that the Group's affiliation to the organization implies respect for a contract freely entered into, as well as respect for decisions taken in congress.
3) The number of militants in a Group is limited to a maximum of 12.

## The Local Federation

1) The Groups of one locality are under an obligation to form themselves into a Local Federation.
2) The General Assembly of the militants of one locality is the forum for evaluation of ideas and action plans. It should meet fairly frequently (at least once each month) and it has sole collective decision-making powers at the local level.
3) Every militant is required to attend the Plenary Assemblies of his Local Federation on a regular basis. Three consecutive, unexplained absences may entail his exclusion from the organization.
4) In the event of non-unanimity on an action plan, the latter must secure the support of 3/4 (three-fourths) of the militants present at the General Assembly before it can be put into effect in the organization's name. Those not in agreement shall refrain from all external counter-propaganda, but may engage in action based upon different criteria, though not conflicting with the action of the organization, and with the later's endorsement.
5) The two basic officers of the Local Federation are: the organizing Secretary and the Propaganda Coordinating Secretary. Appointed to serve from one General Assembly to the next, they may have their mandate renewed for a maximum of one year. After a six month interval, they may be re-appointed to one of these offices.
6) Other officers may be appointed on a temporary basis, should this be felt necessary.

## The Regional Federation

1) The Groups of one region are under an obligation to form themselves into a Regional Federation.
2) A region may not be formed with Groups from under 3 (three) different localities.
3) The Regional Assembly of the delegates from each Group must be held fairly regularly (at least once every three months) and performs the same functions at regional level as the General Assembly of militants does at local level.
4) The role of Regional Liaison Commission, in charge of internal communications, the Regional Treasury and coordinating Propaganda, is to be vested in

one Group from the Region. Holding office from one Regional Assembly to the next, this group may find its mandate renewed for a maximum of one year. After an interval of 6 (six) months, it may again be entrusted with that office.
5) Should the need arise, other Regional Commissions may be established on a temporary basis.

## The Plenum

1) The plenum is the general assembly of the delegates from each Regional Liaison Commission.
2) The Plenum meets as convened by the National Collective or at the prompting of half of the Regional Liaison Commissions. It is not required to meet regularly.
3) Its object is to monitor the activity of the National Collective, to assist it in making decisions for the organization should certain unforeseen events necessitate rapid decision-making when pressure of time precludes the convening of an Extra-ordinary Congress.
4) A 3/4 (three fourths) vote is required for a Plenum decision, each Regional liaison Commission casting as many votes as there are Groups in its Regional Federation. The National Collective may not participate in the voting.
5) The Plenum may suspend the National Collective from its duties and convene an Extra-ordinary Congress, but it may not admit or expel anyone.
6) Any militant of the organization may attend a Plenum as the delegated observer from his Group.

## The Congress

1) Since all decisions must of necessity be made by the rank and file, the Congress amounts to the General Assembly of all the organization's Groups: it is therefore empowered to take all decisions governing the life of the organization.
2) Prepared at Group level, through the Internal Bulletin and through the Regional Assemblies, the Congress is a working session and proceeds in camera.
3) The Congress agenda, drafted on the basis of proposals from the Groups and the National Collective, should be communicated to the Groups at least two months in advance of the Congress date. Voting may proceed only on the specific items featured on the agenda. Thus, no decision compromising the organization's ideological line may be taken without its having first been debated in the Groups. On each item of the agenda, delegates' first contribution is limited to a maximum of 30 (thirty) minutes, and their second to five.
4) Only delegates duly mandated by their Groups participate in the organization's Congress. Observers' mandates may be issued to militants from the Groups who wish to attend the proceedings.
5) Only if it has more than five militants is a Group entitled to a say in the Congress proceedings. Only one delegate per Group is empowered to participate

in the voting. He represents the entire membership of his Group: the vote may not be split. However, as the technicality of the business at hand may necessitate a range of expertise, several delegates from the same Group may take part in the Congress.

6) Should the militants from the same Group not have managed to overcome their differences, nor reached a clear majority feeling on a given point, the Group may abstain when the vote is taken.

7) The Chairman of the Proceedings, and his assessors. appointed by Congress at the start of business, proceed to sample opinion and determine the outcome by adding up the number of votes cast. Decisions are reached by a 3/4 (three fourths) majority and a minute is drafted which Congress then ratifies. The Chairman of the proceedings and his assessors may not speak in the debates: as they will, of necessity be members of Groups, it will be for their Group's delegates to represent them.

8) As the implementation of decisions reached in Congress requires the continuous presence of the collective expression of the organization, the Congress appoints a National Collective charged with coordinating and carrying out the decisions it has reached.

9) This National Collective comprises five officers plus an equal number of deputies in case they might no longer be capable of performing their duties:
- an organizing Secretary (internal Relations).
- an External Relations Secretary.
- a Secretary for International Relations.
- a Propaganda Coordinating Secretary.
- a Treasurer.

10) These various secretaries should all be drawn from the same region, but they may not hold any office in their Local and Regional Federations.

11) Holding office from one Congress to the next, the officers may not belong to the National Collective for more than two consecutive years. After an interval of one year, they can again take up a position on the National Collective.

12) Excepting in the case of certain unforeseen events which require speedy decision-making, the National Collective may not take initiatives and make decisions except where these accord with the organization's ideological line as laid down in Congress. It is answerable for its actions before a Plenum or the next Congress.

13) Congresses are held every year and each time in a different geographical location, as far as possible. Should the need arise, an Extra-ordinary Congress may meet if summoned by the National Collective, a Plenum or at the prompting of half of the organization's Groups.

## National Office

1) The National Propaganda Council, charged with issuing the organization's Newspaper and various Reviews, publishing books, pamphlets and posters

destined for nationwide distribution, comprises a Publications Committee and a Steering Committee.

2) The Publications Committee is appointed by Congress, the Steering Committee by the National Collective. The Propaganda Coordinating Secretary is the National Collective's representative on the National Propaganda Council.

3) The National Collective is responsible for directing and managing the National Propaganda Council.

4) It is desirable that the members of the NPC should be drawn from the same region as the members of the National Collective.

5) The members of the NPC may not hold any office in their Local and Regional Federations.

## The Treasury

1) It is left to the Group and to the Regional Federation to determine the rate of dues.

2) Regional or national activities are funded by the Regional Federation or the organization as a whole, proportionately with the number of militants per Group. Thus it is the task of the Regional Liaison Commission or the National Collective to collect the funds and co-ordinate activities.

3) To fund the activities of the National Collective, there is a national levy payable 12 (twelve) times a year: the minimum amount of this is prescribed by Congress in the light of the anticipated requirements of the National Collective.

4) There is a solidarity fund, into which funds not raised from dues (special demonstrations, donations, etc.) are paid. This fund is used to cover the organization's debts as well as the purchase of propaganda material for those Groups which might not have the wherewithal to procure their own.

5) In the event of its failing to regularize its dues payments prior to Congress, a Group may be denied admission to the latter. A repeat offense may entail expulsion.

## The Internal Bulletin

1) The Internal Bulletin (IB) is placed under the supervision of the organizing Secretary. It is monthly and involves at the least reports on the activities of each Group and from the members of the National Collective and NPC.

2) The publication date, format and print-run of the IB are determined by Congress. Two IBs are run off per Group and five for the national archives. The IBs are the property of the Groups and not of the militants.

3) In order to spread the bulk of the work around all of the Groups, in order to ensure that the organization as a whole can continually monitor the serious business of each Group, in order to avert all censorship, it is the Groups themselves that roneo their submissions to the IB. Thus the work of the organizing Secretary consists merely of reprinting the pages submitted and passing on the IBs thereby compiled to the various Groups.

4) It is essentially through the IB that the minority in the organization finds expression.

5) A Group not contributing regularly to the IB may be deemed to have lost interest in the organization and, as such, incur expulsion.

## Security

1) For reasons of security, a militant on his travels will at all times carry a letter of introduction signed by the organizing Secretary of his Local Federation.

2) Also on security grounds, the organizing Secretary of each Local Federation keeps on him a list of the names and addresses of the militants of his locality. He can thus confirm for officers at various levels, at a moment's notice, whether a given individual is or is not a member of the organization.

## Admissions

1) There is no individual affiliation to the organization. Every new member must belong to a Group or, if none exists in his area, he must be in touch with the nearest Group, in anticipation of a Group being formed in his area.

2) Every new member belonging to a Group will be precluded from representing it for the period of one year, and from holding any office at any level. He will still be able to attend Congress, with the consent of his Group, as observer-delegate.

3) Before it is accepted, a Group that has sued for admission will have to wait until the organization has been able to check that it conforms to the movement's ethic. To that end, it shall submit its monthly report on its activities as well as copies of its handbills and pamphlets, will take part on the same footing as the organization's Groups in the distribution of the Newspaper (cash on delivery) and will scrutinize the Ideological and organizational Contracts to see if they suit it.

4) In the event of militants trained in the organization being behind the formation of a new Group, there shall be an exception to the preceding rule. It is for the organization's Congresses to endorse or reject affiliation of a new Group (by unanimity minus 10 percent).

## Expulsions

1) Any individual or Group that is in breach of contract with the collectivity will thereby exclude itself from the organization.

2) As far as the individual is concerned, it is for the Group to which he belongs to decide for itself upon exclusion (with a 3/4 majority of votes cast on an individual basis).

The excluded militant may appeal to the Regional assembly which will decide in the last instance (on a 3/4 majority of votes cast by Group). The militant whose expulsion is annulled by the Regional Federation may join another Group or form a new Group around himself.

3) In the case of the Group, it is for the Regional Assembly to determine exclusion (on a 3/4 majority). The expelled Group may appeal to Congress which will decide in the last resort (on a 3/4 majority).

4) During the appeal period, and pending the decision of the organization, the appellant militant or Group, shall suspend activities with regard to the latter.

## Amendment of the Organizational Contract

1) The present organizational Contract reflects the organization's current circumstances and will require amendment as these evolve.

2) Any amendment to the organizational Contract will be possible only in Congress (unanimity minus 10 percent).

## ADDENUM
## THE CONTRIBUTION OF THE JULES VALLES GROUP, PARIS, TO THE DRAFTING OF THE ORGANIZATIONAL CONTRACT

As a stepping stone to revolution and thus to libertarian communism, we have opted for the creation of a Revolutionary Anarchist organization (ORA), which is to be the driving force behind mass movements against authoritarian systems, said organization being the coalition of persons united by the prior theoretical considerations of:

- ideological unity
- tactical unity
- collective responsibility.

The problem which then arises is that of individuals' affiliation to the organization, the problem of the manner in which those who start out as sympathizers with the ORA are to be gradually incorporated into the organization.

## The Need for Induction Procedures

Generally, individuals wishing to militate in our ranks lack the minimal grounding in theory, and in practice too, which are required for the achievement of effective work.

Then again, the commitment that we demand of militants requires that these be as well-briefed as possible upon the broad tenets of the ORA: so it is essential that we offer a members' "apprenticeship" through what we term a "Front Libertaire Circle."

## The Front Libertaire Circles

Thus, the role of the Front Libertaire Circles is primarily to offer training to ORA sympathizers/prospective militants, but also they must devise propaganda and a libertarian communist policy line.

The Front Libertaire Circles are, consequently, launched initially by one or by several ORA militants, or the nearest ORA Group and are made up of ORA sympathizers.

These Circles, besides theoretical training through the Newspaper and above all printed pamphlets or local talks, are also engaged in practical activities (publishing handbills, posters, bulletins, selling the newspaper, etc.) and should allow the sympathizer to develop his feeling for self-organization and self-management.

Thus, the Front Libertaire Circles are autonomous of the ORA in the sense that they do not implicate the ORA in the activities they might possibly carry out, have a budget of their own, furnished by the sympathizers, and are autonomously managed.

The Circles are merely extensions of the ORA through the ORA militants in the locality, either the ORA Group or, in the case of geographical isolation in the provinces, through the local federations, regionally organized.

Ultimately, in these Circles, the ORA is merely the driving force, the chief theoretical contribution coming through the Newspaper and the *Manifesto* [the ORA's fundamental text — note by A. Skirda].

### Establishing the Circles

These Circles, which are a practical necessity for the Libertarian Front policy which we mean to devise, should be established wheresoever revolutionary propaganda is needed.

There can be Circles in firms, faculties, high schools and even around campaign organizations such as tenants' associations, consumers' associations, the peace movement, and, at a later stage, clandestine circles inside the army: in short, no sector of struggle should be overlooked.

### Definitive Incorporation

In the final analysis, it will be the ORA militants and the local regional that will pronounce upon the definitive incorporation into the ORA of a Circle member, or of an entire Circle, if need be, such incorporation being effected on the basis of subscription to the drive to achieve:
- a sense of collective responsibility.
- personal commitment.

The militant should be a theorist, an agitator and a propagandist as well (without of course lapsing into intellectualism or escapism).

Inside the ORA, the affiliate bears full responsibility, and little by little the difference between the militant and the affiliate should fade away.

# LIST OF BIBLIOGRAPHIC NAMES

**Abos Serena, Miguel**. Aragonese anarcho-syndicalist unfairly blamed for the fall of Zaragoza to the fascists in 1936. A militant of some stature from the teen years of this century, he was on the CNT national committee at the start of 1936 and encouraged CNT supprters to vote in the February 1936 elections. Escaped from Zaragoza in 1937, only to be interned by his CNT colleagues. Served in the 127th Mixed Brigade and died in France in 1940.

**Allemane, Jean** (1843–1935). Involved in the Paris Commune and deported to New Caledonia. Returning in 1880, he joined Guesde's POF and followed the possibilists' breakaway, heading their working-class wing while Brousse headed the intellectuals. Allemane and his colleagues launched the POSR — Revolutionary Socialist Workers' Party — in 1890. The so-called "Allemanists" espoused anti-authoritarian policies and worked for socialist unity. In 1905 the POSR amalgamated with the SFIO — French Section of the Workers' International (Socialist Party). Allemane took issue with the Leninist line on trade unions.

**Armand, Ernest** (1872–1962). Tireless propagandist of Christian then atheist anarchism of the individualist school.

**Arru, André** (born 1911). French anarchist, real name Jean-René Sauliére. Refused mobilization in 1939 and moved to Marseilles to form an underground and multi-national anarchist group of which Voline was a member. Sometime general secretary of the SIA (International Anifascist Solidarity).

Arshinov, Piotr (1887–193?). Ukrainian Bolshevik worker who became an anarchist terrorist before the 1917 revolution. Associate of Makhno in the Ukrainian insurgent movement during and after the Russian revolution. Returned to Russia in the 1932, working as a proof-reader until 1937. Believed killed in a purge.

Ascaso, Francisco (1901–1936). Spanish anarchist activist, inseparable companion of Durruti. Killed in the routing of the Francoist revolt in Barcelona in July 1936.

Azev, Yevno. Social Revolutionary and Okhrana agent who rose to head the SR's Fighting Section. He permitted the SR assassination of tsarist Interior minister Plehve in 1904 and ensured that almost all delegates to the Fighting Section congress in 1906 were arrested. Exposed by Burtsev as a police spy.

Babeuf, François "Gracchus" (1760–1797). French revolutionary and early communist: leader of the Conspiracy of the Equals. Executed by the Directory.

Bakunin, Mikhail (1814–1876). Russian anarchist, focus of the anti-authoritarian elements in the First International opposed to Marx's centralism.

Barmash, Vladimir. Russian anarchist, one-time émigré. A member of the secretariat of the universalist anarchists during the Russian Revolution of 1917, he was sentenced to death and then expelled from the Soviet Union along with Yartchuk, Maximoff, etc. in 1921.

Bastien, Georges. French anarchist active in the textile unions of the Amiens region. Co-founder of the Libertarian Communist Federation of the Nord region in 1920. Edited *Le Libertaire* for a time.

Bellegarricue, Anselme (born c. 1820–?). Involved in the 1848 overthrow of the July monarchy in France, he launched a newspaper in 1850, called *L'Anarchie*, subtitled "a journal of order."

Berkman, Alexander (1870–1936). Russian Jewish anarchist active in the United States before returning to Russia after the Bolshevik revolution, there to record his disillusionment with Bolshevik authoritarianism. Committed suicide in 1936.

Berneri, Camillo (1897–1937). Italian anarchist professor of philosophy and antifascist. Murdered in Barcelona in May 1937 by Stalinists during inter-Republican fighting.

**Besnard, Pierre**. French railroad worker and syndicalist who helped resist the absorption of the French CGTU into the Profintern. Later founded the anarcho-syndicalist CGT-SR affiliated to the Berlin syndicalist international (IWA). Besnard was secretary of the IWA during the civil war in Spain, clashing with the CNT on a number of issues. Wrote influential books setting out the ethics and vision of syndicalism.

Blanqui, Louis Auguste (1805–1881). French revolutionary socialist and vigorous agitator, involved in the earliest upheavals in France from 1831 onwards. Frequently arrested, he spent many years in prison.

Boétie, Etienne de la (1530–1563). French writer who at the age of eighteen wrote *Discourse of Voluntary Servitude* a denunciation of tyranny and the complicity through which it survives.

Bonnot, Jules (1876–1912). Outstanding mechanic active in anarchist and syndicalist circles. Around 1910 he went over to "illegalist" theory, formed a gang and carried out a number of robberies and murders. There was real hysteria about the "Bonnot Gang" until he was killed in a police operation in 1912.

Bonnot Gang. A gang of anarchist illegalists active in France in 1911–1913. Included Jules Bonnot, Raymond Callemin, Octave Garnier, Edouard Carouy, André Soudy, René Valet and Elie Monier.

Borghi, Armando (1882–). Anarchist from an early age and active in the labor movement. When the leaders of the USI (Italian Syndicalist Union). came out in favor of Italian intervention in the Great War, Borghi led the majority which disowned them and he was made secretary of the organization. He was a great friend of Malatesta. Under the fascists Borghi was forced to leave Italy, first for France and then the United States.

Borovoy, Aleksei. Russian academic and individualist anarchist at the time of the 1917 revolution.

Brassens, Georges. French poet and singer, a stalwart of the French Anarchist Federation in charge of organization and helping to run *Le Libertaire*.

Broutchoux, Benoit. French working-class anarchist forged in the struggles of the miners of the north of France. Member of the wartime Syndicalist Defense Committee (CDS).

Brousse, Paul (1844–1912). A member of the First International's libertarian wing from 1872, and involved with the Jura Federation in Switzerland. Deported from Switzerland to France in 1880 he joined Guesde's POF, but broke away with the "possibilists," becoming their leader. Espoused a very reformist, electoralist line.

Burtsev, Vladimir. Russian Social Revolutionary, regarded as expert on operations of the secret police. Ran a revolutionaries' counter-espionage operation against the Okhrana. Later sided with the Whites in the Russian Civil war.

Cabet, Etienne (1788–1856). French utopian socialist. Wrote about an imaginary ideal society in *Voyage to Icaria* (1840). Icarian settlements were founded in the United States in Texas and Illinois in 1848 and 1849 respectively.

Cafiero, Carlo (1846–1892). From a wealthy family of the nobility, he began a career in diplomacy but turned to social studies and political economy. On his travels he met and married the Russian revolutionary Olimpia Kutuzov. He first came into contact with revolutionaries in Paris in 1867 and met the founders of the First International, striking up a relationship with Marx. He became one of the chief propagandists for the IWMA in Italy and a correspondent of F. Engels. In 1971 he met Bakunin in Switzerland and became an anarchist. He was involved in the Rimini convention in 1872 when the decision was made to launch a (libertarian) Italian chapter of the International. Used his wealth to fund a number of insurrections, ranging from the 1874 revolt in Bologna to the Benevento revolt of 1877. While jailed in 1877–1878, translated *Das Kapital* into Italian. In the 1880s he suffered a mental breakdown and died in an asylum in 1892.

Carbo, Eusebio C. (1883–1958). Well-travelled Spanish anarchist noted as a public speaker and writer. Early critic (1921) of the dictatorship of the proletariat. Held a post in the Generalitat during the civil war before recovering his ideological integrity in exile, refusing a ministry in the Republican government-in-exile in 1945.

Caserio, Sante (1874–1894). Italian anarchist who attempted the life of French president Sadi Carnot in 1894. Executed by guillotine.

Chapelier, Emile. French anarchist involved in a range of activities, not least the "L'Expérience" commune in Boitsfort.

Cherkessoff, Varlam (1846–1925). Active revolutionary implicated in the April 1865 attempt on the life of Tsar Alexander II and in the Nechaev plot. Escaped from Tomsk in 1876 and fled abroad. Became a friend of Kropotkin in London, helping to found *Freedom*. Sided with Kropotkin in supporting the Allies in the Great War. Returned to Georgia once the Russian revolution came but was forced to leave by the Bolshevik take-over.

Coeurderoy, Ernest (1825–1862). French republican, socialist and anarchist. Fulminated against authority and in favor of internationalism in numerous books.

Cornelissen, Christian (b. 1864). Dutch anarchist collaborator with Nieuwenhuis on the paper *Recht voor Allen*. A former teacher, Cornelissen was a well-known writer on economic and syndicalist affairs. Signed the *Manifesto of the Sixteen* on the outbreak of the Great War.

Cottin, Emile (1896–1936). French anarchist who attempted the life of French premier Clemenceau in 1919 because of the latter's ban on anarchist meetings. Sentenced to death and reprieved: served 10 years in prison. Died in combat during the Spanish Civil War.

Degayev, Piotr. Russian revolutionary member of the "People's Will" organization. "Turned" by the Okhrana's Lt. Col. Sudeikin, he betrayed numerous comrades to the tsarist authorities before assassinating Sudeikin. Degayev began a new life as professor Alexander Pell in U.S. universities.

Dejacque, Joseph (1821–1876). French internationalist socialist who moved to London and thence to the United States where he edited a paper called *Le Libertaire* and subscribed to anarchist communism.

Delesalle, Paul (1870–1948). Mechanic who became an anarchist after travels in Catalonia and Belgium. Active in the trade unions from 1884 on and deputy to Jean Grave at Temps Nouveaux. Deputy secretary of the Federation of Bourses du Travail 1898–1908. Helped draft the Charter of Amiens. Acting secretary of the CGT while Yvetot was jailed in 1911. Became a bookseller and publisher after 1907.

Duclos, Jacques (1896–1975). Member of the French Communist Party from 1921 and leader of the Communist parliamentary party in France after the second world war. Notoriously close to Moscow and once accused by Trotsky of being a "long-time agent" of Moscow.

Dumoulin, Georges (1877–1963). French miner and revolutionary syndicalist prior to the Great War: during and after the war, he became identified with the reformist line in the CGT.

Durruti, Buenaventura (1896–1936). Legendary Spanish anarchist activist and international revolutionary. Embodiment of the commitment and vigour of Spanish anarchism. Killed in the defense of Madrid in 1936.

Duval, Clément (1850–1935). Famous French illegalist anarchist. Driven by poverty into a life of crime. Mechanic and thief who turned to anarchism and devoted himself to a career of "individual reappropriation," funding various movement activities with the proceeds. Arrested and sentenced to death in 1887, his sentence was then commuted to life imprisonment in Guyana. He escaped from Devil's Island after 14 years. Reached the United States and died in New York. His memoirs were published by Luigi Galleani.

Fabbri, Luigi (1877–1935). One of the most active of Italian anarchists. He joined the movement in his teens in 1897 and soon came into contact with Errico Malatesta who was publishing *L'Agitazione* in Ancona. In 1903 in Rome he launched the review *Il Pensiero* along with Pietro Gori. It ceased to appear in December 1911. He was an active contributor to *Volonta*, a weekly launched by Malatesta in Ancona in 1913. He was among the founders and contributors of the anarchist daily *Umanita Nova* and contributed to *Pensiero e Volonta,* a magazine run by Malatesta in Rome (1924–1926). Harassed by the fascists (having declined, as a teacher, to pledge allegiance to the regime as required by the education authorities) he left Italy. In Paris he launched *Lotta Umana* (1927–1929). Deported from France and from Belgium, he fled to Uruguay and in Montevideo he launched *Studi Sociali* in 1930, running the paper until his death on June 24, 1935. He was a prolific writer and used the pen names of Catalina, Quand-même and L. Sclosser among others.

Faure, Sébastien (1858–1942). French anarchist and former Jesuit seminarian. Ran for parliament for the Guesdist POF in 1885. From 1888 (when he was a delegate to the Third National Congress of the National Federation of Unions) onwards a propagandist for libertarian communism. Joint founder of *Le Libertaire*. Active on behalf of Dreyfus. Founded and ran La Ruche, a coeducational experimental school. The "Grand Old Man" of French anarchism.

Fedeli, Ugo (aka Hugo Treni). Italian anarchist, arrested during the Great War for anti-war activities. In 1924, from Paris he ran the Political Victims' Support Committee, helping antifascists. Deported to Belgium in 1929 after pressure from the Italian government. Later he went to Uruguay from where he was deported to Italy and banished to the island of Ponza in 1933. After 1944 he helped revive the Italian Anarchist Federation (FAI). Author of numerous articles on anarchist history and biographies of anarchists.

Feneon, Felix (1861–1947). French writer, part of the school of artistic anarchism.

Fleshin, Senya (1894–1981). Ukrainian-born. Immigrated to the USA and became anarchist in 1913, working with the *Mother Earth* team. Returned to Russia in 1917 and worked with the *Golos Truda* group in Petrograd. Joined the Nabat federation. Arrested by the Cheka in 1918, 1920 and 1922 and banished to Siberia. Expelled from Russia in 1923. Lived in Berlin, then Paris, escaping the latter after the German invasion. Left for Mexico in 1941.

Fontenis, Georges. French anarchist. Sometime secretary of the French Anarchist Fedration. Later formed the Libertarian Communist Federation (FCL).

Fourier, Charles (1772–1837). Utopian French socialist who offered a minutely detailed description of the operation of a "scientifically"-run society. Recommended ideal communities called Phalansteries, made up of 1,800 likeminded individuals.

Frémont, René (1902–1940). Leading member of the French UACR (Revolutionary Anarchist Communist Union) and UA (Anarchist Union). Editor of *Le Libertaire* from October 1934 to May 1935. General secretary of the UA in 1939. Called up into the French army and killed in June 1940.

Fribourg, Paul (1868–?). French railway worker socialist of the Allemanist school and revolutionary syndicalist. Advocate of the general strike and anti-militarist.

Friedeberg, Dr. Raphael (b. 1863). German social democrat turned anarchist. Active in anarcho-syndicalist spheres in 1904–1908. Abandoned this activity due to ill health.

Garcia, Oliver Juan (?–1980). Spanish anarchist activist. Associate of Ascaso and Durruti. Minister of Justice in the Caballero government in 1936–1937, representing the CNT (and, unofficially, the FAI).

Girault, Ernest (1871–1933). French anarchist activist and chemist. After the Great War he set up a soviet in Argenteuil. In 1920 he joined the French Communist Party.

Goldman, Emma (1869–1940). American anarchist of Russian extraction. Returned to Russia after the Bolshevik revolution and documented the Bolshevik perversion of the people's revolutionary aspirations. Notorious in her younger day as free-loving, iconoclastic "Red" Emma.

Grave, Jean (1854–1939). French anarchist shoemaker and journalist. Author of numerous anarchist works.

Griffuelhes, Victor (1874–1923). One-time Blanquist who became general secretary of the French CGT 1902–1909 — before the Great War. Primarily an activist, he supported the Sacred Union in 1914 but gradually broke away, sympathizing with the revolutionary syndicalist minority.

Guérin, Daniel (1904–1988). French anti-colonialist and socialist. Moved from Trotskyist Marxism towards a hybrid libertarian communism illuminated by the insights of anarchism.

Guesde, Jules (1845–1922). Sympathizer with Bakunin and the anarchists inside the First International, but went over to Marxism in his thirties, becoming its pioneer in France. Founder the POF (French Workers' Party). Entered the cabinet of the government of Sacred Union in 1914 and was Minister of State.

Stuck with the SFIO after the Communist Party broke away from it in 1920. A former libertarian, he espoused a particularly pedantic form of socialism.

**Guillaume, James** (1844–1916). Swiss prominent in the Jura Federation. He preferred to be described as a collectivist rather than "anarchist," regarding the latter term as somewhat extreme.

**Henry, Emile** (1872–1894). French anarchist, executed for terrorist bomb attacks including indiscriminate bombing of a middle-class cafe.

**Hervé, Gustave** (1871–1944). French rabble-rousing anti-militarist and anti-patriot editor of *La Guerre Sociale* prior to the Great War, he turned into a super-patriot after it broke out, changing the name of his paper to *La Victoire*.

**Herzig, Georges** (1857–1921). Genevan Swiss writer who took over the running of *Le Révolté* from Kropotkin and later wrote for the bilingual Swiss anarchist paper *Le Réveil-Il Risveglio* on social hypocrisy. Scathing critic of bureaucratization in Swiss trade unions.

**Jacob, Alexandre (Marius)** (1879–1954). Leader of a gang of anarchist housebreakers that operated in France, Spain, Italy and Switzerland. Jacob admitted 106 "jobs" that netted the equivalent of five million gold francs. Ten percent of his proceeds went to anarchist organizations, causes and publications. Convicted in 1905 and freed from penal servitude in 1925.

**Janvion, Emile.** French anarchist syndicalist active in the CGT before the Great War, co-founder of the International Anti-Militarist Association (1904). Obsessively anti-Masonic and anti-Semitic, campaigned against Masonic influence in the CGT. Took the line that bourgeois politicians had used the Dreyfus Affair as a ploy to rally revolutionaries behind the Republic and began to espouse an anti-Republican line that led to flirtations with Action Française.

**Jaurès, Jean** (1859–1914). Dreyfusard and co-founder of the French SFIO socialist party, Jaurès believed in evolutionary socialism. In 1914 he was assassinated by a French right-winger, Raoul Villain, who considered that Jaurès had left France ill-equipped to face the war with Germany.

**Jouhaux, Léon** (1879–1954). One-time anarchist who became general secretary of the French CGT in 1909, holding that post until 1940. During the Great War he embraced the Sacred Union and after the war he worked closely with the Socialist minister Albert Thomas and the International Labor Office.

**Jover Cortes, Gregorio** (1891–1964). Member of the *Los Solidarios* group, closely associated with Garcia Oliver. During the civil war he served with the Ascaso Column. A revolutionary of the old school, street-fighter and activist.

**Joyeux, Maurice** (1910–). French anarchist, first convicted at the age of 13. Headed the Unemployed Council of the CGTU. Involved in the factory seizures in France in June 1936. Helped re-launch the French Anarchist Federation after 1944. Prolific author and believer in direct action.

**Kropotkin, Peter** (1842–1921). Russian anarchist geographer. Leading advocate of anarcho-communism and federalism.

Lapeyre, Aristide and Paul. French anarchist brothers. Printers of *L'Espagne antifasciste* in Bordeaux from September to November 1937. Aristide (1889–1974) became an anarchist through his friendship with Sébastien Faure. Very active in freethought and anti-clerical circles (using the pen-name "Lucifer"). He was on the staff of *Le Combat syndicalste* in 1936 and ran the French section of the CNT-FAI propaganda operation in Barcelona. Jailed in France during the Occupation and narrowly escaped execution.

Latapie, Jean French metalworker, syndicalist and anti-militarist active in the CGT and close to Aristide Briand.

Léauthier, Jules (1874–1894). Assassinated the Serbian amassador in Paris in 1893. Sentenced to penal servitude for life, he was shot dead by warders a few weeks after arrival on Devil's Island during a convicts' revolt.

Lecoin, Louis (1888–1971). French anarchist and pacifist. Active in the unions, he led the campaign against affiliation of the CGTU to the Profintern. Led campaigns in favor of Sacco, Vanzetti, Durruti, Ascaso and Jover. Co-founder of the Committee for Free Spain in 1936 and of the SIA (International Anifascist Solidarity). Issued a "Peace Now" statement in 1939 and jailed until 1941. Credited with winning recognition of conscientious objector status in France following a hunger strike in 1962. Nominated for a Nobel Peace Prize 1964 and 1966.

Lefrancaise, Gustave. French Communard and communist from the 1848 revolution.

Lepetit (1889–1921). French anarchist syndicalist and laborer. In 1915 he was secretary of the International Action Committee against the Great War. Sentenced in 1917 for bringing out an underground edition of the banned *Le Libertaire*. Sent on a fact-finding mission to Soviet Russia, he was less than impressed and disappeared at sea off Murmansk on the return journey along with his companion, Vergeat.

Leroux, Pierre (1797–1871). French follower of Saint-Simon, helped proclaim the Republic in Paris in 1848.

Leval, Gaston (1895–1978). Pseudonym of Frenchman Pierre Robert Piller, who fled to Spain in 1915 to escape the Great War. In 1921 he was the anarchist groups' delegate seconded to the CNT delegation sent to the Profintern foundation congress in Moscow. His report did much to open CNT eyes to the reality of Bolshevism. Spent some time in Argentina in the 1920s. Collected data on collectivization during the Civil war in Spain. Returning to France he was a prolific writer on anarchism.

Levy, Albert. Member of the CGT leadership and treasurer of the Federation of Bourses du Travail. Resigned after a quarrel with Griffuethes.

Libertad, Albert (1875–1908). Charismatic orator and center for many years of the Parisian individualist anarchist scene. Launched the weekly *L'Anarchie* in 1905.

Lorulot, Andre (Andre Roulot). French anarchist, one-time editor of *L'Anarchie* (Paris) before Victor Serge. Initially encouraged illegalism. Active on the freethought wing of French anarchism.

Louvet, Louis (1899–1971). French anarchist active in the Proofreaders' Union in which he held office in the 40s, 50s and 60s. Author of *A World History of Anarchy* and driving force behind a number of French libertarian publications.

Makhno, Nestor (1889–1934). Ukrainian anarchist revolutionary and guerrilla leader. Leader of the "free soviet" peasant insurgents opposed to the Whites and to the Bolsheviks. Died in exile in Paris.

Malatesta, Errico (1853–1932). Italian anarchist and revolutionary. Early Internationalist and later anarcho-communist.

Malato, Charles (1857–1938). French anarchist son of a Communard father. Anarchist publicist. One of the signatories to the "Manifesto of the Sixteen" during the Great War.

Malinovsky, Roman. Russian Bolshevik leader and Okhrana agent. In 1912 Lenin elevated Malinovsky to the Bolshevik Central Committee.

Malon, Benoit (1841–1893). Nineteenth-century French socialist and Communard. Originally influenced by the libertarian school he later helped form the Possibilists. Espoused a non-sectarian, humanistic brand of socialism.

Martin, Constant (1839–1906). French Blanquist then anarchist involved in the Paris Commune. Collaborator with Pouget.

Martin, Pierre. French anarchist teacher, one of a number of conscientious objectors who refused the call-up in 1939 and were imprisoned as a result.

Marty, André (1886–1956). French communist who came to fame as leader of the Black Sea mutineers in 1919. Inspector of the International Brigades during the Spanish Civil War, he was a notorious Stalinist. Expelled from the French CP in 1953.

Mauricius (René Hemme, aka Vandamme). French individualist anarchist. Made anti-war propaganda during the Great War and was later an enthusiast of what appeared to be the libertarian revolution in Russia in 1917.

Mazzini, Giuseppe (1805–1872). Italian patriot and founder of the Young Italy organization. Republican agitator and rebel, he was attacked by Bakunin as an authoritarian, a theologian and a conservative. Many of Mazzini's followers went over to Bakunin and the International.

Mera Sanz, Cipriano (1897–1975). Anarcho-syndicalist bricklayer largely responsible for the CNT breakthrough in the Madrid region under the Republic. Very successful military commander, he attained the rank of lieutenant colonel in charge of the Fourth Army Corps. In 1939 he destroyed the Communists' attempt to mount a coup.

Meric, Victor. French writer of libertarian, pacifist inclinations who devised the International League of Fighters Against War, founded in 1926. Helped encourage the spread of War Resisters' International, founded in Holland in 1921.

Merlino, Francesco Saverio (1856–1930). Italian lawyer who joined the First International while very young. Acted as defense counsel to numerous anarchists including Malatesta. In 1889 he quit the anarchist movement and joined the Italian Socialist Party although he remained temperamentally an anarchist. In 1899 he launched the Rivista Critica del Socialismo in Rome. He was a very close friend to Malatesta and vehemently antifascist.

Merrheim, Alphonse (1871–1925). French revolutionary syndicalist leader. Alert to the necessity to educate the workers in economics. Led opposition to the Sacred Union in the Great War and participated in the Zimmerwaid Conference. Anti-communist.

Mett, Ida. Author of The Kronstadt Uprising (1938) and wife of Belgian anarcho-syndicalist Nicolas Lazarevitch. In 1928 she was deported from France for holding meetings to expose conditions for the working class in the USSR, to the annoyance of French Communists. In 1931 visited Spain when the monarchy collapsed.

Michel, Louise (1835–1905). Initially a follower of Blanqui, she was an active participant in the Paris Commune and was deported to New Caledonia as a result. She became an anarchist on the long outward journey. Returned to France after the 1880 amnesty and became an anarchist propagandist. Helped Sébastien Faure launch Le Libertaire. Died while on a lecture tour in 1905.

Monatte, Pierre (1881–1960). Dreyfusard socialist who quickly became an anarchist and syndicalist, helping Benoit Broutchoux to build up the miners' union in the Nord coalfields. Resigned from the French CGT'S steering commission in 1914 in protest at its acquiescence in the Sacred Union policy. Helped launch the revolutionary CGTU in 1921, but opposed the anarchist tendency. He was a communist presence in the CGTU and then was expelled from the French CP as a Trotskyist in 1924. Launched the revolutionary syndicalist newsaper La Révolution prolétarienne.

**Nacht, Siegfried**. German anarchist who did much to publicize the potential of French syndicalist practices.

Nettlau, Max (1865–1944). Vienna-born enthusiast and historian of anarchist ideas and activities. Made well-documented examinations of the lives and thought of Bakunin, Elisée Reclus, Malatesta and other anarchist thinkers. Coming from a wealthy family, he was able to devote his time to painstaking research, but his circumstances were greatly reduced by inflation following the First World War. Although he carried on with his research, he had to earn a living now from his articles for newspapers and reviews. His major works are a three volume Mikhael Bakunin: A Biography (London 1896–1900), A Bibliography of Anarchy (Brussels 1897), The Early Spring of Anarchy (Berlin 1925), Anarchism, from Proudhon to Kropotkin (Berlin 1931) and Life of Malatesta (1922) and Elisée Reclus (Berlin 1928).

Niel, Louis (1872–1952). French anarchist and syndicalist who helped marry the Bourse du Travail and the CGT. Moved in the direction of cautious reformism, a matter of change of pace rather than of objectives. Later joined the French socialist party, the SFIO. Compositor and, initially, anarchist. He became a reformist and replaced Griffuelhes in 1900 as secretary of the CGT. He was forced to resign on May 28, 1909, by the revolutionary syndicalist opposition. Became town clerk of Toulouse in 1935.

Nieuwenhuis, Domela (1846–1909). Former Protestant minister who became leader of Dutch social democrats and moved towards anarchism in the 1880s. Especially active as an anti-militarist.

Novomirsky (Kirilovsky). Russian anarchist, one-time editor of Novy Mir. Active terrorist in 1905–1906, he became an opponent of terrorism and advocate of anarcho-syndicalist action. Later joined the Bolshevik party and became a Comintern official.

Odeon, Pierre. French anarchist, friend of Louis Lecoin, refused the draft in 1929. Later organized transport for aid shipments to Spain during the civil war.

Orobon Fernandez, Valeriano (1901–1936). Asturian anarchist whose premature death robbed the CNT of a potential leader. Drafted the resolution on Federations of Industry at the CNT congress in 1919. Alert to the danger posed by fascism (after time spent working in Germany) he was especially vocal in calling for a Revolutionary Labor Alliance. Died of TB in June 1936.

Paepe, César de (1841–1917). Belgian Proudhonist then collectivist member of the First International. Active in the anti-authoritiarian International until 1877, then reverted to more conventional trade unionism.

Paraf-Javal. French individualist anarchist and Freemason, associate of Albert Libertad. Opposed syndicalism and campaigned against militarism. Later fell into a feud with Libertad.

Pelloutier, Fernand (1867–1901). At first a socialist and advocate of the general strike, Pelloutier became an anarchist in 1893, becoming treasurer and then secretary of the Federation of Bourses du Travail by 1895. Died of tuberculosis at the age of 35. Regarded as the "father" of French revolutionary syndicalism.

Perio, Juan (1887–1942). Spanish anarcho-syndicalist. Signed the *treintista* manifesto protesting FAI interference in CNT business. Represented the CNT in the Caballero government in 1936. Handed over to Francoists after the fall of France and executed for refusal to cooperate with Falangist national syndicalism.

Pierrot, Marc (1871–1950). Associated with the Temps nouveaux circle prior to the Great War. Signed the pro-Entente *Manifesto of the Sixteen* in 1916. Editor and leading light of the *Plus Loin* anarchist review after 1922.

Pini, Vittorio. Italian anarchist illegalist in France in the nineteenth century. He funded movement activity and propaganda with the proceeds of his criminal activities. Convicted in 1889 and sentenced to 20 years hard labor.

Pouget, Emile (1860–1931). French anarchist and syndicalist helped form Textile Workers' Union. Publisher renowned for his satirical newspaper *Le Père Peinard*. Fled to England in 1894 to escape an anti-anarchist crackdown, returning to France in 1895. Turned towards syndicalism, running the CGT's official mouthpiece *La Voix du Peuple* and rising to deputy secretary of the CGT. Withdrew from militant activity after 1908.

Prieto, Horacio Martinez (1902–19??). Spanish anarcho-syndicalist, former "pure anarchist" who came to prominence with the Spanish Republic. General secretary of the CNT for a time in 1936. Negotiated the CNT's incorporation into the Caballero government.

Prudhommeaux, André (1902–1968). French agronomist and anarchist, worked closely with Voline. Publisher of *Terre Libre* (1937–1939) and during the Spanish Civil War published *L'Espagne Nouvelle*. Active in the French anarchist movement, favoring a "spontaneist" approach on which Marxists and anarchists could agree.

Ramus, Pierre (1882–1942). Real name Rudolf Grossman. Began his political career writing for the German Social Democratic newspaper in New York. Soon disagreed with social democratic thinking and methods and became an anarchist. Became involved with the labor movement in Austria. Moved to London in 1933. Later he focused on the spreading of anti-militarist and Tolstoyan ideas. Interned at the start of World Wat II. Died in August 1942 on board a ship bound for Mexico.

**Ratchkovsky, Piotr**. Russian Okhrana operative who destroyed the last émigré press of the "People's Will" group in Geneva in 1886. His sensational "discovery" of Russian revolutionaries with bombs in Paris in 1890 helped reduce French sympathy for Russian revolutionaries.

Ravachol or François Koeningstein (1895–1892). Socialist, then anarchist. Joined the ranks of believers in "propaganda by deed." Carried out a number of outrageous acts (including killing an old man for his savings). Guillotined in 1892.

Reclus, Elie (1827–1904). Brother of Elisee Reclus. Supporter of the Paris Commune and anarchist.

Reclus, Elisee (1830–1905). French geographer and anarchist theoretician. Obliged to leave France after his opposition to the coup of December 2, 1851, he toured Europe and America. On his return (1857) he embarked upon geographical research, traveling through Italy, Sicily, Spain, etc., and published *The Earth: A Description of the Phenomena of the Life of the World (1867–1868)*. A member of the First International, he was involved in publication of *Le Cri du peuple* (1869). In 1871 he was sentenced to be deported to New Caledonia as a member of the Paris Commune, but sentence was commuted to 10 years banishment. Settling in Switzerland, Reclus collaborated with *Le Révolté* and managed the newspaper *L'Etendard révolutionnaire* (1882) and edited the Universal Geography which earned him a position at the free university in Brussels.

He was a tireless traveler and published his anarchist book *Evolution, Revolution and the Anarchist Ideal* (1898) and, in conduction with his brother Onésime, geographical studies on *Southern Africa* (1901) and China *The Middle Empire* (1902).

Reclus, Paul (1858–1941). Nephew of Elisée Reclus. At one time, editor of *La Révolte*. Worked for a time in Edinburgh and helped his uncle with his geographical writings.

Robin, Paul (1837–1912). French anarchist educationist. Briefly in 1870 a member of the First International's General Council — proposed by Karl Marx — but dropped once his libertarian beliefs became known. Director of the Cempuis orphanage and advocate of "integral education."

Rocker, Rudolf (1873–1958). German-born anarchist introduced to anarchism by Johann Most. In 1892 he was deported from Germany for "written propaganda," moving to Paris before deportation to London. Active from 1893 on in the Jewish libertarian workers' movement in London, editing its newspaper *Frei Arbeiter Stimme*. Opposed the 1914–1918 war before deportation to Germany in 1918. There he was deported again. Returned to Berlin when the German revolution erupted, only to be jailed by Noske. On his release he helped organize the German anarcho-syndicalists whose 1919 congress laid the foundations for the revival of the anarchist International Workers' Association (Berlin International). Moved to the U.S. after the advent of Nazism.

Rogdaev, Nikolai (?–1932). Russian anarchist who became a commissar in the post–1917 soviet health service. He died in 1932 while in exile in Tashkent.

Rosmer, Alfred (1877–1964). French left-wing communist with syndicalist sympathies. Expelled from the French Communist Party in 1924, he became a Trotskyist and a close friend of Trotsky.

Rühle, Otto (1874–1943). German Marxist schoolteacher and lecturer. Elected to the Reichstag as a Social Democrat in 1912. Joined with K. Liebknecht in voting against war credits in 1915. Left the party in 1916 and led the revolutionaries in Dresden in 1918. Advocated anti-parliamentary council communism. Helped launch the KAPD. Wrote "The Revolution Is Not a Party Matter" and was expelled from the KAPD. Emigrated to Prague and thence to Mexico after 1933. Friend but not follower of Trotsky.

Saint-Simon, Claude (1760–1825). French utopian socialist and advocate of managerial socialism.

Santillan, Diego Abad de (1898–). Spanish anarchist active in the FORA in Argentina in the 1920s. Returned to Spain in the 1930s, becoming a force in anarchist and CNT circles. One of the advocates of collaboration with other antifascists in Catalonia in 1936, he came to revise his opinion.

Schapiro, Alexander (?–1946). Active in Jewish anarchist circles in London at the turn of the century. Returned to Russia after the revolution, imprisoned and released on condition that he never return, following pressure on his behalf by French anarcho-syndicalists. Helped found and lead the IWMA (Berlin International).

Serge, Victor. (Pen name of Victor Kibaitchich) (1890–1947). French individualist anarchist of Russian extraction who collaborated with the Bolsheviks before demurring at Stalinist excesses. Died in Mexico.

Souchy, Augustin (1892–1984). German anarchist active in the Berlin-based revolutionary syndicalist International founded in the 1920s and a specialist in revolutions from below through workers' control and collectivization.

Steimer, Mollie (Pseudonym of Marthe Alperine) (1897–1980). Ukrainian-born anarchist active in the Yiddish-language movement in the U.S. prior to WW1. Deported to Russia in 1921 and expelled in 1923. Arrested and interned in France in 1940 but escaped to Mexico. Partner of Senya Fleshin.

Stirner, Max. (Pen name of Kaspar Schmidt) (1806–1856). German philosopher-anarchist, author of *The Ego and His Own*.

Tchorbadjifeff, Nikolas (1900–1994). Bulgarian anarchist who helped launch the Bulgarian Anarchist Federation in 1918. Involved in the abortive uprising there in 1923, later moving to Paris. Bulgarian representative in the Committee for Free Spain. Interned along with Arthur Koestler who mentions him in *Scum of the Earth*. Member of the French Resistance. One of the founders of *Iztok*, the Paris-based libertarian East European review. Returned to Bulgaria a month before his death there in 1994.

Tikhomirov, Lev (1850–1922). Russian revolutionary associated with the "Land and Liberty" and "People's Will" groups.

Tolain, Henri-Louis (1828–1897). Pioneer of the French labor movement and member of the First International. Became reformist and was expelled by the International for his hostility to the Commune in Paris. Later a senator.

Turner, John (1864–1934). Financial secretary of the Socialist League, 1886. Helped form the United Shop Assistants' Union in 1889 and was its president until 1898. Worked with The Commonweal Group and the Freedom Group. He was the official publisher of *Freedom* from May 1895 until September 1897. Helped publish *Voice of Labor* in 1907. Helped re-launch *Freedom* in May 1930 after its predecessor had been wound up.

Vaillant, Auguste (1861–1894). French anarchist who threw a bomb into the Chamber of Deputies in 1893. Executed by guillotine.

Vaillant, Edouard (1840–1915). French socialist, Marxist, member of the First International and Communard. Leader of the Second International.

Villain, Raoul. Right-wing youth who shot Jean Jaurés dead in 1914, holding him to blame for France's defenselessness in the face of German aggression. The courts treated Villain very leniently.

Vivancos, Miguel Garcia (1895–1972). Founding member of the *Los Solidarios* group in 1922. Driver to Garcia Oliver during the civil war. Served with the Aguiluchos column and was adjutant to Jover. Gained renown as a naive painter after the Second World War.

Voline. (Pen name of Vsevolod M. Eichenbaum) (1882–1945). Russian Social Revolutionary, then, from 1911, anarchist. Involved in 1905 revolution. Managed the Russian anarcho-syndicalist paper *Golos Truda*. Later joined Makhno in the Ukraine. Differed with Makhno over the Arshinov Platform proposal. Opposed CNT-FAI entry into Spanish Republican government. Helped relaunch the French anarchist movement after World War II.

Walter, Karl (1880–1965). Started working with the Freedom Group in London in 1904. In 1908, went to the United States where he wrote for *Mother Earth*. Wrote the Freedom Press-published report on the International Anarchist Congress in Amsterdam in 1907. Wrote sporadically for anarchist papers when he returned to England.

Yudin. Russian anarchist: at the time of the Russian revolution he was a member of the united students.

Yvetot, Georges (1868–1942). French anarchist and revolutionary syndicalist specialising in anti-militarist action. His pacifist activity persisted into the Second World War.

Zabrezhnev, Vladimir. Russian anarchist, attended the Amsterdam Congress in 1907. Later joined the Communist Party and the editorial staff of the *Moscow Izvestia*.

Zhelyabov, Andrei (1850–1881). Russian revolutionary, born a serf and later leader of the combat wing of the "People's Will" organization. Assassinated Tsar Alexander II in 1881.

Zhitomirsky, David. Russian revolutionary and Okhrana spy. Close friend with Lenin in Paris after 1908. Remained friend of Lenin — despite warnings from Burtsev — until 1915.

Zorkine, Paul (?–1962). French anarchist involved with the magazine *Noir et Rouge*, the organ of the GAAR (Anarchist Revolutionary Action Groups) from 1956 until his death in an accident in 1962.

## KATE SHARPLEY LIBRARY

Comrades and Friends —

No doubt some of you will be aware of the work of the Kate Sharpley Library and Documentation Centre, which has been in existence for the last eight years. In 1991 the Library was moved from a storage location in London to Northamptonshire, where we are now in the process of creating a database of the entire collection. At the same time, a working group has been formed to oversee the organisation and running of the Library. The catalogue of the Library material will be published by AK Press (Edinburgh).

The Library is made up of private donations from comrades, deceased and living. It comprises several thousand pamphlets, books, newspapers, journals, posters, flyers, unpublished manuscripts, monographs, essays, etc., in over 20 languages, covering the history of our movement over the last century. It contains detailed reports from the IWA (AIT/IAA), the Anarchist Federation of Britain (1945–50), the Syndicalist Workers Federation (1950–1979) and records from the anarchist publishing houses, Cienfuegos Press, ASP and others. Newspapers include near complete sets of *Black Flag, Freedom, Spain and the World, Direct Actions* (from 1945 onwards), along with countless others dating back 100 years. The Library also has a sizeable collection of libertarian socialist and council communist materials which we are keen to extend.

The Kate Sharpley Library is probably the largest collection of anarchist material in England. In order to extend and enhance the collection, we ask all anarchist groups and publications worldwide to add our name to their mailing list. We also appeal to all comrades and friends to *donate* suitable material to the Library. *All* donations are welcome and can be collected. The Kate Sharpley Library (KSL) was named in honour of Kate Sharpley, a First World War anarchist and anti-war activist — one of the countless "unknown" members of our movement so ignored by "official historians" of anarchism. The Library regularly publishes lost areas of anarchist history.

Please contact us if you would like to use our facilities. To receive details of our publications, send a stamped addressed envelope to:

KSL
BM Hurricane
London WC1N 3XX
England

Kate Sharpley Library
PMB #820
2425 Channing Way
Berkeley, CA 94704
USA
www.katesharpleylibrary.org

**THE KATE SHARPLEY LIBRARY**

# Other Titles of Interest from AK Press

**Orgasms of History: 3000 Years of Spontaneous Revolt**
Yves Fremion, Drawings by Volny
$18.95/£12.00 • pb • 1 902593 34 0
272 pages

Every now and then, things explode. Riots, uprisings, revolutions, new and bizarre social groups spring up seemingly from nowhere. Our standard histories tend to treat these as oddities, if treated at all, or as misguided responses to hard times, limited by lack of responsible leadership. For the first time in English, here's a People's History to puncture that balloon. From the Cynics & Spartacus through the Levelers, Diggers & Ranters to the Revolution of the Carnation, the San Francisco Diggers, Red Guard of Shenwulian, Brethren of the Free Spirit, Guevara, the Provos & the Metropolitan Indians. Nearly 100 episodes of revolt and utopia which popped up without a plan or a leader from the ancient Greeks to the present. Includes Volny's and original artwork and sketches throughout of the characters involved in the greatest, most inspiring events of all time.

Fremion lives in Paris where he participated in the May '68 orgasm.

**Reinventing Anarchy, Again**
Howard J. Ehrlich, Ed.
$24.95/£13.95 • pb • 1 873176 88 0
398 pages

This book brings together the major currents of social anarchist theory in a collection of some of the most important writers from the United States, Canada, England and Australia.

The book is organized into eight sections: What is Anarchism?, The State and Social Organization, Moving Toward Anarchist Society, Anarchafeminism, Work, The Culture of Anarchy, The Liberation of Self, and, finally, Reinventing Anarchist Tactics.

## No Gods No Masters: Book One
Daniel Guérin (ed)
$18.95/£11.95 • pb • 1 873176 64 3
304 pages

This is the first English translation of Guérin's monumental anthology of Anarchism. It details, through a vast array of hitherto unpublished documents, writings, letters and reports, the history, organization and practice of the anarchist movement — its theorists, advocates and activists.

Book 1 includes the writings of Max Stirner, Pierre-Joseph Proudhon, Mikhail Bakunin, James Guillaume, Max Nettlau, Peter Kropotkin, Emma Goldman and Cesar de Paepe amongst others - traversing through 'The Ego And His Own', 'Property Is Theft', 'God And The State', 'The International Revolutionary Society Or Brotherhood', the controversy with Marx and the First International, The Paris Commune, Worker Self-Management, The Jura Federation and more....

## No Gods No Masters: Book Two
Daniel Guérin (ed)
$16.95/£11.95 • pb • 1 873176 69 4
288 pages

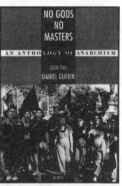

Book 2 includes work from the likes of Malatesta, Emile Henry, Emile Pouget, Augustin Souchy, Gaston Leval, Voline, Nestor Makhno, the Kronstadt sailors, Luigi Fabbri, Buenaventura Durruti and Emma Goldman - covering such momentous events as the Anarchist International, French 'propaganda by the deed', the General Strike, collectivization, The Russian Revolution, the Nabat, The Insurgent Peasant Army of the Ukraine, the Kronstadt Uprising, and the Spanish Civil War and Revolution.

---

## Ordering Information:

**AK Press** 674-A 23rd Street, Oakland, CA 94612-1163, USA
Phone: (510) 208-1700 / E-mail: akpress@akpress.org / URL: www.akpress.org
Please send all payments (checks, money orders, or cash at your own risk) in US dollars. Alternatively, we take VISA and MC.

**AK Press** PO Box 12766, Edinburgh, EH8 9YE, Scotland
Phone: (0131) 555-5165 / E-mail: ak@akedin.demon.uk / URL: www.akuk.com
Please send all payments (cheques, money orders, or cash at your own risk) in UK pounds. Alternatively, we take credit cards.

For a dollar, a pound or a few IRCs, the same addresses would be delighted to provide you with the latest complete AK catalog, featuring several thousand books, pamphlets, zines, audio products and stylish apparel published & distributed by AK Press. Alternatively, check out our websites for the complete catalog, latest news and updates, events, and secure ordering.

## The Struggle Against The State And Other Essays
Nestor Makhno
$9.95/£7.95 • pb • 1 873176 78 3
128 Pages

   Nestor Makhno became an anarchist after the Russian Revolution of 1905. Sentenced to death for armed struggle, his sentence was commuted to life imprisonment. Liberated in 1917, he organized an army of anarchist resistance against both the Bolsheviks and the White counterrevolutionaries.

   Throughout his period of struggle, he consistently advocated the creation of anarchist communism in the most difficult and impractical of conditions. Forced to flee by the Bolsheviks, he eventually ended up in exile in Paris. Nestor Makhno wrote occasional essays in self-vindication and in vindication of the peasant insurgent movement that bore his name. He remained politically active, contributing to Delo Truda and other papers, and helped create the Organizational Platform Of The Libertarian Communists. Makhno was determined that the next time anarchism, acting in the light of experiences dearly bought, revamped and more disciplined thanks to its Organizational Platform, might reap the rewards proportionate with the commitment and sacrifice of its activists. Makhno died from tuberculosis on July 25, 1934, aged 44. The essays in this volume date from his period in exile.

## The Friends Of Durruti Group: 1937-1939
Agustin Guillamón
$9.95/£7.95 • pb • 1 873176 54 6
128 Pages

   "Revolutions without theory fail to make progress. We of the 'Friends Of Durruti' have outlined our thinking, which may be amended as appropriate in great social upheavals but which hinges upon two essential points which cannot be avoided. A program, and rifles."— El Amigo del Pueblo, No. 5, July 20, 1937.

   Spain 1936-1939: This is the story of a group of anarchists engaged in the most thoroughgoing social and economic revolution of all time. Essentially street fighters with a long pedigree of militant action, they used their own experiences to arrive at the finest contemporary analysis of the Spanish Revolution. In doing so they laid down essential markers for all future revolutionaries. This study — drawing on interviews with participants and synthesizing archival information — is THE definitive text on these unsung activists.

   This volume is translated, edited and introduced by Paul Sharkey, acknowledged internationally as the foremost expert on the Friends Of Durruti Group.

## The Spanish Anarchists:
## The Heroic Years 1868-1936
Murray Bookchin
$19.95/£13.95 • pb • 1 873176 04 X
322 Pages

A long-awaited new edition of the seminal history of Spanish Anarchism. Hailed as a masterpiece, it includes a new prefatory essay by the author.

"I've read The Spanish Anarchists with the excitement of learning something new. It's solidly researched, lucidly written and admirably fair-minded.... Murray Bookchin is that rare bird today, a historian."
–DWIGHT MACDONALD

"I have learned a great deal from this book. It is a rich and fascinating account.... Most important, it has a wonderful spirit of revolutionary optimism that connects the Spanish Anarchists with our own time." –HOWARD ZINN

Murray Bookchin has written widely on politics, history and ecology. His books *To Remember Spain: The Anarchist And Syndicalist Revolution Of 1936* and *Social Anarchism Or Lifestyle Anarchism: An Unbridgeable Chasm* are both published by AK Press.

## Anarchism, Marxism and the
## Future of the Left
Murray Bookchin
$19.95/£13.95 • pb • 1 873176 35 X
352 Pages

Murray Bookchin has been a dynamic revolutionary propagandist since the 1930s when, as a teenager, he orated before socialist crowds in New York City and engaged in support work for those fighting Franco in the Spanish Civil War.

Now, for the first time in book form, this volume presents a series of exciting and engaged interviews with, and essays from, the founder of social ecology.

This expansive collection ranges over, amongst others, Bookchin's account of his teenage years as a young Communist during the Great Depression; his experiences of the 1960s and reflections on that decade's lessons; his vision of a libertarian communist society; libertarian politics; the future of anarchism; and the unity of theory and practice. He goes on to assess the crisis of radicalism today and defends the need for a revolutionary Left. Finally he states what is to be valued in both anarchism and Marxism in building such a Left, and offers guidelines for forming a new revolutionary social movement.

## Beneath the Paving Stones: Situationists and the Beach, May 68
Dark Star Collective (ed)
$15.00/£9.00 • pb • 1 902593 38 3
120 Pages

An anthology of the three classic Situationist pamphlets - *The Poverty of Student Life, Totality for Kids,* and *The Decline and Fall of the Spectacular Commodity Economy,* plus an eyewitness account of the Paris May 68 events. Much of the Situ creed was produced in pamphlet form - and these 3 were crucial in creating the Situationist legend. Indeed, these works by Guy Debord, Raoul Vaneigem and the Strasbourg Students were the most widely translated, distributed and influential pamphlets of the Situationist International available in the 60s. Easier to read than *Society of the Spectacle,* and a provocatively seductive invitation to a life of freedom and revolt, this compendium offers the reader not only a concise introduction to the ideas of the Situationists, but also an insight into what Situationist material was readily available in the late sixties. *Beneath The Paving Stones: Situationists And The Beach* in addition includes numerous documents, photographs, poster art and graffiti originating from Paris in 1968. A beautiful book — probably worth investing in a new coffee-table just to display it properly! As the Situationists continue to have an historical and contemporary relevance, we are proud to offer this anthology to young people of all ages who refuse to knuckle down.

## Obsolete Communism: The Left-Wing Alternative
Daniel & Gabriel Cohn-Bendit
$17.95£12.00 • pb • 1 902593 25 1
240 Pages

"Their nightmares are our dreams"
In May 68 a student protest at Nanterre University spread to other universities, to Paris factories and in a few weeks to most of France. On May 13 a million Parisians marched. Ten million workers went out on strike.

At the center of the fray from the beginning was Daniel Cohn-Bendit, expelled from Nanterre for his agitation. Obsolete Communism was written in 5 weeks immediately after the French state regained control, and no account of May 68 or indeed of any rebellion can match its immediacy or urgency.

Daniel's gripping account of the revolt is complemented by brother Gabriel's biting criticism of the collaboration of the state, the union leadership and the French Communist Party in restoring order, defusing revolutionary energy & handing the factories back to the capitalists. Leninism & the unions come under fire as top-down bureaucracies whose need to manage and control are always at odds with revolutionary action.

"Daniel Cohn-Bendit is the most dangerous scoundrel in France." — President Charles deGaulle

# THE ALEXANDER PRINCIPLE

'The Alexander Technique ... all the things
we have been looking fo... ...m of physical
education: relief from ... to maladjustment,
and constant impro... physical and mental
health. We canno... from any system; nor,
if we seriously d... ...er human beings in a
desirable dire... ...we ask any less.'
*Aldous Huxley*

'Mother Nature is sometimes stupid, says Wilfred
Barlow in his beautifully written, *The Alexander
Principle*. The tension of modern living produces
tension and, says Barlow, it is within the power of
everyone to correct tension habits. I hope this book
will rejuvenate a sadly neglected area of study.'
*The Times Educational Supplement*

'The truth of the matter is that I would be in a
frightful pickle now if I had never been to Barlow.
I think that what he teaches belongs to that
particular corpus of ideas which gives us some hope
of being less mechanical than we otherwise would
be and, therefore, gives us a glimpse of another
kind of freedom.'
*Colin Davis*

'The Alexander Technique has given me a glimpse
of the possibility of harmony.'
*Edna O'Brien*

'Alexander's work is of first class importance and
investigation by the medical profession is imperative.'
*British Medical Journal*

*Wilfred Barlow*

# THE ALEXANDER PRINCIPLE

ARROW BOOKS

Arrow Books Limited
17-21 Conway Street, London W1P 6JD

An imprint of the Hutchinson Publishing Group

London Melbourne Sydney Auckland
Johannesburg and agencies throughout
the world

First published by Gollancz 1973
Arrow edition 1975
Reprinted 1979, 1981 and 1984

Printed and bound in Great Britain by
Anchor Brendon Limited, Tiptree, Essex

ISBN 0 09 910160 2

# CONTENTS

# NOTE

Text references to photographs are given with the term "plate" followed by a number and a facing or following page number. Text references to drawings and diagrams are given with the term "figure" or "fig.".

# LIST OF PLATES

# TO MARJORY

# Chapter 1

## THE ALEXANDER PRINCIPLE

JUST BEFORE THE war, in 1938, I came across a very remarkable man. Seventeen years later, when I wrote his obituary in *The Times*, I called him a genius, and I still see no reason to go back on this. Unfortunately, Alexander was also somewhat of a rogue. His roguery was innocent and patent for all to see and enjoy—he was an entertainer, trained on the stage, as well as a scientist—but it held up full acceptance of his principle in his lifetime.

There is no need here to enlarge on the complex personality of this delightful man, except to marvel that such an earthy character could have come up with such a principle. The confidence-man who discovers that he has a method for making genuine gold-bricks is up against it if he wishes to convince the scientific world that the method is sound; particularly so if he has no scientific language but only the ways of the ordinary world.

Alexander's gold brick was, in fact, HEALTH. His attempts to convince the scientific world did not succeed during his lifetime, but in recent years his principles have been accepted in almost every sphere of human activity. Men and women who are pre-eminent in their various spheres of medicine, science, education, religion, music, politics, art, architecture, industry, literature, philosophy, psychology, the stage and television have gladly accepted the help that the Alexander principle has to offer them: perhaps more important, younger people who came upon it earlier in life are now showing in their successful life-styles just what it has to offer.

This book is a commentary on the thirty years' work which I have done since I met Alexander. It is motivated by a feeling of urgency that, in the present mess and muddle in which we find ourselves, his principle can provide a new touchstone for most of us. It can not only provide a criterion for evaluating our own actions but a criterion for assessing the actions of other people and the value of new popular trends and new popular leaders. It also provides a way of looking at those well-established and time-honoured dogmas which, in the words of Paracelsus, "are not worth a goose's turd".

Alexander's main problem was to persuade people that he had something to offer. The problem still exists, to some extent, but, since the pendulum is now swinging the other way, the problem for most people will be to get hold of someone who knows about the principle and who has not been brought up in the gold-brick atmosphere which dogged Alexander all his life. He has sometimes been poorly served by his followers and many of them so far have found the brick too hot to handle. It is fair to say that only in recent years has the principle found its rightful place in medicine and education. Sufficient numbers of teachers who have been well trained in the principle are only now beginning to appear.

Just one statistic. Since Alexander started working seventy-five years ago when he was 30, more than one hundred teachers of his method have been trained in this country. Of these, only four have died,* including Alexander himself aged 87, and his first assistant, Ethel Webb aged 94: no coronaries, no cancers, no strokes, no rheumatoid arthritis, no discs, no ulcers, no neurological disorders, no severe mental disorder, just occasionally some rather unlikely behaviour; accidents inevitably, but recovery to good functioning and no accident-proneness. By and large, a standard of day-to-day health and happiness which most people encounter only in their earliest years.

This statistic is almost unbelievable. The gold-brick is too good to be true, but it is in fact true, and it is not insufferable arrogance to say that this principle is a MUST. It is by now a plain brute fact that the Alexander principle works. It is also a plain brute fact that over 99% of the population need it but know nothing of it: I hope that, provided the writing of this book does not make me the fifth mortality, I can get across some of its importance to the general reader.

### The Principle

So much for preliminary encouragement. Plenty of this is needed if we are to look at things in a completely different way. What does the Alexander Principle say? The Alexander principle says that

* I do not include U.S. teachers.

> USE AFFECTS FUNCTIONING

The old negro preacher who was asked for the secret of his success, said, "First, ah tells them what ah's gonna say: then ah says it: then ah tells them what ah's just said." So here it is again

> USE AFFECTS FUNCTIONING

What sort of use? What sort of functioning? This is what we need to consider.

*Use*

You are sitting somewhere, perhaps lying somewhere, reading this book. Are you aware of how your hand is holding the book? If you direct your attention to your hand, you will become aware of the pressure of your fingers taking the weight of the book. How are you sitting? Are your knees crossed? Is the weight of your body more on one buttock than the other? Where are your elbows? As you run your eyes over the page, does your head move to alter your eye position, or do just your eyes move? Where are your shoulder-blades? How much muscle tension are you creating in your chest and forearms and generally throughout your body?

USE means the way we use our bodies as we live from moment to moment. Not only when we are moving but when we are keeping still. Not only when we are speaking but when we are thinking. Not only when we are making love but when we are feeling or refusing to feel pleasure. Not only when we are communicating by actual gestures and attitudes but when, unknown to ourselves, our whole bodily mood and disposition tells people what we are like and keeps us that way whether we like it or not. Not only when we are searching and manipulating our surroundings but when we are letting our surroundings manipulate us like puppets: liking what we get, instead of getting what we like.

USE is the theme of this book. Its variety will be described in the chapters which follow.

*Functioning*

FUNCTIONING is also the theme of this book. All of us are functioning—adequately, inadequately, happily, unhappily, healthily, unhealthily. A few case-histories will give an idea of the sort of wrong FUNCTIONING which can go with wrong USE. It may not be immediately clear why these people's USE was the first thing which needed tackling: it is the purpose of this book to indicate the connection and the remedy.

## The Physician

Dr James P, a chest physician, has been worried for some time by increasing depression and a constant pain in his neck. He assuages it with liberal doses of alcohol and by the thanks of his grateful patients. He is a scholarly man who knows all about depression and psychosomatic pains in the neck. His own neck still hurts, and it is getting him down.

About twenty years ago, when he was a timid medical student, he opted for a rather pompous manner which involved straightening his neck, pulling his chin down on to his throat and occasionally belching—the sort of gentle belching which is a common form of parlance in aristocratic clubs, preceded by a slight swallowing of air to provide the necessary ammunition.

A few years later, he refined the head posture to include a deprecatory twist of his head to one side and a puffing-out of his chest in front. A few years later, he was making these movements even when he was alone and sitting quite still: the belching had become a habit, and, in between belching, he tightened his throat and restricted his breathing.

Dr P had already consulted his psychiatric colleagues and he had reluctantly cut down on much of his work since he found it impossible to concentrate. There was not the remotest possibility of him getting rid of his neck pain until his strange muscular usages had been sorted out. Some of his problems are dealt with in Chapter 6 (Use and Disease).

## The Student

Jane B, a pretty 19-year-old, had been reading English Literature at one of the new universities. At school she very nearly didn't take her A levels—she was basically a "good" girl, and was one of the two girls in her sixth form who had never smoked nor lost her virginity. After two days at university, she turned up at home saying she couldn't stand it, but reluctantly agreed to go back—her parents later on rather wished that they had abided by their daughter's instinctive rejection.

She found herself painfully unable to talk with other people and she withdrew more and more into herself. At this point, like many others, she could have chosen to fall in with the general permissive scene, and like many others, if her temperament had been suited to it, she might have sickened of it and made stable enjoyable relationships which used the social anti-depressant drugs as an occasional pleasure rather than a constant haven.

Jane B instead cracked up. She wept almost continuously, not just with tears from her eyes, but with an agonised contraction through her whole body. Her stomach contracted, her hands twisted and tensed, her eyes and head dropped down on her chest, and her shoulders lifted up towards her ears. The psychiatrists said it was "reactive depression" and treated her with shock therapy and anti-depressant drugs. It was not until her USE was considered that the breakthrough to improved functioning became possible. The relationship of USE to Mental Functioning is described in Chapters 7 (Mental Health) and 12 (Applying the Principle).

## The Journalist

Mrs Hermione X used to be well known in the world of women's magazines—wittily informed and human, identifiably plagued with the problems of her wittily informed and human readers. A good degree had neither kept her in the Shades of Academe nor precipitated her into the world of giggling revolutionaries. At the age of 45, married, with grown-up children and time to spare, she suddenly started to wonder what it was all about. She came to me ostensibly for help with her hobby of flute-playing—her breathing and her fingering were totally unpredictable—but a whole range of psychosomatic symptoms were soon being presented to me for appraisal. It soon became apparent that her main trouble was her sex-life. It has been said that at any given time you are in trouble because you are worrying about your sex life: or you are in real trouble because you are not worrying about your sex-life.

Hermione's problem was fairly clear. She felt constantly very sexy, and could be triggered off into sexual excitement by quite small things: but when she began to engage in actual love-making, she would go cold and dead. The harder she worked towards orgasm, the more irritated and less responsive she became.

The whole range of sexual problems in which muscular usage plays a prime part are dealt with in Chapter 8 (The Psycho-mechanics of Sex) but it should not be thought that these are simply the problems of the tense pelvis—Reich's "Frozen Pelvis". Each of us will have elaborated our own minutely variegated system of muscular usages not only in our pelvis but throughout the whole of our bodies—usages which are suddenly thrown up to demand their share of the picture at the most inconvenient moment, and to interfere with the balanced functioning which we expect from our bodies.

### The Schoolboy

Edward P is 11 years old. Two years ago he felt a curious "thumping" at the back of his head, and when his mother became worried by what he told her, he started to get very upset himself. The school doctor could not explain it, nor could a whole battery of neurologists, orthopaedic surgeons and ear, nose and throat specialists who were consulted. The young boy by now was becoming extremely hypochondriacal about it and would argue at length with his mother about how he had said the symptoms felt at such and such a time. Their GP became heartily sick of it all, and a new GP had little extra to offer. A close friend had heard of an osteopath who could do wonders, so the poor little boy went to the osteopath to have his neck cricked week after week, and the "thumping" was quite a convenient reason not to undertake school activities when there was stress around. As so often happens, however—and as may have been the case all along—Edward's pattern of muscular use began to deteriorate in an alarming way.

When he came to see me with his young mother, he could not keep his neck and shoulders still for more than a few seconds, and I was fascinated to see that his mother participated fully in this pattern of muscular twisting and wriggling. They communicated with each other by fractional shifts of muscular adjustment, in which one of them would counter the hints or suggestions of the other by a movement which in its turn had to be countered. This game of muscular ping-pong between the two was quite unconscious and it reminded me of a Jungian psychotherapist who had a habit of establishing rapport with her patients by a series of knowing wriggles and nods of her head which seemed to herself like an exhibition of friendliness, but which must have felt like an irritating intrusion to the patient. The psychotherapist—whom I was treating for a muscle-tension state—said that when I taught her a balanced state of rest, she felt as if she wasn't establishing proper rapport with her patients, although in fact they seemed to find it easier to talk to her.

Edward P was not untypical of boys of his age and such problems of growth are described in Chapter 9 (Personal Growth). By the age of 11, 70% of all boys and girls will already show quite marked muscular and posture deficiencies. Mostly these defects show themselves as passing inefficiencies and difficulties in learning: they become accentuated in emotional situations, and they presage an uneasy adolescence in which childhood faults become blown up into fully fledged defects. By the age of 18, only 5% of the population are free from defects, 15% will have slight defects, 65% will have quite severe defects and 15% will have very severe defects. These figures are based on my published surveys of boys and girls from secondary schools and students from physical training, music and drama colleges, some of whom might reasonably be expected to have a higher physical standard than the rest of the population. It is almost certain that you, the reader of this book, have quite marked defects of which you yourself are unconscious, and which your doctors or teachers or parents did not notice or did not worry about or accepted as an inevitable part of the way you are made.

\*         \*         \*

These case-histories all say the same thing, that USE affects FUNCTIONING. The physician with his neck-pain, the student with her depression, the journalist with her muscular frigidity, the schoolboy with his habit-spasm—all had been pathetically mishandled by their doctors. Diagnosis in their case had been inadequate, not only because of a mistaken idea of what diagnosis should involve, but because of a failure to observe and to understand what is meant by USE. Chapter 5 (Medical

Diagnosis) and 6 (Use and Disease) show where the Alexander
Principle fits into the medical picture, not just in the isolated
examples I have given above, but in the whole wide spectrum
of ill health as it affects us all.

By the time we reach adult life, if not before, most of us will
have developed tension habits which are harmful. The habits
at first may show themselves only as trifling inconsistencies of
behaviour, or perhaps as occasional muscular pain or clumsiness. Frequently, however, they show themselves as infuriating
blockages which prevent us from giving our best just when we
most need to, whether it be in the everyday business of personal
relations, or in the more exacting situations of competitive
sport, public speaking, making music or making love. In any
situation, in fact, in which our FUNCTIONING is affected by our
USE.

## Matthias Alexander

The Alexander Principle sounds at first deceptively simple. I
have called it the Alexander Principle because, as far as I
know, he was the first person to state it, and I have endeavoured
in this book to give an account which will be helpful to someone
who has never heard of him.

Much that is inaccurate has been written about Matthias
Alexander. I knew him intimately for over ten years, married
into his family and have edited the *Alexander Journal* for many
years. In his later years, he asked my wife and me to be responsible for the future of his work, and at his request, I founded the
Alexander Society of Teachers, with this in view. I know as well
as anyone his personal idiosyncrasies—they wear extremely
well now that he is dead, however much they may have upset
people in his lifetime. I suspect that if Alexander were alive today he would be found to be speaking very clearly to our
present condition: his predictions of our present personal and
social unhappinesses have come about very much as he fore-
told.

I should perhaps briefly mention the contact which I myself
had with him and his ideas before and after the war. He had
come to London in 1904, aged 34, from Sydney, where he
had been the director of the "Sydney Dramatic and Operatic
Conservatorium". His concept of USE was not very clearly
formulated at that time, but between 1904 and 1955 he pub-

lished four books, of which the shortest and perhaps most to the point was *The Use of the Self* (Methuen, 1932). This book aroused considerable interest on the part of doctors and teachers and many others, especially in the 1930's. For example, George Bernard Shaw, Aldous Huxley, Stafford Cripps, and Archbishop William Temple were his pupils.

I first heard of him through reading Aldous Huxley's *Ends and Means* in 1937. Almost everything he was saying made sense to me, and I decided to study under him to learn to teach his methods. We struck a very close bond and he certificated me as a teacher in 1940, just after the outbreak of war.

Working in war-time London became difficult and he was evacuated to America with his school in the summer of 1940. It looked at that time as though his work and his principle could easily become lost—nearly all of his teachers were in the services. I myself spent a few boring years as a Regimental medical officer seeing little either of the enemy or medicine. It did, however, give me the opportunity to carry out research on large groups of young men and women who were under great emotional and physical stress: and in the process to confirm many of Alexander's observations on USE.

The widespread application and importance of his principle was not immediately obvious in the first half of this century. He had found it at first in his study of the *act of speaking*, and he had made the fairly trite observation that the way people use their muscles affects the way their voices function. Trite, because many schools of speech training, speech therapy and drama now devote themselves to just such a study of the mechanics of voice function. What was not trite about his observation was the minuteness of his analysis of the physical and psychological factors which are involved in USE, and his realisation that by his method of detailed analysis, a large number of psychological and physical disorders—disorders unconnected with the voice—would appear in a completely new light. He realised that in his lifetime he had only touched the fringe of the new possibilities which his approach had opened up.

## An Evolutionary Hypothesis

The Alexander Principle is a hypothesis: it is not claimed as an established, absolute truth, but as a new way of looking at things, a new way of organising oneself. It may be that it will be proved to be false—human evolution is a story of successful and unsuccessful trying—but it may be that it will be proved to be one of the most important evolutionary hypotheses which human beings have ever thought up for themselves.

The Principle proposes a quite different way of living and of seeing one's life; not different in the sense of making its users into oddities but different in that its users can learn to adopt a different yardstick for themselves and for the people they live with. Different in that its users—over the thirty years I have observed it—seem to be able to adapt more successfully than most people in their social, artistic, and biological spheres: and, most important of all, they appear to live longer and more healthily.

The Alexander Principle states that there are ways of using your body which are better than certain other ways. That when you lose these better ways of using your body, your functioning will begin to suffer—in some important respects. That it is useful to assess other people by the way they use themselves. That however clever or powerful a man may seem to be, however well-endowed a woman may be with beauty and charm, however rich people may be in cash and in contacts, they are suspect if their USE is suspect.

This approach is not a fringe-medicine, a neo-progressive education, a religious escape, or a quack science. It is a difficult disciplined approach to personal living which leads, through discipline, to a personal freedom and health which is possible to some extent for most people at most ages.

There are few people who would not find something useful in what Alexander had to say. He had much to say to the individual, and he had much to say to the educational profession: but he was also laying the foundations for a whole new science of USE, and he was opening up a whole new field for medical enquiry.

Chapters 2, 3 and 4 will discuss his basic principles of USE, BALANCE and REST and to these we must now turn.

# Chapter 2

## USE

MOST OF US are fatalistic about our bodies. According to the luck of the draw, we expect to grow up tall, short, plump, thin, weak, muscular, graceful or clumsy. We expect when we are young that we will grow up and grow old, and we expect that as we grow to middle-age, we will deteriorate. We think that our structural faults lie in our stars and in our parents, not in ourselves: that our body-potential is immutably limited by our initial genetic programme.

To some extent we are right, but to say this is not to have said much more than that the game of chess is boringly limited by the black and white squares.

The Alexander Principle insists that our will is potentially free: that it is what we do with our genetic inheritance which will determine our future structure and performance in nearly all the ways that matter. It starts at a relatively crude level by drawing attention to the ways in which we use and misuse our bodies in such simple matters as standing, sitting, and lying down, and it says that even at this crude level there is USE which is beneficial and USE which is harmful. It goes on from this relatively crude observation of mechanical mis-use to show how the basic structure of the personality, at its minutest and most intimate level, is fashioned from our BODY-USE.

William Harvey, in 1616, described the circulation of the blood, and thereby revolutionised medical thought. This did not mean that prior to this time the blood had not circulated and that it suddenly started circulating there and then; it had circulated for aeons of time before Harvey first described, albeit imperfectly, what was going on. In the same way, the type of USE which Alexander described, has been present for aeons of time. Before Alexander, much was known about it but not in a way which could helpfully be applied to man's health.

It is a long way from William Harvey to Christiaan Barnard. What is written here will no doubt seem elementary in a hundred years' time, and indeed, since Alexander's death, his procedures have been constantly refined; no doubt many more false leads will be attempted and have to be abandoned. It has to be stated clearly that the type of USE which I describe in this book cannot be considered as THE ONLY RIGHT WAY: the USE which I describe is the best I have been able to discover, and, as I describe it, it works. But no doubt far better ways will be found eventually of describing and refining this new approach.

## Alexander's discovery of Wrong Use

Alexander was born in 1868, in rural Australia. To judge by his reviews, he was a successful young actor, in Sydney, until he was increasingly plagued by voice trouble. In the nineteenth century little was known of speech training or speech therapy as we now know it, and Alexander's recurrent loss of voice brought his stage career to an untimely close.

In desperation, and with little medical or physiological knowledge, he decided that he must observe minutely, in a mirror, the way he was using his muscles when he spoke. It is a common observation that when people speak, they are liable to carry out quite inappropriate movements throughout the whole of their body: a glance at a television screen will often show announcers and commentators who have persistent mannerisms when they speak. Alexander was particularly struck by curious movements which took place around his neck and head as he spoke: and although the types of curious movement which can take place in this region are numerous, he picked out the most common one, which consists of a tightening of the head backwards on the neck and downwards into the chest.

At this point—and indeed for the remainder of his life—he became concerned with the types of muscular usage which arise when people react to a stimulus. He was, in fact, a child of his times, with its Stimulus-Response psychology and the Behaviourism which Pavlov and his dogs helped to foster. Fortunately Alexander's initial observations provided enough impetus to enable him to develop and refine his methods until the end of his days. It is necessary to understand—and not to be daunted by—the exuberance which he showed about his initial discovery: a reasonable exuberance, since his voice problems cleared up when he had learned how to stop pulling his head back and down.

### The Primary Control

Alexander's observation of his unconscious mis-use of the neck and head led him to term his improved USE "The Primary Control". He wrote in *The Lancet*: "When I was experimenting with various ways of using myself in an attempt to improve the functioning of my vocal organs, I discovered that a certain use of the head in relation to the neck and of the neck in relation to the torso . . . constituted a '*Primary Control*' of the mechanisms as a whole."

Alexander and some of his supporters at one time seemed to impute an almost magical significance to the "Primary Control" and some of his medical friends gave him information about "controlling centres" in the mid-brain in terms which seemed to imply a subjective awareness of such a centre, which could exert a "Primary Control" over the rest of the body. Shades of Descartes and his Pineal Body!

Few people would find it helpful nowadays to talk about a "Primary Control", although in the past the phrase did emphasise the prime importance of a proper USE of the head and neck, at a time when anatomists and physiologists had no very clear account to give of the factors underlying balance. And fortunately the "Primary Control" hypothesis did not restrict the development of Alexander's practical teaching methods, although it certainly affected the emphasis of his teaching.

### Head Retraction

Alexander wrote further of his observations as follows:[1]

> If you ask someone to sit down, you will observe, if you watch their actions closely, that there is an alteration in the position of the head, which is thrown back, whilst the neck is stiffened and shortened.

This is as good a place as any to begin and soon after I became interested in Alexander, I thought I would see if what he said about this was in fact true. I had the opportunity to carry out an experiment with 105 young men, aged between 17 and 22. It is an experiment which can be tested by anyone. Plate 1 (facing page 12) shows a young man and a girl sitting

down. It can be seen that both of them are throwing their heads
backwards in the process. When I tested the 105 young men, I
fixed a tape-measure to the back of their heads, and made an
ink mark over the prominent vertebra where the neck joins
the chest at the back (fig. 1a). I then asked them to sit down

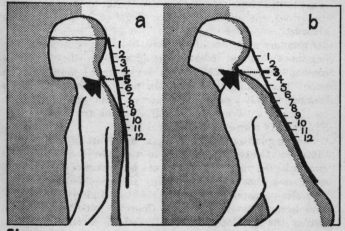

Figure 1

and whilst they were sitting down I observed how much the
tape-measure moved down over the ink mark (fig. 1b).

Out of the 105, only one did not pull back his head and move
the tape downwards; 56 moved it down two inches or more, 43
between one and two inches, and 9 under an inch. The younger
ones pulled their heads back-and-down less than the older
ones. What was even more interesting was that when I asked
them to prevent this, only 11 of them were able to stop contracting their heads into their shoulders, however hard they
tried.

Sir Charles Sherrington, the neurophysiologist, who drew
encouraging attention to Alexander's work in the 1930's,
pointed out what a complicated thing it is to do even such a
simple thing as sitting down:[2]

To execute it must require the right degree of action of a great many muscles and nerves, some hundreds to thousands of nerve fibres, and perhaps a hundred times as many muscle fibres. Various parts of my brain are involved in the co-ordinative management of this, and in so doing, my brain's rightness of action rests on receiving and despatching thousands of nerve messages, and on registering and adjusting pressures and tensions from various parts of me.

It is not surprising that most of these young men could not alter their habitual head-movement simply by trying not to. We cannot alter our habitual way of doing things simply by deciding to do them some other way. Our will is potentially free, but to free it for effective action, we need certain principles of USE on which to base our actions.

## The Use of the Head

Of the 105 young men, 104 showed this particular use of the head in which the skull was pulled back on the neck. The first thing to decide is whether such a habitual use of the head and neck is important. Let us simply say that according to the Alexander principle plate 2a is a MIS-USE. In the last analysis, it will be a matter of taste whether people prefer some other forms of USE to Alexander-USE: indeed whether they would prefer to be sick rather than healthy, to be in pain rather than comfortable.

To me it is self-evident that the state of the child in plate 2c is better than in plate 2b: that plate 14c looks better than plate 14a: that something is amiss if children emerge from adolescence looking like 3b: that the slumped appearance of the two students in plate 4 is aesthetically unpleasing and harmful, amongst other things, to their ability to breathe. Yet such states of slump and head retraction are nowadays the rule, in homes, in classrooms, and in lecture halls; in theatres, in cars and public transport, and, of course, in mental institutions and parliament; and in church as well.

## The Sedentary Life

Few of us will spend more than an hour or so at a time without sitting down. Many people spend more of their working day sitting down than moving, except of course for young children who, once they can walk, can only be made to sit still for a short time by being restrained in high chairs and seat harnesses, or by their mother's hands and arms. The young child instinctively moves and explores and communicates as soon as it wakes and it will continue to do this until it is tired, or until it has been rebuked or restricted into a stillness which is socially more convenient. Such restriction is an inevitable feature of school life, and eventually the growing child may well be sitting at the desk for hours on end, in a class with perhaps forty other children. Most of the children in the classroom will be sitting in a collapsed state, with the weight of the trunk supported through the elbows and the shoulders. The sedentary life has begun.

If then, so much of our life is spent in a sedentary position—and most of the "top" men and women in government, industry medicine, law, music and education and so on will have spent many years sitting down whilst they equipped themselves for their job—it would seem important to consider how we use ourselves in that position.

## Sitting Down

How do we usually set about getting ourselves "sat-down"? Over 99% of us, as exemplified by the 105 young men—and confirmed by studies on all age groups from puberty upwards—pull the back of the skull down into the back of the neck as we sit down and stand up. Usually—unless we are actors or dancers—we are relatively unaware of how we use our bodies as we carry out our daily activities. When we want to sit down, we walk to the available seat, rapidly gauge the seat height, and plant our bottoms without further ado, in such a way as to avoid other people and other objects and without showing too much thigh. In the process, the head usually pulls back and the spine becomes curved. When the seat has been reached there are a few shuffles and wriggles to eliminate the creeping and crinkling of clothing and then the body is allowed to collapse whilst the head and neck are kept in a position which will allow social intercourse or reading or writing. This more often than not involves using the arms and shoulders as struts to support the collapsed body. For eating, the face drops down towards the plate. For tele-viewing, once the initial hypnosis has been induced, the body is collapsed to the lowest point of slump at which the eyes can look ahead out of their sockets. The miracle is that human beings survive it at all: the tragedy is that they know no better and that by the time their body begins to cry out "Enough, Enough", they are set in their ways and in their social commitments.

## Neck Collapse

Sitting-down has been mentioned first because so much of our time is spent using ourselves in this position, and also because the mis-use in this position is so obvious. When Alexander studied his head movements and positions during speech, the mis-use was not so obvious, although plates 5a and 5b show

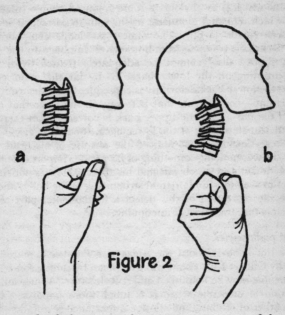

a                                                                 b

## Figure 2

only too clearly how gross the wrong movements of the head can be. And if we consider the picture of a dentist in plate 6 and observe his head and neck position as he bends over a patient, it is clear that his mis-use consists of a dropping of his neck forwards, and a collapse of his upper back into a curve. The movement can be illustrated by the hand and wrist (fig. 2a). The dropping forward of the wrist corresponds to the dropping forward of the neck, and this is shown on a skull in figure 2b. They can be perhaps more clearly seen in X-rays of the neck, plates 7a and 7b. There are a myriad nuances of possible muscular mis-use, but these most common and obvious mis-uses need first to be emphasised: pulling the head back and down is almost universal in our culture.

What follows from this collapse of the neck and upper back? It means the gradual development of a persistent HUMP at the base of the neck, and it means that the rest of the body, if it is to balance itself, has to be wrongly compensated elsewhere. Thus the collapsed neck leads to a throwing-in of the back—the lordosis which is so obvious in some coloured people (plate 8) and which remedial gymnasts try in vain to correct in school children (plate 9a–9b). The almost pandemic complaint of low back pain (ranging from housewives' lumbago to the out-right slipped disc) cannot be adequately treated by simply concentrating on the lower back. In by far the majority of cases, the lower back deformity is consequent on a deformity in the Hump—consequent, that is to say, in the sense that only when the mis-use in the upper back is corrected can there be an efficient stabilising of the lower back. (See also fig. 22f.)

When Alexander first noticed the mis-use of his head and neck, he was noticing something of far greater importance than simply something which affected his speech. He was noticing a defect in the most fundamental structuring of the body, and he made the correction of this defect a fundamental part of his principle that USE affects Functioning.

### What is a Principle?

Since this book is about the Alexander *Principle*, a statement here by Gilbert Ryle about what we mean by calling something a principle may be helpful.[3] Gilbert Ryle says: "A question is a question of principle when it is much more important than most other questions. The relative importance of questions can be explained on these lines: that when, given the answer to one question, it is at once clear what the answers to an *expanding* range of questions are (whilst the answers to any of these other questions do not in the same way throw light on the first question) then the first question is a *question of principle* relative to the latter. Or when, in the case of a range of questions, it is clear that none of them could be answered, or perhaps, even be clearly formulated, before some anterior question is answered, then this anterior question is a question of principle relative to them. The notion of a principle is simply that of one question being logically prior or cardinal to a range of other questions. It is tempting, but it would be too rash to say that there is one absolutely first question."

I have quoted Ryle at length, since it bears on the primacy of Alexander's principle of "The Primary Control". The mis-use of the head and neck is prior to mis-use elsewhere, according to his principle. Mis-use elsewhere can only be adequately dealt with after the correction of mis-use of the head and neck. To paraphrase Ryle, "When, in the case of a range of problems of bodily mis-use, it is clear that none of them can be dealt with or, perhaps, even clearly formulated, before some anterior problem is dealt with, then the need to solve this anterior problem can be termed a principle."

It will be clear from this that we have to start by asking the *right* questions about our body: and we have to find the answers to an expanding range of questions which are thereby thrown up. Alexander's observation of mis-use during speaking opened up just such a new and expanding range of questions.

## The Hump

Most parts of the body have two sorts of names—an everyday common-usage name and an anatomical name (or group of names). For example the names "Elbow" or "Wrist" or "Shoulder" are understood by us all, although in fact they are not very clearly defined anatomical areas: the wrist is, for most of us, a vague area between the hand and the forearm which is liable to get strained: the shoulder is sometimes thought of as the shoulder-blade, or as the top of the upper arm, or as the shoulder-joint itself. The same thing applies to most common body terms—the knee, the stomach, the chest, the back, the neck, and so on—and for most purposes we get on fairly well with these vague terms and we would be lost without them.

The astonishing thing is that the most important USE-area we possess, from the Alexander point of view, has no common name. My task of describing USE would be greatly simplified if there were a simple commonly accepted name for the area of the body in which Alexander first detected a fundamental mis-use, an area which is indeed the Clapham Junction of USE.

It is the region of the body where the back of the neck joins the upper back, and it is a prominent area in everyone because here the shape of the neck vertebrae alters and the spinous processes become more prominent. Figure 3 shows it in profile and plates 10a, 10b and 10c show it in a young child, a lady, and a middle-aged man.

Figure 3

This whole region at the base of the neck, both back and front, is a veritable maelstrom of muscular co-ordination. It is here that those most inadequate evolutionary adaptations—the shoulders and upper arms—will exert their distorting influence during the many activities in which we engage. It is here that faulty patterns of breathing throw the muscles of the lower neck and upper ribs into excessive spasm: it is here that mechanisms of speech and swallowing require a reasonably good vertebral posture if the oesophagus and trachea and associated vocal structures are to function well. It is close to here that blood vessels and nerves of great importance and complexity will pass— blood vessels to the base of the brain, nerve ganglia which affect breathing and heart rate and blood pressure, nerve roots which with increasing age become more and more liable to compression: it is here that 85% of the readers of this book will have arthritis by the time they are 55 (and many of them much younger than that): and it is from here that the head itself—the structure which carries man's most important sensory equipment of sight and hearing, taste and smell, and balance—has to be co-ordinated at rest and in movement.

And it is here that mis-use most frequently starts: it is here that we have to start if we are to correct the multitudinous mis-uses which the rest of the body can throw up. In terms of the Alexander Principle, it is only when this primary mis-use is dealt with that we shall see the answers to an expanding range of questions.

In the past, the hump has been thought of as a dull, inert, fleshy region, with little of interest to offer except to the painter

or shot-putter or dowager pearl-wearer: and indeed, when
improved use has been established, the hump-region simply
provides a context within which other functioning can take
place.

What produces the hump? The short answer is excessive and
wrongly distributed muscle tension. By habitually moving and
keeping still in certain ways, we gradually alter our physique.
Our manner of USE, at rest and during movement, contains a
tangible record of all the basic habits which we have laid down
over the years. In most people, the HUMP is a tangible witness to
a lifetime of mis-use.

The phenomenon of head retraction which Alexander first
noticed is a symptom of pre-existent muscle tension, not the
cause of it. Alexander, with simple clarity, proposed that if
only people could stop pulling their heads back whenever they
reacted, all would be well, and he concentrated his efforts on
training both himself and his pupils to stop doing just this.
Fortunately for him, there was enough novelty and truth in this
fact to help himself, his teachers and his pupils for a whole lifetime: there was enough in it to improve very considerably the
functioning of those who understood the discipline: there was
enough in it to infuriate some members of the medical, educational and other learned professions, since they could not
decide what he was getting up to—H. G. Wells rudely called
it "swanning", others called it quackery and were astonished
that men of the calibre of Professor Dewey, Professor Raymond
Dart, Archbishop Temple, Stafford Cripps, and large numbers
of doctors could be such enthusiastic supporters.

It was inevitable—and still is inevitable—that, once some of
the main features of Alexander-USE were described, people
would find themselves boringly lost in cul-de-sacs which had to
be explored before further roads could be taken. This early
phase of Alexander's work was an inevitable progression from
the work of the early anatomists and anthropologists, who were
concerned with balance and the upright posture, and we must
turn our attention in the next chapter to this question of balance
and posture.

# Chapter 3

## BALANCE

AMONGST THE BOSOMS and bottoms of seaside-front picture postcards, there used to be one of a decrepit old man, standing unsteadily in a doctor's surgery, legs splayed out, holding on to the furniture and saying, "Well, doctor, how do I stand?", and receiving the inevitable answer, "Honestly, I can't imagine". When I look at the hunched backs, twisted spines, fixed pelvises and hopelessly inadequate legs and feet which trudge through my clinic, I also often find it hard to imagine just how they manage to stay upright at all!

The fact is that, for most people, balance is not a question of tight-rope perfection, of ski-jumping precision, of the pas-de-deux or the coolness of the mountaineer. It is possible to sit, stand and walk and indeed to perform highly skilled tasks and yet to be wrongly balanced. The skater in plate 11 can do something which most people would find impossible. She earns her living by bending double and then skating backwards in order to pick up a handkerchief from the ice with her teeth. Obviously she has a keenly developed co-ordination for this and similar activities, but yet her balanced USE of herself is wrong.

Close analysis of the photographs shows that her rib cage is twisted over to one side, not only when she bends but when she is standing still. Had it not been for the fact that she eventually developed pain in her back whilst skating, she would have been totally unaware of this imbalance in her back. Indeed her dance teacher, her doctor and an orthopaedic specialist had not noticed the twist, and she was unable to stop her pain until she learned how to use her back with a more symmetrical balance. Like most people, the dancer took it for granted that her body was a reliable instrument, that it had its own unconscious "wisdom", and that as long as she could do the work for which she was trained, her mode of balance was adequate.

### Body Wisdom

One of the legacies of the last century, with its accent on the God-given perfection of the human frame, was what W. B.

Cannon later called the "Wisdom of the Body".[4] Cannon
suggested that there are certain balanced states of the body
which are natural and normal and to which, in its wisdom, the
body will return after disturbance and stress. Such "body
wisdom" was taken to apply not only to muscular balance, but
to the organic constituents of the body. Illness, on this analysis,
is accompanied by states of imbalance—the sugar in the blood
is constantly raised, the bowel constantly overfull, the vital
capacity of the lungs constantly diminished. On this view, the
physiological wisdom of the body has to be restored by appropriate medical treatment and care, until a more normal
resting balance can be maintained—with or without drugs.
More and more drugs begin to be needed to keep the blood
pressure down, the heart beat regular, the sleep pattern toler-
able. A mental "resting-state of balance" is likewise to be
achieved by more and more drugs to stop anxiety and depression, or else by the cultivation of a Nirvana state by meditation
or other spiritual disciplines.

It is now clear that the "Wisdom-of-the-Body" story is a
fallacy. Increasing dependence on therapeutic drugs—however
wisely and cleverly they may be prescribed—is proof that most
people's body wisdom has gone astray. Somewhere along the
line, the whole story of physiological wisdom has gone off the rails.

Nowhere is this more clear than in the muscular balancing
mechanisms which underlie USE. In recent years, deservedly
popular books like Desmond Morris's *The Naked Ape*[5] have
made people aware of the mechanical problems which the
upright posture produces. Many nineteenth-century anatomists
had assigned varying importance to the upright posture and its
accompanying blessings. Amongst some of them, it was
customary to see something partially divine in being upright—
"that majestic attitude which announces man's superiority
over all the inhabitants of the globe". The Naked Angel, in
fact, rather than The Naked Ape.

In the first quarter of this century, it was still thought that our
spines were perfectly fashioned for the upright posture, but that
the world we lived in was to blame. Sir Arthur Keith,[6] who was
the authority on posture in the 1920's, thought that postural
defects were caused by "the monotonous and trying positions
which are entailed by modern education and modern industry".

But in the second quarter of this century, the new speciality of orthopaedics came increasingly to the view that it was not man's environment but his imperfect adaptation to it that was at fault. Man was seen more and more as a made-over animal, with muscles forced by the adoption of unnatural stances to suffer enormous inequalities in the distribution of labour.[7]

In the second half of this century, a new speciality called Ergonomics turned its gaze on how to fit machines to man and man to the machine. Chairs, car seats, beds, desks, and all sorts of complex machinery have been designed to give correct elbow room and leg length, to give better positioning of pedals, levers and display panels and proper seat dimensions. It was hoped thereby to minimise the fatigue and strain of unnecessary movement in faulty positions.

However, owing to the lack of an adequate concept of muscular balance, the ergonomic approach has not paid off the expected dividends. The working man still arrives home fatigued. Pain in the back affects most of the population, often with crippling severity. 75% of our dentists develop troublesome back pain, over 80% of our secretaries develop headaches —they have not been helped very much by better designed equipment. It is their USE which needs redesigning.

Posture both in the home and in the work place, is as poor as ever it was—and indeed, my figures for adolescents show a deterioration over the past twenty years. Even in the most perfect environment which the ergonomists can construct, the "Wisdom-of-the-Body" cannot apparently resolve the conflict between those parts of the body which are needed for doing an actual job, and those parts which are needed to support the general functioning of the body. Mis-use, in our time, persists and increases.

## Living Anatomy

This lack of an adequate concept of muscle balance came originally from the dissecting-room. Anatomy, as studied in the corpse, does not bring out the complexity of muscular mis-use in the living man.

The identical sameness of the muscles of any man and woman can indeed be demonstrated in the dissecting room without a shadow of doubt, and students can learn in great detail the names and actions of hundreds of muscles which pull on various body levers throughout the body. But this is the anatomy of the dead, the anatomy of sameness.

A living anatomy has to start with the living body and with the infinite variety of each of us. To give them their due, the ergonomists have always understood the need to study muscle action in the living: but unfortunately they took *mis-used* man as their norm, and much of the equipment which they designed was designed for mis-used man. Only rarely did such equipment encourage really good use, and then only in a most superficial sense. The typist may sit in the statistically perfect chair, but her basic habits of mis-use still persist.

The early anatomists and ergonomists have set the stage for a real understanding of the problem. We now know that man's body is not majestically divine. The "Naked Ape" has replaced Rousseau's "Noble Savage" and Wordsworth's "Nature's Priest". We now know that we are faced with an evolutionary problem of combining the potentiality of an intelligent angel with the impulses of an irascible ape.

Alexander, born into the last quarter of the nineteenth century, was plunged straight into this evolutionary argument. When Darwin and Huxley made their onslaught on the first book of Genesis, their evolutionary man had still to compete with the image of the divinely created man. He could not be allowed the simple animality of the ape, but he had to have a splendour and grace of his own: his body had to have a natural goodness and wisdom. In this way, Wordsworth's "Nature's Priest" (who by the vision splendid, was on his way attended), could hold his head high in competition with the divine image.

It is interesting that Alexander's first book was entitled *Man's Supreme Inheritance*. He was inevitably caught up with the notion of a basic perfection which is lost by a combination of environmental stress and personal stupidity. His theme during his lifetime was of an endowment of properly functioning reflexes, which the corporeal sin of mis-use (induced by the overstimulating newness of the environment) has clouded over. On this view, a system of perfectly adequate reflexes had to be restored by learning to inhibit wrongly acquired conditioned reflexes. Or in the words of a recent cleric, by stopping off "ugly contradictions in the true nature of man".

The "vision splendid" has now no need to postulate the

perfect God-given or gene-given templet—one correct shape, and one only which is appropriate for our human stance. We have no "true nature", beset with "ugly contradictions". To know and to be what we "truly" are, we have to *find out* what we are; and we have to construct what we are to be.

The Alexander Principle suggests that by getting our USE in the right order, there is a chance of a new personal evolution. There is no reason to suppose that we are born with a perfectly ordered set of pre-existent natural reflex patterns, and that, by refraining from interfering with them, all will be as well as it can be. The next step in our evolution has to be learned by each one of us, ourselves. *Personal selection has to replace natural selection.* Instead of relying on what the environment can winkle out from our possibilities by natural selection, it becomes a question of what we can winkle out of our possibilities by personal selection.

What sort of balance should we personally select?

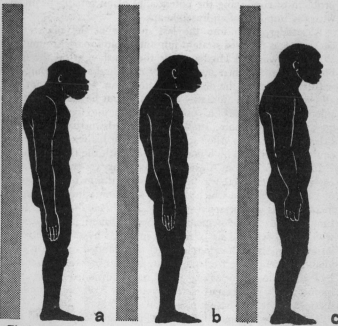

Figure 4

## The Upright Balance

The earliest man-like creatures had a short neck and a well developed "hump". Figure 4 shows diagrammatically an evolution from (a) Proconsul man 2 million years ago, to (b) Pekin man 500,000 years ago, to (c) Neanderthal man 100,000 years ago, to (d) Mount Carmel man 40,000 years ago via (e) Modern man to what I might perhaps call (f) Alexander man! One of the most striking features is the way in which the neck is gradually lengthened and the "hump" has become less prominent. In the process, the centre of gravity has shifted backwards, and the point of skull-balance (the occipital condyles) has come back until the body's centre of gravity now can pass through this point.[8, 9]

As a result, Modern man's neck has become more free to move, but unfortunately a freely moving neck—although giving him a wide ranging ability to turn his gaze and his sensory attention around and about himself—also allows him to

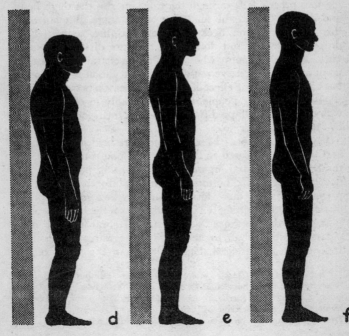

collapse the vertebrae of his neck and his spine. His longer neck allows him more potential freedom, but it also allows him to use certain muscles for activities and postures in which they should play no part. Speaking, swallowing and even ordinary breathing are often made to involve muscle groups in the neck and hump which contribute nothing to the act being performed. The more flexible balance which should be possible is often not actualised: indeed, the potentially free muscles are held fixed in a mis-used balance.*

Alexander balance is selected with a view to promoting the most efficient functioning. Just why it is thought to promote the most efficient functioning will be considered later. At present let us notice in what respect it differs from the balance which most people adopt in the standing position.

The first thing to notice in Alexander balance (fig. 4f) is that, compared with Modern man (fig. 4e), the whole vertebral column is carried much further back. A plumb line from the mastoid process falls through the trochanter of the thigh bone and slightly behind the malleolus of the ankle. But not only this: instead of the neck vertebrae and lumbar vertebrae dropping forward and downward, they are directed up-and-back. Not to the point where they are overstrained, but to a point at which excessive muscle tension in the neck and lower back is released. The effect of this is to increase a person's height slightly in younger people, and considerably in older people, who often have collapsed two inches from their younger height by the time they are 50.

It will also be noticed that the knees are held slightly flexed and the pelvis released so that the pubis points more towards the front. The sexual organs, instead of being pointed to the floor, with associated buttock tension (the "frozen pelvis"), are presented slightly more forward—not by swaying the pelvis forward, but by tipping the pelvis slightly on the lumbar spine.

In this balance, the surfaces of the vertebral joints tend to separate, rather than to be contracted towards each other. Indeed, the Alexander balance throughout the whole of the

---

* See W. Le Gros Clark, *The Antecedents of Man* (Edinburgh University Press, 1959), in which he calculates the position of the condyles geometrically, giving a rating of 30 for Pekin man, 40 for Australopithecus, and 80 for Modern Man. Also B. Campbell, *Human Evolution* (University of Chicago Press, 1967), in which he shows the same process in primates.

body—shoulder blades, shoulders, elbows and hands, hips, knees, ankles and feet—seeks to establish a resting position in which all the joint surfaces are lengthening away from each other. And since it is more and more realised now by neurophysiologists that awareness of muscle balance derives from an awareness of the *lengthening* of muscle, a newly-ordered "Wisdom of the Body" is likely to be facilitated by such lengthening.

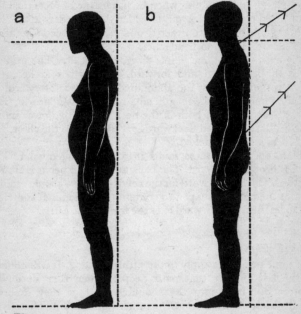

## Figure 5

Plate 12 shows a patient who suffered from tension headaches: it shows him before and after he had learned to apply the Alexander Principle. 12a and 12b show him in profile, 12c and 12d show him photographed on the same occasion from the back view. The most obvious change is that he is taller: and he is wider across the shoulders. Contracted shortened muscles have lengthened.

In 12a his weight is thrown forward: his neck is dropped
forward and his back is arched. In 12b his back is better
although still too arched. Observe the small triangle made
by the lines of the grid in front of his throat, and observe how
the triangle grows as his neck comes back.

Plate 12c shows him from the back. Observe the lines of
muscle contraction at the back of his neck: the raised tensed
shoulders and the tightened buttocks with exaggerated dimp-
ling. Plate 12d shows him when he has learned to lengthen the
contracted neck muscles and to widen the shoulders apart. His
buttocks are now uncontracted and he is appreciably taller.
And free from tension headaches.

Figure 5 makes these points diagrammatically. The neck in
5a is dropped down and forward, the back is arched, the
pelvis is tipped so that the abdominal contents fall forward. In
5b, the direction of the lengthening has been sketched in. The
lines are *up* and *back*, both in the neck and in the lower spine.
The head is not pulled backwards and down into the chest: the
shoulders are not hunched.

Plate 10c shows these faults in a middle-aged man. The
neck is dropped forward. The back arches, the pelvis is tipped
forward. The French word for the pelvis—*bassin*—should remind
us that the pelvis is shaped to contain the abdominal contents,
not to let them slop forward over the front of the *bassin*.

## Sitting Balance

The same principles apply to the sitting position. It was noticed
in the last chapter that most people, when they sit down,
contract the head into the shoulders and as they descend
usually arch the back and thrust their bottoms out. There is of
course the alternative method of hurling the body precipitately
into an easy chair, with the back flexed into a round ball so
that the buttocks land on the front of the seat and the backbone
curves along the rest of the seat and up the back of it.

But notice what happens when you sit down slowly. What
should happen is that—with the heels apart from each other
and toes turned out—the knee cap should move continuously
forward over the line of the foot (pointing approximately
between the big toe and the second toe). As the knees move
forward the body will begin to descend.

At this point (plates 1 and 2a) most people (fig. 6a) will:

  (i) pull their heads back
 (ii) throw the lower chest forward
(iii) throw the pelvis backwards.

Instead the body should descend between two vertical lines (as in fig. 6b). The pelvis should not push back and the lower chest should not push forward.*

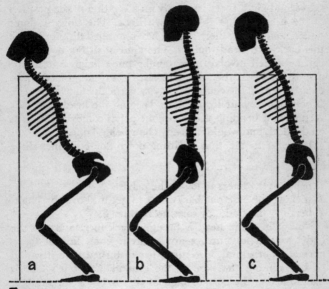

# Figure 6

Depending on the height of the chair, the vertical axis of the body can then move backwards in space. Most people at this point fear that they will lose their balance and fall backwards if they continue on downwards. This, however, will not happen, provided that the head is not allowed to tighten back. Instead it must be directed forward at the top of the neck. When the

* This whole movement can perhaps be better understood by reference to a similar movement of the back when placed against a wall, as described in Chapter 9, figure 25.

USE is very wrong, it may be necessary (fig. 6c) to bend slightly
forward at the hip-joint. This movement is shown in plate 13a.

Now for most people this is not at first easy, except perhaps in
drama and movement colleges, where they have to think about
such body mechanics in detail. An amusing note from one of
my patients puts most of the difficulties in a nut-shell. He wrote:

There seem to be two kinds of sitting down—falling into a
chair and the kind that can be halted. You point out that in
the second kind, there is usually an alteration in the position
of the head so that it is thrown back. The thing I don't
understand is why there should be an implied disapproval of
this backward head motion. The kind of sitting down that
can be halted involves maintaining one's balance until the
arse is firmly on the seat, and *that*, in my misguided view,
entails keeping the centre of gravity vertically above the feet.
If one follows your instructions, keeping the head and back
vertical and bending the knees, the pelvis comes downwards
on the heels and would miss any chair behind one.

It seems to me that in sitting down one combines three
actions:

1. bending the knees to lower the pelvis
2. sticking the arse out backwards to get it above the chair.
3. bending the body forwards to counter 2.

Now if in 3 the head is brought back in relation to the
body, several advantages are secured: one's line of sight,
normally horizontal, is so much less disturbed than it would
be by pointing the nose to the ground, and one's face is
maintained at the normal angle of view to one's companions.

In short it seems to me that there are the soundest reasons
for pulling the head back on sitting down in the controlled,
as distinct from falling, manner. However, on seeing you on
your feet or in a chair I'm completely convinced that you
have "got something", without a doubt. But I can't see any
reason for suggesting that we should not pull our head back
when sitting down.

I was able to show this patient that, if he constantly drew his
head back into his shoulders when he sat down, then he would
arrive in a wrong seated position in which the head was held

hunched into the shoulders as in plates 4 and 28 and that this would lead to "hump" formation and the associated muscle tension and mis-use which this implies: and that, by moving in this way, the spine gradually comes to be shortened, rather in the way which a string of beads (fig. 7a) is straight when lengthened, but goes into curves when it is shortened (fig. 7b). I was also able to show that in fact he could plant his "arse" perfectly well in the manner which I described, provided he kept his knees moving forward and let the vertical axis of his body displace back. And that it was then a simple matter, if necessary, to sit further back in the seat.

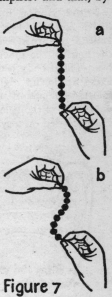

Figure 7

### Head Balance

It should not be thought that the Alexander head balance is simply a matter of idiosyncratic choice. There can be few anatomists and physiologists who do not now accept—in theory at least—the importance of head-position, but the lay reader may be interested in the vestibular apparatus in the inner ear which gives us much information about our balance and about variations in pressures which act on our bodies.

The vestibular apparatus (fig. 8) lies inside the skull, internal to the mastoid process, and it registers variations in pressure both from the outside and from inside the body. When we stop or start moving, when we lean on things, or when we fix one part of our body closer to another part, this apparatus should help to tell us what is happening. Likewise it gives us information about our spatial orientation and about the way we are supporting our body against gravity on various surfaces—our feet on the ground, our buttocks on a seat, our back when lying down.

It does this by means of built-in spirit-levels—the so-called "labyrinth". The names of the particular parts do not matter; the essence of it is that there are cavities placed at right angles in three planes in the skull, which are filled with a heavy

gelatinous fluid, and in contact with this fluid there are a
number of hairs projecting from the cavity walls, the "maculae".

The weight of the fluid drags on the hairs in accordance with
the head position, and, as we move or rotate our bodies, the
inertia of the fluid jogs the fluid up and down against the hairs.
Indeed, posture in relation to gravity is *continuously* registered on
the hairs of the maculae. All of this sends information to the
brain about body positionings in the vertical and longitudinal
axes—up/down, right/left, front/back—and it also gives
information about acceleration and deceleration, by displacement of the gelatinous fluid. It does this more accurately
if it is carried on a symmetrically balanced head.

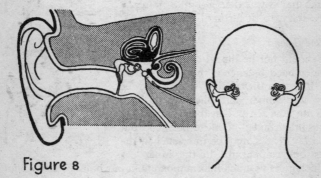

Figure 8

As well as the vestibular apparatus, the skull of course carries
the eyes, which also give a sense of position and acceleration.
But in modern civilisation, the eyes are frequently being
dropped to read or to write or to perform manual tasks. This
dropping of the eyes very soon involves a habit of dropping the
head forward from the hump, and this position may be held
for long periods. As a result, when the eyes are raised (see fig.
22c, Chapter 9), the tendency is for the head to pull back at the
point where the neck joins the skull: and thus the hump is
perpetuated and the head is further encouraged to be held
retracted at the top of the neck.

A correct resting head balance, in which the vestibular
apparatus can be carried on an even keel, provides a stable
platform from which the special senses—eyes, mouth, nose and

ears—can all work. All too often, the vestibular apparatus sacrifices its primary position to the demands of the other senses—the eyes to focus on (or reject) certain sights, the ears to pick up (or to block out) certain sounds, etc. Our precariously evolved head balance is easily disturbed by the bombardments of the modern world and by our incessant desire to pick up or reject information through our special senses. It becomes a prime necessity that we should re-establish a balanced resting position for the head.

## Slump

Alexander-USE suggests then that, if adequate functioning is to be maintained, the head balance should not be upset and it follows from this that the back should not be allowed to slump (plate 14a) when sitting. This for civilised man is a tall order— at first many people find it hard to maintain a lengthening balance when seated. Lengthening is often wrongly interpreted as the need to sit up (plate 14b) over-straight, with the back arched and the chest pushed out and with the weight carried through the upper thigh instead of through the ischial tuberosities—the two small knuckles of bone at the back of the pelvis. Yet, in fact, a correct lengthening balance (plate 14c) is restful and efficient, and soon comes to feel comfortable, once the habit has been acquired.

Not only when sitting up straight but when leaning forward to eat or to write or to read, the back should not be collapsed forward from the hump but should be lengthened and then pivoted forward from the hip joints so that the pelvis moves with the rest of the back. In this way, there will be no excessive slumping in the lower back and the whole trunk will not collapse forward.

In addition to the lengthened use of the trunk, the knees should never be crossed when sitting. Whenever it is socially possible and there is enough room, the knees should be pointed away from each other. Most forms of lower back pain will be benefited by directing the knees away from each other, and this particularly applies to sedentary workers, who sit at desks all day long.

Once you have sat down, it is usually best to move your pelvis deep into the back of the chair seat: this applies to almost all seats: cinema seats, buses, trains, dining chairs and easy chairs whenever the leg-length allows it. Unfortunately many modern chairs—particularly those with a marked curve between the upright and the horizontal—make good USE almost impossible.

The television habit has led to a great deterioration in children's sitting posture. Television, whether we like it or not, is with us to stay, in one form or another It should not be too difficult for parents to encourage their children not to collapse and slump as they watch the screen. If children are too tired for this—after school for example—it is best to arrange for them to lie down with their backs supported, rather than to sit slumping.

Children, when shown, are able to maintain the balance I have been describing without strain and effort, and they will become less tired by their school work as a result. The forces in their environment do however conspire to teach them to mis-use their bodies: the nature of these forces will be elaborated in the chapter on Personal Growth.

Alexander-balance may at first sound as if it entails an immense effort. The learning of it when it has been lost will certainly entail effort; but, when learned, most people find it feels so good and easy that they would not willingly throw it away.

### Balanced Wisdom

The up-shot of the matter is that not only are we poorly designed for achieving balance—poor, in the sense that it does not come easily and automatically to us—but also we have had little instruction in how to get the best out of our particular model. Secretaries and car-drivers have had plenty of scientific investigation into the design of their desks and chairs and their car seats: but in common with all of us, they have been expected to know how to make the best they can out of the body-work which they got from Mum and Dad. And even though they may cast envious eyes at the muscular and bustular torsos which fill their screens and newspapers, they have not learnt to feel an envious thrill at the sight of a properly poised pelvis or a sensibly seated sacrum. They may appreciate the fact that a Dressage rider needs to sit well so that he can control his horse by his buttock-adjustment: but a sensitively poised sitting position has not seemed important to them in the idle boredom of their office, or during the stupefying collapse of politicians on their Parliamentary benches and in their committees. And even the most famous of athletes do not seem, when sitting, immune from a state of collapse which ages them prematurely and eventually nullifies their potentialities just when their skill and experience should be bearing further fruit.

It may sound as though Alexander-USE is simply an elaboration of all the good advice on posture which has been poured out for years in physical education manuals, health and beauty movements, and, more recently, in westernised meditation regimes. But what I have written is only the beginning of a study which involves our most personal and most intimate adjustments in every day living—a study which begins to make sense of phrases like "the whole man" and "psycho-somatic integration".

The further implications of Alexander-USE involve a consideration of the meaning of REST, and to this we must turn in the next chapter.

# Chapter 4

## REST

ALL OF US, in the past few decades, have been through a period which has been characterised by immense change—a change in our means of living as well as a change in our modes of living. During this period, the *tempo* of change, already quickening in the first half of the century, has accelerated at a pace quite out of proportion to the pace of man's earlier evolution. Human relations in almost every sphere have become characterised by speed, by too many things being done far too quickly, without sufficient time being possible for the necessary evolution of biological sequences. No one is immune. Frank Sinatra recently put it well when he spoke of "The need which every thinking man has for a fallow period in which to seek a better understanding of the vast transforming changes now taking place everywhere in the world."

Under these circumstances—to which the customary phrase "the stress of civilisation" scarcely does justice—a consideration of the meaning of REST has become of vital importance. Indeed, the diagnosis of the problem which confronts civilised man is not new. It is, essentially, the need of every man to find biological harmony in a world far removed from conditions suitable for adequate biological functioning. This is a problem which we all of us face—how to live in a confusing and quickly changing world without losing our biological harmony, and without losing satisfaction in our daily living. Such "biological harmony" is impossible without the ability to achieve a balanced state of rest, as opposed to the state of "dis-ease" and fatigue which for most people follows a stress-activity.

There has been a tendency recently to speak as if the main battle against disease and ill health has already been won, and to suggest that an extension of our present methods of prevention and cure would solve the problems of health. It is easy to point with pride to the decline in infant and maternal mortality rates, to the mastery of most of the infections and to our greatly increased expectation of life as compared with a hundred years ago. But it is unduly naive to believe that increases in

height or weight or in length of life, are proof that the day-to-day
health is satisfactory. Certainly the dramatic forms of disease,
such as cholera, smallpox, and typhoid, have been almost
eliminated in Western civilisation. But we are left with the less
dramatic states of "dis-ease", of departures from normal health
and from a balanced state of rest. The medical profession has
scarcely begun to explain what it is that distinguishes an
individual in full health from an individual with "no demonstrable disease".

Health involves many things at many levels but full health
is impossible unless we can maintain a balanced equilibrium in
the face of forces which tend to disturb us. And this is where the
Alexander Principle comes in. Alexander drew attention for
the first time to the structural conditions in which a balanced
equilibrium is possible, as opposed to those in which it is
bound to be impossible. He also showed how most of us are
encouraged and even taught to move and react in an unbalanced manner, until eventually we reach a state of affairs where
we not only cannot recognise how we are mis-using ourselves,
but do not even *want* a different USE when it conflicts with our
habitual social attitudes. A state of affairs where we do not
know how to achieve a balanced state of rest.

*Posture*

Unfortunately, a markedly wrong imbalance may not affect
biological functioning in an obvious way at first, and this
accounts for the bizarre variations in posture which come to be
accepted as normal and suitable for particular social situations
and surroundings.

There is no one single social criterion of what is a good
posture—it has many different meanings to different people.
The barrack square sergeant, the nanny, the anthropologist, the
dancer, the gynaecologist, the sculptor, the actor, the Buddhist
monk—these and many more will all have their particular ideas
of what is right: the adolescent thinks it essential to adopt the
typical slouch: the model shows off her clothes with grotesquely
thrown forward pelvis: the shop assistant and the bar-drinker
relax with weight on one leg: the professional beauty queen
arches her back and pushes out her bosom: and so on through
the whole range of body-language which we may think suitable
and appropriate. None of these postures would matter too much

if their perpetrators had some idea of a postural norm to which they could return when the immediate pressure of the social moment was over. But these distortions *become* each person's own norm, and feel so right that a properly balanced use of the body may feel unnatural. Momentary attitudes in time become habitual dispositions and the body soon becomes moulded into fixed patterns which to a large extent will determine future performance and future functioning.

It is clear that we cannot rely on a *social* criterion of what constitutes good USE. *It is from their effect on biological functioning that the variety of body uses must be judged.* There are many alternative possibilities in the mechanical use of the body at any given time, but there is, for any given situation, a way of using the body which makes for the best functioning, for the least wear and tear, and for the sweetest running engine, just as there is a USE which leads to waste of energy and undue fatigue.

Many writers before Alexander have written of this need for ease and economy of effort. Schopenhauer[10] considered that the USE was good if every movement was performed and every position assumed in the easiest, most appropriate and convenient way—"the pure adequate expression of intention without any superfluity which might exhibit itself in aimless meaningless bustle". Unfortunately the "easiest and most convenient way", although perhaps socially appropriate and convenient, is not necessarily biologically appropriate. Herbert Spencer[11] perhaps came nearer to it when he spoke of "movements which are effected with economy of force, and postures which are maintained within this economy". Likewise Marcus Aurelius wrote: "The body ought to be stable and free from all irregularity whether in rest or in motion. All this should be without any element of affectation." Thomas Aquinas in *Summa Theologica* thought that good use consisted in "due proportion, for the sense delights in things duly proportioned: delight springs from evidence of ease in the performer".

Yes indeed, but what is Easeful USE? When mis-use patterns are never relinquished, but are present even at rest, we are confronted with a state of pervading dis-ease and strain which stops life from being lived as it should be. The fact is that the majority of people do not really know how to achieve an easeful state of muscular rest in their bodies. When their childhood remedy of a good night's sleep fails to restore them to full enjoyable energy, they seek for artificial sleep and artificial tension-release: and the drugs which they use to relax their muscle-tension produce a state of dullness which is a mockery of what living should be.

## Dystonia

The medical name for faulty muscular tension patterns is "dystonia", and it will simplify description if I refer to such patterns of muscular mis-use as "dystonic" patterns.

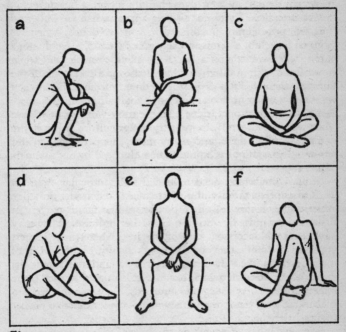

## Figure 9

Dystonic patterns arise and produce an unbalanced resting-state in many ways. They are particularly obvious in the positionings and postures which we adopt when we are keeping still. Over one thousand such body positions have been listed, all of them variations of sitting and lying and standing and kneeling. Some of them seem unusual to western eyes, but the deep squat (fig. 9a) and the tailor squat (fig. 9c) employ a far better USE of the back than, say, the familiar adolescent postures of figure 9d and figure 9f. Figure 9e in which the legs are not crossed is functionally far better than the familiar crossed-knee position of figure 9b.

Dystonic patterns also arise in the simple mechanical actions which we carry out all day and every day when we move ourselves and move objects in our surroundings: moving a fork, a book, a paper, a telephone: moving a dish cloth, an oven door, an electric switch: moving a gear handle, a coin, a bus ticket . . . the list is endless. Dystonic mis-uses appear when we walk and run: when we jump, hurdle, swim, throw, dance; when we swing a golf club, a tennis racket, a cricket bat, a conductor's baton: when we ride on a horse, or a bus, or a bicycle: when we sit slumped in a dinghy or huddled over a text book in the library: when we lift a dish or a dictionary from a shelf: when we stand at a bar or in a shop or at a football match: when we carry out surgical operations or laboratory work or dentistry: when we work manually in industry or agriculture or just in the garden. In all of these, and many more, our performance and our liability to fatigue is bound to be influenced by our manner-of-use.

In activities which need a special skill, muscular dystonia leads to unpredictability of performance. To consider only one athletic sphere, most of our top-class women tennis-players in Britain never quite live-up to their earlier promises. They may have isolated successes, but often, just when their biggest opportunity comes, they become pathetically erratic. Most of them show marked dystonic patterns around the shoulders, upper back and neck, which become accentuated as they come under pressure. As the game proceeds, they can be seen to accentuate their tension, and they do not come back to a proper resting balance.

Of course in the midst of any game—or indeed of any intense activity—there has to be a concentration of effort and expectancy on the matter in hand. But such concentration need not produce dystonia, and we are faced with two questions:

(a) how are we not to mis-use our bodies when we start to do something, and

(b) when we stop, how are we to release the muscular contractions which we have just been making.

Such a muscular control will only become possible if we can start from a properly balanced state of rest, and if we know how to return to (and maintain) such a steady state of muscular rest when we stop. Alexander's concept of USE implied a conscious awareness of such a steady state.

## Postural Homeostasis*

About twenty years ago, I suggested the phrase "postural homeostasis"[12] to describe the steady state in which the body keeps itself balanced. Postural Homeostasis involves a most intricate and delicate interplay of muscular co-ordinations and adjustments throughout the body, to bring the body close to a balanced state.

The balance which results from this inter-play is in what the physicists call "a steady resting state", and in a healthy person these muscular adjustments will mesh together to give a balanced whole: a juggler who balances a number of objects on a pole is maintaining them in a "steady resting state". Work is being done to maintain balance around a central point of stillness. This central point is not fixed. Oscillation takes place around it, with smaller, or bigger swings. Balance can be achieved in all manner of ways—many of them markedly inefficient, with too big an oscillation away from the central resting point.

Such oscillation is characteristic of all our muscular activities. If you look at yourself in a mirror you will see that you are swaying slightly. More obviously if you place a piece of string down the mirror and stand back about ten feet and line up your nose with the piece of string, you will notice as you walk towards the mirror that your nose oscillates a great deal from one side of the string to the other.

Even, when standing still, a pin point of light photographed on the top of the skull (fig. 10) will show a great deal of sway around the central point. Eysenck has confirmed that in neurotic people[13] such swaying oscillations are much larger than in healthy people: indeed, excessive sway is one of the clearest indications of conflict in people's personality.

* This section (from page 51–62), although essential for a full understanding of the Alexander Principle, may be skipped if necessary.

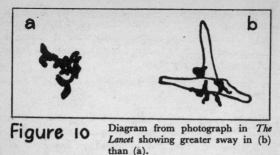

**Figure 10**  Diagram from photograph in *The Lancet* showing greater sway in (b) than (a).

*Muscular Feed-back*

What governs the amount of oscillation in our muscular adjustments? Think of a simple movement (fig. 11) like moving the tip of the right index finger (X) to touch the tip of the left index finger (Y). The distance between X and Y has to be assessed by our brains rather as a cat gauges how to jump from a window ledge to a parapet.

The distance between X and Y is known in cybernetic jargon as the "error". Information about the "error" XY is fed back

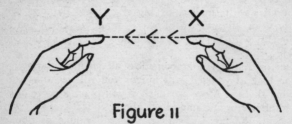

**Figure 11**

to the brain where it is unconsciously checked against a pre-existing model (the receptor element R, in figure 12). According to the construction which we place upon the information received action takes place in the muscles (the effector element M, in figure 12) to move from X to Y. In other words to close the gap and to eliminate the error.

Figure 12 is the prototype of a homeostatic circuit, and it involves what is known as "negative feed-back". Negative feed-back keeps a system oscillating very close to a central resting state, and when there is too big a movement away from the resting position, it brings it back by a compensatory movement.

The receptor element R represents our idea of what—for one reason or another—we consider to be a normal resting state. Through it, we receive information and compute it against our previously stored experience. A useful way of saying this is to say that we all have a "body-construct", made up of all of our previous learned experience of our body, and that we construe

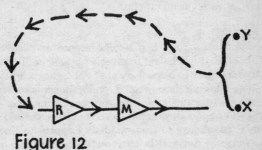

## Figure 12

(put-a-construction-on) what happens to us by reference to this "body-construct".

We can also think of "error" as being the difference between the way we construe things to be and the way we want them to be. And of course we all of us may construe things—and alter our perception of them—to make them seem to be the way we want them to be.

The feed-back circuit in figure 12 is similar to the scanning mechanism which is used in television and radar. The muscles are scanned as one might scan a printed page in search of a word. A thermostat is another example: when it corrects an error, it makes a new one: this too it corrects by making a further but smaller error. It is in fact in a state of "steady motion". When the self-correcting mechanism overshoots the mark, oscillation will occur.

Riding a bicycle is another example. When the rider falls slightly to the right, he turns his front wheel to the right which stops his fall but leads to his being thrown to the left, and he corrects this by turning his wheel to the left, and so on. The net result is a steady resting state in his body, as he uses his arms and his legs to steer and to pedal.

If our "use" is to be accurately balanced, four things at least are needed. Firstly, we need to get adequate information from

our muscles (and from the other parts concerned with movement). Secondly, we need to receive this information accurately
in our brains without obscuring it. Thirdly, we need to activate
our muscles so that they do what we want, with a minimum of
mis-use. And fourthly, we need to know how to come back to—
and maintain—a balanced resting use of our bodies which will
interfere least with our functioning.

*Muscle Physiology*

In a book of this nature, it is totally impossible to give a full
account of all that is relevant in muscle physiology. In the time
since I took a degree in physiology at Oxford, the complex study
of nerve and muscle has become yearly more complex; but
except at a fairly crude level of neuromuscular injury or pathology, it is still almost impossible to relate either the old or the
new muscle physiology to what actually happens to "normal"
human beings at rest and in movement. Perhaps I can cover
myself with those who find my account too simple by recommending R. A. Granit's *The Basis of Motor Control*[14] and
T. Roberts' *Basic Ideas in Neurophysiology*[15] for more detailed
study.

I know of no other sphere of physiology in which acutely
intelligent minds have laboured with more imagination and
skill. But, in spite of this fine physiological work and speculation,
the task of teaching muscular control to actual people in their
actual daily affairs has not yet been greatly facilitated. What I
have to say about muscle control fits the facts as I know them;
and if it is argued that this or that piece of muscle physiology
points in another direction, then, rather like Samuel Johnson, I
would reply by saying "I refute you thus", by showing them
what actually happens in living human beings in the clinical
situation.

Muscle can either shorten or lengthen. It contracts by means
of a molecular shortening which pulls on elastic elements in the
muscle fibre: and the contraction is produced by nerve impulses, synchronised in numerous relay-stations in the brain and
spinal cord. The resultant impulse to a muscle fibre, delivered
at a certain intensity to a muscle in a more or less receptive
state, makes it contract, i.e., shorten.

But what happens when muscle lengthens? Is it simply that
the nerve impulses which made it contract stop firing, so that it

returns back to its original resting length? Unfortunately it is not as easy as that.

We have two systems (fig. 13) by which our muscles are controlled by motor nerves (i.e., nerves which go to the muscle from the brain). The first system—and until recently thought to be the only system—works by making muscle-fibres contract and shorten. 55% of motor-nerves look after this activity. The second system, which uses the remaining 45% of the motor nerves, works on a quite different basis. The nerves from this system do not go directly to actual muscle itself—to the actual biceps muscle or thigh muscle which you can touch with your hand—but to a complex structure called a muscle-spindle, lying within the belly of the anatomical muscles. Many thousands of these lie length-ways in the muscles: they are about 8 mm long, bulging in the middle and tapered at the ends. They are concerned more with the lengthening of muscle than with its contraction.

The muscle-spindle has its own set of internal muscles (plate 15) and in addition to the motor nerves which go *to* it from the brain and spinal cord, it has sensory nerves which go back *from* it to the brain and spinal cord. The spindle is a much more sensitive adjuster of muscle than is the actual overlying muscle itself. Its register of length works in parallel with the overlying muscle not only to damp down excessive oscillations during actual activity, but also *to induce a lengthening of contracted muscle after activity*. In the words of P. A. Merton, it "constitutes a follow-up servo, the muscle length tending to follow changes in spindle length".[16]

The whole mechanism is extremely complex: but from the point of view of someone who is attempting to learn a properly balanced use of his body, two major points arise. Firstly, over-contraction and shortening of anatomical muscle may result in the muscle-spindle going silent, i.e., failing to feed-back information to the brain about how much the muscles are contracting. A spindle stops discharging when over-shortening of the main muscle occurs. And secondly, lengthening of anatomical muscles can be brought about not simply by stopping off the activity which originally made that muscle contract, *but by learning voluntarily to lengthen muscles until they achieve a better resting length*.

It would appear that the muscle-spindle plays a very large

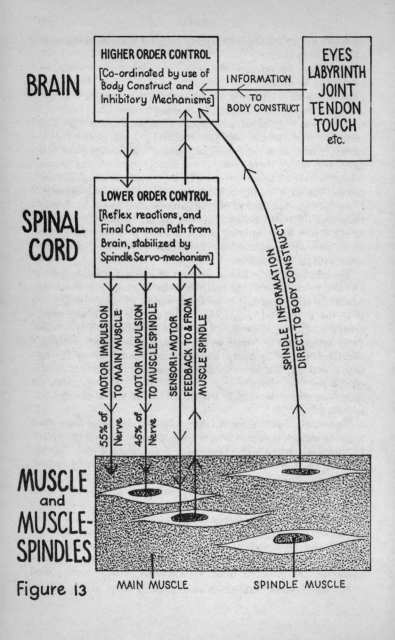

Figure 13

part in this production of length in contracted muscle: and it should be mentioned that spindles are connected not only with the cerebral cortex (through which we control our actions) but with the reticular formation (the nerve-network in our brain which is responsible for our conscious awareness of the world about us).

We can accordingly learn consciously to lengthen tense muscles, not just by stopping the action which made them contract, but as a definite act of will, by which we can release and re-lengthen contracted muscle.

This, of course, is a much simplified account, and it must be, since any nervous pathway we can trace in the brain ultimately connects up, directly or indirectly, with muscles or muscle-spindles. Any frequently repeated use of a particular nervous pathway is likely to lead to the slow development of a "cell-assembly"—a diffuse structure of cells in the cortex and mid-brain and basal ganglia, capable of acting as an enclosed "memory" system which influences other systems and is influenced by other systems; but this sort of detail is not in place here—the cross-correlations of motor and sensory nerves to and from a vast number of motor units and spindles in a large number of muscles, via the spinal cord and all levels of the brain, is fully described in textbooks. The territory of Cybernetics and Information Theory is already well trodden. But after ploughing through the writings of Wiener, Lashley, Craik, Grey Walter, Von Neumann, McCullough, Shannon *et alia*, my brain still reels at the complexity of it. Marvellous phrases like "Signal/noise discrimination", "Error-minimising neuronal networks" and "Negative contingent variability", jostle round my skull. My own simplified version of how muscular feed-back works seems to me adequate without doing damage to the facts. Broadbent,[17] in his introduction to the recent *British Medical Bulletin on Cognitive Psychology* (Sept., 1971), reckons that Psychology has only now reached the point when "it can usefully tackle many problems nearer to ordinary human concerns". No doubt the Alexander Principle will before long be greatly clarified and refined by new paradigms of associative mechanisms in perception: but meanwhile the practical business of detecting and re-educating faulty use-patterns can proceed quite satisfactorily with the simplified view which I am suggesting.

*Faulty Resting Balance*

The patient in plate 16 shows a dystonic pattern both when she is standing upright and when she sits down. The slight twist of her pelvis to the right when she stands becomes much greater when she sits down: and it can be seen that when she sits down she makes an excessive muscle contraction on the left side of her

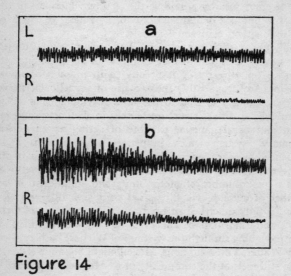

Figure 14

back (just above her pants) which is an accentuation of a similar contraction when she was standing.

Such muscle patterns can be recorded electrically. Figure 14 is a diagram from a recording which I published some years ago in *The Lancet* (2, 659, 1955). In A, the left side of the back shows considerably more activity than the right. In B, when she is moving, there is activity on both sides of the back but more in the left. Her back, in fact, shows a dystonic pattern which distorts the posture of the back, and, in her case, produced pressure on one of her lumbar discs. But, in addition, her resting position was an unbalanced position. Her balance around a central resting point showed excessive oscillations, because of the asymmetry in her muscular resting position.

Figure 15 is a recording of the neck muscles of a violinist who
consulted me because of painful cramps at the base of his neck
when he was playing fast passages.* In figure 15a the muscle is
relatively quiet; in figure 15b he picks up his bow and puts it
down. In figure 15c he again picks it up and puts it down, but

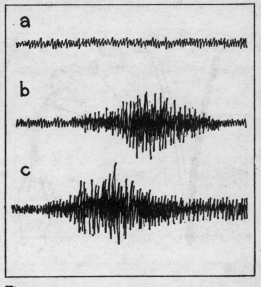

## Figure 15

this time the muscle continues to be in a state of activity even
when he is doing nothing. His feed-back mechanism has gone
wrong, and, at this point, he has no idea of how to release the
contraction, but has to rely on it eventually subsiding—an
impossibility while he is giving a concert. It is clear that he needs
to be taught how to return at will to a properly balanced resting
state.

As a simple illustration of the resting state principle—a
patella hammer (fig. 16a) which has a heavy head on a flexible
wooden handle, will, if agitated, oscillate around a resting
point (fig. 16b): application of an external force (fig. 16c) will

* This diagram is taken from a recording in "Posture and the Resting
State".[18]

deform it, and, after removal of this force, it will either return to its original resting state or it will remain to a greater or less degree deformed (fig. 16d). In time, repeated application of such a force will lead to structural alteration or, at any rate, to a predisposition to bend more easily, just as a piece of paper, once folded, tends to bend more easily in that direction.

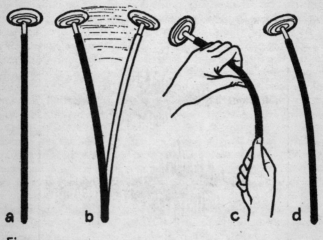

## Figure 16

Dystonic mis-use is present when we do not know how to return to a balanced resting state after reacting to a given situation. Such over-active states in time become habitual and a predisposition to adopt them will persist even when they temporarily disappear.

In time, not only does the resting state of the muscle become wrongly balanced, but it begins to modify the bones and joints on which it works and also the circulatory system which traverses it. The bony framework becomes warped and cramped and stretched by the stresses and strains which are put on it by persistent over-contraction of muscle. These states of over-contraction, large and small, gradually leave their mark on us until our resting state is in its various ways as deformed as the patella hammer in fig. 16.

## Relaxation

There have been many recipes for getting rid of such unwelcome tension: and most people can get by for quite long
periods by one means or another, even though they begin to
show persistent dystonia. Most people, by the time their
adolescence is over, if not before, begin to feel that something is
amiss, and they may already be showing mental or physical
disturbances which either produce symptoms or impair their
performance.

As we grow older, the resting state which we all of us learn
to adopt is either a balanced or an unbalanced one, according
to the degree of mal-distributed muscle tension. Muscular
hypertension is the residual tension and postural deformity
which remains after stress activity—or after any activity which
leaves behind residual muscle tension. Such residual tension
should, ideally, be resolved by returning to a balanced resting
state; but usually it is only partially relaxed, without the
dystonic pattern being resolved. In the latter case the tension
remains latent in an unbalanced resting state, so that it may
only require the idea of moving to re-activate the muscular
hypertension, usually in the form of anticipatory tension or
"set".

Two alternatives therefore are possible. Firstly, the muscle
tension can be relaxed a little without resolving the underlying
dystonic pattern, which remains latent until the conditions for
its renewal occur. Secondly—and this is what is needed—the
tension can be resolved by a return to a balanced resting state,
leaving no unconscious residue.

Owing to a lack of understanding of what is entailed by a
balanced resting state, most people, with or without the help of
their doctor, resort to the first procedure. Under such titles as
relaxation, rest-cure, tranquillising or simply by such expedi-
ents as alcohol, nicotine and slump-collapse at weekends, a
temporary diminution of disagreeable tension may be obtained.
And, by avoiding a stress situation or the memory of it, a
sufficient number of "funk-holes" may be discovered by which
activation of latent tension is avoided. The resultant lack of
vitality, creativity, and enjoyment of forward planning (which
would activate the tension state) eventually becomes the normal
way such people spend their lives.

Why is it that the balanced resting state should be so difficult to attain? Firstly, there is widespread ignorance of what it entails. Secondly—and this will be the topic of later chapters—when someone is in a tension state, there is fear of return to a state of rest. Our preferred self-picture is usually sustained by USING ourselves in a habitual way. By maintaining an unbalanced USE we can maintain self-deception.

The relationship of USE to Mental Health will be discussed in greater detail in Chapter 7, but the significance of Alexander's discovery must first be seen in the sphere of General Medicine. To understand the Medical niche into which his discoveries fit, the concept of Diagnosis itself must be considered: against this background, it will then be possible to detail some of the physical disorders in which USE is particularly relevant.

# Chapter 5

## MEDICAL DIAGNOSIS

THE WHOLE WORLD of medicine and disease is fraught with fear. The television revolution may have taught us that doctors are fallible human beings, but in moments of dire need, the sheer fear of illness and pain invests one's doctor with super-human faculties and wisdom. The patient who, say, is unable to pass water and whose full bladder is a screaming agony, would give at that moment, much of his personal fortune to someone who can relieve him. Most doctors will have experienced from such patients a depth of gratitude which affirms them in a view of themselves as basically useful people.

The doctor, with his *therapeutic* skill, will always be loved, feared and respected. But such rewarding therapeutic moments do not happen very often. A vast amount of general medical practice is concerned with humdrum palliative meas-ures, with relatively dissatisfied and grumbling sick people, and with a mixture of kindness and counselling, or, in bad doctors, of brusqueness and dogmatism. Patients in these circumstances tend to be labelled with a convenient diagnosis which serves to fob them off with a satisfactory explanation, and to touch off a stream of routine therapy.

Hospital practice likewise has its rewarding moments of therapeutic skill, in the accident wards, in the labour wards, in the intensive care units, and sometimes in the skilful handling of modern drugs which can stem the acute infection and the acute depression. But much of the hospital doctor's time is likewise spent in bowing down to the great god Diagnosis. If we are to understand the connection between USE and Disease, we need to be quite clear about what is meant by "a diagnosis", and in the process discover what a disease isn't.

When you walk into a doctor's consulting room, he begins right away to label you. At first his labelling is a rough one—you look "ill". If he is to decide what sort of "ill" you are, he has to examine a few more of your characteristics.

In all of us, at any time, there are a vast number of physio-logical events taking place. Our kidneys are filtering out

fluids, our stomachs and our intestines are setting about any
food which comes their way, our hearts are pumping, our senses
are sensing, our brains are thinking, and our muscular reflexes
are doing their best to handle our postures and our movements,
our words and our desires: the body is a complex whole in a
state of perpetual process. A vast number of interacting events
and interpenetrating processes are going on in all of us all the
time—a veritable "flux of events". Your doctor would like to
know which of these "events" are not functioning as they
should.

The processes which contribute to our organised make-up are
interfused and interdependent, but in spite of the inter-
dependence, it is possible to select some of the distinguishable
processes and "events" for measurement. By dint of various
examinations and laboratory tests it is possible to obtain details
of some of the malfunctioning processes and at this point the
business of Diagnosis begins. The individual events are collected together into a "bundle of events" and this bundle is the
Diagnosis. The doctor is already logically in very deep water
indeed.

A doctor learns many things in his medical training. Philosophy is not one of them. He may, it is true, become what is
called a philosopher, but this is in the practical sense rather
than in the academic sense of the word. Of all stables which
currently require a philosophical spring-clean, the medical
stable is one of the first on the list. The most appalling logical
blunders are being perpetrated daily in the minds and in the
consulting rooms of the medical fraternity: and, in our hospital
wards and Out-patient departments, all manner of procedures
are being carried out in the name of diagnosis. Patients are
having needles of various shapes and sizes thrust, with varying
degrees of accuracy, into almost every portion of their anatomy.

Why, you may ask, as you lie there writhing, why does this
red-faced and perspiring young doctor thrust not once but
twice and thrice into my lower back with a thing like a minia-
ture rapier? Why does he say "Sister, Sister, give me a tube",
and proceed to withdraw from you fluids which you can ill
spare? Why is it important to him? Why is it important to you?
And then, as night comes on and you review the situation, a
horrible doubt assails you. Does he know why it is important?
Does he really understand why he is sticking needles into you?

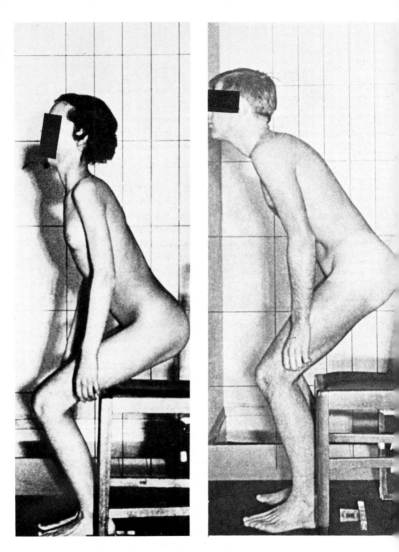

1a 1b Head pulling back into shoulders as in fig. 1.

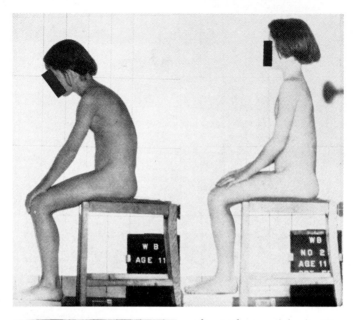

2b and 2c (*above*) Slump versus balanced USE.

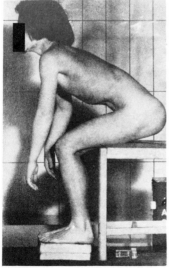

2a Head pulled back, body thrown forward, pelvis thrown back as in fig. 6.

3a 3b Infant alertness versus adolescent collapse.

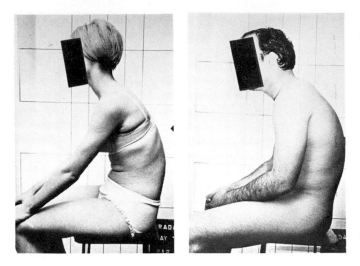

4 Typical slumped sitting positions.

5 Two types of head retraction.

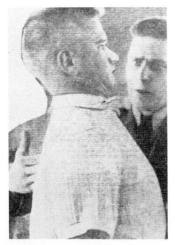 

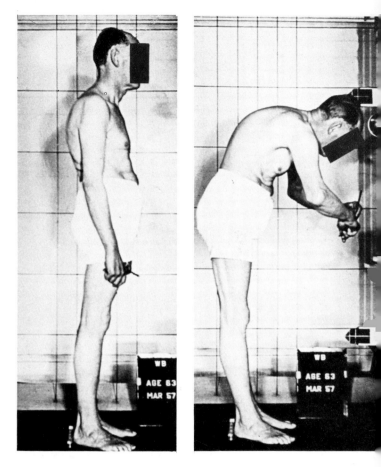

6 Dentist's hump produced by years of bending over patients, and pulling head back.

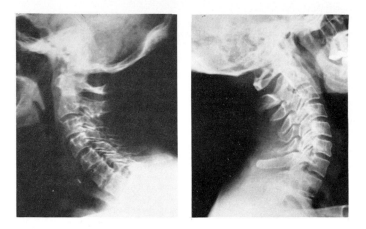

7a 7b X-ray of heads pulling back, and neck constantly arched too much forward as in plate 2a.

8 Athlete with back slumped when sitting, over-arched when standing: excessive tension in back muscles.

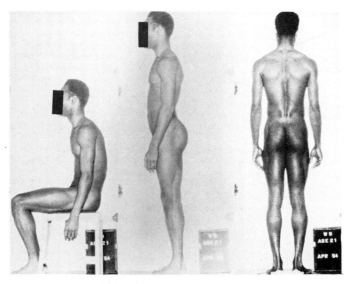

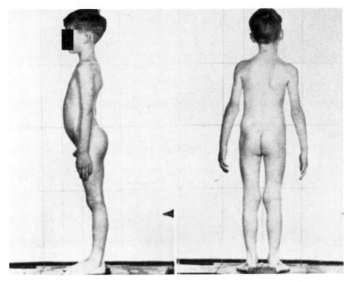

9 Lordosis in schoolchildren. Note neck twist in boy (c. X-ray plate 22)

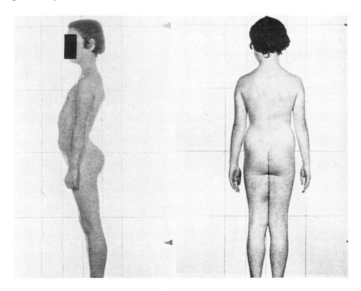

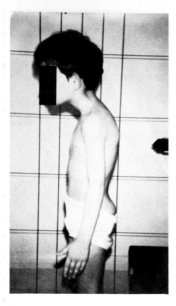
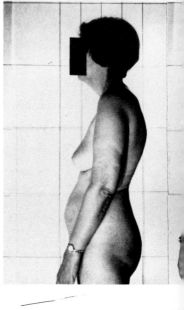

10a, b c Hump in child, woman and man. Back arched, stomach dropped forward. See fig. 5 and fig. 22e.

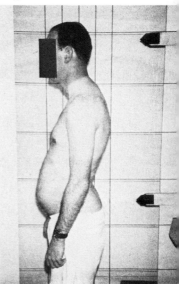

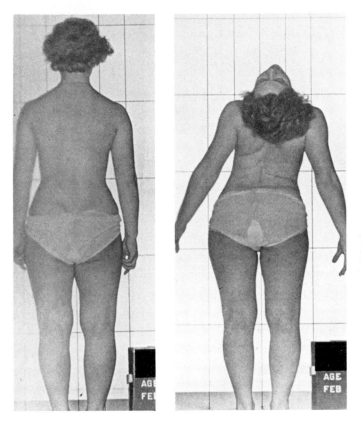

11 Dancer unconsciously twisting her back when bending.

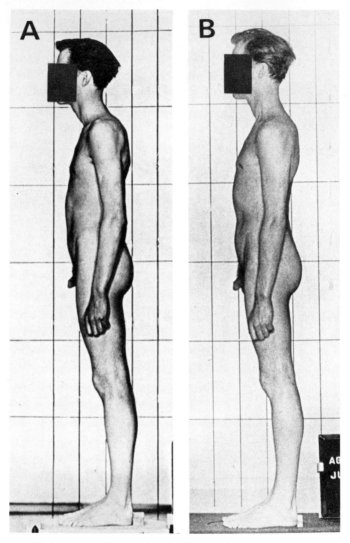

12a. Neck dropped forward as in X-ray plate 7.

  b. Neck lengthening as in fig. 5b.

  c. Back view of 12a. Note tension in neck, shoulders and buttocks.

  d. Back view of 12b. Less tension in neck, shoulders and buttocks.

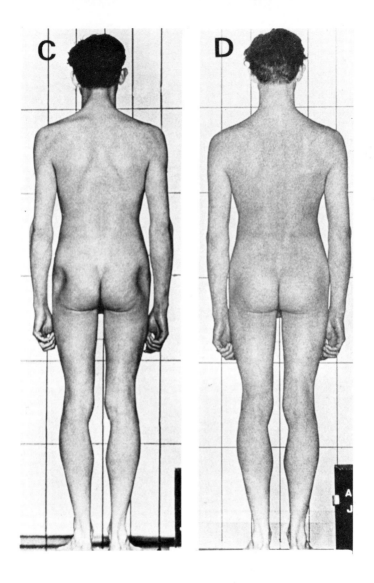

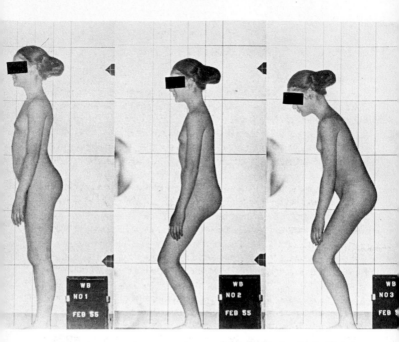

13a (*above*) Alexander's "position of mechanical advantage".

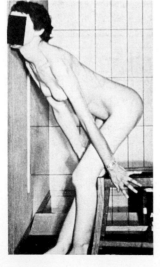

13b Head retraction into position of mechanical disadvantage in sitting down.

So next morning you beckon him to your side, and you say, "Doctor, why did you stick that needle in my back yesterday? It wasn't to make me better, was it?"

He will regard you sternly, and if he is talkative, he may say: "We want to diagnose your condition. We want to know what you are a case of. We want to know what disease is causing your pain. The doctor who sent you to hospital thought it might be sciatica, but we want to be sure about the cause. You surely want us to explain your symptoms by finding out what it really is?"

The young doctor spoke frankly and fairly. Diagnosis, he has been taught, is the be-all and end-all of his work. He must affix to each patient a label which will touch off a routine stream of therapy, a stream which is determined by experience of previous patients with similar labels.

You, the patient, have a pain down your thigh: it is a sharp pain, excruciatingly painful, in fact. You want two things. First of all you want the pain to stop and then you want to know what produced it and how to stop it happening again. When you go to your doctor, you are given two things, a treatment and a label. The treatment may be almost anything; the immediate label, in this case, may be "sciatica". You go home with the impression that sciatica has caused your pain. Not only have you "got" sciatica, but sciatica has "got" you.

The power of a word is tremendous. The mysterious quality of illness has made it all too easy for the patient—and often the doctor—to imagine that diseases do actually exist in the way that a table exists.

To Sydenham, in the seventeenth century, each disease was an entity apart from the patient who displayed it. Sydenham viewed symptoms as having behind them some objective entity —something displayed by, but independent of, the patient. This medical fallacy grew strong in the days when medicine was based predominantly on the post-mortem. The post-mortem was, and is, an invaluable method of observing the condition of the dead body and it is quite obvious that certain organs and tissues do show marked changes which must have been present during life. Likewise tissues and tissue fluids which are removed from the living people may show disturbances in their chemical and physical reactions and appearance. In this way, the disease which the patient has "got" comes to be thought of in terms of these changes in organs and tissues and chemical functioning.

The chemical and physical disturbances (events) which a doctor discovers in the body by his various forms of examination and testing are collected together and grouped into a "bundle of events". For example, when you had an acute pain in your leg, your doctor may have discovered that the muscles were wasted and that certain sensations were altered. An X-ray of your back may have shown that certain vertebrae were too close together. These observations of individual "events" were then grouped together into a bundle and given the label "Sciatica" or, more probably, "Prolapsed Intervertebral Disc (P.I.D.)".

It happens to be the case that we cannot in our language refer to events which are going on somewhere without introducing a name, a word, or phrase which appears to stand for something which is producing them. But since most of us still have the primitive belief that to every name an underlying real entity must correspond, it becomes only too easy for the patient to think that an "event" such as muscle-wasting is produced, by some underlying "morbid entity"—by "Sciatica" or the "P.I.D.", even though these are merely *words* used for labelling. The same principle applies to such labels as Multiple Sclerosis, or Schizophrenia or Leukaemia, which the patient is thought to have "got" and which are thought to be responsible for his symptoms. It leads to statements like "We thought he was Schizophrenic, but he is really a case of reactive Depression". There is a parallel to this in the field of Law where the "is it really an X" problem is always coming up: when, to put it in a stylised form, the accepted criteria of applicability of the word "X" are, say, a, b, c, d and e, and then we find a situation in which, a, c, d, and e are present but not b: and we ask mis-leadingly, "Is it really an X?" In law this question is a request for a decision rather than for a descriptive classification. The question should be "Will it be useful to class it as one?"

This point of view begins to look quite obvious when put in this way and most doctors would reckon to diagnose on the basis of "Will it be useful to label it as one?" But labels have a way of gaining a spurious objectivity, and leading a life of their own.

The bundles of events (diagnostic labels) into which individual events (tissue and chemical changes, etc.) are grouped, do not exist in the same way that the individual events themselves may be said to exist. "Sciatica" does not exist in the way that "muscle-wasting" exists. The process of bundling together events into diagnostic labels is simply a form of classification, adopted from constant usage, embodying the cumulative experience of many doctors. The classifications do not have an independent existence in their own right: they are not there, like the North Pole, waiting to be discovered. They are not "natural" kinds of grouping, in the Platonic sense of "natural" kinds of group, in which things are so-and-so in some absolute sense, so that one point of view, and one only, must be the right one. Leukaemia does not "cause" a raised white cell count: schizophrenia does not "cause" hallucinations. How can a classification "cause" anything except a disturbance in the mind of someone who happens to hear it uttered?

To say this is not to deny the immense usefulness and convenience of a pathological diagnosis. It is simply that diseases are labels—words. There are no diseases—only sick people. What doctors call diseases are states of functioning of many people, no two alike, but similar enough for general concepts to be formed. However, it is only too easy, once doctors have got hold of a recognised disease label, to begin to attribute a false materiality to it—what Whitehead called "the fallacy of misplaced concreteness". By speaking as if disease-labels are morbid entities, doctors are indulging in a sort of medical metaphysics: and all too often they become satisfied merely by pinning on a respectable diagnostic label, a label which satisfies them and their obedient patients.

This obsession with explanatory diagnosis is to a certain extent responsible for the impersonal treatment which patients encounter, whether it be in hospital or from their General Practitioners. The "patient-as-a-person" is easily lost in a too facile labelling process, by which over-importance is given to a "real" pathological lesion which can explain the illness. In the words of T. S. Eliot:

There is, it seems to me
At best, only a limited value
In the knowledge derived from experience.
The knowledge imposes a pattern, and falsifies.

Bad doctors, who are subsequently shown to have made inaccurate observations on their patients, are doctors who have been determined to make what they find in their patients "match" certain preconceived diagnoses with which they are familiar. They make their perception of the patient fit in with what they think it ought to be. Their knowledge "imposes a pattern, and falsifies". In this, they are often encouraged by patients who will grasp at anything which gives them hope, and which makes them feel that their state is a familiar one which doctors know all about.

## Descriptive Falsification

But we are concerned here not with bad, ignorant and hide-bound doctors, who, if pressed, will excuse over-simplification on the grounds of pressure of work. What matters are the good doctors—doctors who with great personal dedication and effort and intelligence are trying to help.

Why is the diagnostic label, as it is used at present, only of limited value and how does it falsify? Consider the case of John G, an insurance broker, aged 42, who was admitted to hospital in the middle of the night with a gastric ulcer which had perforated. He was already known to the hospital and had been treated there four months previously. I only knew him as a social friend and not in a medical capacity, but it was clear that he was creating a tension state in himself which was certain to produce symptoms again of some kind. His work with Lloyds involved sitting cooped-up in a small area in which he was constantly besieged by demands for quotations—demands which needed a very quick response often involving huge sums of money, and requiring the brain of a computer, the tact of a diplomat, and the nerves of a tight-rope walker.

When he had been previously in hospital with a complaint of abdominal pain, he was fully investigated and a barium meal had shown that an ulcer crater was present in his stomach. The diagnosis of "Gastric Ulcer" was made and after a period of treatment with diet and various medicaments, he had lost his pain and returned home: after a short convalescence he returned to his work.

Why was such a diagnosis of "Gastric Ulcer" inadequate, since it was clearly the correct explanation of his pain? Because, when we classify the patient as "a case of gastric ulcer", we are referring not merely to the ulcer crater but to the whole patient, his whole history, his whole personal and social nexus. The patient is not a "gastric ulcer". The diagnosis "gastric ulcer" does not exist in the same sense that the observed ulcer crater might be said to exist. The preoccupation with the label and the ulcer crater dominated John G's doctors to such an extent that they were content simply to have eradicated the ulcer, the pathological explanation of his illness. The fact that John G broke down again, with a perforation 4 months later, shows that the whole concept of Diagnosis had slipped up somewhere. It was not enough to have sent him home with a diet and drugs and a diagnosis which *explained* his ulcer. What was needed was a diagnosis which could *predict* the future course of his illness.

Unfortunately, the word used for a *predictive* diagnostic label is often identical with the word used for an *explanatory* label, and this is usually the name of a specific local lesion or disorder of functioning—"Gastric Ulcer", or "Prolapsed Intervertebral Disc", or "Bronchitis". The muddle arises most insidiously, because the same diagnostic label has to perform the two different roles of explanation and prediction. This muddle is so deep-seated that many doctors will feel in their bones that it is crazy not to admit that "Diabetes"causes a raised blood-sugar, or that "Bronchitis" causes purulent sputum, or that "Depression" causes depression: yet they are not very different from the patient who says, "It's me gastric stomach what's worrying me again, Doctor."

Of course, at first, the patient and his doctor need a satisfactory explanation of the symptom which is troubling him. If a patient starts vomiting, is it due to the lunch-time oysters or is it due to a brain tumour starting to press on centres in the brain? (to take an extreme example). When John G started vomiting blood in the middle of the night, the likely explanation was his old ulcer crater. So far, so good. The ulcer crater is an event, and correct explanation is always in terms of events—oysters, ulcer-craters, intra-cranial pressure. However, once an "event-explanation" has been arrived at, the more difficult matter then arises of constructing the predictive diagnosis which will suggest ways of handling the patient in the future. Explanation and prediction are two quite separate matters.

This means that a predictive label must include more events

than those needed for the immediate explanation. Lack of amines in the brain may, of course, sometimes produce depression, but the predictive-label "Depression" must include many more alterable events than amine-lack. Lack of insulin may, of course, produce a high blood-sugar, but the predictive-label "Diabetes" must include more alterable events than insulin-lack. Bronchial inflammation (bronchitis) may of course produce purulent sputum, but the predictive-label "Bronchitis" must include many more alterable events than bronchial inflammation. The label "Gastric Ulcer" must include many more alterable events than the actual gastric ulceration; and so on.

Medicine is just about the only science left which still clings to hopes of finding a "true explanation". We should label to predict, and not merely to give a "true explanation" of what is causing the trouble.

If I see an animal in a field, I may label it "dangerous bull" and modify my action accordingly, whilst the farmer labels it as "my best Shorthorn", and his dealings with it differ from mine: his is not necessarily a truer view of the animal. Likewise, John G in the ward may be to the house physician "a case of gastric ulcer", to the night nurse "two Soneryls at 10", to the hospital secretary "bed 22 occupied", to the hospital news-vendor "a *Daily Mail*", whilst the poet in the next bed may be thinking "Pale death knocks impartially, Pallida mors impar", and making a predictive diagnosis, almost certainly wrong, that pale death is about to knock. All of these people adopt labels which may help their view of John G during his hospital stay, and which predict what may happen in their relationship to him over that relatively short period.

We can improve the predictive value of our diagnostic label by learning to include more and more events in the "bundle of events" which makes it up. The events can be collected at all levels from the patient—physical, chemical, bacteriological, cells, tissues, organs, and so on up to the higher mental functions and to his personal and social behaviour. It is not that events at the physical and chemical levels are to be seen as an *explanation* of events at another "higher" level, but simply that, when we come to apply a diagnostic label, we should make up bundles of events from whatever levels may help us to predict the patient's future and to handle him accordingly.

*Description and Prescription*

One event which had not been observed in John G's case was his habitually tense USE. This event should always be considered when making a selection of events to be included in the "bundle of events" which makes up a diagnosis. Any diagnosis which has not considered it is liable to fall down—sometimes to a lesser, usually to a greater degree. John G's ulcer might well not have perforated if, during his first hospital stay, his USE had been noticed and tackled.

If, then, USE is to be included in the making of a diagnosis, we must realise that a diagnosis should encompass two things. It should contain a *description* and it should contain a *prescription* —a description of events which are malfunctioning and a prescription of principles for future amelioration and prevention.

Diagnosis has for too long only looked for descriptive explanations (whether they be "dispositional" explanations, "efficient-cause" explanations, or "final-cause" explanations).* Such descriptive-diagnosis may satisfy the desire for pigeonholing, but it does not necessarily carry implications for long-term prevention. A descriptive-diagnosis tends to see the patient in a deterministic manner, at the mercy of his genes, his chemistry, his reflexes and his social commitments. Patients tend to be seen as objects lacking free-will, and not as persons. In the preoccupation with pathological minutiae, the patient-as-a-person is lost.

This "descriptivism" (as it is termed by the philosophers)[19] can, of course, be counter-balanced, and in many doctors it is counter-balanced, by art and understanding: but it often happens that doctors have less intuitive understanding than ordinary unschooled people. From his earliest days in the dissecting room, the medical student has to stifle troublesome feelings which may be stirred up, say, by handling a corpse. He soon learns, in this and many other situations, to filter out his ordinary feelings and to lock himself in a scientific enclosure in which he denies himself the ordinary reactions of the outside world. By so doing, he is able to see his patients as objects for scientific scrutiny, and not personally in a way which might require over-involvement. Such an approach may give him

* See Chapter 7, p. 111.

confidence and a tranquil mind, but it is a confidence purchased at the price of great psychological blindness.

Such *descriptivism* is naïvely deterministic. It does not take sufficient account of the patient's freewill. *Prescriptivism*, on the contrary, says that, as long as people are willing to make up their minds about what to do next, they can be free. But in making up their minds about future action, they have to make a prediction about the future—an opinion, a hypothesis, a diagnosis of what seems likely to happen or desirable to make happen. Such a "prescriptive-diagnosis" does not imply that all future events are or could be predictable. In the realm of health, it simply seeks to include in its diagnostic "bundle" such events as seem likely to affect the patient's health in the future. It seeks not simply to describe the present, but to prescribe action for the future. And it prescribes such action on the basis of principles, of priorities.

The Alexander Principle says that USE will always affect FUNCTIONING. It says that USE should always be included in a prescriptive diagnosis. It says that it will always be important for anyone anywhere to know how to sustain a good manner of USE, in sickness or in health. It seeks to replace the concept of CURE by the concept of PREVENTION.

*Preventive Medicine*

From the patient's point of view, all medicine is preventive medicine. Preventing what it is feared might happen as well as what is actually happening. Preventing pain, preventing a lump from growing and spreading: preventing headache, insomnia, agitation, depression: preventing cough, fatigue, giddiness: preventing an arm or leg from behaving abnormally: stopping overweight, stopping underweight: preventing the hazards of childbirth, preventing even the child being born: preventing the aching back, the tingling fingers, and so on.

*Health*, for most of us, implies that we are able to do, without strain, the things we expect to be able to do: and that we are able to *be* without strain the way we like to *be*. Restoration to contented functioning is what most people mean by being healthy. But when we come to worry about the presence of possible *disease*, we are concerned in the main about *what may happen next*. We are concerned to prevent future trouble either in the immediate or distant future.

The general scientific and technological explosion which got under way in the 1920's has dominated medical thought and training for the past half century. But the explosion is now becoming a spent force. The gains are immense: the new medical skills and medical tools have undeniably altered our whole concept of how to deal with severe illness. Many conditions whose progress could not be adequately prevented before can now be checked. But in the words of Professor Sir Macfarlane Burnet OM, FRS:

"The contribution of laboratory science to Medicine has virtually come to an end: almost none of modern basic research in the medical sciences has any direct or indirect bearing on the *prevention* of disease or the improvement of medical care."

Most readers of this book will know that this is true. They know that they have good reason to thank Medicine for taking the terror out of acute illness: but they also know that it is rare nowadays to find a really healthy happy human being—and one who sustains such health over most of a lifetime. They accept that many symptoms can be managed by the use of powerful psychotropic drugs or by powerful antibiotics, but they are also aware that medicine has little to offer them in certain other conditions in which their functioning is not as good as they might like it to be.

The Duke of Edinburgh, speaking to the British Medical Association, had something to say about this:

Much of the progress in medicine has inevitably been made at the price of deeper and narrower specialization, but the individual is still one unit, and so far as his personal health is concerned a unique unit at that. I am all for studying bits and pieces, but I hope that treatment will remain directed to the whole. The . . . cure of disease is a laudable object but it can be followed blindly. Medical science has to face the fact that remedies for one problem may give rise to others. Of one thing I am quite sure, and that is that the Common Health is more than figures showing improved birth rates, death rates, and the incidence of disease.

*The British Journal of Hospital Medicine* makes the same point (November 1971):

> Advances have brought most acute infections under control but the frequency of chronic disease has increased in both relative and absolute terms . . . The doctor's new role is often an uncomfortable one, since he must continue to care for patients whose disease he cannot cure . . . The sense of responsibility has to be extended from care of the sick to care also for the *potentially* sick.

### The Use—Diagnosis

If I am right—and I think I am—that USE is the single most important factor which remains to be dealt with by medical science, one reason for the lack of help which the average person gets from the average doctor in certain cases is apparent. *Doctors—through no fault of their own—have not been trained to observe in detail the variegated patterns of mis-use which are going on in all of their patients.*

To say all of this is not to claim that the faulty manner of use is the main cause of most unexplained malfunctioning (although in many cases there is a clear causal connection): it is simply to say that although most other types of diseased functioning come under the scrutiny of the medical eye, USE is usually ignored: it is not one of the "events" which is considered when putting together the diagnostic "bundle-of-events". And since those whose USE is reasonably good seem to avoid or at least postpone many of the ills to which human beings are prone, any diagnosis which does not consider this factor is incomplete. Fundamental to the preventive care of a patient. s the teaching of improved habits of life, and, at core, this means teaching an improved USE.

Such a conception goes right beyond our present regimes of medical attention. It in no way precludes the need for an accurate pathological descriptive-diagnosis: but it means that no prescription for treatment is complete until a person's USE has been taken into account.

# Chapter 6

## USE AND DISEASE

IF USE IS indeed the single most important factor which remains to be dealt with by medical science, then it would be reasonable to expect that its relevance would be most obvious in those medical conditions which, excluding minor coughs and colds, are far and away the greatest cause of general ill-health in our present society.

Two types of disorder stand at the top of all the illness league tables—mental disorders and rheumatic disorders. If we consider only the working population (excluding adolescents, housewives, the elderly and chronic disabled who contribute to the bulk of mental disorder), we find that 36 million working days are lost each year from mental disorders. The rheumatic disorders are responsible for almost as many—35 million days lost by the working population each year. The relationship between USE and Mental Health will be taken up in the next chapter, but in this chapter the relevance of USE to certain physical disorders—in particular the rheumatic disorders—will be considered.

### Rheumatism

The term "rheumatism" is a rag-bag which includes a vastly differing range of conditions. It was introduced in medieval times by Galen from the Greek word "rheo" (flow), at a time when medicine believed in the four "humours" of the body whose "flow" was liable to be deranged: in rheumatism, through "acrimony of the humours", abnormal flow was thought to take place into various body cavities: in gout, there were thought to be abnormal drops of humour (guttae) in the joints. It became the practice to refer to any sort of shifting pain as "rheumatism", although in the eighteenth century the term was applied mainly to the muscles. It was recognised that the joints could be involved, but secondarily to a muscular disorder.

In 1827 Scudamore, in a comprehensive treatise on rheumatism, thought that the fleshy parts of muscle were not affected, but that the pain came from tendons and their fibrous insertions into bone. In 1904 Gowers[20] thought that muscular pain came from what he called "fibrositis"—a local inflammation of muscle, although other workers blamed either rigidity or weakness of muscle. At this time Alexander began to expound his concept of mis-use, in which he proposed that attention should be paid to the *general* muscular co-ordination, and not simply to the local site of the pain in the muscle or joint. He also suggested—in majestic language—that the basic fault was psychophysical, and that it lay in "faulty preconceived ideas", "debauched kineasthesia", "inaccurate sensory appreciation".

His ideas received support when, in 1937, Halliday[21] found that of 145 cases of rheumatism, 33% were psycho-neurotic as well: of the cases which went on for more than 2 months, 60% were considered psycho-neurotic. This was confirmed by several other leading rheumatologists—Ellman[22] in 1942 suggested that "the muscles serve as a means of defence and attack in the struggle for existence: if the external expression of aggressiveness is inhibited, muscular tension may result which is felt as pain": and he found that in 50 cases of muscular rheumatism, 70% suffered from psychological disorders.

As electromyography came to be used, many people showed (Hench[23] 1946) that "psychogenic rheumatism is one of the commonest causes of generalised or localised aches and pains". I stressed at this time that we should not use the term "psychogenic": that it was not a question of the "psyche" generating disorder in the body, or the body generating disorder in the "psyche", but rather that the rheumatism and the psychoneurosis are *both* manifestations of an underlying failure to achieve a balanced "resting state" of USE after stress.

Subsequently I published a study of students[24] in which the 10% who complained of persistent muscular pain all manifested a severely disturbed postural balance: and Eysenck,[25] in his book *The Dimensions of Personality*, found a definite and fundamental correlation between neuroticism and an unbalanced postural balance. The "neurotic" will invariably be found to have poorly balanced USE, and the worse the imbalance the greater the likelihood of pain.

I suggested at that time that we should not talk about Misuse as being a psychosomatic disorder but rather that it would be considered as a "stress disorder": a stress disorder being one which habitually involves bodily systems beyond the relevant ones, and in which the organism does not return to a balanced resting state after activity. I suggested that bodily systems could be involved at four levels:

1. Physiological changes
2. Emotional changes
3. Behavioural changes
4. Structural changes

and that all levels might be affected at the same time in the composite disorder of "Mis-use". "Rheumatism" in fact, as I saw it (and still see it), should never be considered simply in terms of the local part of the body which is malfunctioning, but should be taken in the context of the mis-use of the whole body, involving as it does, physiological changes, emotional changes, behavioural changes and structural changes.

Part and parcel of this "USE" concept of rheumatism (and indeed of many other bodily disorders) is my disbelief in the "wisdom of the body". The body is not wise: it is frequently stupid. Perhaps I might digress for a moment to stress what I mean by its stupidity, and how it is that the body may be "wise" about *ends* but not about *means*.

### The Stupidity of the Body

For a human being to remain alive, certain "variables" must remain within definite limits. Many variables in our bodies—the length of our hair or the length of our nails—are not essential to life (except in a social sense): but the temperature and acidity of our blood, the amount of oxygen, sugar, salt, protein, fat and calcium are of vital importance and a matter of life and death. They are kept constant by a ceaseless interplay of adjustments. Even if we don't drink for three days, the amount of water in the blood will change very little. If we then drink six quarts of water in six hours the blood volume still won't change much, although the kidneys have to work over-time to pour it out into the bladder. These mechanisms are on a stimulus/response basis. If there is too much swing away from the desired norm, the body (in its stimulus/response "wisdom") is stimulated to use one of its many systems to restore the balance. If its systems cannot come up trumps, it searches its environment for the necessary constituents—salt for the sweating miner, heroin for the junkie's transient "steady" state, alcohol for the liver which can no longer convert other food properly, nicotine for the quick energy of sugar release, sexual discharge for the irritable restless gonads, colour and music to restore momentary peace to the restless brain.

This might seem like the wisdom of the body, but it is wisdom at a low level. It is the wisdom of end-gaining.

Consider another "essential variable"—your blood pressure. If by some mischance the part of your brain which usually regulates it is knocked out, another part of the brain will take over the job. If this part is knocked out, various ganglia outside the brain take over. If these ganglia are knocked out, the blood vessels themselves attempt, by contracting or enlarging, to regulate the pressure of the blood they contain.

The body, in fact, usually has several alternative ways of doing things. In carpentry terms, it is a bodger. An artful bodger and an end-gaining bodger. There are certain things it wants—so much sugar in the blood, so much salt, so much oxygen, so much protein, such and such a familiar sense of muscular equilibrium, such and such a state of mental calm— and if its easiest ways of getting them don't work, it bodges around with its other systems or muscles to knock something together which will do, until finally, it runs out of alternatives and begins to seize up. This is "end-gaining"—the determination to get short-term ends on a reflex stimulus/response basis, without ensuring that there are no harmful by-products.

Reflex end-gaining does not pause to see whether the alternatives will be constructive or destructive in the long run. Such destructive alternativism is not "wisdom". The badly burned body will recklessly pour out its body fluids through the burnt surface until it dies from fluid loss. The asthmatic in his end-gaining anxiety to take in more and more air will use muscles in the upper chest in such a way that he cannot release them properly to let the used air out.

Bodging, which uses potentially destructive procedures, is always a risky business, although much of our fortuitous evolution to date has been a case of "artful bodging". We our-selves have it in us to decide our future in the spheres which we consider important. With all our short-comings and conflicting systems and desires, we can still act by deliberate intention, exercising our mind. Instead of being at the mercy of a bodgedup system of physico-chemical reactions or muscular reflexes, we have it in us to become self-adjusting. We have it in us to live by principles which we ourselves have personally selected— a life of "constructive alternativism", using a new body-construct, rather than a life of destructive alternativism.

## Use and Rheumatism

Nowhere is the "stupidity" of the body more apparent than in the case of the rheumatic disorders. Let us take as an example the condition of osteo-arthritis of the hip-joint. I am not here concerned with the factors which may have led to its development—although I suggest that mis-use is one of the most important—but with what happens when the condition is beginning to show itself. The earliest sign is a narrowing of the width of the joint, a narrowing which leads to a shortening of the distance between the hip and the ground. This shortening usually leads to a further faulty distribution of body weight so that it is mainly carried through the affected hip. The result of this wrong distribution of weight is that the arthritic condition progresses and further shortening takes place on the affected side: this leads to putting further weight on the affected hip-joint, and so on, until the familiar picture of distortion and leg-shortening presents itself.

Such arthritis of the hip cannot be considered purely as a local event, although, of course, the point may come when local surgery is needed in dealing with the local condition. From a prevention or rehabilitation point of view, the use of the whole body has to be considered. When the early condition is starting to show itself, attention must be given to the *general* use, to see that the balance is not thrown more and more on to the affected side.

This principle applies equally to such relatively slight but infuriatingly persistent conditions as "tennis elbow", painful stiff shoulders ("frozen shoulder"), and minor aches and pains in neck, chest, back and legs. Such conditions may certainly disappear after rest or rubbing or injection or physiotherapy. But often they persist and become a source of worry and dissatisfaction with medical care. More often than not, such conditions will be associated with a small but un-diagnosed disorder of the general USE—plate 17 shows a young girl with just such a persistent leg pain whose tendency to stand with her weight wrongly distributed was only noticed when she was accurately photographed against a grid.

But these are usually small pains and pin-pricks. Of far greater importance are the major USE-disorders of the spinal column. The need for good USE-training in the various postural deformities of the spine—kyphosis, lordosis and scoliosis—is apparent; and even in spines which are severely affected, as in polio or idiopathic scoliosis, a great deal of help can usually be given to correct some of the deformity and to prevent its increase. But by far the greatest number of patients seen in a Rheumatology Clinic (excluding the trivia, and arthritis affecting the limbs) will be one of two conditions. The first is what is known as cervical spondylosis; the second is the almost pandemic pain-in-the-back. These conditions are so prevalent and often so unresponsive to medical treatment that they each need special consideration here, since it is in these two conditions that the Alexander Principle has much to offer.

### Cervical Spondylosis

Since the head-neck balance was thought by Alexander to be the primary seat of mis-use, he had much to say about symptoms which arise from such mis-use. The varieties of mis-use in the head-neck region are infinitely complex. If we look at only a tiny sample of mis-used necks (plates 18a, b, c, d, e) we see how much they vary: and yet an X-ray report on them never mentions even the *presence* of mis-use, much less the *type* of mis-use. Added to which, a "still" picture of a neck gives only slight indication of the nuances of muscular usage which are going on all the time, whether they be produced by speech, or swallowing, or gesturing, or emoting or searching the surroundings with the eyes or the ears.

The commonest of these mis-uses involves a drop forward of the middle of the neck, and this is accompanied by a pulling of the head back on the top of the neck. Plates 18a, 18b and 18c give examples of this: plate 18d shows the same thing, although in time the neck has become so collapsed into the hump that it may not at once be obvious just how much collapse has taken place.

This collapse will involve a tension of the muscles which go up into the back of the skull—not only the big external muscles (fig. 17a, b, c) but also the smaller internal sub-occipital

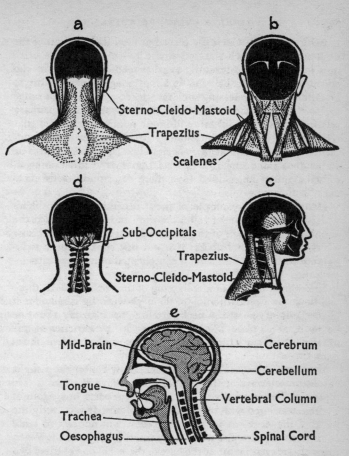

## Figure 17

Only the external and internal muscles of the neck are depicted—certain intermediary muscles are omitted. The sub-occipital muscles play a part in fine skull movements. The other muscles which relate the skull to the neck are mainly inserted into the back of the skull. There is great disparity in strength between the anterior (flexor) muscles and the posterior (extensor) muscles. In the upright posture, strong extensors encourage pulling-back of the head. To carry out relatively automatic functions of mastication, swallowing, breathing and phonation whilst the body is held erect is a complex task. (See Raymond Dart: *The Attainment of Poise*. S. Afr. Med. J., 1947, 21, 74.)

muscles (fig. 17d) which are placed around the junction of the neck and head. Much was—ill-advisedly—made of these small muscles by some of Alexander's earlier medical supporters who encouraged him in a belief in an almost magical potentiality to be obtained from releasing such muscles so as to give full range to his "Primary Control". One doctor wrote "The primary relation upon which all more ultimate relations depend is that relation established by the small group of muscles which comprise the atlas-occipital, axis-occipital, atlas-axis system. The stupendous importance of this relation in the functioning of muscles cannot be realised by a mere description of its existence."

Here is another example of the "stupendous" atmosphere which dogged Alexander in his life-time and which masked the actual factual analysis of the immensely varied forms of misuse which affect so many necks: it is not just *one* type of muscle-balance which is at fault, but a complicated network of muscle-pulls throughout the neck.

Sometimes, instead of a collapsing of the neck forward, there will be an over-straightening of the neck with slight movement of the body of one of the neck vertebrae backwards on the one below it, as in plate 18e. These cases, in my experience, are usually associated with really intractable neck, head or facial pain.

If we look at the neck from the back, we will often see a slight curvature sideways at the base of the neck, in the hump (see plate 22). This is usually ignored in X-ray reports, but, again, it is often associated with intractable symptoms. If you study the back of the neck, as in plate 12c, you will notice two tense contracted muscles just where they insert into the skull. When there is a sideways twist at the base of the neck, one of these two muscles will be more prominent than the other and the resultant tension imbalance is even harder to release than the more symmetrical type of faulty tension.

These and many more types of mis-use will always be found in the condition of cervical spondylosis (head and neck arthritis) or cervical disc pressure. These conditions affect 85% of us in our 50's, and most doctors will agree that they are difficult to treat and are long lasting.

The usual symptom, at first, is numbness or tingling in the fingers of one hand, due to pressure on nerve-roots from the compressed and fore-shortened neck vertebrae. Sometimes the first symptom is severe pain in the neck, shoulder or arm, which typically is worse in the early hours of the morning, when the warmth of bedclothes has perhaps produced a congestion in the already narrowed passages which carry nerves outward from the spinal cord. Sufferers find that they have to get up, or place their arm outside the bedclothes, or in some new position to relieve the pain.

Re-education of the faulty USE which accompanies cervical spondylosis will usually produce a relief of symptoms.

### Pain in the Back

Over half the adult population experience severe lower back and sciatic pain. Of the £190 million estimated annual cost of the rheumatic disorders, a high and increasing proportion are due to back pain. Middle-aged workers with back trouble stay away from work for an average of five months, and since a large number of them will be off work for less time than this, it means, on the other hand, that a sizeable proportion will be away for more than a year.

In most cases there may be some obvious immediate cause for the acute pain—a prolapsed disc or ankylosing spondylitis: but most of the people with painful backs will find themselves given a diagnostic label such as lumbo-sacral strain, sacro iliac strain, postural backache, ligamentous strain, fibrositis; plus, from osteopaths, sophisticated labels like "facet-block" or the un-sophisticated label of an "osteopathic lesion".

Over 1,000 possible reasons for back pain are cited in one American text book. USE is not to be found amongst them. The failure to cope medically with back pain is exactly what might be expected where there is widespread ignorance of what con-stitutes a properly used back. My own experience, *quite categorically*, is that most forms of back pain, even after there has been unsuccessful surgery, are best treated by making USE re-education a prime necessity. *Of course*, there may be allevia-tion by manipulation, or physiotherapy, injection, traction, corsets and so on: but the basic problem remains, that these procedures do not alter the general manner of USE, and this general manner of USE constitutes a Damoclean sword which is liable to fall when external or internal stress builds up.

Only too frequently such disabling back pain attacks men

and women of very high calibre who are making a big contribution in their chosen sphere. Often they will be under thirty years
of age, and they face a prospect of crippling pain which will impose a restrictive pattern on their lives, whether it be in a rearing
of their children or in the development of their working life.
Eventually, after casting around for any conceivable therapy
that might help, they resign themselves to a greatly restricted
existence, propped up by corsets and aspirins and loving
relations and friends: and very often they become profoundly
depressed, since the mis-use pattern which led to their back
trouble will, more often than not, contain a depressive-slump
element in its components.

It cannot be emphasised too strongly, so I will write it in
capitals. IT IS WRONG TO TREAT A PAINFUL BACK AS A LOCAL
CONDITION. BACK PAIN IS ALWAYS ACCOMPANIED AND PRECEDED
BY GENERAL MIS-USE.

This general mis-use will have many variations. But almost
always three things can be seen to be wrong. The thorax (chest
cage) will be thrown over to one side (and may be slightly
rotated on the lumbar spine) (plate 19). The shoulder-blades
will be raised, so that much of the muscular supporting work
of the back is being done by the shoulders instead of the mid-
back (plate 19). And the breathing pattern will be seen to
involve a slight arching forward of the lumbar spine and the
predominant habit of breathing-in with the front of the chest
and the abdomen. There will be many other associated
tensions, depending on the type of pain. An acute disc lesion
will probably show flattening and rigidity, a chronic back may
be hyper-lordotic. But, strange as it may at first-sight appear, a
painful lower back should always first be dealt with by sorting
out the mis-use patterns in the Neck and Hump, since only
when an improved co-ordination can be maintained in the
upper part of the back, can there be an improved USE in the
lower back and legs.

*Arthritis*

Before leaving this discussion of rheumatic disorders, a mention
must be made of the condition of rheumatoid arthritis. It differs
from osteo-arthritis in that it is a general joint disease. It affects
at least 1% of all males and 3% of all females: in mild cases
there is little disability but severe cases show advanced crippling

and deterioration of many joints and tendons. It is another example of the "stupidity" of the body in that the "adaptive" response of the body is a major cause of the disease.

A study of 400 cases in 1952 by the social workers of Peto Place (now the Arthur Stanley Institute) left no doubt that in at least 60% of cases of rheumatoid arthritis, there had been a preceding stress. Over 95% of a series of cases which I reported at the Royal Society of Medicine in 1964 occurred after what I considered to be preceding stress.

A typical history, as written by one of my patients, was:

My mother was taken to hospital with her second stroke aged 73: I went backwards and forwards for 16 months to Mile End, sometimes at 10 o'clock at night, sometimes 8 o'clock in the morning, sitting with her for hours, then rushing home and on to work. After she died I woke one morning, my feet felt funny and couldn't walk. I thought it was chilblains. It got worse till I had to borrow shoes too big for me, then I came on to you.

Or another one:

We were living under very crowded conditions for five to six years, in premises that had been condemned by the Council due to overcrowding.

Or again, from an intelligent librarian:

It became necessary to assume the responsibility of providing and sharing a house with a parent, thereby changing my way of life. This venture had to be undertaken on a strictly limited income, and making ends meet gave rise to anxiety. The curtailment of my personal freedom was realised with regret. The situation was accepted, there being no question of escape, rather of anxiety to fulfil duties.

I doubt if anyone who has worked in this field would wish to deny this stress factor, but one is still faced with the question of why one person reacts with rheumatoid arthritis and another person doesn't: indeed, the same question applies to most illnesses—most of us can cite quite appalling psychological traumata or physical strains in our youth and maturity, which we weather in one way or another. Stress, in the event, seems to depend on what seems like a stress to any one of us: in other words, on our body construct, the way we "construe" our situation, and the way we "structure" our response to it through our manner of USE.

"Rheumatoid" patients exhibit in their USE a degree of muscular agitation which is not present in other rheumatic patients. I first noticed this in relation to excessive head movements made during speaking, but closer analysis showed a wriggling movement not only in the muscles of the spine but also in the limbs. Rheumatoid patients in the early stages of their condition, generally tend to be "wrigglers", in a state of muscular agitation: and if they are not, it is either because the pathology has led to fixation, or because pain and discomfort have led them to keep more still, or because they seek to control their agitation by excessive tension. It is particularly in the communication-situation that this muscular agitation becomes apparent and it may serve as an early diagnostic pointer.

Many of them are shy, sensitive people whose feelings are easily hurt—people with difficulty in communicating. This difficulty might account for the meticulous, orderly conscientious life which they like to lead, since they like an environment in which learned stereotyped responses will suffice. It has struck me when dealing with them that through this feeling of inadequacy, in the communication situation, they make exaggerated muscular agitation. Many of them, by a sort of puppy-dog wriggling, put up a false front of niceness which belies their preferred disposition. It does not seem to me outside the bounds of possibility that this constant muscular restlessness may lead to joint dysfunction: and it cannot but be helpful to teach them a muscular resting-state in which their exaggerated homeostatic swings are damped down.

## Physical Medicine and Physiotherapy

Most hospital Rheumatology departments in the past combined their function with what is known as "Physical Medicine"—that is to say, the use of *physical* methods as opposed to *chemical* methods of treatment. This sharing of functions has grown up from the fact that Rheumatologists share with Physical Medicine specialists the need for the use of physiotherapists, trained in such physical methods. Nowadays most Physical Medicine specialists prefer to think of themselves as predominantly Rheumatologists, mainly because of the link which this gives them with general medicine, and also because the physiotherapist, who carries out the actual day-to-day treatment on the patient, comes to know a great deal more about the vagaries of muscle than they do.

Much of a physiotherapist's time—when it is not used in various methods involving electricity—is spent on the educating and re-educating of muscle. A major part of their time will be spent on the various rheumatic disorders but they will also be involved in exercises of various kinds—pre-natal and post-natal exercises, breathing exercises, mobilising and strengthening exercises for the back, mobilising fixed shoulders and knees and hips, correcting such postural defects as flat feet, knock-knees, winged shoulders, lordotic backs. Much time is spent in the after-care of people who have broken their bones, suffered amputation or nerve injury, or who have undergone serious orthopaedic surgery to backs or hips or other regions: both before and after an operation patients in the wards are helped to become active sooner than they might if left to their own desires. Much time is spent on the rehabilitation of patients who have had a stroke or suffer from long-lasting nervous diseases, like multiple sclerosis or cerebral palsy. And, of course, a major part of the time is spent on "placebo" therapy in which the friendliness of the physiotherapist and the comfort of massage and heat and so on, is a major part of the treatment. The varieties of procedures are immense but unfortunately they rarely include a knowledge of Alexander's work, which throws a completely new light on exercise-procedures.

Many physiotherapy departments also have personnel trained in manipulative procedures which used to be the preserve of the osteopath and the chiropractor. And many of them use relatively gross manipulative methods in the form of traction to the neck or the spine or the limbs. Such manipulative methods are often a feature of "health farms" which have taken over much of the work that used to be done in the past by spas. In the old days the spas provided an amiable outlet for the wealthy to spend their cash in pleasant surroundings. Now that the spas have been nationalised in Britain, the "health farms" likewise provide a pleasant health-giving holiday for the wealthy

or hypochrondriacal, and enable various forms of physiotherapy, etc., to be carried out in pleasant surroundings.

Very few physiotherapists in the NHS or in private practice,
have at present an understanding of Alexander's conception of
USE. Alexander himself attacked them ferociously, since much
of what they did was, in his opinion, based on the "end-gaining"
principle and they did not seem to understand the need to treat
*local* lesions on a *general* basis.

Physiotherapists have been slower to learn Alexander's ideas
than the modern physical educationists. There is no doubt that
before long the pressure of demand from patients will make it
necessary for physiotherapy training schools to wake up to these
ideas.

In all the types of situation mentioned above in which
physiotherapy is given—the rheumatic disorders, the spinal
disorders, postural disorders, neurological disorders, breathing
disorders, ante-natal and post-natal care, general ward care
and rehabilitation, the Alexander Principle has much to
offer. The only limiting factor is availability of time and the
capacity of the sick or elderly patient to co-operate. Restoration
to the type of adequate functioning which is envisaged in this
book is not at present achieved by our present hospital care,
either in the wards or under out-patient care. To say this is not
to decry the patient and devoted work which the physiotherapists and occupational therapists are carrying out: it is simply
that, as things are at present, there is a gap in their training and
in their working procedures.

*Breathing Disorders*

Nowhere is this more apparent than in the treatment of breathing disorders. To take one obvious example, asthma deaths are
increasing, in spite of modern drugs which can counteract the
acute attack. It is no good simply blaming increased environmental stress, mites in the house dust, or the increased use of
steroid drugs and inhalers which give temporary relief. Something is still missing from the story: and, as usual, this something
is the "use"-explanation, which tends to be overlooked. *The
asthmatic needs to be taught how to stop his wrong way of breathing.*
Breathing exercises have, of course, frequently been given by
physiotherapists for this and for other breathing conditions but
the fact is that breathing exercises do not help the asthmatic

greatly—in fact, recent studies show that after a course of "breathing exercises", the majority of people breathe less efficiently than they did before they started them.

There is no shortage of information about the *physiology* of breathing—most of us know that too little oxygen or too much carbon dioxide will make us want more air and we know that various reflex mechanisms in the brain, blood vessels and lung will work automatically to keep the breathing process going. This is what starts happening when we are born. This is what stops happening when we die. But this physiological account of reflex breathing does not tell us much about *how to breathe*. It is not only in the sphere of medicine that there is this lack of knowledge. Actors, singers, speech teachers, and speech therapists have a special need to know about breathing, as, of course, have all teachers of physical education. Yet in all of these fields —medicine, communications and physical education—there is a paucity of information about wrong breathing habits. The asthmatic does not need breathing exercises—he needs breathing *education*. He needs a minute analysis of his faulty breathing habits and clear instruction on how to replace them by an improved use of his chest. Such chest-use cannot be separated out from a consideration of the general manner of use. *All* patients with chronic bronchitis and asthma have a significantly high score in the Eysenck personality inventory, and the Cattell self-analysis test. These personality disorders increase as the chest trouble increases: and to repeat it again, there is a very high correlation between personality disorder and mis-use.

I have for some years given some very simple instructions to patients about their breathing, and these are reprinted in Chapter 11. As with all such written instructions, however, five minutes practical instruction is worth any amount of reading about it.

*Stress Diseases*

I have so far mentioned in this chapter many of the types of medical condition in which the Alexander Principle is most obviously needed. To this list should be added the diseases of civilisation—the so-called "stress" diseases. Whilst one would hope that knowledge of the Principle will lessen the incidence of these conditions, for the most part its role will be in the lives of people who have already acquired a "stress" condition and who are needing to change their whole *modus vivendi*.

High on the list is Hypertension—raising of the blood pressure to the point at which there is a risk of cardiac damage or stroke. It is well known that emotional factors play a large part in raising the blood pressure: frequently a patient's pressure will fall considerably when he is resting in hospital or simply when he is less afraid of the medical situation in which he finds himself. I have found blood pressure to drop by as much as 30 points after a half-hour re-educational session in which tense muscles were relaxed: and it seems reasonable to suggest that since most blood vessels traverse or are surrounded by muscles, any over-contraction of the muscle is bound to squeeze the lumen of the blood vessel and thereby make it more difficult for the blood to be pumped through them by the heart. The less the obstruction to the blood flow, the less the pressure.

I see a good number of people who have had a coronary thrombosis. I have never yet seen a case in which the upper chest was not markedly raised and over-contracted. The "powerful" tycoon impression is often accompanied by the blown up, over-filled chest. I regard it as essential that such patients should be taught to release their chest tension and to do so in a way that is accompanied by an improvement in their general USE.

Gastro-intestinal conditions figure high in the list of stress conditions, whether it be gastric and duodenal disorders, "spastic" colon, ulcerative colitis, rectal spasm, or anorexia nervosa in the young. Along with these there are less easily defined symptoms of abdominal discomfort—compulsive air-swallowing, abdominal bloating and belching, and just simple constipation. And there is, of course, the undiagnosed pain in the stomach. The tenth most common cause of admission to hospital in males (and the sixth most common in females) is abdominal pain which remains unexplained after investigation. In children and adolescents it tends to be low down on the right side: in middle-aged people it tends to be higher up in the centre. Children do not grow out of these pains—they have been shown still to be present twenty years later. Many of these patients have their appendix taken out but this does not diminish the re-admission rate to hospital, which is high. It stands to reason that the fullest investigation must be carried out to see if there is pathological change: but where full investigation has been completed and treatment has not resolved the condition, it is often useful to tackle the mis-use which invariably accompanies these conditions. These patients with unexplained abdominal pain also have a high Eysenck neuroticism score—and this, as we know, correlates closely with postural imbalance. More often than not these patients will be found to have a slight sideways displacement of the thorax on the lower back and often a rotary twist of the dorso-lumbar spine with associated muscle spasm. This should always be looked for in cases of unexplained abdominal discomfort.

I am often asked to see migraine sufferers and it is rare to find one who cannot be helped by learning to release faulty tension around the head, neck and face. Whilst there may well be a constitutional predisposition to migraine, in the form of arterial spasm which is hormonally precipitated, there is nevertheless always an added factor of excessive neck tension, which perpetuates a condition, often for days, which should resolve in a few hours. This has been realised by Migraine Clinics, but owing to their lack of an understanding of the complexity of the muscular tensions in the neck and "hump", they have not been very successful in their relaxation therapy.

I see a number of epileptics and petit-mal sufferers, and, provided they are willing to undergo re-education—many of them have a temperament which is impatient unless they are filled up with drugs—it is often possible to reduce markedly the incidence of attacks, to the point of complete disappearance in a number of cases.

A certain number of gynaecological conditions can be helped by the USE approach: dysmenorrhoea, retroversion of the uterus and vaginismus can be helped. The application of the Principle to sexual functioning will be discussed in detail in Chapter 8. A knowledge of how to maintain a stable integrated pattern of USE is also invaluable at the menopause—a time when the awareness of the postural model (the body construct) may often become disturbed, with resultant feelings of unreality and depersonalisation.

Perhaps the most obvious field for application is in the therapy of the various muscular tics and cramps, which can vary from the "occupational palsies" such as writers' and telephonists' cramp, to severe conditions like spasmodic torticollis and persistent spasm of the shoulders and trunk. I should mention here the condition of "atypical facial pain"—acute pain, usually across the nose, cheek and eyes, differing from trigeminal neuralgia in that it usually occurs in young adults. Anyone who has seen these patients—and the ineffectual way in which they have been treated—would not be surprised that out of a group of six of my patients (it is a relatively rare condition) four had made suicide attempts because of the pain: one of them after her jaw had been bound together by wire to immobilise the spasm. Re-education is arduous and takes many months but all of the six cases became free from pain.

It is interesting that Alexander in his writings described torticollis and trigeminal neuralgia as two conditions which he had been able to help markedly: and one must remember that in the past the Alexander Principle has often been the last-ditch approach, when everything else had been tried, and the patients were severely distressed and disturbed by the chronicity of their condition: and, of course, sceptical of getting relief from yet one more suggested approach.

One further category which should be mentioned is accident-proneness, whether it be in motor-cars or in the clumsiness of handling objects and one's general movements in everyday life. The well-integrated person is less accident prone. Indeed, it seems obvious that the better balanced person is going to do himself less accidental damage and be less vulnerable to the unexpected incident or fault in his environment.

*Local versus General*

This chapter has touched on a hotch-potch of medical processes; but then the body itself is a hotch-potch of inter-connecting processes and usages.

It is clear that such a conglomeration of bodily processes and uses must be integrated by a Principle—a principle which permits of order and hierarchical structure: a hierarchy in which isolated parts of the body are not permitted to gain dominance over the well-being of the whole on an end-gaining basis. The Alexander Principle says that it is time to understand just how USE can be regulated to produce a stable equilibrium: and it lays down procedures by which the conglomeration of potentially conflicting use-patterns can be integrated into a hierarchical structure. It embodies this hierarchical structure in a newly learned body-construct, through which reflex "stupidity" comes under the influence of the "wisdom" of the brain.

Part of the objection to Alexander's work, in his lifetime, was that some people felt he was claiming to teach people to control their functioning directly with their conscious mind. He never suggested—and it is not suggested here—that we know enough about our physico-chemical processes to attempt to control them by will, except perhaps on a research basis (rats can influence their heart rate, blood pressure, intestine movements and urine formation; human beings likewise can be trained to reduce their blood pressure, by conditioning their autonomic control of blood vessels). Such isolated control is at present more of a curiosity than a clinical tool. It is rather that by establishing a principle of *chosen order* in the body's muscular USE, the autonomic system does not remain so disordered after stress. A balanced resting state of use—in which individual parts do not gain dominance over other parts to which they should be subservient in the total hierarchy—appears to modify the development of persisting autonomic imbalance.

The Alexander Principle applies right across the medical field. When someone gets ill, the sick part of his body is, of course, important; but just as important are the things which he does with the rest of his body in response to the sickness of that part. The patient feels ill because he has, say, an acute sinus infection, but at the same time he will feel ill because he is using himself badly. The use-patterns which he has developed over the years provide a context which both predisposes him to his illness and also diminishes his resilience and capacity to adapt to the stress of the present illness. But all of this tends to be ignored by his doctor. The doctor thinks the patient is ill, say, because of his sinus, and the whole rigmarole of medical investigation is switched on to this. The sinus may indeed be making him feel ill, but a vast amount of the feeling of "illness" is based on bad USE. As soon as it is feasible, the patient's USE needs as much attention as does the specific pathology.

When and if the sinus trouble eventually clears up, the doctor will drop out of the picture, and from his point of view the patient is, for the time being, restored to normal health. The doctor will only have seen him on a few isolated occasions, but the patient has to live with himself always, and he has to live with his persisting habits of wrong USE. His doctor finds "no demonstrable disease": no descriptive disease-label may now be pinned on him. But in spite of this, wrong habits of USE persist and lead the patient to feel continuously fatigued and unwell, to the point when the strain of making any extra effort outside of his everyday life may far outweigh any personal gain or social pleasure.

Investigations which were carried out at the Peckham Health Centre showed that, out of 1,666 normal individuals who were examined, there were 1,505 cases of classifiable disease: but, in addition to this, the investigators found a widespread condition of "de-vitalisation", characterised by an overwhelming sense of fatigue and loss of vitality.

Nowadays it is popular to have general "health screening" of men and women over the age of 50 to exclude serious illness, but, alas, as yet such health screening does not include an analysis of their mis-use. Any investigation into problems of "dis-ease" and "de-vitalisation" must take into account the persistent influence of USE in every reaction and during every moment of life. Any diagnosis which ignores this influence is incomplete. Any plan of treatment which fails to take it into account must leave behind a predisposition to disease and malfunctioning.

*Recommended Steps*

So I make the following suggestions for the use of the Alexander Principle in medicine:

1. Preventively: during the school years (at least), Doctors, PE instructors, dance teachers and school teachers should be aware of mis-use in the children under their care. Some notice should be made on the child's record and any deterioration noted.

2. Therapeutically: the USE-factor should be included in the various systems which are expected to be examined by doctors. Not merely, as at present, as a cursory analysis of joint mobility, integrity of the reflexes, muscular power and so on; but as a bodily system in its own right, as important as any other bodily system. No medical student should complete his training without being given some knowledge of the the USE-factor.

3. In hospital medicine, there must be a new concept of rest, so that the patient who is lying in bed supposedly resting is not setting up excessive dystonic patterns.

4. Specifically, it must be used in the care of rheumatic, ortho-paedic, neurological, psychosomatic and mental disorders.

5. In order to do this, nurses and physiotherapists should be instructed about USE. Not only will it help them in handling their patients, but it will give them personally an additional way of coping with the stresses and strains of hospital life; and heaven knows, there is plenty of stress for nurses in a world in which trival matters are often apt to gain too much importance, a world full of rigid rules and hierarchy, a world in which the personality has to be constantly adapted to suit different patients, and yet a world in which there is lack of scope for initiative.

6. In industry, by an extension of the present work of ergonomic scientists and factory doctors so that they can learn to detect working conditions which encourage mis-use and to observe correctable mis-use in workers.

7. On a larger scale, the preventive implications of the Alex-ander Principle must be plugged by those interested in health education everywhere. The resources of television, radio and published articles must be used to make these facts more widely known.

8. To make all of the foregoing possible, people must be trained specifically in teaching the Principle, in order to help those who fall into the above categories. The size of the problem should not be allowed to prevent the start being made. Sooner or later, a wide-scale attack on these needs will have to be attempted.

# Chapter 7

## MENTAL HEALTH

IT HAS BEEN suggested that if a concept could be found in the field of Mental Health which would be as basic as is the concept of MASS in physics, then the whole subject would be revolutionised. USE may well be just that basic concept.

It cannot be emphasised too strongly that it is not ideas which are responsible for neurosis. It is the way in which we react to our ideas with our dystonic use-patterns which constitutes the neurosis. The reason why this has not seemed obvious in the past is that, prior to Alexander's work, there has never been an adequate micro-analysis of dystonic use-patterns. Until his concept of USE was established, no criterion could be adopted which would tell us in what ways a mentally sick person was departing from good USE.

Much behaviour which passes for normal already contains traces of neurotic mis-use. Such pre-neurotic mis-use patterns are usually ignored or not recognised until they have developed to the point of seeming definitely odd. Before the development of such odd behaviour, the mis-used person may have been thought simply to have the "normal abnormalities" which go to make up most people's personality. It is only after improved use-patterns have been developed that it becomes clear just how much the previous mental disorder was based on an inadequate manner of use: and such a manner of use will be seen to return if the neurotic pattern returns.

Much of what I write about mental health is clearly at odds with much that is currently said and done. But there are no cut-and-dried absolute verities in this field. Psychiatrists, behaviour therapists, psychotherapists of every shade and complexion hold views which not only conflict with other groups but with other members of their own groups. I have been a member for many years of the Society for Psychosomatic Research, and the Philosophy of Science Group: anyone who has attended meetings of these august bodies will recall an atmosphere of disputation which is fine for Science but which does not necessarily bode well for the handling of patients.

By adopting an innocent attitude, which says "This is how is seems to me: I may be wrong", I might appear to be attempting to buy off criticism. But the passion to prove and disprove theories in a rigorous scientific manner is not compatible with the immediate clinical handling by one man of a sufficient number of patients. Once I had established—in as rigorous a scientific manner as I could[26, 27]—that a method did exist which could reliably alter USE, it seemed to me more important in my own lifetime to employ that method over the large range of medical and mental problems which were referred to me by other doctors, in the expectation that I would gradually come to an understanding of the possibilities and limitations of the approach. If my account appears simplistic, it conceals an all too willing disposition to take on all comers on my home ground.

## Anxiety and Muscle Tension

I spent the greater part of ten years working very closely with Alexander, often just with himself and myself and one patient in the room, and it soon became clear to me that his work could provide a way of detecting and observing "mental" states which no other process could throw up in such tangible form. Behind his theories of the "Primary Control" and a seemingly gymnastic preoccupation with getting people to sit-down and stand-up without upsetting the tension balance of their necks and backs, lay a constant preoccupation with the "chosen" and "unchosen" components of behaviour.

One of the earliest medical articles which I wrote on his work, in 1947, was entitled "Anxiety and Muscle Tension",[28] and it was clear to me then that his approach was very relevant to the handling of neurotic disorders.

The connection between anxiety states and muscle tension is now generally accepted, and the drug firms have been quick to fill the doctor's letter-box with expensive circulars which purport to show just how anxiety can be relieved by using their tension-relaxing drugs. But in 1944 the general psychiatric opinion was that "in anxiety states there is no known structural or chemical variation which accompanies the all too obvious symptoms"[29] and, that "if we consider the long list of psycho-neurotics with their hysterias, anxieties, obsessions and states of inexplicable fatigue and depression, there is no characteristic physical accompaniment which can be detected by present methods". It was clear to me at that time, from Alexander's work, that there was indeed a very definite physical accompaniment, i.e., muscular over-activity and mis-use, which accompanied psycho-neurosis.

In the succeeding years it became clearer, by the use of electrical methods of recording muscle tension, just how close the correlation could be between mental states and muscular states. For example, arm tension was found to be connected with hostility: buttock and thigh tension with sexual problems. In many other ways, it became clear that the mentally sick were physically tense. One of the most striking observations at that time was made by Wolff[30] who found that over 90% of headache-sufferers produced their pain, albeit unwittingly, by "marked sustained contraction in the muscles of the neck", and that such muscular contraction was associated with "emotional strain, dissatisfaction, apprehension and anxiety".

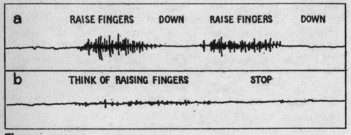

Figure 18

Over the past twenty years, many people have followed up these observations on Mind and Muscle. A recording which I made many years ago illustrates the point (fig. 18). It shows (a) the electrical activity in a person's forearm when an actual movement of the hand is being made, but also (b) the activity which occurs when the hand movement is only being *thought* of. This is an astonishing indication of the link between mind and muscle, and various people of the behaviourist school have suggested that it is impossible even to *think* of an activity without causing small contractions in the muscles which would produce the actual movement in reality. It has been claimed indeed, by some people, that thinking itself is always carried out by such small muscular movements. Small movements of the vocal muscles or of the muscles of the eyes were considered likely vehicles by the early behaviourists. It is tempting to follow up such ideas, but it seems to me more likely that the undoubted over-activity which occurs in certain muscles when most of us are engaged in thinking, is in fact an unnecessary mis-use, and simply gives further indication of how easily most of us will produce unresolved dystonic patterns in response to quite minor ideas.

Gilbert Ryle likewise deprecates, from a philosophical point of view (*Royal Institute of Philosophy Lectures*, vol. 1, 1966–1967), such an equation of mind with muscle, so that mind is even made to include such things as "the tennis-player's wrist and eye movements, the conversationalist's tongue movements and ear-prickings: the typist's finger movements and so on". His paper should be consulted.

But even if muscle is not regarded as a "vehicle" for mind, it is indisputable that tiny muscular use-patterns do frequently occur when we engage in thought (over and above tonic action-currents in muscle). In the words of R. C. Davis: "One has but to observe them on a set of recording instruments to believe that they are by far the most numerous responses of the organism. It is clear that any overt response, vocal utterance, or bodily movement, is surrounded by a wide penumbra of them."[31]

## Tension during Communication

The more I worked with Alexander, the clearer it became to me that the tension patterns which arise during movement are quite different from those which are triggered off by the process of communication. The processes of searching and selecting so as to connect-up and communicate with other people are deeply embedded in our character structure and may not be at once apparent as obvious mis-use patterns. Communication does of course take place in a most obvious way by word and by gesture; bodily "mood-signs" are the stock in trade of any actor, and easy to observe. But, in addition to these *obvious* gestures and postures, we find in most people tiny use-patterns which unconsciously, automatically, and whether they like it or not, transmit a certain mood, often quite contrary to their intention of expressing themselves in such a way.

Recent writings on "body language" and "body awareness" have stressed the importance of such non-verbal communication. But many of these forms of USE can only be observed under the conditions of minute analysis which Alexander was the first to employ. One of Alexander's greatest contributions lay in his method of minutely observing tiny dystonic patterns and in his realisation that most of them will only show up *when a patient is asked to learn something new*. Above all, he observed them without introducing tiresome instrumentation and within the context of an acceptable everyday learning situation.

Many of us will be aware of a slight clenching of our hands when we are angry, or a hunching of our shoulders and fixing our chest when we are afraid, or fidgeting movements when we are anxious. But many other tension states occur which are below the level of our consciousness, although contributing a great deal to the general background of our personal awareness. Such patterns may be amongst the most delicate and sensitive means of communication which we have at our disposal, even though they so easily become irrelevant, unchosen, unconscious habits.

Often these tensions include fragments of some role which was significant in the past but which is now irrelevant. They may appear suddenly at quite inappropriate moments, and they may evoke from those around us reactions we do not want. Unless there is knowledge of a basic balanced resting-state of USE, such tensions are liable to build up into attitudes which undermine our interpersonal relationships, without our knowing it.

In many cases the emotional tension may be quite obvious and land us in trouble there and then—for example in the sudden muscular cramps which affect writers, carpenters, musicians, cow-milkers, dentists, golfers (at the top of the back swing), billiard-players (so that they cannot bring the cue forward) and many others, including a recent patient of mine who, when lifting a glass or a tea cup, would get stuck with his cup half-way towards his mouth.

These tension states often occur in a setting in which there is emotional strain. Writer's cramp has been attributed to anger which is unexpressed or denied—anger which leads first to a clenching of the forearm and hand and then to the adoption of increasingly bizarre shoulder and neck postures in an attempt to counteract the arm clenching. In the same way, unwanted sexual feeling may be counteracted by making excessive leg and pelvic tensions.

In most of these dystonic patterns it is not easy to separate a physical reason from a psychological reason. The way in which we construe our surroundings, the way in which we seek to *construct* our surroundings to our taste, is a psychophysical act, in which Mind cannot be separated from Muscle for long.

## Mind and Muscle

In spite of his old fashioned stimulus/response approach, Alexander was throughout insistent on psycho-physical related-ness. The relation of Mind to Muscle had usually simply been thought of as "mens sana in corpore sano" (and its corollary "mens insana in corpore insano"). This sort of uncomplicated cheeriness appeared in a popular book by Goldthwaite, entitled *Body Mechanics* (1934).[32] "When the body is used rightly, all of the structures are in such adjustment that there is no particular strain in any part. The physical processes are at their best, the mental functions are performed most easily, and the personality or spirit of the individual possesses its greatest strength." There are reminders here of William James: "Thus the sovereign voluntary path to cheerfulness, if our spontaneous cheerfulness is lost, is to sit up cheerfully, to look round cheerfully, to act and speak as if cheerfulness were already there."

To which one can only say, "Yes, indeed, would that it were so easy." Unfortunately such an approach begs the whole question, which is how such a "sitting-up" is to be obtained. The slumped posture is not the opposite of sitting up straight. There are a myriad ways of slumping and a myriad ways of straightening the various parts of the body. The body is not simply a system of mechanical levers, to be adjusted into differ-ent positions like a mechanical crane. It is a subtle organ of expression, in which emotional states modify and are modified by muscular tension states. William James indeed knew all about this when he wrote: "By the sensations that so incessantly pour from the over-tense excited body, the over-tense excited habit of mind is kept up: and the sultry threatening exhausting thunderous inner atmosphere never quite clears away." His sovereign remedy of "sitting up cheerfully" is unlikely to get rid of the "thunderous inner feelings", as long as unresolved dy-stonic patterns persist.

Nevertheless, one should not forget the role of Courage in the Mind/Muscle relationship. Courage is clearly present in four minute milers, in mountaineers, in riders from Ghent to Aix, and even in the everyday man who exerts will power to take the plunge into a cold bath or the sea. We are familiar with the stories of paralysed and amputated heroes learning to walk, painfully, step by muscular step; much of it admirable and much of it truly heroic, and to be seen daily in rehabilitation departments throughout the country.

But in the everyday world, the "courageous" use of muscle has tended recently to fall into disrepute except as part of the Saturday gladiatorial scene on football pitch or athletic arena. A recoil to the shuffling discothèque has followed: but there has also followed an interest in the less violent use of muscle—a use which will permit and not preclude clarity of thought and emotion. It is with such less violent use of muscle that Alexander was concerned.

## Attitude and Emotion

Darwin in his book *The Expression of the Emotions in Man and Animals* (1872)[33] used the term "expressive action" to denote movements, gestures and attitudes from which the existence of an underlying state can be inferred, and he considered that "such movements of expression reveal the thoughts of others more truly than do words which may be falsified". More recently phrases like "non-verbal communication" and "body language" have appeared, and it has become a commonplace that emotional attitudes of, say, fear and aggression are mirrored immediately in muscle; such moods as happiness, excitement and evasion are thought to have their characteristic muscular patterns and postures.

There is nothing very new in this thought. St Augustine wrote in the fifth century, "Hoc autem eos velle ex motu corporis aperiebatur: tanquam verbis naturalibus omnium gentium." (Their intention became apparent through their bodily movement, as it were the natural language of all peoples), *Confessions*, 1.

It is a commonplace that most of us tend to adopt the attitude of those we are with and especially of those we love: even in the cinema we may mimic those we identify with (which may account for vigorous feelings which come on after a James Bond picture). A family posture is often the expression of a basic family mood. Rejection of the family mood may lead to rejection of the family posture—"I can't stand like that, it feels just like the way my mother looks", as one girl with a chronic back pain said to me after her posture had been temporarily corrected. She preferred her pain to her parent's posture.

And indeed to change such engrained postures is bound to have repercussions on interpersonal relationships. Plate 20 shows a civil servant who had severe shoulder pain as a result of an engrained attitude of cringing. It was possible to get him to release the tension by which he was deforming himself and in his new state he was free from pain. Such, however, was his attitude of cringing in front of superiors that he would sooner lose what he had been taught, and give himself a pain, rather than not appear "humble". It was not until he eventually had a flaming row with his boss and "stood up for himself" that he was able to maintain his improved pain-free attitude.

Such deforming attitudes of cringing and evasiveness eventually lead to structural change: the evasive action of turning the gaze away by rotating the head will eventually set up a permanent twist in the neck: and this in its turn makes evasiveness more easy.

The *Attitude Theory of the Emotions*[34] is fine as far as it goes, but its observations are mostly still at a crude behavioural level. The cases I cited above—which could be multiplied almost indefinitely—do indeed say that the body has its language and that we have for too long neglected the important messages which are sent out in that language. But the crude James-Lange approach which says that the attitude *is* the emotion does not do justice to the facts. Almost any emotion can get latched on to almost any habitual muscle tension trick. The named emotions—anger, fear, jealousy, evasion, cowardice, courage and so on—are only a fraction of the multitudes of shades of emotional feeling which go on in all of us. Most of these feelings have no particular names. They are part of the background of our general awareness—a background which is sustained by our particular use.

And even at this crude macroscopic level of observable "body language", the message may not be an immediate one. *Many habitual postures do not represent an immediate expression of an emotion, but are rather a position from which certain actions and emotions can be possible.* The slumped collapsed adolescent is confused at first if he adopts an improved USE, because most of his favoured inter-personal reactions become impossible with this new use. It is only from his old slumped and twisted state that he feels able to communicate with those he likes: his old slumped posture is the position from which he can express certain emotions and from which he cannot express other reactions. His particular posture is not necessarily to be acquainted with any particular emotion, although eventually a state of depression will be only too easily induced by a state of slump.

Many of these postures indeed do not start as an emotional response, but rather from the way we use our bodies in recurrent work situations. The office worker, the conveyor-belt engineer, the lorry driver, the mum-bent-over-baby, the dentist, the pianist, carry out certain occupations for so long that they eventually will hold themselves partially contracted even when they are not involved in the actual pressures and resistances of their jobs. This residual tension may not be conscious but eventually it is maintained most of the time. The summation of their various temporary attitudes eventually finds its expression in a posture—or in a limited repertoire of postures—which come to dominate a person's character. These deforming postures are the result of the gain in strength in certain specific muscles which have never been properly released, until eventually it becomes easier to rest and to move within the familiar deformed structure. In small and at first unobtrusive ways we become enslaved to our past.

### The Restructuring of Use

Alexander saw, as many have seen, that what was needed was a better way to help a person to reconstruct his life so that he need not be a victim of his past. But he attempted such a restructuring at the fundamental level of USE, on a general rather than a specific basis; and in a way not attempted by other forms of psychological treatment. No one could claim that drugs or shock treatment restructure a person's USE, except in the crudest sense. The alternatives of individual or group psychotherapy in which a person's ideas and constructs are examined and worked through, is, when available, an advance on crude physical treatments; but the inescapable fact remains that all neurotic people mis-use themselves. I have never yet seen a neurotic person who did not show dystonic patterns. Accordingly, the Alexander Principle asserts that, in the therapy of neurotic disorders, any form of drug treatment or psychotherapy which ignores the USE factor is inadequate.

The Alexander approach reverses the psychotherapeutic approach. The psychotherapist says "you will only get rid of your unwanted behaviour in a satisfactory way when your mental attitudes have been sorted out". The Alexander Principle says "It will be impossible to sort out your mental attitudes in a satisfactory way as long as you persist with that faulty manner of use." Not that I do not applaud the insights of psychotherapy and psycho-analysis: but if we recognise mis-use as a comprehensive attempt to deal with our personal experience of emotional distress, there is no need to give priority to discovering a psychological cause of that mis-use. The priority must be given to learning an improved manner of use, so that from this vantage point, the mis-use patterns can be detected, and resolved when they arise.

Psychotherapy seeks to give us insight into why we have taken up this or that attitude. This, however, can be only one of the aspects of the formation of tension habits. It may well be that a given muscle-tension habit started at some specific time, maybe as the result of some severe trauma, maybe as a casual unimportant accidental trick which was discovered and seemed to fit a given circumstance, at a time when the general use-pattern was already becoming disturbed. But at whatever time and however these tension habits were learned, an adult will have elaborated them (and many other tricks) until they are closely meshed in with all of his behaviour throughout his whole day as part of his habitual use. Release there may be from insight into the situation which led to the setting up of a defensive dystonia, but after a time this insight will have exhausted its possibilities for beneficial change. The inertia, the necessity, the comfort (however slight) of the established way of life will continue to provoke tension habits and to keep them in existence: and they will stay in existence until a thorough re-education of mis-use patterns has taken place. With the best will and the best insight from the best psychiatrists in the world, we can only eventually tackle our tension habits by unlearning them at each actual moment of behavioural reaction and this means the establishment of a CONSCIOUSLY STRUCTURED PATTERN OF USE.

*The Direction of Use*

It is at this point that many people have been baffled in the past by Alexander. It is here that the Alexander Principle emerged as a truly novel approach.

The novelty arises around what Alexander called "directing" or "ordering". He was asking for something completely novel from himself and also from his pupils: and the trouble was that he did not make very clear to them what it was that he wanted, so that innumerable versions—or none—of this part of his work began to appear.

Let us take the re-educational situation of the Alexander teacher who is giving instruction to a new patient or pupil. The actual re-educational process is described in detail in Chapter 10, but, briefly, two things are involved. The first is a gentle adjustment of the patient—manually—by the teacher, in such a way as to coax misused muscles to a better co-ordination. Secondly, the patient (or pupil, in an educational context) has to play his part in the proceedings *by consciously projecting to himself a sequence of thought which matches closely the occurrences which his teacher is inducing in his musculature.*

Now this is a totally novel way of going on. Behaviour-therapists certainly have their modes of muscle training, with punishments and rewards. Massage techniques, stroking techniques, body contact techniques likewise involve close body contact between therapist and patient. I have surveyed some of these methods in *Modern Trends in Psychosomatic Medicine*,[26] and I made the point there that Alexander's approach was quite different from any of them. He demanded a minutely sensitive attention on the part of the patient to the setting up of a new *ordered structure* in his body: *ordered* in the sense of being consciously projected as a command to the muscles: and *ordered* in the sense of giving sequential attention to the body in a certain 1, 2, 3, 4, 5, etc., order.

To put it another way. A conductor consulted me on account of a pain in his right arm, his baton arm. Not only was his shoulder fixed and painful, but his elbow also—a condition akin to a tennis elbow. After I had started to give him instruction, he asked me to a rehearsal and to subsequent performances. I had already observed that, even when he lay still on my couch, his whole upper back tended to pull over to the right and that his rib cage was rotating more on the right side. It became apparent when he started to conduct that the movements of his right side became completely dominant over the demands of the rest of his body. He reacted to the needs of his baton by losing command of the general co-ordination of his trunk. His head pulled back and sideways, his shoulders hunched, his chest rotated to the right side; in particular, his baton movements were not made simply from point X to point Y, but after reaching point Y would jerk excessively back again towards point X, rather in the manner of a reflex knee jerk.

The conductor was reacting muscularly in the wrong order. Instead of maintaining the central co-ordination of his back as a "core-structure", he was becoming totally involved in the peripheral movements of his arms, so that the structure of his trunk was distorted and his basic balance upset. His resting posture became more and more twisted, and by the end of the concert he was losing touch not only with himself but with his orchestra and choir. His muscles were reacting in the wrong order.

It is perhaps a play on words to speak of "ordering" in two senses—getting the muscles to react in the right order, and giving "orders". For this reason it is perhaps better to talk of giving "directions" to oneself. Even this may—to some people—smack too much of vitalism and mind/body dualism. It does not really matter much. If it is preferred, this activity can be called "projecting a pattern", "employing a new bodily construct", "ordering", or simply remembering to release and relengthen muscle during and after movment in a certain sequence. Whatever the activity is called, the patient can learn an actual formal construction of words which he learns to link on to the new desired USE, until, in time, the new verbal pattern can be "directed", "projected", "thought", in such a way as to bring the body back into the desired resting homeostasis.

Under conditions of stress this becomes the patient's conscious possession. One of my patients, a well known concert pianist who had a hatred of flying, tells the story of flying back to London from Amsterdam, sitting nervously with a paper bag in front of his mouth, prepared for the worst, and of the man in the seat next to him saying, "I don't mind you being sick, but I do wish you would stop saying *head-forward-and-up, back-lengthen-and-widen*."

Each patient will make his own method of "directing",

which, with or without the help of a teacher, he can learn to link up with the new desired USE-structure. One patient tells me that he phrases the orders in the form of a question to himself, enquiring in sequence of his body whether it corresponds to his desired USE-structure, in the way that a laboratory technician might test the colour of a sample of blood against his haemoglobin standard colours. The "order" presents a standard against which muscle-information can be matched, so that, by feed-back, the "mis-match" signals are eliminated and muscular matching obtained.

## Directed Awareness

It is this aspect of the Alexander Principle which has in the past excited the interest of theologians, philosophers, artists, and of course the crankiest of cranky mind-over-matter merchants. It is a source of somewhat wry amusement to deal in one morning, as I once did, with a Nobel prize winner, a famous and dim-witted television beauty, and a young spastic boy, and to be told by all three of them that they approved of what I was doing because I was "speaking their language". (The spastic boy told his mother that he felt he understood me completely.) It does not seem to matter much if the teacher finds himself transported to the wilder shores of meditation, Sufism, Subud, Gurdjieff, Noöspherism, Jungian Yinning and Yanging, Reichian genitalism and so on, provided that the patient can visibly be seen to be linking up a new "direction" with the new improved manner of use. I would not presume to be derogatory of any of these things—their proponents as I have met them are, in the main, highly evolved and sensitive people: but they leave me with the impression that since my Alexander-training is so acceptable to them and so enlarging to their concepts of mental health, then the Alexander Principle of USE may indeed be as fundamental to Psychology as MASS is to Physics. And this impression is confirmed by the acceptability of the principle to a broad range of psychiatrists, psychotherapists, academic psychologists and behaviour therapists.

## The Inscape

The poet Gerard Manley Hopkins coined the word "inscape" to describe our personal internal "landscape" and this may appeal more to many people than phrases like "body image" and "body construct". The "inscape" which Alexander sought, as a teacher, to construct for his patients and pupils was made up of a formal sequence of words, which, if they did nothing more, reminded the person who projected them to himself of the Alexander experience which had been built into them so far. But the Alexander "inscape" is designed to do more than this. It specifically sets out to counteract such states as anxiety and depression: and to counteract them not simply by inducing a self-hypnotic mental Nirvana but by influencing the actual muscular structuring of the body.

Plate 21 shows a woman who has been taught just such a new "inscape". Her face, which cannot be shown, was one of typical depression: likewise her posture was collapsed and heavy. Her mental depression found its counterpart in her physical collapse. The second picture shows her after only a few weeks of re-education: the third picture shows her six months later, during which time she had received no further re-education at the hands of a teacher, but had worked on her own as she had been taught. The improvement has clearly been dramatic.

There is no need to go on about the typically dejected and collapsed posture of patients in a depressive illness—in or out of mental hospitals it is clear for all to see. But it is sad that amongst the typical physical functions which are held to be most usually disturbed in depression—sleep, appetite, libido, weight, etc.,—there is no mention of USE. And since USE is ignored, it is not surprising that four out of five people with a depressive illness relapse—and go on relapsing with increasing frequency as they grow older. Certainly anti-depressant drugs and shock therapy may help the immediate impossible situation; but depressive illnesses nowadays differ little from the way they were fifty years ago and—as things are shaping at present— they will look much the same in fifty years' time unless people wake up to the factor of USE. In Hopkins' words (in "The Leaden Echo and the Golden Echo"):

No, nothing can be done
To keep at bay
Ruck and wrinkle, dropping, dying, death's worst,
    winding sheets
Tombs and worms and tumbling to decay;
So be beginning, be beginning to despair.

One influential neuro-psychiatrist in the 1960's, when asked what could be done to avoid depression, replied, "I don't think that the individual can do a tremendous lot to avoid illness, except in palpably suicidal situations like smoking and over-drinking." When asked "Would it count as a great progress in medical theory and practice if you could simply give a man a shot of the right mixtures that would do the whole trick", he replied, "Naturally one would prefer the short and effective aid: experience has taught me that this is so very much more predictably effective." And, in the same interview, he was quoted as saying, "It can be an awful nuisance to have an intelligent patient."

The Alexander Principle is addressed to intelligent people and intelligent patients who are sick of being treated like morons and filled up with drugs. Some at least have begun to realise that a drugged half-life—even if it means that certain long-stay mental patients can be put out of hospital into circulation—is degrading to their dignity and to their potentialities. Such people are casting around for other answers, even though they know that such answers can never be easy.

It will now be clear that the Alexander Principle is not easy. Most people who have had practical experience of it see it as obvious, but never easy. But most people accept with avidity an approach which will give them a chance of long-term mental health, however difficult that approach may be. It is no easy panacea, but it is a major possibility of escape for many—an escape from dependence on doctors and drugs, an escape from the boringness of habitual patterns of thought and behaviour.

## The Cause of Mental Disorder

A diagnosis, as Chapter 5 has stressed, is needed both for an explanation and for a prediction. For tackling the present existing situation and for planning a "better future". How can USE be seen as an explanation, a cause, of mental disorder? How can a knowledge of USE be used for planning the future?

First we need to understand what a "cause" is—there are all sorts of causes.

If you throw a stone at a brittle glass window it will break, and under similar circumstances it would always break. But there are more causes than the actual stone. If I hadn't *wished* to throw the stone, the window would still be intact; if it had been a ping-pong ball, the window would still be intact; if the window had been as tough as a car windscreen, it might not have shattered. Three sorts of causes: 1. My wish. 2. The stone. 3. The brittleness of the window.

These are usually called:

1. Final-cause motivation: i.e., my wish for a certain end, or for the consequences-which-flow from that end, e.g., so that I can steal a diamond bracelet from the window.
2. The "efficient (or effector) cause": i.e., the actual moving factor which does it: in this case, the stone.
3. The "dispositional cause": i.e., the circumstances which make it possible—the brittleness of the glass, the absence of policemen. This disposition of the glass is a latent capacity which exhibits itself when the circumstances arise.

Let me take another example. I am frying an egg for breakfast, in a frying-pan, over a gas flame. The final cause (my motivation) is that I want the end (i.e., a fried egg).

The efficient (effector) cause is the actual gas flame: I turned on the gas—the first step: lit it, and now it burns merrily. I would not have turned it on without some sort of decision to do so—the decision, born of my "final cause".

And lastly there is the dispositional cause. An egg is disposed to coagulate when heated, because of its chemical composition.

### Which Cause?

Which of these three types of cause are we to blame for a mental disorder? Which of them can we alter?

When people put forward several explanations of something, the explanations are not really *rival* explanations—they are answers to different questions. There are as many sorts of explanations as there are questions: it is simply a matter of priorities. The causes (antecedents) which matter are the one which can be altered and usually the chief causes tend to be the one which one particular speaker thinks *should* be altered.

If, say, a car has hit a pedestrian, there are innumerable antecedents without which the accident could not have occurred. The pedestrian who was hit says it was the driver's bad brakes: the driver says the cause was the pedestrian's carelessness in stepping out into the road without looking. There may be no disagreement about the facts; both may agree that the brakes were bad and that the pedestrian did not look soon enough, and that if either of these things had been otherwise, there would have been no accident.* In the law courts we have to decide who was to blame. In medicine we not only "blame" but we seek to prescribe measures which will prevent it going on or happening again.

This stylised pedestrian/driver situation can be paralleled in disputes about the cause of mental disorder. Disputes among psychiatrists about causes could more realistically be listed as disputes about treatments. The true cause lies deep in the psyche (psychotherapy needed): the true cause lies in the brain chemistry (drugs needed): the true cause lies in conditioned reflexes (behaviour therapy needed).

These three rivals may not be clear-cut and may overlap in their methods at times, but, by and large, they remain distinct. Three different causes are postulated: three different approaches are recommended.

These three different schools of psychiatric thought range themselves around the three "causes" which I have mentioned —"dispositional causes", "final causes", and "efficient causes". The dispositionists search for a chemical or physical pre-disposition in the brain which may lead to abnormal behaviour: and since at present they only have crude chemical notions of what this might be, they use crude blunderbuss chemicals with which to alter the brain chemistry, and do not mind if they alter other chemistry, which is not faulty, at the same time. Alternatively they may use crude physical methods such as ECT or leucotomy to alter engrained brain dispositions.

The "final-causists" (the various schools of psychotherapy) work to find the decision which was once taken to "throw the stone or fry the egg", a decision which perhaps was once consciously chosen and deemed appropriate, but has now become unchosen and inappropriate. And indeed, if we try to sort out neurotic mis-use in terms of such final cause motivation, we can perhaps find out eventually (over months, years or even decades) what the patient's "game" was which started that particular tension manifestation. But by now the tension trick is so much part of him that it will not be released simply by him

* I am indebted to Anthony Flew (personal communication) for this example.

discovering why he started it. The patient may come to terms with it, but much of it remains embodied in the whole life pattern which he has evolved, and the muscular usages through which he expresses it.

The third cause—the "efficient" cause—has as its champions the schools of behaviour therapists, and right manfully do they battle, in seeking to alter the conditioned reflexes which have become embedded in the life pattern, whatever the original reason for the conditioning. But they are at a disadvantage—an unnecessary disadvantage. They do not know enough about mis-use, and they work with an ethology of *macro*-behaviour— relatively gross observable behaviour—and not at the all-important *micro*-analysis of USE.

The writers'-cramps and phobias which they tackle by aversion-therapy and deconditioning are crude stuff indeed. Their operant conditioning techniques often appear terrifyingly aggressive to anyone used to the subtlety of the Alexander concept of muscular use.

Three types of cause for mental ill-health: final cause, efficient cause, dispositional cause; ideas, muscular behaviour, physical predisposition.

The Alexander Principle—the teaching and learning of which is considered in Chapter 10—takes all three into account. Final cause—the choice—is dealt with by the remaking of the body-image, and by teaching the new faculty of "ordering". The efficient cause—the muscular reaction—is dealt with by a minuteness of muscular analysis which is undreamed of by the behaviourists.

The dispositional cause is what we have referred to in Chapter 4 as the "resting-state", which may be either unbalanced or balanced. This resting state is manifested in the patient's *general use pattern* and it is dealt with over a period of time—by a gradual re-education of the postural attitude and disposition—and not by instantaneous chemical or physical onslaught. Through it, a new disposition, based on a new USE-structure, can be built up. The Alexander re-educational procedure occupies itself with all three "causes" in its practical learning situation.

### The Alexander Approach to Mental Health

The Alexander Principle is no cure-all; but it does provide, for someone who is prepared to undertake a considerable discipline, a chance of health where previously there was only despair.

I said at the start of this chapter that much of what I would say would be at odds with the current treatment of mental disorder. The Alexander Principle makes the following points:

1. No psychological diagnosis is complete unless it takes your USE into account.
2. You may get help and insight from psychotherapy, but such insight will not in itself alter your habits of USE. Your unchanged habits of USE will provide a soil on which further mental disorder can grow.
3. Insights which you may get when in a very disturbed state of USE are not necessarily to be trusted.
4. Accordingly, it should be a priority in mental treatment to obtain the best possible resting state of balanced USE before embarking on treatment. The same applies to group therapy.
5. The success of any given treatment (whether by psychotherapy, behaviour therapy, drugs or shock treatment) should be assessed by its effect on the general USE and not just by its success in putting the patient back into circulation. There is as much USE-insanity in the streets as in the wards of our hospitals.

*Conclusion*

This chapter has taken us to the most fundamental aspect of Alexander's work—its basis in personal direction and choice, and its construction of a basic "inscape" or core-structure from which choice can be possible. It should now be clear that the Alexander Principle is neither predominantly psychological nor predominantly physical but *psycho-physical*, bridging the gap between the analysts and the behaviour therapists, between the prayers and the drugs, between psyche and soma.

The Alexander Principle proposes that if you will acquire a more balanced USE, you will be able to go into new surroundings and accept new experiences (or old experiences which have previously thrown you) without the old degree of strain. Not right away, but gradually you will find new ways of connecting up with things and people, without fear or stress.

Nowhere is this more relevant than in the sphere of Sexual Functioning, and this topic will be pursued in the next chapter.

# Chapter 8

## THE PSYCHO-MECHANICS OF SEX

SEX, WHEN RIGHT, is for most of us the most pleasant desire-able, enjoyable activity in which any of us will have the luck to engage. It takes a lifetime of study and sensitivity to explore its possibilities; it goes devastatingly wrong for all of us at times; it goes miraculously right for most of us, often when we least seem to expect or deserve it; and, like everything else, it is facilitated and it is hindered by the sensitivity of our manner of use. It is exacting and it is mysterious: we can never quite know what will switch the current off or on.

In sexual matters, there is nowadays no firm agreement about what is right and good. Variegated guilt-free sex with many partners, aided if necessary by drugs which are believed to be relatively harmless, is set against long-lasting "normal" sex, in which the same male organ is more often than not in apposition with the same female organ. On the one hand, "magic" is sought from technical variety and drugs: on the other, from an experience which can grow and develop over a lifetime of "normal" intercourse with one partner. Both sides see the other side as wrong: "obscene" on the one hand, "old-fashioned" on the other. Both seem to desire a "good" which is incompatible with the "good" which the other wants.

In a scientific society, no doubt some sociologist-cum-anthropologist-cum-psychologist could eventually produce evidence to show that matched controls—just imagine trying to get sufficient numbers, let alone following them up for at least twenty years—were happier following a variegated sex-life than the old-fashioned "normal" or vice-versa. In the absence of such unobtainable evidence, all that can be suggested are certain immediate biological principles, which will hold good for sexual behaviour whatever the culture.

Such is the power of our early training that most of us are cautious about where our sexual feelings may take us. The young adolescent girl who had been told by her mother that she must never let a man touch her, and thereafter sat rigid in buses in case a man should accidentally come into contact, seems ridiculous to us: but the initial explosion of sex at adolescence makes most people wary of where their sexual reflexes may carry them, and they may soon learn to stifle even the slightest stirrings.

The psycho-analysts have not helped in this matter. Until recently it has been thought undesirable for an analyst to have any physical contact with the patient who is being analysed, and my own re-educational work, which involves almost continuous handling and adjustment and training of the body, has seemed to some analysts to be inviting disastrous transference situations. Yet this does not take place in any harmful sense. Not only is it necessary for patients to be handled in order to learn how to use themselves properly; it is positively beneficial for them to realise that in this situation they can be touched and adjusted without fear and danger: that they are not going to be raped or feel the need to make instant onslaught on whoever happens to be around.

In *Eros denied*[35] Wayland Young has pointed out how it is that "around the thought and act of sex there hangs a confusion and a danger, a tension and a fear which far exceed those hanging over any other normal and useful part of life in our culture". In the 1970's the sexual revolution which Reich preached, has tried hard to get under way, but the revolution has been, in the main, concerned with the *physical* mechanics of sex: sex supermarkets, school instruction, the pill, easier abortion, less reluctance to make love, less social censure, better facilities for sexual voyeurism. But it is one thing to have the means and mechanics for sex: it is quite another to practice an art which can encompass the ugliness of the jerking dog and the beauty of Marcus Perennius. Plastic-doll nudity, on stage and screen, with simulated coition, tells us little or nothing about the all-important psycho-mechanics of sex which are as invisible as our breathing, as subtle as the tiny brush strokes of a Chinese calligrapher.

## Sexual Manners of Use

Sexual activity involves the sharpening of all the senses. In it, the human faculties of searching, selecting and interconnecting are employed with an intensity which is scarcely matched in any other sphere of life—at any rate for the ordinary man or woman who do not spend much time in the creative arts. In it, the workaday system of role-playing and payment for work-done no longer has any real validity: payment and acceptance, giving and rewarding, are instantaneous.

The key word is responsiveness—the responsiveness of our own body to touch and movement, the sensed response of the partner: but mainly our responsiveness to our own feelings.

We have seen from previous chapters that muscular responsiveness is a matter of "feed-back", by which our perception of sensation is adjusted and controlled by a "body construct"—by the way in which we "construe" what is happening and "construct" the muscular reaction which we would prefer.

Feed-back can be of two kinds—*negative* feed-back, in which, like a thermostat, mechanisms of balanced sensitivity adjust the temperature so that it doesn't get out of hand: or *positive* feed-back, in which each fresh stimulus adds to the intensity of the muscular reaction which is providing the stimulus, so that it provokes yet more of the stimulus: the atomic explosion is the prototype of positive feed-back, in which a chain reaction of stimulus and response becomes uncontrollable in a matter of milliseconds.

Sexual responsiveness likewise, quite obviously, involves both negative and positive feed-back. By negative feed-back, sexual stirrings are not allowed to go over too soon into an uncontrollable positive feed-back situation. But such is the cultural fear of positive feed-back that even the slightest stirrings of sexual pleasure may come to be stifled, and the opposite poles of sexual deadness and sexual explosion come to constitute an "either-or" situation, which leaves a vast intermediate territory unsensed and unexplored.

## Erotism

Our language has a shortage of words which refer to this vast intermediate territory and there are few words in our language for experiencing the erotic pleasure which does not lead to immediate orgasmic discharge. To feel "sexy" or "randy" implies a state of lust which already sounds either naughty or reprehensible. Far be it from me to decry the whole language and lore of the dirty story which we learn from our earliest school-days and which remain, graffiti scribbled on the walls of our cerebral cortex, long after more important and beautiful ideas have disappeared. The young lady of Spain is with me for life, along with snatches of the Prayer Book, reiterated in youth, not heard recently but easily evoked: the night-time prayer against the devil who "like a roaring lion walketh about seeking whom he may devour, which of ourselves we cannot resist".

The erotic words which we do not seem to possess are words for experiences which do not nightly devour us with passion and which we have no particular need to resist. To talk, for example, of "eroticism" already brings in a boudoir tinge of a sensuality, far from the everyday pleasure in our muscles and skin which should be part of our moment-to-moment bodily awareness. "Erotism" seems to me perhaps a better word, if it can be freed from the overtones of guilt which the Freudian phrase "auto-erotism" gave it. Words may not seem all that important, but words are signposts, and we sorely need words for this realm of awareness and bodily pleasure which may have no immediate sexual implication, although it is a part of the sexual spectrum.

## Muscular Texture

Erotism is concerned as much with the *texture* of bodily experiences as with its *structure*. When we lose texture, we lose livingness in our bodies: we feel blunted or deadened: we may feel action occurring (action to gain ends), but the satisfaction lies more in the achievement than in the actual doing. The accent is on specific objects, isolated from their background, instead of on the texture of the background.

The Gestalt psychologists, although out of fashion nowadays, encouraged us to think of perception in terms of "figure" and "ground". To take a simple example—a countryman who comes up to London finds the traffic noise deafening, the filthy streets disgusting. The noise and the dirt stand out as "figure" against the groundwork of his expectations. But a Londoner has long since lost the traffic noise in a general background—he does not notice it. Instead he notices perhaps the number of an approaching bus or other "figures" important to himself. A police-car siren may stand out momentarily as a "figure", or perhaps a jet-plane, but even these soon may become background for more immediate figures.

In the control of sexual perception we are dealing very much with such a "figure-ground" situation, in which, by thought and by movement we can turn our attention from one part to another, from one "figure" to another, until by muscular sensitivity and feed-back we gradually build up a generally heightened awareness of bodily texture. We should not be simply concerned with structure, but with the development and recognition of texture.

Texture—as the computers have proved, whether it be in the micro-analysis of a painting or of a fabric—is based on *order*; and it is based on the repetition of order, in a certain progression along certain hierarchies. If hierarchical order is lost, texture is lost. If a picture is painted in the wrong order, not only is integrated texture lost, but paint which is applied too late may run and "weep" because its molecular structure will not marry with the paint already applied.

Texture in the context of sexual perception is built up of a repetitive order which gives an on-going progression from one state to the next. In sexual perception, as in everyday living, the textural quality of our muscular experience is obtained by a correct order of the structural USE of our body, and by a refusal to fix the on-going progression of movement by muscular tension. Texture is destroyed by tension.

Such tension may be a deliberate defence, or it may be unconscious although once deliberate. When sexual feeling begins to invade the texture of our muscular experience, it may not always be welcome. Negative feed-back is usually adequate to regulate and enjoy the more everyday felicities of Erotism (although even these may be blocked by over-tension): but when there is transition to an on-going sexual progression, in which positive feed-back begins to take over, muscle-tension brakes are liable to be clamped right down.

Characteristic of the beginnings of such on-going sexual feelings are sensations which can be described as "floating" or "falling", or "lightness" or even of gluey "heavyness". Many of us are afraid of such sensations. The sensation of being anaesthetised gives something of such a sense of progressive falling into ourselves; and most of us will have experienced certain situations in which, momentarily, all visible means of support disappear and we feel ourselves falling.

It needs a certain courage not to attempt to counteract such feelings of falling or floating. To "let go" into someone's arms may be infinitely reassuring, but it does not mean that, once the weight is off the feet, it becomes possible to let go all the habitual dystonic patterns of our lifetime. Even the most erudite employer of the most erudite sexual skills and approaches will find that both he and his partner are thrown out of gear and out of pleasure by dystonic patterns which seem to appear for no apparent reason and which may effectively kill off feeling and desire and the natural progression towards orgasm: or may modify both the quality and the timing of feelings so that both are unsatisfactory.

It would be a mistake to make it sound as if most people are making heavy weather of their loving most of the time; but it would be rare to find someone who does not occasionally run into trouble, and there are some people for whom love-making is never very satisfactory and in whom the onward "textural" progression of muscular release is constantly replaced by feelings of tension. Instead of erotic feelings of floating and lightness, hey will experience feelings of trying hard and effort—indeed there may be cramp and pain—or there may be a deadening and blunting of sensation.

When texture is replaced by tension, sexual responsiveness may come to be equated with relatively violent movement. Many women feel that they must exhibit by the intensity of their body movements and the wildness of their breathing and voice that they are in no way frigid: they may even persuade themselves in so doing that this is what it is all about.

Sexual responsiveness is not a matter of wild movement except in so far as positive feed-back releases the reflexes. It is a matter of the handling of subtle differential feelings of expansion and swelling, of systole and diastole, throughout the whole body. In a word, it is about the balancing of muscular reactions, and it is about the correct "ordering" of muscular reactions, to produce texture.

## The Order of Reaction

The ordering of muscular reactions was discussed in the previous chapter; and, just like the orchestral conductor who allowed the demands of his baton to over-ride the needs of the rest of his body, many people, by over-concentration on specifically genital movements and sensations, begin to induce in themselves a general fixation and rigidity which in its turn restricts the natural progression through the many phases of love making. (In passing, it is nice to remember that according to

the fourteenth-century Cabalists the total number of angels is
301,655,722. This number is not surprising when we recall that
the different phases of love making were considered to have
forty-seven different angels, each responsible for each developing phase: and that it was recommended that appropriate, if
brief, acknowledgement should be paid to each angel in passing
from one phase to the next. This certainly is appropriate to
what might be termed "centimetre" sex, as opposed to the ten
second sprinters.)

Such "angel-ology"[36] does not imply a lack of spontaneity.
But it does see the highest pleasure as involving the mind as well
as the perineum, and it has lessons for those who think that
sexual functioning can safely be left to our instinctive drives and
desires. It is fondly believed by some that love-making has its
own natural progressions which will work automatically in a
reasonably satisfying manner. Yet doctor's clinics, marriage
guidance clinics and the divorce courts are full of examples of
failed sexual co-operation, of impotence and frigidity: and even
when one partner gets by, the other partner may be putting a
brave face on a lack of orgastic satisfaction.

The orgasm has sometimes been called the "white woman's
burden", since failure to achieve it is thought to be shameful,
carrying with it a stigma of inadequacy and insensitivity. This
in its turn leads to a disparaging of the orgasm—it has been
likened by some to an involuntary sneeze—and to an almost
Victorian acceptance by some women of the uncompleted
sexual act. And this in turn leads to a more and more one-sided
masculine performance, and to a tendency to shut off—by
excessive muscular tension—the early stirrings of erotic feeling
which experience has shown usually to be frustrated. And since
erotic feelings take a lot of shutting off, there has to be a
correspondingly vigilant creation of muscular over-contraction
until such contractions become part and parcel of the character
structure. Love-making, quite categorically, does not necessarily work properly just by the light of nature; and where that
"Nature" is distorted by mis-use, there is liable to be a corresponding lack of lasting satisfaction.

*Sexual Perception*

It is possible to have the largest library of sexual information
that the literate world can produce and comprehensive access

to the facilities required, and yet still to misfire. It is the familiar story of the differrence between knowing *how* and knowing *that*. Sexual performance is in no way different from any other skill in its ultimate dependence on practice rather than theory. The stage may be set: the dating, the soft lights; the marriage, the desire; the adjuncts and the adjuvants; the reflexes which carry their rhythms from swamp and forest to the comfort of the civilised bedroom; and yet something is still needed. Civilised man needs to make his sexual experience new not every time, but every moment of every time.

How is each sexual moment to be creatively different? How can two people avoid the silly traps into which their more stupid reflexes will lead them? In the language of the Alexander Principle—how can awareness of USE be adapted into a subtle instrument of sexual communication?

There are helpful parallels to be drawn between our approach to works of art and our engagement in love-making. The thing which distinguishes a work of art from kitsch is that it is something to which we can return again and again, noticing new aspects, revising initial impressions, discovering intricacies and nuances.

Some very obvious parallels suggest themselves—as many people have noted—in the world of music. An immature listener may at first be able to pick out from a Beethoven symphony only certain melodic passages, rhythmic patterns and dominant instruments.*[37] As he grows more experienced, he will begin to notice variations in themes or patterns, including perhaps some inversions, abbreviated versions or transposed sections; he will be able to concentrate on different instruments and follow their development through the piece or through extended passages. He will have sufficient patience to listen to each movement in its sequence, and to notice difference in moods.

As he becomes a more accomplished listener he will be able to discern relationships between disparate sections, and he will have a heightened freedom which allows him to focus now on one, now on another aspect of rhythm, melody, harmony and instrumentation, and perhaps to focus on several of these

---

* This example is prompted by Howard Gardner in "Figure and Ground in Aesthetic Perception", *British Journal of Aesthetics*, Winter 1972, although he does not draw a parallel with sexual experience.

aspects at the same time. Eventually he comes to know it so well that he can re-create it in his mind, criticise certain perform-ances of it, anticipate its implications and possibilities. In spite of such sophistication, he may at times employ only a primitive perception, and focus merely on the melody and the rhythm, ignoring other aspects; but unlike less developed listeners, he has the option of returning to a more differentiated and articulated apprehension of the piece, if he desires.

In discussing such a sensitive musical appreciator, I don't think that I need draw heavy-handed parallels with sex-appreciation, except perhaps to point out that, in sexual activity, one is more in the position of the orchestral player, producing as well as listening to the sound, than of a member of an audience: and that for many of us, this will be about the most creative and artistic act in which we will engage.

## The Background to Sexual Activity

Three parts of the body, besides the actual sex organs, need to be thought about during love-making, since all three areas may produce unhelpful tension. All three have to be thought about in different ways, since all three can inhibit sexual flow. The three parts are the muscles of the head and neck; the muscles of the chest and abdomen as they affect breathing; and the muscles of the lower back, pelvis and thighs as they affect genital movement. (The arms and legs obviously can also become tense and mis-used in sexual activity; but, by and large, they will behave fairly well so long as the pelvis is free, and so long as the shoulder, hip and knee joints will actually move.

We have considered to some extent the tensions which arise in the head and neck region (Alexander's "Primary Control"). It may be helpful to consider the dystonic patterns which can arise around the activity of breathing. Not only during sexual activity but in many other ways, breathing is inseparable from the handling of the emotional life of each one of us.

The connection between sexual feeling and breathing has been frequently stressed before. Ancient Yoga disciplines pre-scribed complicated—and to all intents impossible—regimes of taking in air through one nostril down to the genital area where it was to be circulated around before being brought up to be expelled through the other nostril. Recently breathing tech-niques have again come into prominence with the work of

Wilhelm Reich. I first encountered Reich's ideas in the US in 1949, and was impressed then by his account of "muscle-armouring"—states of tension which prevent the full experience of sexuality.

Reich's account of the stages of the orgasm was masterly, but he sadly mis-fired over his concept of breathing. Lacking an adequate concept of USE, he laid down a number of muscular and breathing techniques which, after the first novelty wears off, are apt to leave basic dystonic patterns scarcely altered. The violence of his breathing and pelvic movements—although perhaps giving brief emotional release to some really frozen-up and unresponsive people—are too disconnected from the every-day living of these people to be of basic usefulness. The subtlety of Reich's written work does not seem to be matched by a corresponding subtlety in practice.

Indeed, similar breathing techniques are to be found even in the folk-lore of middle-class England. One crude way of inducing sexual feeling is to breathe out several times deeply from the upper chest to the genital area whilst at the same time slightly contracting the thighs and buttocks, and something like this was described by Reich. I am reliably informed by a splendid headmistress that when she was young, in the girls' dorm at her particular school, they used to say "Come on, girls, let's URGE", and this was accomplished by breathing out and contracting somewhat in the manner described. This preceded Reich by at least twenty years. I would back Roedean against Reich any day of the week, and no doubt the folk-lore of many countries contains similar and such-like advice to young maidens and men.

I have no such esoteric advice to give, but simply the advice that one must learn not to fix the breathing through excessive or wrongly-distributed muscle-tension: and that if one is emotion-ally disturbed either by flaws in the sexual flow or other matters, it is always helpful to try to introduce order into the sequence of breathing. It is important not to *start* to breathe in by a move-ment which raises the upper chest and breast-bone, although this region will normally be raised a little at the *end* of breathing in; and it is helpful to learn to release tension in the shoulders and upper chest as you begin to *breathe out*—this is the only point in the breathing-cycle at which upper-chest tensions can be released without upsetting the cycle. And the more that breathing can be thought of as an activity of the middle of the back, and of the back and sides of the abdomen, the less the opportunity for harmful tension.

*How to Lie Down*

Sex-manuals are filled with innumerable varieties of coital positions: sitting, standing, lying, kneeling, this way and that. But, by and large, most love-making involves at least one partner in lying down: and usually one or the other's legs are going to be relatively straightened out at the hip joint.

It is interesting that, in the past, when people have talked about the evolution of the "upright" posture, they are usually thinking about standing or sitting upright. But few animals except man can *lie* with their legs straightened-out from the pelvis. We do not automatically know how to lie down properly with our legs out straight, any more than we know how to stand and sit upright properly. If there is to be an adequate and subtle adjustment of the pelvis and its muscles during coitus, more needs to be known about a balanced resting position of the pelvis, when lying down.

A few points may help self-analysis.

*Lie down on the back (see fig. 32) with the elbows out to the side and the knees pointing upwards towards the ceiling. In this position there should be no arch in the lower back. It should be impossible to insert a hand between the lower back and the surface beneath. If in fact the back is arched in this position, it will be due to two things: the front of the chest at its lowest point is being pushed forward too much and the whole chest cage needs to lie much flatter against the supporting surface, with the shoulder-blades widening apart; or, the second, and more common reason, is that the pelvis is arching forwards towards the thighs. If the fingers are placed about one and a half inches from the navel on either side and then run down towards the pelvis, they will strike a jutting-out piece of the pelvis on each side. These "spines" of the pelvis, when the back is arched, will be too close to the thighs. The buttocks need to be dropped slightly down and away from the middle of the back—this may be quite a big adjustment if it is very arched at rest—and in so doing the pelvic spines will drop slightly towards the abdominal cavity. If the fingers are kept on the spines as this movement is made, there will be an impression that the spines are slightly separating away from each other. The movement I have been describing—as will be apparent—is very much concerned in the approximation of genital surfaces. During coitus such a movement by both men and women when accompanied by a slight buttock contraction will constitute the inwards sexual connection: the slight releasing of tension the outward movement.*

*The composite movement of moving the pelvis forward, which involves a slight flattening of the back, will also correspond to a widening across the back of the chest which takes place when breath is taken in. The slight tilting of the pelvis back as the genitals are separated is accompanied by breathing out and a slight relaxation of vaginal musculature or perineal musculature in the man.*

*The correction of an unduly arched pelvis and back is of course a much larger adjustment than the minuscule "plateau" movements of coitus. But it will be clear that, given a range of movement from A to B, the resting position should be about half way between A and B. If—as in the case of the arched back—the resting position is much closer to A than to B, then the potentiality for muscular relaxation and contraction, lengthening and shortening, is markedly limited. And if certain muscles around the pelvis are held almost permanently over-contracted, the scope for progressional movement is small. The muscles which are usually found to be over-contracted are the buttock muscles themselves, plus the muscles of the front and inside of the upper thigh.*

*When lying down as I have described, with the fingers on the spines of the pelvis, one side may be found to be higher, i.e., closer to the ceiling than the other: or one spine may be raised up closer to the chest on one side. If this is the case, it is likely that the weight is being distributed more along one side of the back than the other. It should be relatively easy to distribute the weight equally, and this will predispose to a better release of tension in the buttocks and back.*

### Muscular Blocks and Interferences

Sexual activity, like breathing, is not "about" anything. It can of course be said that it is about producing children or pleasure one with another, just as breathing can be used for producing speech. But the basic processes of sex and breathing are not about anything. A process is going on and a process is something which you must let happen—not interfere with. There are no rules for the right way to engage in these processes: only, perhaps, rules for what not to do. In our moment-to-moment living, we too often make this mistake of *doing* some fixed thing, instead of engaging in some process: we *Read, copulate, eat, speak,* instead of engaging in a *process* of reading, a *process* of copulating, a *process* of eating, a *process* of speaking.

As human beings, we are so constructed that we work best when we concern ourselves with process. When we are concerned with *ends* rather than *means*, our bodies don't function as well. The human organism is built for process-operation, not for end-gaining.

As we engage in a process, something unexpected may happen and if we are not end-gaining, we can notice it and adjust ourselves to it. The psycho-mechanics of sex must learn not to interfere with processes and rhythms which arise and develop spontaneously: if there are to be new perceptions, it must learn to regulate without interference.

Interference takes place at two levels. At the gross mechanical level, postures which have been developed over many years will limit mobility either because the surrounding joints have become stiff with mis-use, or because sexual leverages produce pain and cramp in already over-tense muscles. It is not surprising that mis-used man has in recent years embarked on a variety of sexual practices which need involve only a bare minimum of mechanical mobility. When the lower back, pelvis and limbs can move freely, there is surely enough potential sexual experience here to last several lifetimes.

At a more subtle level, muscular tension patterns of great complexity interfere with the quality of sensation which is fed back to the brain from the on-going processes of muscular movement and contraction. The mechanisms of balanced sensitivity (which have already been touched on in the previous chapter) are liable to become blocked by tension, and any attempt to unblock a feeling of deadness by specific action or movement is liable to fail. Under such circumstances the capacity to give orders and directions to the main core-structure, i.e., the head, neck, back and breathing, is the quickest way to unblock a purely local tension. We have seen that a writer's cramp cannot be adequately treated by concentrating on releasing the muscles of the wrist and hand, but there must first be attention to the co-ordination of the neck and shoulder. In the same way pelvic tensions—once they have become maldistributed—require a release of tension first in the neck and shoulders and then an improved use of the middle of the back and thorax.

*Arthur K. was a pianist of 52 who had been married for three years but had never managed to consummate his marriage. He had previously been receiving psychotherapy and he told me that his only experience of orgasm had been in his late teens when he had been severely reproved for masturbating. He assured me that since that time there had been no sexual outlet, and that his psycho-therapist blamed his deadness on his unsatisfactory early experience.*

*He had been referred to me primarily for treatment of a painful arm and shoulder and it was several weeks before he admitted to his sexual problem. I had already begun to tackle with him the excessive and mal-distributed tension patterns around his lower back and legs and he was gradually learning to release some of the tension. He progressed to the point when I was able to show him a co-ordination of his lower back and pelvis in which his use became normally balanced. At this point he blurted out "I can't do that; it makes me think of the sexual act."*

*We persevered to familiarise him with the new co-ordination in the easy safety of my training conditions, and he arranged to see me the following week. When he returned, he told me an extraordinary story of returning home and seeing a nude photograph in one of the colour magazines which aroused him greatly to the point when he was able thereupon to consummate his marriage—history does not relate what his wife thought about it—and thereafter he had been able to repeat the experience.*

This strange story illustrates the fact that we may know quite well what the factors were which led us in the past to set up a muscular defensive block: but insight into the origin will not necessarily untie muscular blocks which over a period of years have become incorporated into our whole basic manner of use. In this case it was only after the blocks had been undone and the patient felt reassured and at ease in the unblocked state, that he was able to respond without blocking when away from me.

Such stories which arise again and again in the re-educational situation, usually illustrate the fear which people have of unusual feelings. Most muscular blocks and defences were chosen, at the time, for what seemed to be a good reason— usually to avoid pain or rebuke (the so-called "traumatic avoidance response"); rather like the child who learns to call fire a "No-No", after being scared from it by being burnt and by his parents shouting. The on-going sexual sensation of free movement and flowing can also become a "No-No".

Such a patient has to learn to disregard his usual body construct: he has to learn no longer to construe his feelings as a "No-No". He can learn through the Alexander Principle to occupy his thinking with the projection of a new body-construct, which in its turn will feed back new sensations to his brain—sensations which will have no fear-connotation.

## Sexual Disorders

The late Joan Malleson wrote to me about the relevance which she saw in such an approach to such sexual tensions as vaginismus: this is another of the muscular blocks which can come to lead a life of its own, outside of its place in the general muscular hierarchy. Similarly, a pre-existent muscular dystonia can lead to such disorders as premature ejaculation and can be helped by a general re-ordering of the body-construct. Such "re-ordering" is relevant not only to the actual timing and performance of a sexual act, but to the role which habit and compulsion play in the desire for sexual outlet, and in the mental states of preparations and "guilty longing" which occupy many people's thoughts to a greater or lesser degree. (A recent survey indicated that most young adults think about sex once every 15 minutes.)

But many people never get to the point of even attempting the sexual act. In our present "free society", shyness and loneliness still abound. Much has been written about the tragedy of being "taken unprepared", but there is the even greater tragedy of being prepared but never allowing oneself to be taken. Many people seem to spend their time putting their money into the telephone box, going through all the work of dialling the number they want but at the critical moment, when they have only to "press Button A" to get in contact, they press Button B to get their money back. And even when they can hear "their own true love" speaking at the other end, urging them to press Button A, their nerve fails and they press Button B again.

However free the social opportunities may seem, shyness and loneliness continue to be induced by muscular blocks and defences which prevent the making and taking of opportunity.

## Freedom-in-thought

Alexander was dead before what the 1970's called "The Permissive Society" was upon us. But his views on Freedom were often expressed: that *external* freedom to carry out certain actions (freedom-*of*-thought-and-action) is far less important than our own personal freedom *in* thought and action. He rightly saw that, even when we have the most perfect conditions of environment, company, and cash, our happiness is still determined by our capacity to think newly and freely; and that such a capacity is limited by our manner of use.

It is a great improvement that young (and old) people can now find easier sexual outlets without guilt, and without the feeling that someone will disapprove. The sexual drive is of basic strength: the human body is prodigal of sexual functioning. Not only are millions of spermatozoa made available for a task which one alone can complete, but some degree of sexual pleasure is available even to a severely sick person. The brain is claimed to be the last region of the body to die, but the gonads must run it a pretty close second. The sick man, the evil man, the old man, do not easily lose their sexual pleasure.

I remember, when working as a house surgeon to the late Kenneth Walker, being summoned out of bed to the private ward in the middle of the night by an elderly clergyman whose prostate had been removed and who found to his dismay that he could not obtain an erection. He was not himself, of course, and a few weeks later must have blushed at the thought. He was pacified by my reassurance, but it does indicate how persistent is the sexual urge, and why moral codes and punishments have seemed necessary in the past to curb such a persistent urge: and why the individual may feel the social need to adopt blocking tactics.

Innumerable treatises have been written on moral philosophy, on free-will and choice. Innumerable theologies have presented views on the good life; about heavens and abominations and the wrath to come. You would think that out of all this lot, somewhere someone would be able to give a young (or old) person really useful advice about whether or not, and when, to indulge in sexual activity. Ninety-five per cent of us masturbate or have masturbated at some time: a considerable number will be wondering in the future whether or not to masturbate. Dry textbooks of moral philosophy would surely become best-sellers if they genuinely considered, say, this one sexual dilemma.

But most of the treatises on moral philosophy are about such things as why I decide to cross the road to go to a tobacconist's

shop, or what it means to call a strawberry a "good strawberry".
They do not tell a young man, who feels guilt after masturbating, much about this fascinating stimulus-response situation in
which free-will and determinism are on opposite sides of the
pitch.

Perhaps I have an exaggerated view of its importance. The
English public school system—the one I know—insisted on little
adolescent boys jumping out of bed at 7.00 a.m., and, at my
particular establishment, pyjamas had to be removed, and there
was a quick run down the stairs to an icy cold shower where—
observed by jeering older boys—a jet of cold water played over
the anatomy. Now it was an observable fact that most of the
small adolescents were in a state of modified erection:
modified that is to say by the icy dash. One boy indeed kept
his father's large hunter watch by his bed, and applied it to his
genitals in the hope of taking the impetus out of his tumescence
before the embarrassing run was made. Many of the boys—
such of them as one talked to—were plagued by guilt. Others
made a thorough Portnoy of their situation; and one of them
reckoned to achieve two orgasms—watched by an admiring
group of friends—between the ringing of the bell for prayers and
turning up spick and span in hall two minutes later for the
benediction.

For what it is worth—and as the sympathetic recipient of
countless "confessions" from worried patients—I have never
seen anyone whose sexual apparatus was harmed in the process,
nor do massive masturbators seem eventually to fail more than
less frequent performers to achieve successful coitus: it is just
that a few of them may lose the exploratory drive which the
demand of an unsatisfied sexual urge would give them. And
most of them are perpetually worried by the problem of "shall
I, shan't I".

The only observation I can make about the morals of whether
to have sex or not with or without a sexual partner, and when,
is the phrase which I culled from Professor Sparshott's excellent
monograph *An Enquiry into Goodness*.[38] He puts forward the view
that "To say that a thing is good is to say that it is such as to
satisfy the desires and needs of the person or persons concerned". It takes Professor Sparshott a whole book to sort out
the implications of this one sentence, but the advantage is that
it does refer to other people as well as to oneself and it can also

include oneself not only as one is today, here and now, but oneself in a month's time, a year's time, five years' time. Oneself at a later date is very much one of the persons whose needs have to be thought about—obviously oneself in five years' time with syphilis or a genital stricture or a fatherless child has to be considered, as also has oneself with a "frozen" insensitive sexual orientation due to over-caution and timidity. As with most things though—unfortunately—we don't know till we have tried; but at any rate, one can try to avoid making the same mistakes too often and one can try to avoid being frightened off by one or two bad experiences with unsuitable people. One can avoid, say, labelling oneself homosexual after one or two disastrous fumblings with the opposite sex or after one or two enjoyable experiences with the same sex. And, perhaps, one can learn, from a knowledge of the Alexander Principle, that if the USE of certain partners is muddled and disorganised, they may be pleasant companions over a short period, but the unpleasant and difficult habits which are already observable in their USE, will make life miserable for both partners over a long period. Alternatively, on the obverse side of this particular coin, we may perhaps find it easier to salvage something out of a relationship which still has much to commend it, *if we can learn to attend to our own mis-use patterns*: or if this does not help, a more stable manner-of-use may give the courage to make, or take, the break-up.

# Chapter 9

## PERSONAL GROWTH

THE TWENTIETH CENTURY has seen an increasing sophistication into the possibilities and perils of up-bringing. The Freudian and Kleinian emphasis on the importance of the child's early years has led some parents to instant guilt, since it appears that, no matter what we do, even our everyday encounters with our children can lead to far-reaching consequences. I knew one otherwise intelligent philosopher who put himself, his wife and his three children all under psycho-analysis—the oldest child was six—and such was the intensity of his belief in it that, when one child fell from a tree and cut himself badly, it was a toss up whether they would go first to a casualty department (to have the cut sewn up) or to the analyst (to have the right slant put on it all).

Latterly Winnicott, in a revulsion from such instant guilt, was at pains to emphasise that "mother knows best", and that parents should follow their natural expertise. One of my patients expressed this view nicely when she was writing to me about the similarity of my handling of a patient and the parent's handling of a child.

Years ago my husband took a film of me putting our second son aged five months into a pram. When I saw the film afterwards I was struck by the obviously deft skilled way I handled the child. I was staggered because I had never thought of myself in this way nor had I realised that a mother's relationship with the child bore a relationship to that of any craftsman to his material. It is fascinating to watch the positive *going with* his material that the carpenter or potter etc., develop through constant contact with it. Mothers and their babies can achieve this: and I in my capacity as a patient with you can be quite content to become absorbed in my body as a material that has a particular grain or plasticity in it, if one can eliminate the need to *react*. In my case this is the key to the success of it. In everyday life I am a powerful reactor and in the sessions I am content to become a material, reacting only to the teacher.

This "natural dexterity" line contains a certain amount of truth, but just as with love-making, natural *dexterity* (along with the other wisdoms of the body) becomes only too often a natural *stupidity*, when it is based on end-gaining. It may be that some mothers do have an inborn dexterity in handling the young infant but many other factors soon come in. The sad fact is that if a mother is herself an end-gainer and the possessor of faulty tension patterns, she will very soon begin to influence her child in the wrong direction.

From the moment of birth the helpless child is dependent on the handling and the ideas of its mother. It is picked up jerkily or smoothly, crossly or kindly: its head and back are supported carefully or ignorantly. It lies face down or face up, according to fashion. It is allowed to yell or it is picked up on demand. It connects with the mother, on breast or bottle, and as it suckles, it likes to gaze long and deep into the mother's eyes, with a unified visual connection which it may never know again. But in the main, its connection is kinaesthetic, through muscles and movement, and it is quick to pick up feelings of tension, timidity or rejection from the bodily rather than the visual contact: and especially from the mother's hands, since another person's hands are a most powerful stimulus towards good or bad USE.

As the nervous system develops, the stage of sitting up is reached. One American "Alexander" teacher, Alma Frank, carried out a painstaking study of how children first sit up, and she showed that if children are made to sit up before their nervous systems have adequately matured, they loll about, with the beginnings of mis-use, and their backs develop a side-ways curvature. She took some beautiful pictures of children who were left to adopt the sitting-up position on their own, at their own chosen time. She showed that if they were left alone, they would adopt a balanced upright position of the back, with the head in the position of Alexander's "Primary Control".

The child should be left to initiate movements in its own time. To pull a child up by the arms too soon is to ask for mis-use. By the age of twelve months, over 90% of children will have developed a sideways curvature in their backs. The urge to place a child on a pot and leave it sitting there hopefully should be restrained, until such time as it can support its own back properly without lolling and collapsing. Likewise, the various landmarks of standing and taking the first steps to walk should not be hurried: the child should not be "stood-up" or encouraged to walk until its *own* balanced USE enables it to do so.

## The Standing Child

There are few more beautiful sights than the well-used child standing with legs slightly flexed in the Alexander balance and with the vertebral column well back, counter-balanced by the head. But by the age of 2½ or 3 years, things are already beginning to go sadly wrong.

The child at this age will have adopted many of the tempos and tensions of the parents. The family mood—or the mood of one dominant parent—will already be inducing its associated posture in the child. This process will continue with us for all our lives, since, if we are to share the constructions which people we admire put on things, we are eventually forced to share something of their manner of USE—a "posture-swapping", in which they may also adopt something of our posture. We imitate the attitudes of those we admire in order to make contact easier: it is through USE that we construe our surroundings and since a major part of our connecting-up with other people consists of an attempt to share the construction which they put on things, we have to adapt our USE to theirs. In a situation in which we are dominant, they will adapt their own USE to ours: "posture-swapping" is rarely fifty-fifty; it tends to favour the dominant person.

The effect on the child of this projective posture-swapping will begin to be a personally idiosyncratic mixture of tensions and predispositions of structures and potential attitudes, an amalgam of nature and not-so-much nurture as selective-preference on the part of the *child* as he brings up his parents as best he can!

## Schooling

The child is not long under the sole influence (good or bad) of its parents, nor are they for long the sole objects of the child's influence. Much has been written on the stages of physical and psychological growth from the primary schooling stage up-wards: too much to summarise in such a short chapter as this by someone as medically orientated as myself. But even to a relative outsider to the educational scene it is obvious that much more is known nowadays about the various stages of personal growth during the school years. Piaget's views on cognitive development have led to wide-spread curriculum changes. Psychologists in general are providing much better ways of assessing the individual child's possibilities and hindrances. Gesell has detailed the stages through which a child's personality will mature, and Tanner[39] has put a welcome emphasis on the widely different speeds at which children grow up and mature.

But, behind all these facts and statistics, the fact remains that each one of us is an individual, and we each of us have our own unique way of seeing things. It might at first seem an impossible task to generalise about personal growth, since every waking moment of every waking child's life is uniquely its own: it has its own unique parents, its own unique home: its own unique reactions to school and learning: its own unique physical possibilities and barriers: and, eventually, its own unique way of connecting-up with things and people.

The story of personal growth has indeed progressed far from the stimulus/response psychology of the behaviourists and the hell-fire of the churchmen. But, *pace* Freud, Gesell, Piaget, Winnicott *et alia*, it has had little to say so far about USE. And since USE is the compendious Gladstone-bag within which the Freudian Unconscious, the maturation processes of Gesell, the cognitive development of Piaget, and the "natural" behaviour of Winnicott, must lie; and since USE is observable—and alterable—by both the child and his teacher or parent (once they know how) it must be given as high a priority in education as in medicine: higher, indeed, since the problem is one of preventive medicine in the widest sense.

*Use Analysis*

What sort of things should we be on the look out for when we look at the USE of a child or adolescent? It will be clear from the previous chapters that many of the subtle forms of mis-use are not at all obvious on a superficial examination. Nevertheless, repeated attitudes—mental and physical—soon begin to leave an obvious mark on a person. So let us as systematically as possible consider some of the most common and obvious mis-uses which can be detected by almost anyone if they look.

## The Head and Neck

Let us take a schematic head and look at it sideways on (fig. 19a). Let us take the 7 neck vertebrae which connect it to the chest (fig. 19b). Now let us look again at the collection of sideways X-rays of the head and neck (plate 18). The most common mis-use involves a pull of the head back and a drop forward of the neck (plate 18a, b, c, d and fig. 19c) but there are many variations. Sometimes there is an over-straightening of the neck (plate 18e, and fig. 19d).

Let us look at a head and neck from the *back* and add a few more vertebrae—those in the "hump" at the upper part of the chest at the back (fig. 19e).

Many people will be able to see in a mirror that they have developed a habit of slightly pulling one ear down towards the shoulder (fig. 19f), as shown by the level of the lobe of the ear. If this occurs it leads to a compensatory twist in the neck, usually in the lower part of the neck and the "hump".

It happens to be a fact that this is a difficult place to X-ray, at least in routine X-rays of the neck and chest: either the neck is X-rayed or the chest is X-rayed—the junction area tends to be ignored. Quite small twists in this area (a cervico-dorsal scoliosis) tend to be ignored, but they indicate quite considerable

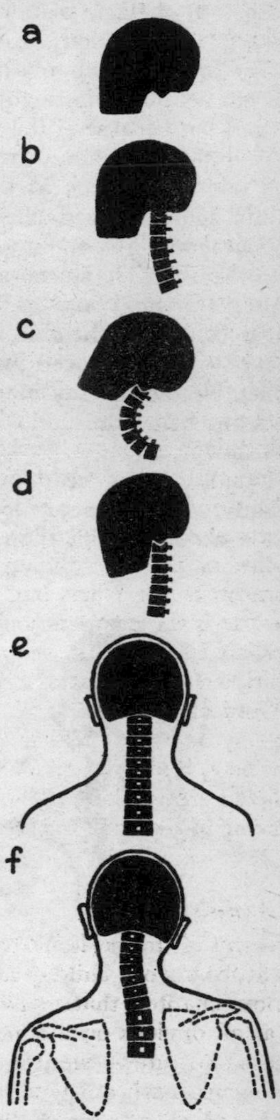

Figure 19

upsets in the muscle balance in the neck (X-ray plate 22).

Look at the line of muscles as they come out of the neck towards the shoulder (figure 20 and plate 19b).

The line will probably be lower on one side than the other, not just because being right or left-handed has made the muscle bigger, but because of the structural mis-use—the scoliosis.

With this imbalance, there will probably be more tension on one side of the neck at the back than on the other side—a fruitful source of headache and neck tension pain: or there will be more tension in one sterno-mastoid muscle, in front, than on the other side. The sterno-mastoid is the thin muscle which runs from the mastoid bone to the top of the breast bone—it will be felt to contract if the chin is pulled down on to the throat, and if the fingers are placed just above the inner ends of the collar bones. Needless to say many other muscles on the sides of the neck and below the chin will contract if the chin is pulled down like this.

Usually, if the head pulls to one side, it will also rotate slightly, so that someone looking from the back would see more of the jaw on one side than the other. An established rotation or

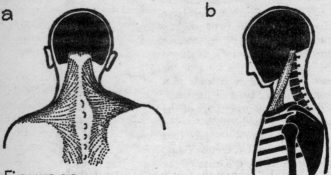

Figure 20

sideways contraction of the head will lead to an asymmetry in the face and perhaps to slight occlusion troubles, since the jaw will be opening sideways. And to that most distressing symptom, the clicking jaw.

Whilst we are discussing the head, look at the eyes. Is there a frown? Wrinkles there may be, according to age, but a deeply fixed frown can usually be released a little without loss of social seriousness (if indeed this type of frowning seriousness is ever needed). And the jaws may be held too tightly together—leading in some cases to teeth grinding. The tension will relax if the lower jaw is dropped rather in the drooling manner of the village idiot. When the jaws are closed, the lower teeth should not touch the upper teeth, but should lie just behind them. When the jaw opens it should first drop a very small distance down and then should move slightly forward, in the manner in which a bull dog holds his lower teeth pushed forward. Many jaws are permanently held in an "undershot" position, held back into the throat, not because it was inherited, but because it is held there by habit. And, of course, some people reckon that their chins are big and ugly and hold them in to try to make them look smaller—a dubious cosmetic advantage for which high cost is paid in terms of tension and fixation.

Whilst on the topic of jaws, a word must be said about stammering. In recent years, leading speech therapists have realised and acknowledged how fundamental the Alexander Principle is in their re-educational work, and I have seen many intractable stammerers greatly helped by re-education along these lines. Most of the leading speech training colleges in Britain now know about and use the Principle as a fundamental part of their training.

### The Chest

We have already seen that it is easy to develop a sideways twist where the neck joins the back (fig. 20). This is usually accompanied by a throwing of the chest sideways in the opposite direction to the head. The chest (and collar bones in front) which should lie something like figure 21a instead lies as in figure 21b (see page 140).

The collar bone on the side to which it is pushed over may be slightly higher than the other (although *both* collar bones may already be too high because of shoulder tension). The angle between the ribs will be sharper on one side than the other, and in fact the chest may be not so much inflated on that side as on the other, and the cartilage which joins the front of the lower ribs may be felt pushing more forward than on the other side.

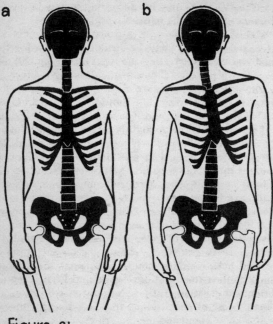

Figure 21

Such chest twists and rotations are frequently unobserved by doctors, and many patients suffer from distressing pain in the chest—sometimes labelled "pleurodynia" or "intercostal neuralgia"—which does not respond to physiotherapy, and leaves lurking doubts that there may be heart or lung pathology in spite of all tests showing them to be clear. (Everything I write presupposes that the usual obvious medical examinations are carried out to make sure that there is no gross pathology. But, of course, even if there is pathology, it can rarely do anything but good to also consider the manner of use.)

*The Abdomen*
When looking frontways on, it may perhaps be noticed that one

side of the abdomen is straighter than the other—that there is less "waist" on one side than the other. This follows on from the displacement of the thorax sideways (fig. 21b).

The abdominal muscles will be over-stretched and over-straightened on the side to which the thorax has moved, and shortened and "waisted" on the opposite side. And often when this happens, the pelvis on the shortened side will be contracted up towards the chest.

Such twists are often blamed by osteopaths on a short leg, and usually they say this because an X-ray of the pelvis is found to be tilted up more on one side than on the other. There are indeed *some* shortened legs—markedly so in some cases after fractures or polio or arthritis, etc.—but usually an inaccurate measurement of the *true* length of the leg will have been made (i.e., it was measured from the wrong bony points), and the remedy of building up the shoe to lengthen the supposedly short leg will do little to correct an imbalance which stems from a sideways displacement of the neck and chest.

An over-contraction of muscles may also be found in the front of the abdomen: in addition to acting as a form of "muscular armour" which, by continued contraction, attempts to counter-act feelings of butterflies or anxiety or sexual stirrings, the over-contraction will occasionally give rise to abdominal pain. The diagnosis of "spastic colon" is very often accompanied by such unnoticed abdominal mis-use, and many people with this distressing condition can be helped, and may avoid needless and fruitless abdominal surgery.

Abdominal laxity and general flabbiness is more often the rule in the middle aged, and to understand this, we need to look once more at our spines and our stance sideways on.

### The Spine

Plate 23 shows three secondary school children standing with stomachs collapsed forward. Plate 24 shows a young girl collapsing when she sits. This is the rule, not the exception, in most schools. Alertness at first is made possible by the natural on-going vitality of most of us: but for many school-children, the hours in class are hours of unmitigated boredom, punctuated by bouts of fear and aggression. Added to which the accent on learning to read and to write involves provision of a desk, towards which the eyes and head will tend to drop.* This encourages the formation of an exaggerated hump where the neck joins the chest, plus a slumping of the lower back, and collapse of the rib-cage (fig. 22a).

The slumped head posture becomes habitual so that when the eyes are raised to look ahead this has to be accomplished by an increase in the forward curve in the neck (fig. 22b). But the habit of holding the eyes down may persist until eventually the back of the skull begins to be *held* contracted back into the upper neck in order to look straight ahead (fig. 22c).

In other words the plane of the eyes is altered more by moving the level of the head than by moving the eyes (although they will move a little).

What happens when the child stands up? When it stands up it cannot simply keep a continuous rounded curve down the back, which it had when sitting, since it would produce the impossible (fig. 22d).

So, instead of the good USE in figures 22f, it makes the necessary (but wrong) compensation in the lower back; and this, if we add on the head compensation, gives us figure 22e, the familiar picture of the arched-in lower back, which is so common in school-children over the age of 5, a picture which we saw in plates 9 and 23. And from the back-view we see the sideways scoliotic twists which start in the neck (plate 22) and are compensated wrongly in the chest and lower back.

This combination of lordosis (arched-in back) plus scoliosis (sideways curvature) will persist into adult life and will usually be present when there is chronic back pain (usually it is only in the *acutely* painful back that the lumbar curve is flattened by spasm—a fact which has led some orthopaedic surgeons to try to overcome such flattening and to encourage back-arching). The pathetic picture in plate 25a shows one such patient (who has already undergone a back operation) being encouraged to do just those things which will make his already poor posture much worse. Plate 25b shows a physiotherapist practising this type of exercise.

* A nice verbatim account by Crispin aged nine, "Nearly all the children at school sit with their spines all curled up. That can't be good, can it? Sometimes the teacher tells us to sit up straight and when we ask her why her own back is all curved she says she is relaxing."

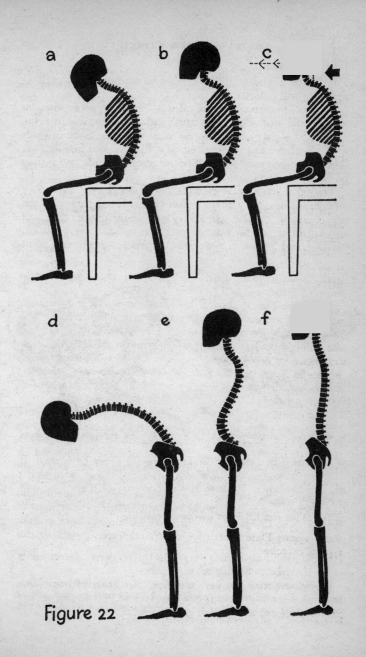

Figure 22

*Pelvis and Legs*

The pelvis is a most difficult bone to visualise to oneself as figure 23 will indicate.

By far the commonest general mis-use of the pelvis involves pulling the buttocks backwards and upwards towards the lower back—part of the process of arching the back inwards which we have already noticed. But in addition, just like the skull, the pelvis may be tilted up more on one side and it may be rotated back on one side.

The pelvic muscles are extremely complex; on the inside they include the muscles which connect up the lower back with the perineum and legs (fig. 24a and b) and on the outside the small and big muscles which are responsible for standing, walking, running and jumping. One should perhaps make the point

## Figure 23     a                b

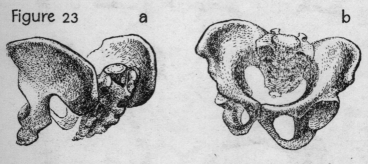

Pelvis three-quarter view back       Pelvis three-quarter view front

again that, when sitting, the knees should never be crossed. If they are crossed it will involve a mis-use of the muscles which connect the lower back to the upper part of the thigh, and the thigh with the pelvis. (figs. 24c and d). A crossing of the ankles is far less likely to involve a mis-use.

*Standing and Walking*

The following instructions may help the reader to detect faults in the USE when standing and walking.

*If you stand with your back to a wall (fig. 25a), with your heels about two inches in front of it and feet about 18 inches apart, you can begin to notice and identify some of your defects.*

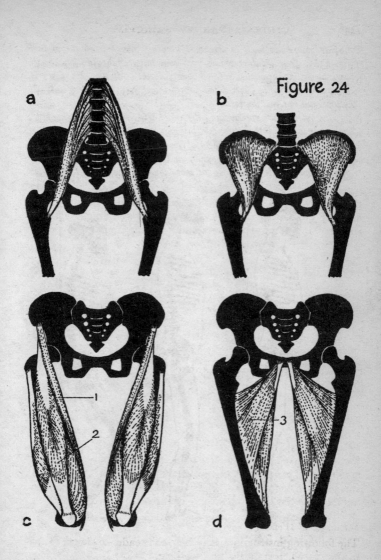

**Figure 24**

The ilio-psoas muscle has been divided for clarity into two parts (a. Psoas, b. Iliacus). The thigh muscles shown are 1, Sartorius; 2, Quadriceps; 3, Adductors.

*Sway your body back to the wall keeping your toes on the ground (fig. 25b). Your shoulder-blades and your buttocks should hit the wall simultaneously. If you are rotated, one side will hit the wall first; if your pelvis is usually carried too far forward, your shoulders will hit the wall but not your buttocks.*

*If the buttocks are not touching the wall, bring them back to the wall. You may notice now that there is a big gap between your lower back and the wall. This gap will disappear if you bend both your knees forward (keeping your heels on the ground) and at the same time drop your buttocks and tip the sexual organs more towards the front, rather than*

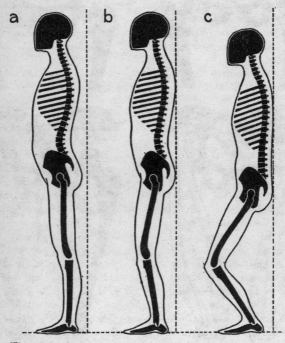

a     b     c

Figure 25

*towards the floor (fig. 25c). If you find this position tiring after quite a short time, then you are indeed in a mis-used state! But you will be gratified to notice that your flabby dropped stomach has taken up a slimmer appearance. You may also find that the back of your skull is touching the wall. This is a mis-use—Alexander's basic fault of "head retraction", as described in Chapter 2.*

*Notice, in this position, whether the arches of your feet are flattened. You can probably unflatten them if, with the knees still bent, you turn your knee-caps outwards, rather as the eye-balls could be squinted out at the sides. This will also tend to correct bow-leg (tibial torsion).*

*Now slowly straighten your knees but do not brace them back when standing fully erect.* The knees should never be braced back when standing, *but should always be slightly bent: the same applies to walking.*

*There should now only be a slight arch in the lower back, depending on your particular build and avoirdupois. You can now bring your body away from the wall, keeping your feet where they were. In bringing the body thus forward, the head should lead the movement, not the chest or abdomen.*

*If you now bring the feet together, you are in a position to detect faults in your walking pattern. Place two high-backed chairs in front of you, figure 26a, and hold them with the tips of the fingers and thumb and with the elbows well out. Begin to walk with the right leg by raising the right knee slightly so that the right heel leaves the ground. But as you do this there will begin to be slight transfer of weight to the left leg to enable the right foot to leave the ground. Many people will find that instead of getting the right foot off the ground by bending the right knee, they instead pull the right side of the pelvis up towards the right side of the chest (fig. 26b). You will detect this happening by the excessive pressure which is felt through one of the hands which is holding the chair. There should be no disturbance of the upper body and arms when this initial movement of bending the knee is made (fig. 26c).*

*The next stage of walking is simply to go on bending the knee until only the tip of the big toe is left touching the ground (fig. 26d): then as the whole body moves forward, the foot leaves the ground, and should be placed on the ground in front with the* heel *touching the ground just before the sole of the foot touches (Fig. 26e). The knee should not be braced back, as in a "goose-step": and if the sole hits the ground first, it will usually have involved too much arching of the lower back. With a heel–toe action it is possible to maintain a use of the lower back in which it is not arched.*

*Such a manoeuvre is not intended to teach you how to walk but simply, at this stage, how to detect faults in your walking pattern. A fully integrated pattern of walking would involve very close attention to the upper part of the body, not just to the legs. It is, of course, easier if you*

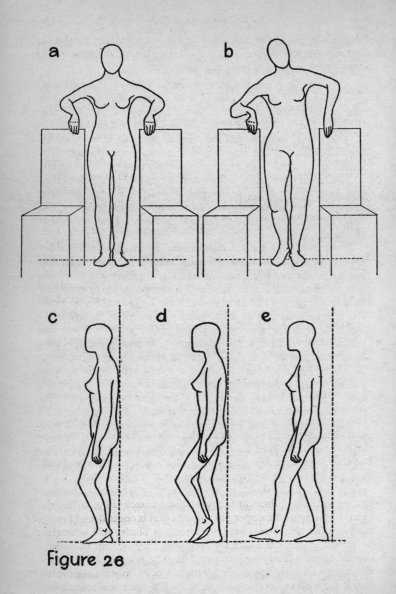

Figure 26

*have the help of a teacher who can show you how to hold the top of each*
*chair between your fingers and hands, in such a way as not to create*
*undue tension in the head, neck, shoulders and arms.*

## Shoulders and Arms

There is no particular reason except convenience for leaving a
consideration of shoulders and arms to this point. Indeed, they
are, for most people an important site of mis-use, since they are
involved in so much of the life of civilised men. Figure 27 shows
the muscles which often distort the USE of the shoulder-blades.

In most people the shoulder-blades are drawn up towards the
back of the neck during movement and, eventually, even at
rest. They will often also be too much pulled together, either
because of wrong instruction at school, to "pull your shoulders
together": or else because in the sedentary un-energetic life
which most people lead, the chest cage is relatively unexpanded
and the shoulder-blades—which should lie flat and widened
across the back of the properly expanded chest—tend to come
together and to become winged when the chest is unexpanded.
The bottom end of one shoulder-blade may be felt to be sticking
out if the other hand is put behind the back and stretched
across to touch the opposite shoulder-blade at the back.

The winged position of the shoulder-blades can be temporarily counteracted by raising the hands and arms forward. This
movement (which takes place when holding the top of a chair,
as previously described) will usually cause the shoulder blades
to lie flat on the back of the chest—a position in which they
should lie even when the arms hang to the side. When holding a
chair in this manner, the elbows should be turned well away
from the body, the cubital fossa (the bend of the elbow) facing
the side of the body. This position may feel round-shouldered,
but this is because the "hump" is now more obvious and no
longer disguised by a spurious squaring of the shoulders.

A pulling of the shoulder blades together is usually accompanied by holding them up too tightly at the back of the neck and
hump: and since the upper part of the chest is conical and more
narrow than the lower chest, the shoulder blades will wrongly
be pulled inwards towards the hump as they rise up over the
conical chest. Clearly such tension has to be released by a slight
dropping and widening of the shoulder blades: but most people
find it difficult to do this without slumping their lower back at

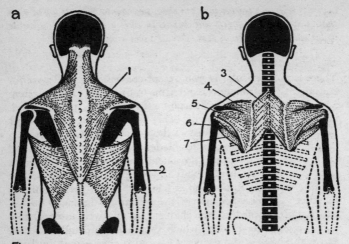

## Figure 27

1. Trapezius; 2; Latissimus Dorsi; 3. Rhomboids;
4. Supraspinatus; 5. Infraspinatus; 6. Teres Minor;
7. Teres Major.

the same time. So not only do the shoulders have to be released and widened, but the back has, at the same time to lengthen (without arching) and to widen to support the shoulders; a process which is facilitated if the chest cage is expanded to widen across the back. Plate 26 shows such a widening, with chest expansion. Plate 27 shows the slow improvement in the right (but not left) shoulder tension.

A great deal of emotional tension is expressed in the shoulders. Dorothy Tutin told me that she played Joan of Arc with the shoulders slightly raised and fixed to give a feeling of defiance. A whole range of most subtle emotions are manifested in the shoulders—shrugs, aggressive threatenings, or resignation and nostalgia from, say, a slight release of the upper chest muscles as they insert into the upper arm in the armpit.

### The Arms

The bend of the elbow should not be facing forwards when standing: indeed, the upper arm should turn slightly inwards, so that the elbow turns slightly out and away from the body. If the shoulders are collapsed, the upper arms will also usually be held too close to the body.

The front of the elbow is a place where most people hold themselves far too fixed, so that the fore-arm may be flexed, at rest, too much towards the upper arm. We use our arms for many of our activities of daily living, and we gradually come to adopt a resting position in which the fore-arm is too clenched, the elbow a little too bent, and the hand not sufficiently straightened out. The line from the inside of the elbow (which can be drawn down, via the inner border of the wrist, to the end of the thumb) should be almost straight, so that the fingers, at rest, can be straightened and turned slightly away from the thumb. Driving a car, playing a musical instrument, handling tools and objects of all kinds, can be most economically carried out from this resting position, which will also involve a broadening of the palm of the hand and a separating of the fingers. One should endeavour to adjust the height and position of desks, musical instruments, display-panels on work-benches etc., so that such good use of the arm and hand is not hampered. And in writing and typewriting, there should not be too much deviation from the use of the shoulders, arms and hands which I have described. And of course in such all too frequent medical conditions as the stiff "frozen" shoulder, tennis elbow, and "tenosynovitis" of the wrist, it is of paramount importance to establish correct habits of using the whole upper limb, and to ensure adequate postural support for it from the trunk. Likewise in various games and athletic activities, it is essential to learn a basic resting use of the arms and shoulders: a consideration of such mis-uses may give a clue to persistent putting-errors or slicing of the golf ball, or patches of erratic serving and smashing in tennis, and so on.

This brief account of some of the more obvious mis-uses scarcely touches the fringe of the problem. It is easier to demonstrate these things on living persons—it took a long weekend at an adult education college in which I gave six lectures, demonstrated for four hours on local school-children and individually analysed all those taking the course, before I reckoned I had established all the structural points I wished to make. Plate 28 shows most of the common defects—the slumped sitting position, head pulled back when standing-up, dropping of the shoulder and arm with thorax displacement, neck dropped forward, prominent hump, arched back, knees too braced back. And all in the same young man, aged 23.

## The Incidence of Mis-Use

A given individual not only at the macroscopic level but much more importantly at the microscopic level will create his own permutations and combinations out of the many alternative mis-uses. A neat classification of mis-use is not at present possible, but in spite of this, it is possible, using broad categories, to get some idea of the extent of the problem.

Various physical education colleges and local education authorities have, over the years, allowed me to carry out studies on their students and school children, and I was the medical member of the National Committee on Movement Training a few years ago, in which we attempted to assess the physiological effects of various types of physical education.

The pro forma, figure 28, has proved a useful guide in assessing a given person's defects, and it has been adopted by educational authorities in their remedial work. It can be scored on a simple basis of one, two, or three marks according to the severity of the defect. Most of these "posture studies" have been carried out with the help of Professor Tanner from the Institute of Child Health. His book *Growth and Adolescence* (*op. cit.*), will give an indication of the detail in which such studies are carried out.

Surveys were carried out at some of our leading physical education colleges, where a high physical standard is required at entry, and which draw on some of the best athletes and games players in the country. It can be reasonably claimed that this group of students have applied themselves from an early age to the development of their bodies, and they are destined to become physical education teachers all over the country.

When analysing their faults by photography, a definite pattern appeared (fig. 29) of well defined categories—those scoring 0–3 who have excellent USE, those scoring 4–5 who have some slight defects, those between 6–9 who show severe defects, those between 10–14 who show very severe defects and those over 15 who show really gross deformity. In a group of 112 physical education students (fig. 29b) the majority, 62%, showed severe defects, 11·5% showed slight defects and 26·5%

| Region | Faults | Score | Faults | Score |
|--------|--------|-------|--------|-------|
| HEAD | Poked | | Tilted | |
| | Retracted | | Pulled Down | |
| SHOULDERS | Raised | | Rotated | |
| | Dropped | | Pulled Together | |
| PELVIS | Tilt | | Forward Carriage | |
| | Rotated | | Gluteal Asymmetry | |
| SPINE | Scoliosis | | Thorax Displacement | |
| | Kyphosis | | Lordosis | |
| STANCE | Hyperextended Knees | | Forward Inclination | |
| | Internal Rotation Knees | | Symmetry | |
| TENSION | Specific | | | |
| | General | | | |

**Figure 28**  Form for recording postural faults

showed very severe defects. Similar figures were obtained from groups of male, (fig. 29a) and female (fig. 29c) drama students.

On the basis of such studies it is clear that whatever methods are being used in our schools, the end-results even in the best students are not good. The idea that a healthy natural outdoor

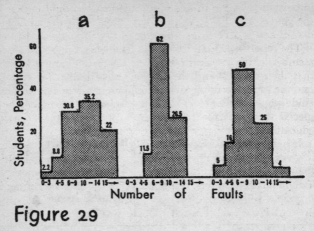

Figure 29

life with plenty of fresh air and exercise will ensure a reasonably good USE is simply not true—we see how high is the incidence of defects in physical education students. However, even if it were true, the main problem would still be how to establish a USE which would stand up to the strain of living in a civilisation in which the healthy life may not be easily available.

The figures of wrong USE in students are alarming but equally alarming were the figures which were obtained by the National Committee for Movement Training of the USE of children in secondary schools. This study was carried out in schools in Hertfordshire and, in addition to a whole battery of physiological and psychological tests, I carried out a survey of postural and tension defects.[40] It was encouraging that the committee's comments at the end of the study were: "The main hope for the future seems to be the kind of measurements and ratings that Dr Barlow and his colleagues can make."

In a world survey of physical education methods, which was carried out in the UK, in the US, Australia, and the USSR, the report was concluded by an account of the work which Professor Tanner and I have carried out, and the report quoted me as follows: "At present, Physical Education training does not leave its pupils with either the knowledge or the desire to maintain healthful activity in advancing years. The problems of adult deterioration under civilised conditions is far more important than the problem of providing healthful outlets for the young. Physical Education has failed unless the adult both desires and is able to maintain good USE throughout his life."

The report concludes: "Both these doctors are in touch with members of the Physical Education Association, and it is hoped that their interest and their wider opportunities for research into the problems of physical development and movement may guide physical educators in their educational work and be of special help to those responsible for corrective physical education."[41]

It is difficult, unaided, to learn the Principle, and accordingly it is vital that this knowledge should eventually be available at the school level. Just how it is to be fitted in will be a matter for individual headmasters. It is tempting to feel that the Alexander Principle will be too strong a medicine for some schools at present. However, through the patience and skill of certain Alexander teachers, who have quietly worked to prove to other school staff just how valuable their contribution can be, it does seem now that the Principle can be acceptably incorporated into many schools and that this process will be mutually helpful on both sides.

In recent years Alexander teachers have been taken on to the staff of four colleges—the Royal College of Music (where most of my early research was done), the Royal Academy of Dramatic Art, New College of Speech and Drama, and Guildhall. The Inner London Education Authority has recognised the Alexander Institute for provision of major county awards—a move which may do something to satisfy the huge increase in demand for trained teachers. But, in the main, most Alexander training is still carried out by individual teachers who work privately. It has often been the case in the past that when a new educational need has arisen, it has at first had to be dealt with in the private sector, rather than by the state. It is only when the evidence has become incontrovertible that the institutions join in.

The evidence now is quite incontrovertible. We are witnessing a widespread deterioration in USE which begins at an early age, and which present educational methods are doing little to prevent. Most people have lost good USE by the time they are past early childhood. Not all the time, but in most of their activities and when they are resting. Nobody bothers about it because nobody notices until the defects have become severe. Many family situations are bound to produce tensions in children, but it is difficult enough even for the lucky ones whose parents provide a balanced environment. It is difficult for children to "keep their heads" when "all around" them they are surrounded by people who are monstrous monuments of mis-use.

Alexander devised a method for teaching improved habits of USE, and this has become widely known as "The Alexander Technique". The next chapter will explain some of the concepts that underlie his technique and will describe procedures carried out in an Alexander lesson.

# Chapter 10

## TEACHING THE PRINCIPLE

> Some come in hope and others come in fear,
> Diverse in shape the multitude appear.
>
> POPE

ALEXANDER INSTRUCTION IS, at first, an individual matter, one-to-one: it cannot be skimped. Unless it is detailed, it is nothing. The Alexander teacher will have his subjects with him for between half an hour and an hour, during which time there is a continuously absorbing preoccupation with the development of new USE. For most people this will involve at least fifteen sessions: for many it will involve very many more. Relatively stereotyped procedures of physiotherapy or manipulation may produce a greater turn-over of patients, and with less effort. This can never be the case with Alexander instruction. A teacher can only deal with a comparatively small number of people in a working day.

Learning a better general USE is no different in kind from learning any other specific skill, but with or without a teacher, it will involve working at two simultaneous levels—a mental "labelling" level, and a psycho-physical "experiencing" level. To illustrate these two levels, let us think of someone who is blindfolded and who is trying to make out what an object (A) in front of him is:

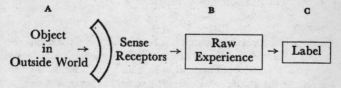

His sense-receptors may tell him first that it is heavy, smooth, cold, rounded, etc.,: he is getting from the senses a "Raw" unformulated experience (B). Very soon he will think he recognises it and may give it a label (C): a "jug", perhaps.

The labelling process, C, involves discrimination and recognition according to what we know already about jugs, etc. The label is *not* the experience: the word is not the object. The two levels must not be confused, although one leads to the other.

An animal in the forest has, presumably, a fairly simple labelling process: if it is a monkey, which is in ever-present danger of being eaten by a tiger, the important thing is to be able to detect the tiger before it actually arrives. A scent on the breeze—level B, is associated in a flash with the thought, level C, of a tiger, and this stimulates an immediate response—probably shinning up a tree with all the other monkeys. However, it would be useless for a well-meaning stranger to shout "Look-out! Tiger, Tiger!", because the verbal label "Tiger" would mean nothing, whereas the scent on the breeze would mean everything. Words and ideas by themselves, are not a sufficient form of education in anything which involves the senses, and they can only become effective when they have been linked to a raw experience by a learning procedure. Thus, in time, a monkey might be trained to get up a tree whenever someone shouted "Tiger".

If a new USE is to be learned, it is necessary for many new experiences of USE, level B, to come to be associated with new labels, level C: and the new labels will, in time, come to induce the improved USE. In human beings, the new USE-label cannot be as simple as that of the conditioned animal: but a simple association must first be set up between the names of various USES and the actual USES themselves. A grammar of the body has to be learned—a grammar not to be triggered into action by some external cry of "Tiger, Tiger", but by being projected personally as and when one wishes.

*Grammar*

An electrical recording which has been obtained from a muscle during re-education shows this procedure clearly. Figure 30 shows a recording from neck muscles which are being trained to release, whilst, at the same time, the patient repeats to himself a verbal direction "neck release". In (a) there is much initial tension in the neck: in (b) the tension becomes momentarily less, but returns as soon as the teacher stops his gentle adjustment of the head. In (c) the improved balance is obtained sooner, but still it returns when the teacher stops his adjustment and likewise in (d). In (e) the patient is now able to maintain

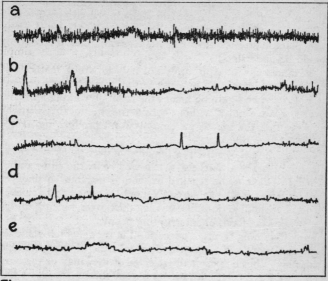

# Figure 30

the state of lessened tension and, in time, will be able to evoke this state simply by running over the "orders".

A sequence of such verbal directions is taught whilst a better tensional balance is obtained all over the body; the sequence is designed to scan the body in serial order, much as a television camera scans its object or as one scans a telephone directory in search of a number. The sequence of directions thus provides a model with both spatial and temporal co-ordinates. Such a sequence fulfils the function of checking the development of too much tension and of restoring a resting state when it has been disturbed. If kept in mind during performances, it will ensure that deviations from the resting state are not excessive.

However, to learn such a "Body-Grammar" is not in itself enough. Two other factors are needed. First, the subject must learn not to "End-gain": and this will require what Alexander called "Inhibiting".

## End-gaining

Most people prepare for action by creating unnecessary muscle

tension and one of the most interesting and original ideas which
Alexander put forward to explain such unnecessary tension was
his concept of "End-gaining". In order to understand what
takes place in an Alexander lesson it is essential that this concept
should be understood.

Alexander meant it to apply not only to wrong methods of
teaching and learning a new USE but on a much more general
basis. Briefly, end-gaining means the habit of working for ends,
targets, goals, results, without considering the means: without
ensuring that the means we employ won't produce too many
harmful by-products.

End-gaining shows itself in the form of over-quick and over-
energetic reactions. Targets—when we live by the end-gaining
principle—have to be reached as soon as possible, so that yet
another target can be achieved. Not only big goals and achievements: but small actions like turning the tap on, picking things
up, swallowing food, or interrupting people.

In end-gaining terms, a successful life is one which achieves
more and more goals, and the devil take the hindmost. These
goals may either be personally selected or they may be the ones
which we have been encouraged by our society to select: but
whether they be the goals of the "organisation man" or the
lonely pioneer, "end-gaining" implies that proper consideration
is not being given to the USE involved in gaining the end.

This concept of end-gaining was taken up with avidity by
John Dewey, the American educational philosopher,[42] who saw
it as a way in which children could become more interested in
what they were actually doing than in the pat-on-the-back
which they hoped to get from exam success or from being top of
the form. It was also taken up by Aldous Huxley who wrote a
book—*Ends and Means*[43]—about it:

> We are all, in Alexander's phrase, end-gainers. We have
> goals towards which we hasten without ever considering the
> means whereby we can best achieve our purpose. The ideal
> man is one who is non-attached. All education must ulti-
> mately aim at producing non-attachment.

Modern interest in meditation has led some writers to see in
Alexander's "end-gaining" the same fault which they themselves are trying to eliminate. For this reason some of the writing

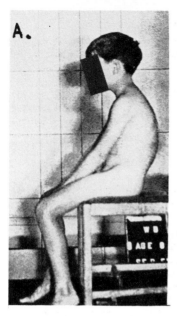

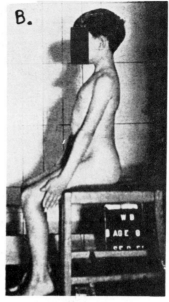

14a Slumping.

14b Sitting too straight.

14c Balanced.

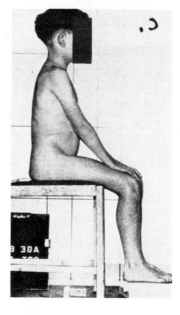

15 Muscle-spindle lengthwise (above). Cut through vertically (below) to show small internal muscles and large external muscles.

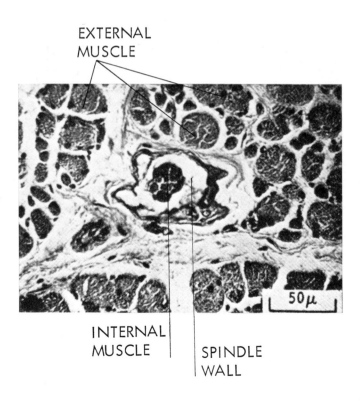

EXTERNAL
MUSCLE

INTERNAL
MUSCLE

SPINDLE
WALL

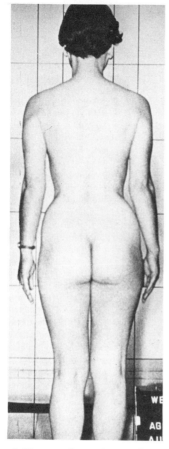

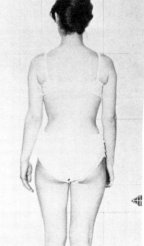

16 Note neck tension at back. Raised right shoulder. Tension left side of lower back. Pelvis twisting to right.

17 Patient standing on right leg. Central upright of grid should pass through middle of back and pelvis.

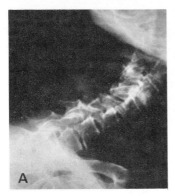

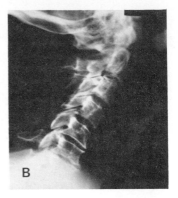

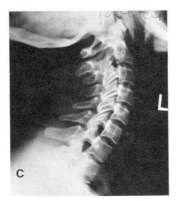

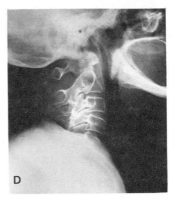

18a, b, c, d, e
a. Neck collapsed forward.
b. Head back, Upper neck
forward, lower neck back. c.
Head pulled back. d. Lower
neck collapsed out of sight. e.
Overstraightened neck. Fourth
vertebra slipped forward on
fifth.

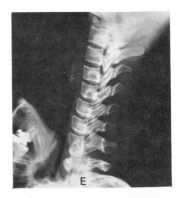

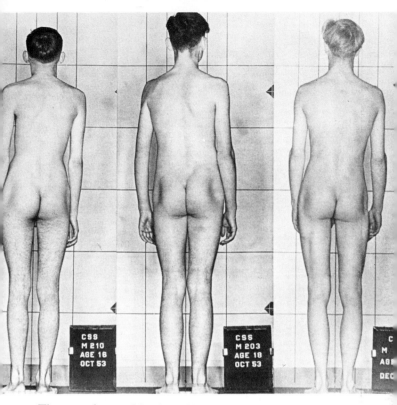

19a Three students with chest displaced to side. Note middle student, right shoulder back.

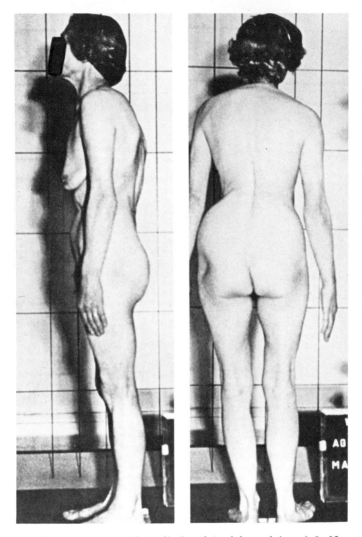

19b Elderly woman. Chest displaced to right, pelvis to left. Note neck collapse and tense sterno-mastoid muscle.

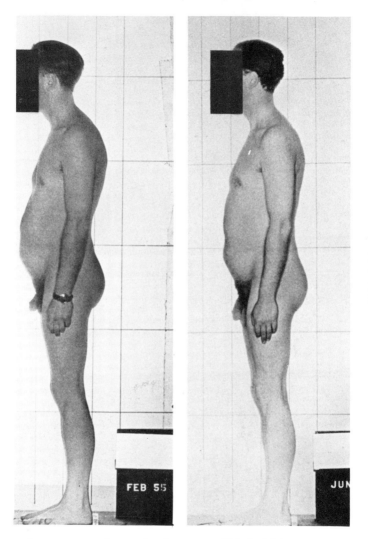

20 Improvements in emotional state, paralleled with improvement in attitude.

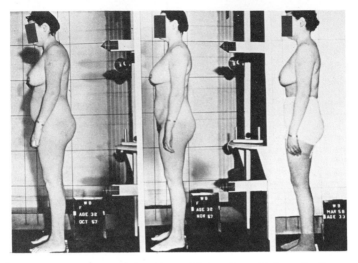

21 Collapse and depression. Loss of depression with loss of collapse.

22 Sideways twist at base of neck. See plate 9 (left) and plate 19a.

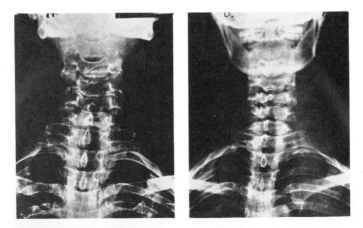

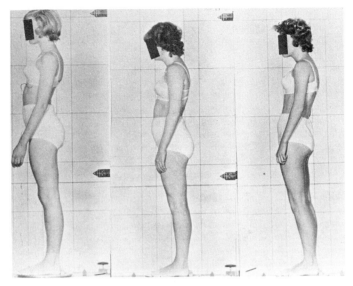

23 Three schoolgirls selected at school as having "good posture" Note multiple severe defects—sway-backs, lordosis, lump formation and head poking.

24 Typical schoolchild posture. Spine curved as in fig. 7, neck dropped forward, head back.

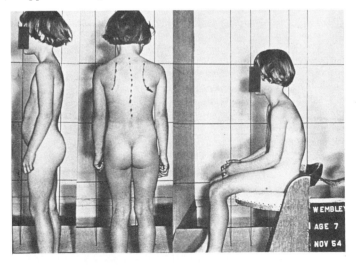

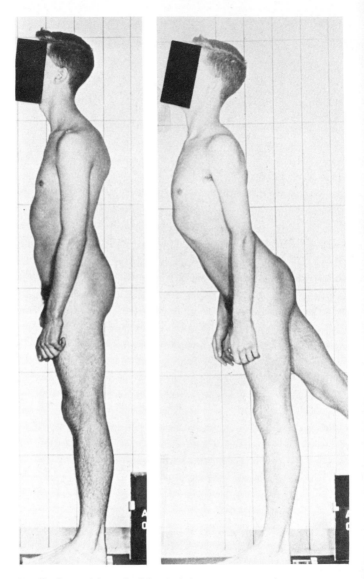

25a Patient with arched back doing wrong exercise.

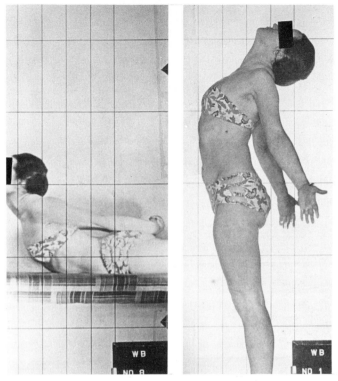

25b Physiotherapist showing wrong back-tensing exercises.

27 Back straighter and right shoulder widening after re-education.

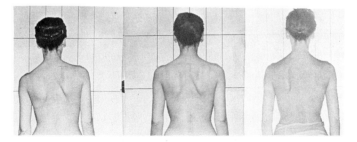

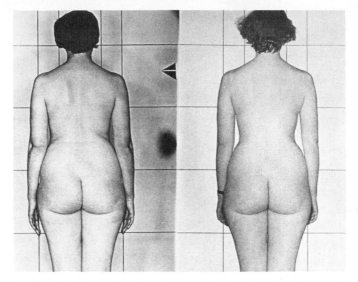

26 Widening of shoulder-blades apart. Note loss of skin fold in b after re-education.

28 Most of the possible defects! Slump, head retraction, lordosis, scoliosis, shoulder raised, right hand dropped, tibial torsion.

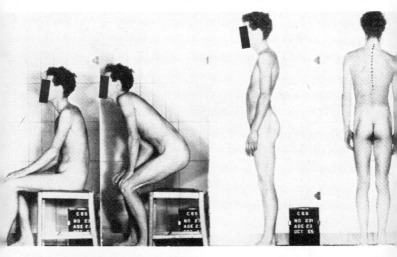

about Alexander has had a mystical flavour, not to say a sentimentality. Experiences which can come from what Alexander called "inhibiting" such end-gaining have been seen by some people as more important than any of the other effects of Good USE.

*Inhibiting*
"Inhibiting" as Alexander suggested it, is not to be confused with repression and unresponsiveness as understood by the psychotherapists. Alexander had a fairly simple stimulus/response psychology and his behaviour diagram went something like this:

| Input | → | Throughput | → | Output |

He rightly saw that end-gaining was a reflex action which tended to by-pass the reasoning brain and that most end-gainers are reacting automatically on an input/output basis, so that activity is directed towards satisfying the input as soon as possible, whether or not the habitual way of doing this is appropriate. He accordingly insisted that on the receipt of a stimulus, there must be an "inhibition" of the immediate muscular response, so that by "throughput", there could be adequate preparation for the succeeding activity. Such inhibition became a cornerstone of his re-educational methods.

This is an important and basic observation; but the snag which may arise from a rigorous determination to refuse to react and to register sensations is that curious states of disorientation may be induced in this way and, like the philosopher who stood on a river bank watching someone drown whilst he tried to decide whether human life was valuable, the use of inhibition has led some Alexander adherents in the past to a state of passivity in which they prefer not to respond at all in case their dystonic patterns should reappear. Such "sensory deprivation"—which may come from over-zealous inhibition—must clearly be used with care. This snag, however, disappears if the period of inhibition is seen merely as a stage of preparatory choice in which the eventual muscular USE can be decided on—a stage which leads on to activity or to a state of freedom whilst at rest.

There will be much to say about "inhibiting" in Chapter 11 (Learning the Principle). Consideration can now be given to the Alexander Technique and a specimen Alexander "lesson".

## The Alexander Technique

The Alexander Technique, briefly, is a method of showing people how they are mis-using their bodies and how they can prevent such mis-uses, whether it be at rest or during activity. This information about USE is conveyed by manual adjustment on the part of the teacher, and it involves the learning of a new Body-Grammar—a new mental pattern in the form of a sequence of words which is taught to the pupil, and which he learns to associate with the new muscular use which he is being taught by the manual adjustment. He learns to project this new pattern to himself not only whilst he is being actually taught but when he is on his own.

This procedure is *not* a method of manipulation in which the subject is a passive recipient and goes out none the wiser about how to stop himself getting into a tension-state again. It is a method by which he is taught to work on himself to prevent his recurrent habits of mis-use, and by which he can learn to build up a new use-structure.

It is *not* a form of hypnosis, by which the mind is conditioned to obey commands which some other person has planted there. It could perhaps be described, in its initial phase, as a *de*-conditioning, since it aims to teach the pupil to recognise when he is making faulty tension: but it is not akin to the deconditioning procedures of behaviour-therapy, in which, say, the tension of a writer's cramp is punished by giving an electric shock every time the pen is held wrongly. Instead, it involves throughout a conscious attention and learning by the patient, and no adjustments are considered useful unless they can be built up into a new conscious body-construct, to be used consciously by the patient afterwards.

It is *not* a form of relaxation therapy. Certainly the pupil will learn to release tension which was previously unconscious, but in all probability the pupil will be expected to replace unnecessary tensions by additional work in other muscle groups which previously had been under-developed. Many people, for example, having picked up the bad habit of slumping and cross-ing their knees, will find that they will have to put more work into their lower back and thighs if they are to release excessive tension which they have been making in their neck and shoulders. The over-tension of their neck and shoulders will be replaced by more tone in the lower back and thighs; but, of course, each of us has his individual patterns, and each of us will have different patterns of wrong muscle tension which need to be redistributed.

### Exercise Therapy

How is this learning to be brought about?

Not by "exercises" as they are ordinarily understood—the "stretching" and "strengthening" exercises of physiotherapy and physical education are valueless in dealing with this problem.* It might be argued that from its original use (*ex-arcere* meaning to "break-out" from a "shut-in" state) the word exercise would be appropriate for a procedure which seeks to release dystonic patterns. But since the hardest problem of all in such re-education is to stop people "doing" too much, the word "exercise" is probably best confined to such phrases as "Directive Exercise". The word "Practise" is not so suspect, so long as it is not divorced from a real-life context.

### Defective Awareness

Even so, it might be thought that once a proper USE-diagnosis has been made, learning should be easy. Given that people are interfering with their USE in a certain way, all that is necessary, surely, is to show them what is right and get them to practise it: then all will be well.

Unfortunately the problem is not so easy. When people have grown accustomed to a certain manner-of-use, no matter how twisted or crooked it may be, it will have come to feel "right" to them even though it may also be producing pain and inefficiency and clumsiness. Our sense of "rightness" is a very precious possession to most of us—it is, after all, the outcome of our whole experience of living to date, and our whole nature is bound up with the pattern of movement and posture which we have developed. Indeed, our whole memory pattern is closely tied-in

* W. Barlow, Proceedings of the Royal Society of Medicine, *op. cit.* Over a twelve-month period, students who were given such "exercises" had developed more postural defects than they started with.

with the substratum of muscle-tone which underlies our USE. A sense of the space co-ordinates of our postural system pervades all our behaviour. We *are* our posture.

This means that, the moment we try to carry out a basic re-education of USE, we very rapidly run up against our attachment to our old feeling of ourselves. We can be shown in detail what are our defects, and most of us will readily admit that they need altering, and that our general feeling of ourselves must be inaccurate for us to have got into such a mis-used state. In spite of this, however, most people try to correct their mis-uses by deliberately taking up some new position which they think is what is now required. In the process they will only create yet another set of dystonic patterns: and it will not be long before they revert to the old habitual pattern, particularly when they start to move. It may be recalled that out of my group of 105 young men (Chapter 2) only 11 out of the 105 were able to alter their habits at will and then only at the immediate moment of supervision.

### The Alexander Lesson

Alexander himself has described how he managed to teach himself a new body-construct, and to associate this with a new manner-of-use.[44] But this is a laborious business on one's own, and, in common with most skills, it is all far easier with the help of a good teacher.

It may be helpful to describe an Alexander lesson, although of course each teacher will have worked out his own ways of presenting the necessary information as clearly as he can.

An initial examination by the teacher will have indicated that there are certain forms of wrong USE which are deeply established. These uses will be showing themselves in the disposition and alignment of the bones of the vertebral column and limbs, and they will be showing themselves in a disposition to react with the muscles in certain habitual ways. It is taken that the pupil has been sufficiently persuaded by this diagnosis to accept the type of instruction which is being given.

The pupil will be asked to lie down on a fairly hard surface— the usual medical or physiotherapy couch is a good height. The head will need about 1 inch of firm support under it, although up to 3 inches may be needed if the Hump has become fixed and very bent forward. The pupil will be told not to do anything—in other words to "inhibit" any reflex movement which tends to take place when he is handled or moved.

The teacher will place both of his hands at the sides of the neck and will ask the pupil to say to himself the words, "NECK FREE, HEAD FORWARD AND OUT". He will perhaps explain that "FORWARD" means the opposite of pushing the skull back into the support under the head, and that "OUT" is the opposite of retracting the skull, like a tortoise, into the hump and the chest. (When standing or sitting, the instruction may be "FORWARD AND UP", which amounts to the same thing.) The teacher will repeat these words as he gently adjusts the head in such a way as to release neck tensions which are preventing it from going forward-and-out. These neck tensions will be manifold and different in each one of us. The neck X-rays (plate 18) showed just a few of the sorts of contortions into which we can get our necks and heads. All such contortions are gently corrected—to some extent—by the teacher as he takes the head forward-and-out. Obviously the tensions and distortions of a lifetime won't come undone in one magic moment: and equally obviously, the somewhat improved balance which is initially attained in this way cannot be taken to be the one final and right answer. Over a period of days and weeks, the pupil will gradually become familiarised with an improving and changing use of the head and neck.

This familiarisation with a new USE would not, in itself, be of much value. It is also necessary for the pupil to learn how to maintain such an improving use when he starts to react.

At first, the teacher will present only quite a small stimulus. He might suggest that, the pupil should let him turn his head by rotating it to one side. Many people—most people, in fact—when such a movement is suggested, will not be able to let the teacher carry out the movement for them, but will start to do it themselves. The pupil will therefore be told not to do the movement, but, in Alexander phraseology, to "inhibit". In terms of our Input-Throughput-Output diagram (page 161) when a stimulus (the Input) is received, it is necessary not to respond with an immediate muscular Output, but instead to enage in Throughput—that is to say, the projection to oneself of the words, "Head forward and out". Whilst these words are projected (and provided the pupil will "inhibit" the doing of the movement which the teacher says he is going to carry out) it becomes possible to detect just when tension is created in the neck and around the head and throat.

At some point in this procedure, the teacher will have emphasised the importance of the direction "NECK FREE", so that the pupil will come to associate with the direction "NECK FREE, HEAD FORWARD AND OUT", not only a spatial positioning of the skull in relationship to the chest and hump, but also a releasing of neck and throat tensions which have become apparent.

When the teacher adjusts the head, he is able to release quite a lot of tension in the neck and hump: but the pupil will also notice that some slight force is being exerted on the back of the chest and the lower back. When this occurs, the teacher will give the verbal direction "BACK LENGTHEN AND WIDEN", whilst in various and devious ways he achieves such a co-ordination. In lengthening the back, he will be at pains not to produce an undue arch in the middle of the back, and, indeed, by adjustment of the chest and pelvis, he will see to it that the lower back becomes almost completely flat on the couch. As he continues with this procedure, he will insist that the new verbal direction should be in the right order. If, as he adjusts the lower back, the pupil should stiffen his neck, the teacher will insist that the pupil should emphasise to himself the order, "Head forward and out", until it is clearly perceived, and then add on to it the direction to the back to "lengthen and widen". With his hands he will repeat the muscular experiences in the right order—a task which sounds complex when written down in this way, but fairly obvious in practice when undertaken by a skilled instructor.

There are many more such "orders" to be added to the new body-grammar. The teacher may now say that he wishes to move one of the legs so that the hip flexes and the knee points towards the ceiling. He will again insist on the pupil "inhibiting" any doing of the movement, and he will ask him to continue to project the orders to the neck, head and back, and to add on to them such an order as "KNEE OUT OF THE HIP" or perhaps "HIP FREE", or "KNEE TO THE CEILING". (There is no right or wrong about the actual verbal phrasing of such orders, but merely a sequence in which it is best to give attention to the body.) * 45, 46, 47

Teachers may vary as to the point at which they will tackle the shoulders and arms. I personally think they should very soon be linked up with the instruction to free the neck, since many neck and chest tensions will not release until the whole shoulder girdle—comprising the shoulder-blade and collar-bone—is adjusted. I usually suggest the order "SHOULDER RELEASE AND WIDEN", and since this is always a dramatic adjustment at first, I find it helpful to do this in the first session, since a most obvious feeling of bodily re-adjustment usually takes place and even the dimmest of pupils (kinaesthetically, that is to say) will usually notice when one shoulder now lies two inches wider and lower than the one on the other side. And since the trapezius muscle goes from the back of the head, down the side of the neck, into the shoulder girdle, it is possible to give the subject an easy and obvious demonstration that, unless he thinks of his head going "forward-and-out" as his shoulder is adjusted, his head will simply pull down with the shoulder because of the trapezius contraction. Most people, during this procedure will realise that by giving their attention (in the form of the verbal "orders") they can maintain an improved head-neck-shoulder balance.

But again, the varieties of shoulder-use are considerable: all that can be looked for is a gradual transition to an anatomical norm. And it is explained again and again to the patient that what he is learning is a neutral "resting position" of balance of the various parts of his body—rather like the "neutral" of a car to which one can return after one has been in gear. And it is stressed throughout that for any given position or activity there is a due amount of muscle tension needed. More muscle work will be needed for sitting than for lying: more work for lifting a hammer than a tooth-brush: but that the increase in muscular activity should be undertaken on a general and not a local basis.

* Professor G. E. Coghill whose *Anatomy and the Problem of Behaviour* was considered a classic in its time by such people as Le Gros Clark and J. Z. Young explained that the correct sequence was Cephalo-caudad, from head-to-tail. His book, along with Judson Herrick's biography *G. E. Coghill: Naturalist and Philosopher*, is useful reading since he gave whole-hearted backing to Alexander. I touched on Coghill's account of sequential ordering in an article in *The Lancet*, entitled "Psychosomatic problems in postural re-education".

Increased forearm work should not be produced in a way which involves a hunching of the shoulders and a tensing of one side of the neck. Lack of interference with Alexander's "Primary Control" of the head and neck is taken to be of prime importance at rest and during activity.

It is unlikely that, in the initial session or two, much more can be done than to familiarise the patient with the words of his new body-grammar, and to get him used to being handled in a certain way and a certain sequence: but the impact of this whole procedure is considerable and most people will realise that they are being asked to set about things in a way which is quite novel and individual to themselves. I have had quite young children describing to me—in their later years—the immense impression which such "lessons" had upon them, and the feeling of security and individual attention which they remember.

It is indeed on this fundamental basis of practical attention and instruction that the patient/pupil will eventually be prepared to let go more deep-seated and unconscious tension patterns. It can be frightening to surrender our familiar sense of balance to someone else, and most of us—as I have noted in Chapter 7—have a multitude of tricks of muscle-armouring by which we defend ourselves from contact which we fear to be harmful. The release of tension may lead to anxiety—or tears, or laughter or anger: anything to distract one's attention away from the unfamiliar experiences of releasing tension. This goes for seemingly quite normal people, as well as for those who are in a state of apprehension or distress.

A well-constructed Alexander lesson will not have the effect of making the subject feel that he is being "got at", but that both he and the teacher are learning together how to sort out the mis-use problems. It is not that there is one master-key—Alexander's Primary Control—which will unlock the prison, but rather that there is a key-blank, out of which, by using the Alexander Principle, an individual key can be constructed: a key which can be used to unlock our unnecessary defences and to open up a way of dealing with future buffetings. Life will always buffet us, if we are to live fully.

*Sitting and Standing*

Many Alexander teachers prefer not to begin instruction

lying down, but in the more active situations of sitting and standing. The subject may be asked to take up a standing position, and it will be emphasised that he is not to "do" the new body-pattern, but simply to project it to himself. He must never "do" the orders: just think them. It will be explained that such "ordering" is always a "pre-" activity: that when we receive an outside stimulus (or an inside one from some idea which has sprung up or which we have cooked up) we are all of us liable to react with preparatory tension: that we are liable to get "set" in preparation for what we are going to do, and that such an anticipatory pre-set usually triggers us off into far too much effort when we initiate a movement.*

When the subject is standing quite still, the teacher will obtain as good a pre-set as he can by his gentle manual adjustment, and he will then ask the subject to continuously project the new body-pattern as the knees are bent forward to sit down. This is an unfamiliar experience at first, in which the usual balance may seem to be alarmingly upset. In time, however, it becomes familiar, and in this specific situation of sitting-down and standing-up, it is possible for much insight to be gained into faulty tensional habits and into the maintenance of the new pattern under stress. Likewise, when in the sitting position, small movements of the trunk backward and forward from the hip-joint (whilst maintaining the improved direction of head, neck and back) can be used to teach the subject how to attend to his USE. It should be explained that in such activities, the subject is not learning a correct way to sit and stand but how to attend to his USE so as to prevent unnecessary tension. Such learning carries over into other situations.

Alexander wrote frequently of a "position of mechanical advantage". An easy way to achieve this is to slide the back down the wall, as described in Chapter 9, at the same time putting the knees apart and flexing the pelvis so that the whole

---

* A body sliding along a surface is restricted by *friction*: but to start moving along a surface, it is necessary to overcome what engineers call "stiction": we have to get a car moving by using low gears, to overcome the initial inertia. In much the same way, our joints exhibit this property of "stiction". They tend to get relatively stuck when held still and fixed for a time, and an extra effort may be needed to initiate movement. The moral of this is not to allow ourselves to become fixed when at rest, and to let out the clutch slowly when we get up out of a chair or any other movement involving change of position.

back is flat against the wall. If the entire spine from head to pelvis is now kept lengthening, it can be inclined forward from the wall, with the buttocks still touching the wall (fig. 31). In this position the directions are "Head forward and up; back lengthen and widen; knees forward and apart", and in addition, the neck can be directed to lengthen "Up-and-back" and the lumbar spine likewise up-and-back (as in fig. 5b).

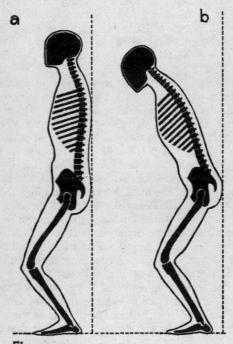

## Figure 31

Throughout this manœuvre, attention is given to inhibiting and projecting the new body construct, which includes orders to the knees and ankles and elbows and hands.

Such detailed attention leads to a heightened awareness o the co-ordination of the whole body, and most subjects will experience an exhilarating feeling of lightness and "up-ness" in their bodies as they begin to engage their minds in such a manner.*[48] Such an experience, although unfamiliar, will often convince people that they are engaging in something of great value.

## The Alexander Teacher

Alexander teachers, naturally, vary in their approaches, but unlike other teaching situations, they all have one thing in common: they will have to obey their own educational demands if they are to influence their pupils. There is no trick, however clever, by which this fact can be evaded. It is for this reason that the training of Alexander teachers has always insisted on first improving their own USE to a point at which they not only have a high standard but one which they can sustain when they are under full teaching pressure. This does not mean that, in order to teach well, it is necessary for the teacher to be in some ineffable state of "directive lightness". At the other end of the scale, the teaching can never become automatic and rule of thumb, since each pupil presents his own personal problems and difficulties.

A detached form of teaching which relies on a pedagogic, professorial, didactic attitude, is simply not possible. It is intensely boring if during a lesson the teacher gives the impression that he is seeking to expound a thesis or to prove a case, and makes the pupil feel he is being reproved if his attention wanders or if for a moment he disagrees.

But the pupil also must realise that the learning process involves a most detailed attention on his part: that his organism is being "re-calibrated", and brought back to true: that ideally, he will eventually need to give attention to his USE all day long, so that not only will he become freer whilst interacting with the outside world, but will know how to return to a balanced state of rest after such interaction. And both he and his teacher can never forget what a tall order it is to ask him to disobey habit.

It follows that, during a training programme, various emotions may be "transferred" to the teacher. There is often an initial "honeymoon" period of great pleasure in having discovered not only something which explains previous troubles, but which also offers a solution. Some people continue their happy honeymoon into a long and successful "marriage" with

* Many mystical experiences include an "UP" component (*Ecstasy*, Marghanita Laski, Cresset Press, 1961).

the new idea and practices. But for many—and probably most people—there are bound to be "break-down" periods which lead to a certain amount of depression and to a feeling of dissatisfaction that a given Alexander teacher is not being clear or helpful enough. Also, to see oneself as one really is must usually involve some cutting down on, or alteration in, outside commitments, at least for a time. Few people can expect to make such big changes in themselves without experiencing periods of anxiety and depression, and they may find that they are not able to meet the new need and challenge of the Alexander Principle without abandoning, at least for a time, the effort to pursue some other relationship. Added to this, most people feel slightly stupid with their new USE at first, because the new USE-components have not yet been incorporated into familiar sequential rhythms. Ease comes from a feeling of on-going sequence—we can all remember our difficulties in first learning to drive or ski. The new Alexander-USE has no clear place at first in our sequential organisation. When however, the new patterns become incorporated into newly-timed sequences, we get a feeling of ease and a motivation to use the new patterns— an ease which at first can only be experienced when the teacher is giving us help. The enjoyable feeling of "lightness" which comes after working with a good teacher is evanescent at first: and if there is not to be an undue dependence on the teacher who can give us this "lightness"—and with such dependence, all the concomitant problems of the transference situation—then the pupil must learn to work independently, on his own.

At present the majority of Alexander pupils are adults and adolescents who have found their way to a teacher, either through the guidance of their doctors or educational friends, or simply by word of mouth. They form an immensely variegated cross-section of the population, and their problems are equally variegated. There can be no one correct way to learn the Principle—each will find his own way on the basis of his own education and Alexander instruction. I have found in the past that the question and answer approach is a useful way of dealing with so many different attitudes, and in the next chapter this method will be used.

Obviously most of the people who read this chapter will not have had personal Alexander instruction but this is not essential for understanding it.

# Chapter 11

## LEARNING THE PRINCIPLE

THIS CHAPTER TAKES the form of a series of questions by a pupil or prospective pupil, and answers from an Alexander teacher.

*     *     *

*Just what sort of work am I expected to do on my own in order to achieve a balanced regulation of my body?*

The Alexander Technique aims to teach a pupil to associate a new sequence of thought with a new manner of using the body. You may already have found that when running over the new sequence of thought you can become aware of much unnecessary tension at rest, and unnecessary pressure during movement.

*That sounds fine, but under the almost incessant stimulation of my busy life, I don't seem to have much time or inclination to think about this sort of thing. I realise that I need to alter my old habits but just where am I to begin?*

The situations which, in the majority of people, produce muscle tension, and take them away from a balanced resting state are:

*a.* Talking to other people, especially to people you know well, particularly when your job or life situation requires you to establish rapport with them.

*b.* The stimulus of handling familiar objects around you—the toothbrush, door-handle, articles of clothing, typewriter, gear-lever, piano, food, and indeed the whole range of biological activities from swallowing to excreting.

*c.* The commitments in which you are already engaged, e.g., the tennis player in his team, the office boy who has to be obsequious, the business executive who feels he has to adopt a forceful attitude, the dancer or physical educationist who has to make movements which involve maldistributed tension, the teacher who has to fit her teaching to a curriculum and get things done in a certain time.

*d*. The emotional gusts: waves of irritation, fear, sexual excitement, crying, and sentimental eye moistening, depression, suspicion, excitability.

*e*. Obsessional repetitive mental states: day dreaming, recurrent tunes in the head, self conversation, etc. Such states occur as a background to tension which is already present, and the attempt to control them may lead to further tension.

*f*. Excessive desire for the smoke, the drink, the chocolate, etc.: it is not suggested that such things are harmful in moderation, but many people find themselves in a state of tension and conflict for which these are a poor form of palliation.

*g*. Fatigue: after making excessive tension there is a temptation to collapse and "slump". It is a mistake to slump in a chair—far better to lie horizontally if one is tired.

*h*. The feeling of unfamiliarity with the new conditions; feeling, for example, "stuck up" or different when employing the new body-construct.

*i*. Rush: the need (or imagined need) to get things done quickly.

*j*. Frustration: civilisation usually implies delay between desire and satisfaction, and under these conditions, tension may mount up unless one consciously regulates it.

*But how am I expected to alter these habits?*

In your lessons so far, you will have realised the importance of inhibition—"stopping off" an immediate reaction to the stimuli which your teacher has given you. You will have found that, unless you "inhibit" the stimulus, say, of sitting down or standing up, you react in the tense and distorted way which it is necessary to change: but you will have found that, by "inhibiting" and employing the new form of "direction", you can usually prevent this happening. In the same way it should now be possible for you to check you immediate reaction to many of the situations outlined above; and even if you find it impossible to maintain the improved tension-balance, you are at any rate aware when it has been lost, and are able to return to a better resting equilibrium when the immediate stress is over.

*Am I expected to think of this all day long?*

In the beginning stages it is most unlikely that you will be able to work at it all day long. Start with the simplest activities, and set aside special periods when you work at this and this only. There are, in addition, very many hours during the day when one must perforce keep still in one place, e.g., waiting for a bus, or many other times when overt activity is prevented or frustrated.

*How, then, am I to work in these special periods?*

You will probably have learned from your lessons that "realisation" is more important than "trying". Intense concentration for only short periods of time will not produce permanent change in your manner-of-use, but it will begin to build up and to carry over continually into your everyday life. It is a good idea to make a habit of working for short periods in the following way:

i  Find somewhere where you are not likely to be disturbed, and where you can lie down if necessary—the floor with a book under your head will do.

ii Lying down with a book under your head and with your knees pointing to the ceiling, decide consciously to keep quite still, i.e., don't wriggle or scratch, and don't follow irrelevant patterns of thought. Give to yourself the following verbal directions:

(*a*) "Neck release, head forward and out." As you give this sequence of thought, at first you will not "realise" what the direction means but as you continue, you will begin to associate it with an awareness of your neck and your head. If you are out of touch with yourself, you will begin to regain the degree of awareness which you may previously have had, either when working well on yourself or during a lesson. By "awareness" is meant what should be a normal sense of "being-in-yourself", as opposed to the state of mind-body split which is so often present in adults, if not in children.

(*b*) While preserving, by direction, this awareness of the head and neck—an awareness in which your verbal order will be part-and-parcel of the actual perception as the organising component of it—add on the verbal direction to "lengthen and widen your back". Your lessons will already have made you familiar with the meaning of this phrase, although it is likely that fresh meaning and fresh simplification will accrue as you run over the sequence to yourself. For example, the whole of the back may be realised as lengthening in one unit instead of thinking of the upper back as separate from the lower back: or perhaps the "widening" of the back may suddenly be noticed to include a releasing of the shoulder blades and arm-pit. At this point, your interest in the new realisation may be found to have caused you to "lose" the head direction, and it will be necessary to re-inforce this before returning to the lengthening and widening direction. (c) This process of adding together the direction to the head and the direction to the back may take several minutes or even longer: indeed, if it seems to take less time, you will almost certainly have been making a muscular change by direct movement, instead of sticking to realising the meaning of the orders. Remember that we do not move our bodies in the same way as we pick up an external object—a brush or a pen or a pail. To "move" our forearm is not the same as to move a spoon. Moving ourselves and bits of ourselves—as opposed to moving external objects—is always a question of *allowing* movement to take place, rather than of picking-up and putting somewhere else. Allowing the movement, say, of an arm, should involve a total general awareness of the body in which the active process involved in the arm movement is small compared with the active process of awareness which is going on in the whole of the body all of the time. Similarly, a movement of standing up after sitting down—a movement which mainly involves a leg adjustment—does not require only the leg activity, but primarily a maintenance of the awareness of the rest of the body whilst allowing the necessary leg movement to take place.

*When I was thinking about it yesterday I noticed certain muscular changes taking place. You have told me I should be wary of trusting my feeling, and also that I should not "do". Was I "doing" this muscular change I felt: in fact was I working the wrong way?*

If you were "ordering", it is possible that changes did take place. Most people, however, when they notice such things beginning to happen, stop "ordering" and get interested in helping the changes by "doing". When you notice something beginning to happen, it is more important than ever to "think" and not to "do". It will be found, however, that if you move after having "ordered" for quite a long time, muscular over-tension will release as you move, provided that you continue ordering as you move. In other words, the directions which you have learned to give to yourself affect the "pre-set" (the preparatory tension) in your muscles.

*Does it help if I visualise what you are teaching me?*

No. The kinaesthetic (muscular) sense is separate from the visual sense. Visual imagery, which is almost certainly associated with old, wrong muscular sensations, is liable to lead to confusion between these old muscular sensations and the new ones you have to learn. It is far safer to use a brand new symbolism to link up with the improved new kinaesthetic sense —a new "body construct" made up of the body-grammar which you have learned.

*Could you explain what you mean by "body-construct" more clearly?*

In the past there has been many terms suggested for the mental model which we have of ourselves. In 1911, Henry Head used the term "Postural model" and wrote: "by means of a perpetual alteration in posture, we are always building up a postural model of ourselves which constantly changes". He also spoke of "Body-memory" which modifies our perceptions at an unconscious level, so that our spatial consciousness is always bound to be influenced by what has happened before.

The term "body-image" was used by Schilder for the visual, mental and memory images which we may have of our bodies. Macdonald Critchley used the term in a similar way, and for many years neuro-physiologists have sketched out a "homunculus"—a little-man image in the brain cortex—which is taken to represent various areas of the body.

The term "Body-concept" has been used for when people think that they are too tall or too short or that their breasts are too large or their bottoms too big.

Other writers have spoken of the "body percept", by which they mean the momentary perceptions we may have of our body at any given time, irrespective of the construction which we may put upon perceptions, or of the mental factors which led us to obtain that particular perception.

For many reasons I prefer the term "body construct",[49] a term which implies not only the way we "construe" things but also the way we "construct" our responses and organise outside things so that they will appear the way we want them to be. Such a "body construct" produces (and is based on) our habitual USE of our bodies, and it forms the background to our perceptions.

It is a common experience that once we are set and readied for a given course of action, it is impossible to think of doing anything else. Our preparatory "set" affects our observations so that we see everything in conformity to it. We will all of us have had the experience, when waiting to carry out some activity, of being triggered off into action by some quite inappropriate stimulus, some accidental resemblance to the configuration which we are waiting for, or, when we are very strung up, something which bears no resemblance to it whatever. If we are to check such reactions and only release our response when the time is right, we need to have control over our preparatory state. Our subjective experience of this preparatory state is what I understand by our "body construct".

*Does this mean that the new "body construct" will eventually become unconscious?*

No. A human being is not a one-way system, unconsciously reacting on a stimulus/response basis according to previous conditioning. We ourselves search out from our surroundings the stimuli which we prefer to perceive. We don't sit around waiting to salivate when a dinner gong may ring: we are constantly concerned with the "organisation of preferred perceptions". Such preferences make up the "body construct" and are embedded in our habitual resting state. The way we use our body is the way we perceive and construe our world. The organisation of our preferred perception has its basis in the use of our muscles whether they be used in posture, movement or communication.

Such preferences are usually at an unchosen, unconscious level: our characteristic preferences are embodied in our muscular tension patterns. The Alexander Principle suggests that our "body construct" must be used consciously and that this will involve us in "inhibiting" our habitual responses.

The repeated use of such "inhibiting" and projecting a conscious body construct would be an impossibility in everyday life, unless some degree of amalgamative learning had taken place. At first, the new details of muscular USE may have to be "thought-out": but in time, this becomes a state of "thoughtful movement", rather than of "thought-out action".

To understand how this happens, let us consider the learning of some special skill like learning to drive a car. The way in which driving a car becomes "second nature" is familiar to many of us—the painstaking need to at first remember a right order for doing each movement, until this grows into a familiar routine which does not have to be thought-out each time. And not only a familiar routine: the outline of the car will eventually become an extension of our personal body boundaries. The body-construct has matured, and we can now release the "thinking-out" part of our brain for the moment-to-moment control of the car in traffic. There will no longer be the need to "think-out" each detail: but there will still be the need for "thoughtful-movement"—thought which concerns itself with the general USE, as well as with arm and feet movements.

A new "body construct", once learned, can be used to put oneself into a state of "thoughtful movement": but there will always have to be a decision to switch it on. It has to be made, and made afresh, according to the circumstances. It may not be immediately accessible to us at a conscious level, as part of our ordinary awareness, but has to be "directed".

*Will working in this way help me to cope better with things?*
Yes, but only if you are prepared to work hard at it and show considerable initiative. There are bound to be discouragements which tempt you back to your familiar pattern, and there may be a period in which you manage certain aspects of your life less effectively because of the need to develop the new pattern: just as a tennis player, cricketer or golfer may have to re-learn his technique in order to get the "bugs" out of it, and may for a time be less efficient. Indeed, working in this new way may lead at first to discomfort-plus-desire-for-change, rather than comfort-plus-coping-better-with-the-present. Nevertheless, conditions of physical pain may clear up fairly soon, although a temporary situation may well arise in which the pain clears up provided one works in this new unfamiliar manner, but the pain returns when one adopts a familiar "comfortable" pattern, e.g., slumping, crossing the knees, or reacting in an over-excited manner.

*Can you give me some advice about my breathing?*

It is easier to detect the more subtle faults of breathing when lying down, but first take a look at yourself standing. Preferably remove all your clothing and stand in front of a long mirror, arms hanging down. Are the tips of your fingers at the same level?

If one hand is lower than the other, look at your shoulders. One will be lower than the other. Look at the line of your neck. It will be longer on the dropped side than on the other side.

Now imagine a perpendicular dropping from the outer edge of the lower shoulder towards the floor (fig. 32a). It will probably fall through your thigh. Now look at the perpendicular from the other shoulder. It will probably miss the thigh by about an inch. Why?

Look at your whole chest cage. It is because your chest is displaced sideways (see plate 19) that your hand and shoulder are lower. This sideways displacement will affect breathing on the dropped side, and the breathing may also be further affected by a rotation of the chest backward on one side.

Now look at yourself sideways on (fig. 32b). Observe the base of the neck at the back. If the neck vertebrae are dropping too far forward and the spine at the back of the chest is bent forward, this produces an excessive hump. The forward dropping of the neck will exert pressure on the trachea. It is necessary to carry the head on the neck in such a way that the forward curve of the neck is corrected.

Now look at your lower back. If your back is arched (figs. 32b and 32c) and your abdomen is protruding, your chest cage in front will, usually, be pushed forward, and in most people the angle between the ribs in front will be narrowed. It is difficult to get full breathing movement unless the arching of the back is corrected. This must be corrected in such a way as not to accentuate the hump at the base of the neck.

Lie on your back on a hard surface with your knees pointing upward and a support under your head. Observe the bend of your elbows. The funny bone should be turned outward from the body and the inside of the elbow towards the body, so as to widen the armpit and upper arm away from the sides of the chest. If, in this position, your forearms and hands will not lie flat on the surface (fig. 32c), your shoulder girdles are too tense and need to be released from the base of the neck.

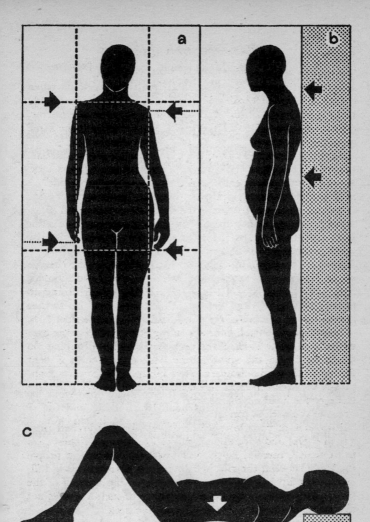

## Figure 32

Figure 32a shows dropped left shoulder and arm, thorax displaced to right, pelvis raised on left. 32b shows neck dropped forward and back unduly arched. 32c shows back wrongly arched off surface and forearm not lying flat.

Are you breathing? Many people, when studying or concentrating, hold their breath for long periods. Don't. At rest breathe at least ten to twelve times a minute.

Are you moving your chest and abdomen in front when you start to breathe in? Breathing in is a *back* activity. If you start breathing in by raising your upper chest in front, it is like trying to open an umbrella by pulling on the cover from the outside at the top. It can be done, but it is inefficient.

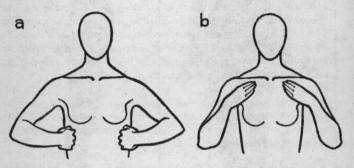

a    b

## Figure 33

Place the backs of your hands against the sides of your chest (fig. 33a). Imagine the gills of a fish half-way down your back on each side. Breathing in should start there, and the ribs should move out sideways against your hands. If your chest cage is displaced sideways, one side will move more than the other. Is the bottom of the rib cage nearer to your pelvis on one side than the other?

Place your hands on the upper chest (fig. 33b), just below the collar bones on each side, and almost touching the breast bone. When you start to breathe out, there should be a slight release of tension as the upper chest and breast bone drop. If you are very tense, a sigh will give you the feeling of the upper chest releasing. Don't raise the chest when you start to breathe in.

Breathing out, at rest, should last at least twice as long as breathing in. As you finish breathing out, you will feel your stomach muscles contract slightly. In order to get the next breath into your back, you will first have to release this stomach contraction. Many breathing difficulties come from keeping the upper chest and abdominal muscles too tense in front even at rest.

Look at your nostrils. Is one less dilated than the other? If you touch it, it will spring out slightly. Where is your tongue? At rest it should not press on the roof of the mouth but should lie flat on the floor of the mouth. The dilated nostril and flattened tongue will give you a better airway.

Think about your throat. When a baby screams, or when you attempt to defaecate, you will notice a tightening in the throat. Some people, when they breathe in, tighten in this region and do not release it completely when breathing out. This leads to fixation of the upper chest—an attitude often betokening fear of aggression. This tension can be relaxed, on breathing out, by releasing the throat and dropping the upper chest very slightly.

Look at your shoulders. The shoulder-blades should never be pulled together at the back—there has been much faulty teaching about this in the past—but they should lie flat on the chest cage (plates 12d and 26).

*I cannot help feeling, from what you have written that you think that no one, in the long run, can be really happy or healthy unless they use the Alexander Principle. Most medical and educational innovations tend to be "over-sold" when they are first put forward. Don't you think that you have spoiled your case by saying such things as, "This seems to me to be the single most important problem which medicine now has to deal with."*

The objection would certainly be valid if I had suggested that the Alexander Principle was a "cure-all". But this isn't the point which I am making. The recognition of the widespread presence of bacteria was not a "cure-all"—it simply pointed the way in which research had to be directed. It is the same with the mis-use: its manifestations need to be tabulated as carefully as were the types of bacteria. The recognition of the widespread presence of mis-use opens up a whole new field of Preventive Medicine, whilst at the same time indicating certain medical conditions—notably the rheumatic and mental disorders—in which immediate application can be made.

It would indeed be unhelpful to hold out something which in fact cannot be provided: or to promise great prospects to people who theoretically might be capable of working in this way, but who, when it comes down to it, will be quite incapable of it. There is so much that is clear and valuable in this approach that it would be silly to claim too much. The influence of USE on mental and physical functioning (and, therefore, on "health and happiness") is quite clear: what we can never be so clear about is the extent of the trainability of any given person, and their willingness to use what we can teach them. There is, however, in the majority of people an area, however small, in which their USE can be improved, with consequent improvement in their functioning (though not the "cure" of their "disease").

In the educational sphere, there is no question of over-selling the Alexander Principle. The training of teachers of it has been recognised by the Inner London Education Authority and selected students at the Alexander Institute are eligible for training grants. The problem is to make a sufficient number of well-trained teachers available to satisfy the demand.

# Chapter 12

## APPLYING THE PRINCIPLE

Why are we so fagged, so fashed, so cogged, so cumbered,
When the thing we freely forfeit is kept with fonder a care?

HOPKINS (*The Golden Echo*)

MOST POLEMICAL BOOKS—and this book is intended, at least in part, to be polemical—are strong on the diagnosis of predicament, but not so strong on solution. The Alexander Principle poses a new sort of predicament: it proposes an inclusive hypothesis-bag into which to stuff several of our present-day predicaments. It says that it is better to live by a difficult principle which unifies, than by a series of lower-order rules which constantly come into conflict with each other.

Like all hypotheses it has its limitations and it needs testing and refining: but a sufficient number of people have lived successfully by it for a sufficient number of years to indicate that it is a viable proposition.

### The Mature Rebellion

There comes a time in most people's lives when they feel the need to take a hard look at their pattern of living. Adolescent rebellion is, in the main, a rebellion against external life-forces —parents, teachers, employers and politicians who are blamed for the difficulties and inequities which become only too clear once childhood is over. The vast impersonal world moves implacably on, and the desire for someone at least to take some notice of us, plus the desire to be rid of adult deceit and the desire not to be "grey", leads us, in adolescence, to upheaval and disruption. The young are living and growing and life is to be sensed and enjoyed. They are no longer willing to put up with the barrack-square attitude "You'll bloody well do as you're bloody well *told*, same as I do" (a choice morsel which floated through the windows of my Medical Inspection room during the war). They wish to be rid of the deadening junk of the past, the customs which enslave them, and the false respect which stupid people seem to demand from them.

But one can't go on blaming the older people and the outside world for ever. A more mature rebellion stops saying "The world is making me grey: they hate me without cause", and starts to say instead, "The buck stops here with me: just exactly what is the matter with me: why don't I do as well as I know I can, why does my back ache, why is my sex a muddle, why am I ten different people: how can I begin to take responsibility for my own problems?"

This *internal* rebellion is a request for valid Principles, not for a revolution. The rebel is not necessarily a revolutionary. The rebel is determinedly unsubdued by the pressure of external authority, but this does not lead him to a revolutionary world of terror. The rebel has no wish to exploit anyone, but simply a desire to escape from the deadening octopus of mediocrity which tells him to be as dull as everyone else.

If he is to escape from his dullness he needs a plan of action: he needs principles with which to escape the "system".

There is no dearth of helpful suggestions. The priest, the psychiatrist, the poet, the novelist have much to say about the inner-life: the sociologist and doctor can recommend job-change, wife-change, recreation-change, diet-change, medicine and drugs. But individual men and women, in the main, still lead lives of quiet desperation, in spite of 2,000 years of religion, art and science. They have periods of great humour and joy, excitement and success; but, by and large, far too many people's plans go awry, their health and happiness deteriorate, their drive peters out in frustrated boredom. They live two lives: a Personal Life, based on the home and family, where at least they feel real, if miserable; and the Working Life, with its values of money-seeking and social status, where they experience a quite different reality: and if they are un-unemployed, doing a mundane job for lack of anything better, they become un-real people, in bondage to a life of tedium.

This is the lot of many apparently "normal" people. But even "normal" people will become disorganised and eventually break down when they are faced with seemingly insoluble situations. And when they become depressed and "got-down" by the complexity of it all, they begin to accentuate their latent habits of mis-USE.

*The Core-Structure*

I have used the phrase "core-structure" to indicate the development of a personal standard of good USE which can stop us from being "got-down" and by means of which we can preserve our onward momentum and vitality even when external stress makes stability difficult: a core-structure which will sustain us also when long periods of necessary learning have not yet given us skill and confidence.

Amidst the give-and-take of personal relationship, with its "posture-swapping" and role-taking, such a core-structure enables due respect to be given to other people's needs and attitudes without us having to copy their mis-USE. It does away with the need for the "conformity-deformities" by which we are expected to show loyalty to our tribe; but it also gives a capacity to reconcile, by giving a capacity to maintain our own stability in the presence of conflict, and in the presence of unpleasant end-gainers. In a world in which we may have little in common with some people, it helps us to find common ground.

Most especially it helps in the moment-to-moment regulation of unwanted emotion. One of my patients expressed the help which she gets from it in the following way.

Often I get a feeling of being *unsafe*: it is not an easy feeling to describe exactly, but it must date right back to childhood. The feeling is caused by other people and comes on quite suddenly. A look or a word is enough to start the feeling, which hits me in my midriff and it makes me feel knotted up and apprehensive. Since working with you I have discovered that physically I contract the part of my body which lies just below my ribs (this must be the region the ancients called the solar plexus) and it also has the effect of making me arch the middle of my back. This seems to be the way in which I produce feelings of unsafety in myself. If I can catch myself in time before this contraction sets in, the unsafe feeling only lasts for a moment. I have discovered that if I can remember to give my "orders" when I begin to get this feeling, I can stop it getting a grip. It stops me going into this quite dotty feeling of insecurity, in which I feel as if everyone is getting at me in a threatening way. "Ordering" seems to make me able to adjust to the other person, not necessarily very well, but at least not stupidly. I can react from a secure feeling of widening across my back and shoulders, instead of from a panic feeling in my stomach. It also makes me often able to see that no reaction is called-for, and that if I stay quite calm, with a feeling of being supported in my back, I can cope perfectly well with what is going on. I can see when it is appropriate to react, and when I needn't.

Feelings of safety or lack of security date from our earliest childhood, and are based on our feeling of our USE. A loving serene home atmosphere with plenty of warm physical contact, can certainly help to make a child feel secure. Unfortunately this feeling of security usually also includes a copying of the parents postures and moods and corresponding mis-uses. The feeling of "right" and the feeling of security which we get from this posture may serve us well on the home-ground (and many never leave the home-ground) but it cannot be appropriate for other situations which we must explore if we are to grow. Without a manner of USE which we can make basic to *all* situations, we are liable to feel insecurity and to confine ourselves within the bounds of what we know already—the recipe for a humdrum life.

If parents know something about the principles of good USE, the child's feeling of security can be based on such good USE, and with it a loving, communicative and non-aggressive relationship.

*The Reasonable Man*

The patient mentioned above, with her feelings of insecurity and stomach-panic, said she could prevent it happening if she "gave her orders". Just what exactly was she talking about?

I described in Chapters 10 and 11 the teaching and learning of a sequence of "orders", which gradually comes to be associated with a better resting-state of balance, and with a core-structure which gives a more secure balance during movement and communication. Alexander considered that by teaching people this ordering-process, he was putting them, as he expressed it, "into communication with their reason", as opposed to the panic and insecurity which may come when we react by instinctive end-gaining.

"Reason" has had a poor press in recent years. The ways and habits of the reasonable man have been at a discount, along with the image of the "good" man. The holocaust of violence which was unleashed in World War II, plus the threat of the nuclear-bomb poised above our heads, has produced an "eat, drink and be irrational" mood—a mood of despair that our religions and our reason should have led us to the abyss.

This has also been the half-century of the "common man": the depressed classes have become more literate and more vocal, but often not sufficiently educated to find and express their own reason. And one curious phenomenon has been a widespread acceptance of the dominant postural mood of the socially-deprived classes—a posture of sullen collapse, plus an aggressive muscular contraction of the shoulders and arms: a posture which has come to be adopted by large numbers of middle-class adolescents as a way of connecting-up with those they sympa-thise with, and as an escape from the rigid strait-jacket of the army and the genteel.

Caught between a Victorian ethic which believed in reason and self-help, and a Freudian ethic which says that reason and self-help are bound to founder on the shoals of the unconscious, modern man has had few principles which he can use intelli-gently: and instead he has fallen back on the *ad hoc* satisfaction of his needs, as and when they arise. In this he relies mainly on instinct and on the habits with which he has got by in the past.

Instinct and habit have one thing in common: they mean that we react only to *one* specific aspect of the general situation which confronts us. Reason on the other hand implies that as many as possible of our relevant needs are taken into account before we react: and accordingly it has seemed essential that the rational man should know as much as possible about his "relevant desires and needs". Years and years of school and university education are devoted to learning such relevant reasons, so that, in theory, we can become free to work out suit-able alternatives, and to set up our own "oughts" and impera-tives.

But the gulf between theory and practice remains to be bridged. Reason, when learned only at this level, has proved inadequate: and this inadequacy has led, in part, to the present discontent, to the demand even for "de-schooling".

And it has led to a growing need for the Alexander Principle. In Huxley's words:[50]

It is now possible to conceive of a totally new type of educa-tion, affecting the entire range of human activity, from the physiological, through the intellectual, moral and practical, to the spiritual—an education which, by teaching them proper Use, would preserve children and adults from most of the diseases and evil habits that now affect them: an education whose training would provide men and women with the psycho-physical means for behaving rationally.

Reason, as taught in school and in university will always be liable to founder, unless the reasoning faculty can be used in an additional way, TO DIRECT OUR DECISIONS. Alexander—and of course many, many people before him—realised that the reasoning *deciding* part of our consciousness could also be employed to give directions (orders) to ourselves. But, prior to Alexander, such "directing" had never been applied to USE in anything like the detail which he showed to be necessary: indeed, it could not be, because not enough was known about the sort of USE to which such reasoning direction could be applied. Direction-of-Use is the missing tool which Reason requires, if it is not to "founder on the shoals of unconscious habit".

### Thinking-in-Activity

However simple something may be in practice, to describe it is not so simple, and it may require familiarity with quite small detail if it is to be understood. "Directing" the manner-of-use is a simple single activity, but the description is complicated by the varieties of human mis-use.

Because of this difficulty, the Alexander Principle has been over-simplified by some people into the need just to sit up straight or to adopt an improved standing-posture: but these postures are only the outward visible signs of an inwardly directed tensional balance. They are an essential long-term part of the reasoning man's equipment—no more and no less: and it is clear that when, say, we are collapsed down in a state of physical depression, it will be hard to get the ideas which will indicate a way out, and even harder to act on them. But there is much more to applying the Principle than sitting up straight.

Let us postulate a perfect environment—a sort of scientific monastery in which the world is not too much with us: a world in which both reason and faith are considered valid: faith, to let go of the known, reason to work for the unknown: a world which seeks to work by principle and not by habit.

This perfect environment is provided to some extent in an Alexander training-group, although of necessity only for a few hours a day, and not far from the customary pressures of money and family and the future. If I first describe such ideal training conditions, in which Alexander-work has been fined down to its most accurate and most intimate, we can then proceed to "trim" a little from this ideal setting, to see what is possible for everyday man in everyday life.

Under such conditions—whether or not a teacher is giving personal instruction at any given moment—there will be a pre-occupation with thought and movement. End-gaining—action which does not pay heed to the manner-of-use—is less likely to occur under such conditions, because there are none of the raucous stimuli of the bustling world to demand instant response. Subjectively, the distinction will begin to emerge between the "content" of the thought, and the actual "function" of thinking (in the sense that a car must be actually functioning before it can go to this place or that): and it will come to be appreciated that there is more to thinking than manipulating ideas; more than doing sums, more than making sex-plans, more than letters and loving and music and how to arrange the furniture. There will be a growing awareness of another type of thinking, a thinking which is part of movement and stillness, belonging with them and underlying them.

It is with this type of thinking that the Alexander "student" will concern himself within his training group. A state of bodily stillness will be sought in which there is a personal organisation of the Use-perception. This personal organisation ("directing") may be found to involve a very slight muscular activity, an adjustment which is present both at rest and during action. Muscular activity, as we have seen, is never still: it may be fined-down and fined-down, but the gradation between stillness and activity is only one of degree. Slight oscillation (Chapter 3) is always present, even in the balanced resting-state.

Under such conditions of directed thinking, the student will become increasingly aware of the muscular matrix of his decision, and of the part he can play in attending to the small shifts of muscle-tension which will accompany both his emotions and his insights. The appreciation of these shifts is as delicate as the finest touch of the violinist, and such directed thinking is at first a tenuous thing—any fatigue or lessening of attention can put an end to it.

We have usually taken it for granted that we can only use our minds in two deliberate ways—content-thinking (i.e., with words, sentences, music, images, etc.,) and behaviour-control. But between content-thinking and overt behaviour there is another sphere of personal life, a vast world of existence to be managed by awareness and attention (although "managed" is too forceful a term for the attentive living which is implied).

This sort of work has been going on for many years in Alexander groups. It does, however, pre-suppose a degree of peace and quiet which may not be easily available, except perhaps in a hospital, a school or a university. For the average patient (or pupil) who studies the Alexander Principle on his own such detailed application to "directing" is difficult in our present economy. With increasing leisure it should be easier, and most of us are in fact far less busy than our "office hours" mighti mply. Certainly in the initial learning-phase, it is essential to have some freedom from intrusion: but even when there are others around, most people already have a way of keeping up their own "silent soliloquy": and this soliloquy could more profitably be used occasionally in Use-direction. We cannot escape from our function of being attentive human beings, except by living in a deadening state of passivity. A critical sifting process is going on, to a greater or lesser degree, in all of our normal perception. Giving "directions" is like setting the focus and speed of a camera. If the focus is wrong, a blurred picture will result, which can be misinterpreted in many ways. Time spent in directing is never wasted. A far more appropriate response is possible if the focus of perception has been sharpened by directing.

## The Sense of Reality

Such increased self-awareness is bound to interfere with some of our social shams and to compel us to face up to reality.*⁵¹

At core, most of us want reality: but when we are in a mis-

---

* Pasternak: "The great majority of us are required to live a life of constant duplicity. Your health is bound to be affected if, day-after-day, you say the opposite of what you feel, if you grovel before what you dislike." *Dr Zhivago.* Collins, 1958.

used state, we may have to be *taught* reality. In the Alexander teaching-situation, a teacher can give us a glimpse of reality through the teaching-process—there is usually a chink through which a start can be made.

However, at first it may only be a glimpse: much of the early learning stages will be vague and we may have to content ourselves with an intellectual confidence in the diagnosis and in the procedures.

The process of slowly laying foundations may at first give only a sense of "un-realised potential" rather than one of "real actuality". This state of unrealised potential is distasteful to many of us, and we therefore may prefer the actuality of our old mis-use, however un-real it may be. The discarding of this un-real actuality may seem like a loss at first, and loss of anything familiar is sad: we will find that we are profoundly attached to our old mis-uses and the moods they maintain.

We fear new things, because we fear that we may lose our familiar command of the situation. By learning a familiar command of our USE, we can acquire an abiding sense of consistency, and dispense with the need for an external familiarity. There has to be a willingness to accept the unfamiliar—a deeply implicit feeling that life is open to be changed.

Routines of course will always be needed—all sensible life is based on personally-selected routines; but routines can always be changed, whereas habits can too easily outlive their usefulness and lead us into unreality.

The discarding of such unreality must go on. To *be* what we can be, we have to find out what we are. *Being* what we are means being alive, happy and adjusted to our day-to-day life: in other words, being "all-there". This "all-there" sense of reality is easier for children, who live in a restricted environment where their vivid sensibility allows them to "find-out" all the time. Unless we, as adults find out what we are up to with our USE—and continue to find out about our USE as things change—we will have an increasing sense of un-reality, of not being all-there.

To find out what we are is, however, only to find out the ordinariness, not the supernatural. Reality, when we find it, is ordinary and everyday—but an ordinariness in which our heightened senses can delight. It is not a question of going from the prosaic to the "miraculous", but from unreality to reality.

The Alexander Principle proposes that we can achieve a more real state if we will learn to direct a free manner-of-use. Such a new sense of reality will not occur immediately, except in glimpses: but if the desired pattern is constantly held in mind during the long period of learning, it begins to take over and to take its part in the inevitable processes of growth and change.

Such detailed directing is not easy for most people in every-day life: but such detail is not needed all the time. There is a difference between learning and living (although the fullest life will always be one which seeks to learn something from the next thing we do). However, when we are, for a time, away from the actual pressures of living—whether it be because we have broken down mentally or physically, or because we have deliberately put ourselves in a restricted learning environment —living and learning can become synonymous.

## Hypnosis and Relaxation

I am often asked why I don't use hypnosis in order to help people to release their unconscious tensions. Recently a young woman suggested to me that since she was prepared to accept that her neck and chest tensions were due to some infantile trauma, might she not be able to recall the original traumatic incident if she was hypnotised? And that if she were subsequently told of this forgotten reason, might she not then more easily release the tension (a combination of pre-hypnosis and hypnosis)?

I made the following points to her:

The snag with all such approaches is that your chest-armouring is not now one single specific mis-use, although it may have started as a specific mis-use. Over the intervening years, a most elaborate system of compensating mis-uses has been established, and the discovery of one original "trigger" cause, will not now release your other compensations. Indeed your chest tensions could only have become so firmly established because your *general* manner-of-use at the original time was already disturbed. The soil was there already. Most of us have been through many incidents of extreme fear and stress when young and if our manner-of-use is good we throw them off. The same thing applies to the extremes of stress which we encounter when we are adults.

There is no need to bring in hypnosis—it can only add another factor of unconscious dependence. Instead of searching for the old context, it is more useful to construct a *new* context, in the light of which the old attitude will be seen now to be insignificant. During your Alexander instruction you will have many insights, once you have begun to establish a resting-state of calmer USE. In such a resting-state, almost anything can serve to remind you of forgotten incidents. Seeing an advertisement on the underground, a chance facial expression, a line of poetry or an overheard remark can serve to flood your awareness with a realisation of some forgotten attitude.

This forgotten attitude was previously manifested in your old mis-use pattern. With Alexander instruction, you have for a time lost the old mis-use pattern, but it will have been triggered into reappearance by, say, the underground poster. Against the background of your newly-found awareness of better USE, you are then able to detect the abrupt transition back to your old familiar (but previously un-felt) state of mis-use.

It follows that when you are having Alexander instruction and are thinking a good deal about it, you should observe quite fleeting insights, and endeavour to think them through, both on your own and with your teacher. An insight may be extremely tenuous and may not necessarily be formulated as a clear attitude to this or that person or situation. It may take the form of a sensation of some new release of muscle-tension, or of some new spatial awareness of how, say, your chest joins on to your lower back; or of how the pelvis can move or release in an integrated manner.

When the fog of mis-use begins to clear, the impact is considerable, and there will be a desire to employ the fog-clearing mechanisms whenever the fog has descended again: as descend it will, although it will now descend on someone who has hope and a method for coping with it.

What has been said about hypnosis applies equally to "relaxation" therapy. I read in a recent treatise on relaxation that "The exercises are not difficult—in fact they are very simple." In a sense this is true. They are simple and ineffectual, except at a trivial level. How possibly could tension habits which have been built up over many years be altered by some simple rule-of-thumb procedure? There has been an alarming vogue recently among psychotherapists of trying to get their patients to relax by various forms of body-contact and gentle handling. The therapist has usually picked up these techniques after a very few instructional sessions from this or that pundit. I am not surprised that the whole subject has got a reputation for being dangerous. The technical problems of teaching a balanced resting-state of USE are teasingly difficult: I was myself nearly ten years in training before I reckoned that it would be sensible to work without supervision.

There cannot be a place for such simple relaxation-therapy, at any serious level. It can never be a question of detecting faulty tension patterns once and for all, de-conditioning them by hypnosis or relaxation, and seeing them disappear. It is rather a matter of continually having to notice the tensions, in countless different situations, and gradually finding out the compensatory-tensions, which, like layers of an onion, manifest themselves when succeeding layers have been stripped off. Just how far the stripping should go will depend on time and inclination, and it is essential that the psychotherapist or teacher should know exactly what he is doing and how much can be tolerated.

USE must not be ignored, whatever the psychotherapeutic situation. Modern linguistics has an adage "Don't ask for The Meaning, ask for the Use"—implying that words should not be studied in isolation from the various sentences in which they take part. In the same way, we should say "Don't look for the memory, look for the Use". The grammar of the body has to be studied in action, in living Use, not dormant in dreams or on the dissecting-table. The meaning of a memory belongs with its present-moment Use: when a mis-use is reconciled back into a directive resting-state, the harmful memory has gone.

The unconscious is irrelevant when we learn to live more consciously—a tautology, but the one must imply the other. Body-use *is* the "unconscious" for most people. As USE becomes more conscious, the unconscious habit can lose its grip.

*An Alexander Life-style*

It will be clear from this chapter that the Alexander Principle can be applied at many levels. Only a few people at present have the time or inclination to embark on a detailed research into it, and indeed much of the work already done has produced information which can be passed on without similar effort. Many people—probably the majority—will be content, and thankful, to use it for the alleviation of ill-health: the body is resilient, and it can get along fairly well without having to be in some ideally-used state of directive detachment all day long, provided that certain clear general principles of good-use are sustained. There is a distinction of degree between the medical and the educational needs: doctors, by and large, tend to see bacteria rather than infinity in a "grain of sand". It is not an ignoble use of the Principle to remove pain and suffering, as some Alexander adherents have seemed to imply.

But few people will, or can, apply the Principle without sorting out at least some of their basic living-habits: and many, in time, come to value it much more for its effect on their general life-style than for its effect on their corns.

A Principle which seeks to change habit at the very moment of reaction is bound to have an impact on anyone who attempts it, and there have been many and varied attempts by different people to give it a style which fitted their own temperament. Huxley's "non-attachment", Dewey's brand of Pragmatism, Bernard Shaw's Life-force, Ludovici's "race of mental giants", the rationalism of a few minor rationalists, the opportunism of a score of European and American "therapists", who thought it was a band-wagon, but found it was a bed of nails: the short-cutters in the world of speech-training and PE, who listened impatiently to all the talk about "end-gaining": and above all, the crackpots, carnivorous, herbivorous, astrologising, worshipping, finding a haven in Alexander's "Nil a me alienum puto, so long as you keep quiet and don't pull your head back." He once said to me, "If there is a crack-pot within 50 miles, he will find his way to me."

It is a miracle that it survived some of this bunch, and since, in the early days, anyone who was dim-witted or cross at his own learning-difficulties could call it a load of rubbish, Alexander was at the mercy of malevolents, since there was no one to contradict them. It was a buyer's market for most of his life, and it is not surprising that he accepted gratefully the plaudits of any minor "authority" who was prepared to say that his work was valuable. And it is not surprising that he was distrustful of much of the human race—"lowly evolved swine" was one of his epithets in later years, and I can personally vouch that it is true that he kept a blunderbuss in his room with which to scare off itinerant musicians and street-criers—a splendid spectacle of Edwardian outrage. And he used it metaphorically on those who would have liked him to be their "little man round the corner who is a *wizard*".

Fortunately there has always been a hard core of common sense at the back of it all. The actual practical teaching procedures have gone on, individually and in groups, in an almost total separation from what anyone might be saying about it (and as they will continue to go on, relatively undisturbed by anything which I am writing about it).

This is not to say that most of Alexander's early supporters were off-the-beam. John Dewey, Aldous Huxley, Raymond Dart, Canon Shirley, Irene Tasker, Lord Lytton, Isobel Cripps, Dr Peter Macdonald, Fred Watts (his publisher)—all of them were major figures who gave the Principle an essential impetus at various times. And, latterly there have been many others who have seen that the Principle should play an integral part in their Institutions, and who have struggled to make a place for it: along with a large number of non-professional people who have seen that it should play an integral part in their personal living.

They have discovered that what Alexander called the "means-whereby" approach, works for them also. That they can tackle most of their problems by working out the "means": that if they will content themselves with a potential which cannot be immediately cashed, then almost any problem can be broken down into the "next thing" to do: and that a combination of tiny grains of sand eventually makes quite a tidy beach.

### Alexander

There were, as I have pointed out, two sides to Alexander's character. He himself never quite escaped the need for the "media". He had to get the ball rolling somehow. He had to make enough money to sustain his own scientific life: and since he was originally an actor, he needed applause, and he thought that others would gauge his success by the extent of that applause.

Yet for at least eight hours of each working day, none of this mattered. He would be working, with a detailed intensity, at the moment-to-moment re-education of his pupils and his groups, with humour and intelligence, giving all the time in the world to the needs of the particular person in front of him. This seemed to me to be genius: no one had ever done just this type of work before.

In common with most doctors, my life has brought me into contact with many very intelligent people—many of them people of the highest talent. For what it is worth, I must place on record that I found in Alexander an imaginative genius and an adherence to scientific method which I have not seen outmatched by anyone. I think he transformed the human condition, although as yet on a tiny scale.

# CONCLUSION

Myself when young did eagerly frequent
Doctor and Saint and heard great Argument
About it and about:
But evermore came out
By that same door wherein I went.

EDWARD FITZGERALD

ALEXANDER WAS NO saint, but he saw his Principle as a major hope for most of us. Many people have found that his Principle has opened a new door for them: not necessarily the door to wealth and success, but an escape-hatch and a possible way through to what might seem an impossible personal evolution.

Fagged, fashed, cogged, cumbered, stuck in a dreary set of commitments and habits—some evolution must be attempted if a life is to be made with style and with pleasure. A very few people have over the ages chosen to explore something quite different. We have had a half-century of the common man, of the individual doing-his-own-thing. Perhaps we can now have a next half-century of the extra-vidual, the man who not only has freed himself from the compulsions of society, but who has a way of freeing himself from his own compulsions: a way which by the cultivation of an attentive resting-state of USE can move him towards the life of the "whole man". Such a man, *capax universi*, will find a world of infinite charm and variety in that which Alexander has to offer.

# APPENDICES

# A SHORT BIOGRAPHY OF ALEXANDER

*Some of this material is taken from an unpublished autobiographical
fragment*

FREDERICK MATTHIAS ALEXANDER was born in 1869 at
Wynyard on the north-west coast of Tasmania, the oldest son of
John and Betsy Alexander. His grandfather, Matthias Alexander, owned a large property which included Table Cape,
between the sea and River Inglis. He spent his childhood in
country pursuits, and in particular the training and management of horses.

At the age of 17, he started working in the Mount Bischoff
Tin Mining Company—"with deep regret I finished the way of
life I had enjoyed up to that time, the outdoor experience in the
fields, the sea and the beaches". Whilst at Mount Bischoff his
main interests were "teaching myself to play the violin and
taking part in amateur dramatic performances".

At the age of 20, he went to Melbourne with £500 which he
had saved up, and lived with his uncle, James Pearce. "For
3 months or so, I was chiefly interested in seeing and hearing all
that was best in the theatre, the art galleries and in music. By
this time I had decided to train myself for a career as a Reciter."

Alexander kept himself in Melbourne by taking various jobs
—he mentions an estate agency, a department store and a firm
of tea merchants—whilst he studied the violin and was "much
occupied in the evenings in acting and producing plays."

His interest in reciting increased—"during this time, I did
all that was possible to prepare myself for a career as a Reciter,
with a small selected Repertoire of dramatic and humorous
pieces". But he was already much worried by "hoarseness and
lowered vitality", and he had begun his research into his USE:
"I considered that the source of my trouble lay in the USE of my
vocal organs."

In spite of his vocal trouble, he embarked on a career as a
reciter and appears to have had a considerable immediate
success, performing in various cities in Tasmania and Australia.
But he was increasingly hampered by his voice, and began to

search for a method to prevent his trouble. A full account of his research appears in his book *The Use of the Self* and in *The Alexander Journal*, No. 7, 1972.

Once he had cleared up his vocal trouble, Alexander settled in Auckland, where he combined his reciting career with teaching the method he had discovered—"employing a technique that enabled one to change and improve USE". During his time in Auckland he decided to make the teaching of his method his main career and he moved to Melbourne in 1894 to do this.

He continued to give recitals in Melbourne and built up a teaching practice, giving both individual and group instruction. In 1899 he moved to Sydney, where he became firmly established as a teacher of his method—"my teaching was basically one of changing and controlling reaction"—and he became director of the Sydney Dramatic and Operatic Conservatorium between 1900 and 1904.

One of his friends in Sydney, Dr McKay, encouraged him to go to London to teach his method. The decision to move was not easy—"I would be taking a serious risk in an attempt to build up a practice in London, where competition was considerable and where I would be unknown." In 1904—with no quick air or sea travel—Australia was a long way indeed from England both culturally and in actual miles. Nevertheless, "the desire to take the plunge grew rapidly and I decided to take it."

It was a large gamble to take, and he was immediately in some financial trouble—trouble which was with him to some extent for most of his life. Perhaps unfortunately he became interested in betting—horses had always been a passion with him—and on one occasion when "the financial aspect was the one remaining difficulty", he was given a tip for a double on the Newmarket Handicap and the Australia Cup at 150–1, which won him £750 when he was down to his last £5. This appears to have been a turning point in getting himself settled in London.

In the years before World War I, he worked mainly with actors—Henry Irving, Viola Tree, Lily Langry, Constance Collier, Oscar Asche, and Matheson Lang were among his pupils—and he wrote his first book *Man's Supreme Inheritance*, which was published in 1910.

From 1914 to 1924 he spent half of his time in the US and half of his time in England, writing two further books *Conscious Control* and *Constructive, Conscious Control of the Individual*, which had a preface by John Dewey, the American educational philosopher.

In spite of his considerable teaching success, his money troubles appear to have continued—perhaps connected with his habit at this time of spending the months between May and October "resting and racing"! When I first met him in 1938, he was an undischarged bankrupt, although maintaining his teaching practice at 16 Ashley Place in London. I accepted at the time that he had become a bankrupt rather than pay a debt which he considered unfair, but he never quite sorted out the economics of his role in a satisfactory manner, and he tended to get himself involved in a complicated network of financial and social transactions.

After World War I, he was fortunate in having the help of two teachers, Ethel Webb and Irene Tasker. A class for children was started in 1924 in London, and subsequently a school in Penhill in Kent, where his method was made fundamental to the whole school curriculum.

In 1930 a teachers' training class was established in his rooms in London at 16 Ashley Place, and it was carried on there until 1940 when he took his school to America. Whilst in America, his fourth book, *The Universal Constant in Living*, was published.

His time in the US from 1940 to 1943 was not a very happy one. It looked at that time as though his work and his Principle could easily become lost—nearly all of his teachers were in the services.

Eventually Alexander could stand the separation from England no longer, and he returned to London in the summer of 1943. He was now becoming an old man and he was embittered by the refusal of medicine and education to recognise his ideas. The very qualities which had led him to his scientific discoveries—single-mindedness and questioning—tended now towards suspiciousness. This was not helped by an attack on his work in South Africa, culminating in a libel action which he brought successfully against the South African Government in 1948.

He won large damages in the case, but the summing up was fair: briefly that his method was sound but that his presentation

of it was misleading. Fortunately the judges saw past his mode
of presentation to the value of what he was actually doing.

Alexander in his old age retained to the last his immense
teaching skill and patience: but in the years before his death,
his hard life had taken its toll, and he began to despair of his
ideas ever being accepted without being watered down.

After he returned from the US to England in 1943, a
teachers' training course was started once more in London in
1945. In 1948, as noted by Sir Stafford Cripps at a dinner which
was later held to celebrate Alexander's eightieth birthday,
"there was set up the Society of Teachers, as a central body for
the furtherance of the teaching and for the upholding of
proper professional standards. To these teachers, Alexander has
entrusted the carrying-on of his work in the form in which he
has passed it on to them."

Alexander died in 1955, still at work, at Ashley Place. The
subsequent years have seen an increasing interest in his Principle. Unfortunately, some people who claim to be teaching it
will not necessarily have undergone an adequate training.
Membership of the Society of Teachers of the Alexander
Technique (STAT) or the possession of a certificate signed by
Alexander is proof that a three-year training has been taken at a
training establishment approved by the Society. If there is any
doubt about the qualification of a teacher, it would be prudent
to enquire about this.

These brief biographical details can be amplified by reference
to back numbers of *The Alexander Journal* (published by STAT)
which contains articles by many of the teachers and doctors
who knew Alexander well. Perhaps the clearest account ever
given appears in the Memorial lecture which my wife, Marjory
Alexander Barlow, gave at the Medical Society of London in
1965 and this was subsequently reprinted by the Alexander
Institute.

No one person can give a full account of Alexander. Most
people made contact with him through the medium of his
teaching, i.e., mainly through non-verbal communication. So
much depended upon his presence, his hands, and the whole
circumstance of his re-educational situation that one might
well despair of giving a clear account of him to a third person.
The memory of the man resides in the skill which he was able
to pass on to succeeding generations of teachers.

# GLOSSARY

BEHAVIOUR

1. *Stimulus/Response:* Lifting a telephone receiver after hearing its bell ring.
2. *Operant:* Lifting a telephone receiver to call someone.
3. *Directed:* Letting telephone ring a little longer, whilst pausing to check over-quick reflex reaction, and then attending to the USE whilst lifting the receiver and responding.
4. *Feed-back:* Allowing behaviour to be influenced by knowledge of results rather than by expectations.
5. *Conditioned:* Behaviour adopted in the past by conscious choice or training but which has become unconscious and unchosen.

BODY-CONSTRUCT

A person's perceptive framework (made up of previous learned experience) by means of which he *construes* what he perceives and edits it to obtain (by his muscular USE) his preferred perception.

CORE-STRUCTURE

A directed USE in which the co-ordination of the head, neck and back is not disturbed by the limbs, the breathing, the use of the special senses, the act of communicating or the various biological functions.

DIAGNOSIS

1. *Descriptive:* The classification of reports on events in a person's past and present life.
2. *Prescriptive:* A diagnosis which carries implications for preventive action.

DIRECTING

Used in two senses:

1. Projecting verbal directions which have both an anatomical and a functional component, e.g., "Shoulder Release". The anatomical direction ("Shoulder") is a signal to put attention on the shoulder: the functional component ("Release") is a signal to release any faulty USE which the anatomical direction may have made apparent.
2. Pointing in a certain direction, e.g., the shoulder should release in a sideways "widening" direction, and not by being dropped inwards across the back of the chest.

DOING

Making unnecessary muscle-tension in an attempt to "do" the Alexander directions. Non-doing = allowing the muscles to act in response to direction. Undoing = releasing unnecessary muscle tension.

DYSTONIA

Use which involves excessive and/or wrongly distributed muscular tension.

ELECTROMYOGRAPHY

The recording of small amounts of muscular activity by placing electrodes in or over a muscle.

END-GAINING

Carrying out actions to attain ends without attending to the USE (the "means") and without gauging the amount of pressure and tension required to start a given activity. On a larger scale, any form of behaviour which does not permit the feed-back of information except that which relates to the one specific end desired.

ERGONOMICS

The study of USE and posture in a working or social environment, and the design of equipment to facilitate functioning.

HOMEOSTASIS

The capacity of certain bodily systems to achieve a relatively steady neutral balance, with a greater or lesser degree of oscillation around a central resting point, to which the system seeks to return after stress.

INHIBITING

1. Checking over-quick reflex activity, to give the possibility of choice.
2. In a more sophisticated Alexander sense, it means deliberately taking a moment to stop and say "No" to an action which one has decided in advance to carry out.

KINAESTHESIA

The perception of USE.

KYPHOSIS

An excessive "hump" anywhere between the lower neck and the middle back.

LORDOSIS

An unduly arched-in lower back.

MIS-USE

Use which involves an inappropriate relationing of one (or many) parts of the body to the rest of the body, either through too much or too little muscle-tension.

NEGATIVE FEED-BACK

The elimination of error by means of a servo-mechanism.

POSTURE

The external shape of the body, at rest and in movement, as observed by another person. Produced by the effect of good or bad USE on the genetic physique.

PRIMARY CONTROL
  Alexander's phrase to describe the relationing of the skull to the neck, and of the skull-and-neck to the rest of the body.

PRINCIPLE
  A hypothesis which is adopted as being logically prior to a range of other questions. An answer which is not itself contained in some prior answer.

REFLEX
  A bodily reaction which is almost invariably initiated by the same type of stimulus.

SCOLIOSIS
  A sideways curvature of the spine.

SERVO-MECHANISM
  A system which is influenced by the consequences of its own behaviour.

SPONDYLOSIS
  Arthritis of a part of the vertebral column.

STIMULUS
  An event which is followed by a behavioural response.

USE
  The characteristic and habitual way of using and moving the body. The relationing of one part of the body to another part in response to circumstances and the environment.

# REFERENCES

1. W. Barlow, "An Investigation into Kinaesthesia", *Medical Press Circular* 215, 60, 1946.
2. C. Sherrington, *Man on his Nature*, Cambridge University Press 1951.
3. G. Ryle, *Collected Papers*, Hutchinson 1971.
4. W. Cannon, *The Wisdom of the Body*, Kegan Paul 1932.
5. D. Morris, *The Naked Ape*, Jonathan Cape 1967.
6. Sir A. Keith, "Man's Posture: Its Evolution and Disorders", *British Medical Journal* I, 451, 1923.
7. E. Hooton, "Why Men behave like Apes and Vice Versa", *Science* 83, 271, 1936.
8. W. Le Gros Clark, *The Antecedents of Man*, Edinburgh University Press 1959.
9. B. Campbell, *Human Evolution*, Chicago University Press 1967.
10. A. Schopenhauer, *The World as Will and Idea*, Kegan Paul 1883.
11. H. Spencer, "Gracefulness" in *Essays*, Williams 1857.
12. W. Barlow, "Postural Homeostasis", *Annals of Physical Medicine* 1, No. 3, 1952.
13. H. J. Eysenck, *Dimensions of the Personality*, Routledge and Kegan Paul 1947.
14. R. A. Granit, *The Basis of Motor Control*, London and New York Academic Press 1970.
15. T. Roberts, *Basic Ideas in Neurophysiology*, Butterworth 1966.
16. P. A. Merton, "Nervous Gradation of Muscular Contraction", *British Medical Bulletin* 12, 214–18, 1956.
17. D. E. Broadbent, "Introduction", *British Medical Bulletin on Cognitive Psychology* 1971.
18. W. Barlow, "Posture and the Resting State", *Annals of Physical Medicine* vol. II, No. 4 1954.
19. R. M. Hare, *Freedom and Reason*, Oxford University Press 1963.
20. W. R. Gowers, "Lumbago: its lessons and analogues", *British Medical Journal* 1, p. 117, 1904.
21. J. L. Halliday, "Psychological factors in Rheumatism", *British Medical Journal* 1, p. 213, 1937.
22. I. P. Ellman, "Fibrositis", *Annals of the Rheumatic Diseases* 3, p. 56, 1942.
23. P. Hench, "The Management of Chronic Arthritis and other

Rheumatic diseases among soldiers of the U.S. Army", *Annals of the Rheumatic Diseases* 5, p. 106, 1946.

24. W. Barlow, "Anxiety and Muscle-Tension Pain", *British Journal of Clinical Practice* vol. 13, No. 5, p. 339, 1959.

25. H. J. Eysenck, "Dimensions of the Personality", *op. cit.*

26. W. Barlow, in *Modern Trends in Psychosomatic Medicine*, Butterworths, 1954.

27. W. Barlow, "Postural Deformity", *Proceedings of Royal Society of Medicine* vol. 49, No. 9, p. 670, 1956.

28. W. Barlow, "Anxiety and Muscle Tension", *British Journal of Physical Medicine* 10, 81, 1947.

29. A. Gregg, "What is Psychiatry?", *British Medical Journal* 5, i, 551, 1944.

30. H. Wolff, *Headache*, Oxford University Press 1948.

31. Davis, Buchwold and Frankmann, "Autonomic & Muscular Responses and their relation to simple Stimuli", *Psychological Monographs* No. 405, p. 69, 1955.

32. J. E. Goldthwaite, *Body Mechanics*, Lippincott 1952.

33. C. Darwin, *The Expression of the Emotions in Man and Animals*, Reprinted: Thinkers Library, Watts 1945.

34. M. Bull, "Attitude Theory of the Emotions", *New York Nervous Disease Monograph* 1951.

35. W. Young, *Eros denied*, Corgi 1967.

36. L. Corbin, *Avicenna*, Routledge and Kegan Paul 1960.

37. H. Gardner, "Figure and Ground in Aesthetic Perception", *British Journal of Aesthetics* 1972.

38. Prof. T. Sparshott, *An Enquiry into Goodness*, University of Toronto Press 1958.

39. J. M. Tanner, *Growth at Adolescence*, Oxford, Blackwell Scientific Publications 1962.

40. W. Barlow, "Rest and Pain", *Proceedings of IV International Congress of Physical Medicine, Excerpta Medica International*, Series 107, p. 494, 1964.

41. M. Swain, "Survey of Physical Education", *Australian Journal Physical Education*, June 1961.

42. J. Dewey, *Experience and Nature*, Open Court 1925.

43. Aldous Huxley, *Ends and Means*, Chatto & Windus 1937.

44. F. M. Alexander, *The Use of the Self*, Methuen 1932.

45. Prof. G. E. Coghill, *Anatomy and the Problem of Behaviour*, Cambridge University Press 1929.

46. Judson Herrick, *G. E. Coghill: Naturalist and Philosopher*, Chicago University Press 1949.

47. W. Barlow, "Psychosomatic Problems in Postural re-education", *The Lancet*, p. 659, 2 Sept., 1955.

48. Marghanita Laski, *Ecstasy*, Cresset Press 1961.

49. Mair & Bannister, *The Evaluation of Personal Constructs*, Academic Press 1968.
50. Aldous Huxley, "End-gaining and Means Whereby", *Alexander Journal*, No. 4, p. 19, 1965.
51. B. Pasternak, *Dr Zhivago*, Collins 1958.

# INDEX

# INDEX
## by H. E. Crowe